AF779693

College Accounting

fifteenth edition

College Accounting

Chapters 1–13

JOHN ELLIS PRICE, Ph.D., CPA
Professor of Accounting (Retired)
University of North Texas
Denton, Texas

M. DAVID HADDOCK JR., Ed.D., CPA
Professor of Accounting (Retired)
Chattanooga State Community College
Chattanooga, Tennessee

MICHAEL J. FARINA, MBA, CPA, CGMA
Professor of Accounting
Cerritos College
Norwalk, California

Mc Graw Hill Education

COLLEGE ACCOUNTING, FIFTEENTH EDITION

Chapters 1–13

Published by McGraw-Hill Education, 2 Penn Plaza, New York, NY 10121. Copyright © 2017 by McGraw-Hill Education. All rights reserved. Printed in the United States of America. Previous editions © 2015, 2012, and 2009. No part of this publication may be reproduced or distributed in any form or by any means, or stored in a database or retrieval system, without the prior written consent of McGraw-Hill Education, including, but not limited to, in any network or other electronic storage or transmission, or broadcast for distance learning.

Some ancillaries, including electronic and print components, may not be available to customers outside the United States.

1 2 3 4 5 6 7 8 9 DOW 21 20 19 18 17 16

ISBN 978-1-259-63111-5 (chapters 1–30)
MHID 1-259-63111-7 (chapters 1–30)
ISBN 978-1-259-99516-3 (chapters 1–13)
MHID 1-259-99516-X (chapters 1–13)

Chief Product Officer, SVP, Products & Markets: *G. Scott Virkler*
Vice President, General Manager, Products & Markets: *Marty Lange*
Managing Director: *Tim Vertovec*
Marketing Director: *Natalie King*
Executive Brand Manager: *Steve Schuetz*
Director, Product Development: *Rose Koos*
Director of Digital Content: *Peggy Hussey*
Associate Director of Digital Content: *Kevin Moran*
Lead Product Developer: *Kris Tibbetts*
Product Developer: *Michael McCormick*
Senior Marketing Manager: *Michelle Williams*
Market Development Manager: *Erin Chomat*
Digital Product Analyst: *Xin Lin*
Director, Content Design & Delivery: *Linda Avenarius*
Program Manager: *Daryl Horrocks*
Content Project Managers: *Lori Koetters, Angela Norris*
Senior Buyer: *Laura Fuller*
Design: *Matt Diamond*
Content Licensing Specialists: *Ann Marie Jannette, Shannon Manderscheid*
Cover Image: © *Satoshi Muramastu/Getty Images*
Compositor: *SPi Global*
Printer: *R. R. Donnelley*

All credits appearing on page or at the end of the book are considered to be an extension of the copyright page.

Library of Congress Control Number: 2016946641

The Internet addresses listed in the text were accurate at the time of publication. The inclusion of a website does not indicate an endorsement by the authors or McGraw-Hill Education, and McGraw-Hill Education does not guarantee the accuracy of the information presented at these sites.

mheducation.com/highered

About the Authors

Courtesy of John Ellis Price

JOHN ELLIS PRICE recently retired as professor of accounting at the University of North Texas. Dr. Price has more than 36 years of experience in higher education with over half of those years serving in key leadership positions including as founding president and professor of accounting at the University of North Texas at Dallas. Dr. Price has previously held positions of professor and assistant professor, as well as chair and dean, at the University of North Texas, Jackson State University, and the University of Southern Mississippi. Dr. Price has also been active in the Internal Revenue Service as a member of the Commissioner's Advisory Group for two terms and as an Internal Revenue agent.

Professor Price is a certified public accountant who has twice received the UNT College of Business Administration's Outstanding Teaching Award and the university's President's Council Award. Majoring in accounting, he received his BBA and MS degrees from the University of Southern Mississippi and his PhD in accounting from the University of North Texas.

Dr. Price is a member of the Mississippi Society of Certified Public Accountants, the American Accounting Association, and the American Taxation Association (serving as past chair of the Subcommittee on Relations with the IRS and Treasury). Dr. Price has also served as chair of the American Institute of Certified Public Accountants Minority Initiatives Committee and as a member of the Foundation Trustees.

Courtesy of M. David Haddock Jr.

M. DAVID HADDOCK JR. recently retired from his role as director of training for LBMC, PC, one of the top 50 CPA firms in the United States. He has transitioned his professional role to coaching consultant and CPE instructor. In a 35-year career in higher education, Dr. Haddock served in faculty and administrative roles at Auburn University at Montgomery, the University of Alabama in Birmingham, the University of West Georgia, and Chattanooga State Community College. At his retirement from higher education, he was professor of accounting and associate vice president for academic affairs at Chattanooga State Community College in Tennessee. In addition to his teaching, he also maintained a sole proprietorship accounting and tax practice for 20 years prior to joining LBMC.

He received his BS in accounting and MS in adult education from the University of Tennessee and the EdD degree in administration of higher education from Auburn University. He is a licensed CPA in Tennessee.

Dr. Haddock served as chair of the Tennessee Society of CPAs and the Educational & Memorial Foundation of the TSCPAs for 2012–2013 and a member of AICPA Council. He is a frequent speaker for Continuing Professional Education programs.

Courtesy of Michael J. Farina

MICHAEL J. FARINA is professor of accounting and finance at Cerritos College in California. Prior to joining Cerritos College, Professor Farina was a manager in the audit department at a large multinational firm of certified public accountants and held management positions with other companies in private industry.

He received an AA in business administration from Cerritos College; a BA in business administration from California State University, Fullerton; and an MBA from the University of California, Irvine. Professor Farina is a member of Beta Gamma Sigma, an honorary fraternity for graduate business students. He is a licensed certified public accountant in California and a member of the American Institute of Certified Public Accountants and the California Society of Certified Public Accountants. Professor Farina is also a Chartered Global Management Accountant, a designation bestowed by a joint venture of the American Institute of Certified Public Accountants and the Chartered Institute of Management Accountants.

Professor Farina has received two Outstanding Faculty awards from Cerritos College. Professor Farina was the co-chair of the Accounting and Finance Department at Cerritos College for over 20 years.

Price/Haddock/Farina

© Satoshi Muramastu/Getty Images

For students just embarking on a college career, an accounting course can seem daunting, like a rushing river with no clear path to the other side. As the most trusted and readable text on the market, *College Accounting* by Price, Haddock, and Farina presents material in a way that will help students understand the content better and more quickly. Through proven pedagogy, time-tested and accurate problem material, and a straightforward approach to the basics of accounting, Price/Haddock/Farina **bridges the rushing river**, offering first-time accounting students a path to understanding and mastery.

Whether a student is taking the course in preparation for a four-year degree or as the first step to a career in business, Price/Haddock/Farina guides him or her over the bridge to success. The authors represent the breadth of educational environments—a community college, a career school, and a four-year university—ensuring that the text is appropriate for all student populations. Throughout, they have adhered to a common philosophy about textbooks: they should be readable, contain many opportunities for practice, and be able to make accounting relevant for all.

New to the Fifteenth Edition

- **Chapter openers** have been revised featuring companies such as: Apple, AT&T, Bed, Bath & Beyond, Boeing, JP Morgan Chase & Co., Costco, Deloitte, Dr Pepper Snapple, Facebook, Ford, H&R Block, S&P Global, Southwest, Starbucks, Uber, and UPS, and the Financial Accounting Standards Board.
- **Real-world examples** throughout the text have been updated.
- **End-of-chapter** exercises, problems, and critical thinking problems have been revised and updated throughout the text.
- **Mini-Practice Sets** have been revised and updated.
- **Financial Statement Analysis Questions** have been updated to include the latest financial data in the Business Connections section.
- **Student quizzes** have been updated and are now available in Connect.
- **Chapter 9 NEW** appendix on the perpetual inventory system, complete with exercises and problems focused on perpetual inventory.
- **Chapter 10** Updates for the latest earnings base for the Social Security tax and minimum hourly rate of pay added. Sidebar comments revised for the Affordable Care Act, and sidebar alert added on the 2016 overtime changes to the Fair Labor Standards Act.
- **Chapter 11** The section on reporting and paying state unemployment taxes has been completely revised.

McGraw Hill Education **connect**®

Required=Results

©Getty Images/iStockphoto

McGraw-Hill Connect®
Learn without Limits

Connect is a teaching and learning platform that is proven to deliver better results for students and instructors.

Connect empowers students by continually adapting to deliver precisely what they need, when they need it, and how they need it, so your class time is more engaging and effective.

Connect's Impact on Retention Rates, Pass Rates, and Average Exam Scores

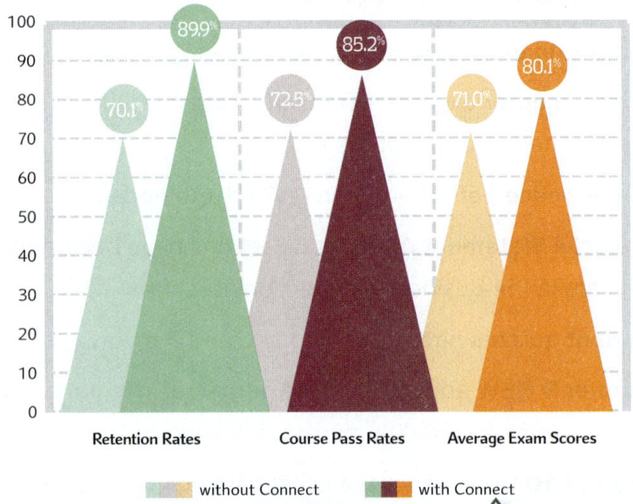

Using **Connect** improves passing rates by **12.7%** and retention by **19.8%.**

73% of instructors who use **Connect** require it; instructor satisfaction **increases** by 28% when **Connect** is required.

Analytics

Connect Insight®

Connect Insight is Connect's new one-of-a-kind visual analytics dashboard that provides at-a-glance information regarding student performance, which is immediately actionable. By presenting assignment, assessment, and topical performance results together with a time metric that is easily visible for aggregate or individual results, Connect Insight gives the user the ability to take a just-in-time approach to teaching and learning, which was never before available. Connect Insight presents data that helps instructors improve class performance in a way that is efficient and effective.

Impact on Final Course Grade Distribution

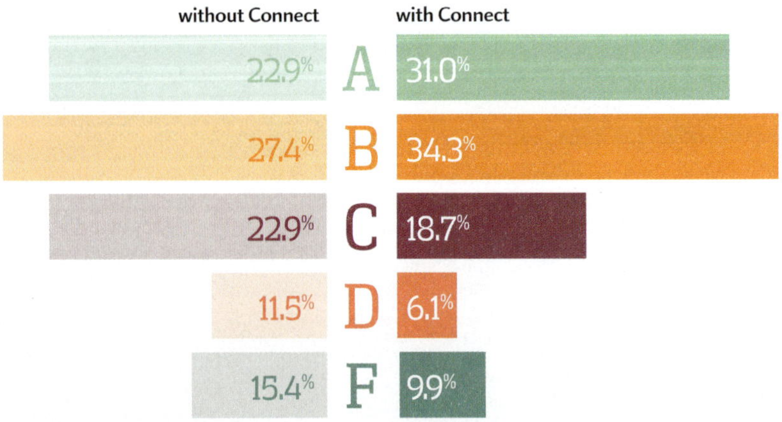

Adaptive

©Getty Images/iStockphoto

THE **ADAPTIVE** **READING EXPERIENCE** DESIGNED TO TRANSFORM THE WAY STUDENTS READ

More students earn **A's** and **B's** when they use McGraw-Hill Education **Adaptive** products.

SmartBook®

Proven to help students improve grades and study more efficiently, SmartBook contains the same content within the print book, but actively tailors that content to the needs of the individual. SmartBook's adaptive technology provides precise, personalized instruction on what the student should do next, guiding the student to master and remember key concepts, targeting gaps in knowledge and offering customized feedback, and driving the student toward comprehension and retention of the subject matter. Available on smartphones and tablets, SmartBook puts learning at the student's fingertips—anywhere, anytime.

Over **5.7 billion questions** have been answered, making McGraw-Hill Education products more intelligent, reliable, and precise.

www.mheducation.com

STUDENTS WANT SMARTBOOK®

95% of students reported **SmartBook** to be a more effective way of reading material

100% of students want to use the Practice Quiz feature available within **SmartBook** to help them study

100% of students reported having reliable access to off-campus wifi

90% of students say they would purchase **SmartBook** over print alone

95% reported that **SmartBook** would impact their study skills in a positive way

Mc Graw Hill Education

*Findings based on a 2015 focus group survey at Pellissippi State Community College administered by McGraw-Hill Education

Acknowledgments

The authors are deeply grateful to the following accounting educators for their input during development of *College Accounting*. The feedback from these knowledgeable instructors provided the authors with valuable assistance in meeting the changing needs of the college accounting classroom.

Cornelia Alsheimer,
Santa Barbara City College

Julia Angel,
North Arkansas College

James R. Armbrester,
Lawson State Community College–Bessemer Campus

Laura Bantz,
McHenry County College

Victoria Bentz,
Yavapai College

Anne Bikofsky,
College of Westchester

David Bland,
Cape Fear Community College

Patrick Borja,
Citrus College

Kathy Bowen,
Murray State College

Gerald Caton,
Yavapai College

Steven L. Christian,
Jackson Community College

Marilyn Ciolino,
Delgado Community College

Jean Condon,
Mid-Plains Community College Area (Nebraska)

Joan Cook,
Milwaukee Area Technical College

Gisela Dicklin,
Edmonds Community College

Michael Discello,
Pittsburgh Technical Institute

Sid Downey,
Cochise College

Steven Ernest,
Baton Rouge Community College

Ann Esarco,
McHenry County College

Paul Fisher,
Rogue Community College

Allen Ford,
Institute for the Deaf, Rochester Institute of Technology

Jeff Forrest,
Saint Louis Community College

David Forsyth,
Palomar College

Mark Fronke,
Cerritos College

Nancy Goehring,
Monterey Peninsula College

Renee Goffinet,
Spokane Community College

Jane Goforth,
North Seattle Community College

Lori Grady,
Buck County Community College

Gretchen Graham,
Community College of Allegheny County

Marina Grau,
Houston Community College

Chad Grooms,
Gateway Community and Technical College

David Grooms,
Maui Community College

Sue Gudmunson,
Lewis-Clark State College

Becky Hancock,
El Paso Community College

Christina Hata,
Miracosta College

Scott Hays,
Central Oregon Community College

Mary Jane Hollars,
Vincennes University

R. Stephen Holman,
Elizabethtown Community and Technical College

Ray Ingram,
Southwest Georgia Technical College

Dennis Jirkovsky,
Indiana Business College

Stacy Johnson,
Iowa Central Community College

Jane Jones,
Mountain Empire Community College

Dmitriy Kalyagin,
Chabot College

Norm Katz,
National College–Stow

Sandra Kemper,
Front Range Community College

Patty Kolarik,
Hutchinson Community College

Elida Kraja,
Saint Louis Community College–Flors Valley

Greg Lauer,
North Iowa Area Community College

David Laurel,
South Texas College

Thomas E. Lynch,
Hocking College

Josephine Mathias,
Mercer County Community College

Roger McMillian,
Mineral Area College

Jim Meir,
Cleveland State Community College

Michelle Meyer,
Joliet Junior College

John Miller,
Metropolitan Community College

Lora Miller,
Centura College

Peter Neshwat,
Brookline College

Marc Newman,
Hocking Technical College

Anthony Newton,
Highline Community College

Kenneth Newton,
Cleveland State Community College

Jon Nitschke,
Montana State University

Joel Peralto,
University of Hawaii–Hawaii Community College

Shirley Powell,
Arkansas State University

Carol Reinke,
Empire College

Barbara Rice,
Gateway Community and Technical College

Reynold Robles,
Texas State Technical College–Harlingen

Morgan Rockett,
Moberly Area Community College

Joan Ryan,
Clackamas Community College

Patricia Scales,
Brookstone College

Michael Schaub,
Shasta College

Tom Snavely,
Yavapai College

Rick Street,
Spokane Community College

Domenico Tavella,
Pittsburgh Technical Institute

Judy Toland,
Bucks County Community College

Donald Townsend,
Forsyth Technical Community College

Patricia Walczak,
Lansing Community College

Linda Whitten,
Skyline College

Thank You . . .

WE ARE GRATEFUL for the outstanding support from McGraw-Hill Education. In particular, we would like to thank Tim Vertovec, managing director; Steve Schuetz, executive brand manager; Michael McCormick, product developer; Lori Koetters and Angela Norris, content project managers; Laura Fuller, buyer; Matt Diamond, designer; and Ann Marie Jannette and Shannon Manderscheid, content licensing specialists.

Finally, we would like to thank our supplement authors and accuracy checkers: Helen Roybark, Radford University; David Krug, Johnson County Community College; Mark McCarthy, East Carolina University; Debra Johnson, Cerritos College; Anna Boulware, St. Charles Community College; Linda Muren, Cuyahoga Community College; Jeanine Metzler, Northampton Community College; Dominique Svarc, William Rainey Harper College; Jeannie Folk, College of DuPage; Kathleen O'Donnell, Onongada Community College; Jason Bess, Stautzenberger College; Beth Woods; Carol Yacht; Linda Flowers, Houston Community College; Matt Lowenkron; Renee Goffinet, Spokane Community College; and Teresa Alenikov, Cerritos College.

John Price • David Haddock • Michael Farina

> The Price *College Accounting* textbook is a well-written and planned-out approach to a college accounting approach. It goes into more detail and coverage of topics than most college accounting textbooks that I have seen. Each chapter includes great examples and transactional analysis as the topics progress.
>
> —Roger McMillian
> Mineral Area College

Brief Contents

Contents

Chapter 3

Chapter 4

Accounting: The Language of Business

Chapter 1

www.uber.com

© MikeDotta/Shutterstock

How do you get from the airport to your hotel when traveling on business? How do you get home from a party when it is not safe for you to drive? How do you get into the downtown business district for a meeting when parking is difficult and expensive? How do you get to any destination when taking your own vehicle is not convenient or possible? Taxis are not always available or affordable and public transportation is difficult when in an unfamiliar city. Uber is an alternative.

Uber is a smartphone app used to summon personal transportation on an as-needed basis. Started in 2009 in San Francisco, California, as an alternative to taxis, consumers install an app on their smartphone that allows them to request transportation from Uber drivers, who use their own vehicles. Uber quickly spread across the United States and expanded internationally in 2012. By the spring of 2015, Uber was available in over 300 cities and 50 countries. By late 2015, Uber was estimated to have a net worth over $50 billion.

In 2015, Uber drivers are estimated to earn $10.8 billion, of which Uber keeps 20% as its revenue, making its estimated revenue in 2015 approximately $2 billion. As Uber continues to grow and seek additional investment funding, accountants are pivotal in tracking and reporting the company's financial results and position in terms of revenues earned, expenses used, assets owned, and liabilities owed as well as calculating the company's net income (revenues − expenses) and net worth (assets − liabilities). Accountants are essential to the company's continued growth and success by providing financial information necessary for decision making.

thinking critically

Can you think of any organizations that would be interested in how Uber is performing?

LEARNING OBJECTIVES

1-1 Define accounting.

1-2 Identify and discuss career opportunities in accounting.

1-3 Identify the users of financial information.

1-4 Compare and contrast the three types of business entities.

1-5 Describe the process used to develop generally accepted accounting principles.

1-6 Define the accounting terms new to this chapter.

NEW TERMS

- accounting
- Accounting Standards Codification
- Accounting Standards Update
- accounting system
- auditing
- auditor's report
- certified public accountant (CPA)
- corporation
- creditor
- discussion memorandum
- economic entity
- entity
- exposure draft
- financial statements
- generally accepted accounting principles (GAAP)
- governmental accounting
- international accounting
- management advisory services
- managerial accounting
- partnership
- public accountants
- separate entity assumption
- social entity
- sole proprietorship
- Statements of Financial Accounting Standards
- stock
- stockholders
- tax accounting

Section 1

SECTION OBJECTIVES	TERMS TO LEARN
>> 1-1 Define accounting. WHY IT'S IMPORTANT Business transactions affect many aspects of our lives. >> 1-2 Identify and discuss career opportunities in accounting. WHY IT'S IMPORTANT There's something for everyone in the field of accounting. Accounting professionals are found in every workplace from public accounting firms to government agencies, from corporations to nonprofit organizations. >> 1-3 Identify the users of financial information. WHY IT'S IMPORTANT A wide variety of individuals and businesses depend on financial information to make decisions.	accounting accounting system auditing certified public accountant (CPA) financial statements governmental accounting management advisory services managerial accounting public accountants tax accounting

What Is Accounting?

Accounting provides financial information about a business or a nonprofit organization. Owners, managers, investors, and other interested parties need financial information in order to make decisions. Because accounting is used to communicate financial information, it is often called the "language of business."

The Need for Financial Information

Suppose a relative leaves you a substantial sum of money and you decide to carry out your lifelong dream of opening a small sportswear shop. You rent space in a local shopping center, purchase fixtures and equipment, purchase goods to sell, hire salespeople, and open the store to customers. Before long you realize that, to run your business successfully, you need financial information about the business. You probably need information that provides answers to the following questions:

- How much cash does the business have?
- How much money do customers owe the business?
- What is the cost of the merchandise sold?
- What is the change in sales volume?
- How much money is owed to suppliers?
- What is the profit or loss?

As your business grows, you will need even more financial information to evaluate the firm's performance and make decisions about the future. An efficient accounting system allows owners and managers to quickly obtain a wide range of useful information. The need for timely information is one reason that businesses have an accounting system directed by a professional staff.

>> 1-1 OBJECTIVE
Define accounting.

Accounting Defined

Accounting is the process by which financial information about a business is recorded, classified, summarized, interpreted, and communicated to owners, managers, and other interested parties. An **accounting system** is designed to accumulate data about a firm's financial affairs, classify the data in a meaningful way, and summarize it in periodic reports called **financial statements.** Owners and managers obtain a lot of information from financial statements. The accountant:

- establishes the records and procedures that make up the accounting system,
- supervises the operations of the system,
- interprets the resulting financial information.

Most owners and managers rely heavily on the accountant's judgment and knowledge when making financial decisions.

Accounting Careers

>> **1-2 OBJECTIVE**
Identify and discuss career opportunities in accounting.

Many jobs are available in the accounting profession, and they require varying amounts of education and experience. Bookkeepers and accountants are responsible for keeping records and providing financial information about the business. Generally, bookkeepers are responsible for recording business transactions. In large firms, bookkeepers may also supervise the work of accounting clerks. Accounting clerks are responsible for the recordkeeping part of the accounting system—perhaps payroll, accounts receivable, or accounts payable. Accountants usually supervise bookkeepers and prepare the financial statements and reports of the business.

Newspapers and websites often have job listings for accounting clerks, bookkeepers, and accountants:

- Accounting clerk positions usually require one to two accounting courses and little or no experience.
- Bookkeeper positions usually require one to two years of accounting education plus experience as an accounting clerk.
- Accountant positions usually require a bachelor's degree but are sometimes filled by experienced bookkeepers or individuals with a two-year college degree. Most entry-level accountant positions do not have an experience requirement. Both the education and experience requirements for accountant positions vary according to the size of the firm.

Accountants usually choose to practice in one of three areas:

- public accounting
- managerial accounting
- governmental accounting

Table 1.1 shows a list of occupations with job duties that are similar to those of accountants and auditors.

PUBLIC ACCOUNTING

Public accountants work for public accounting firms. Public accounting firms provide accounting services for other companies. Usually they offer three services:

- auditing
- tax accounting
- management advisory services

The largest public accounting firms in the United States are called the "Big Four." The Big Four are Deloitte & Touche, Ernst & Young, KPMG, and PricewaterhouseCoopers.

Many public accountants are **certified public accountants (CPAs).** To become a CPA, an individual must have a certain number of college credits in accounting courses, demonstrate good personal character, pass the Uniform CPA Examination, and fulfill the experience requirements of the state of practice. CPAs must follow the professional code of ethics.

Auditing is the review of financial statements to assess their fairness and adherence to generally accepted accounting principles. Accountants who are CPAs perform financial audits.

ABOUT **ACCOUNTING**

Accounting Services
The role of the CPA is expanding. In the past, accounting firms handled audits and taxes. Today accountants provide a wide range of services, including financial planning, investment advice, accounting and tax software advice, and profitability consulting. Accountants provide clients with information and advice on electronic business, health care performance measurement, risk assessment, business performance measurement, and information system reliability.

TABLE 1.1 Occupations with Similar Job Duties to Accountants and Auditors

Occupation	Job Duties	Entry-Level Education
Bookkeeping, Accounting, and Auditing Clerks	Bookkeeping, accounting, and auditing clerks produce financial records for organizations. They record financial transactions, update statements, and check financial records for accuracy.	High school diploma or equivalent
Budget Analysts	Budget analysts help public and private institutions organize their finances. They prepare budget reports and monitor institutional spending.	Bachelor's degree
Cost Estimators	Cost estimators collect and analyze data to estimate the time, money, resources, and labor required for product manufacturing, construction projects, or services. Some specialize in a particular industry or product type.	Bachelor's degree
Financial Analysts	Financial analysts provide guidance to businesses and individuals making investment decisions. They assess the performance of stocks, bonds, and other types of investments.	Bachelor's degree
Financial Managers	Financial managers are responsible for the financial health of an organization. They produce financial reports, direct investment activities, and develop strategies and plans for the long-term financial goals of their organization.	Bachelor's degree
Management Analysts	Management analysts, often called management consultants, propose ways to improve an organization's efficiency. They advise managers on how to make organizations more profitable through reduced costs and increased revenues.	Bachelor's degree
Personal Financial Advisors	Personal financial advisors give financial advice to people. They help with investments, taxes, and insurance decisions.	Bachelor's degree
Postsecondary Teachers	Postsecondary teachers instruct students in a wide variety of academic and vocational subjects beyond the high school level. They also conduct research and publish scholarly papers and books.	Doctoral or professional degree
Tax Examiners and Collectors, and Revenue Agents	Tax examiners and collectors, and revenue agents ensure that governments get their tax money from businesses and citizens. They review tax returns, conduct audits, identify taxes owed, and collect overdue tax payments.	Bachelor's degree
Top Executives	Top executives devise strategies and policies to ensure that an organization meets its goals. They plan, direct, and coordinate operational activities of companies and public or private-sector organizations.	Bachelor's degree

Source: Bureau of Labor Statistics, U.S. Department of Labor, *Occupational Outlook Handbook,* 2014–15 Edition, Accountants and Auditors, on the Internet at http://www.bls.gov/ooh/business-and-financial/accountants-and-auditors.htm (visited September 23, 2015).

Tax accounting involves tax compliance and tax planning. *Tax compliance* deals with the preparation of tax returns and the audit of those returns. *Tax planning* involves giving advice to clients on how to structure their financial affairs in order to reduce their tax liability.

Management advisory services involve helping clients improve their information systems or their business performance.

MANAGERIAL ACCOUNTING

Managerial accounting, also referred to as *private accounting,* involves working for a single business in industry. Managerial accountants perform a wide range of activities, including:

- establishing accounting policies,
- managing the accounting system,
- preparing financial statements,
- interpreting financial information,
- providing financial advice to management,
- preparing tax forms,
- performing tax planning services,
- preparing internal reports for management.

GOVERNMENTAL ACCOUNTING

Governmental accounting involves keeping financial records and preparing financial reports as part of the staff of federal, state, or local governmental units. Governmental units do not earn profits. However, governmental units receive and pay out huge amounts of money and need procedures for recording and managing this money.

Some governmental agencies hire accountants to audit the financial statements and records of the businesses under their jurisdiction and to uncover possible violations of the law. The Securities and Exchange Commission, the Internal Revenue Service, the Federal Bureau of Investigation, and Homeland Security employ a large number of accountants.

Users of Financial Information

>> **1-3 OBJECTIVE**
Identify the users of financial information.

The results of the accounting process are communicated to many individuals and organizations. Who are these individuals and organizations, and why do they want financial information about a particular firm?

OWNERS AND MANAGERS

Assume your sportswear shop is in full operation. One user of financial information about the business is you, the owner. You need information that will help you evaluate the results of your operations as well as plan and make decisions for the future. Questions such as the following are difficult to answer without financial information:

- Should you drop from the product line the long-sleeved pullover that is not selling well, or should you just reduce the price?
- How much should you charge for the denim jacket that you are adding to the product line?
- How much should you spend on advertising?
- How does this month's profit compare with last month's profit?
- Should you open a new store?

SUPPLIERS

A number of other people are interested in the financial information about your business. For example, businesses that supply you with sportswear need to assess the ability of your firm to pay its bills. They also need to set a credit limit for your firm.

BANKS

What if you decide to ask your bank for a loan so that you can open a new store? The bank needs to be sure that your firm will repay the loan on time. The bank will ask for financial information prepared by your accountant. Based on this information, the bank will decide whether to make the loan and the terms of the loan.

TAX AUTHORITIES

The Internal Revenue Service (IRS) and other state and local tax authorities are interested in financial information about your firm. This information is used to determine the tax base:

- Income taxes are based on taxable income.
- Sales taxes are based on sales income.
- Property taxes are based on the assessed value of buildings, equipment, and inventory (the goods available for sale).

The accounting process provides all of this information.

REGULATORY AGENCIES AND INVESTORS

If an industry is regulated by a governmental agency, businesses in that industry have to supply financial information to the regulating agency. For example, the Federal Communications Commission receives financial information from radio and television stations. The Securities and Exchange Commission (SEC) oversees the financial information provided by publicly owned corporations to their investors and potential investors. Publicly owned corporations trade their shares on stock exchanges and in over-the-counter markets. Congress passed the Securities Act of 1933 and the Securities Exchange Act of 1934 in order to protect those who invest in publicly owned corporations.

The SEC is responsible for reviewing the accounting methods used by publicly owned corporations. The SEC has delegated this review to the accounting profession but still has the final say on any financial accounting issue faced by publicly owned corporations. If the SEC does not agree with the reporting that results from an accounting method, the SEC can suspend trading of a company's shares on the stock exchanges.

Major changes were made to the regulatory environment in the accounting profession with the passage of the Public Company Accounting Reform and Investor Protection Act of 2002 (also known as the Sarbanes-Oxley Act) that was signed into law by President George W. Bush on August 2, 2002. The Act was the most far-reaching regulatory crackdown on corporate fraud and corruption since the creation of the Securities and Exchange Commission in 1934.

The Sarbanes-Oxley Act was passed in response to the wave of corporate accounting scandals starting with the demise of Enron Corporation in 2001, the arrest of top executives at WorldCom and Adelphia Communications Corporation, and ultimately the demise of Arthur Andersen, an international public accounting firm formerly a member of the "Big Five." Arthur Andersen was found guilty of an obstruction of justice charge after admitting that the firm destroyed thousands of documents and electronic files related to the Enron audit engagement. Although on May 31, 2008, the Supreme Court of the United States reversed the Andersen guilty verdict, Arthur Andersen has not returned as a viable business. As a result of the demise of Arthur Andersen, the "Big Five" are now the "Big Four."

The Act significantly tightens regulation of financial reporting by publicly held companies and their accountants and auditors. The Sarbanes-Oxley Act created a five-member Public Company Accounting Oversight Board. The Board has investigative and enforcement powers to oversee the accounting profession and to discipline corrupt accountants and auditors. The Securities and Exchange Commission oversees the Board. Two members of the Board are certified public accountants, to regulate the accountants who audit public companies, and the remaining three must not be and cannot have been CPAs. The chair of the Board may be held by one of the CPA members, provided that the individual has not been engaged as a practicing CPA for five years.

Major provisions of the Act include rules on consulting services, auditor rotation, criminal penalties, corporate governance, and securities regulation. The Act prohibits accountants from offering a broad range of consulting services to publicly traded companies that they audit and requires accounting firms to change the lead audit or coordinating partner and the reviewing partner for a company every five years. Additionally, it is a felony to "knowingly" destroy or create documents to "impede, obstruct or influence" any existing or contemplated federal investigation. Auditors are also required to maintain all audit or review work papers for seven years. Criminal penalties, up to 20 years in prison, are imposed for obstruction of justice and the Act raises the maximum sentence for defrauding pension funds to 10 years.

Chief executives and chief financial officers of publicly traded corporations are now required to certify their financial statements and these executives will face up to 20 years in prison if they "knowingly or willfully" allow materially misleading information into their financial statements. Companies must also disclose, as quickly as possible, material changes in their financial position. Wall Street investment firms are prohibited from retaliating against analysts who criticize investment-banking clients of the firm. The Act contains a provision with broad new protection for whistle-blowers and lengthens the time that investors have to file lawsuits against corporations for securities fraud.

By narrowing the type of consulting services that accountants can provide to companies that they audit, requiring auditor rotation, and imposing stiff criminal penalties for violation of the Act, it appears that this legislation will significantly help to restore public confidence in financial statements and markets and change the regulatory environment in which accountants operate.

CUSTOMERS

Customers pay special attention to financial information about the firms with which they do business. For example, before a business spends a lot of money on a new computer system,

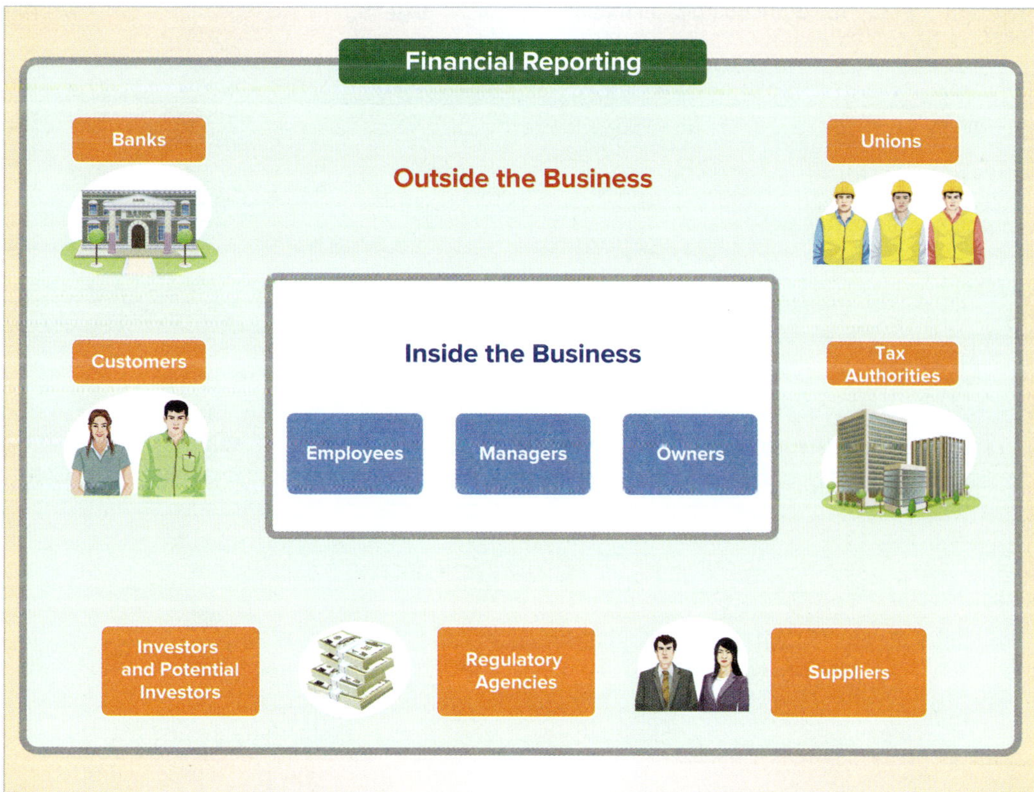

FIGURE 1.1

Users of Financial Information

the business wants to know that the computer manufacturer will be around for the next several years in order to service the computer, replace parts, and provide additional components. The business analyzes the financial information about the computer manufacturer in order to determine its economic health and the likelihood that it will remain in business.

EMPLOYEES AND UNIONS

Often employees are interested in the financial information of the business that employs them. Employees who are members of a profit-sharing plan pay close attention to the financial results because they affect employee income. Employees who are members of a labor union use financial information about the firm to negotiate wages and benefits.

Figure 1.1 illustrates different financial information users. As you learn about the accounting process, you will appreciate why financial information is so important to these individuals and organizations. You will learn how financial information meets users' needs.

Section 1 Self Review

QUESTIONS

1. What are the names of three accounting job positions?
2. Why is accounting called the "language of business"?
3. What are financial statements?

EXERCISES

4. Which organization has the final say on financial accounting issues faced by publicly owned corporations?
   a. Securities and Exchange Commission
   b. Federal Trade Commission
   c. U.S. Treasury Department
   d. Internal Revenue Service
5. One requirement for becoming a CPA is to pass the:
   a. Final CPA Examination
   b. SEC Accounting Examination
   c. Uniform CPA Examination
   d. State Board Examination

ANALYSIS

6. As the owner of a small business, you have decided to expand your locations. In order to expand, you must apply for a loan. What type of information will you need to provide to the lender?

(Answers to Section 1 Self Review are on page 18.)

Section 2

SECTION OBJECTIVES	TERMS TO LEARN
>> 1-4 Compare and contrast the three types of business entities. WHY IT'S IMPORTANT Each type of business entity requires unique legal and accounting considerations. >> 1-5 Describe the process used to develop generally accepted accounting principles. WHY IT'S IMPORTANT Accounting professionals are required to use common standards and principles in order to produce reliable financial information.	Accounting Standards Codification Accounting Standards Update auditor's report corporation creditor discussion memorandum economic entity entity exposure draft generally accepted accounting principles (GAAP) international accounting partnership separate entity assumption social entity sole proprietorship Statements of Financial Accounting Standards stock stockholders

Business and Accounting

The accounting process involves recording, classifying, summarizing, interpreting, and communicating financial information about an economic or social entity. An **entity** is recognized as having its own separate identity. An entity may be an individual, a town, a university, or a business. The term **economic entity** usually refers to a business or organization whose major purpose is to produce a profit for its owners. **Social entities** are nonprofit organizations, such as cities, public schools, and public hospitals. This book focuses on the accounting process for businesses, but keep in mind that nonprofit organizations also need financial information.

Types of Business Entities

>> 1-4 OBJECTIVE
Compare and contrast the three types of business entities.

The three major legal forms of business entity are the sole proprietorship, the partnership, and the corporation. In general, the accounting process is the same for all three forms of business. Later in the book you will study the different ways certain transactions are handled depending on the type of business entity. For now, however, you will learn about the different types of business entities.

SOLE PROPRIETORSHIPS

A **sole proprietorship** is a business entity owned by one person. The life of the business ends when the owner is no longer willing or able to keep the business going. Many small businesses are operated as sole proprietorships.

The owner of a sole proprietorship is legally responsible for the debts and taxes of the business. If the business is unable to pay its debts, the **creditors** (those people, companies, or government agencies to whom the business owes money) can turn to the owner for payment. The owner may have to pay the debts of the business from personal resources, including personal savings. When the time comes to pay income taxes, the owner's income and the income of the business are combined to compute the total tax responsibility of the owner.

It is important that the business transactions be kept separate from the owner's personal transactions. If the owner's personal transactions are mixed with those of the business, it will be difficult to measure the performance of the business. The term **separate entity assumption** describes the concept of keeping the firm's financial records separate from the owner's personal financial records.

PARTNERSHIPS

A **partnership** is a business entity owned by two or more people. The partnership structure is common in businesses that offer professional services, such as law firms, accounting firms, architectural firms, medical practices, and dental practices. At the beginning of the partnership, two or more individuals enter into a contract that details the rights, obligations, and limitations of each partner, including:

- the amount each partner will contribute to the business,
- each partner's percentage of ownership,
- each partner's share of the profits,
- the duties each partner will perform,
- the responsibility each partner has for the amounts owed by the business to creditors and tax authorities.

The partners choose how to share the ownership and profits of the business. They may share equally or in any proportion agreed upon in the contract. When a partner leaves, the partnership is dissolved and a new partnership may be formed with the remaining partners.

Partners are individually, and as a group, responsible for the debts and taxes of the partnership. If the partnership is unable to pay its debts or taxes, the partners' personal property, including personal bank accounts, may be used to provide payment. It is important that partnership transactions be kept separate from the personal financial transactions of the partners.

Under the Limited Liability Partnership Act of most states, a Limited Liability Partnership (LLP) may be formed. An LLP is a general partnership that provides some limited liability for all partners. LLP partners are responsible and have liability for their own actions and the actions of those under their control or supervision. They are not liable for the actions or malfeasance of another partner. Except for the limited liability aspect, LLPs generally have the same characteristics, advantages, and disadvantages as any other partnership.

important!

Separate Entity Assumption

For *accounting* purposes, all forms of business are considered separate entities from their owners. However, the corporation is the only form of business that is a separate *legal* entity.

CORPORATIONS

A **corporation** is a business entity that is separate from its owners. A corporation has a legal right to own property and do business in its own name. Corporations are very different from sole proprietorships and partnerships.

Stock, issued in the form of stock certificates, represents the ownership of the corporation. Corporations may be *privately* or *publicly* owned. Privately owned corporations are also called *closely held* corporations. The ownership of privately owned corporations is limited to specific individuals, usually family members. Stock of closely held corporations is not traded on an exchange. In contrast, stock of publicly owned corporations is bought and sold on stock exchanges and in over-the-counter markets. Most large corporations have issued (sold) thousands of shares of stock.

An owner's share of the corporation is determined by the number of shares of stock held by the owner compared to the total number of shares issued by the corporation. Assume that Hector Flores owns 600 shares of Sample Corporation. If Sample Corporation has issued 2,000 shares of stock, Flores owns 30 percent of the corporation (600 shares ÷ 2,000 shares = 0.30 *or* 30%). Some corporate decisions require a vote by the owners. For Sample Corporation, Flores has 600 votes, one for each share of stock that he owns. The other owners have 1,400 votes.

> **Subchapter S corporations, also known as S corporations, are entities formed as corporations that meet the requirements of Subchapter S of the Internal Revenue Code to be treated essentially as a partnership so the corporation pays no income tax. Instead, shareholders include their share of corporate profits, and any items that require special tax treatment, on their individual income tax returns. Otherwise, S corporations have all of the characteristics of regular corporations. The advantage of the S corporation is that the owners have limited liability and avoid double taxation.**

One of the advantages of the corporate form of business is the indefinite life of the corporation. A sole proprietorship ends when the owner dies or discontinues the business. A partnership ends on the death or withdrawal of a partner. In contrast, a corporation does not end when ownership changes. Some corporations have new owners daily because their shares are actively traded (sold) on stock exchanges.

Corporate owners, called **stockholders** or *shareholders,* are not personally responsible for the debts or taxes of the corporation. If the corporation is unable to pay its bills, the most stockholders can lose is their investment in the corporation. In other words, the stockholders will not lose more than the cost of the shares of stock.

The accounting process for the corporate entity, like that of the sole proprietorship and the partnership, is separate from the financial affairs of its owners. Usually this separation is easy to maintain. Most stockholders do not participate in the day-to-day operations of the business.

Table 1.2 summarizes the business characteristics for sole proprietorships, partnerships, and corporations.

Generally Accepted Accounting Principles

The Securities and Exchange Commission has the final say on matters of financial reporting by publicly owned corporations. The SEC has delegated the job of determining proper accounting standards to the accounting profession. However, the SEC sometimes overrides decisions

TABLE 1.2

Major Characteristics of Business Entities

Characteristic	Type of Business Entity		
	Sole Proprietorship	Partnership	Corporation
Ownership	One owner	Two or more owners	One or more owners, even thousands
Life of the business	Ends when the owner dies, is unable to carry on operations, or decides to close the firm	Ends when one or more partners withdraw, when a partner dies, or when the partners decide to close the firm	Can continue indefinitely; ends only when the business goes bankrupt or when the stockholders vote to liquidate
Responsibility for debts of the business	Owner is responsible for the firm's debt when the firm is unable to pay	Partners are responsible individually and jointly for the firm's debts when the firm is unable to pay	Stockholders are not responsible for the firm's debts; they can lose only the amount they invested

the accounting profession makes. To fulfill its responsibility, the accounting profession has developed, and continues to develop, **generally accepted accounting principles (GAAP).** Generally accepted accounting principles must be followed by publicly owned companies unless they can show that doing so would produce information that is misleading.

>> **1-5 OBJECTIVE**
Describe the process used to develop generally accepted accounting principles.

THE DEVELOPMENT OF GENERALLY ACCEPTED ACCOUNTING PRINCIPLES

Generally accepted accounting principles are developed by the Financial Accounting Standards Board (FASB), which is composed of five full-time members. Prior to 2009, the FASB issued 168 **Statements of Financial Accounting Standards.** The FASB developed these statements and, before issuing them, obtained feedback from interested people and organizations.

First, the FASB wrote a **discussion memorandum** to explain the topic being considered. Then public hearings were held where interested parties could express their opinions, either orally or in writing. The groups that consistently expressed opinions about proposed FASB statements were the SEC, the American Institute of Certified Public Accountants (AICPA), public accounting firms, the American Accounting Association (AAA), and businesses with a direct interest in a particular statement.

The AICPA is a national association for certified public accountants. The AAA is a group of accounting educators. AAA members research possible effects of a proposed FASB statement and offer their opinions to the FASB.

After public hearings, the FASB released an **exposure draft,** which described the proposed statement. Then the FASB received and evaluated public comment about the exposure draft. Finally, FASB members voted on the statement. If at least four members approved, the statement was issued.

important!

GAAP

The SEC requires all publicly owned companies to follow generally accepted accounting principles. As new standards are developed or refined, accountants interpret the standards and adapt accounting practices to the new standards.

The above process was used until 2009. Effective July 1, 2009, the source of authoritative U.S. GAAP is the FASB **Accounting Standards Codification,** which are communicated through an **Accounting Standards Update (Update).** The Codification reorganizes U.S. GAAP pronouncements into approximately 90 accounting topics. It also includes relevant U.S. Securities and Exchange Commission guidance that follows the same topical structure in separate sections in the Codification.

Updates are now published on these accounting topics for all authoritative U.S. GAAP promulgated by the FASB, regardless of the form in which such guidance may have been issued prior to the release of the FASB Codification. An Update summarizes the key provisions of the project that led to the Update, details the specific amendments to the FASB Codification, and explains the basis for the Board's decision.

Accounting principles vary from country to country. **International accounting** is the study of the accounting principles used by different countries. In 1973, the International Accounting Standards Committee (IASC) was formed. Recently, the IASC's name was changed to the International Accounting Standards Board (IASB). The IASB deals with issues caused by the lack of uniform accounting principles. The IASB also makes recommendations to enhance comparability of reporting practices.

THE USE OF GENERALLY ACCEPTED ACCOUNTING PRINCIPLES

Every year, publicly traded companies submit financial statements to the SEC. The financial statements are audited by independent certified public accountants. The CPAs are called *independent* because they are not employees of the company being audited and they do not have a financial interest in the company. The financial statements include the auditor's report. The **auditor's report** contains the auditor's opinion about the fair presentation of the operating results and financial position of the business. The auditor's report also confirms that the financial information is prepared in conformity with generally accepted accounting principles. The financial statements and the auditor's report are made available to the public, including existing and potential stockholders.

MANAGERIAL IMPLICATIONS <<

FINANCIAL INFORMATION

- Managers of a business make sure that the firm's accounting system produces financial information that is timely, accurate, and fair.
- Financial statements should be based on generally accepted accounting principles.
- Each year a publicly traded company must submit financial statements, including an independent auditor's report, to the SEC.
- Internal reports for management need not follow generally accepted accounting principles but should provide useful information that will aid in monitoring and controlling operations.
- Financial information can help managers to control present operations, make decisions, and plan for the future.
- The sound use of financial information is essential to good management.

THINKING CRITICALLY

If you were a manager, how would you use financial information to make decisions?

Businesses and the environment in which they operate are constantly changing. The economy, technology, and laws change. Generally accepted accounting principles are changed and refined as accountants respond to the changing environment.

Section 2 Self Review

QUESTIONS

1. What are generally accepted accounting principles?
2. Why are generally accepted accounting principles needed?
3. How are generally accepted accounting principles developed?

EXERCISES

4. A nonprofit organization such as a public school is a(n):
   a. social unit
   b. economic unit
   c. social entity
   d. economic entity
5. You plan to open a business with two of your friends. You would like to form a corporation, but your friends prefer the partnership form of business. What are some of the advantages of the corporate form of business?
6. An organization that has two or more owners who are legally responsible for the debts and taxes of the business is a:
   a. social entity
   b. partnership
   c. sole proprietorship
   d. corporation

(Answers to Section 2 Self Review are on page 18.)

Review and Applications

1 Chapter REVIEW Chapter Summary

Accounting is often called the "language of business." The financial information about a business is communicated to interested parties in financial statements.

Learning Objectives

1-1 Define accounting.

Accounting is the process by which financial information about a business is recorded, classified, summarized, interpreted, and communicated to owners, managers, and other interested parties. Accurate accounting information is essential for making business decisions.

1-2 Identify and discuss career opportunities in accounting.

- There are many job opportunities in accounting.
- Accounting clerk positions, such as accounts receivable clerk, accounts payable clerk, and payroll clerk, require the least education and experience.
- Bookkeepers usually have experience as accounting clerks and a minimum of one to two years of accounting education.
- Most entry-level accounting positions require a college degree or significant experience as a bookkeeper.
- Accountants usually specialize in one of three major areas: public, managerial, or governmental accounting.
  - Some accountants work for public accounting firms and perform auditing, tax accounting, or management advisory functions.
  - Other accountants work in private industry where they set up and supervise accounting systems, prepare financial reports, prepare internal reports, or assist in determining the prices to charge for the firm's products.
  - Still other accountants work for government agencies. They keep track of public funds and expenditures, or they audit the financial records of businesses and individuals to determine whether the records are in compliance with regulatory laws, tax laws, and other laws. The Securities and Exchange Commission, the Internal Revenue Service, the Federal Bureau of Investigation, and Homeland Security employ many accountants.

1-3 Identify the users of financial information.

All types of businesses need and use financial information. Users of financial information include owners and managers, employees, suppliers, banks, tax authorities, regulatory agencies, and investors. Nonprofit organizations need similar financial information.

1-4 Compare and contrast the three types of business entities.

- A sole proprietorship is owned by one person. The owner is legally responsible for the debts and taxes of the business.
- A partnership is owned by two or more people. The owners are legally responsible for the debts and taxes of the business.
- A corporation is a separate legal entity from its owners.
- Note that all three types of business entities are considered separate entities for accounting purposes.

1-5 Describe the process used to develop generally accepted accounting principles.

- The SEC has delegated the authority to develop generally accepted accounting principles to the accounting profession. The Financial Accounting Standards Board handles this task. A series of steps used by the FASB includes issuing a discussion memorandum, an exposure draft, and a statement of principle.
- The SEC oversees the Public Company Accounting Oversight Board that was created by the Sarbanes-Oxley Act. The Board regulates financial reporting by accountants and auditors of publicly held companies.
- Each year, firms that sell stock on stock exchanges or in over-the-counter markets must publish audited financial reports that follow generally accepted accounting principles. They must submit their reports to the SEC. They must also make the reports available to stockholders.

1-6 Define the accounting terms new to this chapter.

Glossary

Accounting (p. 2) The process by which financial information about a business is recorded, classified, summarized, interpreted, and communicated to owners, managers, and other interested parties

Accounting Standards Codification (p. 12) The source of authoritative U.S. GAAP

Accounting Standards Update (p. 12) Changes to Accounting Standards Codification are communicated through Accounting Standards Update covering approximately 90 topics

Accounting system (p. 2) A process designed to accumulate, classify, and summarize financial data

Auditing (p. 3) The review of financial statements to assess their fairness and adherence to generally accepted accounting principles

Auditor's report (p. 12) An independent accountant's review of a firm's financial statements

Certified public accountant (CPA) (p. 3) An independent accountant who provides accounting services to the public for a fee

Corporation (p. 10) A publicly or privately owned business entity that is separate from its owners and has a legal right to own property and do business in its own name; stockholders are not responsible for the debts or taxes of the business

Creditor (p. 10) One to whom money is owed

Discussion memorandum (p. 12) An explanation of a topic under consideration by the Financial Accounting Standards Board

Economic entity (p. 9) A business or organization whose major purpose is to produce a profit for its owners

Entity (p. 9) Anything having its own separate identity, such as an individual, a town, a university, or a business

Exposure draft (p. 12) A proposed solution to a problem being considered by the Financial Accounting Standards Board

Financial statements (p. 3) Periodic reports of a firm's financial position or operating results

Generally accepted accounting principles (GAAP) (p. 12) Accounting standards developed and applied by professional accountants

Governmental accounting (p. 5) Accounting work performed for a federal, state, or local governmental unit

International accounting (p. 12) The study of accounting principles used by different countries

Management advisory services (p. 5) Services designed to help clients improve their information systems or their business performance

Managerial accounting (p. 5) Accounting work carried on by an accountant employed by a single business in industry

Partnership (p. 10) A business entity owned by two or more people who are legally responsible for the debts and taxes of the business

Public accountants (p. 3) Members of firms that perform accounting services for other companies

Separate entity assumption (p. 10) The concept of keeping a firm's financial records separate from the owner's personal financial records

Social entity (p. 9) A nonprofit organization, such as a city, public school, or public hospital

Sole proprietorship (p. 9) A business entity owned by one person, who is legally responsible for the debts and taxes of the business

Statements of Financial Accounting Standards (p. 12) Accounting principles established by the Financial Accounting Standards Board

Stock (p. 10) Certificates that represent ownership of a corporation

Stockholders (p. 11) The owners of a corporation; also called shareholders

Tax accounting (p. 5) A service that involves tax compliance and tax planning

Comprehensive **Self Review**

1. What is the purpose of accounting?
2. What does the accounting process involve?
3. What is the purpose of the auditor's report?
4. What are the three types of business entities?
5. How is the ownership of a corporation different from that of a sole proprietorship?

(Answers to Comprehensive Self Review are on page 18.)

Discussion Questions

1. What types of people or organizations are interested in financial information about a firm, and why are they interested in this information?
2. Why is it important for business records to be separate from the records of the business's owner or owners? What is the term accountants use to describe this separation of personal and business records?
3. What are the three types of business entities, and how do they differ?
4. What are the major functions or activities performed by accountants in private industry?
5. What is tax planning?
6. What types of services do public accountants provide?
7. What are the three major areas of accounting?
8. What is the purpose of the Financial Accounting Standards Board?
9. What groups consistently offer opinions about proposed FASB statements?
10. What is the function of the Securities and Exchange Commission?
11. What led to the passage of the Public Company Accounting Reform and Investor Protection Act of 2002?
12. What is the purpose of the Public Company Accounting Oversight Board?

PROBLEM

Critical Thinking Problem

Which Type of Business Entity?

Since graduating from college five years ago, you have worked for a national chain of men's clothing stores. You have held several positions within the company and are currently manager of a local branch store.

Over the past three years, you have observed a pattern in the purchases of men's suits. You establish that the majority of men's suit purchases are black, brown, blue, gray, and olive. You also noticed that French cuff shirts are now fashionable, but few stores carry a wide color selection. Since you have always wanted to be in business for yourself, you decide to open a shop that will sell suits that are black, brown, blue, gray, and olive and to carry a wide array of colors of French cuff shirts. Your store will also sell fashionable ties and cuff links. You have decided that your store will brand itself for focusing on men's fashion; therefore, the name for your store will be "The Style Shop." You have discussed your plan with a number of people in the industry and they believe your idea is a viable one and have encouraged you to pursue your dream of becoming an entrepreneur.

A new upscale outdoor shopping mall is opening nearby, and you have decided that now is the time to take the plunge and go into business for yourself. After developing a comprehensive business plan that includes marketing strategies and financial projections, you decide to open The Style Shop in the new mall.

One of the things you must decide in the process of transforming your idea into reality is the form of ownership for your new business. Should it be organized as a sole proprietorship, a partnership, or a corporation?

What advantages or disadvantages are there to each choice? What do you think of the proposed name for the business, The Style Shop? Use the chart below to organize your thoughts.

Business Entity	Advantages	Disadvantages
Sole Proprietorship		
Partnership		
Corporation		

BUSINESS CONNECTIONS

Know Accounting

Managerial | FOCUS

1. As an owner or manager of a business, what questions would you ask to judge the firm's performance, control operations, make decisions, and plan for the future?
2. Why is financial information important?
3. Besides earning a profit, what other objectives might a business have? Can financial information play an important role in these objectives?
4. What kind of problems can you foresee if a business owner and/or manager does not have a basic knowledge of accounting?
5. What would you tell a small business owner who says he does not see a need for an accounting system in his business because he closely supervises the day-to-day operations and knows exactly what is happening with the business?
6. What is the role of the manager versus the accountant?
7. Does a business owner/manager need to worry about the separate entity assumption? Why or why not?
8. Why are international accounting standards important to management?

To Tell or Not to Tell

Ethical | DILEMMA

You are employed as an accountant for Innovative Computing. Your company is in the process of signing a large contract with an electronics components supplier. You have a personal friend who works for the electronics components supplier, and you have personal knowledge that it has trouble paying its bills. Should you report this to your employer before the purchase?

Notes to Financial Statements

Financial Statement | ANALYSIS

Within a company's annual report, a section called "Notes to Consolidated Financial Statements" offers general information about the company along with detailed notes related to its financial statements.

Analyze Online: On the American Eagle Outfitters, Inc., website (www.ae.com), click on About AEO located at the bottom of the page. Then click on AE Investment Information.

Analyze:

1. What types of merchandise does this company sell?
2. Who are the potential users of the information presented? Why would this information be helpful to these users?

3. What age consumer does the company target?
4. Would American Eagle Outfitters, Inc., be considered an economic entity or a social entity? Why?

Determining Information

TEAMWORK

Restful Sleep Mattress Company is planning to expand into selling bedroom furniture. This expansion will require a loan from the bank. The bank has requested financial information. Discuss, in a group, the information the bank would require. What information, if any, would you not provide the bank?

FASB—What Is It?

Internet CONNECTION

Go to the FASB website at www.FASB.org. How many Accounting Standards Updates were issued in the current year? How are they cited?

Answers to **Self Reviews**

Answers to Section 1 Self Review

1. Clerk, bookkeeper, and accountant.
2. The results of the accounting process—financial statements—communicate essential information about a business to concerned individuals and organizations.
3. Periodic reports that summarize the financial affairs of a business.
4. **a.** Securities and Exchange Commission
5. **c.** Uniform CPA Examination
6. Current sales and expenses figures, anticipated sales and expenses, and the cost of the expansion.

Answers to Section 2 Self Review

1. Accounting standards that are changed and refined in response to changes in the environment in which businesses operate.
2. GAAP help to ensure that financial information fairly presents a firm's operating results and financial position.
3. The FASB develops proposed statements and solicits feedback from interested individuals, groups, and companies. The FASB evaluates the opinions received and votes on the statement.
4. **c.** social entity
5. The shareholders are not responsible for the debts and taxes of the corporation. Corporations can continue in existence indefinitely.
6. **b.** partnership

Answers to Comprehensive Self Review

1. To gather and communicate financial information about a business.
2. Recording, classifying, summarizing, interpreting, and communicating financial information about a business.
3. To obtain the objective opinion of a professional accountant from outside the company that the statements fairly present the operating results and financial position of the business and that the information was prepared according to GAAP.
4. Sole proprietorship, partnership, and corporation.
5. A sole proprietorship is a business entity owned by one person. A corporation is a separate legal entity that has a legal right to own property and do business in its own name.

Analyzing Business Transactions

Chapter 2

© AP Photo/Marcio Jose Sanchez.

www.southwest.com

Rollin King and Herb Kelleher had a simple notion when they got into the airline business: "If you get your passengers to their destinations when they want to get there, on time, at the lowest possible fares, and make darn sure they have a good time doing it, people will fly your airline."

Today, Southwest has become one of the most profitable airlines—posting a profit for the 43rd consecutive year in a row! However, running an airline is no easy task. Think of all of the financial transactions that take place on a daily basis. The airline has to buy planes, equipment, and supplies—like those peanuts we are so fond of. It also has to pay employees, pay for repairs on its equipment, and buy insurance, just to name a few expenses. Then, it has to sell enough tickets in order to be able to generate money to pay for all of these things. Yikes. That is a lot of cash coming in and going out. With an emphasis on customer service, Southwest has a reputation of being fun and quirky and having a sense of humor. You never know what might happen when you board a Southwest flight, but you know you'll have a good time.

thinking critically

How does Southwest keep track of all of these transactions so that it can continue to run its airline profitably?

LEARNING OBJECTIVES

2-1 Record in equation form the financial effects of a business transaction.

2-2 Define, identify, and understand the relationship between asset, liability, and owner's equity accounts.

2-3 Analyze the effects of business transactions on a firm's assets, liabilities, and owner's equity and record these effects in accounting equation form.

2-4 Prepare an income statement.

2-5 Prepare a statement of owner's equity and a balance sheet.

2-6 Define the accounting terms new to this chapter.

NEW TERMS

- accounts payable
- accounts receivable
- assets
- balance sheet
- break even
- business transaction
- capital
- equity
- expense
- fair market value
- fundamental accounting
- equation
- income statement
- liabilities
- net income
- net loss
- on account
- owner's equity
- revenue
- statement of owner's equity
- withdrawals

Section 1

SECTION OBJECTIVES	TERMS TO LEARN
>> 2-1 Record in equation form the financial effects of a business transaction. WHY IT'S IMPORTANT Learning the fundamental accounting equation is a basis for understanding business transactions. >> 2-2 Define, identify, and understand the relationship between asset, liability, and owner's equity accounts. WHY IT'S IMPORTANT The relationship between assets, liabilities, and owner's equity is the basis for the entire accounting system.	accounts payable assets balance sheet business transaction capital equity liabilities on account owner's equity

Property and Financial Interest

The accounting process starts with the analysis of business transactions. A **business transaction** is any financial event that changes the resources of a firm. For example, purchases, sales, payments, and receipts of cash are all business transactions. The accountant analyzes each business transaction to decide what information to record and where to record it.

>> 2-1 OBJECTIVE
Record in equation form the financial effects of a business transaction.

Beginning with Analysis

Let's analyze the transactions of Eli's Consulting Services, a firm that provides a wide range of accounting and consulting services. Trayton Eli, CPA, has a master's degree in accounting. He is the sole proprietor of Eli's Consulting Services. Sergio Sanchez, the office manager, has an associate's degree in business and has taken 12 semester hours of accounting. The firm is located in a large office complex.

Every month, Eli's Consulting Services bills clients for the accounting and consulting services provided that month. Customers can also pay in cash when the services are rendered.

STARTING A BUSINESS

Let's start from the beginning. Trayton Eli obtained the funds to start the business by withdrawing $100,000 from his personal savings account. The first transaction of the new business was opening a checking account in the name of Eli's Consulting Services. The separate bank account helps Eli keep his financial interest in the business separate from his personal funds.

When a business transaction occurs, it is analyzed to identify how it affects the equation *property equals financial interest.* This equation reflects the fact that in a free enterprise system, all property is owned by someone. In this case, Eli owns the business because he supplied the property (cash).

Use these steps to analyze the effect of a business transaction:

1. Describe the financial event.
   - Identify the property.
   - Identify who owns the property.
   - Determine the amount of increase or decrease.

2. Make sure the equation is in balance.

Property	=	Financial Interest

BUSINESS TRANSACTION

Trayton Eli withdrew $100,000 from personal savings and deposited it in a new checking account in the name of Eli's Consulting Services.

ANALYSIS

a. The business received $100,000 of ***property*** in the form of cash.

a. Eli had a $100,000 ***financial interest*** in the business.

Note that the equation *property* equals *financial interest* remains in balance. The total of one side of the equation must always equal the total of the other side.

Property		=	Financial Interest
	Cash	=	Trayton Eli, Capital
(a) Invested cash	**+$100,000**		
(a) Increased equity			**+$100,000**
New balances	$100,000	=	$100,000

An owner's financial interest in the business is called **equity,** or **capital.** Trayton Eli has $100,000 equity in Eli's Consulting Services.

PURCHASING EQUIPMENT FOR CASH

The first priority for office manager Sergio Sanchez was to get the business ready for opening day on December 1.

BUSINESS TRANSACTION

Eli's Consulting Services issued a $5,000 check to purchase a computer and other equipment.

ANALYSIS

b. The firm purchased new property (equipment) for $5,000.

b. The firm paid out $5,000 in cash.

The equation remains in balance.

	Property			=	Financial Interest
	Cash	+	Equipment	=	Trayton Eli, Capital
Previous balances	$100,000			=	$100,000
(b) Purchased equipment		+	**$5,000**		
(b) Paid cash	**−5,000**				
New balances	$95,000	+	$5,000	=	$100,000

Notice that there is a change in the composition of the firm's property. Now the firm has cash and equipment. The equation shows that the total value of the property remains the same, $100,000. Trayton Eli's financial interest, or equity, is also unchanged. Note that property (Cash and Equipment) is equal to financial interest (Trayton Eli, Capital).

These activities are recorded for the business entity Eli's Consulting Services. Trayton Eli's personal assets, such as his personal bank account, house, furniture, and automobile, are kept separate from the property of the firm. Nonbusiness property is not included in the accounting records of the business entity.

PURCHASING EQUIPMENT ON CREDIT

Sanchez purchased additional office equipment. Office Plus, the store selling the equipment, allows Eli's Consulting Services 60 days to pay the bill. This arrangement is called buying **on account.** The business has a *charge account,* or *open-account credit,* with its suppliers. Amounts that a business must pay in the future are known as **accounts payable.** The companies or individuals to whom the amounts are owed are called *creditors.*

BUSINESS TRANSACTION

Eli's Consulting Services purchased office equipment on account from Office Plus for $6,000.

ANALYSIS

c. The firm purchased new property (equipment) that cost $6,000.
c. The firm owes $6,000 to Office Plus.
The equation remains in balance.

	Property			=	Financial Interest		
	Cash	+	Equipment	=	Accounts Payable	+	Trayton Eli, Capital
Previous balances	$95,000	+	$ 5,000	=			$100,000
(c) Purchased equip.		+	**6,000**	=			
(c) Incurred debt					**+$6,000**		
New balances	$95,000	+	$11,000	=	$6,000	+	$100,000

Office Plus is willing to accept a claim against Eli's Consulting Services until the bill is paid. Now there are two different financial interests or claims against the firm's property—the creditor's claim (Accounts Payable) and the owner's claim (Trayton Eli, Capital). Notice that the total property increases to $106,000. Cash is $95,000 and equipment is $11,000. Trayton Eli, Capital stays the same, but the creditor's claim increases to $6,000. After this transaction is recorded, the left side of the equation still equals the right side.

When Ben Cohen and Jerry Greenfield founded Ben & Jerry's Homemade Ice Cream, Inc., in 1978, they invested $8,000 of their own funds and borrowed funds of $4,000. The equation *property equals financial interest* is expressed as

Property	=	Financial Interest
cash	=	*creditors' claims*
		+ *owners' claims*
$12,000	=	$ 4,000
		+ 8,000
		$12,000

ABOUT ACCOUNTING

History

For as long as people have been involved in business, there has been a need for accounting. The system of accounting we use is based upon the works of Luca Pacioli, a Franciscan monk in Italy. In 1494, Pacioli wrote about the bookkeeping techniques in practice during his time.

PURCHASING SUPPLIES

Sanchez purchased supplies so that Eli's Consulting Services could start operations. The company that sold the items requires cash payments from companies that have been in business less than six months.

BUSINESS TRANSACTION

Eli's Consulting Services issued a check for $1,500 to Office Delux, Inc., to purchase office supplies.

ANALYSIS

d. The firm purchased office supplies that cost $1,500.

d. The firm paid $1,500 in cash.

The equation remains in balance.

	Property					=	Financial Interest		
	Cash	+	Supplies	+	Equipment	=	Accounts Payable	+	Trayton Eli, Capital
Previous balances	$95,000			+	$11,000	=	$6,000	+	$100,000
(d) Purchased supplies		+	**$1,500**						
(d) Paid cash	**$1,500**								
New balances	$93,500	+	$1,500	+	$11,000	=	$6,000	+	$100,000

Notice that total property remains the same, even though the form of the property has changed. Also note that all of the property (left side) equals all of the financial interests (right side).

PAYING A CREDITOR

Sanchez decided to reduce the firm's debt to Office Plus by $2,500.

BUSINESS TRANSACTION

Eli's Consulting Services issued a check for $2,500 to Office Plus.

ANALYSIS

e. The firm paid $2,500 in cash.

e. The claim of Office Plus against the firm decreased by $2,500.

The equation remains in balance.

	Property					=	Financial Interest		
	Cash	+	**Supplies**	+	**Equipment**	=	**Accounts Payable**	+	**Trayton Eli, Capital**
Previous balances	$93,500	+	$1,500	+	$11,000	=	$6,000	+	$100,000
(e) Paid cash	**−$ 2,500**								
(e) Decreased debt							**−$2,500**		
New balances	$91,000	+	$1,500	+	$11,000	=	$3,500	+	$100,000

RENTING FACILITIES

In November, Sanchez arranged to rent facilities for $4,000 per month, beginning in December. The landlord required that rent for the first two months—December and January—be paid in advance. The firm prepaid (paid in advance) the rent for two months. As a result, the firm obtained the right to occupy facilities for a two-month period. In accounting, this right is considered a form of property.

BUSINESS TRANSACTION

Eli's Consulting Services issued a check for $8,000 to pay for rent for the months of December and January.

ANALYSIS

f. The firm prepaid the rent for the next two months in the amount of $8,000.

f. The firm decreased its cash balance by $8,000.

The equation remains in balance.

	Property							=	Financial Interest		
	Cash	+	**Supplies**	+	**Prepaid Rent**	+	**Equipment**	=	**Accounts Payable**	+	**Trayton Eli, Capital**
Previous balances	$91,000	+	$1,500			+	$11,000	=	$3,500	+	$100,000
(f) Paid cash	**−$8,000**										
(f) Prepaid rent					**+$8,000**						
New balances	$83,000	+	$1,500	+	$8,000	+	$11,000	=	$3,500	+	$100,000

Notice that when property values and financial interests increase or decrease, the total of the items on one side of the equation still equals the total on the other side.

Property		=	Financial Interest	
Cash	$ 83,000		Accounts Payable	$ 3,500
Supplies	1,500		Trayton Eli, Capital	100,000
Prepaid Rent	8,000			
Equipment	11,000			
Total	$103,500		Total	$103,500

The balance sheet is also called the ***statement of financial position.*** **Caterpillar Inc. reported assets of $78.5 billion, liabilities of $63.6 billion, and owners' equity of $14.9 billion on its statement of financial position at December 31, 2015.**

Assets, Liabilities, and Owner's Equity

>> 2-2 OBJECTIVE

Define, identify, and understand the relationship between asset, liability, and owner's equity accounts.

Accountants use special accounting terms when they refer to property and financial interests. For example, they refer to the property that a business owns as **assets** and to the debts or obligations of the business as **liabilities.** The owner's financial interest is called **owner's equity.** (Sometimes owner's equity is called *proprietorship* or *net worth.* Owner's equity is the preferred term and is used throughout this book.) At regular intervals, Trayton Eli reviews the status of the firm's assets, liabilities, and owner's equity in a financial statement called a **balance sheet.** The balance sheet shows the firm's financial position on a given date. Figure 2.1 shows the firm's balance sheet on November 30, the day before the company opened for business.

The assets are listed on the left side of the balance sheet and the liabilities and owner's equity are on the right side. This arrangement is similar to the equation *property equals financial interest.* Property is shown on the left side of the equation, and financial interest appears on the right side.

The balance sheet in Figure 2.1 shows:

- the amount and types of property the business owns,
- the amount owed to creditors,
- the owner's interest.

This statement gives Trayton Eli a complete picture of the financial position of his business on November 30.

FIGURE 2.1 **Balance Sheet for Eli's Consulting Services**

Eli's Consulting Services
Balance Sheet
November 30, 2019

Assets		*Liabilities*	
Cash	83 000 00	*Accounts Payable*	3 500 00
Supplies	1 500 00		
Prepaid Rent	8 000 00	*Owner's Equity*	
Equipment	11 000 00	*Trayton Eli, Capital*	100 000 00
Total Assets	103 500 00	*Total Liabilities and Owner's Equity*	103 500 00

Section 1 Self Review

QUESTIONS

1. What is a business transaction?
2. Describe a transaction that increases an asset and the owner's equity.
3. What does the term "accounts payable" mean?

EXERCISES

4. Kathryn Carter purchased a computer for $3,350 on account for her business. What is the effect of this transaction?
   a. Equipment decrease of $3,350 and accounts payable increase of $3,350.
   b. Equipment increase of $3,350 and accounts payable increase of $3,350.
   c. Equipment increase of $3,350 and cash increase of $3,350.
   d. Cash decrease of $3,350 and owner's equity increase of $3,350
5. Jane Nelson began a new business by depositing $130,000 in the business bank account. She wrote two checks from the business account: $19,000 for office furniture and $6,000 for office supplies. What is her financial interest in the company?
   a. $105,000
   b. $111,000
   c. $130,000
   d. $124,000

ANALYSIS

6. Persian Import Co. has no liabilities. The assets and owner's equity balances are as follows. What is the balance of "Supplies"?

Cash	$ 75,000
Office Equipment	$ 25,000
Supplies	????
Fred Walker, Capital	$110,000

(Answers to Section 1 Self Review are on page 48.)

Section 2

SECTION OBJECTIVES	TERMS TO LEARN
>> 2-3 Analyze the effects of business transactions on a firm's assets, liabilities, and owner's equity and record these effects in accounting equation form. WHY IT'S IMPORTANT Property will always equal financial interest. >> 2-4 Prepare an income statement. WHY IT'S IMPORTANT The income statement shows the results of operations. >> 2-5 Prepare a statement of owner's equity and a balance sheet. WHY IT'S IMPORTANT These financial statements show the financial condition of a business.	accounts receivable break even expense fair market value fundamental accounting equation income statement net income net loss revenue statement of owner's equity withdrawals

The Accounting Equation and Financial Statements

The word *balance* in the title "balance sheet" has a special meaning. It emphasizes that the total on the left side of the report must equal, or balance, the total on the right side.

The Fundamental Accounting Equation

>> **2-3 OBJECTIVE**
Analyze the effects of business transactions on a firm's assets, liabilities, and owner's equity and record these effects in accounting equation form.

In accounting terms, the firm's assets must equal the total of its liabilities and owner's equity. This equality can be expressed in equation form, as illustrated here. The amounts are for Eli's Consulting Services on November 30.

Assets	=	Liabilities	+	Owner's Equity
$103,500	=	$3,500	+	$100,000

The relationship between assets and liabilities plus owner's equity is called the **fundamental accounting equation.** The entire accounting process of analyzing, recording, and reporting business transactions is based on the fundamental accounting equation.

If any two parts of the equation are known, the third part can be determined. For example, consider the basic accounting equation for Eli's Consulting Services on November 30, with some information missing.

	Assets	=	Liabilities	+	Owner's Equity
1.	?	=	$3,500	+	$100,000
2.	$103,500	=	?	+	$100,000
3.	$103,000	=	$3,500	+	?

In the first case, we can solve for assets by adding liabilities to owner's equity ($3,500 + $100,000) to determine that assets are $103,500. In the second case, we can solve for liabilities by subtracting owner's equity from assets ($103,500 – $100,000) to determine that liabilities are $3,500. In the third case, we can solve for owner's equity by subtracting liabilities from assets ($103,500 – $3,500) to determine that owner's equity is $100,000.

important!

Revenues increase owner's equity. Expenses decrease owner's equity.

EARNING REVENUE AND INCURRING EXPENSES

Eli's Consulting Services opened for business on December 1. Some of the other businesses in the office complex became the firm's first clients. Eli also used his contacts in the community to identify other clients. Providing services to clients started a stream of revenue for the business. **Revenue,** or *income,* is the inflow of money or other assets that results from the sales of goods or services or from the use of money or property. A sale on account does not increase money, but it does create a claim to money. When a sale occurs, the revenue increases assets and also increases owner's equity.

An **expense,** on the other hand, involves the outflow of money, the use of other assets, or the incurring of a liability. Expenses include the costs of any materials, labor, supplies, and services used to produce revenue. Expenses cause a decrease in owner's equity.

A firm's accounting records show increases and decreases in assets, liabilities, and owner's equity as well as details of all transactions involving revenue and expenses. Let's use the fundamental accounting equation to show how revenue and expenses affect the business.

SELLING SERVICES FOR CASH

During the month of December, Eli's Consulting Services earned a total of $36,000 in revenue from clients who paid cash for accounting and bookkeeping services. This involved several transactions throughout the month. The total effect of these transactions is analyzed below.

ANALYSIS

g. The firm received $36,000 in cash for services provided to clients.

g. Revenue increased by $36,000, which results in a $36,000 increase in owner's equity.

The fundamental accounting equation remains in balance.

	Assets							=	Liabilities	+	Owner's Equity		
	Cash	+	Supplies	+	Prepaid Rent	+	Equipment	=	Accounts Payable	+	Trayton Eli, Capital	+	Revenue
Previous balances	$ 83,000	+	$1,500	+	$8,000	+	$11,000	=	$3,500	+	$100,000		
(g) Received cash	**+$36,000**												
(g) Increased owner's equity by earning revenue												+	**$36,000**
New balances	$119,000	+	$1,500	+	$8,000	+	$11,000	=	$3,500	+	$100,000	+	$ 36,000
	$139,500								$139,500				

Notice that revenue amounts are recorded in a separate column under owner's equity. Keeping revenue separate from the owner's equity will help the firm compute total revenue more easily when the financial statements are prepared.

SELLING SERVICES ON CREDIT

Eli's Consulting Services has some charge account clients. These clients are allowed 30 days to pay. Amounts owed by these clients are known as **accounts receivable.** This is a new form of asset for the firm—claims for future collection from customers. During December, Eli's Consulting Services earned $11,000 of revenue from charge account clients. The effect of these transactions is analyzed as follows:

ANALYSIS

h. The firm acquired a new asset, accounts receivable, of $11,000.

h. Revenues increased by $11,000, which results in an $11,000 increase in owner's equity.

The fundamental accounting equation remains in balance.

	Assets									=	Liab.	+	Owner's Equity		
	Cash	+	Accts. Rec.	+	Supp.	+	Prepaid Rent	+	Equip.	=	Accts. Pay.	+	Trayton Eli, Capital	+	Rev.
Previous balances	$119,000			+	$1,500	+	$8,000	+	$11,000	=	$3,500	+	$100,000	+	$36,000
(h) Received new asset—accts. rec.			**+$11,000**												
(h) Increased owner's equity by earning revenue														+	**$11,000**
New balances	$119,000	+	$11,000	+	$1,500	+	$8,000	+	$11,000	=	$3,500	+	$100,000	+	$47,000
	$150,500										$150,500				

COLLECTING RECEIVABLES

During December, Eli's Consulting Services received $6,000 on account from clients who owed money for services previously billed. The effect of these transactions is analyzed below.

ANALYSIS

i. The firm received $6,000 in cash.

i. Accounts receivable decreased by $6,000.

The fundamental accounting equation remains in balance.

	Assets									=	Liab.	+	Owner's Equity		
	Cash	+	Accts. Rec.	+	Supp.	+	Prepaid Rent	+	Equip.	=	Accts. Pay.	+	Trayton Eli, Capital	+	Rev.
Previous balances	$119,000	+	$11,000	+	$1,500	+	$8,000	+	$11,000	=	$3,500	+	$100,000	+	$47,000
(i) Received cash	**+$6,000**														
(i) Decreased accounts receivable			**−$6,000**												
New balances	$125,000	+	$5,000	+	$1,500	+	$8,000	+	$11,000	=	$3,500	+	$100,000	+	$47,000
	$150,500										$150,500				

In this type of transaction, one asset is changed for another asset (accounts receivable for cash). Notice that revenue is not increased when cash is collected from charge account clients. The revenue was recorded when the sale on account took place (see entry **(h)**). Notice that the fundamental accounting equation, *assets equal liabilities plus owner's equity,* stays in balance regardless of the changes arising from individual transactions.

PAYING EMPLOYEES' SALARIES

So far Eli has done very well. His equity has increased by the revenues earned. However, running a business costs money, and these expenses reduce owner's equity.

During the first month of operations, Eli's Consulting Services hired an accounting clerk. The salaries for the new accounting clerk and the office manager are considered an expense to the firm.

BUSINESS TRANSACTION

In December, Eli's Consulting Services paid $8,000 in salaries for the accounting clerk and Sergio Sanchez.

ANALYSIS

j. The firm decreased its cash balance by $8,000.

j. The firm paid salaries expense in the amount of $8,000, which decreased owner's equity.

The fundamental accounting equation remains in balance.

	Assets									=	Liab.	+	Owner's Equity				
	Cash	**+**	**Accts Rec.**	**+**	**Supp.**	**+**	**Prepaid Rent**	**+**	**Equip.**	**=**	**Accts. Pay.**	**+**	**Trayton Eli, Capital**	**+**	**Rev.**	**−**	**Exp.**
Previous balances	$125,000	+	$5,000	+	$1,500	+	$8,000	+	$11,000	=	$3,500	+	$100,000	+	$47,000		
(j) Paid cash	**−$8,000**																
(j) Decreased owner's equity by incurring salaries exp.																	**+ $8,000**
New balances	$117,000	+	$5,000	+	$1,500	+	$8,000	+	$11,000	=	$3,500	+	$100,000	+	$47,000	−	$8,000
	$142,500										$142,500						

Notice that expenses are recorded in a separate column under owner's equity. The separate record of expenses is kept for the same reason that the separate record of revenue is kept—to analyze operations for the period.

PAYING UTILITIES EXPENSE

At the end of December, the firm received a $650 utilities bill.

BUSINESS TRANSACTION

Eli's Consulting Services issued a check for $650 to pay the utilities bill.

ANALYSIS

k. The firm decreased its cash balance by $650.

k. The firm paid utilities expense of $650, which decreased owner's equity.

The fundamental accounting equation remains in balance.

	Assets									=	Liab.	+	Owner's Equity				
	Cash	+	Accts. Rec.	+	Supp.	+	Prepaid Rent	+	Equip.	=	Accts. Pay.	+	T. Eli, Capital	+	Rev.	−	Exp.
Previous balances	$117,000	+	$5,000	+	$1,500	+	$8,000	+	$11,000	=	$3,500	+	$100,000	+	$47,000	−	$8,000
(k) Paid cash	**−$650**																
(k) Decreased owner's equity by utilities exp.																+	**$650**
New balances	$116,350	+	$5,000	+	$1,500	+	$8,000	+	$11,000	=	$3,500	+	$100,000	+	$47,000	−	$8,650
	$141,850										$141,850						

EFFECT OF OWNER'S WITHDRAWALS

On December 30, Eli withdrew $5,000 in cash for personal expenses. **Withdrawals** are funds taken from the business by the owner for personal use. Withdrawals are not a business expense but a decrease in the owner's equity.

BUSINESS TRANSACTION

Trayton Eli wrote a check to withdraw $5,000 cash for personal use.

ANALYSIS

I. The firm decreased its cash balance by $5,000.

I. Owner's equity decreased by $5,000.

The fundamental accounting equation remains in balance.

	Assets									=	Liab.	+	Owner's Equity				
	Cash	+	Accts. Rec.	+	Supp.	+	Prepaid Rent	+	Equip.	=	Accts. Pay.	+	Trayton Eli, Capital	+	Rev.	−	Exp.
Previous balances	$116,350	+	$5,000	+	$1,500	+	$8,000	+	$11,000	=	$3,500	+	$100,000	+	$47,000	−	$8,650
(l) Withdrew cash	**−$5,000**																
(l) Decreased owner's equity												−	**$ 5,000**				
New balances	$111,350	+	$5,000	+	$1,500	+	$8,000	+	$11,000	=	$3,500	+	$95,000	+	$47,000	−	$8,650
	$136,850										$136,850						

SUMMARY OF TRANSACTIONS

Figure 2.2 summarizes the transactions of Eli's Consulting Services through December 31. Notice that after each transaction, the fundamental accounting equation is in balance. Test your understanding by describing the nature of each transaction. Then check your results by referring to the discussion of each transaction.

FIGURE 2.2 Transactions of Eli's Consulting Services Through December 31, 2019

	Assets					= Liab.	+ Owner's Equity		
	Cash	+ Accts. Rec.	+ Supp.	+ Prepaid Rent	+ Equip.	= Accts. Pay.	+ T. Eli, Capital	+ Rev.	− Exp.
(a)	+$100,000						+ $100,000		
Balances	100,000					=	100,000		
(b)	−5,000				+ $5,000				
Balances	95,000				+ 5,000	=	100,000		
(c)					+ 6,000	+ $6,000			
Balances	95,000				+ 11,000	= 6,000	+ 100,000		
(d)	−1,500		+ $1,500						
Balances	93,500		+ 1,500		+ 11,000	= 6,000	+ 100,000		
(e)	−2,500					− 2,500			
Balances	91,000		+ 1,500		+ 11,000	= 3,500	+ 100,000		
(f)	−8,000			+ $8,000					
Balances	83,000		+ 1,500	+ 8,000	+ 11,000	= 3,500	+ 100,000		
(g)	+36,000							+ $36,000	
Balances	119,000		+ 1,500	+ 8,000	+ 11,000	= 3,500	+ 100,000	+ 36,000	
(h)		+ $11,000						+ 11,000	
Balances	119,000	+ 11,000	+ 1,500	+ 8,000	+ 11,000	= 3,500	+ 100,000	+ 47,000	
(i)	+6,000	− 6,000							
Balances	125,000	+ 5,000	+ 1,500	+ 8,000	+ 11,000	= 3,500	+ 100,000	+ 47,000	
(j)	−8,000								+$8,000
Balances	117,000	+ 5,000	+ 1,500	+ 8,000	+ 11,000	= 3,500	+ 100,000	+ 47,000	− 8,000
(k)	−650								+650
Balances	116,350	+ 5,000	+ 1,500	+ 8,000	+ 11,000	= 3,500	+ 100,000	+ 47,000	− 8,650
(l)	−5,000						− 5,000		
Balances	$111,350	+ $5,000	+ $1,500	+ $8,000	+ $11,000	= $3,500	+ $95,000	+ $47,000	− $8,650
	$136,850					$136,850			

>> **2-4 OBJECTIVE**
Prepare an income statement.

The Income Statement

To be meaningful to owners, managers, and other interested parties, financial statements should provide information about revenue and expenses, assets and claims on the assets, and owner's equity.

The **income statement** shows the results of business operations for a specific period of time such as a month, a quarter, or a year. The income statement shows the revenue earned and the expenses of doing business. (The income statement is sometimes called a *profit and loss statement* or a *statement of income and expenses.* The most common term, income statement, is used throughout this text.) Figure 2.3 shows the income statement for Eli's Consulting Services for its first month of operation.

The income statement shows the difference between revenue from services provided or goods sold and the amount spent to operate the business. **Net income** results when revenue is greater than the expenses for the period. When expenses are greater than revenue, the result is a **net loss.** In the rare case when revenue and expenses are equal, the firm is said to **break even.** The income statement in Figure 2.3 shows a net income; revenue is greater than expenses.

recall

Financial Statements

Financial statements are reports that summarize a firm's financial affairs.

Eli's Consulting Services		
Income Statement		
Month Ended December 31, 2019		
Revenue		
Fees Income		*47 000 00*
Expenses		
Salaries Expense	*8 000 00*	
Utilities Expense	*650 00*	
Total Expenses		*8 650 00*
Net Income		*38 350 00*

FIGURE 2.3

Income Statement for Eli's Consulting Services

The three-line heading of the income statement shows *who, what,* and *when.*

- Who—the business name appears on the first line.
- What—the report title appears on the second line.
- When—the period covered appears on the third line.

The third line of the income statement heading in Figure 2.3 indicates that the report covers operations for the "Month Ended December 31, 2019." Review how other time periods are reported on the third line of the income statement heading.

Period Covered	Third Line of Heading
Jan., Feb., Mar.	Three-Month Period Ended March 31, 2019
Jan. to Dec.	Year Ended December 31, 2019
July 1 to June 30	Fiscal Year Ended June 30, 2019

Note the use of single and double rules in amount columns. A single line is used to show that the amounts above it are being added or subtracted. Double lines are used under the final amount in a column or section of a report to show that the amount is complete. Nothing is added to or subtracted from an amount with a double line.

Some companies refer to the income statement as the *statement of operations.* American Eagle Outfitters, Inc., reported $3.52 billion in sales on consolidated statements of operations for the fiscal year ended January 30, 2016.

The income statement for Eli's Consulting Services does not have dollar signs because it was prepared on accounting paper with ruled columns. However, dollar signs are used on income statements that are prepared on plain paper, that is, not on a ruled form.

The Statement of Owner's Equity and the Balance Sheet

>> 2-5 OBJECTIVE

Prepare a statement of owner's equity and a balance sheet.

The **statement of owner's equity** reports the changes that occurred in the owner's financial interest during the reporting period. This statement is prepared before the balance sheet so that the amount of the ending capital balance is available for presentation on the balance sheet. Figure 2.4 shows the statement of owner's equity for Eli's Consulting Services. Note that the statement of owner's equity has a three-line heading: *who, what,* and *when.*

- The first line of the statement of owner's equity is the capital balance at the beginning of the period.
- Net income is an increase to owner's equity; net loss is a decrease to owner's equity.
- Withdrawals by the owner are a decrease to owner's equity.

FIGURE 2.4

Statement of Owner's Equity for Eli's Consulting Services

Eli's Consulting Services		
Statement of Owner's Equity		
Month Ended December 31, 2019		
Trayton Eli, Capital, December 1, 2019		100,000.00
Net Income for December	38,350.00	
Less Withdrawals for December	5,000.00	
Increase in Capital		33,350.00
Trayton Eli, Capital, December 31, 2019		133,350.00

- Additional investments by the owner are an increase to owner's equity.
- The total of changes in equity is reported on the line "Increase in Capital" (or "Decrease in Capital").
- The last line of the statement of owner's equity is the capital balance at the end of the period.

If Trayton Eli had made any additional investments during December, this would appear as a separate line on Figure 2.4. Additional investments can be cash or other assets such as equipment. If an investment is made in a form other than cash, the investment is recorded at its fair market value. **Fair market value** is the current worth of an asset or the price the asset would bring if sold on the open market.

The ending balances in the asset and liability accounts are used to prepare the balance sheet.

	Assets										=	Liab.	+	Owner's Equity				
	Cash	+	Accts. Rec.	+	Supp.	+	Prepaid Rent	+	Equip.		=	Accts. Pay.	+	T. Eli, Capital	+	Rev.	−	Exp.
New balances	$111,350	+	$5,000	+	$1,500	+	$8,000	+	$11,000		=	$3,500	+	$95,000	+	$47,000	−	$8,650
	$136,850											$136,850						

important!

Financial Statements

The balance sheet is a snapshot of the firm's financial position on a specific date. The income statement, like a movie or video, shows the results of business operations over a period of time.

The ending capital balance from the statement of owner's equity is also used to prepare the balance sheet. Figure 2.5 shows the balance sheet for Eli's Consulting Services on December 31, 2019.

The balance sheet shows:

- Assets—the types and amounts of property that the business owns,
- Liabilities—the amounts owed to creditors,
- Owner's Equity—the owner's equity on the reporting date.

In preparing a balance sheet, remember the following:

- The three-line heading gives the firm's name (who), the title of the report (what), and the date of the report (when).
- Balance sheets prepared using the account form (as in Figure 2.5) show total assets on the same horizontal line as the total liabilities and owner's equity.
- Dollar signs are omitted when financial statements are prepared on paper with ruled columns. Statements that are prepared on plain paper, not ruled forms, show dollar signs with the first amount in each column and with each total.
- A single line shows that the amounts above it are being added or subtracted. Double lines indicate that the amount is the final amount in a column or section of a report.

Figure 2.6 shows the connections among the financial statements. Financial statements are prepared in a specific order:

- income statement
- statement of owner's equity
- balance sheet

FIGURE 2.5 Balance Sheet for Eli's Consulting Services

Eli's Consulting Services Balance Sheet December 31, 2019			
Assets		*Liabilities*	
Cash	111,350.00	Accounts Payable	3,500.00
Accounts Receivable	5,000.00		
Supplies	1,500.00		
Prepaid Rent	8,000.00	*Owner's Equity*	
Equipment	11,000.00	Trayton Eli, Capital	133,350.00
Total Assets	136,850.00	Total Liabilities and Owner's Equity	136,850.00

FIGURE 2.6

Process for Preparing Financial Statements

Step 1: Prepare the Income Statement

Eli's Consulting Services Income Statement Month Ended December 31, 2019		
Revenue		
Fees Income		47,000.00
Expenses		
Salaries Expense	8,000.00	
Utilities Expense	650.00	
Total Expenses		8,650.00
Net Income		38,350.00

Net income (or loss) is transferred to the statement of owner's equity.

Step 2: Prepare the Statement of Owner's Equity

Eli's Consulting Services Statement of Owner's Equity Month Ended December 31, 2019		
Trayton Eli, Capital, December 1, 2019		100,000.00
Net Income for December	38,350.00	
Less Withdrawals for December	5,000.00	
Increase in Capital		33,350.00
Trayton Eli, Capital, December 31, 2019		133,350.00

The ending capital balance is transferred to the balance sheet.

Step 3: Prepare the Balance Sheet

Eli's Consulting Services Balance Sheet December 31, 2019			
Assets		*Liabilities*	
Cash	111,350.00	Accounts Payable	3,500.00
Accounts Receivable	5,000.00		
Supplies	1,500.00		
Prepaid Rent	8,000.00	*Owner's Equity*	
Equipment	11,000.00	Trayton Eli, Capital	133,350.00
Total Assets	136,850.00	Total Liabilities and Owner's Equity	136,850.00

MANAGERIAL IMPLICATIONS <<

ACCOUNTING SYSTEMS

- Sound financial records and statements are necessary so that businesspeople can make good decisions.
- Financial statements show:
  - the amount of profit or loss,
  - the assets on hand,
  - the amount owed to creditors,
  - the amount of owner's equity.
- Well-run and efficiently managed businesses have good accounting systems that provide timely and useful information.
- Transactions involving revenue and expenses are recorded separately from owner's equity in order to analyze operations for the period.

THINKING CRITICALLY

If you were buying a business, what would you look for in the company's financial statements?

Net income from the income statement is used to prepare the statement of owner's equity. The ending capital balance from the statement of owner's equity is used to prepare the balance sheet.

The Importance of Financial Statements

Preparing financial statements is one of the accountant's most important jobs. Each day millions of business decisions are made based on the information in financial statements.

Business managers and owners use the balance sheet and the income statement to control current operations and plan for the future. Creditors, prospective investors, governmental agencies, and others are interested in the profits of the business and in the asset and equity structure.

Section 2 Self Review

QUESTIONS

1. What are withdrawals and how do they affect the basic accounting equation?
2. If an owner gives personal tools to the business, how is the transaction recorded?
3. What information is included in the financial statement headings?

EXERCISES

4. Interior Designs has assets of $240,000 and liabilities of $90,000. What is the owner's equity?
   a. $50,000
   b. $30,000
   c. $150,000
   d. $110,000
5. U Fix It Hardware had revenues of $210,000 and expenses of $120,000. How does this affect owner's equity?

ANALYSIS

6. What information is contained in the income statement?
   a. revenues and expenses for a period of time
   b. assets, liabilities, and owner's equity for a period of time
   c. revenue and expenses on a specific date
   d. assets, liabilities, and owner's equity on a specific date

(Answers to Section 2 Self Review are on page 48.)

Chapter 2

Review and Applications

REVIEW Chapter Summary

Accounting begins with the analysis of business transactions. Each transaction changes the financial position of a business. In this chapter, you have learned how to analyze business transactions and how they affect assets, liabilities, and owner's equity. After transactions are analyzed and recorded, financial statements reflect the summarized changes to and results of business operations.

Learning Objectives

2-1 **Record in equation form the financial effects of a business transaction.**

The equation *property equals financial interest* reflects the fact that in a free enterprise system all property is owned by someone. This equation remains in balance after each business transaction.

2-2 **Define, identify, and understand the relationship between asset, liability, and owner's equity accounts.**

The term *assets* refers to property. The terms *liabilities* and *owner's equity* refer to financial interest. The relationship between assets, liabilities, and owner's equity is shown in equation form.

Assets	=	Liabilities	+	Owner's Equity
Owner's Equity	=	Assets	−	Liabilities
Liabilities	=	Assets	−	Owner's Equity

2-3 **Analyze the effects of business transactions on a firm's assets, liabilities, and owner's equity and record these effects in accounting equation form.**

1. Describe the financial event.
   - Identify the property.
   - Identify who owns the property.
   - Determine the amount of the increase or decrease.
2. Make sure the equation is in balance.

2-4 **Prepare an income statement.**

The income statement summarizes changes in owner's equity that result from revenue and expenses. The difference between revenue and expenses is the net income or net loss of the business for the period.

An income statement has a three-line heading:

- who
- what
- when

For the income statement, "when" refers to a period of time.

2-5 **Prepare a statement of owner's equity and a balance sheet.**

Changes in owner's equity for the period are summarized on the statement of owner's equity.

- Net income increases owner's equity.
- Added investments increase owner's equity.
- A net loss for the period decreases owner's equity.
- Withdrawals by the owner decrease owner's equity.

A statement of owner's equity has a three-line heading:

- who
- what
- when

For the statement of owner's equity, "when" refers to a period of time.

The balance sheet shows the assets, liabilities, and owner's equity on a given date.

A balance sheet has a three-line heading:

- who
- what
- when

For the balance sheet, "when" refers to a single date.

The financial statements are prepared in the following order.

1. Income Statement
2. Statement of Owner's Equity
3. Balance Sheet

2-6 **Define the accounting terms new to this chapter.**

Glossary

Accounts payable (p. 22) Amounts a business must pay in the future

Accounts receivable (p. 28) Claims for future collection from customers

Assets (p. 25) Property owned by a business

Balance sheet (p. 25) A formal report of a business's financial condition on a certain date; reports the assets, liabilities, and owner's equity of the business

Break even (p. 32) A point at which revenue equals expenses

Business transaction (p. 20) A financial event that changes the resources of a firm

Capital (p. 21) Financial investment in a business; equity

Equity (p. 21) An owner's financial interest in a business

Expense (p. 28) An outflow of cash, use of other assets, or incurring of a liability

Fair market value (p. 34) The current worth of an asset or the price the asset would bring if sold on the open market

Fundamental accounting equation (p. 27) The relationship between assets and liabilities plus owner's equity

Income statement (p. 32) A formal report of business operations covering a specific period of time; also called a profit and loss statement or a statement of income and expenses

Liabilities (p. 25) Debts or obligations of a business

Net income (p. 32) The result of an excess of revenue over expenses

Net loss (p. 32) The result of an excess of expenses over revenue

On account (p. 22) An arrangement to allow payment at a later date; also called a charge account or open-account credit

Owner's equity (p. 25) The financial interest of the owner of a business; also called proprietorship or net worth

Revenue (p. 28) An inflow of money or other assets that results from the sales of goods or services or from the use of money or property; also called income

Statement of owner's equity (p. 33) A formal report of changes that occurred in the owner's financial interest during a reporting period

Withdrawals (p. 31) Funds taken from the business by the owner for personal use

Comprehensive **Self Review**

1. What is the difference between buying for cash and buying on account?
2. If one side of the fundamental accounting equation is decreased, what will happen to the other side? Why?
3. Describe a transaction that will cause Accounts Payable and Cash to decrease by $1,200.
4. What effect does revenue and expenses have on owner's equity?
5. In what order are the financial statements prepared? Why?

(Answers to Comprehensive Self Review are on page 49.)

Discussion Questions

1. What is revenue?
2. What are expenses?
3. How is net income determined?

4. How does net income affect owner's equity?
5. Describe the effects of each of the following business transactions on assets, liabilities, and owner's equity.
   a. Bought equipment on credit.
   b. Paid salaries to employees.
   c. Sold services for cash.
   d. Paid cash to a creditor.
   e. Bought furniture for cash.
   f. Sold services on credit.
6. What is the fundamental accounting equation?
7. What are assets, liabilities, and owner's equity?
8. What information does the balance sheet contain?
9. What information does the income statement contain?
10. What information does the statement of owner's equity contain?
11. What information is shown in the heading of a financial statement?
12. Why does the third line of the headings differ on the balance sheet and the income statement?

APPLICATIONS

Exercises

Determining accounting equation amounts.

Exercise 2.1
Objectives 2-1, 2-2

Just before Johnson Laboratories opened for business, Howard Johnson, the owner, had the following assets and liabilities. Determine the totals that would appear in the firm's fundamental accounting equation (Assets = Liabilities + Owner's Equity).

Cash	$49,500
Laboratory Equipment	77,500
Laboratory Supplies	10,800
Loan Payable	15,200
Accounts Payable	11,375

Completing the accounting equation.

Exercise 2.2
Objectives 2-1, 2-2

The fundamental accounting equations for several businesses follow. Supply the missing amounts.

Assets	=	Liabilities	+	Owner's Equity
1. $32,350	=	$6,720	+	$?
2. $28,900	=	$6,380	+	$?
3. $48,075	=	$?	+	$12,300
4. $?	=	$5,700	+	$33,876
5. $54,000	=	$?	+	$29,200

Exercise 2.3
Objectives 2-1, 2-2, 2-3

▶ Determining the effects of transactions on the accounting equation.

Indicate the impact of each of the transactions below on the fundamental accounting equation (Assets = Liabilities + Owner's Equity) by placing a "+" to indicate an increase and a "–" to indicate a decrease. The first transaction is entered as an example.

	Assets	=	Liabilities	+	Owner's Equity
Transaction 1	–				–

TRANSACTIONS

1. Paid $2,100 for utilities.
2. Performed services for $10,500 on account.
3. Received $6,500 from charge account customers.
4. Paid salaries of $4,500 to employees.
5. Paid $8,000 to a creditor on account.
6. Owner invested $90,000 in the business.
7. Purchased $26,700 of supplies on account.
8. Purchased equipment for $21,000 cash.
9. Paid $6,000 for rent (in advance).
10. Performed services for $7,800 cash

Exercise 2.4
Objectives 2-1, 2-2, 2-3

▶ Determining balance sheet amounts.

The following financial data are for the dental practice of Dr. Donna Wells when she began operations in July. Determine the amounts that would appear in Dr. Wells's balance sheet.

1. Owes $21,000 to the Allen Equipment Company.
2. Has cash balance of $15,500.
3. Has dental supplies of $5,650.
4. Owes $6,180 to Contemporary Furniture Supply.
5. Has dental equipment of $28,550.
6. Has office furniture of $10,000.

Exercise 2.5
Objectives 2-1, 2-2, 2-3

▶ Determining the effects of transactions on the accounting equation.

The Copy Center had the transactions listed below during the month of June. Show how each transaction would be recorded in the accounting equation. Compute the totals at the end of the month. The headings to be used in the equation follow.

		Assets			=	Liabilities	+	Owner's Equity				
Cash	+	Accounts Receivable	+	Equipment	=	Accounts Payable	+	John Amos, Capital	+	Revenue	–	Expenses

TRANSACTIONS

1. John Amos started the business with a cash investment of $60,000.
2. Purchased equipment for $22,000 on credit.
3. Performed services for $3,100 in cash.

4. Purchased additional equipment for $4,600 in cash.
5. Performed services for $5,050 on credit.
6. Paid salaries of $4,450 to employees.
7. Received $3,200 cash from charge account customers.
8. Paid $13,000 to a creditor on account.

Computing net income or net loss.

Exercise 2.6
Objective 2-4

The Computer Store had the following revenue and expenses during the month ended July 31. Did the firm earn a net income or incur a net loss for the period? What was the amount?

Fees for computer repairs	$46,800
Advertising expense	8,100
Salaries expense	20,500
Telephone expense	1,080
Fees for printer repairs	6,730
Utilities expense	1,710

Identifying transactions.

Exercise 2.7
Objectives 2-1, 2-2, 2-3

The following equation shows the effects of a number of transactions that took place at Brock Auto Repair Company during the month of July. Describe each transaction.

	Assets					=	Liabilities	+	Owner's Equity				
	Cash	+	Accounts Receivable	+	Equipment	=	Accounts Payable	+	Horace Brock, Capital	+	Revenue	−	Expenses
Bal.	$82,000	+	$8,000	+	$60,000	=	$40,000	+	$110,000	+	0	−	0
1.	+12,000										+$12,000		
2.	−7,800				+7,800								
3.	4,200						−4,200						
4.	−6,910												+$6,910
5.	+1,800		−1,800										
6.			+13,380								+13,380		
7.	−4,320												+4,320

Preparing an income statement.

Exercise 2.8
Objective 2-4

At the beginning of September, Selena Cantu started Cantu Wealth Management Consulting, a firm that offers financial planning and advice about investing and managing money. On September 30, the accounting records of the business showed the following information. Prepare an income statement for the month of September 2019.

Cash	$ 66,200	Fees Income	155,800
Accounts Receivable	8,000	Advertising Expense	13,000
Office Supplies	6,800	Salaries Expense	32,000
Office Equipment	75,000	Telephone Expense	1,600
Accounts Payable	11,400	Withdrawals	18,000
Selena Cantu, Capital, September 1, 2019	53,400		

Computing net income or net loss.

Exercise 2.9
Objective 2-4

On December 1, Kate Holmes opened a speech and hearing clinic. During December, her firm had the following transactions involving revenue and expenses. Did the firm earn a net income or incur a net loss for the period? What was the amount?

Paid $3,100 for advertising.
Provided services for $2,800 in cash.
Paid $800 for telephone service.
Paid salaries of $2,600 to employees.
Provided services for $3,000 on credit.
Paid $450 for office cleaning service.

Exercise 2.10 ▶ **Preparing a statement of owner's equity and a balance sheet.**

Objective 2-5

CONTINUING >>> Problem

Using the information provided in Exercise 2.8, prepare a statement of owner's equity for the month of September and a balance sheet for Cantu Wealth Management Consulting as of September 30, 2019.

PROBLEMS

Problem Set A connect

Problem 2.1A ▶ **Analyzing the effects of transactions on the accounting equation.**

Objectives 2-1, 2-2, 2-3

On July 1, Tommy Wrigley established Wrigley Home Appraisal Services, a firm that provides expert residential appraisals and represents clients in home appraisal hearings.

INSTRUCTIONS

Analyze the following transactions. Record in equation form the changes that occur in assets, liabilities, and owner's equity. (Use plus, minus, and equals signs.)

TRANSACTIONS

1. The owner invested $100,000 in cash to begin the business.
2. Paid $20,250 in cash for the purchase of equipment.
3. Purchased additional equipment for $15,200 on credit.
4. Paid $12,500 in cash to creditors.
5. The owner made an additional investment of $25,000 in cash.
6. Performed services for $9,750 in cash.
7. Performed services for $7,800 on account.
8. Paid $6,000 for rent expense.
9. Received $5,500 in cash from credit clients.
10. Paid $7,550 in cash for office supplies.
11. The owner withdrew $12,000 in cash for personal expenses.

Analyze: What is the ending balance of cash after all transactions have been recorded?

Problem 2.2A ▶ **Analyzing the effects of transactions on the accounting equation.**

Objectives 2-1, 2-2, 2-3

Harold Joseph is a painting contractor who specializes in painting commercial buildings. At the beginning of June, his firm's financial records showed the following assets, liabilities, and owner's equity.

Cash	$ 72,000	Accounts Payable	15,300
Accounts Receivable	18,500	Harold Joseph, Capital	107,250
Office Furniture	42,500	Revenue	65,800
Auto	27,500	Expenses	27,850

INSTRUCTIONS

Set up an accounting equation using the balances given above. Record the effects of the following transactions in the equation. (Use plus, minus, and equals signs.) Record new balances after each transaction has been entered. Prove the equality of the two sides of the final equation on a separate sheet of paper.

TRANSACTIONS

1. Performed services for $7,200 on credit.
2. Paid $1,820 in cash for new office chairs.
3. Received $13,800 in cash from credit clients.
4. Paid $910 in cash for telephone service.
5. Sent a check for $5,200 in partial payment of the amount due creditors.
6. Paid salaries of $10,580 in cash.
7. Sent a check for $1,285 to pay electric bill.
8. Performed services for $12,900 in cash.
9. Paid $2,660 in cash for auto repairs.
10. Performed services for $13,800 on account.

Analyze: What is the amount of total assets after all transactions have been recorded?

Preparing a balance sheet.

◀ **Problem 2.3A**
Objective 2-5

Taylor Equipment Repair Service is owned by Jason Taylor.

INSTRUCTIONS

Use the following figures to prepare a balance sheet dated February 28, 2019. (You will need to compute the owner's equity.)

Cash	$ 68,600	Equipment	156,000
Supplies	12,760	Accounts Payable	48,000
Accounts Receivable	26,400		

Analyze: What is the net worth, or owner's equity, at February 28, 2019, for Taylor Equipment Repair Service?

Preparing an income statement, a statement of owner's equity, and a balance sheet.

◀ **Problem 2.4A**
Objectives 2-4, 2-5

The following equation shows the transactions of Cotton Cleaning Service during May. The business is owned by Taylor Cotton.

	Assets							=	Liab.	+	Owner's Equity				
	Cash	+	Accts. Rec.	+	Supp.	+	Equip.	=	Accts. Pay.	+	T. Cotton, Capital	+	Rev.	−	Exp.
Balances, May 1	15,000	+	3,000	+	5,800	+	33,800	=	7,000	+	50,600	+	0	−	0
Paid for utilities	−980														+980
New balances	14,020	+	3,000	+	5,800	+	33,800	=	7,000	+	50,600	+	0	−	980
Sold services for cash	+4,980												+4,980		
New balances	19,000	+	3,000	+	5,800	+	33,800	=	7,000	+	50,600	+	4,980	−	980
Paid a creditor	−2,100								−2,100						
New balances	16,900	+	3,000	+	5,800	+	33,800	=	4,900	+	50,600	+	4,980	−	980
Sold services on credit			+2,900										+2,900		
New balances	16,900	+	5,900	+	5,800	+	33,800	=	4,900	+	50,600	+	7,880	−	980
Paid salaries	−8,900														+8,900
New balances	8,000	+	5,900	+	5,800	+	33,800	=	4,900	+	50,600	+	7,880	−	9,880
Paid telephone bill	−314														+314
New balances	7,686	+	5,900	+	5,800	+	33,800	=	4,900	+	50,600	+	7,880	−	10,194
Withdrew cash for personal expenses	−3,000										−3,000				
New balances	4,686	+	5,900	+	5,800	+	33,800	=	4,900	+	47,600	+	7,880	−	10,194

INSTRUCTIONS

Analyze each transaction carefully. Prepare an income statement and a statement of owner's equity for the month. Prepare a balance sheet for May 31, 2019. List the expenses in detail on the income statement.

Analyze: In order to complete the balance sheet, which amount was transferred from the statement of owner's equity?

Problem Set B

Problem 2.1B ▶ Analyzing the effects of transactions on the accounting equation.

Objectives 2-1, 2-2, 2-3

On September 1, Sarah Dodd opened Tailor Made Tutoring Service.

INSTRUCTIONS

Analyze the following transactions. Use the fundamental accounting equation form to record the changes in property, claims of creditors, and owner's equity. (Use plus, minus, and equals signs.)

TRANSACTIONS

1. The owner invested $36,000 in cash to begin the business.
2. Purchased equipment for $16,000 in cash.
3. Purchased $6,000 of additional equipment on credit.
4. Paid $3,000 in cash to creditors.
5. The owner made an additional investment of $6,000 in cash.
6. Performed services for $4,200 in cash.
7. Performed services for $3,650 on account.
8. Paid $2,600 for rent expense.
9. Received $2,500 in cash from credit clients.
10. Paid $3,150 in cash for office supplies.
11. The owner withdrew $5,000 in cash for personal expenses.

Analyze: Which transactions increased the company's debt? By what amount?

Problem 2.2B ▶ Analyzing the effects of transactions on the accounting equation.

Objectives 2-1, 2-2, 2-3

Rhonda Johnson owns Johnson's Consulting Service. At the beginning of September, her firm's financial records showed the following assets, liabilities, and owner's equity.

Cash	$ 76,000	Accounts Payable	20,000
Accounts Receivable	24,000	Rhonda Johnson, Capital	99,600
Supplies	25,600	Revenue	104,000
Office Furniture	48,000	Expenses	50,000

INSTRUCTIONS

Set up an equation using the balances given above. Record the effects of the following transactions in the equation. (Use plus, minus, and equals signs.) Record new balances after each transaction has been entered. Prove the equality of the two sides of the final equation on a separate sheet of paper.

TRANSACTIONS

1. Performed services for $16,000 on credit.
2. Paid $5,760 in cash for utilities.
3. Performed services for $20,000 in cash.
4. Paid $3,200 in cash for office cleaning service.
5. Sent a check for $9,600 to a creditor.

6. Paid $3,840 in cash for the telephone bill.
7. Issued checks for $28,000 to pay salaries.
8. Performed services for $22,400 in cash.
9. Purchased additional supplies for $4,000 on credit.
10. Received $12,000 in cash from credit clients.

Analyze: What is the ending balance for owner's equity after all transactions have been recorded?

Preparing a balance sheet.

Problem 2.3B
Objective 2-5

Ronald Thomas is opening a tax preparation service on December 1, which will be called Ronald's Tax Service. Thomas plans to open the business by depositing $25,000 cash into a business checking account. The following assets will also be owned by the business: furniture (fair market value of $7,500) and computers and printers (fair market value of $8,500). There are no outstanding debts of the business as it is formed.

INSTRUCTIONS

Prepare a balance sheet for December 1, 2019, for Ronald's Tax Service by entering the correct balances in the appropriate accounts. (You will need to use the accounting equation to compute owner's equity.)

Analyze: If Ronald's Tax Service had an outstanding debt of $8,000 when the business was formed, what amount should be reported on the balance sheet for owner's equity?

Preparing an income statement, a statement of owner's equity, and a balance sheet.

Problem 2.4B
Objectives 2-4, 2-5

The equation below shows the transactions of Kathryn Proctor, Attorney and Counselor at Law, during August. This law firm is owned by Kathryn Proctor.

	Assets							=	Liab.	+	Owner's Equity				
	Cash	+	Accts. Rec.	+	Supp.	+	Equip.	=	Accts. Pay.	+	K. Proctor, Capital	+	Rev.	−	Exp.
Balances, Aug. 1	7,200	+	1,800	+	5,400	+	10,000	=	1,200	+	23,200	+	0	−	0
Paid for utilities	−600														+600
New balances	6,600	+	1,800	+	5,400	+	10,000	=	1,200	+	23,200	+	0	−	600
Performed services for cash	+6,000												+6,000		
New balances	12,600	+	1,800	+	5,400	+	10,000	=	1,200	+	23,200	+	6,000	−	600
Paid a creditor	−600								600						
New balances	12,000	+	1,800	+	5,400	+	10,000	=	600	+	23,200	+	6,000	−	600
Performed services on credit			+4,800										+4,800		
New balances	12,000	+	6,600	+	5,400	+	10,000	=	600	+	23,200	+	10,800	−	600
Paid salaries	−5,400														+5,400
New balances	6,600	+	6,600	+	5,400	+	10,000	=	600	+	23,200	+	10,800	−	6,000
Paid telephone bill	−600														+600
New balances	6,000	+	6,600	+	5,400	+	10,000	=	600	+	23,200	+	10,800	−	6,600
Withdrew cash for personal expenses	−1,200										−1,200				
New balances	4,800	+	6,600	+	5,400	+	10,000	=	600	+	22,000	+	10,800	−	6,600

INSTRUCTIONS

Analyze each transaction carefully. Prepare an income statement and a statement of owner's equity for the month. Prepare a balance sheet for August 31, 2019. List the expenses in detail on the income statement.

Analyze: In order to complete the statement of owner's equity, which amount was transferred from the income statement?

Critical Thinking Problem 2.1

Financial Statements

The following account balances are for William Giese, Certified Public Accountant, as of April 30, 2019.

Cash	$60,000
Accounts Receivable	24,000
Maintenance Expense	9,200
Advertising Expense	7,780
Fees Earned	53,600
William Giese, Capital, April 1	?
Salaries Expense	26,000
Machinery	42,000
Accounts Payable	26,400
William Giese, Withdrawals for April	13,600

INSTRUCTIONS

Using the accounting equation form, determine the balance for William Giese, Capital, April 1, 2019. Prepare an income statement for the month of April, a statement of owner's equity, and a balance sheet as of April 30, 2019. List the expenses on the income statement in alphabetical order.

Analyze: What net change in owner's equity occurred during the month of April?

Critical Thinking Problem 2.2

Accounting for a New Company

Richard Harris opened a gym and fitness studio called Body Builders Fitness Center at the beginning of November of the current year. It is now the end of December, and Harris is trying to determine whether he made a profit during his first two months of operations. You offer to help him and ask to see his accounting records. He shows you a shoe box and tells you that every piece of paper pertaining to the business is in that box.

As you go through the material in the shoe box, you discover the following:

a. A receipt from Galloway Properties for $9,000 for November's rent on the exercise studio.

b. Bank deposit slips totaling $7,500 for money collected from customers who attended exercise classes.

c. An invoice for $40,000 for exercise equipment. The first payment is not due until December 31.

d. A bill for $2,100 from the maintenance service that cleans the studio. Harris has not yet paid this bill.

e. A December 19 parking ticket for $75. Harris says he was in a hurry that morning to get to the Fitness Center on time and forgot to put money in the parking meter.

f. A handwritten list of customers and fees for the classes they have taken. As the customers attend the classes, Harris writes their names and the amount of each customer's fee on the list. As customers pay, Harris crosses their names off the list. Fees not crossed off the list amount to $3,200.

g. A credit card receipt for $600 for printing flyers advertising the grand opening of the studio. For convenience, Harris used his personal credit card.

h. A credit card receipt for $700 for four warm-up suits Harris bought to wear at the studio. He also put this purchase on his personal credit card.

Use the concepts you have learned in this chapter to help Harris.

1. Prepare an income statement for the first two months of operation of Body Builders Fitness Center.
2. How would you evaluate the results of the first two months of operation?
3. What advice would you give Harris concerning his system of accounting?

BUSINESS CONNECTIONS

Interpreting Results

Managerial | FOCUS

1. After examining financial data for a monthly period, the owner of a small business expressed surprise that the firm's cash balance had decreased during the month even though there was substantial net income. Do you think this owner is right to expect cash to increase because of a substantial net income? Why or why not?
2. Is it reasonable to expect that all new businesses will have a net income from the first month's operations? From the first year's operations?
3. Why should managers be concerned with changes in the amount of creditors' claims against the business?
4. How does an accounting system help managers control operations and make sound decisions?

To Record or Not to Record

Ethical | DILEMMA

You are Julia, a new accounts receivable clerk for Nixon Paper and Office Supply. Toward the end of the month, Carol Reed, a very personable sales associate, tells you that the previous A/R clerk always recorded a sales invoice when she got a verbal agreement from a customer to buy paper or office supplies. She has a verbal order from her favorite customer for $10,000 of paper and wants you to create a sales invoice today. You know that in order to create a sales invoice you need a purchase order from the customer. You also know that Ms. Reed receives a monthly bonus based on the monthly sales. If her sales are above $20,000, she gets a 10 percent bonus. Would you agree to record the sales of products before receiving the purchase order from the customer? What effect would it have on the customer, on the sales associate, on the company, and on the job?

Income Statement

Financial Statement ANALYSIS

Review the following excerpt from the 2015 consolidated statement of income for Southwest Airlines Co. Answer the questions that follow.

Southwest Airlines Co.
Consolidated Statement of Income
Years Ended December 31, 2015 and 2014

		2015	2014
Operating Revenues (in millions):			
Passenger		*$18,299*	*$17,658*
Freight		*179*	*175*
Other		*1,342*	*772*
Total operating revenues		*19,820*	*18,605*
Net Income		*$2,181*	*$1,136*

Analyze:

1. Although the format for the heading of an income statement can vary from company to company, the heading should contain the answers to who, what, and when. List the answers to each question for the statement presented above.
2. What three types of revenue are reflected on this statement?
3. The net income of $2.181 billion reflected on Southwest Airlines Co.'s consolidated statement of income for 2015 will be transferred to the next financial statement to be prepared. Net income is needed to complete which statement?

Analyze Online: Find the *Investor Relations* section of the Southwest Airlines Co. website (www.southwest.com) and answer the following questions.

4. What total operating revenues did Southwest Airlines Co. report for the most recent quarter?
5. Find the most recent press release posted on the website. Read the press release, and summarize the topic discussed. What effect, if any, do you think this will have on company earnings? Why?

Internet | CONNECTION

Selling on Internet

Go to the Federated Corporation website at www.federated-fds.com. What companies are included in this corporation? Can you see a link to purchase items online? What transaction, if any, would you record when an item is ordered from the Internet? Does the website include job offerings? What jobs would be available in Finance (go to Support operations, finance to find the requirements for a job)?

TEAMWORK

Working to Provide Accurate Data

Gloria's Fabrics is a large fabric provider to the general public. The accounting office has three employees: accounts receivable clerk, accounts payable clerk, and full charge bookkeeper. The accounts receivable clerk creates the sales invoices and records the cash receipts, the accounts payable clerk creates and pays the purchase orders, and the full charge bookkeeper reconciles the checking account. Assign each group member one of the three jobs. Identify the accounts and describe the transactions that would be recorded by that assigned job. What effect would each transaction have on each account? How would each member of the accounting department work together to present accurate information for the decision makers?

Answers to **Self Reviews**

Answers to Section 1 Self Review

1. A financial event that changes the resources of the firm.
2. An example is the initial investment of cash in a business by the owner.
3. Amounts that a company must pay to creditors in the future.
4. **b.** Equipment is increased by $3,350 and accounts payable is increased by $3,350.
5. **c.** $130,000.
6. $10,000.

Answers to Section 2 Self Review

1. Funds taken from the business to pay for personal expenses. They decrease the owner's equity in the business.
2. As an additional investment by the owner recorded on the basis of fair market value.
3. The firm's name (who), the title of the statement (what), and the time period covered by the report (when).
4. **c.** $150,000.
5. $90,000 increase.
6. **a.** revenue and expenses for a period of time

Answers to Comprehensive Self Review

1. Buying for cash results in an immediate decrease in cash; buying on account results in a liability recorded as accounts payable.
2. The opposite side of the accounting equation will decrease because a decrease in assets results in a corresponding decrease in either a liability or the owner's equity.
3. The payment of $1,200 to a creditor on account.
4. Revenue increases owner's equity. Expenses decrease owner's equity.
5. The income statement is prepared first because the net income or loss is needed to complete the statement of owner's equity. The statement of owner's equity is prepared next to update the change in owner's equity. The balance sheet is prepared last.

Analyzing Business Transactions Using T Accounts

Chapter 3

www.att.com

© AP Photo/Marcio Jose Sanchez

When Alexander Graham Bell invented the telephone in 1876, and gave birth to the company that would become AT&T, he had no idea that a century and a half later, millions of people worldwide would be relying on his "name-sake" to call, text, and e-mail the people in their lives. Since being formed in 1877, AT&T has broadened its offerings through new-product development and diversification. Recognized as one of the leading worldwide providers of IP-based communications services to business, AT&T also offers the greatest number of phones that work in most countries, the largest Wi-Fi network in the United States, and the largest number of high-speed Internet access subscribers in the United States.

Keeping track of the multitude of transactions initiated by these services has been the job of the accountant. However, because the accounting equation-table is just too clumsy to be used in a company that has thousands upon thousands of transactions every month, accountants use a more streamlined recordkeeping approach. Accountants throughout the world rely instead on a double-entry system of debits and credits.

thinking critically

How might accountants in 1877 have recorded The Bell Telephone Company's first telephone service revenue transaction? How did this transaction affect the fundamental accounting equation?

LEARNING OBJECTIVES

- **3-1** Set up T accounts for assets, liabilities, and owner's equity.
- **3-2** Analyze business transactions and enter them in the accounts.
- **3-3** Determine the balance of an account.
- **3-4** Set up T accounts for revenue and expenses.
- **3-5** Prepare a trial balance from T accounts.
- **3-6** Prepare an income statement, a statement of owner's equity, and a balance sheet.
- **3-7** Develop a chart of accounts.
- **3-8** Define the accounting terms new to this chapter.

NEW TERMS

- account balance
- accounts
- chart of accounts
- classification
- credit
- debit
- double-entry system
- drawing account
- footing
- normal balance
- permanent account
- slide
- T account
- temporary account
- transposition
- trial balance

Section 1

SECTION OBJECTIVES	TERMS TO LEARN
>> 3-1 Set up T accounts for assets, liabilities, and owner's equity. WHY IT'S IMPORTANT The T account is an important visual tool used as an alternative to the fundamental accounting equation.	account balance accounts classification footing normal balance T account
>> 3-2 Analyze business transactions and enter them in the accounts. WHY IT'S IMPORTANT Accountants often use T accounts to help analyze and classify business transactions.	
>> 3-3 Determine the balance of an account. WHY IT'S IMPORTANT Accurate account balances contribute to a reliable accounting system.	

Transactions That Affect Assets, Liabilities, and Owner's Equity

In this chapter, you will learn how to record the changes caused by business transactions. This recordkeeping is a basic part of accounting systems.

Asset, Liability, and Owner's Equity Accounts

The accounting equation is one tool for analyzing the effects of business transactions. However, businesses do not record transactions in equation form. Instead, businesses establish separate records, called **accounts,** for assets, liabilities, and owner's equity. Use of accounts helps owners and staff analyze, record, classify, summarize, and report financial information. Accounts are recognized by their **classification** as assets, liabilities, or owner's equity. Asset accounts show the property a business owns. Liability accounts show the debts of the business. Owner's equity accounts show the owner's financial interest in the business. Each account has a name that describes the type of property, the debt, or the financial interest.

Accountants use T accounts to analyze transactions. A **T account** consists of a vertical line and a horizontal line that resemble the letter **T.** The name of the account is written on the horizontal (top) line. Increases and decreases in the account are entered on either side of the vertical line.

The following are T accounts for assets, liabilities, and owner's equity:

ASSETS		=	LIABILITIES		+	OWNER'S EQUITY	
+ Record increases	– Record decreases		– Record decreases	+ Record increases		– Record decreases	+ Record increases

RECORDING A CASH INVESTMENT

>> **3-1 OBJECTIVE**
Set up T accounts for assets, liabilities, and owner's equity.

Asset accounts show items of value owned by a business. Trayton Eli invested $100,000 in the business. Sergio Sanchez, the office manager for Eli's Consulting Services, set up a ***Cash*** account. Cash is an asset. Assets appear on the left side of the accounting equation. Cash increases appear on the left side of the ***Cash*** T account. Decreases are shown on the right side. Sanchez entered the cash investment of $100,000 **(a)** on the left side of the ***Cash*** account.

T accounts normally do not have plus and minus signs. We show them to help you identify increases (+) and decreases (−) in accounts.

recall

The Accounting Equation
Assets = Liabilities + Owner's Equity

Cash	
+	−
(a) 100,000	

Sergio Sanchez set up an account for owner's equity called ***Trayton Eli, Capital.*** Owner's equity appears on the right side of the accounting equation (Assets = Liabilities + Owner's Equity). Increases in owner's equity appear on the right side of the T account. Decreases in owner's equity appear on the left side. Sanchez entered the investment of $100,000 **(a)** on the right side of the ***Trayton Eli, Capital*** account.

Trayton Eli, Capital	
−	+
	(a) 100,000

>> **3-2 OBJECTIVE**
Analyze business transactions and enter them in the accounts.

Use these steps to analyze the effects of the business transactions:

1. Analyze the financial event.
   - Identify the accounts affected.
   - Classify the accounts affected.
   - Determine the amount of increase or decrease for each account.
2. Apply the left-right rules for each account affected.
3. Make the entry in T-account form.

BUSINESS TRANSACTION

Trayton Eli withdrew $100,000 from personal savings and deposited it in the new business checking account for Eli's Consulting Services.

ANALYSIS

a. The asset account ***Cash*** is increased by $100,000.
a. The owner's equity account, ***Trayton Eli, Capital,*** is increased by $100,000.

LEFT-RIGHT RULES

LEFT Increases to asset accounts are recorded on the left side of the T account. Record $100,000 on the left side of the ***Cash*** T account.

RIGHT Increases to owner's equity accounts are recorded on the right side of the T account. Record $100,000 on the right side of the ***Trayton Eli, Capital*** T account.

T-ACCOUNT PRESENTATION

Cash	
+	−
(a) 100,000	

Trayton Eli, Capital	
−	+
	(a) 100,000

RECORDING A CASH PURCHASE OF EQUIPMENT

Sergio Sanchez set up an asset account, ***Equipment,*** to record the purchase of a computer and other equipment.

BUSINESS TRANSACTION

Eli's Consulting Services issued a $5,000 check to purchase a computer and other equipment.

ANALYSIS

b. The asset account ***Equipment*** is increased by $5,000.

b. The asset account ***Cash*** is decreased by $5,000.

LEFT-RIGHT RULES

LEFT Increases to asset accounts are recorded on the left side of the T account. Record $5,000 on the left side of the ***Equipment*** T account.

RIGHT Decreases to asset accounts are recorded on the right side of the T account. Record $5,000 on the right side of the ***Cash*** T account.

T-ACCOUNT PRESENTATION

Equipment	
+	−
(b) 5,000	

Cash	
+	−
	(b) 5,000

Let's look at the T accounts to review the effects of the transactions. Sanchez entered $5,000 **(b)** on the left (increase) side of the ***Equipment*** account. He entered $5,000 **(b)** on the right (decrease) side of the ***Cash*** account. Notice that the ***Cash*** account shows the effects of two transactions.

Equipment	
+	−
(b) 5,000	

Cash	
+	−
(a) 100,000	(b) 5,000

RECORDING A CREDIT PURCHASE OF EQUIPMENT

Liabilities are amounts a business owes its creditors. Liabilities appear on the right side of the accounting equation (Assets = Liabilities + Owner's Equity). Increases in liabilities are on the right side of liability T accounts. Decreases in liabilities are on the left side of liability T accounts.

BUSINESS TRANSACTION

The firm bought office equipment for $6,000 on account from Office Plus.

ANALYSIS

c. The asset account ***Equipment*** is increased by $6,000.

c. The liability account ***Accounts Payable*** is increased by $6,000.

LEFT-RIGHT RULES

LEFT Increases to asset accounts are recorded on the left side of the T account. Record $6,000 on the left side of the ***Equipment*** T account.

RIGHT Increases to liability accounts are recorded on the right side of the T account. Record $6,000 on the right side of the ***Accounts Payable*** T account.

T-ACCOUNT PRESENTATION

Equipment +	Equipment −
(c) 6,000	

Accounts Payable −	Accounts Payable +
	(c) 6,000

important!

For liability T accounts

- right side shows increases,
- left side shows decreases.

Let's look at the T accounts to review the effects of the transactions. Sanchez entered $6,000 **(c)** on the left (increase) side of the ***Equipment*** account. It now shows two transactions. He entered $6,000 **(c)** on the right (increase) side of the ***Accounts Payable*** account.

Equipment +	Equipment −
(b) 5,000	
(c) 6,000	

Accounts Payable −	Accounts Payable +
	(c) 6,000

The balance sheet of Avery Dennison Corporation at January 1, 2016, showed net property, plant, and equipment of $847.9 million.

RECORDING A CASH PURCHASE OF SUPPLIES

Sergio Sanchez set up an asset account called ***Supplies.***

BUSINESS TRANSACTION

Eli's Consulting Services issued a check for $1,500 to Office Delux Inc. to purchase office supplies.

ANALYSIS

d. The asset account ***Supplies*** is increased by $1,500.

d. The asset account ***Cash*** is decreased by $1,500.

LEFT-RIGHT RULES

LEFT Increases to asset accounts are recorded on the left side of the T account. Record $1,500 on the left side of the ***Supplies*** T account.

RIGHT Decreases to asset accounts are recorded on the right side of the T account. Record $1,500 on the right side of the ***Cash*** T account.

T-ACCOUNT PRESENTATION

Supplies +	Supplies −
(d) 1,500	

Cash +	Cash −
	(d) 1,500

Sanchez entered $1,500 **(d)** on the left (increase) side of the ***Supplies*** account and $1,500 **(d)** on the right (decrease) side of the ***Cash*** account.

Supplies +	Supplies −
(d) 1,500	

Cash +	Cash −
(a) 100,000	(b) 5,000
	(d) 1,500

Notice that the ***Cash*** account now shows three transactions: the initial investment by the owner (**a**), the cash purchase of equipment (**b**), and the cash purchase of supplies (**d**).

RECORDING A PAYMENT TO A CREDITOR

On November 30, the business paid $2,500 to Office Plus to apply against the debt of $6,000 shown in ***Accounts Payable.***

BUSINESS TRANSACTION

Eli's Consulting Services issued a check in the amount of $2,500 to Office Plus.

ANALYSIS

e. The asset account ***Cash*** is decreased by $2,500.

e. The liability account ***Accounts Payable*** is decreased by $2,500.

LEFT-RIGHT RULES

LEFT Decreases to liability accounts are recorded on the left side of the T account. Record $2,500 on the left side of the ***Accounts Payable*** T account.

RIGHT Decreases to asset accounts are recorded on the right side of the T account. Record $2,500 on the right side of the ***Cash*** T account.

T-ACCOUNT PRESENTATION

Accounts Payable −	Accounts Payable +
(e) 2,500	

Cash +	Cash −
	(e) 2,500

Let's look at the T accounts to review the effects of the transactions. Sanchez entered $2,500 **(e)** on the right (decrease) side of the ***Cash*** account. He entered $2,500 **(e)** on the left (decrease) side of the ***Accounts Payable*** account. Notice that both accounts show the effects of several transactions.

Accounts Payable	
–	+
(e) 2,500	(c) 6,000

Cash	
+	–
(a) 100,000	(b) 5,000
	(d) 1,500
	(e) 2,500

RECORDING PREPAID RENT

In November, Eli's Consulting Services was required to pay the December and January rent in advance. Sanchez set up an asset account called ***Prepaid Rent.***

BUSINESS TRANSACTION

Eli's Consulting Services issued a check for $8,000 to pay rent for the months of December and January.

ANALYSIS

f. The asset account ***Prepaid Rent*** is increased by $8,000.
f. The asset account ***Cash*** is decreased by $8,000.

LEFT-RIGHT RULES

LEFT Increases to asset accounts are recorded on the left side of the T account. Record $8,000 on the left side of the ***Prepaid Rent*** T account.

RIGHT Decreases to asset accounts are recorded on the right side of the T account. Record $8,000 on the right side of the ***Cash*** T account.

T-ACCOUNT PRESENTATION

Prepaid Rent	
+	–
(f) 8,000	

Cash	
+	–
	(f) 8,000

Let's review the T accounts to see the effects of the transactions. Sanchez entered $8,000 **(f)** on the left (increase) side of the ***Prepaid Rent*** account. He entered $8,000 **(f)** on the right (decrease) side of the ***Cash*** account.

Notice that the ***Cash*** account shows the effects of numerous transactions. It shows initial investment **(a)**, equipment purchase **(b)**, supplies purchase **(d)**, payment on account **(e)**, and advance rent payment **(f)**.

Prepaid Rent	
+	–
(f) 8,000	

Cash	
+	–
(a) 100,000	(b) 5,000
	(d) 1,500
	(e) 2,500
	(f) 8,000

>> 3-3 OBJECTIVE

Determine the balance of an account.

Account Balances

An **account balance** is the difference between the amounts on the two sides of the account. First add the figures on each side of the account. If the column has more than one figure, enter the total in small pencil figures called a **footing.** Then subtract the smaller total from the larger total. The result is the account balance.

- If the total on the right side is larger than the total on the left side, the balance is recorded on the right side.
- If the total on the left side is larger, the balance is recorded on the left side.
- If an account shows only one amount, that amount is the balance.
- If an account contains entries on only one side, the total of those entries is the account balance.

Let's look at the ***Cash*** account for Eli's Consulting Services. The left side shows $100,000. The total of the right side is $17,000. Subtract the footing of $17,000 from $100,000. The result is the account balance of $83,000. The account balance is shown on the left side of the account.

Cash	
+	−
(a) 100,000	(b) 5,000
	(d) 1,500
	(e) 2,500
	(f) 8,000
	17,000 ← Footing
Bal. 83,000	

Usually account balances appear on the increase side of the account. The increase side of the account is the **normal balance** of the account.

The following is a summary of the procedures to increase or decrease accounts and shows the normal balance of accounts.

ABOUT **ACCOUNTING**

Law Enforcement

The FBI and other law enforcement agencies recruit accountants to investigate criminal conduct. Perhaps the most famous use of accounting by law enforcers is the conviction of Al Capone for tax evasion after he could not be jailed for his ties to organized crime.

ASSETS		=	LIABILITIES		+	OWNER'S EQUITY	
+ Increase (Normal Balance)	Decrease		− Decrease	+ Increase (Normal Balance)		− Decrease	+ Increase (Normal Balance)

Figure 3.1 shows a summary of the account balances for Eli's Consulting Services. Figure 3.2 shows a balance sheet prepared for November 30, 2019.

In equation form, the firm's position after these transactions is:

Assets							=	Liabilities	+	Owner's Equity
Cash	+	Supp.	+	Prepaid Rent	+	Equip.	=	Accounts Payable	+	Trayton Eli, Capital
$83,000	+	$1,500	+	$8,000	+	$11,000	=	$3,500	+	$100,000

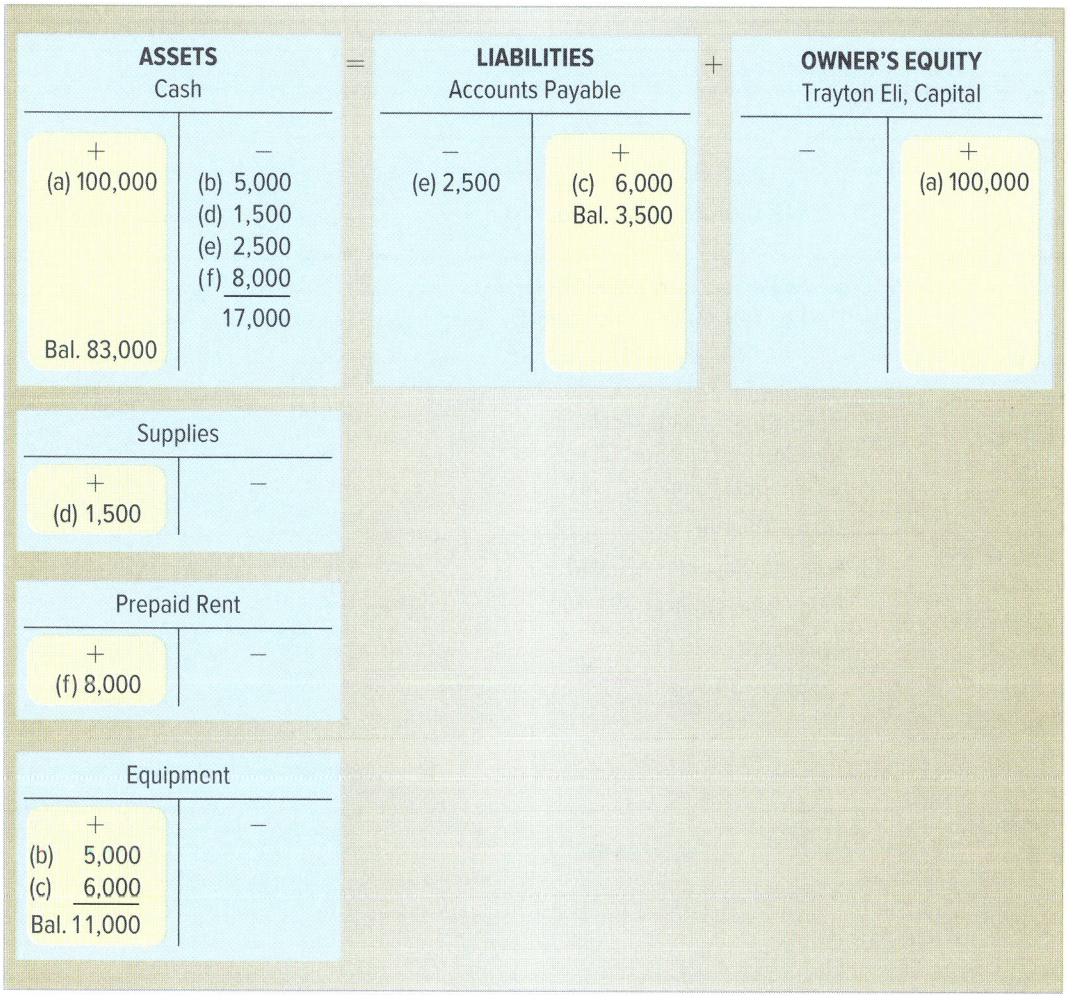

FIGURE 3.1

T-Account Balances for Eli's Consulting Services

FIGURE 3.2 **Balance Sheet for Eli's Consulting Services**

Eli's Consulting Services			
Balance Sheet			
November 30, 2019			
Assets		*Liabilities*	
Cash	83 0 0 0 00	*Accounts Payable*	3 5 0 0 00
Supplies	1 5 0 0 00		
Prepaid Rent	8 0 0 0 00	*Owner's Equity*	
Equipment	11 0 0 0 00	*Trayton Eli, Capital*	100 0 0 0 00
Total Assets	103 5 0 0 00	*Total Liabilities and Owner's Equity*	103 5 0 0 00

Notice how the balance sheet reflects the fundamental accounting equation.

Section 1 Self Review

QUESTIONS

1. Increases are recorded on which side of asset, liability, and owner's equity accounts?
2. What is a footing?
3. What is meant by the "normal balance" of an account? What is the normal balance side for asset, liability, and owner's equity accounts?

EXERCISES

4. The Richey Company purchased new equipment for $40,400 from Office Supplies, Inc., to be paid in 30 days. Which of the following is correct?
   a. ***Equipment*** is increased by $40,400. ***Accounts Payable*** is decreased by $40,400.
   b. ***Equipment*** is increased by $40,400. ***Accounts Payable*** is increased by $40,400.
   c. ***Equipment*** is decreased by $40,400. ***Accounts Payable*** is increased by $40,400.
   d. ***Equipment*** is increased by $40,400. ***Cash*** is decreased by $40,400.
5. From the following accounts, show that the fundamental accounting equation is in balance. All accounts have normal balances.

   Cash—$15,400

   Accounts Payable—$10,000

   Todd Dodd, Capital—$30,000

   Equipment—$20,000

   Supplies—$4,600

ANALYSIS

6. Foot and find the balance of the ***Cash*** account.

Cash	
+	–
36,000	12,000
22,000	5,000
	5,200
	2,350

   a. 58,000
   b. 32,000
   c. 33,450
   d. 24,100

(Answers to Section 1 Self Review are on page 84.)

Section 2

SECTION OBJECTIVES	TERMS TO LEARN
>> 3-4 Set up T accounts for revenue and expenses. WHY IT'S IMPORTANT T accounts help you understand the effects of all business transactions. >> 3-5 Prepare a trial balance from T accounts. WHY IT'S IMPORTANT The trial balance is an important check of accuracy at the end of the accounting period. >> 3-6 Prepare an income statement, a statement of owner's equity, and a balance sheet. WHY IT'S IMPORTANT Financial statements summarize the financial activities and condition of the business. >> 3-7 Develop a chart of accounts. WHY IT'S IMPORTANT Businesses require a system that allows accounts to be easily identified and located.	chart of accounts credit debit double-entry system drawing account permanent account slide temporary account transposition trial balance

Transactions That Affect Revenue, Expenses, and Withdrawals

Let's examine the revenue and expense transactions of Eli's Consulting Services for December to see how they are recorded.

Revenue and Expense Accounts

Some owner's equity accounts are classified as revenue or expense accounts. Separate accounts are used to record revenue and expense transactions.

RECORDING REVENUE FROM SERVICES SOLD FOR CASH

During December, the business earned $36,000 in revenue from clients who paid cash for bookkeeping, accounting, and consulting services. This involved several transactions. Sergio Sanchez entered $36,000 **(g)** on the left (increase) side of the asset account ***Cash.***

Cash	
+	−
Bal. 83,000	
(g) 36,000	

>> **3-4 OBJECTIVE**
Set up T accounts for revenue and expenses.

How is the increase in owner's equity recorded? One way would be to record the $36,000 on the right side of the ***Trayton Eli, Capital*** account. However, the preferred way is to keep revenue separate from the owner's investment until the end of the accounting period. Therefore, Sanchez opened a revenue account for ***Fees Income.***

Sanchez entered $36,000 (**g**) on the right side of the ***Fees Income*** account. Revenues increase owner's equity. Increases in owner's equity appear on the right side of the T account. Therefore, increases in revenue appear on the right side of revenue T accounts.

Fees Income	
−	+
	(g) 36,000

The right side of the revenue account shows increases and the left side shows decreases. Decreases in revenue accounts are rare but might occur because of corrections or transfers.

Let's review the effects of the transactions. Sanchez entered $36,000 (**g**) on the left (increase) side of the ***Cash*** account and $36,000 (**g**) on the right (increase) side of the ***Fees Income*** account.

Cash	
+	−
Bal. 83,000	
(g) 36,000	

Fees Income	
−	+
	(g) 36,000

At this point, the firm needs just one revenue account. Most businesses have separate accounts for different types of revenue. For example, sales of goods such as clothes are recorded in the revenue account ***Sales.***

RECORDING REVENUE FROM SERVICES SOLD ON CREDIT

In December, Eli's Consulting Services earned $11,000 from various charge account clients. Sanchez set up an asset account, ***Accounts Receivable.***

ANALYSIS

h. The asset account ***Accounts Receivable*** is increased by $11,000.

h. The revenue account ***Fees Income*** is increased by $11,000.

LEFT-RIGHT RULES

LEFT Increases to asset accounts are recorded on the left side of the T account. Record $11,000 on the left side of the ***Accounts Receivable*** T account.

RIGHT Increases in revenue appear on the right side of the T account. Record $11,000 on the right side of the ***Fees Income*** T account.

T-ACCOUNT PRESENTATION

Accounts Receivable	
+	−
(h) 11,000	

Fees Income	
−	+
	(h) 11,000

Let's review the effects of the transactions. Sanchez entered $11,000 **(h)** on the left (increase) side of the ***Accounts Receivable*** account and $11,000 **(h)** on the right (increase) side of the ***Fees Income*** account.

Accounts Receivable	
+	−
(h) 11,000	

Fees Income	
−	+
	(g) 36,000
	(h) 11,000

RECORDING COLLECTIONS FROM ACCOUNTS RECEIVABLE

Charge account clients paid $6,000, reducing the amount owed to Eli's Consulting Services.

ANALYSIS

i. The asset account ***Cash*** is increased by $6,000.

i. The asset account ***Accounts Receivable*** is decreased by $6,000.

LEFT-RIGHT RULES

LEFT Increases to asset accounts are recorded on the left side of the T account. Record $6,000 on the left side of the ***Cash*** T account.

RIGHT Decreases to asset accounts are recorded on the right side of the T account. Record $6,000 on the right side of the ***Accounts Receivable*** T account.

T-ACCOUNT PRESENTATION

Cash	
+	−
(i) 6,000	

Accounts Receivable	
+	−
	(i) 6,000

Let's review the effects of the transactions. Sanchez entered $6,000 **(i)** on the left (increase) side of the ***Cash*** account and $6,000 **(i)** on the right (decrease) side of the ***Accounts Receivable*** account. Notice that revenue is not recorded when cash is collected from charge account clients. The revenue was recorded when the sales on credit were recorded **(h).**

Cash	
+	−
Bal. 83,000	
(g) 36,000	
(i) 6,000	

Accounts Receivable	
+	−
(h) 11,000	(i) 6,000

RECORDING AN EXPENSE FOR SALARIES

Expenses decrease owner's equity. Decreases in owner's equity appear on the left side of the T account. Therefore, increases in expenses (which are decreases in owner's equity) are recorded on the left side of expense T accounts. Decreases in expenses are recorded on the right side of the T accounts. Decreases in expenses are rare but may result from corrections or transfers.

recall

Expense

An expense is an outflow of cash, the use of other assets, or the incurring of a liability.

BUSINESS TRANSACTION

In December, Eli's Consulting Services paid $8,000 in salaries.

ANALYSIS

j. The asset account ***Cash*** is decreased by $8,000.
j. The expense account ***Salaries Expense*** is increased by $8,000.

LEFT-RIGHT RULES

LEFT Increases in expenses appear on the left side of the T account. Record $8,000 on the left side of the ***Salaries Expense*** T account.

RIGHT Decreases in asset accounts are recorded on the right side of the T account. Record $8,000 on the right side of the ***Cash*** T account.

T-ACCOUNT PRESENTATION

Salaries Expense

+	−
(j) 8,000	

Cash

+	−
	(j) 8,000

How is the decrease in owner's equity recorded? One way would be to record the $8,000 on the left side of the ***Trayton Eli, Capital*** account. However, the preferred way is to keep expenses separate from owner's investment. Therefore, Sanchez set up a ***Salaries Expense*** account.

To record the salary expense, Sanchez entered $8,000 **(j)** on the left (increase) side of the ***Salaries Expense*** account. Notice that the plus and minus signs in the ***Salaries Expense*** account show the effect on the expense account, not on owner's equity.

Salaries Expense

+	−
(j) 8,000	

Sanchez entered $8,000 **(j)** on the right (decrease) side of the ***Cash*** T account.

Cash

+	−
Bal. 83,000	(j) 8,000
(g) 36,000	
(i) 6,000	

Most companies have numerous expense accounts. The various expense accounts appear in the Expenses section of the income statement.

RECORDING AN EXPENSE FOR UTILITIES

At the end of December, Eli's Consulting Services received a $650 bill for utilities. Sanchez set up an account for ***Utilities Expense.***

BUSINESS TRANSACTION

Eli's Consulting Services issued a check for $650 to pay the utilities bill.

ANALYSIS

k. The asset account ***Cash*** is decreased by $650.

k. The expense account ***Utilities Expense*** is increased by $650.

LEFT-RIGHT RULES

LEFT Increases in expenses appear on the left side of the T account. Record $650 on the left side of the ***Utilities Expense*** T account.

RIGHT Decreases to asset accounts are recorded on the right side of the T account. Record $650 on the right side of the ***Cash*** T account.

T-ACCOUNT PRESENTATION

Utilities Expense

+	−
(k) 650	

Cash

+	−
	(k) 650

Let's review the effects of the transactions.

Utilities Expense

+	−
(k) 650	

Cash

+	−
Bal. 83,000	(j) 8,000
(g) 36,000	(k) 650
(i) 6,000	

The Drawing Account

In sole proprietorships and partnerships, the owners generally do not pay themselves salaries. To obtain funds for personal living expenses, owners make withdrawals of cash. The withdrawals are against previously earned profits that have become part of capital or against profits that are expected in the future.

Since withdrawals decrease owner's equity, withdrawals could be recorded on the left side of the capital account. However, the preferred way is to keep withdrawals separate from the owner's capital account until the end of the accounting period. An owner's equity account called a **drawing account** is set up to record withdrawals. Increases in the drawing account (which are decreases in owner's equity) are recorded on the left side of the drawing T accounts.

BUSINESS TRANSACTION

Trayton Eli wrote a check to withdraw $5,000 cash for personal use.

ANALYSIS

l. The asset account ***Cash*** is decreased by $5,000.

l. The owner's equity account ***Trayton Eli, Drawing*** is increased by $5,000.

FIGURE 3.3

The Relationship Between Owner's Equity and Revenue, Expenses, and Withdrawals

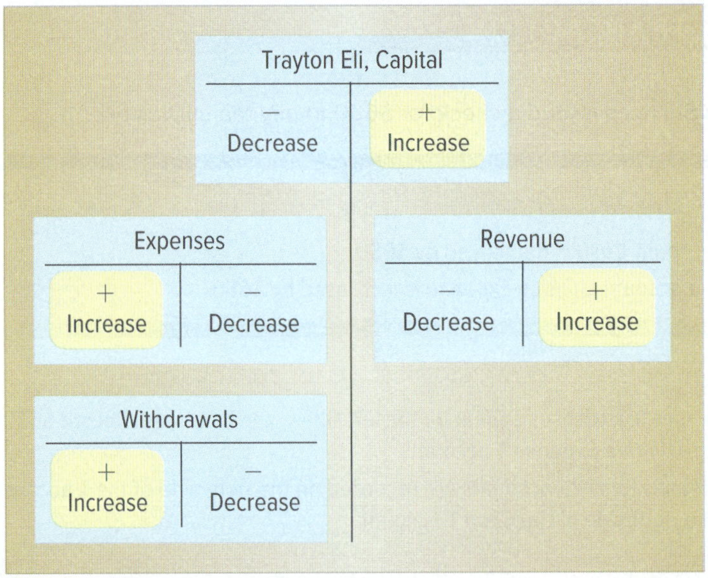

LEFT-RIGHT RULES

LEFT Increases to drawing accounts are recorded on the left side of the T account. Record $5,000 on the left side of the ***Trayton Eli, Drawing*** T account.

RIGHT Decreases to asset accounts are recorded on the right side of the T account. Record $5,000 on the right side of the ***Cash*** T account.

T-ACCOUNT PRESENTATION

Trayton Eli, Drawing	
+	–
(l) 5,000	

Cash	
+	–
	(l) 5,000

Let's review the transactions. Sanchez entered $5,000 **(l)** on the right (decrease) side of the asset account ***Cash*** and $5,000 **(l)** on the left (increase) side of ***Trayton Eli, Drawing.*** Note that the plus and minus signs show the effect on the drawing account, not on owner's equity.

Trayton Eli, Drawing	
+	–
(l) 5,000	

Cash	
+	–
Bal. 83,000	(j) 8,000
(g) 36,000	(k) 650
(i) 6,000	(l) 5,000

Figure 3.3 shows a summary of the relationship between the capital account and the revenue, expense, and drawing accounts.

important!

Normal Balances

Debit:	*Credit:*
Asset	Liability
Expense	Revenue
Drawing	Capital

The Rules of Debit and Credit

Accountants do not use the terms *left side* and *right side* when they talk about making entries in accounts. Instead, they use the term **debit** for an entry on the left side and **credit** for an entry on the right side. Figure 3.4 summarizes the rules for debits and credits. The accounting system is called the **double-entry system.** This is because each transaction has at least two entries—a debit and a credit.

FIGURE 3.4 Rules for Debits and Credits

Account	Debit	Credit
ASSET ACCOUNTS	Debit + Increase Side (Normal Bal.)	Credit − Decrease Side
LIABILITY ACCOUNTS	Debit − Decrease Side	Credit + Increase Side (Normal Bal.)
OWNER'S CAPITAL ACCOUNT	Debit − Decrease Side	Credit + Increase Side (Normal Bal.)
OWNER'S DRAWING ACCOUNT	Debit + Increase Side (Normal Bal.)	Credit − Decrease Side
REVENUE ACCOUNTS	Debit − Decrease Side	Credit + Increase Side (Normal Bal.)
EXPENSE ACCOUNTS	Debit + Increase Side (Normal Bal.)	Credit − Decrease Side

After the December transactions for Eli's Consulting Services are recorded, the account balances are calculated. Figure 3.5 below shows the account balances at the end of December. Notice that the fundamental accounting equation remains in balance (Assets = Liabilities + Owner's Equity).

FIGURE 3.5 End-of-December 2019 Account Balances

ASSETS = LIABILITIES + OWNER'S EQUITY

ASSETS

Cash

	Debit		Credit
Bal	83,000	(j)	8,000
(g)	36,000	(k)	650
(i)	6,000	(l)	5,000
	125,000		13,650
Bal.	111,350		

Accounts Receivable

	Debit		Credit
(h)	11,000	(i)	6,000
Bal.	5,000		

Supplies

	Debit		Credit
Bal.	1,500		

Prepaid Rent

	Debit		Credit
Bal.	8,000		

Equipment

	Debit		Credit
Bal.	11,000		

LIABILITIES

Accounts Payable

	Debit		Credit
		Bal.	3,500

OWNER'S EQUITY

Trayton Eli, Capital

	Debit		Credit
		Bal.	100,000

Trayton Eli, Drawing

	Debit		Credit
(l)	5,000		

Fees Income

	Debit		Credit
		(g)	36,000
		(h)	11,000
		Bal.	47,000

Salaries Expense

	Debit		Credit
(j)	8,000		

Utilities Expense

	Debit		Credit
(k)	650		

FIGURE 3.6

Trial Balance

Eli's Consulting Services		
Trial Balance		
December 31, 2019		
ACCOUNT NAME	DEBIT	CREDIT
Cash	111 3 5 0 00	
Accounts Receivable	5 0 0 0 00	
Supplies	1 5 0 0 00	
Prepaid Rent	8 0 0 0 00	
Equipment	11 0 0 0 00	
Accounts Payable		3 5 0 0 00
Trayton Eli, Capital		100 0 0 0 00
Trayton Eli, Drawing	5 0 0 0 00	
Fees Income		47 0 0 0 00
Salaries Expense	8 0 0 0 00	
Utilities Expense	6 5 0 00	
Totals	150 5 0 0 00	150 5 0 0 00

recall

Financial Statement Headings

The financial statement headings answer three questions:

Who—the company name

What—the report subtitle

When—the date of, or the period covered by, the report

>> 3-5 OBJECTIVE

Prepare a trial balance from T accounts.

The Trial Balance

Once the account balances are computed, a trial balance is prepared. The **trial balance** is a statement that tests the accuracy of total debits and credits after transactions have been recorded. If total debits do not equal total credits, there is an error. Figure 3.6 shows the trial balance for Eli's Consulting Services. To prepare a trial balance, perform the following steps:

1. Enter the trial balance heading showing the company name, report title, and closing date for the accounting period.
2. List the account names in the same order as they appear on the financial statements.
   - Assets
   - Liabilities
   - Owner's Equity
   - Revenue
   - Expenses
3. Enter the ending balance of each account in the appropriate Debit or Credit column.
4. Total the Debit column.
5. Total the Credit column.
6. Compare the total debits with the total credits.

MANAGERIAL IMPLICATIONS <<

FINANCIAL STATEMENTS

- Recording entries into accounts provides an efficient method of gathering data about the financial affairs of a business.
- A chart of accounts is usually similar from company to company; balance sheet accounts are first, followed by income statement accounts.
- A trial balance proves the financial records are in balance.
- The income statement reports the revenue and expenses for the period and shows the net income or loss.
- The statement of owner's equity shows the change in owner's equity during the period.
- The balance sheet summarizes the assets, liabilities, and owner's equity of the business on a given date.
- Owners, managers, creditors, banks, and many others use financial statements to make decisions about the business.

THINKING CRITICALLY

What are some possible consequences of not recording financial data correctly?

UNDERSTANDING TRIAL BALANCE ERRORS

If the totals of the Debit and Credit columns are equal, the financial records are in balance. If the totals of the Debit and Credit columns are not equal, there is an error. The error may be in the trial balance, or it may be in the financial records. Some common errors are:

- adding trial balance columns incorrectly;
- recording only half a transaction—for example, recording a debit but not recording a credit, or vice versa;
- recording both halves of a transaction as debits or credits rather than recording one debit and one credit;
- recording an amount incorrectly from a transaction;
- recording a debit for one amount and a credit for a different amount;
- making an error when calculating the account balances.

FINDING TRIAL BALANCE ERRORS

If the trial balance does not balance, try the following procedures:

1. Check the arithmetic. If the columns were originally added from top to bottom, verify the total by adding from bottom to top.
2. Check that the correct account balances were transferred to the correct trial balance columns.
3. Check the arithmetic used to compute the account balances.
4. Check that each transaction was recorded correctly in the accounts by tracing the amounts to the analysis of the transaction.

Sometimes you can determine the type of the error by the amount of the difference. Compute the difference between the debit total and the credit total. If the difference is divisible by 2, a debit might be recorded as a credit, or a credit recorded as a debit.

If the difference is divisible by 9, there might be a transposition. A **transposition** occurs when the digits of a number are switched (357 for 375). The test for a transposition is:

$$\begin{array}{r} 375 \\ -357 \\ \hline 18 \end{array} \qquad 18/9 = 2$$

Also check for slides. A **slide** occurs when the decimal point is misplaced (375 for 37.50). We can test for a slide in the following manner:

$$\begin{array}{r} 375.00 \\ 37.50 \\ \hline 337.50 \end{array} \qquad 337.50/9 = 37.50$$

Financial Statements

>> **3-6 OBJECTIVE**
Prepare an income statement, a statement of owner's equity, and a balance sheet.

After the trial balance is prepared, the financial statements are prepared. Figure 3.7 shows the financial statements for Eli's Consulting Services. The amounts are taken from the trial balance. As you study the financial statements, note that net income from the income statement is used on the statement of owner's equity. Also note that the ending balance of the ***Trayton Eli, Capital*** account, computed on the statement of owner's equity, is used on the balance sheet.

Chart of Accounts

>> **3-7 OBJECTIVE**
Develop a chart of accounts.

A **chart of accounts** is a list of all the accounts used by a business. Figure 3.8 shows the chart of accounts for Eli's Consulting Services. Each account has a number and a name. The balance sheet accounts are listed first, followed by the income statement accounts. The account number is assigned based on the type of account.

FIGURE 3.7

Financial Statements for Eli's Consulting Services

Eli's Consulting Services
Income Statement
Month Ended December 31, 2019

Revenue		
Fees Income		47 000 00
Expenses		
Salaries Expense	8 000 00	
Utilities Expense	650 00	
Total Expenses		8 650 00
Net Income		38 350 00

Eli's Consulting Services
Statement of Owner's Equity
Month Ended December 31, 2019

Trayton Eli, Capital, December 1, 2019		100 000 00
Net Income for December	38 350 00	
Less Withdrawals for December	5 000 00	
Increase in Capital		33 350 00
Trayton Eli, Capital, December 31, 2019		133 350 00

Eli's Consulting Services
Balance Sheet
December 31, 2019

Assets		*Liabilities*	
Cash	111 350 00	*Accounts Payable*	3 500 00
Accounts Receivable	5 000 00		
Supplies	1 500 00		
Prepaid Rent	8 000 00	*Owner's Equity*	
Equipment	11 000 00	*Trayton Eli, Capital*	133 350 00
Total Assets	136 850 00	*Total Liabilities and Owner's Equity*	136 850 00

Asset Accounts	100–199	Revenue Accounts	400–499
Liability Accounts	200–299	Expense Accounts	500–599
Owner's Equity Accounts	300–399		

Notice that the accounts are not numbered consecutively. For example, asset account numbers jump from 101 to 111 and then to 121, 137, and 141. In each block of numbers, gaps are left so that additional accounts can be added when needed.

Permanent and Temporary Accounts

The asset, liability, and owner's equity accounts appear on the balance sheet at the end of an accounting period. The balances of these accounts are then carried forward to start the new period. Because they continue from one accounting period to the next, these accounts are called **permanent accounts** or *real accounts.*

Revenue and expense accounts appear on the income statement. The drawing account appears on the statement of owner's equity. These accounts classify and summarize changes in owner's equity during the period. They are called **temporary accounts** or *nominal accounts* because the balances in these accounts are transferred to the capital account at the end of the accounting period. In the next period, these accounts start with zero balances.

Eli's Consulting Services Chart of Accounts	
Account Number	**Account Name**
Balance Sheet Accounts	
100–199	**ASSETS**
101	Cash
111	Accounts Receivable
121	Supplies
137	Prepaid Rent
141	Equipment
200–299	**LIABILITIES**
202	Accounts Payable
300–399	**OWNER'S EQUITY**
301	Trayton Eli, Capital
Statement of Owner's Equity Account	
302	Trayton Eli, Drawing
Income Statement Accounts	
400–499	**REVENUE**
401	Fees Income
500–599	**EXPENSES**
511	Salaries Expense
514	Utilities Expense

FIGURE 3.8

Chart of Accounts

important!

Balance Sheet Accounts

The amounts on the balance sheet are carried forward to the next accounting period.

important!

Income Statement Accounts

The amounts on the income statement are transferred to the capital account at the end of the accounting period.

Section 2 Self Review

QUESTIONS

1. What is the increase side for *Cash; Accounts Payable;* and *Trayton Eli, Capital*?
2. What is a transposition? A slide?
3. What is a trial balance and what is its purpose?

EXERCISES

4. Which account has a normal debit balance?
   a. Fees Income
   b. Jim Davis, Drawing
   c. Jim Davis, Capital
   d. Accounts Payable
5. The company owner took $5,000 cash for personal use. What is the entry for this transaction?
   a. Debit *Cash* and credit *Caleb Parker, Capital.*
   b. Debit *Cash* and credit *Caleb Parker, Drawing.*
   c. Debit *Caleb Parker, Drawing* and credit *Cash.*
   d. Debit *Caleb Parker, Capital* and credit *Cash.*

ANALYSIS

6. Describe the errors in the Parker Interiors trial balance.

Parker Interiors
Trial Balance
December 31, 2019

	DEBIT	CREDIT
Cash	15 0 0 0 00	
Accts. Rec.	10 0 0 0 00	
Equip.	7 0 0 0 00	
Accts. Pay.		15 0 0 0 00
C. Parker, Capital		22 0 0 0 00
C. Parker, Drawing		10 0 0 0 00
Fees Income	14 0 0 0 00	
Rent Exp.	2 0 0 0 00	
Supplies Exp.	2 0 0 0 00	
Telephone Exp.	5 0 0 0 00	
Totals	55 0 0 0 00	47 0 0 0 00

(Answers to Section 2 Self Review are on page 84.)

Review and Applications

3 Chapter REVIEW Chapter Summary

In this chapter, you have learned how to use T accounts to help analyze and record business transactions. A chart of accounts can be developed to easily identify all the accounts used by a business. After determining the balance for all accounts, the trial balance is prepared to test the accuracy of total debits and credits after transactions have been recorded.

Learning Objectives

3-1 Set up T accounts for assets, liabilities, and owner's equity.

T accounts consist of two lines, one vertical and one horizontal, that resemble the letter T. The account name is written on the top line. Increases and decreases to the account are entered on either the left side or the right side of the vertical line.

3-2 Analyze business transactions and enter them in the accounts.

Each business transaction is analyzed for its effects on the fundamental accounting equation, Assets = Liabilities + Owner's Equity. Then these effects are recorded in the proper accounts. Accounts are classified as assets, liabilities, or owner's equity.

- Increases in an asset account appear on the debit, or left, side because assets are on the left side of the accounting equation. The credit, or right, side records decreases.
- An increase in a liability account is recorded on the credit, or right, side. The left, or debit, side of a liability account is used for recording decreases.
- Increases in owner's equity are shown on the credit (right) side of an account. Decreases appear on the debit (left) side.
- The drawing account is used to record the withdrawal of cash from the business by the owner. The drawing account decreases owner's equity.

3-3 Determine the balance of an account.

The difference between the amounts recorded on the two sides of an account is known as the balance of the account.

3-4 Set up T accounts for revenue and expenses.

- Revenue accounts increase owner's equity; therefore, increases are recorded on the credit side of revenue accounts.
- Expenses are recorded on the debit side of the expense accounts because expenses decrease owner's equity.

3-5 Prepare a trial balance from T accounts.

The trial balance is a statement to test the accuracy of the financial records. Total debits should equal total credits.

3-6 Prepare an income statement, a statement of owner's equity, and a balance sheet.

The income statement is prepared to report the revenue and expenses for the period. The statement of owner's equity is prepared to analyze the change in owner's equity during the period. Then the balance sheet is prepared to summarize the assets, liabilities, and owner's equity of the business at the end of the period.

3-7 Develop a chart of accounts.

A firm's list of accounts is called its chart of accounts. Accounts are arranged in a predetermined order and are numbered for handy reference and quick identification. Typically, accounts are numbered in the order in which they appear on the financial statements. Balance sheet accounts come first, followed by income statement accounts.

3-8 Define the accounting terms new to this chapter.

Glossary

Account balance (p. 58) The difference between the amounts recorded on the two sides of an account

Accounts (p. 52) Written records of the assets, liabilities, and owner's equity of a business

Chart of accounts (p. 69) A list of the accounts used by a business to record its financial transactions

Classification (p. 52) A means of identifying each account as an asset, liability, or owner's equity

Credit (p. 66) An entry on the right side of an account

Debit (p. 66) An entry on the left side of an account

Double-entry system (p. 66) An accounting system that involves recording the effects of each transaction as debits and credits

Drawing account (p. 65) A special type of owner's equity account set up to record the owner's withdrawal of cash from the business

Footing (p. 58) A small pencil figure written at the base of an amount column showing the sum of the entries in the column

Normal balance (p. 58) The increase side of an account

Permanent account (p. 70) An account that is kept open from one accounting period to the next

Slide (p. 69) An accounting error involving a misplaced decimal point

T account (p. 52) A type of account, resembling a T, used to analyze the effects of a business transaction

Temporary account (p. 70) An account whose balance is transferred to another account at the end of an accounting period

Transposition (p. 69) An accounting error involving misplaced digits in a number

Trial balance (p. 68) A statement to test the accuracy of total debits and credits after transactions have been recorded

Comprehensive **Self Review**

1. What is a chart of accounts?
2. What are withdrawals and how are they recorded?
3. What type of accounts are found on the balance sheet?
4. On which side of asset, liability, and owner's equity accounts are decreases recorded?
5. Your friend has prepared financial statements for her business. She has asked you to review the statements for accuracy. The trial balance debit column totals $91,000 and the credit column totals $104,000. What steps would you take to find the error?

(Answers to Comprehensive Self Review are on page 85.)

Discussion Questions

1. What are accounts?
2. What is the purpose of a chart of accounts?
3. In what order do accounts appear in the chart of accounts?
4. When a chart of accounts is created, number gaps are left within groups of accounts. Why are these number gaps necessary?
5. Accounts are classified as permanent or temporary accounts. What do these classifications mean?
6. How is the balance of an account determined?
7. Indicate whether each of the following types of accounts would normally have a debit balance or a credit balance:
   a. An asset account
   b. A liability account
   c. The owner's capital account
   d. A revenue account
   e. An expense account
8. The terms *debit* and *credit* are often used in describing the effects of transactions on different accounts. What do these terms mean?
9. Why is ***Prepaid Rent*** considered an asset account?

10. Why is the modern system of accounting usually called the double-entry system?
11. Are the following accounts permanent or temporary accounts?
    a. Fees Income
    b. Johnny Jones, Drawing
    c. Accounts Payable
    d. Accounts Receivable
    e. Johnny Jones, Capital
    f. Prepaid Rent
    g. Cash
    h. Advertising Expense
    i. Utilities Expense
    j. Equipment
    k. Salaries Expense
    l. Prepaid Insurance

APPLICATIONS

Exercises

Exercise 3.1 ▶ Setting up T accounts.

Objective 3-1

Anderson Cleaning Service has the following account balances on December 31, 2019. Set up a T account for each account and enter the balance on the proper side of the account.

Cash	$38,000	Accounts Payable	48,400
Equipment	92,000	Charles Anderson, Capital	81,600

Exercise 3.2 ▶ Using T accounts to analyze transactions.

Objective 3-2

Derrick Wells decided to start a dental practice. The first five transactions for the business follow. For each transaction, (1) determine which two accounts are affected, (2) set up T accounts for the affected accounts, and (3) enter the debit and credit amounts in the T accounts.

1. Derrick invested $45,000 cash in the business.
2. Paid $15,000 in cash for equipment.
3. Performed services for cash amounting to $4,500.
4. Paid $1,900 in cash for advertising expense.
5. Paid $1,500 in cash for supplies.

Exercise 3.3 ▶ Determining debit and credit balances.

Objective 3-3

Indicate whether each of the following accounts normally has a debit balance or a credit balance:

1. Equipment
2. Accounts Receivable
3. Salaries Expense
4. Supplies
5. Accounts Payable
6. Fee Income
7. Taylor Brown, Capital
8. Cash

Exercise 3.4
Objective 3-3

Identifying debits and credits.

In each of the following sentences, fill in the blanks with the word *debit* or *credit:*

1. Revenue accounts normally have __?__ balances. These accounts increase on the __?__ side and decrease on the __?__ side.
2. Liability accounts normally have __?__ balances. These accounts increase on the __?__ side and decrease on the __?__ side.
3. Expense accounts normally have __?__ balances. These accounts increase on the __?__ side and decrease on the __?__ side.
4. Asset accounts normally have __?__ balances. These accounts increase on the __?__ side and decrease on the __?__ side.
5. The owner's capital account normally has a __?__ balance. This account increases on the __?__ side and decreases on the __?__ side.

Exercise 3.5
Objective 3-3

Determining account balances.

The following T accounts show transactions that were recorded by Residential Relocators, a firm that specializes in local housing rentals. The entries for the first transaction are labeled with the letter (a), the entries for the second transaction with the letter (b), and so on. Determine the balance of each account.

Cash			
(a)	95,000	(b)	23,000
(d)	15,000	(e)	350
(g)	1,500	(h)	5,500
		(i)	2,500

Equipment			
(c)	40,000		

Accounts Receivable			
(f)	5,000	(g)	1,500

Accounts Payable			
		(c)	40,000

Supplies			
(b)	23,000		

Scott Hamilton, Capital			
		(a)	95,000

Fees Income			
		(d)	15,000
		(f)	5,000

Telephone Expense			
(e)	350		

Scott Hamilton, Drawing			
(i)	2,500		

Salaries Expense			
(h)	5,500		

Exercise 3.6
Objectives 3-5, 3-6
CONTINUING >>> Problem

Preparing a trial balance and an income statement.

Using the account balances from Exercise 3.5, prepare a trial balance and an income statement for Residential Relocators. The trial balance is for December 31, 2019, and the income statement is for the month ended December 31, 2019.

Exercise 3.7
Objective 3-6
CONTINUING >>> Problem

Preparing a statement of owner's equity and a balance sheet.

From the trial balance and the net income or net loss determined in Exercise 3.6, prepare a statement of owner's equity and a balance sheet for Residential Relocators as of December 31, 2019.

Exercise 3.8 ► **Preparing a chart of accounts.**
Objective 3-7

The accounts that will be used by Dad & Sons Moving Company follow. Prepare a chart of accounts for the firm. Classify the accounts by type, arrange them in an appropriate order, and assign suitable account numbers.

Salaries Expense	Office Supplies
Prepaid Rent	Accounts Payable
Fees Income	Cash
Accounts Receivable	Utilities Expense
Telephone Expense	Office Equipment
Nelson Sullivan, Capital	Nelson Sullivan, Drawing

PROBLEMS

Problem Set A

Problem 3.1A ► **Using T accounts to record transactions involving assets, liabilities, and owner's equity.**
Objective 3-1

The following transactions occurred at several different businesses and are not related.

INSTRUCTIONS

Analyze each of the transactions. For each, decide what accounts are affected and set up T accounts. Record the effects of the transaction in the T accounts. Use plus and minus signs before the amounts to show the increases and decreases.

TRANSACTIONS

1. Hunter Thompson, an owner, made an additional investment of $21,000 in cash.
2. A firm purchased equipment for $10,000 in cash.
3. A firm sold some surplus office furniture for $1,700 in cash.
4. A firm purchased a computer for $3,700, to be paid in 60 days.
5. A firm purchased office equipment for $11,200 on credit. The amount is due in 60 days.
6. Nancy Fowler, owner of Fowler Travel Agency, withdrew $6,000 of her original cash investment.
7. A firm bought a delivery truck for $37,000 on credit; payment is due in 90 days.
8. A firm issued a check for $3,500 to a supplier in partial payment of an open account balance.

Analyze: List the transactions that directly affected an owner's equity account.

Problem 3.2A ► **Using T accounts to record transactions involving assets, liabilities, and owner's equity.**
Objectives 3-1, 3-2

The following transactions took place at Calhoun Counseling Services, a business established by Ronald Calhoun.

INSTRUCTIONS

For each transaction, set up T accounts from this list: ***Cash; Office Furniture; Office Equipment; Automobile; Accounts Payable; Ronald Calhoun, Capital;*** and ***Ronald Calhoun, Drawing.*** Analyze each transaction. Record the amounts in the T accounts affected by that transaction. Use plus and minus signs to show increases and decreases in each account.

TRANSACTIONS

1. Ronald Calhoun invested $35,000 cash in the business.
2. Purchased office furniture for $8,500 in cash.
3. Bought a fax machine for $525; payment is due in 30 days.
4. Purchased a used car for the firm for $8,500 in cash.
5. Calhoun invested an additional $5,500 cash in the business.
6. Bought a new computer for $2,000; payment is due in 60 days.
7. Paid $525 to settle the amount owed on the fax machine.
8. Calhoun withdrew $2,500 in cash for personal expenses.

Analyze: Which transactions affected asset accounts?

Using T accounts to record transactions involving revenues and expenses.

Problem 3.3A
Objectives 3-2, 3-4

The following occurred during June at Hicks Family Counseling.

INSTRUCTIONS

Analyze each transaction. Use T accounts to record these transactions and be sure to put the name of the account on the top of each account. Record the effects of the transaction in the T accounts. Use plus and minus signs before the amounts to show the increases and decreases.

TRANSACTIONS

1. Purchased office supplies for $6,000 in cash.
2. Delivered monthly statements; collected fee income of $52,000.
3. Paid the current month's office rent of $10,000.
4. Completed professional counseling; billed client for $8,000.
5. Client paid fee of $4,000 for weekly counseling, previously billed.
6. Paid office salaries of $9,200.
7. Paid telephone bill of $1,160.
8. Billed client for $6,000 fee for preparing a counseling evaluation.
9. Purchased office supplies of $2,200 on account.
10. Paid office salaries of $9,200.
11. Collected $6,000 from client who was billed.
12. Clients paid a total of $18,200 cash in fees.

Analyze: How much cash did the business spend during the month?

Using T accounts to record all business transactions.

Problem 3.4A
Objectives 3-1, 3-2, 3-4

The following accounts and transactions are for Randy Guttery, Landscape Consultant.

INSTRUCTIONS

Analyze the transactions. Record each in the appropriate T accounts. Use plus and minus signs in front of the amounts to show the increases and decreases. Identify each entry in the T accounts by writing the letter of the transaction next to the entry.

ASSETS

Cash

Accounts Receivable

Office Furniture

Office Equipment

LIABILITIES

Accounts Payable

OWNER'S EQUITY

Randy Guttery, Capital

Randy Guttery, Drawing

REVENUE

Fees Income

EXPENSES

Rent Expense

Utilities Expense

Salaries Expense

Telephone Expense

Miscellaneous Expense

TRANSACTIONS

a. Guttery invested $80,000 in cash to start the business.

b. Paid $3,000 for the current month's rent.

c. Bought office furniture for $8,360 in cash.

d. Performed services for $4,100 in cash.

e. Paid $625 for the monthly telephone bill.

f. Performed services for $7,000 on credit.

g. Purchased a computer and copier for $19,000; paid $6,500 in cash immediately with the balance due in 30 days.

h. Received $3,500 from credit clients.

i. Paid $2,000 in cash for office cleaning services for the month.

j. Purchased additional office chairs for $2,900; received credit terms of 30 days.

k. Purchased office equipment for $20,000 and paid half of this amount in cash immediately; the balance is due in 30 days.

l. Issued a check for $4,700 to pay salaries.

m. Performed services for $7,250 in cash.

n. Performed services for $8,000 on credit.

o. Collected $4,000 on accounts receivable from charge customers.

p. Issued a check for $1,450 in partial payment of the amount owed for office chairs.

q. Paid $350 to a duplicating company for photocopy work performed during the month.

r. Paid $610 for the monthly electric bill.

s. Guttery withdrew $4,500 in cash for personal expenses.

Analyze: What liabilities does the business have after all transactions have been recorded?

Problem 3.5A ► Preparing financial statements from T accounts.

Objectives 3-3, 3-5, 3-6

CONTINUING >>> Problem

The accountant for the firm owned by Randy Guttery prepares financial statements at the end of each month.

INSTRUCTIONS

Use the figures in the T accounts for Problem 3.4A to prepare a trial balance, an income statement, a statement of owner's equity, and a balance sheet. (The first line of the statement headings should read "Randy Guttery, Landscape Consultant.") Assume that the transactions took place during the month ended June 30, 2019. Determine the account balances before you start work on the financial statements.

Analyze: What is the change in owner's equity for the month of June?

Problem Set B

Using T accounts to record transactions involving assets, liabilities, and owner's equity.

◀ **Problem 3.1B**
Objectives 3-1, 3-2

The following transactions occurred at several different businesses and are not related.

INSTRUCTIONS

Analyze each of the transactions. For each transaction, set up T accounts. Record the effects of the transaction in the T accounts. Use plus and minus signs to show the increases and decreases.

TRANSACTIONS

1. A firm purchased equipment for $16,000 in cash.
2. The owner, Ana Rodriguez, withdrew $4,000 cash.
3. A firm sold a piece of surplus equipment for $3,000 in cash.
4. A firm purchased a used delivery truck for $12,000 in cash.
5. A firm paid $3,600 in cash to apply against an account owed.
6. A firm purchased office equipment for $5,000. The amount is to be paid in 60 days.
7. Kelvin Newton, owner of the company, made an additional investment of $20,000 in cash.
8. A firm paid $1,500 by check for office equipment that it had previously purchased on credit.

Analyze: Which transactions affect liability accounts?

Using T accounts to record transactions involving assets, liabilities, and owner's equity.

◀ **Problem 3.2B**
Objectives 3-1, 3-2

The following transactions took place at Oilfield Equipment Service.

INSTRUCTIONS

For each transaction, set up T accounts from the following list: ***Cash; Shop Equipment; Store Equipment; Truck; Accounts Payable; Alexander Neal, Capital;*** and ***Alexander Neal, Drawing.*** Analyze each transaction. Record the effects of the transactions in the T accounts. Use plus and minus signs before the amounts to show the increases and decreases.

TRANSACTIONS

1. Alexander Neal invested $20,000 cash in the business.
2. Purchased shop equipment for $1,800 in cash.
3. Bought store fixtures for $1,200; payment is due in 30 days.
4. Purchased a used truck for $10,000 in cash.
5. Neal gave the firm his personal tools that have a fair market value of $3,000.
6. Bought a used cash register for $2,500; payment is due in 30 days.
7. Paid $400 in cash to apply to the amount owed for store fixtures.
8. Neal withdrew $1,600 in cash for personal expenses.

Analyze: Which transactions affect the ***Cash*** account?

Using T accounts to record transactions involving revenue and expenses.

◀ **Problem 3.3B**
Objectives 3-2, 3-4

The following transactions took place at Brown-Huddleston Laundry and Cleaners.

INSTRUCTIONS

Analyze each of the transactions. For each transaction, decide what accounts are affected and set up T accounts. Record the effects of the transaction in the T accounts. Use plus and minus signs before the amounts to show the increases and decreases.

TRANSACTIONS

1. Paid $3,750 for the current month's rent.
2. Performed services for $4,500 in cash.
3. Paid salaries of $3,400.
4. Performed additional services for $6,100 on credit.
5. Paid $790 for the monthly telephone bill.
6. Collected $4,000 from accounts receivable.
7. Received a $190 refund for an overcharge on the telephone bill.
8. Performed services for $4,280 on credit.
9. Paid $475 in cash for the monthly electric bill.
10. Paid $795 in cash for gasoline purchased for the firm's van during the month.
11. Received $3,125 from charge account customers.
12. Performed services for $4,700 in cash.

Analyze: What total cash was collected for Accounts Receivable during the month?

Problem 3.4B ► Using T accounts to record all business transactions.

Objectives 3-1, 3-2, 3-4

The accounts and transactions of Conner McAllister, Counselor and Attorney at Law, follow.

INSTRUCTIONS

Analyze the transactions. Record each in the appropriate T accounts. Use plus and minus signs in front of the amounts to show the increases and decreases. Identify each entry in the T accounts by writing the letter of the transaction next to the entry.

ASSETS

Cash

Accounts Receivable

Office Furniture

Office Equipment

Automobile

LIABILITIES

Accounts Payable

OWNER'S EQUITY

Conner McAllister, Capital

Conner McAllister, Drawing

REVENUE

Fees Income

EXPENSES

Automobile Expense

Rent Expense

Utilities Expense

Salaries Expense

Telephone Expense

TRANSACTIONS

a. Conner McAllister invested $140,000 in cash to start the business.
b. Paid $7,800 for the current month's rent.
c. Bought a used automobile for the firm for $38,500 in cash.

d. Performed services for $10,500 in cash.

e. Paid $1,850 for automobile repairs.

f. Performed services for $11,280 on credit.

g. Purchased office chairs for $6,500 on credit.

h. Received $5,400 from credit clients.

i. Paid $3,800 to reduce the amount owed for the office chairs.

j. Issued a check for $1,590 to pay the monthly utility bill.

k. Purchased office equipment for $22,800 and paid half of this amount in cash immediately; the balance is due in 30 days.

l. Issued a check for $18,900 to pay salaries.

m. Performed services for $7,450 in cash.

n. Performed services for $6,500 on credit.

o. Paid $967 for the monthly telephone bill.

p. Collected $4,200 on accounts receivable from charge customers.

q. Purchased additional office equipment and received a bill for $6,880 due in 30 days.

r. Paid $900 in cash for gasoline purchased for the automobile during the month.

s. Conner McAllister withdrew $8,000 in cash for personal expenses.

Analyze: What outstanding amount is owed to the company from its credit customers?

Preparing financial statements from T accounts.

Problem 3.5B
Objectives 3-3, 3-5, 3-6
CONTINUING >>> Problem

The accountant for the firm owned by Conner McAllister prepares financial statements at the end of each month.

INSTRUCTIONS

Use the figures in the T accounts for Problem 3.4B to prepare a trial balance, an income statement, a statement of owner's equity, and a balance sheet. (The first line of the statement headings should read "Conner McAllister, Counselor and Attorney at Law.") Assume that the transactions took place during the month ended April 30, 2019. Determine the account balances before you start work on the financial statements.

Analyze: What net change in owner's equity occurred during the month of April?

Critical Thinking Problem 3.1

Financial Condition

At the beginning of the summer, Brent Davis was looking for a way to earn money to pay for his college tuition in the fall. He decided to start a lawn service business in his neighborhood. To get the business started, Brent used $3,000 from his savings account to open a checking account for his new business, Emerald Lawn Care. He purchased two used power mowers and various lawn care tools for $1,000, and paid $1,800 for a second-hand truck to transport the mowers.

Several of his neighbors hired him to cut their grass on a weekly basis. He sent these customers monthly bills. By the end of the summer, they had paid him $2,400 in cash and owed him another $1,200. Brent also cut grass on an as-needed basis for other neighbors who paid him $2,000.

During the summer, Brent spent $400 for gasoline for the truck and mowers. He paid $2,000 to a friend who helped him on several occasions. An advertisement in the local paper cost $400. Now, at the end of the summer, Brent is concerned because he has only $1,800 left in his checking account. He says, "I worked hard all summer and have only $1,800 to show for it. It would have been better to leave the money in the bank."

Prepare an income statement, a statement of owner's equity, and a balance sheet for Emerald Lawn Care. Explain to Brent whether or not he is "better off" than he was at the beginning of the summer. (Hint: T accounts might be helpful in organizing the data.)

Critical Thinking Problem 3.2

Sole Proprietorship

Brenda Jo Smith is an architect who operates her own business. The accounts and transactions for the business follow.

INSTRUCTIONS

(1) Analyze the transactions for January 2019. Record each in the appropriate T accounts. Use plus and minus signs in front of the amounts to show the increases and decreases. Identify each entry in the T account by writing the letter of the transaction next to the entry.

(2) Determine the account balances. Prepare a trial balance, an income statement, a statement of owner's equity, and a balance sheet.

ASSETS

Cash

Accounts Receivable

Office Furniture

Office Equipment

LIABILITIES

Accounts Payable

OWNER'S EQUITY

Brenda Jo Smith, Capital

Brenda Jo Smith, Drawing

REVENUE

Fees Income

EXPENSES

Advertising Expense

Utilities Expense

Salaries Expense

Telephone Expense

Miscellaneous Expense

TRANSACTIONS

a. Brenda Jo Smith invested $20,000 in cash to start the business.

b. Paid $2,000 for advertisements in a design magazine.

c. Purchased office furniture for $2,300 in cash.

d. Performed services for $4,550 in cash.

e. Paid $210 for the monthly telephone bill.

f. Performed services for $1,560 on credit.

g. Purchased a fax machine for $325; paid $75 in cash with the balance due in 30 days.

h. Paid a bill for $550 from the office cleaning service.

i. Received $2,130 from clients on account.

j. Purchased additional office chairs for $545; received credit terms of 30 days.

k. Paid $4,000 for salaries.

l. Issued a check for $225 in partial payment of the amount owed for office chairs.

m. Received $2,300 in cash for services performed.

n. Issued a check for $460 for utilities expense.

o. Performed services for $2,150 on credit.

p. Collected $900 from clients on account.

q. Brenda Jo Smith withdrew $2,500 in cash for personal expenses.

r. Paid $600 to Copy Quick for photocopy work performed during the month.

Analyze: Using the basic accounting equation, what is the financial condition of Brenda Jo Smith's business at month-end?

BUSINESS CONNECTIONS

Informed Decisions

Managerial FOCUS

1. In discussing a firm's latest financial statements, a manager says that it is the "results on the bottom line" that really count. What does the manager mean?
2. If a firm's expenses equal or exceed its revenue, what actions might management take?
3. How can management find out, at any time, whether a firm can pay its bills as they become due?
4. How do the income statement and the balance sheet help management make sound decisions?

To Open or Not to Open

Ethical DILEMMA

As the bookkeeper of a new start-up company, you are responsible for keeping the chart of accounts up to date. At the end of each year, you analyze the accounts to verify that each account should be active for accumulation of costs, revenues, and expenses. In July, the accounts payable clerk has asked you to open an account named ***New Expenses.*** You know that an account name should be specific and well defined. You feel that the A/P clerk might want to charge some expenses to that account that would not be appropriate. Why do you think the A/P clerk needs this ***New Expenses*** account? Who needs to know this information and what action should you consider?

Management Letter and Annual Report

Financial Statement ANALYSIS

Annual reports released by publicly held companies include a letter to the stockholders written by the chief executive officer, chairman of the board, or president.

Analyze Online: Locate the Adobe Systems Incorporated website (www.adobe.com). Within *Investor Relations* in the *About Adobe* link in the *Menu,* find the annual report for the current year. Read the letter to the stockholders within the annual report.

Analyze:

1. What types of information can a company's management deliver using the letter to stockholders?
2. What annual revenue did Adobe Systems Incorporated report for fiscal 2015?

3. What amount of cash, cash equivalents, and short-term investments did Adobe have on hand at the end of 2015?
4. Are the financial results presented in the current year more or less favorable than those presented for fiscal 2014?
5. How much in operating cash flows did Adobe generate during fiscal year 2015?

TEAMWORK

Specific Chart of Accounts

A chart of accounts varies with each type of business as well as each company. In a group, compare and contrast the accounts that would appear in Cole's Real Estate Office, Sarah's Clothing Emporium, Neal's Grocery Store, and Tanner Plumbing Service. What accounts would appear in all companies? What accounts would be specific to each business?

Internet CONNECTION

10K Reports

Financial statements can reveal a great deal about a company. Corporations are required to produce a 10K report that includes the income statement and balance sheet. Go to the companies' websites listed below, select investor relations, annual report, and 10K report. From the income statement, decide the most profitable company. From the balance sheet, decide the company with the largest amount of cash available and the one with the most assets. (www.jcpenny.com) (www.honeywell.com)

Answers to **Self Reviews**

Answers to Section 1 Self Review

1. Increases in asset accounts are recorded on the left side. Increases in liability and owner's equity accounts are recorded on the right side.
2. The sum of several entries on either side of an account that is entered in small pencil figures.
3. The increase side of an account. The normal balance of an asset account is on the left side. The normal balance of liability and owner's equity accounts is on the right side.
4. **b.** ***Equipment*** is increased by $40,400. ***Accounts Payable*** is increased by $40,400.
5.

Cash	+	Equipment	+	Supplies	=	Accounts Payable	+	Todd Dodd, Capital
15,400	+	$20,000	+	$4,600	=	$10,000	+	$30,000
				$40,000	=	$40,000		

6. **c.** 33,450

Answers to Section 2 Self Review

1. The increase side of ***Cash*** is the left, or debit, side. The increase side of ***Accounts Payable*** is the right, or credit, side. The increase side of ***Trayton Eli, Capital*** is the right, or credit, side.
2. A transposition is an error in which the digits of a number are switched, for example, when 517 is recorded as 571. A slide is an error in which the decimal point is misplaced, for example, when 317 is written as 3.17.
3. The trial balance is a list of all the accounts and their balances. Its purpose is to prove the equality of the total debits and credits.
4. **b.** ***Jim Davis, Drawing***
5. **c.** ***Caleb Parker, Drawing*** would be debited and ***Cash*** would be credited.
6. ***C. Parker, Drawing***—10,000 should be in the Debit column.

   Fees Income—14,000 should be in the Credit column.

   The new column totals will be 51,000.

Answers to Comprehensive Self Review

1. A list of the numbers and names of the accounts of a business. It provides a system by which the accounts of the business can be easily identified and located.
2. Cash taken from the business by the owner to obtain funds for personal living expenses. Withdrawals are recorded in a special type of owner's equity account called a drawing account.
3. The asset, liability, and owner's equity accounts.
4. Decreases in asset accounts are recorded on the credit side. Decreases in liability and owner's equity accounts are recorded on the debit side.
5. - Check the math by adding the columns again.
   - Determine whether the account balances are in the correct columns.
   - Check the accounts to see whether the balances in the accounts were computed correctly.
   - Check the accuracy of transactions recorded during the period.

The General Journal and the General Ledger

Chapter **4**

Source: Johnson Space Center/NASA

www.boeing.com

Boeing was founded by William Boeing in 1916 as Pacific Aero Products; the company's name was changed to Boeing a year later. In 1917, Boeing employed 28 people; today, Boeing employs more than 165,000 people in more than 65 countries. Boeing also utilizes the talents and skills of hundreds of thousands more people who work for Boeing suppliers worldwide.

Boeing, the world's largest aerospace company, is organized into two business units: Boeing Commercial Airplanes and Boeing Defense, Space & Security. As a top U.S. exporter, the company supports commercial airlines and U.S. and allied government customers in 150 countries. More than 10,000 Boeing-built commercial jetliners are in service worldwide, which is roughly 48 percent of the world fleet. Furthermore, about 90 percent of the world's cargo is transported on Boeing planes.

Boeing derives its income from the sales of products and the sales of services. For the fiscal year ended December 31, 2015, Boeing reported total revenue of $96.1 billion on record commercial deliveries of airplanes. Boeing also reported net earnings of $5.2 billion for the year 2015. Operating cash flow increased to $9.4 billion with strong liquidity of $12.1 billion in cash and marketable securities. Backlog orders remain strong at $489 billion including $83 billion of net orders during 2015. For the 2016 fiscal year, Boeing expects revenue to be between $93 and $95 billion including commercial airplane deliveries between 740 and 745. Operating cash flow for 2016 is expected to be approximately $10 billion.

thinking critically

How do you think Boeing would record the purchase of new manufacturing equipment that will be used for several years?

LEARNING OBJECTIVES	NEW TERMS	
4-1 Record transactions in the general journal.	accounting cycle	general journal
4-2 Prepare compound journal entries.	audit trail	general ledger
4-3 Post journal entries to general ledger accounts.	balance ledger form	journal
4-4 Correct errors made in the journal or ledger.	chronological order	journalizing
4-5 Define the accounting terms new to this chapter.	compound entry	ledger
	correcting entry	posting

Section 1

SECTION OBJECTIVES	TERMS TO LEARN
>> 4-1 Record transactions in the general journal. WHY IT'S IMPORTANT Written records for all business transactions are necessary. The general journal acts as the "diary" of the business. >> 4-2 Prepare compound journal entries. WHY IT'S IMPORTANT Compound entries contain several debits or credits for a single business transaction, creating efficiencies in journalizing.	accounting cycle audit trail chronological order compound entry general journal journal journalizing

The General Journal

The **accounting cycle** is a series of steps performed during each accounting period to classify, record, and summarize data for a business and to produce needed financial information. The first step in the accounting cycle is to analyze business transactions. You learned this skill in Chapter 3. The second step in the accounting cycle is to prepare a record of business transactions.

Journals

Business transactions are recorded in a **journal,** which is a diary of business activities. The journal lists transactions in **chronological order,** that is, in the order in which they occur. The journal is sometimes called the *record of original entry* because it is where transactions are first entered in the accounting records. There are different types of journals. This chapter will examine the general journal. You will become familiar with other journals in later chapters.

> Most corporations use accounting software to record business transactions. Industry-specific software is available for accounting firms, oil and gas companies, construction firms, medical firms, and any other industry-specific business enterprise.

>> 4-1 OBJECTIVE
Record transactions in the general journal.

important!

The Diary of a Business
The general journal is similar to a diary. The general journal details, in chronological order, the economic events of the business.

The General Journal

The **general journal** is a financial record for entering all types of business transactions. **Journalizing** is the process of recording transactions in the general journal.

Figure 4.1 shows the general journal for Eli's Consulting Services. Notice that the general journal has a page number. To record a transaction, enter the year at the top of the Date column. In the Date column, write the month and day on the first line of the first entry. After the first entry, enter the year and month only when a new page is started or when the year or the month changes. In the Date column, write the day of each transaction on the first line of each transaction.

In the Description column, enter the account to be debited. Write the account name close to the left margin of the Description column, and enter the amount on the same line in the Debit column.

Enter the account to be credited on the line beneath the debit. Indent the account name about one-half inch from the left margin. Enter the amount on the same line in the Credit column.

Then enter a complete but concise description of the transaction in the Description column. Begin the description on the line following the credit. The description is indented about one inch from the left margin.

Write account names exactly as they appear in the chart of accounts. This will minimize errors when amounts are transferred from the general journal to the accounts.

FIGURE 4.1

General Journal Entry

GENERAL JOURNAL PAGE 1

	DATE		DESCRIPTION	POST. REF.	DEBIT	CREDIT	
1	2019						1
2	Nov.	6	Cash		100 000 00		2
3			Trayton Eli, Capital			100 000 00	3
4			Investment by owner				4
5							5

Record the year first, then the month and day.

Record the debit first.

Indent about one-half inch and record the credit.

Indent again and write the description.

Leave a blank line between general journal entries. Some accountants use this blank line to number each general journal entry.

When possible, the journal entry description should refer to the source of the information. For example, the journal entry to record a payment should include the check number in the description. Document numbers are part of the audit trail. The **audit trail** is a chain of references that makes it possible to trace information, locate errors, and prevent fraud. The audit trail provides a means of checking the journal entry against the original data on the documents.

important!

Audit Trail

To maintain the audit trail, descriptions should refer to document numbers whenever possible.

RECORDING NOVEMBER TRANSACTIONS IN THE GENERAL JOURNAL

In Chapters 2 and 3, you learned a step-by-step method for analyzing business transactions. In this chapter, you will learn how to complete the journal entry for a business transaction in the same manner. Review the following steps before you continue:

GL

1. Analyze the financial event:
   - Identify the accounts affected.
   - Classify the accounts affected.
   - Determine the amount of increase or decrease for each account affected.
2. Apply the rules of debit and credit:
   a. Which account is debited? For what amount?
   b. Which account is credited? For what amount?
3. Make the entry in T-account form.
4. Record the complete entry in general journal form.

BUSINESS TRANSACTION

On November 6, Trayton Eli withdrew $100,000 from personal savings and deposited it in a new business checking account for Eli's Consulting Services.

Eli's Consulting Services

MEMORANDUM 01

TO: Sergio Sanchez
FROM: Trayton Eli
DATE: November 6, 2019
SUBJECT: Contributed personal funds to the business

I contributed $100,000 from my personal savings to Eli's Consulting Services.

ANALYSIS

a. The asset account ***Cash*** is increased by $100,000.

a. The owner's equity account, ***Trayton Eli, Capital,*** is increased by $100,000.

DEBIT-CREDIT RULES

DEBIT Increases to asset accounts are recorded as debits. Debit ***Cash*** for $100,000.

CREDIT Increases to the owner's equity account are recorded as credits. Credit ***Trayton Eli, Capital*** for $100,000.

T-ACCOUNT PRESENTATION

Cash	
+	−
(a) 100,000	

Trayton Eli, Capital	
−	+
	(a) 100,000

GENERAL JOURNAL ENTRY

GENERAL JOURNAL PAGE 1

	DATE		DESCRIPTION	POST. REF.	DEBIT	CREDIT	
1	2019						1
2	Nov.	6	Cash		100 000 00		2
3			Trayton Eli, Capital			100 000 00	3
4			Investment by owner,				4
5			Memo 01				5

BUSINESS TRANSACTION

On November 7, Eli's Consulting Services issued Check 1001 for $5,000 to purchase a computer and other equipment.

$ 5,000.00	No. 1001
Date November 7, 20 19	
To The Information Technology Store	
For Office Equipment	
	Dollars | Cents
Balance brought forward	100,000 00
Add deposits	
Total	100,000 00
Less this check	5,000 00
Balance carried forward	95,000 00

ANALYSIS

b. The asset account ***Equipment*** is increased by $5,000.

b. The asset account ***Cash*** is decreased by $5,000.

DEBIT-CREDIT RULES

DEBIT Increases to asset accounts are recorded as debits. Debit ***Equipment*** for $5,000.

CREDIT Decreases to asset accounts are recorded as credits. Credit ***Cash*** for $5,000.

T-ACCOUNT PRESENTATION

Equipment	
+	
(b) 5,000	

Cash	
+	−
	(b) 5,000

GENERAL JOURNAL ENTRY

GENERAL JOURNAL PAGE 1

	DATE		DESCRIPTION	POST. REF.	DEBIT	CREDIT	
6	Nov.	7	*Equipment*		5 000 00		6
7			*Cash*			5 000 00	7
8			*Purchased equip., Check 1001*				8

The check number appears in the description and forms part of the audit trail for the transaction.

BUSINESS TRANSACTION

On November 10, Eli's Consulting Services purchased office equipment on account for $6,000.

OFFICE *plus* **INVOICE NO. 2223**

DATE: Nov. 10, 2019
ORDER NO.: P38
SHIPPED BY: n/a
TERMS: 60 days

TO Eli's Consulting Services

QTY.	ITEM	UNIT PRICE	TOTAL
1	Copier	500	500
1	Fax Machine	300	300
4	Computers	1,025	4,100
3	Printers	250	750
2	Scanners	125	250
2	Calculators	50	100
	Total		6,000

ANALYSIS

c. The asset account ***Equipment*** is increased by $6,000.

c. The liability account ***Accounts Payable*** is increased by $6,000.

DEBIT-CREDIT RULES

DEBIT Increases to asset accounts are recorded as debits. Debit ***Equipment*** for $6,000.

CREDIT Increases to liability accounts are recorded as credits. Credit ***Accounts Payable*** for $6,000.

T-ACCOUNT PRESENTATION

Equipment	
+	−
(c) 6,000	

Accounts Payable	
−	+
	(c) 6,000

GENERAL JOURNAL ENTRY

GENERAL JOURNAL PAGE 1

	DATE		DESCRIPTION	POST. REF.	DEBIT	CREDIT	
10	Nov.	10	*Equipment*		6 000 00		10
11			*Accounts Payable*			6 000 00	11
12			*Purchased equipment on*				12
13			*account from Office Plus,*				13
14			*Inv. 2223, due in 60 days*				14

The supplier's name (Office Plus) and invoice number (2223) appear in the journal entry description and form part of the audit trail for the transaction. The journal entry can be checked against the data on the original document, Invoice 2223.

BUSINESS TRANSACTION

On November 28, Eli's Consulting Services purchased supplies for $1,500, Check 1002.

$ 1,500.00 **No. 1002**
Date November 28, 20 19
To Office Delux, Inc.
For Supplies

	Dollars	Cents
Balance brought forward	95,000	00
Add deposits		
Total	95,000	00
Less this check	1,500	00
Balance carried forward	93,500	00

ANALYSIS

d. The asset account ***Supplies*** is increased by $1,500.

d. The asset account ***Cash*** is decreased by $1,500.

DEBIT-CREDIT RULES

DEBIT Increases to asset accounts are recorded as debits. Debit ***Supplies*** for $1,500.

CREDIT Decreases to asset accounts are recorded as credits. Credit ***Cash*** for $1,500.

T-ACCOUNT PRESENTATION

Supplies +	Supplies −
(d) 1,500	

Cash +	Cash −
	(d) 1,500

GENERAL JOURNAL ENTRY

GENERAL JOURNAL PAGE 1

	DATE		DESCRIPTION	POST. REF.	DEBIT	CREDIT	
16	Nov.	28	Supplies		1 5 0 0 00		16
17			Cash			1 5 0 0 00	17
18			Purchased supplies,				18
19			Check 1002				19
20							20

Sergio Sanchez decided to reduce the firm's debt to Office Plus. Recall that the firm had purchased equipment on account in the amount of $6,000. On November 30, Eli's Consulting Services issued a check to Office Plus. Sergio Sanchez analyzed the transaction and recorded the journal entry as follows.

BUSINESS TRANSACTION

On November 30, Eli's Consulting Services paid Office Plus $2,500 in partial payment of Invoice 2223, Check 1003.

$ 2,500.00	No. 1003
Date November 30, 20 19	
To Office Plus	
For Payment on Account	

	Dollars	Cents
Balance brought forward	93,500	00
Add deposits		
Total	93,500	00
Less this check	2,500	00
Balance carried forward	91,000	00

ANALYSIS

e. The asset account ***Cash*** is decreased by $2,500.

e. The liability account ***Accounts Payable*** is decreased by $2,500.

DEBIT-CREDIT RULES

DEBIT Decreases to liability accounts are recorded as debits. Debit ***Accounts Payable*** for $2,500.

CREDIT Decreases to asset accounts are recorded as credits. Credit ***Cash*** for $2,500.

T-ACCOUNT PRESENTATION

Accounts Payable −	Accounts Payable +
(e) 2,500	

Cash +	Cash −
	(e) 2,500

GENERAL JOURNAL ENTRY

GENERAL JOURNAL PAGE 1

	DATE		DESCRIPTION	POST. REF.	DEBIT	CREDIT	
21	Nov.	30	Accounts Payable		2 5 0 0 00		21
22			Cash			2 5 0 0 00	22
23			Paid on account, Office Plus,				23
24			Invoice 2223, Check 1003				24

Notice that the general journal Description column includes three important items for the audit trail:

- the supplier name,
- the invoice number,
- the check number.

In the general journal, always enter debits before credits. This is the case even if the credit item is considered first when mentally analyzing the transaction.

Eli's Consulting Services issued a check in November to pay December and January rent in advance. Recall that the right to occupy facilities is considered a form of property. Sergio Sanchez analyzed the transaction and recorded the journal entry as follows.

BUSINESS TRANSACTION

On November 30, Eli's Consulting Services wrote Check 1004 for $8,000 to prepay rent for December and January.

$ 8,000.00	No. 1004
Date November 30, 20 19	
To Davidson Properties	
For Prepaid Rent	

	Dollars	Cents
Balance brought forward	91,000	00
Add deposits		
Total	91,000	00
Less this check	8,000	00
Balance carried forward	83,000	00

ANALYSIS

f. The asset account ***Prepaid Rent*** is increased by $8,000.

f. The asset account ***Cash*** is decreased by $8,000.

DEBIT-CREDIT RULES

DEBIT Increases to asset accounts are recorded as debits. Debit ***Prepaid Rent*** for $8,000.

CREDIT Decreases to asset accounts are recorded as credits. Credit ***Cash*** for $8,000.

T-ACCOUNT PRESENTATION

Prepaid Rent	
+	−
(f) 8,000	

Cash	
+	−
	(f) 8,000

GENERAL JOURNAL ENTRY

GENERAL JOURNAL PAGE 1

	DATE		DESCRIPTION	POST. REF.	DEBIT	CREDIT	
26	Nov.	30	Prepaid Rent		8 000 00		26
27			Cash			8 000 00	27
28			Paid Dec. and Jan. rent				28
29			in advance; Check 1004				29

RECORDING DECEMBER TRANSACTIONS IN THE GENERAL JOURNAL

Eli's Consulting Services opened for business on December 1. Let's review the transactions that occurred in December. Refer to items **g** through **l** in Chapter 3 for the analysis of each transaction.

1. Performed services for $36,000 in cash.
2. Performed services for $11,000 on credit.
3. Received $6,000 in cash from credit clients on their accounts.
4. Paid $8,000 for salaries.
5. Paid $650 for a utility bill.
6. The owner withdrew $5,000 for personal expenses.

Figure 4.2 shows the entries in the general journal. In an actual business, transactions involving fees income and accounts receivable occur throughout the month and are recorded when they take place. For the sake of simplicity, these transactions are summarized and recorded as of December 31 for Eli's Consulting Services.

>> 4-2 OBJECTIVE
Prepare compound journal entries

PREPARING COMPOUND ENTRIES

So far, each journal entry consists of one debit and one credit. Some transactions require a **compound entry**—a journal entry that contains more than one debit or credit. In a compound entry, record all debits first, followed by the credits.

When Allstate purchased an insurance division of CNA Financial Corporation, Allstate paid cash and issued a 10-year note payable (a promise to pay). Detailed accounting records are not available to the public, but a compound journal entry was probably used to record this transaction.

FIGURE 4.2

General Journal Entries for December

GENERAL JOURNAL PAGE 2

DATE		DESCRIPTION	POST. REF.	DEBIT	CREDIT
2019					
Dec.	31	Cash		36 000 00	
		Fees Income			36 000 00
		Performed services for cash			
	31	Accounts Receivable		11 000 00	
		Fees Income			11 000 00
		Performed services on credit			
	31	Cash		6 000 00	
		Accounts Receivable			6 000 00
		Received cash from credit clients on account			
	31	Salaries Expense		8 000 00	
		Cash			8 000 00
		Paid monthly salaries to employees, Checks 1005–1006			
	31	Utilities Expense		650 00	
		Cash			650 00
		Paid monthly bill for utilities, Check 1007			
	31	Trayton Eli, Drawing		5 000 00	
		Cash			5 000 00
		Owner withdrew cash for personal expenses, Check 1008			

Suppose that on November 7, when Eli's Consulting Services purchased the equipment for $5,000, Trayton Eli paid $2,500 in cash and agreed to pay the balance in 30 days. This transaction is analyzed below.

BUSINESS TRANSACTION

On November 7, the firm purchased equipment for $5,000, issued Check 1001 for $2,500, and agreed to pay the balance in 30 days.

ANALYSIS

The asset account ***Equipment*** is increased by $5,000. The asset account ***Cash*** is decreased by $2,500. The liability account ***Accounts Payable*** is increased by $2,500.

DEBIT-CREDIT RULES

DEBIT Increases to assets are recorded as debits. Debit ***Equipment*** for $5,000.

CREDIT Decreases to assets are credits. Credit ***Cash*** for $2,500. Increases to liabilities are credits. Credit ***Accounts Payable*** for $2,500.

T-ACCOUNT PRESENTATION

Equipment	
+	–
5,000	

Cash	
+	–
	2,500

Accounts Payable	
–	+
	2,500

GENERAL JOURNAL ENTRY

GENERAL JOURNAL PAGE 1

	DATE		DESCRIPTION	POST. REF.	DEBIT	CREDIT	
6	Nov.	7	Equipment		5 000 00		6
7			Cash			2 500 00	7
8			Accounts Payable			2 500 00	8
9			Bought equip. from The				9
10			Information Technology Store,				10
11			Inv. 11, issued Ck. 1001 for				11
12			$2,500, bal. due in 30 days				12

recall

Debits = Credits

No matter how many accounts are affected by a transaction, total debits must equal total credits.

Section 1 Self Review

EXERCISES

1. The part of the journal entry to be recorded first is the:
   - a. asset.
   - b. credit.
   - c. debit.
   - d. liability.
2. A general journal is like a(n):
   - a. address book.
   - b. appointment calendar.
   - c. diary.
   - d. to-do list.

QUESTIONS

3. Why are check and invoice numbers included in the journal entry description?
4. Why is the journal referred to as the "record of original entry"?
5. In a compound journal entry, if two accounts are debited, must two accounts be credited?

ANALYSIS

6. The accountant for Emerald Lawn Care never includes descriptions when making journal entries. What effect will this have on the accounting system?

(Answers to Section 1 Self Review are on page 118.)

Section 2

SECTION OBJECTIVES	TERMS TO LEARN
>> 4-3 Post journal entries to general ledger accounts. WHY IT'S IMPORTANT The general ledger provides a permanent, classified record for a company's accounts.	balance ledger form
>> 4-4 Correct errors made in the journal or ledger. WHY IT'S IMPORTANT Errors must be corrected to ensure a proper audit trail and to provide good information.	correcting entry general ledger ledger posting

The General Ledger

You learned that a journal contains a chronological (day-by-day) record of a firm's transactions. Each journal entry shows the accounts and the amounts involved. Using the journal as a guide, you can enter transaction data in the accounts.

Ledgers

T accounts are used to analyze transactions quickly but are not used to maintain financial records. Instead, businesses keep account records on a special form that makes it possible to record all data efficiently. There is a separate form for each account. The account forms are kept in a book or binder called a **ledger.** The ledger is called the *record of final entry* because the ledger is the last place that accounting transactions are recorded.

The process of transferring data from the journal to the ledger is known as **posting.** Posting takes place after transactions are journalized. Posting is the third step of the accounting cycle.

THE GENERAL LEDGER

Every business has a general ledger. The **general ledger** is the master reference file for the accounting system. It provides a permanent, classified record of all accounts used in a firm's operations.

important!

General Journal and General Ledger

The general journal is the record of *original* entry. The general ledger is the record of *final* entry.

LEDGER ACCOUNT FORMS

There are different types of general ledger account forms. Sergio Sanchez decided to use a balance ledger form. A **balance ledger form** shows the balance of the account after each entry is posted. Look at Figure 4.3. It shows the first general journal entry, the investment by the owner. It also shows the general ledger forms for ***Cash*** and ***Trayton Eli, Capital.*** On the ledger form, notice the:

- account name and number;
- columns for date, description, and posting reference (post. ref.);
- columns for debit, credit, balance debit, and balance credit.

FIGURE 4.3

Posting from the General Journal to the General Ledger

GENERAL JOURNAL PAGE 1

	DATE		DESCRIPTION	POST. REF.	DEBIT	CREDIT	
1	2019						1
2	Nov.	6	Cash	101	100 000 00		2
3			Trayton Eli, Capital	301		100 000 00	3
4			Investment by owner				4
5							5
6							
7							

ACCOUNT Cash ACCOUNT NO. 101

DATE		DESCRIPTION	POST. REF.	DEBIT	CREDIT	BALANCE DEBIT	BALANCE CREDIT
2019							
Nov.	6		J1	100 000 00		100 000 00	

ACCOUNT Trayton Eli, Capital ACCOUNT NO. 301

DATE		DESCRIPTION	POST. REF.	DEBIT	CREDIT	BALANCE DEBIT	BALANCE CREDIT
2019							
Nov.	6		J1		100 000 00		100 000 00

ABOUT **ACCOUNTING**

Careers

How do you get to be the president of a large corporation in the United States? Probably by beginning your career as an accountant. More accountants have advanced to be presidents of large corporations than people with any other background.

>> 4-3 OBJECTIVE

Post journal entries to general ledger accounts.

recall

Normal Balance

The normal balance of an account is its increase side.

POSTING TO THE GENERAL LEDGER

Examine Figure 4.4. On November 7, Sergio Sanchez made a general journal entry to record the purchase of equipment. To post the data from the journal to the general ledger, Sanchez entered the debit amount in the Debit column in the ***Equipment*** account and the credit amount in the Credit column in the ***Cash*** account.

In the general journal, identify the first account listed. In Figure 4.4, ***Equipment*** is the first account. In the general ledger, find the ledger form for the first account listed. In Figure 4.4, this is the ***Equipment*** ledger form.

The steps to post from the general journal to the general ledger follow:

1. On the ledger form, enter the date of the transaction. Enter a description of the entry, if necessary. Usually routine entries do not require descriptions.
2. On the ledger form, enter the general journal page in the Posting Reference column. On the ***Equipment*** ledger form, the **J1** in the Posting Reference column indicates that the journal entry is recorded on page 1 of the general journal. The letter **J** refers to the general journal.
3. On the ledger form, enter the debit amount in the Debit column or the credit amount in the Credit column. In Figure 4.4 on the ***Equipment*** ledger form, $5,000 is entered in the Debit column.
4. On the ledger form, compute the balance and enter it in the Debit Balance column or the Credit Balance column. In Figure 4.4, the balance in the ***Equipment*** account is a $5,000 debit.
5. On the general journal, enter the ledger account number in the Posting Reference column. In Figure 4.4, the account number 141 is entered in the Posting Reference column next to "Equipment."

Repeat the process for the next account in the general journal. In Figure 4.4, Sanchez posted the credit amount from the general journal to the ***Cash*** ledger account. Notice on the ***Cash*** ledger form that he entered the credit of $5,000 and then computed the account balance. After the transaction is posted, the balance of the ***Cash*** account is $95,000.

Be sure to enter the numbers in the Posting Reference columns. This indicates that the entry was posted and ensures against posting the same entry twice. Posting references are part of the audit trail. They allow a transaction to be traced from the ledger to the journal entry, and then to the source document.

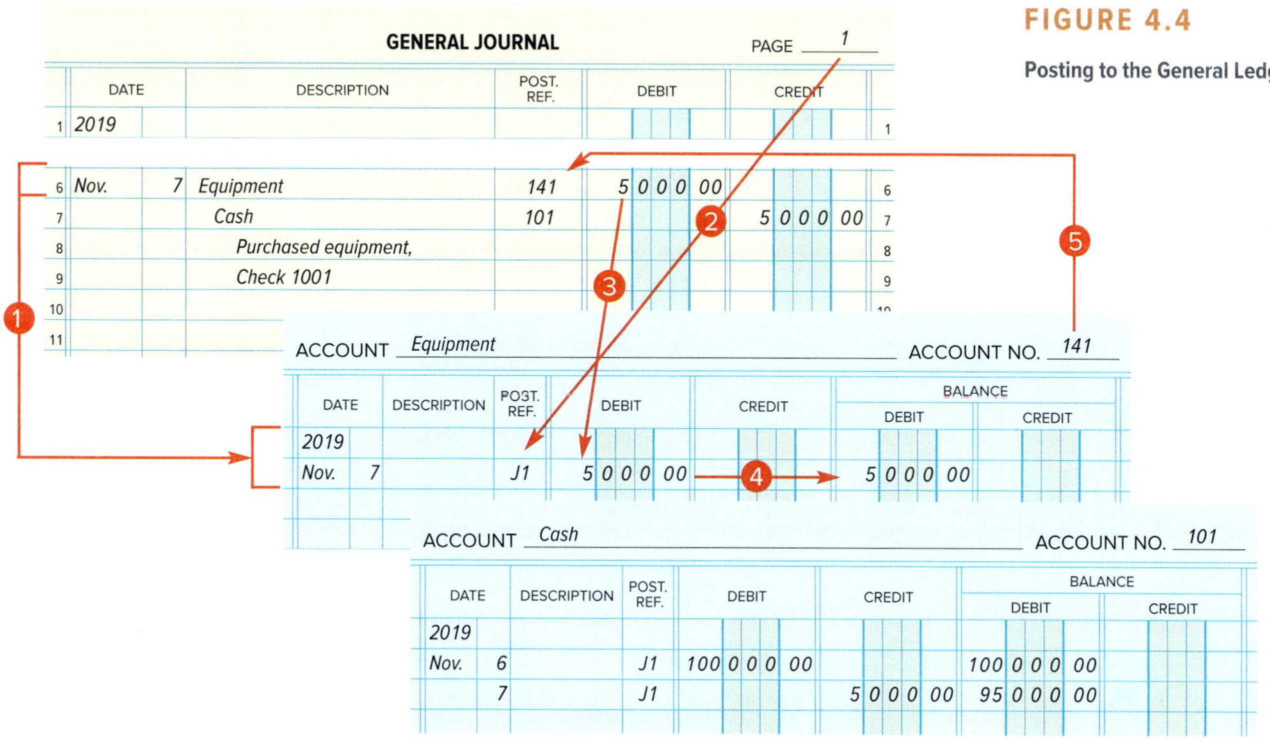

FIGURE 4.4

Posting to the General Ledger

Figure 4.5 shows the general ledger after all the entries for November and December are posted.

Each ledger account provides a complete record of the increases and decreases to that account. The balance ledger form also shows the current balance for the account.

In the general ledger accounts, the balance sheet accounts appear first and are followed by the income statement accounts. The order is:

- assets
- liabilities
- owner's equity
- revenue
- expenses

This arrangement speeds the preparation of the trial balance and the financial statements.

FIGURE 4.5

Posted General Ledger Accounts

ACCOUNT *Cash* ACCOUNT NO. *101*

DATE		DESCRIPTION	POST. REF.	DEBIT	CREDIT	BALANCE DEBIT	BALANCE CREDIT
2019							
Nov.	6		J1	100 000 00		100 000 00	
	7		J1		5 000 00	95 000 00	
	28		J1		1 500 00	93 500 00	
	30		J1		2 500 00	91 000 00	
	30		J1		8 000 00	83 000 00	
Dec.	31		J2	36 000 00		119 000 00	
	31		J2	6 000 00		125 000 00	
	31		J2		8 000 00	117 000 00	
	31		J2		650 00	116 350 00	
	31		J2		5 000 00	111 350 00	

(continued)

FIGURE 4.5 (continued)

ACCOUNT *Accounts Receivable* ACCOUNT NO. *111*

DATE		DESCRIPTION	POST. REF.	DEBIT	CREDIT	BALANCE DEBIT	BALANCE CREDIT
2019							
Dec.	31		J2	11,000 00		11,000 00	
	31		J2		6,000 00	5,000 00	

ACCOUNT *Supplies* ACCOUNT NO. *121*

DATE		DESCRIPTION	POST. REF.	DEBIT	CREDIT	BALANCE DEBIT	BALANCE CREDIT
2019							
Nov.	28		J1	1,500 00		1,500 00	

ACCOUNT *Prepaid Rent* ACCOUNT NO. *137*

DATE		DESCRIPTION	POST. REF.	DEBIT	CREDIT	BALANCE DEBIT	BALANCE CREDIT
2019							
Nov.	30		J1	8,000 00		8,000 00	

ACCOUNT *Equipment* ACCOUNT NO. *141*

DATE		DESCRIPTION	POST. REF.	DEBIT	CREDIT	BALANCE DEBIT	BALANCE CREDIT
2019							
Nov.	7		J1	5,000 00		5,000 00	
	10		J1	6,000 00		11,000 00	

ACCOUNT *Accounts Payable* ACCOUNT NO. *202*

DATE		DESCRIPTION	POST. REF.	DEBIT	CREDIT	BALANCE DEBIT	BALANCE CREDIT
2019							
Nov.	10		J1		6,000 00		6,000 00
	30		J1	2,500 00			3,500 00

ACCOUNT *Trayton Eli, Capital* ACCOUNT NO. *301*

DATE		DESCRIPTION	POST. REF.	DEBIT	CREDIT	BALANCE DEBIT	BALANCE CREDIT
2019							
Nov.	6		J1		100,000 00		100,000 00

ACCOUNT *Trayton Eli, Drawing* ACCOUNT NO. *302*

DATE		DESCRIPTION	POST. REF.	DEBIT	CREDIT	BALANCE DEBIT	BALANCE CREDIT
2019							
Dec.	31		J2	5,000 00		5,000 00	

(continued)

FIGURE 4.5 (continued)

ACCOUNT *Fees Income* ACCOUNT NO. *401*

DATE		DESCRIPTION	POST. REF.	DEBIT	CREDIT	BALANCE DEBIT	BALANCE CREDIT
2019							
Dec.	31		J2		36 000 00		36 000 00
	31		J2		11 000 00		47 000 00

ACCOUNT *Salaries Expense* ACCOUNT NO. *511*

DATE		DESCRIPTION	POST. REF.	DEBIT	CREDIT	BALANCE DEBIT	BALANCE CREDIT
2019							
Dec.	31		J2	8 000 00		8 000 00	

ACCOUNT *Utilities Expense* ACCOUNT NO. *514*

DATE		DESCRIPTION	POST. REF.	DEBIT	CREDIT	BALANCE DEBIT	BALANCE CREDIT
2019							
Dec.	31		J2	650 00		650 00	

Correcting Journal and Ledger Errors

>> **4-4 OBJECTIVE**

Correct errors made in the journal or ledger.

Sometimes errors are made when recording transactions in the journal. For example, a journal entry may show the wrong account name or amount. The method used to correct an error depends on whether or not the journal entry has been posted to the ledger:

- If the error is discovered *before* the entry is posted, neatly cross out the incorrect item and write the correct data above it. Do not erase the error. To ensure honesty and provide a clear audit trail, erasures are not made in the journal.
- If the error is discovered *after* posting, a **correcting entry**—a journal entry made to correct the erroneous entry—is journalized and posted. Do not erase or change the journal entry or the postings in the ledger accounts.

Note that erasures are never permitted in the journal or ledger.

recall

Order of Accounts

The general ledger lists accounts in the same order as they appear on the trial balance: assets, liabilities, owner's equity, revenue, and expenses.

MANAGERIAL IMPLICATIONS <<

ACCOUNTING SYSTEMS

- Business managers should be sure that their firms have efficient procedures for recording transactions.
- A well-designed accounting system allows timely and accurate posting of data to the ledger accounts.
- The information that appears in the financial statements is taken from the general ledger.
- Since management uses financial information for decision making, it is essential that the financial statements be prepared quickly at the end of each period and that they contain the correct amounts.
- The promptness and accuracy of the statements depend on the efficiency of the recording process.
- A well-designed accounting system has a strong audit trail.
- Every business should be able to trace amounts through the accounting records and back to the documents where the transactions were first recorded.

THINKING CRITICALLY

What are the consequences of not having a good audit trail?

Let's look at an example. On September 1, an automobile repair shop purchased some shop equipment for $18,000 in cash. By mistake, the journal entry debited the ***Office Equipment*** account rather than the ***Shop Equipment*** account, as follows.

GENERAL JOURNAL PAGE 16

	DATE		DESCRIPTION	POST. REF.	DEBIT	CREDIT	
1	2019						1
2	Sept.	1	Office Equipment	141	18 000 00		2
3			Cash	101		18 000 00	3
4			Purchased equipment,				4
5			Check 1104				5
6							6
7							7

The error was discovered after the entry was posted to the ledger. To correct the error, a correcting journal entry was prepared and posted. The correcting entry debits ***Shop Equipment*** and credits ***Office Equipment*** for $18,000. This entry transfers $18,000 out of the ***Office Equipment*** account and into the ***Shop Equipment*** account.

GENERAL JOURNAL PAGE 28

	DATE		DESCRIPTION	POST. REF.	DEBIT	CREDIT	
1	2019						1
2	Oct.	1	Shop Equipment	151	18 000 00		2
3			Office Equipment	141		18 000 00	3
4			To correct error made on				4
5			Sept. 1 when a purchase				5
6			of shop equipment was				6
7			recorded as office				7
8			equipment				8
9							9

Suppose that the error was discovered before the journal entry was posted to the ledger. In that case, the accountant would neatly cross out "Office Equipment" and write "Shop Equipment" above it. The correct account (***Shop Equipment***) would be posted to the ledger in the usual manner.

Section 2 Self Review

QUESTIONS

1. Why are posting references made in ledger accounts and in the journal?
2. Are the following statements true or false? Why?
   a. "If a journal entry that contains an error has been posted, erase the entry and change the posting in the ledger accounts."
   b. "Once an incorrect journal entry has been posted, the incorrect amounts remain in the general ledger accounts."
3. What is entered in the Posting Reference column of the general journal?

EXERCISES

4. The general journal organizes accounting information in:
   a. account order.
   b. alphabetical order.
   c. date order.
5. The general ledger organizes accounting information in:
   a. account order.
   b. alphabetical order.
   c. date order.

ANALYSIS

6. Draw a diagram of the first three steps of the accounting cycle.

(Answers to Section 2 Self Review are on page 118.)

Chapter 4

Review and Applications

REVIEW Chapter Summary

In this chapter, you have studied the method for journalizing business transactions in the records of a company. The details of each transaction are then posted to the general ledger. A well-designed accounting system provides for prompt and accurate journalizing and posting of all transactions.

Learning Objectives

4-1 Record transactions in the general journal.

- Recording transactions in a journal is called journalizing, the second step in the accounting cycle.
  - A journal is a daily record of transactions.
  - A written analysis of each transaction is contained in a journal.
- The general journal is widely used in business. It can accommodate all kinds of business transactions. Use the following steps to record a transaction in the general journal:
  - Number each page in the general journal. The page number will be used as a posting reference.
  - Enter the year at the top of the Date column. After that, enter the year only when a new page is started or when the year changes.
  - Enter the month and day in the Date column of the first line of the first entry. After that, enter the month only when a new page is started or when the month changes. Always enter the day on the first line of a new entry.
  - Enter the name of the account to be debited in the Description column.
  - Enter the amount to be debited in the Debit column.
  - Enter the name of the account to be credited on the next line. Indent the account name about one-half inch.
  - Enter the amount to be credited in the Credit column.
  - Enter a complete but concise description on the next line. Indent the description about one inch.
- Note that the debit portion is always recorded first.
- If possible, include source document numbers in descriptions in order to create an audit trail.

4-2 Prepare compound journal entries.

A transaction might require a journal entry that contains several debits or credits. All debits are recorded first, followed by the credits.

4-3 Post journal entries to general ledger accounts.

- Posting to the general ledger is the third step in the accounting cycle. Posting is the transfer of data from journal entries to ledger accounts.
- The individual accounts together form a ledger. All the accounts needed to prepare financial statements are found in the general ledger.
- Use the following steps to post a transaction.
  - On the ledger form:
    1. Enter the date of the transaction. Enter the description, if necessary.
    2. Enter the posting reference in the Posting Reference column. When posting from the general journal, use the letter **J** followed by the general journal page number.
    3. Enter the amount in either the Debit column or the Credit column.
    4. Compute the new balance and enter it in either the Debit Balance column or the Credit Balance column.
  - On the general journal:
    5. Enter the ledger account number in the Posting Reference column.
- To summarize the steps of the accounting cycle discussed so far:
  1. Analyze transactions.
  2. Journalize transactions.
  3. Post transactions.

4-4 Correct errors made in the journal or ledger.

To ensure honesty and to provide a clear audit trail, erasures are not permitted in a journal. A correcting entry is journalized and posted to correct a previous mistake. Posting references in the journal and the ledger accounts cross reference the entries and form another part of the audit trail. They make it possible to trace or recheck any transaction.

4-5 Define the accounting terms new to this chapter.

Glossary

Accounting cycle (p. 88) A series of steps performed during each accounting period to classify, record, and summarize data for a business and to produce needed financial information

Audit trail (p. 89) A chain of references that makes it possible to trace information, locate errors, and prevent fraud

Balance ledger form (p. 97) A ledger account form that shows the balance of the account after each entry is posted

Chronological order (p. 88) Organized in the order in which the events occur

Compound entry (p. 94) A journal entry with more than one debit or credit

Correcting entry (p. 101) A journal entry made to correct an erroneous entry

General journal (p. 88) A financial record for entering all types of business transactions; a record of original entry

General ledger (p. 97) A permanent, classified record of all accounts used in a firm's operation; a record of final entry

Journal (p. 88) The record of original entry

Journalizing (p. 88) Recording transactions in a journal

Ledger (p. 97) The record of final entry

Posting (p. 97) Transferring data from a journal to a ledger

Comprehensive Self Review

1. What is recorded in the Posting Reference column of a general journal?
2. Why is the ledger called the "record of final entry"?
3. How do you correct an incorrect journal entry that has not been posted?
4. Give examples of items that might appear in an audit trail.
5. Which of the following shows both the debits and credits of the entire transaction?
   a. An entry in the general journal
   b. A posting to a general ledger account

Answers to Comprehensive Self Review are on page 119.)

Discussion Questions

1. What is the purpose of a journal?
2. In what order are accounts arranged in the general ledger? Why?
3. What is a ledger?
4. What is posting?
5. What are posting references? Why are they used?
6. What is the accounting cycle?
7. What is a compound journal entry?
8. What is the value of having a description for each general journal entry?
9. What procedure is used to record an entry in the general journal?
10. How should corrections be made in the general journal?
11. What is an audit trail? Why is it desirable to have an audit trail?

APPLICATIONS

Exercises

Analyzing transactions.

Exercise 4.1
Objective 4-1

Selected accounts from the general ledger of the Ray Shipping Service follow. Analyze the following transactions and indicate by number what accounts should be debited and credited for each transaction.

101 Cash
111 Accounts Receivable
121 Supplies
131 Equipment
202 Accounts Payable
301 Richelle Ray, Capital
401 Fees Income
511 Rent Expense
514 Salaries Expense
517 Utilities Expense

TRANSACTIONS

1. Gave a cash refund of $750 to a customer because of a lost package. (The customer had previously paid in cash.)
2. Sent a check for $1,050 to the utility company to pay the monthly bill.
3. Provided services for $7,800 on credit.
4. Purchased new equipment for $4,600 and paid for it immediately by check.
5. Issued a check for $3,500 to pay a creditor on account.
6. Performed services for $15,250 in cash.
7. Collected $6,250 from credit customers.
8. The owner made an additional investment of $25,000 in cash.
9. Purchased supplies for $3,250 on credit.
10. Issued a check for $3,750 to pay the monthly rent.

Recording transactions in the general journal.

Exercise 4.2
Objective 4-1
GL

Selected accounts from the general ledger of Mason Consulting Services follow. Record the general journal entries that would be made to record the following transactions. Be sure to include dates and descriptions in these entries.

101 Cash
111 Accounts Receivable
121 Supplies
131 Equipment
141 Automobile
202 Accounts Payable
301 Zack Mason, Capital
302 Zack Mason, Drawing
401 Fees Income
511 Rent Expense
514 Salaries Expense
517 Telephone Expense

DATE		TRANSACTIONS
2019		
Sept.	1	Zack Mason invested $30,000 in cash to start the firm.
	4	Purchased office equipment for $3,250 on credit from Den, Inc.; received Invoice 9823, payable in 30 days.
	16	Purchased an automobile that will be used to visit clients; issued Check 1001 for $15,000 in full payment.
	20	Purchased supplies for $260; paid immediately with Check 1002.
	23	Returned damaged supplies for a cash refund of $85.
	30	Issued Check 1003 for $2,100 to Den, Inc., as payment on account for Invoice 9823.
	30	Withdrew $1,500 in cash for personal expenses.
	30	Issued Check 1004 for $3,500 to pay the rent for October.
	30	Performed services for $7,325 in cash.
	30	Paid $220 for monthly telephone bill, Check 1005.

Exercise 4.3 ▶ **Posting to the general ledger.**

Objectives 4-1, 4-3

CONTINUING >>> Problem

Post the journal entries that you prepared for Exercise 4.2 to the general ledger. Use the account names shown in Exercise 4.2.

Exercise 4.4 ▶ **Compound journal entries.**

Objective 4-2

The following transactions took place at the Cook Employment Agency during November 2019. Record the general journal entries that would be made for these transactions. Use a compound entry for each transaction.

DATE		TRANSACTIONS
Nov.	5	Performed services for Job Search, Inc., for $20,000; received $9,500 in cash and the client promised to pay the balance in 60 days.
	18	Purchased a graphing calculator for $450 and some supplies for $600 from Office Supply; issued Check 1008 for the total.
	23	Received Invoice 1602 for $2,500 from Automotive Technicians Repair for repairs to the firm's automobile; issued Check 1009 for half the amount and arranged to pay the other half in 30 days.

Exercise 4.5 ▶ **Recording a correcting entry.**

Objective 4-4

On June 10, 2019, an employee of Williams Corporation mistakenly debited ***Telephone Expense*** rather than ***Utilities Expense*** when recording a bill of $2,000 for the May utility service. The error was discovered on June 30. Prepare a general journal entry to correct the error.

Exercise 4.6 ▶ **Recording a correcting entry.**

Objective 4-4

On August 22, 2019, an employee of Bell Company mistakenly debited the ***Repair Expense*** account rather than the ***Truck Expense*** account when recording a bill of $900 for repairs. The error was discovered on October 1. Prepare a general journal entry to correct the error.

PROBLEMS

Problem Set A

Recording transactions in the general journal.

Problem 4.1A
Objective 4-1

The transactions that follow took place at the Desoto Recreation and Sports Arena during September 2019. This firm has indoor courts where customers can play tennis for a fee. It also rents equipment and offers tennis lessons.

INSTRUCTIONS

Record each transaction in the general journal, using the following chart of accounts. Be sure to number the journal page 1 and to write the year at the top of the Date column. Include a description for each entry.

ASSETS
101 Cash
111 Accounts Receivable
121 Supplies
141 Equipment
LIABILITIES
202 Accounts Payable
OWNER'S EQUITY
301 Ellis Carter, Capital
302 Ellis Carter, Drawing

REVENUE
401 Fees Income
EXPENSES
511 Equipment Repair Expense
512 Rent Expense
513 Salaries Expense
514 Telephone Expense
517 Utilities Expense

DATE		TRANSACTIONS
Sept.	1	Issued Check 1169 for $2,000 to pay the September rent.
	5	Performed services for $4,000 in cash.
	6	Performed services for $2,950 on credit.
	10	Paid $900 for monthly telephone bill; issued Check 1170.
	11	Paid for equipment repairs of $1,050 with Check 1171.
	12	Received $1,500 on account from credit clients.
	15	Issued Checks 1172–1177 for $5,200 for salaries.
	18	Issued Check 1178 for $2,700 to purchase supplies.
	19	Purchased new tennis rackets for $3,250 on credit from The Tennis Supply Shop; received Invoice 3108, payable in 30 days.
	20	Issued Check 1179 for $3,820 to purchase new nets. (Equip.)
	21	Received $500 on account from credit clients.
	21	Returned a damaged net and received a cash refund of $570.
	22	Performed services for $3,480 in cash.
	23	Performed services for $5,050 on credit.
	26	Issued Check 1180 for $620 to purchase supplies.
	28	Paid the monthly electric bill of $2,500 with Check 1181.
	30	Issued Checks 1182–1187 for $5,200 for salaries.
	30	Issued Check 1188 for $5,000 cash to Ellis Carter for personal expenses.

Analyze: If the company paid a bill for supplies on October 1, what check number would be included in the journal entry description?

Problem 4.2A ► Journalizing and posting transactions.

Objectives 4-1, 4-2, 4-3

GL

On October 1, 2019, Helen Kennedy opened an advertising agency. She plans to use the chart of accounts listed below.

INSTRUCTIONS

1. Journalize the transactions. Number the journal page 1, write the year at the top of the Date column, and include a description for each entry.
2. Post to the ledger accounts. Before you start the posting process, open accounts by entering account names and numbers in the headings. Follow the order of the accounts in the chart of accounts.

ASSETS
101 Cash
111 Accounts Receivable
121 Supplies
141 Office Equipment
151 Art Equipment

LIABILITIES
202 Accounts Payable

OWNER'S EQUITY
301 Helen Kennedy, Capital
302 Helen Kennedy, Drawing

REVENUE
401 Fees Income

EXPENSES
511 Office Cleaning Expense
514 Rent Expense
517 Salaries Expense
520 Telephone Expense
523 Utilities Expense

DATE		TRANSACTIONS
Oct.	1	Helen Kennedy invested $70,000 cash in the business.
	2	Paid October office rent of $4,000; issued Check 1001.
	5	Purchased desks and other office furniture for $18,000 from Office Furniture Mart, Inc.; received Invoice 6704 payable in 60 days.
	6	Issued Check 1002 for $4,100 to purchase art equipment.
	7	Purchased supplies for $1,670; paid with Check 1003.
	10	Issued Check 1004 for $800 for office cleaning service.
	12	Performed services for $4,200 in cash and $1,800 on credit. (Use a compound entry.)
	15	Returned damaged supplies for a cash refund of $300.
	18	Purchased a computer for $3,000 from Office Furniture Mart, Inc., Invoice 7108; issued Check 1005 for a $1,750 down payment, with the balance payable in 30 days. (Use one compound entry.)
	20	Issued Check 1006 for $9,500 to Office Furniture Mart, Inc., as payment on account for Invoice 6704.
	26	Performed services for $4,800 on credit.
	27	Paid $375 for monthly telephone bill; issued Check 1007.
	30	Received $4,200 in cash from credit customers.
	30	Mailed Check 1008 to pay the monthly utility bill of $1,080.
	30	Issued Checks 1009–1011 for $9,000 for salaries.

Analyze: What is the balance of account 202 in the general ledger?

Recording correcting entries.

◀ **Problem 4.3A**
Objective 4-4

The following journal entries were prepared by an employee of International Marketing Company who does not have an adequate knowledge of accounting.

INSTRUCTIONS

Examine the journal entries carefully to locate the errors. Provide a brief written description of each error. Assume that ***Office Equipment*** and ***Office Supplies*** were recorded at the correct values.

GENERAL JOURNAL PAGE 3

	DATE		DESCRIPTION	POST. REF.	DEBIT	CREDIT	
1	2019						1
2	April	1	Accounts Payable		15 8 0 0 00		2
3			Fees Income			15 8 0 0 00	3
4			Performed services on credit				4
5							5
6		2	Cash		6 0 0 00		6
7			Telephone Expense			6 0 0 00	7
8			Paid for March telephone				8
9			service, Check 1917				9
10							10
11		3	Office Equipment		8 2 0 0 00		11
12			Office Supplies		9 0 0 00		12
13			Cash			9 5 0 0 00	13
14			Purchased file cabinet and				14
15			office supplies, Check 1918				15
16							16
17							17
18							18
19							19
20							20

Analyze: After the correcting journal entries have been posted, what effect do the corrections have on the company's reported assets?

Problem 4.4A ► Journalizing and posting transactions

Objectives 4-1, 4-2, 4-3

GL

Four transactions for Automotive Maintenance and Repair Shop that took place in November 2019 appear below, along with the general ledger accounts used by the company.

INSTRUCTIONS

Record the transactions in the general journal and post them to the appropriate ledger accounts. Be sure to number the journal page 1 and to write the year at the top of the Date column.

Cash	101	Equipment	151
Accounts Receivable	111	Accounts Payable	202
Office Supplies	121	Ryan O'Malley, Capital	301
Tools	131	Fees Income	401
Machinery	141		

DATE		TRANSACTIONS
Nov.	1	Ryan O'Malley invested $60,000 in cash plus tools with a fair market value of $5,000 to start the business.
	2	Purchased equipment for $3,500 and supplies for $700 from Office Depot, Invoice 501; issued Check 100 for $700 as a down payment with the balance due in 30 days.
	10	Performed services for Patricia Reed for $3,200, who paid $1,000 in cash with the balance due in 30 days.
	20	Purchased machinery for $4,000 from Craft Machinery, Inc., Invoice 709; issued Check 101 for $1,500 in cash as a down payment with the balance due in 30 days.

Analyze: What liabilities does the business owe as of November 30?

Problem Set B

Recording transactions in the general journal.

Problem 4.1B
Objective 4-1

The transactions listed below took place at Moore Building Cleaning Service during September 2019. This firm cleans commercial buildings for a fee.

INSTRUCTIONS

Analyze and record each transaction in the general journal. Choose the account names from the chart of accounts shown below. Be sure to number the journal page 1 and to write the year at the top of the Date column.

ASSETS
101 Cash
111 Accounts Receivable
141 Equipment

LIABILITIES
202 Accounts Payable

OWNER'S EQUITY
301 Ruth Moore, Capital
302 Ruth Moore, Drawing

REVENUE
401 Fees Income

EXPENSES
501 Cleaning Supplies Expense
502 Equipment Repair Expense
503 Office Supplies Expense
511 Rent Expense
514 Salaries Expense
521 Telephone Expense
524 Utilities Expense

DATE		TRANSACTIONS
Sept.	1	Ruth Moore invested $65,000 in cash to start the business.
	5	Performed services for $3,000 in cash.
	6	Issued Check 1000 for $3,000 to pay the September rent.
	7	Performed services for $8,500 on credit.
	9	Paid $750 for monthly telephone bill; issued Check 1001.
	10	Issued Check 1002 for $775 for equipment repairs.
	12	Received $2,100 from credit clients.
	14	Issued Checks 1003–1004 for $13,000 to pay salaries.
	18	Issued Check 1005 for $900 for cleaning supplies.
	19	Issued Check 1006 for $1,050 for office supplies.
	20	Purchased equipment for $12,000 from Razor Equipment, Inc., Invoice 1012; issued Check 1007 for $2,000 with the balance due in 30 days
	22	Performed services for $5,200 in cash.
	24	Issued Check 1008 for $1,050 for the monthly electric bill.
	26	Performed services for $7,500 on account.
	30	Issued Checks 1009–1010 for $13,000 to pay salaries.
	30	Issued Check 1011 for $10,000 to Ruth Moore to pay for personal expenses.

Analyze: How many transactions affected expense accounts?

Problem 4.2B ► Journalizing and posting transactions.

Objectives 4-1, 4-2, 4-3

In June 2019, Ian Lee opened a photography studio that provides services to public and private schools. His firm's financial activities for the first month of operations and the chart of accounts appear below.

INSTRUCTIONS

1. Journalize the transactions. Number the journal page 1 and write the year at the top of the Date column. Describe each entry.
2. Post to the ledger accounts. Before you start the posting process, open the accounts by entering the names and numbers in the headings. Follow the order of the accounts in the chart of accounts.

ASSETS

101 Cash

111 Accounts Receivable

121 Supplies

141 Office Equipment

151 Photographic Equipment

LIABILITIES

202 Accounts Payable

OWNER'S EQUITY

301 Ian Lee, Capital

302 Ian Lee, Drawing

REVENUE

401 Fees Income

EXPENSES

511 Office Cleaning Expense

514 Rent Expense

517 Salaries Expense

520 Telephone Expense

523 Utilities Expense

DATE		TRANSACTIONS
June	1	Ian Lee invested $20,000 cash in the business.
	2	Issued Check 1001 for $2,000 to pay the June rent.
	5	Purchased desks and other office furniture for $9,500 from Office Supply, Inc.; received Invoice 5312, payable in 60 days.
	6	Issued Check 1002 for $2,100 to purchase photographic equipment.
	7	Purchased supplies for $550; paid with Check 1003.
	10	Issued Check 1004 for $800 for office cleaning service.
	12	Performed services for $2,600 in cash and $2,600 on credit. (Use one compound entry.)
	15	Returned damaged supplies; received a $180 cash refund.
	18	Purchased a computer for $2,250 from Dallas Office Supply, Invoice 304; issued Check 1005 for a $500 down payment. The balance is payable in 30 days. (Use one compound entry.)
	20	Issued Check 1006 for $2,500 to Office Supply, Inc., as payment on account for office furniture, Invoice 5312.
	26	Performed services for $2,500 on credit.
	27	Paid $632 for monthly telephone bill; issued Check 1007
	30	Received $2,300 in cash from credit clients on account.
	30	Issued Check 1008 to pay the monthly utility bill of $750.
	30	Issued Checks 1009—1011 for $6,550 for salaries.

Analyze: What was the ***Cash*** account balance after the transaction of June 27 was recorded?

Recording correcting entries.

Problem 4.3B
Objective 4-4

All the journal entries shown below contain errors. The entries were prepared by an employee of New Bellmont Corporation who does not have an adequate knowledge of accounting.

INSTRUCTIONS

Examine the journal entries carefully to locate the errors. Provide a brief written description of each error. Assume that ***Office Equipment*** and ***Office Supplies*** were recorded at the correct values.

GENERAL JOURNAL PAGE 1

	DATE		DESCRIPTION	POST. REF.	DEBIT	CREDIT	
1	2019						1
2	Jan.	1	Accounts Payable		1 100 00		2
3			Fees Income			1 100 00	3
4			Performed services on credit				4
5							5
6		2	Cash		750 00		6
7			Telephone Expense			750 00	7
8			Paid for January telephone				8
9			service, Check 1601				9
10							10
11		3	Office Equipment		1 250 00		11
12			Office Supplies		250 00		12
13			Cash			1 300 00	13
14			Purchased file cabinet and				14
15			office supplies, Check 1602				15
16							16

Analyze: After the correcting journal entries have been posted, what effect do the corrections have on the reported assets of the company?

Problem 4.4B ► Journalizing and posting transactions.

Objectives 4-1, 4-2, 4-3

Several transactions that occurred during December 2019, the first month of operation for Wilner's Accounting Services, follow. The company uses the general ledger accounts listed below.

INSTRUCTIONS

Record the transactions in the general journal (page 1) and post to the appropriate accounts.

Cash	101	Furniture & Fixtures	151
Accounts Receivable	111	Accounts Payable	202
Office Supplies	121	Charles Wilner, Capital	301
Computers	131	Fees Income	401
Office Equipment	141		

DATE		TRANSACTIONS
Dec.	3	Charles Wilner began business by depositing $25,000 cash into a business checking account.
	4	Purchased a computer for $2,500 cash.
	5	Purchased furniture and fixtures on account for $7,500.
	6	Purchased office equipment for $2,800 cash.
	10	Rendered services to client and sent bill for $3,200.
	11	Purchased office supplies for $1,050 in cash.
	15	Received invoice for furniture purchased on December 5 and paid it.

Analyze: Describe the activity for account 202 during the month.

Critical Thinking Problem 4.1

Financial Statements

James Wilson is a new staff accountant for Zoie's Beauty Supply. He has asked you to review the financial statements prepared for April to find and correct any errors. Review the income statement and balance sheet that follow and identify the errors Wilson made (he did not prepare a statement of owner's equity). Prepare a corrected income statement and balance sheet, as well as a statement of owner's equity, for Zoie's Beauty Supply.

Zoie's Beauty Supply
Income Statement
April 30, 2019

Revenue		
Fees Income		38 800 00
Expenses		
Salaries Expense	9 500 00	
Rent Expense	2 500 00	
Repair Expense	800 00	
Utilities Expense	1 700 00	
Drawing	4 500 00	
Total Expenses		19 900 00
Net Income		23 600 00

Zoie's Beauty Supply
Balance Sheet
Month Ended April 30, 2019

Assets		*Liabilities*	
Land	12 000 00	*Accounts Receivable*	7 000 00
Building	40 000 00		
Cash	15 000 00	*Owner's Equity*	
Accounts Payable	5 000 00	*Zoie Taylor, Capital, April 1, 2019*	49 200 00
Total Assets	56 200 00	*Total Liabilities and Owner's Equity*	56 200 00

Critical Thinking Problem 4.2

GL

Start-Up Business

On June 1, 2019, Jenna Davis opened the Leadership Coaching Agency. She plans to use the chart of accounts given below.

INSTRUCTIONS

1. Journalize the transactions. Be sure to number the journal pages and write the year at the top of the Date column. Include a description for each entry.
2. Post to the ledger accounts. Before you start the posting process, open the accounts by entering the account names and numbers in the headings. Using the list of accounts below, assign appropriate account numbers and place them in the correct order in the ledger.
3. Prepare a trial balance.
4. Prepare the income statement.
5. Prepare a statement of owner's equity.
6. Prepare the balance sheet.

ACCOUNTS

Accounts Payable	Jenna Davis, Drawing
Office Furniture	Recording Equipment
Accounts Receivable	Rent Expense
Advertising Expense	Salaries Expense
Cash	Supplies
Fees Income	Telephone Expense
Jenna Davis, Capital	Utilities Expense

DATE		TRANSACTIONS
June	1	Jenna Davis invested $40,000 cash to start the business.
	2	Issued Check 201 for $2,000 to pay the June rent for the office.
	3	Purchased desk and other office furniture for $12,000 from Lowe's Office Supply, Invoice 5103; issued Check 202 for a $2,000 down payment with the balance due in 30 days.
	4	Issued Check 203 for $1,700 for supplies.
	6	Performed services for $7,000 in cash.
	7	Issued Check 204 for $3,000 to pay for advertising expense.
	8	Purchased recording equipment for $15,000 from Special Moves, Inc., Invoice 2122; issued Check 205 for a down payment of $5,000 with the balance due in 30 days.
	10	Performed services for $5,500 on account.
	11	Issued Check 206 for $3,000 to Lowe's Office Supply as payment on account.
	12	Performed services for $10,000 in cash.
	15	Issued Check 207 for $6,200 to pay an employee's salary.
	18	Received payments of $4,000 from credit clients on account.
	20	Issued Check 208 for $6,000 to Special Moves, Inc., as payment on account.
	25	Issued Check 209 in the amount of $375 for the monthly telephone bill.
	27	Issued Check 210 in the amount of $980 for the monthly electric bill.
	28	Issued Check 211 to Jenna Davis for $5,000 for personal living expenses.
	30	Issued Check 212 for $6,200 to pay the salary of an employee.

Analyze: How many postings were made to the ***Cash*** account?

BUSINESS CONNECTIONS

Business Records

Managerial | FOCUS

1. How might a poor set of recording procedures affect the flow of information to management?
2. Why should management be concerned about the efficiency of a firm's procedures for journalizing and posting transactions?
3. Why should management insist that a firm's accounting system have a strong audit trail?
4. The owner of a new business recently questioned the accountant about the value of having both a journal and a ledger. The owner believes that it is a waste of effort to enter data about transactions in two different records. How would you explain the value of having both records?

Correcting Entries

Ethical | DILEMMA

As the full-time bookkeeper, your job is to make any corrections to the general ledger accounts. Each correction needs the reason for the change and the effect on each account, whether it is an increase or decrease.

Mesia has come to you for help. For the third time this month, she has recorded a cash receipt twice. She wants you to record a correcting entry that will reverse her mistakes. The correcting entry she wants you to make will record a credit to the ***Cash*** account and a debit to ***Sales.*** What should you investigate before making a decision about the correcting entry? What is happening to the ***Cash*** account? Is this a continual problem for Mesia? Would you accept a dinner offer from Mesia if you fix her mistake?

Balance Sheet

Financial Statement ANALYSIS

Review the following excerpt taken from the Walmart consolidated balance sheet as of January 31, 2016.

Analyze:

Walmart Stores, Inc. Consolidated Balance Sheet January 31, 2016	
(Amounts in millions)	
Property and Equipment:	
Property and Equipment (net)	$110,171
Property Under Capital Leases:	
Property Under Capital Leases (net)	$ 6,345

1. When the accountant for Walmart records a purchase of property and equipment, what type of account is debited? If Walmart purchases equipment on credit, what account might be credited?
2. What type of source document might be reflected in the journal entry to record the purchase of equipment?
3. If the accounting manager reviewed the ***Equipment*** account in the general ledger, what types of information might be listed there?

Analyze Online: Locate the website for Walmart (www.walmartstores.com), which provides an online store for consumers as well as corporate information. Within the website, locate the consolidated balance sheet for the current year.

4. What is the balance reported for cash and cash equivalents at January 31 of the current year?
5. What is the balance reported for inventories at January 31 of the current year?

TEAMWORK

Audit Trail

An audit trail allows an individual to track a transaction from the journal entry to the general ledger through to the financial statements. The audit trail can also find all the transactions that comprise the dollar amount for each account listed on the income statement and balance sheet. Your team has been assigned the duty to diagram the audit trail for your company. In your diagram, show several transactions and how they would be tracked from the journal entry to the financial statement and back to the journal entry.

Internet CONNECTION

Accounting Careers

Enter "Accounting Careers" in a search tool like Google. Select a site that will provide the skills and talents required for an accountant. Also find the salaries for accountants in your local area. Note the amount of experience and education needed to receive the salary you want to be earning in the next five years.

Answers to **Self Reviews**

Answers to Section 1 Self Review

1. **c.** debit
2. **c.** diary.
3. To provide an audit trail to trace information through the accounting system.
4. It is the first accounting record where transactions are entered.
5. No. The only requirement is that the total debits must equal the total credits.
6. The audit trail will be very difficult to follow.

Answers to Section 2 Self Review

1. They indicate that the entry has been posted and ensure against posting the same entry twice.
2. Both statements are false. If an incorrect journal entry was posted, a correcting entry should be journalized and posted. To ensure honesty and provide a clear audit trail, erasures are not permitted in the journal.
3. The ledger account number.
4. **c.** date order.
5. **a.** account order.
6.

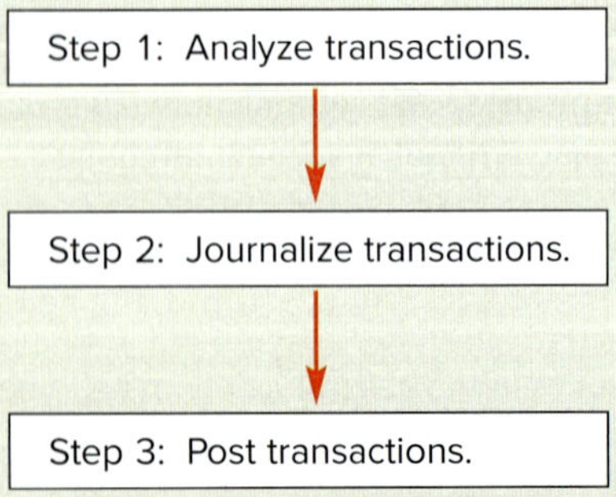

Answers to Comprehensive Self Review

1. The general ledger account number.
2. It is the last accounting record in which a transaction is recorded.
3. Neatly cross out the incorrect item and write the correct data above it.
4. Check number.
   Invoice number for goods purchased on credit from a vendor.
   Invoice number for services billed to a charge account customer.
   Memorandum number.
5. **a.** An entry in the general journal.

Adjustments and the Worksheet

Chapter **5**

© Eden Breitz/Alamy Stock Photo

www.deloitte.com

The financial information prepared by accountants is used by others to make decisions. Users of financial statements may include the company's owners, managers, and employees; creditors; investors; customers; and taxing and regulatory authorities. How do users of the financial information know if what is being reported is a true representation of a company's financial performance? Financial service firms, such as Deloitte Touche Tohmatsu Limited (Deloitte), provide the service of verifying the accuracy and reliability of a company's financial information.

Deloitte consists of thousands of dedicated professionals throughout the world who provide audit, tax, consulting, and other financial-related services to its clients. Deloitte earns its revenue by the time spent performing these financial services. For the fiscal year ended May 31, 2015, Deloitte reported $35.2 billion in revenue. Even though it may not have been paid immediately, Deloitte must recognize the $35.2 billion in revenue at the time the services are performed.

Deloitte also incurs expenses related to earning its revenue. Expenses are the costs necessary to earn revenue. Some examples of the expenses incurred by Deloitte include employees' wages and benefits, training, travel, business insurance, and office and computer supplies. To properly measure the company's financial performance, it is important to ensure that the expenses incurred are recorded in the same year as the revenue generated by the expense. Matching the revenue and expenses within the same year provides Deloitte with the most accurate financial results to evaluate its financial performance and determine the amount of costs necessary to earn its revenue.

thinking critically

Careful recordkeeping is critical to all businesses, large and small. Why does matching these revenues and expenses within the same year matter so much?

LEARNING OBJECTIVES

5-1 Complete a trial balance on a worksheet.

5-2 Prepare adjustments for unrecorded business transactions.

5-3 Complete the worksheet.

5-4 Prepare an income statement, statement of owner's equity, and balance sheet from the completed worksheet.

5-5 Journalize and post the adjusting entries.

5-6 Define the accounting terms new to this chapter.

NEW TERMS

account form balance sheet
adjusting entries
adjustments
book value
contra account
contra asset account
depreciation
prepaid expenses
report form balance sheet
salvage value
straight-line depreciation
worksheet

Section 1

SECTION OBJECTIVES	TERMS TO LEARN
>> 5-1 Complete a trial balance on a worksheet. **WHY IT'S IMPORTANT** Time and effort can be saved when the trial balance is prepared directly on the worksheet. Amounts can be easily transferred to other sections of the worksheet. >> 5-2 Prepare adjustments for unrecorded business transactions. **WHY IT'S IMPORTANT** Not all business transactions occur between separate business entities. Some financial events occur within a business and need to be recorded.	adjusting entries depreciation adjustments prepaid expenses book value salvage value contra account straight-line depreciation contra asset account worksheet

The Worksheet

Financial statements are completed as soon as possible in order to be useful. One way to speed the preparation of financial statements is to use a worksheet. A **worksheet** is a form used to gather all data needed at the end of an accounting period to prepare the financial statements. Preparation of the worksheet is the fourth step in the accounting cycle.

Figure 5.1 shows a common type of worksheet. The heading shows the company name, report title, and period covered. In addition to the Account Name column, this worksheet contains five sections: Trial Balance, Adjustments, Adjusted Trial Balance, Income Statement, and Balance Sheet. Each section includes a Debit column and a Credit column. The worksheet has 10 columns in which to enter dollar amounts.

>> 5-1 OBJECTIVE

Complete a trial balance on a worksheet.

The Trial Balance Section

Refer to Figure 5.2 as you read about how to prepare the Trial Balance section of the worksheet.

1. Enter the general ledger account names.
2. Transfer the general ledger account balances to the Debit and Credit columns of the Trial Balance section.
3. Total the Debit and Credit columns to prove that the trial balance is in balance.
4. Place a double rule under each Trial Balance column to show that the work in that column is complete.

recall

Trial Balance

If total debits do not equal total credits, there is an error in the financial records. The error must be found and corrected.

FIGURE 5.1

Ten-Column Worksheet

Eli's Consulting Services
Worksheet
Month Ended December 31, 2019

	ACCOUNT NAME	TRIAL BALANCE		ADJUSTMENTS	
		DEBIT	CREDIT	DEBIT	CREDIT
1					
2					
3					
4					
5					

FIGURE 5.2 A Partial Worksheet

Eli's Consulting Services
Worksheet
Month Ended December 31, 2019

	ACCOUNT NAME	TRIAL BALANCE		ADJUSTMENTS	
		DEBIT	CREDIT	DEBIT	CREDIT
1	*Cash*	111,350.00			
2	*Accounts Receivable*	5,000.00			
3	*Supplies*	1,500.00			(a) 500.00
4	*Prepaid Rent*	8,000.00			(b) 4,000.00
5	*Equipment*	11,000.00			
6	*Accumulated Depreciation—Equipment*				(c) 183.00
7	*Accounts Payable*		3,500.00		
8	*Trayton Eli, Capital*		100,000.00		
9	*Trayton Eli, Drawing*	5,000.00			
10	*Fees Income*		47,000.00		
11	*Salaries Expense*	8,000.00			
12	*Utilities Expense*	650.00			
13	*Supplies Expense*			(a) 500.00	
14	*Rent Expense*			(b) 4,000.00	
15	*Depreciation Expense—Equipment*			(c) 183.00	
16	*Totals*	150,500.00	150,500.00	4,683.00	4,683.00
17					
18					
19					

Notice that the trial balance has four new accounts: ***Accumulated Depreciation—Equipment, Supplies Expense, Rent Expense,*** and ***Depreciation Expense—Equipment.*** These accounts have zero balances now, but they will be needed later as the worksheet is completed.

The Adjustments Section

>> 5-2 OBJECTIVE

Prepare adjustments for unrecorded business transactions.

Usually, account balances change because of transactions with other businesses or individuals. For Eli's Consulting Services, the account changes recorded in Chapter 4 were caused by transactions with the firm's suppliers, customers, landlord, and employees. It is easy to recognize, journalize, and post these transactions as they occur.

Some changes are not caused by transactions with other businesses or individuals. They arise from the internal operations of the firm during the accounting period. Journal entries made to update accounts for previously unrecorded items are called **adjustments** or **adjusting entries.** These changes are first entered on the worksheet at the end of each accounting period. The worksheet provides a convenient form for gathering the information and determining the effects of the changes. Let's look at the adjustments made by Eli's Consulting Services on December 31, 2019.

ADJUSTED TRIAL BALANCE		INCOME STATEMENT		BALANCE SHEET		
DEBIT	CREDIT	DEBIT	CREDIT	DEBIT	CREDIT	
						1
						2
						3
						4
						5

recall

Trial Balance

On the trial balance, accounts are listed in this order: assets, liabilities, owner's equity, revenue, and expenses.

GL

ADJUSTING FOR SUPPLIES USED

On November 28, 2019, Eli's Consulting Services purchased $1,500 of supplies. On December 31, the trial balance shows a $1,500 balance in the ***Supplies*** account. This amount is too high because some of the supplies were used during December.

An adjustment must be made for the supplies used. Otherwise, the asset account ***Supplies*** is overstated because fewer supplies are actually on hand. The expense account ***Supplies Expense*** is understated. The cost of the supplies used represents an operating expense that has not been recorded.

On December 31, Sergio Sanchez counted the supplies. Remaining supplies totaled $1,000. This meant that supplies amounting to $500 were used during December ($1,500 − $1,000 = $500). At the end of December, an adjustment must be made to reflect the supplies used. The adjustment reduces the ***Supplies*** account to $1,000, the amount of supplies remaining. It increases the ***Supplies Expense*** account by $500 for the amount of supplies used. Notice that the adjustment for supplies is based on actual usage.

Refer to Figure 5.2 to review the adjustment on the worksheet: a debit of $500 to ***Supplies Expense*** and a credit of $500 to ***Supplies.*** Both the debit and credit are labeled ***(a)*** to identify the two parts of the adjustment.

Supplies is a type of prepaid expense. **Prepaid expenses** are items that are acquired and paid for in advance of their use. Other common prepaid expenses are prepaid rent, prepaid insurance, and prepaid advertising. When cash is paid for these items, amounts are debited to ***Prepaid Rent, Prepaid Insurance,*** and ***Prepaid Advertising;*** all are asset accounts. As prepaid expenses are used, an adjustment is made to reduce the asset accounts and to increase the related expense accounts.

ADJUSTMENT

Record the adjustment for supplies.

ANALYSIS

The expense account *Supplies Expense* is increased by $500. The asset account *Supplies* is decreased by $500.

DEBIT-CREDIT RULES

DEBIT Increases to expense accounts are recorded as debits. Debit ***Supplies Expense*** for $500.

CREDIT Decreases to asset accounts are recorded as credits. Credit ***Supplies*** for $500.

T-ACCOUNT PRESENTATION

Supplies Expense	
+	−
500	

Supplies	
+	−
	500

ABOUT **ACCOUNTING**

Accounting Software

The use of accounting software eliminates the need to prepare a worksheet. However, adjusting entries must always be made to properly reflect account balances at the end of a reporting period.

Let's review the effect of the adjustment on the asset account ***Supplies.*** Recall that the ***Supplies*** account already had a balance of $1,500. If no adjustment is made, the balance would remain at $1,500, even though only $1,000 of supplies are left.

Supplies			
+		–	
Bal.	1,500	Adj.	500
Bal.	1,000		

ADJUSTING FOR EXPIRED RENT

On November 30, 2019, Eli's Consulting Services paid $8,000 rent for December and January. The right to occupy facilities for the specified period is an asset. The $8,000 was debited to ***Prepaid Rent,*** an asset account. On December 31, 2019, the ***Prepaid Rent*** balance is $8,000. This is too high because one month of rent has been used. The expired rent is $4,000 ($8,000 ÷ 2 months). At the end of December, an adjustment is made to reflect the expired rent.

ADJUSTMENT

Record the adjustment for expired rent.

ANALYSIS

The expense account ***Rent Expense*** is increased by $4,000. The asset account ***Prepaid Rent*** is decreased by $4,000.

DEBIT-CREDIT RULES

DEBIT Increases to expense accounts are recorded as debits. Debit ***Rent Expense*** for $4,000.

CREDIT Decreases to asset accounts are recorded as credits. Credit ***Prepaid Rent*** for $4,000.

T-ACCOUNT PRESENTATION

Rent Expense	
+	–
4,000	

Prepaid Rent	
+	–
	4,000

Let's review the effect of the adjustment on the asset account ***Prepaid Rent.*** The beginning balance of $8,000 represents prepaid rent for the months of December and January. By December 31, the prepaid rent for the month of December is "used up." The adjustment reducing ***Prepaid Rent*** recognizes the expense of occupying the facilities in December. The $4,000 ending balance represents prepaid rent for the month of January.

Prepaid Rent			
+		–	
Bal.	8,000	Adj.	4,000
Bal.	4,000		

important!

Prepaid Expense

Prepaid rent is recorded as an asset at the time it is paid. As time elapses, the asset is used up. An adjustment is made to reduce the asset and to recognize rent expense.

Refer again to Figure 5.2 to review the adjustment on the worksheet: a debit of $4,000 to ***Rent Expense*** and a credit of $4,000 to ***Prepaid Rent.*** Both parts of the adjustment are labeled ***(b)***.

ADJUSTING FOR DEPRECIATION

There is one more adjustment to make at the end of December. It involves the equipment purchased in November. The cost of long-term assets such as equipment is not recorded as an expense when purchased. Instead, the cost is recorded as an asset and spread over the time the assets are used for the business. **Depreciation** is the process of allocating the cost of long-term assets over their expected useful lives. There are many ways to calculate depreciation. Eli's Consulting Services uses the **straight-line depreciation** method. This method results in an equal amount of depreciation being charged to each accounting period during the asset's useful life. The formula for straight-line depreciation is

$$\text{Depreciation} = \frac{\text{Cost} - \text{Salvage value}}{\text{Estimated useful life}}$$

Salvage value is an estimate of the amount that may be received by selling or disposing of an asset at the end of its useful life.

Eli's Consulting Services purchased $11,000 worth of equipment. The equipment has an estimated useful life of five years and no salvage value. The depreciation for December, the first month of operations, is $183 (rounded).

$$\frac{\$11{,}000 - \$0}{60 \text{ months}} = \$183 \text{ (rounded)}$$

1. Convert the asset's useful life from years to months: 5 years × 12 months = 60 months.
2. Divide the total depreciation to be taken by the total number of months: $11,000 ÷ 60 = $183 (rounded).
3. Record depreciation expense of $183 each month for the next 60 months.

> Conoco Inc. depreciates property such as refinery equipment, pipelines, and deep-water drill ships on a straight-line basis over the estimated life of each asset, ranging from 15 to 25 years.

important!

Contra Accounts

The normal balance for a contra account is the opposite of the related account. ***Accumulated Depreciation*** is a contra asset account. The normal balance of an asset account is a *debit.* The normal balance of a contra asset account is a *credit.*

As the cost of the equipment is gradually transferred to expense, its recorded value as an asset must be reduced. This procedure cannot be carried out by directly decreasing the balance in the asset account. Generally accepted accounting principles require that the original cost of a long-term asset continue to appear in the asset account until the firm has used up or disposed of the asset.

The adjustment for depreciation is recorded in a contra account entitled ***Accumulated Depreciation—Equipment.*** A **contra account** has a normal balance that is opposite that of a related account. For example, the ***Equipment*** account is an asset and has a normal debit balance. ***Accumulated Depreciation—Equipment*** is a **contra asset account** with a normal credit balance, which is opposite the normal balance of an asset account. The adjustment to reflect depreciation for December is a $183 debit to ***Depreciation Expense—Equipment*** and a $183 credit to ***Accumulated Depreciation—Equipment.***

The ***Accumulated Depreciation—Equipment*** account is a record of all depreciation taken on the equipment. The financial records show the original cost of the equipment (***Equipment,*** $11,000) and all depreciation taken (***Accumulated Depreciation—Equipment,*** $183). The difference between the two accounts is called book value. **Book value** is that portion of an asset's original cost that has not yet been depreciated. Three amounts are reported on the financial statements for equipment:

Equipment	$11,000
Less accumulated depreciation	−183
Equipment at book value	$10,817

Refer to Figure 5.2 to review the depreciation adjustment on the worksheet. The two parts of the adjustment are labeled ***(c)***.

ADJUSTMENT

Record the adjustment for depreciation.

ANALYSIS

The expense account ***Depreciation Expense—Equipment*** is increased by $183. The contra asset account ***Accumulated Depreciation—Equipment*** is increased by $183.

DEBIT-CREDIT RULES

DEBIT Increases to expense accounts are recorded as debits. Debit ***Depreciation Expense—Equipment*** for $183.

CREDIT Increases to contra asset accounts are recorded as credits. Credit ***Accumulated Depreciation—Equipment*** for $183.

T-ACCOUNT PRESENTATION

Depreciation Expense—Equipment	
+	−
183	

Accumulated Depreciation—Equipment	
−	+
	183

If Eli's Consulting Services had other kinds of long-term tangible assets, an adjustment for depreciation would be made for each one. Long-term tangible assets include land, buildings, equipment, trucks, automobiles, furniture, and fixtures. Depreciation is calculated on all long-term tangible assets except land. Land is not depreciated.

Notice that each adjustment involved a balance sheet account (an asset or a contra asset) and an income statement account (an expense). When all adjustments have been entered, total and rule the Adjustments columns. Be sure that the totals of the Debit and Credit columns are equal. If they are not, locate and correct the error or errors before continuing. Figure 5.2 shows the completed Adjustments section.

Section 1 Self Review

QUESTIONS

1. What are adjustments?
2. Why are prepaid expenses adjusted at the end of an accounting period?
3. Why is the worksheet prepared?

EXERCISES

4. A firm paid $3,000 for supplies during the accounting period. At the end of the accounting period, the firm had $1,500 of supplies on hand. What adjustment is entered on the worksheet?
   a. ***Supplies*** is debited for $1,500 and ***Supplies Expense*** is credited for $1,500.
   b. ***Supplies Expense*** is debited for $1,500 and ***Supplies*** is credited for $1,500.
   c. ***Supplies*** is debited for $3,000 and ***Supplies Expense*** is credited for $3,000.
   d. ***Supplies Expense*** is debited for $3,000 and ***Supplies*** is credited for $3,000.
5. On January 1, a firm paid $30,000 for six months' rent, January through June. What is the adjustment for rent expense at the end of January?
   a. ***Rent Expense*** is debited for $30,000 and ***Prepaid Rent*** is credited for $30,000.
   b. ***Prepaid Rent*** is debited for $5,000 and ***Rent Expense*** is credited for $5,000.
   c. ***Rent Expense*** is debited for $5,000 and ***Prepaid Rent*** is credited for $5,000.
   d. No adjustment is made until the end of June.

ANALYSIS

6. Three years ago, Overnight Delivery bought a delivery truck for $80,000. The truck has no salvage value and a five-year useful life. What is the book value of the truck at the end of three years?

Answers to Section 1 Self Review are on page 159.)

Section 2

SECTION OBJECTIVES	TERMS TO LEARN
>> 5-3 Complete the worksheet. WHY IT'S IMPORTANT The worksheet summarizes both internal and external financial events of a period. >> 5-4 Prepare an income statement, statement of owner's equity, and balance sheet from the completed worksheet. WHY IT'S IMPORTANT Using a worksheet saves time in preparing the financial statements. >> 5-5 Journalize and post the adjusting entries. WHY IT'S IMPORTANT Adjusting entries update the financial records of the business.	account form balance sheet report form balance sheet

Financial Statements

The worksheet is used to prepare the financial statements. Preparing financial statements is the fifth step in the accounting cycle.

The Adjusted Trial Balance Section

>> 5-3 OBJECTIVE
Complete the worksheet.

The next task is to prepare the Adjusted Trial Balance section.

1. Combine the figures from the Trial Balance section and the Adjustments section of the worksheet. Record the computed results in the Adjusted Trial Balance columns.
2. Total the Debit and Credit columns in the Adjusted Trial Balance section. Confirm that debits equal credits.

Figure 5.3 shows the completed Adjusted Trial Balance section of the worksheet. The accounts that do not have adjustments are simply extended from the Trial Balance section to the Adjusted Trial Balance section. For example, the ***Cash*** account balance of $111,350 is recorded in the Debit column of the Adjusted Trial Balance section without change.

The balances of accounts that are affected by adjustments are recomputed. Look at the ***Supplies*** account. It has a $1,500 debit balance in the Trial Balance section and shows a $500 credit in the Adjustments section. The new balance is $1,000 ($1,500 – $500). It is recorded in the Debit column of the Adjusted Trial Balance section.

Use the following guidelines to compute the amounts for the Adjusted Trial Balance section.

- If the account has a debit balance in the Trial Balance section and a debit entry in the Adjustments section, add the two amounts.

If the Trial Balance section has a:	AND if the entry in the Adjustments section is a:	Then:
Debit balance	Debit	Add the amounts.
Debit balance	Credit	Subtract the credit amount.
Credit balance	Credit	Add the amounts.
Credit balance	Debit	Subtract the debit amount.

FIGURE 5.3 A Partial Worksheet

Eli's Consulting Services
Worksheet
Month Ended December 31, 2019

	ACCOUNT NAME	TRIAL BALANCE		ADJUSTMENTS	
		DEBIT	CREDIT	DEBIT	CREDIT
1	*Cash*	111 350 00			
2	*Accounts Receivable*	5 000 00			
3	*Supplies*	1 500 00			(a) 500 00
4	*Prepaid Rent*	8 000 00			(b) 4 000 00
5	*Equipment*	11 000 00			
6	*Accumulated Depreciation—Equipment*				(c) 183 00
7	*Accounts Payable*		3 500 00		
8	*Trayton Eli, Capital*		100 000 00		
9	*Trayton Eli, Drawing*	5 000 00			
10	*Fees Income*		47 000 00		
11	*Salaries Expense*	8 000 00			
12	*Utilities Expense*	650 00			
13	*Supplies Expense*			(a) 500 00	
14	*Rent Expense*			(b) 4 000 00	
15	*Depreciation Expense—Equipment*			(c) 183 00	
16	*Totals*	150 500 00	150 500 00	4 683 00	4 683 00
17	*Net Income*				

- If the account has a debit balance in the Trial Balance section and a credit entry in the Adjustments section, subtract the credit amount.
- If the account has a credit balance in the Trial Balance section and a credit entry in the Adjustments section, add the two amounts.
- If the account has a credit balance in the Trial Balance section and a debit entry in the Adjustments section, subtract the debit amount.

Prepaid Rent has a Trial Balance debit of \$8,000 and an Adjustments credit of \$4,000. Enter \$4,000 (\$8,000 – \$4,000) in the Adjusted Trial Balance Debit column.

Four accounts that started with zero balances in the Trial Balance section are affected by adjustments. They are ***Accumulated Depreciation—Equipment, Supplies Expense, Rent Expense,*** and ***Depreciation Expense—Equipment.*** The figures in the Adjustments section are simply extended to the Adjusted Trial Balance section. For example, ***Accumulated Depreciation—Equipment*** has a zero balance in the Trial Balance section and a \$183 credit in the Adjustments section. Extend the \$183 to the Adjusted Trial Balance Credit column.

Once all account balances are recorded in the Adjusted Trial Balance section, total and rule the Debit and Credit columns. Be sure that total debits equal total credits. If they are not equal, find and correct the error or errors.

The Income Statement and Balance Sheet Sections

The Income Statement and Balance Sheet sections of the worksheet are used to separate the amounts needed for the balance sheet and the income statement. For example, to prepare an income statement, all revenue and expense account balances must be in one place.

Starting at the top of the Adjusted Trial Balance section, examine each general ledger account. For accounts that appear on the balance sheet, enter the amount in the appropriate column of the Balance Sheet section. For accounts that appear on the income statement, enter the amount in the appropriate column of the Income Statement section. Take care to enter debit amounts in the Debit column and credit amounts in the Credit column.

ADJUSTED TRIAL BALANCE		INCOME STATEMENT		BALANCE SHEET		
DEBIT	CREDIT	DEBIT	CREDIT	DEBIT	CREDIT	
111 350 00						1
5 000 00						2
1 000 00						3
4 000 00						4
11 000 00						5
	183 00					6
	3 500 00					7
	100 000 00					8
5 000 00						9
	47 000 00					10
8 000 00						11
650 00						12
500 00						13
4 000 00						14
183 00						15
150 683 00	150 683 00					16
						17

PREPARING THE BALANCE SHEET SECTION

Refer to Figure 5.4 as you learn how to complete the worksheet. Asset, liability, and owner's equity accounts appear on the balance sheet. The first five accounts that appear on the worksheet are assets. Extend the asset accounts to the Debit column of the Balance Sheet section. The next account, ***Accumulated Depreciation—Equipment,*** is a contra asset account. Extend it to the Credit column of the Balance Sheet section. Extend ***Accounts Payable*** and ***Trayton Eli, Capital*** to the Credit column of the Balance Sheet section. Extend ***Trayton Eli, Drawing*** to the Debit column of the Balance Sheet section.

PREPARING THE INCOME STATEMENT SECTION

Revenue and expense accounts appear on the income statement. Extend the ***Fees Income*** account to the Credit column of the Income Statement section. The last five accounts on the worksheet are expense accounts. Extend these accounts to the Debit column of the Income Statement section.

After all account balances are transferred from the Adjusted Trial Balance section of the worksheet to the financial statement sections, total the Debit and Credit columns in the Income Statement section. For Eli's Consulting Services, the debits (expenses) total $13,333 and the credits (revenue) total $47,000.

Next, total the columns in the Balance Sheet section. For Eli's Consulting Services, the debits (assets and drawing account) total $137,350 and the credits (contra asset, liabilities, and owner's equity) total $103,683.

Return to the Income Statement section. The totals of these columns are used to determine the net income or net loss. Subtract the smaller column total from the larger one. Enter the difference on the line below the smaller total. In the Account Name column, enter "Net Income" or "Net Loss."

In this case, the total of the Credit column, $47,000, exceeds the total of the Debit column, $13,333. The Credit column total represents revenue. The Debit column total represents expenses. The difference between the two amounts is a net income of $33,667. Enter $33,667 in the Debit column of the Income Statement section.

recall

Locating Errors

If total debits do not equal total credits, find the difference between total debits and total credits.

If the difference is divisible by 9, there could be a transposition error. If the difference is divisible by 2, an amount could be entered in the wrong (Debit or Credit) column.

FIGURE 5.4 **A Completed Worksheet**

Eli's Consulting Services
Worksheet
Month Ended December 31, 2019

	ACCOUNT NAME	TRIAL BALANCE DEBIT	TRIAL BALANCE CREDIT	ADJUSTMENTS DEBIT	ADJUSTMENTS CREDIT
1	*Cash*	111,350.00			
2	*Accounts Receivable*	5,000.00			
3	*Supplies*	1,500.00			(a) 500.00
4	*Prepaid Rent*	8,000.00			(b) 4,000.00
5	*Equipment*	11,000.00			
6	*Accumulated Depreciation—Equipment*				(c) 183.00
7	*Accounts Payable*		3,500.00		
8	*Trayton Eli, Capital*		100,000.00		
9	*Trayton Eli, Drawing*	5,000.00			
10	*Fees Income*		47,000.00		
11	*Salaries Expense*	8,000.00			
12	*Utilities Expense*	650.00			
13	*Supplies Expense*			(a) 500.00	
14	*Rent Expense*			(b) 4,000.00	
15	*Depreciation Expense—Equipment*			(c) 183.00	
16	*Totals*	150,500.00	150,500.00	4,683.00	4,683.00
17	*Net Income*				
18					

important!

Net Income

The difference between the Debit and Credit columns of the Income Statement section represents net income. The difference between the Debit and Credit columns of the Balance Sheet section should equal the net income amount.

Net income causes a net increase in owner's equity. As a check on accuracy, the amount in the Balance Sheet Debit column is subtracted from the amount in the Credit column and compared to net income. In the Balance Sheet section, subtract the smaller column total from the larger one. The difference should equal the net income or net loss computed in the Income Statement section. Enter the difference on the line below the smaller total. For Eli's Consulting Services, enter $33,667 in the Credit column of the Balance Sheet section.

Total the Income Statement and Balance Sheet columns. Make sure that total debits equal total credits for each section.

Eli's Consulting Services had a net income. If it had a loss, the loss would be entered in the Credit column of the Income Statement section and the Debit column of the Balance Sheet section. "Net Loss" would be entered in the Account Name column on the worksheet.

Preparing Financial Statements

When the worksheet is complete, the next step is to prepare the financial statements, starting with the income statement. Preparation of the financial statements is the fifth step in the accounting cycle.

>> 5-4 OBJECTIVE

Prepare an income statement, statement of owner's equity, and balance sheet from the completed worksheet.

PREPARING THE INCOME STATEMENT

Use the Income Statement section of the worksheet to prepare the income statement. Figure 5.5 shows the income statement for Eli's Consulting Services. Compare it to the worksheet in Figure 5.4.

If the firm had incurred a net loss, the final amount on the income statement would be labeled "Net Loss for the Month."

ADJUSTED TRIAL BALANCE		INCOME STATEMENT		BALANCE SHEET		
DEBIT	CREDIT	DEBIT	CREDIT	DEBIT	CREDIT	
111,350.00				111,350.00		1
5,000.00				5,000.00		2
1,000.00				1,000.00		3
4,000.00				4,000.00		4
11,000.00				11,000.00		5
	183.00				183.00	6
	3,500.00				3,500.00	7
	100,000.00				100,000.00	8
5,000.00				5,000.00		9
	47,000.00		47,000.00			10
8,000.00		8,000.00				11
650.00		650.00				12
500.00		500.00				13
4,000.00		4,000.00				14
183.00		183.00				15
150,683.00	150,683.00	13,333.00	47,000.00	137,350.00	103,683.00	16
		33,667.00			33,667.00	17
		47,000.00	47,000.00	137,350.00	137,350.00	18

PREPARING THE STATEMENT OF OWNER'S EQUITY

The statement of owner's equity reports the changes that have occurred in the owner's financial interest during the reporting period. Use the data in the Balance Sheet section of the worksheet, as well as the net income or net loss figure, to prepare the statement of owner's equity.

- From the Balance Sheet section of the worksheet, use the amounts for owner's capital; owner's withdrawals, if any; and owner's investments, if any.
- From the Income Statement section of the worksheet, use the amount calculated for net income or net loss.

The statement of owner's equity is prepared before the balance sheet because the ending capital balance is needed to prepare the balance sheet. The statement of owner's equity reports the change in owner's capital during the period ($28,667) as well as the ending capital ($128,667). Figure 5.6 shows the statement of owner's equity for Eli's Consulting Services.

PREPARING THE BALANCE SHEET

The accounts listed on the balance sheet are taken directly from the Balance Sheet section of the worksheet. Figure 5.7 shows the balance sheet for Eli's Consulting Services.

Note that the equipment's book value is reported on the balance sheet ($10,817). Do not confuse book value with market value. Book value is the portion of the original cost that has not been depreciated. *Market value* is what a willing buyer will pay a willing seller for the asset. Market value may be higher or lower than book value.

Notice that the amount for ***Trayton Eli, Capital,*** $128,667, comes from the statement of owner's equity.

FIGURE 5.5

Income Statement

Eli's Consulting Services Income Statement Month Ended December 31, 2019		
Revenue		
Fees Income		*47,000.00*
Expenses		
Salaries Expense	*8,000.00*	
Utilities Expense	*650.00*	
Supplies Expense	*500.00*	
Rent Expense	*4,000.00*	
Depreciation Expense—Equipment	*183.00*	
Total Expenses		*13,333.00*
Net Income for the Month		*33,667.00*

FIGURE 5.6

Statement of Owner's Equity

Eli's Consulting Services Statement of Owner's Equity Month Ended December 31, 2019		
Trayton Eli, Capital, December 1, 2019		*100,000.00*
Net Income for December	*33,667.00*	
Less Withdrawals for December	*5,000.00*	
Increase in Capital		*28,667.00*
Trayton Eli, Capital, December 31, 2019		*128,667.00*

FIGURE 5.7

Balance Sheet

Eli's Consulting Services Balance Sheet December 31, 2019		
Assets		
Cash		*111,350.00*
Accounts Receivable		*5,000.00*
Supplies		*1,000.00*
Prepaid Rent		*4,000.00*
Equipment	*11,000.00*	
Less Accumulated Depreciation	*183.00*	*10,817.00*
Total Assets		*132,167.00*
Liabilities and Owner's Equity		
Liabilities		
Accounts Payable		*3,500.00*
Owner's Equity		
Trayton Eli, Capital		*128,667.00*
Total Liabilities and Owner's Equity		*132,167.00*

The balance sheet in Figure 5.7 is prepared using the report form. The **report form balance sheet** lists the asset accounts first, followed by liabilities and owner's equity. Chapters 2 and 3 illustrated the **account form balance sheet,** with assets on the left and liabilities and owner's equity on the right. The report form is widely used because it provides more space for entering account names and its format is easier to prepare.

> Some companies show long-term assets at a net amount. "Net" means that accumulated depreciation has been subtracted from the original cost. For example, The Boeing Company's consolidated statement of financial position as of December 31, 2015, reflects:
>
> The net amounts for Property, plant, and equipment that appears on the balance sheet for 2015 and 2014 are $12,076 million and $11,007 million, respectively. These amounts are net of accumulated depreciation of $16,286 and $15,689 million for December 31, 2015, and December 31, 2014, respectively.

Figure 5.8A through Figure 5.8G provide a step-by-step demonstration of how to complete the worksheet and financial statements for Eli's Consulting Services.

FIGURE 5.8A Worksheet Summary

The worksheet is used to gather all the data needed at the end of an accounting period to prepare the financial statements. The worksheet heading contains the name of the company (**WHO**), the title of the statement being prepared (**WHAT**), and the period covered (**WHEN**). The worksheet contains 10 money columns that are arranged in five sections labeled Trial Balance, Adjustments, Adjusted Trial Balance, Income Statement, and Balance Sheet. Each section includes a Debit column and a Credit column.

The information reflected in the worksheet below is for Eli's Consulting Services for the period ending December 31, 2019. The illustrations that follow will highlight the preparation of each part of the worksheet.

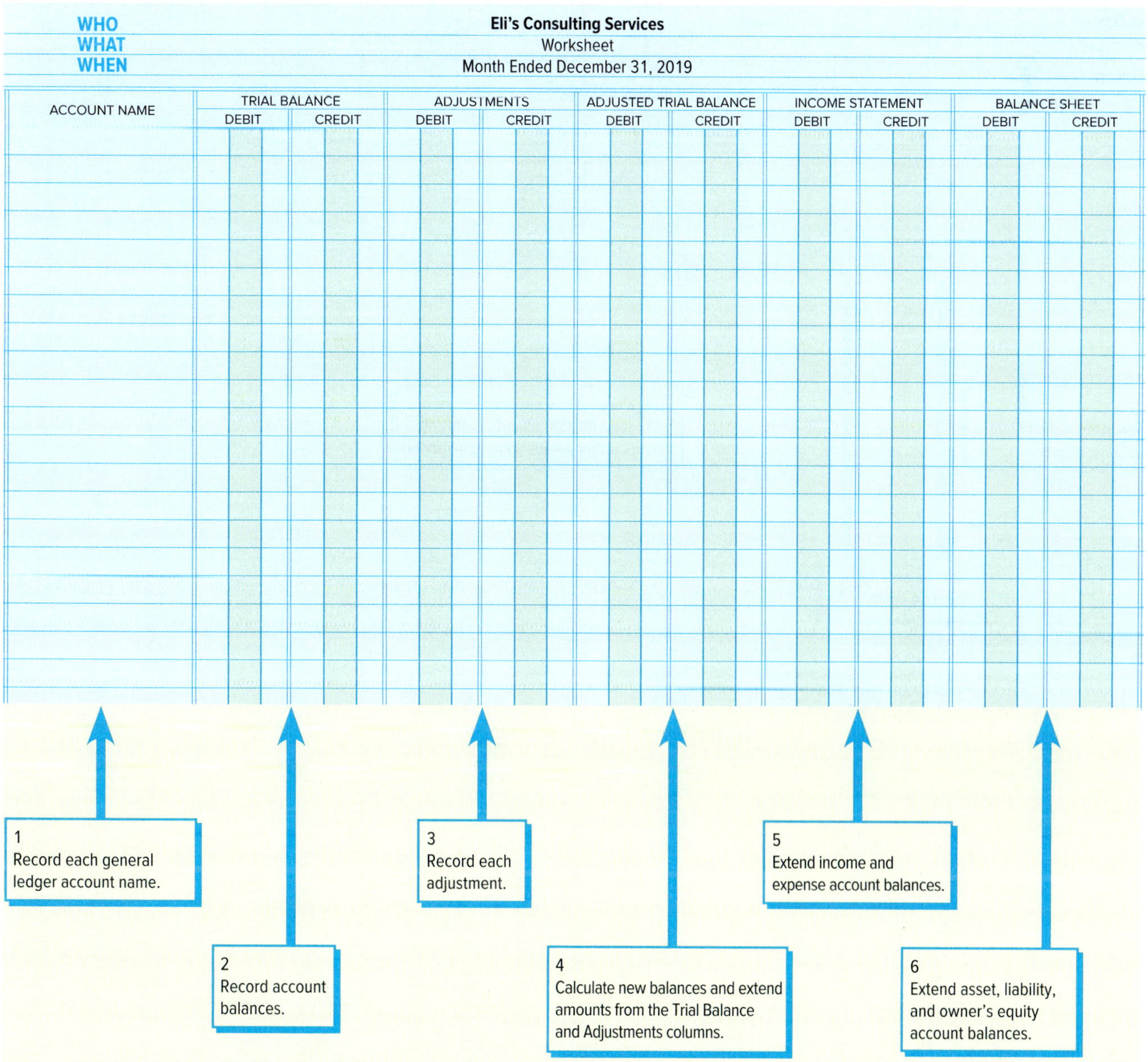

FIGURE 5.8B The Trial Balance Columns

The first step in preparing the worksheet for Eli's Consulting Services is to list the general ledger accounts and their balances in the Account Name and Trial Balance sections of the worksheet. The equality of total debits and credits is proved by totaling the Debit and Credit columns.

Eli's Consulting Services
Worksheet
Month Ended December 31, 2019

ACCOUNT NAME	TRIAL BALANCE		ADJUSTMENTS		ADJUSTED TRIAL BALANCE		INCOME STATEMENT		BALANCE SHEET	
	DEBIT	CREDIT	DEBIT	CREDIT	DEBIT	CREDIT	DEBIT	CREDIT	DEBIT	CREDIT
Cash	111 350 00									
Accounts Receivable	5 000 00									
Supplies	1 500 00									
Prepaid Rent	8 000 00									
Equipment	11 000 00									
Accum. Depr.—Equipment										
Accounts Payable		3 500 00								
Trayton Eli, Capital		100 000 00								
Trayton Eli, Drawing	5 000 00									
Fees Income		47 000 00								
Salaries Expense	8 000 00									
Utilities Expense	650 00									
Supplies Expense										
Rent Expense										
Depr. Expense—Equipment										
Totals	150 500 00	150 500 00								

Draw a single rule to indicate the addition of the Debit and the Credit columns.

Draw a double rule under the totals of a set of Debit/Credit columns to indicate that no further amounts are to be added.

Trial Balance totals must be equal.

FIGURE 5.8C The Adjustments

The data in the general ledger accounts at the end of an accounting period does not present a complete picture of the firm's financial affairs even though transactions have been recorded accurately throughout the period. Certain financial changes have occurred with the business as a result of its operations that have not yet been entered in the accounting records. These changes must be recognized and recorded at the end of the accounting period. The Adjustments section of the worksheet is used to record these changes. The Adjustments section of the worksheet for Eli's Consulting Services reflects three adjustments. Notice that the debit and credit parts of each adjustment are identified by a letter. After all adjustments are entered, the Debit and Credit columns of the Adjustments section are totaled to test that total debits equal total credits.

Eli's Consulting Services
Worksheet
Month Ended December 31, 2019

ACCOUNT NAME	TRIAL BALANCE		ADJUSTMENTS		ADJUSTED TRIAL BALANCE		INCOME STATEMENT		BALANCE SHEET	
	DEBIT	CREDIT	DEBIT	CREDIT	DEBIT	CREDIT	DEBIT	CREDIT	DEBIT	CREDIT
Cash	111 350 00									
Accounts Receivable	5 000 00									
Supplies	1 500 00			(a) 500 00						
Prepaid Rent	8 000 00			(b)4 000 00						
Equipment	11 000 00									
Accum. Depr.—Equipment				(c) 183 00						
Accounts Payable		3 500 00								
Trayton Eli, Capital		100 000 00								
Trayton Eli, Drawing	5 000 00									
Fees Income		47 000 00								
Salaries Expense	8 000 00									
Utilities Expense	650 00									
Supplies Expense			(a) 500 00							
Rent Expense			(b)4 000 00							
Depr. Expense—Equipment			(c) 183 00							
Totals	150 500 00	150 500 00	4 683 00	4 683 00						

Draw a single rule to indicate that the columns are to be added.

Total debits must equal total credits.

Draw a double rule under the Debit/Credit column total.

FIGURE 5.8D **The Adjusted Trial Balance**

The third set of columns is the Adjusted Trial Balance. The balance for the accounts in this set of columns is obtained by combining the amounts in the Trial Balance columns with the amounts in the Adjustments columns. If no adjustment is made to an account, the amount in the Trial Balance column is extended to the appropriate column in the Adjusted Trial Balance section. If an adjustment is made to an account, the adjustment amount is added to or subtracted from the Trial Balance amount and the new total is extended to the appropriate column in the Adjusted Trial Balance section.

Eli's Consulting Services
Worksheet
Month Ended December 31, 2019

ACCOUNT NAME	TRIAL BALANCE		ADJUSTMENTS		ADJUSTED TRIAL BALANCE		INCOME STATEMENT		BALANCE SHEET	
	DEBIT	CREDIT	DEBIT	CREDIT	DEBIT	CREDIT	DEBIT	CREDIT	DEBIT	CREDIT
Cash	111 350 00				111 350 00					
Accounts Receivable	5 000 00				5 000 00					
Supplies	1 500 00			(a) 500 00	1 000 00					
Prepaid Rent	8 000 00			(b)4 000 00	4 000 00					
Equipment	11 000 00				11 000 00					
Accum. Depr.—Equipment				(c) 183 00		183 00				
Accounts Payable		3 500 00				3 500 00				
Trayton Eli, Capital		100 000 00				100 000 00				
Trayton Eli, Drawing	5 000 00				5 000 00					
Fees Income		47 000 00				47 000 00				
Salaries Expense	8 000 00				8 000 00					
Utilities Expense	650 00				650 00					
Supplies Expense			(a) 500 00		500 00					
Rent Expense			(b)4 000 00		4 000 00					
Depr. Expense—Equipment			(c) 183 00		183 00					
Totals	150 500 00	150 500 00	4 683 00	4 683 00	150 683 00	150 683 00				

Draw a single rule to indicate that the columns are to be added.

Total debits must equal total credits.

Draw a double rule under the Debit/Credit column totals.

FIGURE 5.8E The Financial Statement Columns

The accounts from the Adjusted Trial Balance columns are next extended to the columns of the statements on which the accounts will appear. The account balances for the asset, liability, and owner's capital accounts are extended to the Balance Sheet columns. The owner's drawing account balance is extended to the Balance Sheet Debit column and will be used when the formal statement of owner's equity is prepared. The balances of the revenue and expense accounts are extended to the Income Statement columns.

Eli's Consulting Services
Worksheet
Month Ended December 31, 2019

ACCOUNT NAME	TRIAL BALANCE		ADJUSTMENTS		ADJUSTED TRIAL BALANCE		INCOME STATEMENT		BALANCE SHEET	
	DEBIT	CREDIT	DEBIT	CREDIT	DEBIT	CREDIT	DEBIT	CREDIT	DEBIT	CREDIT
Cash	111 350 00				111 350 00				111 350 00	
Accounts Receivable	5 000 00				5 000 00				5 000 00	
Supplies	1 500 00			(a) 500 00	1 000 00				1 000 00	
Prepaid Rent	8 000 00			(b) 4 000 00	4 000 00				4 000 00	
Equipment	11 000 00				11 000 00				11 000 00	
Accum. Depr.—Equipment				(c) 183 00		183 00				183 00
Accounts Payable		3 500 00				3 500 00				3 500 00
Trayton Eli, Capital		100 000 00				100 000 00				100 000 00
Trayton Eli, Drawing	5 000 00				5 000 00				5 000 00	
Fees Income		47 000 00				47 000 00		47 000 00		
Salaries Expense	8 000 00				8 000 00		8 000 00			
Utilities Expense	650 00				650 00		650 00			
Supplies Expense			(a) 500 00		500 00		500 00			
Rent Expense			(b) 4 000 00		4 000 00		4 000 00			
Depr. Expense—Equipment			(c) 183 00		183 00		183 00			
Totals	150 500 00	150 500 00	4 683 00	4 683 00	150 683 00	150 683 00				

Revenue and expense account balances are extended to the Income Statement section.

Asset, liability, capital, and drawing account balances are extended to the Balance Sheet section.

FIGURE 5.8F Determining Net Income or Net Loss

After all account balances have been transferred to the financial statement sections, the columns in the Income Statement and Balance Sheet sections are totaled. The difference between the larger and smaller column totals represents the net income or net loss for the period. In the case of Eli's Consulting Services, the difference of $33,667.00 represents the net income for the period because the smaller column in the Income Statement section is the Debit column. This balance indicates that the firm had more revenue for the period than expenses. Notice that the smaller column in the Balance Sheet section of the worksheet is the Credit column. The net income is added to the smaller column total in the Balance Sheet section because the net income represents an increase of the owner's equity in the business.

After the net income or net loss is recorded on the worksheet, the Income Statement and Balance Sheet columns are totaled again. All pairs of columns should balance.

Eli's Consulting Services
Worksheet
Month Ended December 31, 2019

ACCOUNT NAME	TRIAL BALANCE		ADJUSTMENTS		ADJUSTED TRIAL BALANCE		INCOME STATEMENT		BALANCE SHEET	
	DEBIT	CREDIT	DEBIT	CREDIT	DEBIT	CREDIT	DEBIT	CREDIT	DEBIT	CREDIT
Cash	111 350 00				111 350 00				111 350 00	
Accounts Receivable	5 000 00				5 000 00				5 000 00	
Supplies	1 500 00			(a) 500 00	1 000 00				1 000 00	
Prepaid Rent	8 000 00			(b)4 000 00	4 000 00				4 000 00	
Equipment	11 000 00				11 000 00				11 000 00	
Accum. Depr.—Equipment				(c) 183 00		183 00				183 00
Accounts Payable		3 500 00				3 500 00				3 500 00
Trayton Eli, Capital		100 000 00				100 000 00				100 000 00
Trayton Eli, Drawing	5 000 00				5 000 00				5 000 00	
Fees Income		47 000 00				47 000 00		47 000 00		
Salaries Expense	8 000 00				8 000 00		8 000 00			
Utilities Expense	650 00				650 00		650 00			
Supplies Expense			(a) 500 00		500 00		500 00			
Rent Expense			(b)4 000 00		4 000 00		4 000 00			
Depr. Expense—Equipment			(c) 183 00		183 00		183 00			
Totals	150 500 00	150 500 00	4 683 00	4 683 00	150 683 00	150 683 00	13 333 00	47 000 00	137 350 00	103 683 00
Net Income							33 667 00			33 667 00
							47 000 00	47 000 00	137 350 00	137 350 00

The net income or net loss is the balancing amount for both the Income Statement and Balance Sheet columns. The income or loss will always be added to the smaller column total. If the smaller column is the Debit subtotal, a net income is reported for the period. If the smaller column is the Credit subtotal, a net loss is reported for the period.

FIGURE 5.8G **Preparing the Financial Statements**

The information needed to prepare the financial statements is obtained from the worksheet.

Eli's Consulting Services
Income Statement
Month Ended December 31, 2019

Revenue		
Fees Income		47,000.00
Expenses		
Salaries Expense	8,000.00	
Utilities Expense	650.00	
Supplies Expense	500.00	
Rent Expense	4,000.00	
Depreciation Expense—Equipment	183.00	
Total Expenses		13,333.00
Net Income for the Month		33,667.00

When expenses for the period are less than revenue, a net income results. The net income is transferred to the statement of owner's equity.

Eli's Consulting Services
Statement of Owner's Equity
Month Ended December 31, 2019

Trayton Eli, Capital, December 1, 2019		100,000.00
Net Income for December	33,667.00	
Less Withdrawals for December	5,000.00	
Increase in Capital		28,667.00
Trayton Eli, Capital, December 31, 2019		128,667.00

The withdrawals are subtracted from the net income for the period to determine the change in owner's equity.

Eli's Consulting Services
Balance Sheet
December 31, 2019

Assets		
Cash		111,350.00
Accounts Receivable		5,000.00
Supplies		1,000.00
Prepaid Rent		4,000.00
Equipment	11,000.00	
Less Accumulated Depreciation	183.00	10,817.00
Total Assets		132,167.00
Liabilities and Owner's Equity		
Liabilities		
Accounts Payable		3,500.00
Owner's Equity		
Trayton Eli, Capital		128,667.00
Total Liabilities and Owner's Equity		132,167.00

The ending capital balance is transferred from the statement of owner's equity to the balance sheet.

SUMMARY OF FINANCIAL STATEMENTS

The Income Statement

The income statement is prepared directly from the data in the Income Statement section of the worksheet. The heading of the income statement contains the name of the firm (WHO), the name of the statement (WHAT), and the period covered by the statement (WHEN). The revenue section of the statement is prepared first. The revenue account name is obtained from the Account Name column of the worksheet. The balance of the revenue account is obtained from the Credit column of the Income Statement section of the worksheet. The expenses section of the income statement is prepared next. The expense account titles are obtained from the Account Name column of the worksheet. The balance of each expense account is obtained from the Debit column of the Income Statement section of the worksheet.

Determining the net income or net loss for the period is the last step in preparing the income statement. If the firm has more revenue than expenses, a net income is reported for the period. If the firm has more expenses than revenue, a net loss is reported. The net income or net loss reported must agree with the amount calculated on the worksheet.

The Statement of Owner's Equity

The statement of owner's equity is prepared from the data in the Balance Sheet section of the worksheet and the general ledger capital account. The statement of owner's equity is prepared before the balance sheet so that the amount of the ending capital balance is available for presentation on the balance sheet. The heading of the statement contains the name of the firm (WHO), the name of the statement (WHAT), and the date of the statement (WHEN).

The statement begins with the capital account balance at the beginning of the period. Next, the increase or decrease in the owner's capital account is determined. The increase or decrease is computed by adding the net income (or subtracting the net loss) for the period to any additional investments made by the owner during the period and subtracting withdrawals for the period. The increase or decrease is added to the beginning capital balance to obtain the ending capital balance.

The Balance Sheet

The balance sheet is prepared from the data in the Balance Sheet section of the worksheet and the statement of owner's equity. The balance sheet reflects the assets, liabilities, and owner's equity of the firm on the balance sheet date. The heading of the statement contains the name of the firm (WHO), the name of the statement (WHAT), and the date of the statement (WHEN).

The assets section of the statement is prepared first. The asset account titles are obtained from the Account Name column of the worksheet. The balance of each asset account is obtained from the Debit column of the Balance Sheet section of the worksheet. The balance of each contra asset account, such as accumulated depreciation, is obtained from the Credit column of the Balance Sheet section of the worksheet. The liability and owner's equity section is prepared next. The liability and owner's equity account titles are obtained from the Account Name column of the worksheet. The balance of each liability account is obtained from the Credit column of the Balance Sheet section of the worksheet. The ending balance for the owner's capital account is obtained from the statement of owner's equity. Total liabilities and owner's equity must equal total assets.

Journalizing and Posting Adjusting Entries

>> **5-5 OBJECTIVE**
Journalize and post the adjusting entries.

The worksheet is a tool. It is used to determine the effects of adjustments on account balances. It is also used to prepare the financial statements. However, the worksheet is not part of the permanent accounting record.

After the financial statements are prepared, the adjustments shown on the worksheet must become part of the permanent accounting record. Each adjustment is journalized and posted to the general ledger accounts. Journalizing and posting adjusting entries is the sixth step in the accounting cycle.

For Eli's Consulting Services, three adjustments are needed to provide a complete picture of the firm's operating results and its financial position. Adjustments are needed for supplies expense, rent expense, and depreciation expense.

Refer to Figure 5.4 for data needed to record the adjustments. Enter the words "Adjusting Entries" in the Description column of the general journal. Some accountants prefer to start a new page when they record the adjusting entries. Then journalize the adjustments in the order in which they appear on the worksheet.

After journalizing the adjusting entries, post them to the general ledger accounts. Figure 5.9 shows how the adjusting entries for Eli's Consulting Services on December 31, 2019, were journalized and posted. Account numbers appear in the general journal Posting Reference column because all entries have been posted. In each general ledger account, the word "Adjusting" appears in the Description column.

Remember that the worksheet is not part of the accounting records. Adjustments that are on the worksheet must be recorded in the general journal and posted to the general ledger in order to become part of the permanent accounting records.

FIGURE 5.9

Journalized and Posted Adjusting Entries

GENERAL JOURNAL — PAGE 3

	DATE		DESCRIPTION	POST. REF.	DEBIT	CREDIT	
1	2019		Adjusting Entries				1
2	Dec.	31	Supplies Expense	517	500 00		2
3			Supplies	121		500 00	3
4							4
5		31	Rent Expense	520	4000 00		5
6			Prepaid Rent	137		4000 00	6
7							7
8		31	Depr. Expense—Equipment	523	183 00		8
9			Accum. Depr.—Equipment	142		183 00	9
10							10
11							

ACCOUNT Supplies — ACCOUNT NO. 121

DATE		DESCRIPTION	POST. REF.	DEBIT	CREDIT	BALANCE DEBIT	BALANCE CREDIT
2019							
Nov.	28		J1	1500 00		1500 00	
Dec.	31	Adjusting	J3		500 00	1000 00	

ACCOUNT Prepaid Rent — ACCOUNT NO. 137

DATE		DESCRIPTION	POST. REF.	DEBIT	CREDIT	BALANCE DEBIT	BALANCE CREDIT
2019							
Nov.	30		J2	8000 00		8000 00	
Dec.	31	Adjusting	J3		4000 00	4000 00	

ACCOUNT Accumulated Depreciation—Equipment — ACCOUNT NO. 142

DATE		DESCRIPTION	POST. REF.	DEBIT	CREDIT	BALANCE DEBIT	BALANCE CREDIT
2019							
Dec.	31	Adjusting	J3		183 00		183 00

ACCOUNT Supplies Expense — ACCOUNT NO. 517

DATE		DESCRIPTION	POST. REF.	DEBIT	CREDIT	BALANCE DEBIT	BALANCE CREDIT
2019							
Dec.	31	Adjusting	J3	500 00		500 00	

ACCOUNT Rent Expense — ACCOUNT NO. 520

DATE		DESCRIPTION	POST. REF.	DEBIT	CREDIT	BALANCE DEBIT	BALANCE CREDIT
2019							
Dec.	31	Adjusting	J3	4000 00		4000 00	

ACCOUNT Depreciation Expense—Equipment — ACCOUNT NO. 523

DATE		DESCRIPTION	POST. REF.	DEBIT	CREDIT	BALANCE DEBIT	BALANCE CREDIT
2019							
Dec.	31	Adjusting	J3	183 00		183 00	

MANAGERIAL IMPLICATIONS <<

WORKSHEETS

- The worksheet permits quick preparation of the financial statements. Quick preparation of financial statements allows management to obtain timely information.
- Timely information allows management to:
  - evaluate the results of operations,
  - evaluate the financial position of the business,
  - make decisions.
- The worksheet provides a convenient form for gathering information and determining the effects of internal changes, such as:
  - recording an expense for the use of a long-term asset like equipment,
  - recording the actual use of prepaid items.
- The more accounts that a firm has in its general ledger, the more useful the worksheet is in speeding the preparation of the financial statements.
- It is important to management that the appropriate adjustments are recorded in order to present a complete and accurate picture of the firm's financial affairs.

THINKING CRITICALLY

Why is it necessary to record an adjustment for depreciation?

Section 2 Self Review

QUESTIONS

1. Why is it necessary to journalize and post adjusting entries even though the data are already recorded on the worksheet?
2. What amounts appear on the statement of owner's equity?
3. What is the difference between a report form balance sheet and an account form balance sheet?

EXERCISES

4. ***Accumulated Depreciation—Equipment*** is a(n):
   a. contra liability account.
   b. contra asset account.
   c. liability account.
   d. asset account.
5. On a worksheet, the adjusted balance of the ***Supplies*** account is extended to the:
   a. Balance Sheet Credit column.
   b. Balance Sheet Debit column.
   c. Income Statement Credit column.
   d. Income Statement Debit column.

ANALYSIS

6. Beck Repair Shop purchased equipment for $40,000. ***Depreciation Expense*** for the month is $800. What is the balance of the ***Equipment*** account after posting the depreciation entry? Why?

Answers to Section 2 Self Review are on pages 159–160.)

Review and Applications

5 Chapter REVIEW Chapter Summary

At the end of the operating period, adjustments for internal events are recorded to update the accounting records. In this chapter, you have learned how the accountant uses the worksheet and adjusting entries to accomplish this task.

Learning Objectives

5-1 Complete a trial balance on a worksheet.

A worksheet is normally used to save time in preparing the financial statements. Preparation of the worksheet is the fourth step in the accounting cycle. The trial balance is the first section of the worksheet to be prepared.

5-2 Prepare adjustments for unrecorded business transactions.

Some changes arise from the internal operations of the firm itself. Adjusting entries are made to record these changes. Any adjustments to account balances should be entered in the Adjustments section of the worksheet.

- Prepaid expenses are expense items that are acquired and paid for in advance of their use. At the time of their acquisition, these items represent assets and are recorded in asset accounts. As they are used, their cost is transferred to expense by means of adjusting entries at the end of each accounting period.

  Examples of general ledger asset accounts and the related expense accounts follow:

Asset Accounts	Expense Accounts
Supplies	Supplies Expense
Prepaid Rent	Rent Expense
Prepaid Insurance	Insurance Expense

- Depreciation is the process of allocating the cost of a long-term tangible asset to operations over its expected useful life. Part of the asset's cost is charged off as an expense at the end of each accounting period during the asset's useful life. The straight-line method of depreciation is widely used. The formula for straight-line depreciation is:

$$\text{Depreciation} = \frac{\text{Cost} - \text{Salvage value}}{\text{Estimated useful life}}$$

5-3 Complete the worksheet.

An adjusted trial balance is prepared to prove the equality of the debits and credits after adjustments have been entered on the worksheet. Once the Debit and Credit columns have been totaled and ruled, the Income Statement and Balance Sheet columns of the worksheet are completed. The net income or net loss for the period is determined, and the worksheet is completed.

5-4 Prepare an income statement, statement of owner's equity, and balance sheet from the completed worksheet.

All figures needed to prepare the financial statements are properly reflected on the completed worksheet. The accounts are arranged in the order in which they must appear on the income statement and balance sheet. Preparation of the financial statements is the fifth step of the accounting cycle.

5-5 Journalize and post the adjusting entries.

After the financial statements have been prepared, the accountant must make permanent entries in the accounting records for the adjustments shown on the worksheet. The adjusting entries are then posted to the general ledger. Journalizing and posting the adjusting entries is the sixth step in the accounting cycle.

To summarize the steps of the accounting cycle discussed so far:

1. Analyze transactions.
2. Journalize transactions.
3. Post the journal entries.
4. Prepare a worksheet.
5. Prepare financial statements.
6. Record adjusting entries.

5-6 Define the accounting terms new to this chapter.

Glossary

Account form balance sheet (p. 134) A balance sheet that lists assets on the left and liabilities and owner's equity on the right (see also Report form balance sheet)

Adjusting entries (p. 123) Journal entries made to update accounts for items that were not recorded during the accounting period

Adjustments (p. 123) See Adjusting entries

Book value (p. 127) That portion of an asset's original cost that has not yet been depreciated

Contra account (p. 126) An account with a normal balance that is opposite that of a related account

Contra asset account (p. 126) An asset account with a credit balance, which is contrary to the normal balance of an asset account

Depreciation (p. 126) Allocation of the cost of a long-term asset to operations during its expected useful life

Prepaid expenses (p. 124) Expense items acquired, recorded, and paid for in advance of their use

Report form balance sheet (p. 134) A balance sheet that lists the asset accounts first, followed by liabilities and owner's equity

Salvage value (p. 126) An estimate of the amount that could be received by selling or disposing of an asset at the end of its useful life

Straight-line depreciation (p. 126) Allocation of an asset's cost in equal amounts to each accounting period of the asset's useful life

Worksheet (p. 122) A form used to gather all data needed at the end of an accounting period to prepare financial statements

Comprehensive Self Review

1. The ***Drawing*** account is extended to which column of the worksheet?
2. Why is the net income for a period recorded in the Balance Sheet section of the worksheet as well as the Income Statement section?
3. Is the normal balance for ***Accumulated Depreciation*** a debit or credit balance?
4. Why are assets depreciated?
5. The ***Supplies*** account has a debit balance of $9,000 in the Trial Balance column. The Credit column in the Adjustments section is $3,600. What is the new balance? The new balance will be extended to which column of the worksheet?

(Answers to Comprehensive Self Review are on page 160.)

Discussion Questions

1. Are the following assets depreciated? Why or why not?
   - **a.** Prepaid Insurance
   - **b.** Delivery Truck
   - **c.** Land
   - **d.** Manufacturing Equipment
   - **e.** Prepaid Rent
   - **f.** Furniture
   - **g.** Store Equipment
   - **h.** Prepaid Advertising
   - **i.** Computers

2. How does the straight-line method of depreciation work?
3. Give three examples of assets that are subject to depreciation.
4. Why is it necessary to make an adjustment for supplies used?
5. What are prepaid expenses? Give four examples.
6. What adjustment would be recorded for expired insurance?
7. A firm purchases machinery, which has an estimated useful life of 10 years and no salvage value, for $60,000 at the beginning of the accounting period. What is the adjusting entry for depreciation at the end of one month if the firm uses the straight-line method of depreciation?
8. What effect does each of the following items have on net income?
   a. The owner withdrew cash from the business.
   b. Credit customers paid $3,000 on outstanding balances that were past due.
   c. The business bought equipment on account that cost $15,000.
   d. The business journalized and posted an adjustment for depreciation of equipment.
9. What effect does each item in Question 8 have on owner's equity?
10. Why is it necessary to journalize and post adjusting entries?
11. What three amounts are reported on the balance sheet for a long-term asset such as equipment?
12. What is book value?
13. How does a contra asset account differ from a regular asset account?
14. Why is an accumulated depreciation account used in making the adjustment for depreciation?

APPLICATIONS

Exercises

McGraw Hill Education connect

Exercise 5.1 ► Calculating adjustments.

Objective 5-2

GL

Determine the necessary end-of-June adjustments for Cain Company.

1. On June 1, 2019, Cain Company, a new firm, paid $8,400 rent in advance for a seven-month period. The $8,400 was debited to the ***Prepaid Rent*** account.
2. On June 1, 2019, the firm bought supplies for $10,250. The $10,250 was debited to the ***Supplies*** account. An inventory of supplies at the end of June showed that items costing $5,960 were on hand.
3. On June 1, 2019, the firm bought equipment costing $72,900. The equipment has an expected useful life of 9 years and no salvage value. The firm will use the straight-line method of depreciation.

Exercise 5.2 ► Calculating adjustments.

Objective 5-2

For each of the following situations, determine the necessary adjustments.

1. A firm purchased a three-year insurance policy for $13,500 on July 1, 2019. The $13,500 was debited to the ***Prepaid Insurance*** account. What adjustment should be made to record expired insurance on the firm's July 31, 2019, worksheet?
2. On December 1, 2019, a firm signed a contract with a local radio station for advertising that will extend over a two-year period. The firm paid $36,000 in advance and debited the amount to ***Prepaid Advertising.*** What adjustment should be made to record expired advertising on the firm's December 31, 2019, worksheet?

Worksheet through Adjusted Trial Balance.

Exercise 5.3
Objectives 5-1, 5-2

On January 31, 2019, the general ledger of Palmer Company showed the following account balances. Prepare the worksheet through the Adjusted Trial Balance section. Assume that every account has the normal debit or credit balance. The worksheet covers the month of January.

ACCOUNTS	
Cash	31,500
Accounts Receivable	11,250
Supplies	4.500
Prepaid Insurance	4,100
Equipment	45,750
Accum. Depr.—Equip.	0
Accounts Payable	8,350
Sadie Palmer, Capital	40,975
Fees Income	58,500
Depreciation Exp.—Equip.	0
Insurance Expense	0
Rent Expense	5,300
Salaries Expense	5,425
Supplies Expense	0

Additional information:

a. Supplies used during January totaled $2,850.

b. Expired insurance totaled $1,025.

c. Depreciation expense for the month was $925.

Correcting net income.

Exercise 5.4
Objectives 5-2, 5-3

Assume that a firm reports net income of $45,000 prior to making adjusting entries for the following items: expired rent, $3,500; depreciation expense, $4,100; and supplies used, $1,800.

Assume that the required adjusting entries have not been made. What effect do these errors have on the reported net income?

Journalizing and posting adjustments.

Exercise 5.5
Objective 5-5

Desoto Company must make three adjusting entries on December 31, 2019.

a. Supplies used, $5,500 (supplies totaling $9,000 were purchased on December 1, 2019, and debited to the ***Supplies*** account).

b. Expired insurance, $4,100; on December 1, 2019, the firm paid $24,600 for six months' insurance coverage in advance and debited ***Prepaid Insurance*** for this amount.

c. Depreciation expense for equipment, $2,900.

Make the journal entries for these adjustments and post the entries to the general ledger accounts: Use page 3 of the general journal for the adjusting entries. Use the following accounts and numbers.

Account	No.
Supplies	121
Prepaid Insurance	131
Accum. Depr.—Equip.	142
Depreciation Exp.—Equip.	517
Insurance Expense	521
Supplies Expense	523

PROBLEMS

Problem Set A

Problem 5.1A ▶ Completing the worksheet.

Objectives 5-1, 5-2, 5-3

The trial balance of Neal Company as of January 31, 2019, after the company completed the first month of operations, is shown in the partial worksheet below.

INSTRUCTIONS

1. Record the trial balance in the Trial Balance section of the worksheet.
2. Complete the worksheet by making the following adjustments: supplies on hand at the end of the month, $2,100; expired insurance, $2,750; depreciation expense for the period, $800.

Analyze: How does the insurance adjustment affect ***Prepaid Insurance***?

Neal Company
Worksheet (Partial)
Month Ended January 31, 2019

	ACCOUNT NAME	TRIAL BALANCE		ADJUSTMENTS	
		DEBIT	CREDIT	DEBIT	CREDIT
1	*Cash*	52,500.00			
2	*Accounts Receivable*	10,900.00			
3	*Supplies*	19,700.00			
4	*Prepaid Insurance*	33,000.00			
5	*Equipment*	54,500.00			
6	*Accumulated Depreciation—Equipment*				
7	*Accounts Payable*		12,900.00		
8	*Alexander Neal, Capital*		126,500.00		
9	*Alexander Neal, Drawing*	7,700.00			
10	*Fees Income*		57,100.00		
11	*Depreciation Expense—Equipment*				
12	*Insurance Expense*				
13	*Salaries Expense*	16,100.00			
14	*Supplies Expense*				
15	*Utilities Expense*	2,100.00			
16	*Totals*	196,500.00	196,500.00		

Problem 5.2A ▶ Reconstructing a partial worksheet.

Objectives 5-1, 5-2, 5-3

The adjusted trial balance of University Book Store as of November 30, 2019, after the firm's first month of operations, appears on the next page.

Appropriate adjustments have been made for the following items:

a. Supplies used during the month, $2,900.
b. Expired rent for the month, $3,500.
c. Depreciation expense for the month, $950.

INSTRUCTIONS

1. Record the Adjusted Trial Balance in the Adjusted Trial Balance columns of the worksheet.
2. Prepare the adjusting entries in the Adjustments columns.
3. Complete the Trial Balance columns of the worksheet prior to making the adjusting entries.

Analyze: What was the balance of ***Prepaid Rent*** prior to the adjusting entry for expired rent?

University Book Store Adjusted Trial Balance November 30, 2019		
Account Name	**Debit**	**Credit**
Cash	$ 23,075	
Accounts Receivable	3,812	
Supplies	4,600	
Prepaid Rent	21,000	
Equipment	27,500	
Accumulated Depreciation—Equipment		$ 950
Accounts Payable		9,000
Ruby Darbandi, Capital		41,837
Ruby Darbandi, Drawing	4,000	
Fees Income		48,550
Depreciation Expense—Equipment	950	
Rent Expense	3,500	
Salaries Expense	8,500	
Supplies Expense	2,900	
Utilities Expense	500	
Totals	$100,337	$100,337

Preparing financial statements from the worksheet.

◀ **Problem 5.3A**
Objective 5-4

The completed worksheet for Cantu Corporation as of December 31, 2019, after the company had completed the first month of operation, appears across the tops of pages 152–153.

INSTRUCTIONS

1. Prepare an income statement.
2. Prepare a statement of owner's equity. The owner made no additional investments during the month.
3. Prepare a balance sheet (use the report form).

Analyze: If the adjustment to ***Prepaid Advertising*** had been $3,400 instead of $1,700, what net income would have resulted?

Preparing a worksheet and financial statements, journalizing adjusting entries, and posting to ledger accounts.

◀ **Problem 5.4A**
Objectives 5-1, 5-2, 5-3, 5-4, 5-5

GL

Paula Judge owns Judge Creative Designs. The trial balance of the firm for January 31, 2019, the first month of operations, is shown below.

INSTRUCTIONS

1. Complete the worksheet for the month.
2. Prepare an income statement, statement of owner's equity, and balance sheet. No additional investments were made by the owner during the month.
3. Journalize and post the adjusting entries. Use 3 for the journal page number. Use the following account numbers: Supplies, 121; Prepaid Advertising, 130; Prepaid Rent, 131; Accumulated Depreciation—Equipment, 142; Supplies Expense, 517; Advertising Expense, 519; Rent Expense, 520; Depreciation Expense, 523.

End-of-the-month adjustments must account for the following items:

a. Supplies were purchased on January 1, 2019; inventory of supplies on January 31, 2019, is $1,600.

b. The prepaid advertising contract was signed on January 1, 2019, and covers a four-month period.

Cantu Corporation
Worksheet
Month Ended December 31, 2019

	ACCOUNT NAME	TRIAL BALANCE DEBIT	TRIAL BALANCE CREDIT	ADJUSTMENTS DEBIT	ADJUSTMENTS CREDIT
1	Cash	39 1 0 0 00			
2	Accounts Receivable	6 5 0 0 00			
3	Supplies	6 0 5 0 00			(a) 3 5 0 0 00
4	Prepaid Advertising	10 2 0 0 00			(b) 1 7 0 0 00
5	Equipment	42 5 0 0 00			
6	Accumulated Depreciation—Equipment				(c) 8 5 0 00
7	Accounts Payable		6 5 0 0 00		
8	Selena Cantu, Capital		54 5 0 0 00		
9	Selena Cantu, Drawing	4 1 0 0 00			
10	Fees Income		57 7 5 0 00		
11	Supplies Expense			(a) 3 5 0 0 00	
12	Advertising Expense			(b) 1 7 0 0 00	
13	Depreciation Expense—Equipment			(c) 8 5 0 00	
14	Salaries Expense	8 9 0 0 00			
15	Utilities Expense	1 4 0 0 00			
16	Totals	118 7 5 0 00	118 7 5 0 00	6 0 5 0 00	6 0 5 0 00
17	Net Income				
18					
19					

c. Rent of $2,100 expired during the month.

d. Depreciation is computed using the straight-line method. The equipment has an estimated useful life of 10 years with no salvage value.

Analyze: If the adjusting entries had not been made for the month, would net income be overstated or understated?

Judge Creative Designs
Worksheet (Partial)
Month Ended January 31, 2019

	ACCOUNT NAME	TRIAL BALANCE DEBIT	TRIAL BALANCE CREDIT
1	Cash	36 5 0 0 00	
2	Accounts Receivable	13 6 0 0 00	
3	Supplies	9 7 5 0 00	
4	Prepaid Advertising	12 4 0 0 00	
5	Prepaid Rent	25 2 0 0 00	
6	Equipment	33 6 0 0 00	
7	Accumulated Depreciation—Equipment		
8	Accounts Payable		16 5 5 0 00
9	Paula Judge, Capital		61 0 0 0 00
10	Paula Judge, Drawing	8 0 0 0 00	
11	Fees Income		74 1 0 0 00
12	Advertising Expense		
13	Depreciation Expense—Equipment		
14	Rent Expense		
15	Salaries Expense	10 7 0 0 00	
16	Supplies Expense		
17	Utilities Expense	1 9 0 0 00	
18	Totals	151 6 5 0 00	151 6 5 0 00
19			

ADJUSTED TRIAL BALANCE		INCOME STATEMENT		BALANCE SHEET		
DEBIT	CREDIT	DEBIT	CREDIT	DEBIT	CREDIT	
39 100 00				39 100 00		1
6 500 00				6 500 00		2
2 550 00				2 550 00		3
8 500 00				8 500 00		4
42 500 00				42 500 00		5
	850 00				850 00	6
	6 500 00				6 500 00	7
	54 500 00				54 500 00	8
4 100 00				4 100 00		9
	57 750 00		57 750 00			10
3 500 00		3 500 00				11
1 700 00		1 700 00				12
850 00		850 00				13
8 900 00		8 900 00				14
1 400 00		1 400 00				15
119 600 00	119 600 00	16 350 00	57 750 00	103 250 00	61 850 00	16
		41 400 00			41 400 00	17
		57 750 00	57 750 00	103 250 00	103 250 00	18
						19

Problem Set B

Completing the worksheet.

◄ **Problem 5.1B**

Objectives 5-1, 5-2, 5-3

The trial balance of Martinez Company as of February 28, 2019, appears below.

Martinez Company
Worksheet (Partial)
Month Ended February 28, 2019

	ACCOUNT NAME	TRIAL BALANCE		ADJUSTMENTS	
		DEBIT	CREDIT	DEBIT	CREDIT
1	*Cash*	36 500 00			
2	*Accounts Receivable*	3 200 00			
3	*Supplies*	2 100 00			
4	*Prepaid Rent*	12 000 00			
5	*Equipment*	23 000 00			
6	*Accumulated Depreciation—Equipment*				
7	*Accounts Payable*		6 000 00		
8	*Julie Martinez, Capital*		49 250 00		
9	*Julie Martinez, Drawing*	1 500 00			
10	*Fees Income*		27 000 00		
11	*Depreciation Expense—Equipment*				
12	*Rent Expense*				
13	*Salaries Expense*	3 150 00			
14	*Supplies Expense*				
15	*Utilities Expense*	800 00			
16	*Totals*	82 250 00	82 250 00		
17					

INSTRUCTIONS

1. Record the trial balance in the Trial Balance section of the worksheet.
2. Complete the worksheet by making the following adjustments: supplies on hand at the end of the month, $1,100; expired rent, $1,000; depreciation expense for the period, $500.

Analyze: Why do you think the account ***Accumulated Depreciation—Equipment*** has a zero balance on the trial balance shown?

Problem 5.2B ▶ Reconstructing a partial worksheet.

Objectives 5-1, 5-2, 5-3

The adjusted trial balance of Kelvin Newton, Attorney-at-Law, as of November 30, 2019, after the company had completed the first month of operations, appears below.

Appropriate adjustments have been made for the following items:

a. Supplies used during the month, $7,200.
b. Expired rent for the month, $6,800.
c. Depreciation expense for the month, $1,100.

Kelvin Newton, Attorney-at-Law
Adjusted Trial Balance
Month Ended November 30, 2019

Account Name	Debit	Credit
Cash	$ 70,100	
Accounts Receivable	17,000	
Supplies	13,600	
Prepaid Rent	81,600	
Equipment	132,000	
Accumulated Depreciation—Equipment		$ 1,100
Accounts Payable		34,000
Kelvin Newton, Capital		160,000
Kelvin Newton, Drawing	12,000	
Fees Income		171,400
Salaries Expense	21,600	
Utilities Expense	3,500	
Supplies Expense	7,200	
Rent Expense	6,800	
Depreciation Expense—Equipment	1,100	
Totals	$366,500	$366,500

INSTRUCTIONS

1. Record the adjusted trial balance in the Adjusted Trial Balance columns of the worksheet.
2. Prepare the adjusting entries in the Adjustments columns.
3. Complete the Trial Balance columns of the worksheet prior to making the adjusting entries.

Analyze: Which contra asset account is on the adjusted trial balance?

Preparing financial statements from the worksheet.

◀ **Problem 5.3B**
Objective 5-4

The completed worksheet for JP's Accounting Services for the month ended December 31, 2019, appears on pages 156–157.

INSTRUCTIONS

1. Prepare an income statement.
2. Prepare a statement of owner's equity. The owner made no additional investments during the month.
3. Prepare a balance sheet.

Analyze: By what total amount did the value of assets reported on the balance sheet decrease due to the adjusting entries?

Preparing a worksheet and financial statements, journalizing adjusting entries, and posting to ledger accounts.

◀ **Problem 5.4B**
Objectives 5-1, 5-2, 5-3, 5-4, 5-5

Sam Nix owns Nix Estate Planning and Investments. The trial balance of the firm for June 30, 2019, the first month of operations, is shown below.

Nix Estate Planning and Investments
Worksheet (Partial)
Month Ended June 30, 2019

	ACCOUNT NAME	TRIAL BALANCE DEBIT	TRIAL BALANCE CREDIT	ADJUSTMENTS DEBIT	ADJUSTMENTS CREDIT
1	Cash	39 400 00			
2	Accounts Receivable	12 200 00			
3	Supplies	15 200 00			
4	Prepaid Advertising	28 800 00			
5	Prepaid Rent	72 000 00			
6	Equipment	90 000 00			
7	Accumulated Depreciation—Equipment				
8	Accounts Payable		21 600 00		
9	Sam Nix, Capital		120 200 00		
10	Sam Nix, Drawing	8 000 00			
11	Fees Income		147 600 00		
12	Advertising Expense				
13	Depreciation Expense—Equipment				
14	Rent Expense				
15	Salaries Expense	15 200 00			
16	Supplies Expense				
17	Utilities Expense	2 600 00			
18	Totals	289 400 00	289 400 00		
19					

INSTRUCTIONS

1. Complete the worksheet for the month.
2. Prepare an income statement, statement of owner's equity, and balance sheet. No additional investments were made by the owner during the month.
3. Journalize and post the adjusting entries. Use 3 for the journal page number. Use the account numbers provided in Problem 5.4A.

JP's Accounting Services
Worksheet
Month Ended December 31, 2019

	ACCOUNT NAME	TRIAL BALANCE DEBIT	TRIAL BALANCE CREDIT	ADJUSTMENTS DEBIT	ADJUSTMENTS CREDIT
1	*Cash*	33 900 00			
2	*Accounts Receivable*	4 400 00			
3	*Supplies*	3 000 00			(a) 1 200 00
4	*Prepaid Advertising*	8 000 00			(b) 1 600 00
5	*Fixtures*	36 000 00			
6	*Accumulated Depreciation—Fixtures*				(c) 600 00
7	*Accounts Payable*		15 000 00		
8	*Jackie Peaches, Capital*		60 000 00		
9	*Jackie Peaches, Drawing*	6 000 00			
10	*Fees Income*		62 660 00		
11	*Supplies Expense*			(a) 1 200 00	
12	*Advertising Expense*			(b) 1 600 00	
13	*Depreciation Expense—Fixtures*			(c) 600 00	
14	*Rent Expense*	7 000 00			
15	*Salaries Expense*	37 200 00			
16	*Utilities Expense*	2 160 00			
17	*Totals*	137 660 00	137 660 00	3 400 00	3 400 00
18	*Net Income*				
19					
20					

End-of-month adjustments must account for the following:

a. The supplies were purchased on June 1, 2019; inventory of supplies on June 30, 2019, showed a value of $6,000.

b. The prepaid advertising contract was signed on June 1, 2019, and covers a four-month period.

c. Rent of $6,000 expired during the month.

d. Depreciation is computed using the straight-line method. The equipment has an estimated useful life of five years with no salvage value.

Analyze: Why are the costs that reduce the value of equipment not directly posted to the asset account ***Equipment***?

Critical Thinking Problem 5.1

The Effect of Adjustments

Assume you are the accountant for Austin Industries. Ellis Austin, the owner of the company, is in a hurry to receive the financial statements for the year ended December 31, 2019, and asks you how soon they will be ready. You tell him you have just completed the trial balance and are getting ready to prepare the adjusting entries. Mr. Austin tells you not to waste time preparing adjusting entries but to complete the worksheet without them and prepare the financial statements based on the data in the trial balance. According to him, the adjusting entries will not make that much difference. The trial balance shows the following account balances:

Prepaid Rent	$ 42,000
Supplies	18,000
Building	210,000
Accumulated Depreciation—Building	16,800

ADJUSTED TRIAL BALANCE		INCOME STATEMENT		BALANCE SHEET		
DEBIT	CREDIT	DEBIT	CREDIT	DEBIT	CREDIT	
33 900 00				33 900 00		1
4 400 00				4 400 00		2
1 800 00				1 800 00		3
6 400 00				6 400 00		4
36 000 00				36 000 00		5
	600 00				600 00	6
	15 000 00				15 000 00	7
	60 000 00				60 000 00	8
6 000 00				6 000 00		9
	62 660 00		62 660 00			10
1 200 00		1 200 00				11
1 600 00		1 600 00				12
600 00		600 00				13
7 000 00		7 000 00				14
37 200 00		37 200 00				15
2 160 00		2 160 00				16
138 260 00	138 260 00	49 760 00	62 660 00	88 500 00	75 600 00	17
		12 900 00			12 900 00	18
		62 660 00	62 660 00	88 500 00	88 500 00	19
						20

If the income statement were prepared using trial balance amounts, the net income would be $95,560.

A review of the company's records reveals the following information:

1. Rent of $42,000 was paid on July 1, 2019, for 12 months.
2. Purchases of supplies during the year totaled $18,000. An inventory of supplies taken at year-end showed supplies on hand of $2,720.
3. The building was purchased three years ago and has an estimated life of 30 years.
4. No adjustments have been made to any of the accounts during the year.

Write a memo to Mr. Austin explaining the effect on the financial statements of omitting the adjustments. Indicate the change to net income that results from the adjusting entries.

Critical Thinking Problem 5.2

Worksheet and Financial Statements

The account balances for the Patterson International Company on January 31, 2019, follow. The balances shown are after the first month of operations.

101	Cash	$36,950	401	Fees Income	$61,850
111	Accounts Receivable	6,800	511	Advertising Expense	3,000
121	Supplies	4,300	514	Depr. Expense—Equip.	0
131	Prepaid Insurance	30,000	517	Insurance Expense	0
141	Equipment	48,000	518	Rent Expense	5,000
142	Accum. Depr.—Equip.	0	519	Salaries Expense	13,400
202	Accounts Payable	12,000	520	Supplies Expense	0
301	Roger Patterson, Capital	80,000	523	Telephone Expense	700
302	Roger Patterson, Drawing	4,000	524	Utilities Expense	1,700

INSTRUCTIONS

1. Prepare the Trial Balance section of the worksheet.
2. Record the following adjustments in the Adjustments section of the worksheet:
   a. Supplies used during the month amounted to $2,100.
   b. The amount in the ***Prepaid Insurance*** account represents a payment made on January 1, 2019, for six months of insurance coverage.
   c. The equipment, purchased on January 1, 2019, has an estimated useful life of 10 years with no salvage value. The firm uses the straight-line method of depreciation.
3. Complete the worksheet.
4. Prepare an income statement, statement of owner's equity, and balance sheet (use the report form).
5. Record the balances in the general ledger accounts, then journalize and post the adjusting entries. Use 3 for the journal page number.

Analyze: If the useful life of the equipment had been 12 years instead of 10 years, how would net income have been affected?

BUSINESS CONNECTIONS

Managerial | FOCUS

Understanding Adjustments

1. A building owned by Hopewell Company was recently valued at $850,000 by a real estate expert. The president of the company is questioning the accuracy of the firm's latest balance sheet because it shows a book value of $550,000 for the building. How would you explain this situation to the president?
2. At the beginning of the year, Mandela Company purchased a new building and some expensive new machinery. An officer of the firm has asked you whether this purchase will affect the firm's year-end income statement. What answer would you give?
3. Suppose the president of a company where you work as an accountant questions whether it is worthwhile for you to spend time making adjustments at the end of each accounting period. How would you explain the value of the adjustments?
4. How does the worksheet help provide vital information to management?

Ethical | DILEMMA

Adjustments

The supplies adjustment records the supplies used for the month from a cupboard that is filled at various times of the month. Molly asks you to record a larger supplies adjustment than is indicated from the ending balance in the supplies cupboard. Molly wants to use these supplies at the nonprofit organization she attends. Would you record a higher supplies expense so Molly could take these extra supplies to her charitable organization?

Financial Statement ANALYSIS

Depreciation

DuPont reported depreciation expense of $1,466 million on its consolidated financial statements for the period envded December 31, 2015. The following excerpt is taken from the company's consolidated balance sheet for the same year:

(Dollars in millions, except per share) December 31, 2015	
Property, Plant and Equipment	$24,130
Less: Accumulated depreciation	14,346
Net property, plant, and equipment	9,784

Analyze:

1. What percentage of the original cost of property, plant, and equipment was depreciated *during* 2015?
2. What percentage of property, plant, and equipment cost was depreciated *as of* December 31, 2015?
3. If the company continued to record depreciation expense at this level each year, how many years remain until all assets would be fully depreciated? (Assume no salvage values.)

Analyze Online: Connect to the DuPont website (www.dupont.com). Click on the *Investors* link to find information on quarterly earnings.

4. What is the most recent quarterly earnings statement presented? What period does the statement cover?
5. For the most recent quarter, what depreciation expense was reported?

Matching Expenses with Revenues

TEAMWORK

Edward Foster is a building contractor. He and his customer have agreed that he will submit a bill to them when he is 25 percent complete, 50 percent complete, 75 percent complete, and 100 percent complete. For example, he has a $200,000 room addition. When he has completed 25 percent, he will bill his customer $50,000. The problem occurs when he is 40 percent complete and has incurred expenses but cannot yet bill his customer. How can his revenue and expenses match? Discuss in a group several ways that Edward's accountant could solve this problem. What accounts would be used?

Prepaid Insurance

Internet | CONNECTION

Prepaid insurance is the most common adjusting entry for a company. Use google.com to do a search of the various insurance companies that provide a variety of insurances to business. Try business insurance companies. Which types of insurance do they offer a business?

Answers to **Self Reviews**

Answers to Section 1 Self Review

1. Entries made to update accounts at the end of an accounting period to include previously unrecorded items that belong to the period.
2. To properly reflect the remaining cost to be used by the business (asset) and the amount already used by the business (expense).
3. So that the financial statements can be prepared more efficiently.
4. **b.** ***Supplies Expense*** is debited for $1,500. ***Supplies*** is credited for $1,500.
5. **c.** ***Rent Expense*** is debited for $5,000. ***Prepaid Rent*** is credited for $5,000.
6. $32,000 ($80,000/5 = $16,000 × 3 = $48,000 – $80,000).

Answers to Section 2 Self Review

1. The worksheet is only a tool that aids in the preparation of financial statements. Any changes in account balances recorded on the worksheet are not shown in the general journal and the general ledger until the adjusting entries have been journalized and posted.
2. **(a)** Beginning owner's equity.
   (b) Net income or net loss for the period.
   (c) Additional investments by the owner for the period.
   (d) Withdrawals by the owner for the period.
   (e) Ending balance of owner's equity.

3. On a report form balance sheet, the liabilities and owner's equity are listed under the assets. On the account form, they are listed to the right of the assets.
4. **b.** contra asset account.
5. **b.** Balance Sheet Debit column.
6. $40,000. The adjustment for equipment depreciation is a debit to ***Depreciation Expense*** and a credit to ***Accumulated Depreciation—Equipment.*** The ***Equipment*** account is not changed.

Answers to Comprehensive Self Review

1. Debit column of the Balance Sheet section.
2. Net income causes a net increase in owner's equity.
3. Credit balance.
4. To allocate the cost of the asset to operations during its expected useful life.
5. $5,400 ($9,000 – $3,600). Debit column of the Balance Sheet section.

Closing Entries and the Postclosing Trial Balance

Chapter **6**

www.carnival.com

© Royalty-Free/Corbis

The folks at Carnival Cruise Lines have made it their business to help people enjoy their leisure time. For nearly 40 years, Carnival has made luxurious ocean cruising a reasonable vacation option for many individuals. Often, for under $100 per person per day, passengers can enjoy a seven-day Caribbean cruise on a ship with soaring atriums, expansive spas, children's facilities, and double promenades offering a myriad of entertainment venues.

Since the TSS *Mardi Gras* made its first voyage in 1972, Carnival Corporation has grown to become the most popular cruise line in the world, attracting four million guests annually. Carnival Cruise Lines is the flagship company of Carnival Corporation & plc, the largest cruise vacation group in the world, with a portfolio of cruise brands in North America, Europe, Australia, and Asia. Headquartered in Miami, Florida, and London, England, Carnival Corporation & plc generated $15.7 billion in revenues in 2015 and realized a total net income of over $1.7 billion.

When a company has been around as long as Carnival, much of its success is dependent on being able to compare its revenues and expenses from one year to the next. In order to do this, Carnival needs to separate revenues and expenses into separate accounting periods so that it can "start fresh" each year. This separation enables the company to evaluate how it is performing from one year to the next. It can help the company pinpoint problem areas—for example, higher ship-to-shore excursion costs—but it can also spotlight improvements—for example, increased revenues in the onboard casinos.

thinking critically

How do Carnival's managers use financial statements to evaluate performance? How might these evaluations affect business policies or strategies?

LEARNING OBJECTIVES

- **6-1** Journalize and post closing entries.
- **6-2** Prepare a postclosing trial balance.
- **6-3** Interpret financial statements.
- **6-4** Review the steps in the accounting cycle.
- **6-5** Define the accounting terms new to this chapter.

NEW TERMS

- closing entries
- Income Summary account
- interpret
- postclosing trial balance

Section 1

SECTION OBJECTIVES	TERMS TO LEARN
>> 6-1 Journalize and post closing entries. **WHY IT'S IMPORTANT** A business ends its accounting cycle at a given point in time. The closing process prepares the accounting records for the beginning of a new accounting cycle.	closing entries *Income Summary* account

Closing Entries

In Chapter 5, we discussed the worksheet and the adjusting entries. In this chapter, you will learn about closing entries.

The Closing Process

The seventh step in the accounting cycle is to journalize and post closing entries. **Closing entries** are journal entries that:

- transfer the results of operations (net income or net loss) to owner's equity,
- reduce revenue, expense, and drawing account balances to zero.

THE INCOME SUMMARY ACCOUNT

The ***Income Summary* account** is a special owner's equity account that is used only in the closing process to summarize results of operations. ***Income Summary*** has a zero balance after the closing process, and it remains with a zero balance until after the closing procedure for the next period.

FIGURE 6.1 Worksheet for Eli's Consulting Services

Eli's Consulting Services
Worksheet
Month Ended December 31, 2019

	ACCOUNT NAME	TRIAL BALANCE DEBIT	TRIAL BALANCE CREDIT	ADJUSTMENTS DEBIT	ADJUSTMENTS CREDIT
1	Cash	111,350.00			
2	Accounts Receivable	5,000.00			
3	Supplies	1,500.00			(a) 500.00
4	Prepaid Rent	8,000.00			(b) 4,000.00
5	Equipment	11,000.00			
6	Accum. Dep.—Equipment				(c) 183.00
7	Accounts Payable		3,500.00		
8	Trayton Eli, Capital		100,000.00		
9	Trayton Eli, Drawing	5,000.00			
10	Fees Income		47,000.00		
11	Salaries Expense	8,000.00			
12	Utilities Expense	650.00			
13	Supplies Expense			(a) 500.00	
14	Rent Expense			(b) 4,000.00	
15	Dep. Expense—Equipment			(c) 183.00	
16					
17	Totals	150,500.00	150,500.00	4,683.00	4,683.00
18	Net Income				
19					

Income Summary is classified as a temporary owner's equity account. Other names for this account are *Revenue and Expense Summary* and *Income and Expense Summary.*

STEPS IN THE CLOSING PROCESS

>> 6-1 OBJECTIVE

Journalize and post closing entries.

There are four steps in the closing process:

1. Transfer the balance of the revenue account to the ***Income Summary*** account.
2. Transfer the expense account balances to the ***Income Summary*** account.
3. Transfer the balance of the ***Income Summary*** account to the owner's capital account.
4. Transfer the balance of the drawing account to the owner's capital account.

The worksheet contains the data necessary to make the closing entries. Refer to Figure 6.1 as you study each closing entry.

STEP 1: TRANSFER REVENUE ACCOUNT BALANCES

On December 31, the worksheet for Eli's Consulting Services shows one revenue account, ***Fees Income.*** It has a credit balance of $47,000. To *close* an account means to reduce its balance to zero. In the general journal, enter a debit of $47,000 to close the ***Fees Income*** account. To balance the journal entry, enter a credit of $47,000 to the ***Income Summary*** account. This closing entry transfers the total revenue for the period to the ***Income Summary*** account and reduces the balance of the revenue account to zero.

The analysis of this closing entry is shown below. In this chapter, the visual analyses will show the beginning balances in all T accounts in order to illustrate closing entries.

ADJUSTED TRIAL BALANCE		INCOME STATEMENT		BALANCE SHEET		
DEBIT	CREDIT	DEBIT	CREDIT	DEBIT	CREDIT	
111,350.00				111,350.00		1
5,000.00				5,000.00		2
1,000.00				1,000.00		3
4,000.00				4,000.00		4
11,000.00				11,000.00		5
	183.00				183.00	6
	3,500.00				3,500.00	7
	100,000.00				100,000.00	8
5,000.00				5,000.00		9
	47,000.00		47,000.00			10
8,000.00		8,000.00				11
650.00		650.00				12
500.00		500.00				13
4,000.00		4,000.00				14
183.00		183.00				15
						16
150,683.00	150,683.00	13,333.00	47,000.00	137,350.00	103,683.00	17
		33,667.00			33,667.00	18
		47,000.00	47,000.00	137,350.00	137,350.00	19

CLOSING ENTRY

important!

***Income Summary* Account**

The ***Income Summary*** account does not have an increase or decrease side and no normal balance side.

First Closing Entry—Close Revenue to Income Summary

ANALYSIS

The revenue account ***Fees Income*** is decreased by $47,000 to zero. The $47,000 is transferred to the temporary owner's equity account ***Income Summary.***

DEBIT-CREDIT RULES

DEBIT Decreases in revenue accounts are recorded as debits. Debit ***Fees Income*** for $47,000.

CREDIT To transfer the revenue to the ***Income Summary*** account, credit ***Income Summary*** for $47,000.

T-ACCOUNT PRESENTATION

Fees Income	
−	+
Closing 47,000	Balance 47,000

Income Summary	
	Closing 47,000

GENERAL JOURNAL ENTRY

GENERAL JOURNAL PAGE 4

	DATE		DESCRIPTION	POST. REF.	DEBIT	CREDIT	
1	2019		Closing Entries				1
2	Dec.	31	Fees Income		47 000 00		2
3			Income Summary			47 000 00	3
4							4

Write "Closing Entries" in the Description column of the general journal on the line above the first closing entry.

The Home Depot, Inc. reported sales of $88.52 billion for the fiscal year ended January 31, 2016. To close the revenue, the company would debit the ***Sales*** account and credit the ***Income Summary*** account.

STEP 2: TRANSFER EXPENSE ACCOUNT BALANCES

The Income Statement section of the worksheet for Eli's Consulting Services lists five expense accounts. Since expense accounts have debit balances, enter a credit in each account to reduce its balance to zero. Debit the total of the expenses, $13,333, to the ***Income Summary*** account. This closing entry transfers total expenses to the ***Income Summary*** account and reduces the balances of the expense accounts to zero. This is a compound journal entry; it has more than one credit.

CLOSING ENTRY

Second Closing Entry—Close Expenses to Income Summary

ANALYSIS

The five expense account balances are reduced to zero. The total, $13,333, is transferred to the temporary owner's equity account ***Income Summary.***

DEBIT-CREDIT RULES

DEBIT To transfer the expenses to the ***Income Summary*** account, debit ***Income Summary*** for $13,333.

CREDIT Decreases to expense accounts are recorded as credits. Credit ***Salaries Expense*** for $8,000, ***Utilities Expense*** for $650, ***Supplies Expense*** for $500, ***Rent Expense*** for $4,000, and ***Depreciation Expense—Equipment*** for $183.

T-ACCOUNT PRESENTATION

Income Summary

Closing 13,333	Balance 47,000

Salaries Expense

+	–
Balance 8,000	Closing 8,000

Utilities Expense

+	–
Balance 650	Closing 650

Supplies Expense

+	–
Balance 500	Closing 500

Rent Expense

+	–
Balance 4,000	Closing 4,000

Depreciation Expense—Equip.

+	–
Balance 183	Closing 183

GENERAL JOURNAL ENTRY

GENERAL JOURNAL PAGE 4

	DATE		DESCRIPTION	POST. REF.	DEBIT	CREDIT	
4	Dec.	31	Income Summary		13 333 00		4
5			Salaries Expense			8 000 00	5
6			Utilities Expense			650 00	6
7			Supplies Expense			500 00	7
8			Rent Expense			4 000 00	8
9			Depreciation Expense—Equip.			183 00	9
10							10

recall

Revenue

Revenue increases owner's equity.

recall

Expenses

Expenses decrease owner's equity.

After the second closing entry, the ***Income Summary*** account reflects all of the entries in the Income Statement columns of the worksheet.

Income Summary			
Dr.		Cr.	
Closing	13,333	Closing	47,000
		Balance	33,667

The Home Depot, Inc. reported total operating expenses of $18.49 billion for its fiscal year ended January 31, 2016. At the end of the fiscal year, accountants for Home Depot, Inc. transferred the balances of all expense accounts to the ***Income Summary*** account.

STEP 3: TRANSFER NET INCOME OR NET LOSS TO OWNER'S EQUITY

The next step in the closing process is to transfer the balance of ***Income Summary*** to the owner's capital account. After the revenue and expense accounts are closed, the ***Income Summary*** account has a credit balance of $33,667, which is net income for the month. The journal entry to transfer net income to owner's equity is a debit to ***Income Summary*** and a credit to ***Trayton Eli, Capital*** for $33,667. When this entry is posted, the balance of the ***Income Summary*** account is reduced to zero and the owner's capital account is increased by the amount of net income.

CLOSING ENTRY

Third Closing Entry—Close Income Summary to Capital

ANALYSIS

The ***Income Summary*** account is reduced to zero. The net income amount, $33,667, is transferred to the owner's equity account. ***Trayton Eli, Capital*** is increased by $33,667.

DEBIT-CREDIT RULES

DEBIT To reduce ***Income Summary*** to zero, debit ***Income Summary*** for $33,667.

CREDIT Net income increases owner's equity. Increases in owner's equity accounts are recorded as credits. Credit ***Trayton Eli, Capital*** for $33,667.

T-ACCOUNT PRESENTATION

Income Summary			
Closing	33,667	Balance	33,667

Trayton Eli, Capital			
−		+	
		Balance	100,000
		Closing	33,667

GENERAL JOURNAL ENTRY

GENERAL JOURNAL PAGE 4

	DATE		DESCRIPTION	POST. REF.	DEBIT	CREDIT	
12	Dec.	31	*Income Summary*		33 667 00		12
13			*Trayton Eli, Capital*			33 667 00	13

After the third closing entry, the ***Income Summary*** account has a zero balance. The summarized expenses ($13,333) and revenue ($47,000) have been transferred to the owner's equity account ($33,667 net income).

Income Summary

Dr.		Cr.	
Expenses	13,333	Revenue	47,000
Closing	33,667		
Balance	0		

Income Summary

Dr. –		Cr. +	
		Balance	100,000
		Net Inc.	33,667
		Balance	133,667

STEP 4: TRANSFER THE DRAWING ACCOUNT BALANCE TO CAPITAL

You will recall that withdrawals are funds taken from the business by the owner for personal use. Withdrawals are recorded in the drawing account. Withdrawals are not expenses of the business. They do not affect net income or net loss.

Withdrawals appear in the statement of owner's equity as a deduction from capital. Therefore, the drawing account is closed directly to the capital account.

When this entry is posted, the balance of the drawing account is reduced to zero and the owner's capital account is decreased by the amount of the withdrawals.

recall

Withdrawals

Withdrawals decrease owner's equity.

CLOSING ENTRY

Fourth Closing Entry—Close Withdrawals to Capital

ANALYSIS

The drawing account balance is reduced to zero. The balance of the drawing account, $5,000, is transferred to the owner's equity account.

DEBIT-CREDIT RULES

DEBIT Decreases in owner's equity accounts are recorded as debits. Debit ***Trayton Eli, Capital*** for $5,000.

CREDIT Decreases in the drawing account are recorded as credits. Credit ***Trayton Eli, Drawing*** for $5,000.

T-ACCOUNT PRESENTATION

Trayton Eli, Capital

–		+	
Closing	5,000	Balance	133,667

Trayton Eli, Drawing

+		–	
Balance	5,000	Closing	5,000

GENERAL JOURNAL ENTRY

GENERAL JOURNAL PAGE 4

	DATE		DESCRIPTION	POST. REF.	DEBIT	CREDIT	
15	Dec.	31	*Trayton Eli, Capital*		5 0 0 0 00		15
16			*Trayton Eli, Drawing*			5 0 0 0 00	16

The new balance of the ***Trayton Eli, Capital*** account agrees with the amount listed in the Owner's Equity section of the balance sheet.

Trayton Eli, Drawing			
Dr. +		Cr. −	
Balance	5,000	Closing	5,000
Balance	0		

Trayton Eli, Capital			
Dr. −		Cr. +	
Drawing	5,000	Balance	100,000
		Net Inc.	33,667
		Balance	128,667

Figure 6.2 shows the general journal and general ledger for Eli's Consulting Services after the closing entries are recorded and posted. Note that:

- "Closing" is entered in the Description column of the ledger accounts;
- the balance of ***Trayton Eli, Capital*** agrees with the amount shown on the balance sheet for December 31;
- the ending balances of the drawing, revenue, and expense accounts are zero.

This example shows the closing process at the end of one month. Usually businesses make closing entries at the end of the fiscal year only.

FIGURE 6.2

Closing Process Completed: General Journal and General Ledger

Step 1 Close revenue.

Step 2 Close expense accounts.

Step 3 Close Income Summary.

Step 4 Close Drawing account.

GENERAL JOURNAL PAGE 4

	DATE		DESCRIPTION	POST. REF.	DEBIT	CREDIT	
1	2019		Closing Entries				1
2	Dec.	31	Fees Income	401	47 000 00		2
3			Income Summary	309		47 000 00	3
4							4
5		31	Income Summary	309	13 333 00		5
6			Salaries Expense	511		8 000 00	6
7			Utilities Expense	514		650 00	7
8			Supplies Expense	517		500 00	8
9			Rent Expense	520		4 000 00	9
10			Depreciation Expense—Equip.	523		183 00	10
11							11
12		31	Income Summary	309	33 667 00		12
13			Trayton Eli, Capital	301		33 667 00	13
14							14
15		31	Trayton Eli, Capital	301	5 000 00		15
16			Trayton Eli, Drawing	302		5 000 00	16
17							17

ACCOUNT *Trayton Eli, Capital* ACCOUNT NO. 301

DATE		DESCRIPTION	POST. REF.	DEBIT	CREDIT	BALANCE DEBIT	BALANCE CREDIT
2019							
Nov.	6		J1		100 000 00		100 000 00
Dec.	31	Closing	J4		33 667 00		133 667 00
	31	Closing	J4	5 000 00			128 667 00

ACCOUNT *Trayton Eli, Drawing* ACCOUNT NO. *302*

DATE		DESCRIPTION	POST. REF.	DEBIT	CREDIT	BALANCE DEBIT	BALANCE CREDIT
2019							
Dec.	*31*		*J2*	*5 000 00*		*5 000 00*	
	31	*Closing*	*J4*		*5 000 00*	*–0–*	

ACCOUNT *Income Summary* ACCOUNT NO. *309*

DATE		DESCRIPTION	POST. REF.	DEBIT	CREDIT	BALANCE DEBIT	BALANCE CREDIT
2019							
Dec.	*31*	*Closing*	*J4*		*47 000 00*		*47 000 00*
	31	*Closing*	*J4*	*13 333 00*			*33 667 00*
	31	*Closing*	*J4*	*33 667 00*			*–0–*

ACCOUNT *Fees Income* ACCOUNT NO. *401*

DATE		DESCRIPTION	POST. REF.	DEBIT	CREDIT	BALANCE DEBIT	BALANCE CREDIT
2019							
Dec.	*31*		*J2*		*36 000 00*		*36 000 00*
	31		*J2*		*11 000 00*		*47 000 00*
	31	*Closing*	*J4*	*47 000 00*			*–0–*

ACCOUNT *Salaries Expense* ACCOUNT NO. *511*

DATE		DESCRIPTION	POST. REF.	DEBIT	CREDIT	BALANCE DEBIT	BALANCE CREDIT
2019							
Dec.	*31*		*J2*	*8 000 00*		*8 000 00*	
	31	*Closing*	*J4*		*8 000 00*	*–0–*	

ACCOUNT *Utilities Expense* ACCOUNT NO. *514*

DATE		DESCRIPTION	POST. REF.	DEBIT	CREDIT	BALANCE DEBIT	BALANCE CREDIT
2019							
Dec.	*31*		*J2*	*650 00*		*650 00*	
	31	*Closing*	*J4*		*650 00*	*–0–*	

ACCOUNT *Supplies Expense* ACCOUNT NO. *517*

DATE		DESCRIPTION	POST. REF.	DEBIT	CREDIT	BALANCE DEBIT	BALANCE CREDIT
2019							
Dec.	*31*	*Adjusting*	*J3*	*500 00*		*500 00*	
	31	*Closing*	*J4*		*500 00*	*–0–*	

(continued)

FIGURE 6.2 (continued)

ACCOUNT *Rent Expense* ACCOUNT NO. *520*

DATE		DESCRIPTION	POST. REF.	DEBIT	CREDIT	BALANCE DEBIT	BALANCE CREDIT
2019							
Dec.	*31*	*Adjusting*	*J3*	*4 0 0 0 00*		*4 0 0 0 00*	
	31	*Closing*	*J4*		*4 0 0 0 00*	*- 0 -*	

ACCOUNT *Depreciation Expense—Equipment* ACCOUNT NO. *523*

DATE		DESCRIPTION	POST. REF.	DEBIT	CREDIT	BALANCE DEBIT	BALANCE CREDIT
2019							
Dec.	*31*	*Adjusting*	*J3*	*1 8 3 00*		*1 8 3 00*	
	31	*Closing*	*J4*		*1 8 3 00*	*- 0 -*	

You have now seen seven steps of the accounting cycle. The steps we have discussed are (1) analyze transactions, (2) journalize the transactions, (3) post the transactions, (4) prepare a worksheet, (5) prepare financial statements, (6) record adjusting entries, and (7) record closing entries. Two steps remain. They are (8) prepare a postclosing trial balance and (9) interpret the financial information.

Section 1 Self Review

QUESTIONS

1. What is the journal entry to close the drawing account?
2. How is the *Income Summary* account classified?
3. What are the four steps in the closing process?

EXERCISES

4. After the closing entries are posted, which account normally has a balance other than zero?
   a. *Rent Expense*
   b. *Income Summary*
   c. *Fees Income*
   d. *Capital*
5. After closing, which accounts have zero balances?
   a. asset and liability accounts
   b. liability and capital accounts
   c. liability, drawing, and expense accounts
   d. revenue, drawing, and expense accounts

ANALYSIS

6. The business owner removes supplies that are worth $1,200 from the company stockroom. She intends to take them home for personal use. What effect will this have on the company's net income?

(Answers to Section 1 Self Review are on page 190.)

Section 2

SECTION OBJECTIVES	TERMS TO LEARN
>> 6-2 Prepare a postclosing trial balance. WHY IT'S IMPORTANT The postclosing trial balance helps the accountant identify any errors in the closing process. **>> 6-3** Interpret financial statements. WHY IT'S IMPORTANT Financial statements contain information that can impact and drive operating decisions and plans for the future of the company. **>> 6-4** Review the steps in the accounting cycle. WHY IT'S IMPORTANT Proper treatment of data as it flows through the accounting system ensures reliable financial reports.	interpret postclosing trial balance

Using Accounting Information

In this section, we will complete the accounting cycle for Eli's Consulting Services.

Preparing the Postclosing Trial Balance

>> 6-2 OBJECTIVE
Prepare a postclosing trial balance.

The eighth step in the accounting cycle is to prepare the postclosing trial balance, or *after-closing trial balance.* The **postclosing trial balance** is a statement that is prepared to prove the equality of total debits and credits. It is the last step in the end-of-period routine. The postclosing trial balance verifies that:

- total debits equal total credits;
- revenue, expense, and drawing accounts have zero balances.

On the postclosing trial balance, the only accounts with balances are the permanent accounts:

- assets
- liabilities
- owner's equity

Figure 6.3 shows the postclosing trial balance for Eli's Consulting Services.

FIGURE 6.3

Postclosing Trial Balance

Eli's Consulting Services
Postclosing Trial Balance
December 31, 2019

ACCOUNT NAME	DEBIT	CREDIT
Cash	111 350 00	
Accounts Receivable	5 000 00	
Supplies	1 000 00	
Prepaid Rent	4 000 00	
Equipment	11 000 00	
Accumulated Depreciation—Equipment		183 00
Accounts Payable		3 500 00
Trayton Eli, Capital		128 667 00
Totals	132 350 00	132 350 00

FINDING AND CORRECTING ERRORS

If the postclosing trial balance does not balance, there are errors in the accounting records. Find and correct the errors before continuing. Refer to Chapter 3 for tips on how to find common errors. Also use the audit trail to trace data through the accounting records to find errors.

>> 6-3 OBJECTIVE
Interpret financial statements.

Interpreting the Financial Statements

The ninth and last step in the accounting cycle is interpreting the financial statements. Management needs timely and accurate financial information to operate the business successfully. To **interpret** the financial statements means to understand and explain the meaning and importance of information in accounting reports. Information in the financial statements provides answers to many questions:

- What is the cash balance?
- How much do customers owe the business?
- How much does the business owe suppliers?
- What is the profit or loss?

Managers of The Home Depot, Inc., use the corporation's financial statements to answer questions about the business. How much cash does our business have? What net earnings did our company report this year? For the fiscal year ended January 30, 2016, The Home Depot, Inc., reported an ending cash balance of $2.2 billion and net earnings of nearly $7.0 billion.

Figure 6.4 shows the financial statements for Eli's Consulting Services at the end of its first accounting period. By interpreting these statements, management learns that:

- the cash balance is $111,350,
- customers owe $5,000 to the business,
- the business owes $3,500 to its suppliers,
- the profit was $33,667.

FIGURE 6.4

End-of-Month Financial Statements

Eli's Consulting Services
Income Statement
Month Ended December 31, 2019

Revenue		
Fees Income		47 000 00
Expenses		
Salaries Expense	8 000 00	
Utilities Expense	650 00	
Supplies Expense	500 00	
Rent Expense	4 000 00	
Depreciation Expense—Equipment	183 00	
Total Expenses		13 333 00
Net Income for the Month		33 667 00

Eli's Consulting Services
Statement of Owner's Equity
Month Ended December 31, 2019

Trayton Eli, Capital, December 1, 2019		100 000 00
Net Income for December	33 667 00	
Less Withdrawals for December	5 000 00	
Increase in Capital		28 667 00
Trayton Eli, Capital, December 31, 2019		128 667 00

Eli's Consulting Services
Balance Sheet
December 31, 2019

Assets		
Cash		111 350 00
Accounts Receivable		5 000 00
Supplies		1 000 00
Prepaid Rent		4 000 00
Equipment	11 000 00	
Less Accumulated Depreciation	183 00	10 817 00
Total Assets		132 167 00
Liabilities and Owner's Equity		
Liabilities		
Accounts Payable		3 500 00
Owner's Equity		
Trayton Eli, Capital		128 667 00
Total Liabilities and Owner's Equity		132 167 00

ABOUT **ACCOUNTING**

Professional Consultants

Professionals in the consulting field, such as accountants and lawyers, need to understand accounting so they can bill for services performed. Because clients have different billing rates depending on the service performed, specialized software is used to manage the paperwork and keep track of the billings and payments.

>> 6-4 OBJECTIVE
Review the steps in the accounting cycle.

The Accounting Cycle

You have learned about the entire accounting cycle as you studied the financial affairs of Eli's Consulting Services during its first month of operations. Figure 6.5 summarizes the steps in the accounting cycle.

Step 1. **Analyze transactions.** Analyze source documents to determine their effects on the basic accounting equation. The data about transactions appears on a variety of source documents such as:

- sales slips,
- purchase invoices,
- credit memorandums,
- check stubs.

Step 2. **Journalize the transactions.** Record the effects of the transactions in a journal.

Step 3. **Post the journal entries.** Transfer data from the journal to the general ledger accounts.

Step 4. **Prepare a worksheet.** At the end of each period, prepare a worksheet.

- Use the Trial Balance section to prove the equality of debits and credits in the general ledger.
- Use the Adjustments section to enter changes in account balances that are needed to present an accurate and complete picture of the financial affairs of the business.
- Use the Adjusted Trial Balance section to verify the equality of debits and credits after the adjustments. Extend the amounts from the Adjusted Trial Balance section to the Income Statement and Balance Sheet sections.
- Use the Income Statement and Balance Sheet sections to prepare the financial statements.

Step 5. **Prepare financial statements.** Prepare financial statements to report information to owners, managers, and other interested parties.

- The income statement shows the results of operations for the period.
- The statement of owner's equity reports the changes in the owner's financial interest during the period.
- The balance sheet shows the financial position of the business at the end of the period.

recall

The Accounting Cycle
The accounting cycle is a series of steps performed during each period to classify, record, and summarize data to produce needed financial information.

FIGURE 6.5
The Accounting Cycle

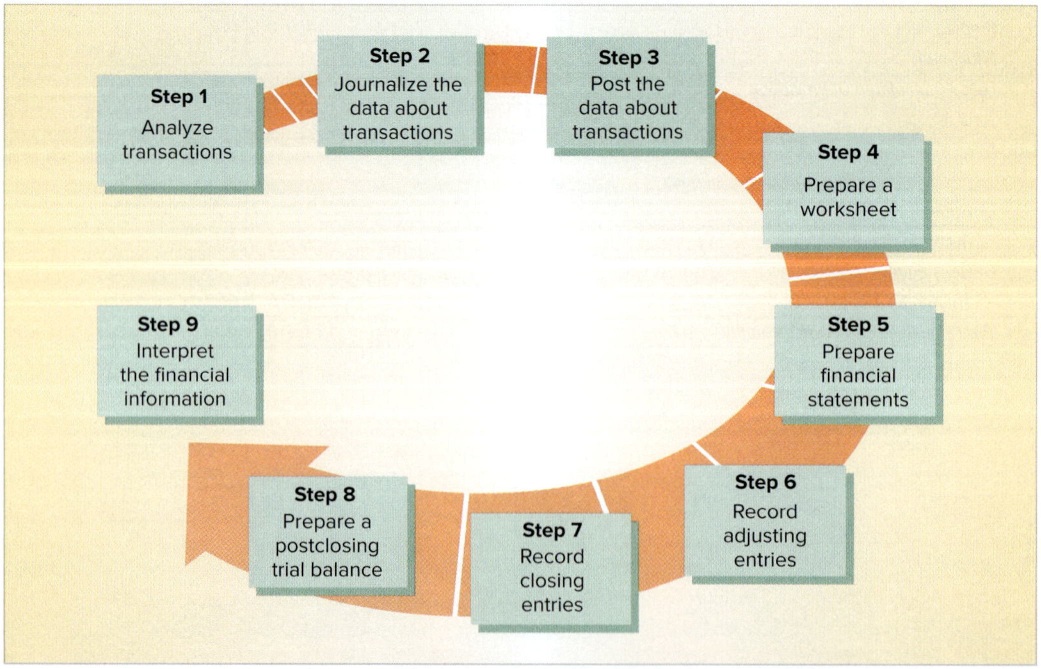

Step 6. **Record adjusting entries.** Use the worksheet to journalize and post adjusting entries. The adjusting entries are a permanent record of the changes in account balances shown on the worksheet.

Step 7. **Record closing entries.** Journalize and post the closing entries to:

- transfer net income or net loss to owner's equity;
- reduce the balances of the revenue, expense, and drawing accounts to zero.

Step 8. **Prepare a postclosing trial balance.** The postclosing trial balance shows that the general ledger is in balance after the closing entries are posted. It is also used to verify that there are zero balances in revenue, expense, and drawing accounts.

Step 9. **Interpret the financial information.** Use financial statements to understand and communicate financial information and to make decisions. Accountants, owners, managers, and other interested parties interpret financial statements by comparing such things as profit, revenue, and expenses from one accounting period to the next.

In addition to financial statements, Adobe Systems Incorporated prepares a Financial Highlights report. This report lists total assets, revenue, net income, and the number of worldwide employees for the past five years.

After studying the accounting cycle of Eli's Consulting Services, you have an understanding of how data flows through a simple accounting system for a small business:

- Source documents are analyzed.
- Transactions are recorded in the general journal.
- Transactions are posted from the general journal to the general ledger.
- Financial information is proved, adjusted, and summarized on the worksheet.
- Financial information is reported on financial statements.

Figure 6.6 illustrates this data flow.

As you will learn in later chapters, some accounting systems have more complex records, procedures, and financial statements. However, the steps of the accounting cycle and the underlying accounting principles remain the same.

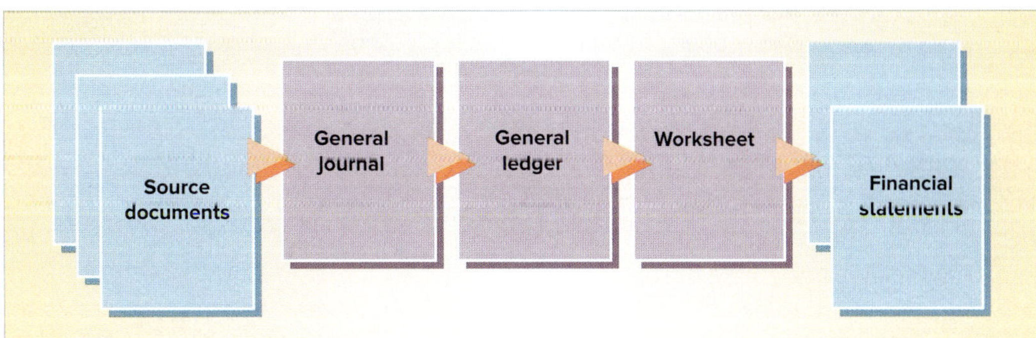

FIGURE 6.6

Flow of Data Through a Simple Accounting System

MANAGERIAL IMPLICATIONS <<

FINANCIAL STATEMENTS

- Management needs timely and accurate financial information to control operations and make decisions.
- A well-designed and well-run accounting system provides reliable financial statements to management.
- Although management is not involved in day-to-day accounting procedures and end-of-period processes, the efficiency of the procedures affects the quality and promptness of the financial information that management receives.

THINKING CRITICALLY

If you owned or managed a business, how often would you want financial statements prepared? Why?

Section 2 Self Review

QUESTIONS

1. What are the last three steps in the accounting cycle?
2. Why is a postclosing trial balance prepared?
3. What accounts appear on the postclosing trial balance?

EXERCISES

4. Which of the following accounts will not appear on the postclosing trial balance?
   a. *Cash*
   b. *J. B. Edwards, Drawing*
   c. *Accounts Payable*
   d. *J. B. Edwards, Capital*
5. After the revenue and expense accounts are closed, *Income Summary* has a credit balance of $60,000. What does this figure represent?
   a. net profit of $60,000
   b. net loss of $60,000
   c. owner's withdrawals of $60,000
   d. increase in owner's equity of $60,000

ANALYSIS

6. On which financial statement would you find the answer to each question?
   - Is there enough cash to purchase new equipment?
   - What were the expenses?
   - Do customers owe money to the business?
   - What were the total fees earned this month?
   - How much money is owed to suppliers?
   - Did the business make a profit?

(Answers to Section 2 Self Review are on page 191.)

REVIEW Chapter Summary

Chapter 6

After the worksheet and financial statements have been completed and adjusting entries have been journalized and posted, the closing entries are recorded and a postclosing trial balance is prepared.

Review and Applications

Learning Objectives

6-1 Journalize and post closing entries.

Journalizing and posting the closing entries is the seventh step in the accounting cycle. Closing entries transfer the results of operations to owner's equity and reduce the balances of the revenue and expense accounts to zero. The worksheet provides the data necessary for the closing entries. A temporary owner's equity account, ***Income Summary,*** is used. There are four steps in the closing process:

1. The balance of the revenue account is transferred to the ***Income Summary*** account.

   Debit ***Revenue***

   Credit ***Income Summary***

2. The balances of the expense accounts are transferred to the ***Income Summary*** account.

   Debit ***Income Summary***

   Credit ***Expenses***

3. The balance of the ***Income Summary*** account—net income or net loss—is transferred to the owner's capital account.

   If ***Income Summary*** has a credit balance:

   Debit ***Income Summary***

   Credit ***Owner's Capital***

   If ***Income Summary*** has a debit balance:

   Debit ***Owner's Capital***

   Credit ***Income Summary***

4. The drawing account is closed to the owner's capital account.

   Debit ***Owner's Capital***

   Credit ***Drawing***

After the closing entries have been posted, the capital account reflects the results of operations for the period. The revenue and expense accounts, with zero balances, are ready to accumulate data for the next period.

6-2 Prepare a postclosing trial balance.

Preparing the postclosing trial balance is the eighth step in the accounting cycle. A postclosing trial balance is prepared to test the equality of total debit and credit balances in the general ledger after the adjusting and closing entries have been recorded. This report lists only permanent accounts open at the end of the period—asset, liability, and the owner's capital accounts. The temporary accounts—revenue, expenses, drawing, and ***Income Summary***—apply only to one accounting period and do not appear on the postclosing trial balance.

6-3 Interpret financial statements.

The ninth step in the accounting cycle is interpreting the financial statements. Business decisions must be based on accurate and timely financial information.

6-4 Review the steps in the accounting cycle.

The accounting cycle consists of a series of steps that are repeated in each fiscal period. These steps are designed to classify, record, and summarize the data needed to produce financial information.

The steps of the accounting cycle are:

1. Analyze transactions.
2. Journalize the transactions.
3. Post the journal entries.
4. Prepare a worksheet.
5. Prepare financial statements.
6. Record adjusting entries.
7. Record closing entries.
8. Prepare a postclosing trial balance.
9. Interpret the financial information.

6-5 Define the accounting terms new to this chapter.

Glossary

Closing entries (p. 162) Journal entries that transfer the results of operations (net income or net loss) to owner's equity and reduce the revenue, expense, and drawing account balances to zero

Income Summary account (p. 162) A special owner's equity account that is used only in the closing process to summarize the results of operations

Interpret (p. 172) To understand and explain the meaning and importance of something (such as financial statements)

Postclosing trial balance (p. 171) A statement that is prepared to prove the equality of total debits and credits after the closing process is completed

Comprehensive Self Review

1. What three financial statements are prepared during the accounting cycle?
2. A firm has the following expenses: ***Rent Expense,*** $3,600; ***Salaries Expense,*** $7,000; ***Supplies Expense,*** $1,500. Give the entry to close the expense accounts.
3. A firm has $90,000 in revenue for the period. Give the entry to close the ***Fees Income*** account.
4. What is the last step in the accounting cycle?
5. Is the following statement true or false? Why? "All owner's equity accounts appear on the postclosing trial balance."

(Answers to Comprehensive Self Review are on page 191.)

Discussion Questions

1. Name the steps of the accounting cycle.
2. What is the accounting cycle?
3. What accounts appear on a postclosing trial balance?
4. Why is a postclosing trial balance prepared?
5. Where does the accountant obtain the data needed for the adjusting entries?
6. Why does the accountant record closing entries at the end of a period?
7. Where does the accountant obtain the data needed for the closing entries?
8. How is the ***Income Summary*** account used in the closing procedure?
9. Briefly describe the flow of data through a simple accounting system.
10. What three procedures are performed at the end of each accounting period before the financial information is interpreted?

APPLICATIONS

Exercises connect

Exercise 6.1 ▶ **Journalize closing entries.**
Objective 6-1

GL

On December 31, 2019, the ledger of Lopez Company contained the following account balances:

Cash	$66,000	Maria Lopez, Drawing	$ 52,000
Accounts Receivable	5,800	Fees Income	107,500
Supplies	4,200	Depreciation Expense	5,500

Equipment	52,000	Salaries Expense	34,000
Accumulated Depreciation	5,000	Supplies Expense	6,000
Accounts Payable	6,000	Telephone Expense	5,200
Maria Lopez, Capital	121,500	Utilities Expense	9,300

All the accounts have normal balances. Journalize the closing entries. Use 4 as the general journal page number.

Exercise 6.2
Objective 6-4

Accounting cycle.

Following are the steps in the accounting cycle. Arrange the steps in the proper sequence.

1. Prepare a worksheet.
2. Record adjusting entries.
3. Analyze transactions.
4. Journalize the transactions.
5. Post the journal entries.
6. Record closing entries.
7. Interpret the financial information.
8. Prepare a postclosing trial balance.
9. Prepare financial statements.

Exercise 6.3
Objective 6-2

Postclosing trial balance.

From the following list, identify the accounts that will appear on the postclosing trial balance.

ACCOUNTS

1. Cash
2. Accounts Receivable
3. Supplies
4. Equipment
5. Accumulated Depreciation
6. Accounts Payable
7. Brianna Celina, Capital
8. Brianna Celina, Drawing
9. Fees Income
10. Depreciation Expense
11. Salaries Expense
12. Supplies Expense
13. Utilities Expense

Exercise 6.4
Objective 6-3

Financial statements.

Managers often consult financial statements for specific types of information. Indicate whether each of the following items would appear on the income statement, the statement of owner's equity, or the balance sheet. Use *I* for the income statement, *E* for the statement of owner's equity, and *B* for the balance sheet. If an item appears on more than one statement, use all letters that apply to that item.

1. Revenue earned during the period
2. Total assets of the business
3. Net income for the period
4. Owner's capital at the end of the period
5. Supplies on hand
6. Cost of supplies used during the period
7. Accounts receivable of the business
8. Accumulated depreciation on the firm's equipment

9. Amount of depreciation charged off on the firm's equipment during the period
10. Original cost of the firm's equipment
11. Book value of the firm's equipment
12. Total expenses for the period
13. Accounts payable of the business
14. Owner's withdrawals for the period
15. Cash on hand

Exercise 6.5 ▶ Closing entries.

Objective 6-1

The ***Income Summary*** and ***Linda Carter, Capital*** accounts for Carter Production Company at the end of its accounting period follow.

ACCOUNT *Income Summary* ACCOUNT NO. *399*

DATE		DESCRIPTION	POST. REF.	DEBIT	CREDIT	BALANCE DEBIT	BALANCE CREDIT
2019							
Dec.	31	Closing	J4		134 000 00		134 000 00
	31	Closing	J4	71 800 00			62 200 00
	31	Closing	J4	62 200 00			– 0 –

ACCOUNT *Linda Carter, Capital* ACCOUNT NO. *301*

DATE		DESCRIPTION	POST. REF.	DEBIT	CREDIT	BALANCE DEBIT	BALANCE CREDIT
2019							
Dec.	1		J1		240 000 00		240 000 00
	31	Closing	J4		62 200 00		302 200 00
	31	Closing	J4	22 000 00			280 200 00

Complete the following statements:

1. Total revenue for the period is __________.
2. Total expenses for the period are __________.
3. Net income for the period is __________.
4. Owner's withdrawals for the period are __________.

Exercise 6.6 ▶ Closing entries.

Objective 6-1

The ledger accounts of AXX Internet Company appear as follows on March 31, 2019:

ACCOUNT NO.	ACCOUNT	BALANCE
101	Cash	$ 40,000
111	Accounts Receivable	29,910
121	Supplies	5,300
131	Prepaid Insurance	12,500
141	Equipment	59,000
142	Accumulated Depreciation—Equipment	20,660
202	Accounts Payable	7,000
301	Aretha Hinkle, Capital	65,000
302	Aretha Hinkle, Drawing	6,500
401	Fees Income	187,230
510	Depreciation Expense—Equipment	10,580

511	Insurance Expense	5,700
514	Rent Expense	16,500
517	Salaries Expense	83,000
518	Supplies Expense	2,800
519	Telephone Expense	3,400
523	Utilities Expense	4,700

All accounts have normal balances. Journalize and post the closing entries. Use 4 as the page number for the general journal in journalizing the closing entries. Use account number 399 for the ***Income Summary*** account.

Closing entries.

◀ **Exercise 6.7**
Objective 6-1

On December 31, the ***Income Summary*** account of Madison Company has a debit balance of $111,000 after revenue of $117,000 and expenses of $228,000 were closed to the account. ***Madison Wells, Drawing*** has a debit balance of $12,000 and ***Madison Wells, Capital*** has a credit balance of $174,000. Record the journal entries necessary to complete closing the accounts. What is the new balance of ***Madison Wells, Capital***?

Accounting cycle.

◀ **Exercise 6.8**
Objective 6-4

Complete a chart of the accounting cycle by writing the steps of the cycle in their proper sequence.

PROBLEMS

Problem Set A

Adjusting and closing entries.

◀ **Problem 6.1A**
Objective 6-1
GL

Consumer Research Associates, owned by Gloria Johnson, is retained by large companies to test consumer reaction to new products. On January 31, 2019, the firm's worksheet showed the following adjustments data: (a) supplies used, $4,680; (b) expired rent, $26,000; and (c) depreciation on office equipment, $9,160. The balances of the revenue and expense accounts listed in the Income Statement section of the worksheet and the drawing account listed in the Balance Sheet section of the worksheet are given below:

REVENUE AND EXPENSE ACCOUNTS	
401 Fees Income	$200,000 Cr.
511 Depr. Expense—Office Equipment	9,160 Dr.
514 Rent Expense	26,000 Dr.
517 Salaries Expense	99,000 Dr.
520 Supplies Expense	4,680 Dr.
523 Telephone Expense	2,700 Dr.
526 Travel Expense	20,780 Dr.
529 Utilities Expense	2,500 Dr.
DRAWING ACCOUNT	
302 Gloria Johnson, Drawing	22,000 Dr.

INSTRUCTIONS

1. Record the adjusting entries in the general journal, page 3.
2. Record the closing entries in the general journal, page 4.

Analyze: What closing entry is required to close a drawing account?

Problem 6.2A ► Journalizing and posting adjusting and closing entries and preparing a postclosing trial balance.

Objectives 6-1, 6-2

A completed worksheet for The King Group is shown below.

INSTRUCTIONS

1. Record balances as of December 31, 2019, in the ledger accounts.
2. Journalize (use 3 as the page number) and post the adjusting entries. Use account number 131 for Prepaid Advertising and the same account numbers for all other accounts shown in Mini-Practice Set 1 for Eli's Consulting Services chart of accounts.
3. Journalize (use 4 as the page number) and post the closing entries.
4. Prepare a postclosing trial balance.

Analyze: How many accounts are listed in the Adjusted Trial Balance section? How many accounts are listed on the postclosing trial balance?

Problem 6.3A ► Journalizing and posting closing entries.

Objective 6-1

On December 31, after adjustments, Gonzalez Company's ledger contains the following account balances:

101	Cash	$ 94,400 Dr.
111	Accounts Receivable	35,600 Dr.
121	Supplies	8,000 Dr.
131	Prepaid Rent	81,200 Dr.
141	Equipment	128,000 Dr.
142	Accumulated Depreciation—Equip.	4,000 Cr.
202	Accounts Payable	17,000 Cr.
301	Emilio Gonzalez, Capital (12/1/2019)	131,240 Cr.
302	Emilio Gonzalez, Drawing	16,400 Dr.

The King Group
Worksheet
Month Ended December 31, 2019

	ACCOUNT NAME	TRIAL BALANCE		ADJUSTMENTS	
		DEBIT	CREDIT	DEBIT	CREDIT
1	*Cash*	93,400.00			
2	*Accounts Receivable*	13,000.00			
3	*Supplies*	8,000.00			(a) 3,400.00
4	*Prepaid Advertising*	32,000.00			(b) 4,000.00
5	*Equipment*	85,000.00			
6	*Accumulated Depreciation—Equipment*				(c) 3,400.00
7	*Accounts Payable*		13,000.00		
8	*Delva King, Capital*		142,000.00		
9	*Delva King, Drawing*	9,400.00			
10	*Fees Income*		103,500.00		
11	*Supplies Expense*			(a) 3,400.00	
12	*Advertising Expense*			(b) 4,000.00	
13	*Depreciation Expense—Equipment*			(c) 3,400.00	
14	*Salaries Expense*	15,400.00			
15	*Utilities Expense*	2,300.00			
16	*Totals*	258,500.00	258,500.00	10,800.00	10,800.00
17	*Net Income*				
18					
19					

401	Fees Income	327,200 Cr.
511	Advertising Expense	11,600 Dr.
514	Depreciation Expense—Equip.	2,000 Dr.
517	Rent Expense	9,200 Dr.
519	Salaries Expense	77,600 Dr.
523	Utilities Expense	15,440 Dr.

INSTRUCTIONS

1. Record the balances in the ledger accounts as of December 31.
2. Journalize the closing entries in the general journal, page 4. Use account number 399 for the ***Income Summary*** account.
3. Post the closing entries to the general ledger accounts.

Analyze: What is the balance of the ***Salaries Expense*** account after closing entries are posted?

Worksheet, journalizing and posting adjusting and closing entries, and the postclosing trial balance.

◄ **Problem 6.4A**

Objectives 6-1, 6-2

GL

A partially completed worksheet for At Home Pet Grooming Service, a firm that grooms pets at the owner's home, follows.

INSTRUCTIONS

1. Record balances as of December 31 in the ledger accounts.
2. Prepare the worksheet.
3. Journalize (use 3 as the journal page number) and post the adjusting entries. Use account number 131 for ***Prepaid Advertising*** and the same account numbers for all other accounts shown in Mini-Practice Set 1 for Eli's Consulting Services chart of accounts.
4. Journalize (use 4 as the journal page number) and post the closing entries.
5. Prepare a postclosing trial balance.

ADJUSTED TRIAL BALANCE		INCOME STATEMENT		BALANCE SHEET		
DEBIT	CREDIT	DEBIT	CREDIT	DEBIT	CREDIT	
93 400 00				93 400 00		1
13 000 00				13 000 00		2
4 600 00				4 600 00		3
28 000 00				28 000 00		4
85 000 00				85 000 00		5
	3 400 00				3 400 00	6
	13 000 00				13 000 00	7
	142 000 00				142 000 00	8
9 400 00				9 400 00		9
	103 500 00		103 500 00			10
3 400 00		3 400 00				11
4 000 00		4 000 00				12
3 400 00		3 400 00				13
15 400 00		15 400 00				14
2 300 00		2 300 00				15
261 900 00	261 900 00	28 500 00	103 500 00	233 400 00	158 400 00	16
		75 000 00			75 000 00	17
		103 500 00	103 500 00	233 400 00	233 400 00	18
						19

At Home Pet Grooming Service
Worksheet
Month Ended December 31, 2019

	ACCOUNT NAME	TRIAL BALANCE DEBIT	TRIAL BALANCE CREDIT	ADJUSTMENTS DEBIT	ADJUSTMENTS CREDIT
1	*Cash*	64 100 00			
2	*Accounts Receivable*	10 900 00			
3	*Supplies*	12 000 00			(a) 4 200 00
4	*Prepaid Advertising*	8 000 00			(b) 3 800 00
5	*Equipment*	42 000 00			
6	*Accumulated Depreciation—Equipment*				(c) 1 160 00
7	*Accounts Payable*		12 000 00		
8	*Shara Johns, Capital*		91 000 00		
9	*Shara Johns, Drawing*	6 000 00			
10	*Fees Income*		53 200 00		
11	*Salaries Expense*	11 600 00			
12	*Utilities Expense*	1 600 00			
13	*Supplies Expense*			(a) 4 200 00	
14	*Advertising Expense*			(b) 3 800 00	
15	*Depreciation Expense—Equipment*			(c) 1 160 00	
16	*Totals*	156 200 00	156 200 00	9 160 00	9 160 00
17					
18					
19					

Analyze: What total debits were posted to the general ledger to complete all closing entries for the month of December?

Problem Set B

Problem 6.1B ► Adjusting and closing entries.

Objective 6-1

Williams Cleaning and Maintenance, owned by Erica Williams, provides cleaning services to hotels, motels, and hospitals. On January 31, 2019, the firm's worksheet showed the following adjustment data. The balances of the revenue and expense accounts listed in the Income Statement section of the worksheet and the drawing account listed in the Balance Sheet section of the worksheet are also given.

ADJUSTMENTS

a. Supplies used, $8,580

b. Expired insurance, $4,440

c. Depreciation on machinery, $3,360

REVENUE AND EXPENSE ACCOUNTS

401 Fees Income	$98,400 Cr.
511 Depreciation Expense—Machinery	3,360 Dr.
514 Insurance Expense	4,440 Dr.
517 Rent Expense	9,000 Dr.
520 Salaries Expense	48,000 Dr.
523 Supplies Expense	8,580 Dr.
526 Telephone Expense	630 Dr.

529 Utilities Expense	1,920 Dr.
DRAWING ACCOUNT	
302 Erica Williams, Drawing	7,200 Dr.

INSTRUCTIONS

1. Record the adjusting entries in the general journal, page 3.
2. Record the closing entries in the general journal, page 4. Use account numbers provided in Mini-Practice Set 1 for any account number not given.

Analyze: What effect did the adjusting entry for expired insurance have on the ***Insurance Expense*** account?

Journalizing and posting adjusting and closing entries and preparing a postclosing trial balance.

◄ **Problem 6.2B**
Objectives 6-1, 6-2

A completed worksheet for Cedar Valley Nursery and Landscape is shown below.

INSTRUCTIONS

1. Record the balances as of December 31 in the ledger accounts.
2. Journalize (use 3 as the page number) and post the adjusting entries. Use account number 131 for ***Prepaid Advertising*** and the same account numbers for all other accounts as shown in Mini-Practice Set 1 for Eli's Consulting Services chart of accounts.
3. Journalize (use 4 as the page number) and post the closing entries.
4. Prepare a postclosing trial balance.

Analyze: What total credits were posted to the general ledger to complete the closing entries?

Journalizing and posting closing entries.

◄ **Problem 6.3B**
Objective 6-1

On December 31, after adjustments, The Dexter Family Farm's ledger contains the following account balances.

101 Cash	$12,750 Dr.
111 Accounts Receivable	10,800 Dr.
121 Supplies	4,500 Dr.
131 Prepaid Rent	34,650 Dr.
141 Equipment	54,000 Dr.
142 Accumulated Depreciation—Equip.	1,350 Cr.
202 Accounts Payable	14,625 Cr.
301 Thomas Dexter, Capital (12/1/2019)	86,175 Cr.
302 Thomas Dexter, Drawing	5,400 Dr.
401 Fees Income	81,000 Cr.
511 Advertising Expense	4,950 Dr.
514 Depreciation Expense—Equip.	1,350 Dr.
517 Rent Expense	3,150 Dr.
519 Salaries Expense	16,200 Dr.
523 Utilities Expense	5,400 Dr.

INSTRUCTIONS

1. Record the balances in the ledger accounts as of December 31.
2. Journalize the closing entries in the general journal, page 4. Use account number 399 for the ***Income Summary*** account
3. Post the closing entries to the general ledger accounts.

Analyze: List the accounts affected by closing entries for the month of December.

Cedar Valley Nursery and Landscape
Worksheet
Month Ended December 31, 2019

	ACCOUNT NAME	TRIAL BALANCE		ADJUSTMENTS	
		DEBIT	CREDIT	DEBIT	CREDIT
1	Cash	32 400 00			
2	Accounts Receivable	6 000 00			
3	Supplies	6 000 00			(a) 3 000 00
4	Prepaid Advertising	9 000 00			(b) 1 200 00
5	Equipment	60 000 00			
6	Accumulated Depreciation—Equipment				(c) 1 500 00
7	Accounts Payable		9 000 00		
8	Scott Jeremy, Capital		82 200 00		
9	Scott Jeremy, Drawing	8 400 00			
10	Fees Income		46 800 00		
11	Supplies Expense			(a) 3 000 00	
12	Advertising Expense			(b) 1 200 00	
13	Depreciation Expense—Equipment			(c) 1 500 00	
14	Salaries Expense	14 400 00			
15	Utilities Expense	1 800 00			
16	Totals	138 000 00	138 000 00	5 700 00	5 700 00
17	Net Income				
18					
19					
20					

Problem 6.4B **Objectives 6-1, 6-2, 6-4**

▶ **Worksheet, journalizing and posting adjusting and closing entries, and the postclosing trial balance.**

A partially completed worksheet for Roy Anderson, CPA, for the month ending June 30, 2019, is shown below.

Roy Anderson, CPA
Worksheet
Month Ended June 30, 2019

	ACCOUNT NAME	TRIAL BALANCE		ADJUSTMENTS	
		DEBIT	CREDIT	DEBIT	CREDIT
1	Cash	31 950 00			
2	Accounts Receivable	11 340 00			
3	Supplies	15 750 00			(a) 2 700 00
4	Computers	28 800 00			
5	Accumulated Depreciation—Computers		2 880 00		(b) 240 00
6	Accounts Payable		12 600 00		
7	Roy Anderson, Capital		62 235 00		
8	Roy Anderson, Drawing	12 000 00			
9	Fees Income		67 950 00		
10	Salaries Expense	37 725 00			
11	Supplies Expense			(a) 2 700 00	
12	Depreciation Expense—Computers			(b) 240 00	
13	Travel Expense	5 400 00			
14	Utilities Expense	2 700 00			
15	Totals	145 665 00	145 665 00	2 940 00	2 940 00
16					
17					

Adjusted Trial Balance		Income Statement		Balance Sheet		
Debit	Credit	Debit	Credit	Debit	Credit	
32,400.00				32,400.00		1
6,000.00				6,000.00		2
3,000.00				3,000.00		3
7,800.00				7,800.00		4
60,000.00				60,000.00		5
	1,500.00				1,500.00	6
	9,000.00				9,000.00	7
	82,200.00				82,200.00	8
8,400.00				8,400.00		9
	46,800.00		46,800.00			10
3,000.00		3,000.00				11
1,200.00		1,200.00				12
1,500.00		1,500.00				13
14,400.00		14,400.00				14
1,800.00		1,800.00				15
139,500.00	139,500.00	21,900.00	46,800.00	117,600.00	92,700.00	16
		24,900.00			24,900.00	17
		46,800.00	46,800.00	117,600.00	117,600.00	18
						19
						20

INSTRUCTIONS

1. Record the balances as of June 30 in the ledger accounts.
2. Prepare the worksheet.
3. Journalize (use 3 as the journal page number) and post the adjusting entries. Use account number 121 for ***Supplies;*** 131 for ***Computers;*** 142 for the ***Accumulated Depreciation*** account; 309 for ***Income Summary;*** 517 for ***Supplies Expense;*** 519 for ***Travel Expense;*** and 523 for ***Depreciation Expense.***
4. Journalize (use 4 as the journal page number) and post the closing entries.
5. Prepare a postclosing trial balance.

Analyze: What is the reported net income for the month of June for Roy Anderson, CPA?

Critical Thinking Problem 6.1

The Closing Process

The Trial Balance section of the worksheet for Contemporary Fashions for the period ended December 31, 2019, appears below. Adjustments data are also given.

ADJUSTMENTS

- **a.** Supplies used, $3,600
- **b.** Expired insurance, $2,400
- **c.** Depreciation expense for machinery, $1,200

INSTRUCTIONS

1. Complete the worksheet.
2. Prepare an income statement.
3. Prepare a statement of owner's equity.

Contemporary Fashions
Worksheet
Month Ended December 31, 2019

	ACCOUNT NAME	TRIAL BALANCE DEBIT	TRIAL BALANCE CREDIT	ADJUSTMENTS DEBIT	ADJUSTMENTS CREDIT
1	*Cash*	40,800.00			
2	*Accounts Receivable*	9,000.00			
3	*Supplies*	7,200.00			(a) 3,600.00
4	*Prepaid Insurance*	10,800.00			(b) 2,400.00
5	*Machinery*	84,000.00			
6	*Accumulated Depreciation—Machinery*				(c) 1,200.00
7	*Accounts Payable*		13,500.00		
8	*Helen Kennedy, Capital*		74,580.00		
9	*Helen Kennedy, Drawing*	6,000.00			
10	*Fees Income*		82,500.00		
11	*Supplies Expense*			(a) 3,600.00	
12	*Insurance Expense*			(b) 2,400.00	
13	*Salaries Expense*	11,100.00			
14	*Depreciation Expense—Machinery*			(c) 1,200.00	
15	*Utilities Expense*	1,680.00			
16	*Totals*	170,580.00	170,580.00	7,200.00	7,200.00
17					
18					
19					

4. Prepare a balance sheet.
5. Journalize the adjusting entries in the general journal, page 3.
6. Journalize the closing entries in the general journal, page 4.
7. Prepare a postclosing trial balance.

Analyze: If the adjusting entry for expired insurance had been recorded in error as a credit to ***Insurance Expense*** and a debit to ***Prepaid Insurance*** for $2,400, what reported net income would have resulted?

Critical Thinking Problem 6.2

Owner's Equity

Demetria Davis, the bookkeeper for Home Interiors and Designs Company, has just finished posting the closing entries for the year to the ledger. She is concerned about the following balances:

Capital account balance in the general ledger:	$97,100
Ending capital balance on the statement of owner's equity:	55,600

Davis knows that these amounts should agree and asks for your assistance in reviewing her work.

Your review of the general ledger of Home Interiors and Designs Company reveals a beginning capital balance of $50,000. You also review the general journal for the accounting period and find the closing entries shown below.

1. What errors did Ms. Davis make in preparing the closing entries for the period?
2. Prepare a general journal entry to correct the errors made.
3. Explain why the balance of the capital account in the ledger after closing entries have been posted will be the same as the ending capital balance on the statement of owner's equity.

GENERAL JOURNAL PAGE 15

	DATE		DESCRIPTION	POST. REF.	DEBIT	CREDIT	
1	2019		Closing Entries				1
2	Dec.	31	Fees Income		98 000 00		2
3			Accumulated Depreciation		8 500 00		3
4			Accounts Payable		33 000 00		4
5			Income Summary			139 500 00	5
6							6
7		31	Income Summary		92 400 00		7
8			Salaries Expense			78 000 00	8
9			Supplies Expense			5 000 00	9
10			Depreciation Expense			2 400 00	10
11			Thomas Richey, Drawing			7 000 00	11
12							12
13							13
14							14

BUSINESS CONNECTIONS

Interpreting Financial Statements

Managerial FOCUS

1. An officer of Westway Corporation recently commented that when he receives the firm's financial statements, he looks at just the bottom line of the income statement—the line that shows the net income or net loss for the period. He said that he does not bother with the rest of the income statement because "it's only the bottom line that counts." He also does not read the balance sheet. Do you think this manager is correct in the way he uses the financial statements? Why or why not?
2. The president of Brown Corporation is concerned about the firm's ability to pay its debts on time. What items on the balance sheet would help her to assess the firm's debt-paying ability?
3. Why is it important that a firm's financial records be kept up-to-date and that management receive the financial statements promptly after the end of each accounting period?
4. What kinds of operating and general policy decisions might be influenced by data on the financial statements?

Timing of a Check

Ethical DILEMMA

On the last day of the fiscal year, Stanley Carpenter comes to you for a favor. He asks that you enter a check for $2,000 to CD Company for Miscellaneous Expense. You notice the invoice looks a little different from other invoices that are processed. Stanley needs the check immediately to get supplies today to complete the project for a favorite customer. You know that by preparing the closing entries tomorrow, Miscellaneous Expense will be set to zero for the beginning of the new year. Should you write this check and record the expense or find an excuse to write the check tomorrow? What would be the effect if the invoice to CD Company was erroneous and you had written the check?

Income Statement

Financial Statement ANALYSIS

In 2015, CSX Corporation, which operates under the name Surface Transportation, reported operating expenses of $8,227 million. A partial list of the company's operating expenses follows. CSX Corporation reported revenues from external customers to be $11,811 million for the year.

Consolidated Income Statement *(Dollars in millions)*	
Revenue	$11,811
Operating Expenses *(Dollars in millions)*	
Labor and Fringe Benefits	$3,290
Materials, Supplies, and Other	2,336
Fuel	957
Depreciation	1,208
Equipment and Other Rents	436

Analyze:

1. If the given categories represent the related general ledger accounts, what journal entry would be made to close the expense accounts at year-end?
2. What journal entry would be made to close the revenue accounts?

Analyze Online: Locate the website for CSX Corporation (www.csx.com). Click on *Investors.* Within the *Annual Report* link, find the most recent annual report.

3. On the consolidated statement of earnings, what was the amount reported for operating expenses?
4. What percentage increase or decrease does this figure represent from the operating expenses reported in 2015 of $8,277 million?

TEAMWORK

Accounting Cycle

Understanding the steps in the accounting cycle is important to get accurate information about the condition of your company. In teams, make strips of paper with the nine steps of the accounting cycle. Give two or three strips to each member of the group. Each team member needs to put his or her strips in the proper order of the nine steps.

Internet CONNECTION

Certified Bookkeeper

Certification in your field indicates you have a certain level of education and training. Go to the American Institute of Professional Bookkeepers website at www.aipb.org. From the certification program icon, determine the three requirements to become a certified bookkeeper.

Answers to **Self Reviews**

Answers to Section 1 Self Review

1. Debit ***Capital*** and credit ***Drawing.***
2. A temporary owner's equity account.
3. Close the revenue account to ***Income Summary.***

   Close the expense accounts to ***Income Summary.***

   Close the ***Income Summary*** account to the capital account.

   Close the drawing account to the capital account.
4. **d.** ***Capital***
5. **d.** revenue, drawing, and expense accounts
6. No effect on net income.

Answers to Section 2 Self Review

1. (7) Record closing entries, (8) prepare a postclosing trial balance, (9) interpret the financial statements.
2. To make sure the general ledger is in balance after the adjusting and closing entries are posted.
3. Asset, liability, and the owner's capital accounts.
4. **b.** ***J.B. Edwards, Drawing***
5. **a.** net profit of $60,000
6. The income statement will answer questions about fees earned, expenses incurred, and profit. The balance sheet will answer questions about the cash balance, the amount owed by customers, and the amount owed to suppliers.

Answers to Comprehensive Self Review

1. Income statement, statement of owner's equity, and balance sheet.
2.

Income Summary	12,100	
Rent Expense		3,600
Salaries Expense		7,000
Supplies Expense		1,500

3.

Fees Income	90,000	
Income Summary		90,000

4. Interpret the financial statements.
5. False. The *temporary* owner's equity accounts do not appear on the postclosing trial balance. The temporary owner's equity accounts are the drawing account and ***Income Summary.***

Mini-Practice Set 1

Service Business Accounting Cycle

Eli's Consulting Services

This project will give you an opportunity to apply your knowledge of accounting principles and procedures by handling all the accounting work of Eli's Consulting Services for the month of January 2020.

INTRODUCTION

Assume that you are the chief accountant for Eli's Consulting Services. During January, the business will use the same types of records and procedures that you learned about in Chapters 1 through 6. The chart of accounts for Eli's Consulting Services has been expanded to include a few new accounts. Follow the instructions to complete the accounting records for the month of January.

Eli's Consulting Services Chart of Accounts	
Assets	**Revenue**
101 Cash	401 Fees Income
111 Accounts Receivable	**Expenses**
121 Supplies	511 Salaries Expense
134 Prepaid Insurance	514 Utilities Expense
137 Prepaid Rent	517 Supplies Expense
141 Equipment	520 Rent Expense
142 Accumulated Depreciation—Equipment	523 Depreciation Expense—Equipment
Liabilities	526 Advertising Expense
202 Accounts Payable	529 Maintenance Expense
Owner's Equity	532 Telephone Expense
301 Trayton Eli, Capital	535 Insurance Expense
302 Trayton Eli, Drawing	
309 Income Summary	

INSTRUCTIONS

1. Open the general ledger accounts and enter the balances for January 1, 2020. Obtain the necessary figures from the postclosing trial balance prepared on December 31, 2019, which appears in Figure 6.3.
2. Analyze each transaction and record it in the general journal. Use page 3 to begin January's transactions.
3. Post the transactions to the general ledger accounts.
4. Prepare the Trial Balance section of the worksheet.
5. Prepare the Adjustments section of the worksheet.
   a. Compute and record the adjustment for supplies used during the month. An inventory taken on January 31 showed supplies of $5,200 on hand.
   b. Compute and record the adjustment for expired insurance for the month.
   c. Record the adjustment for one month of expired rent of $4,000.
   d. Record the adjustment for depreciation of $183 on the old equipment for the month. The first adjustment for depreciation for the new equipment will be recorded in February.
6. Complete the worksheet.
7. Prepare an income statement for the month.
8. Prepare a statement of owner's equity.

9. Prepare a balance sheet using the report form.
10. Journalize and post the adjusting entries.
11. Journalize and post the closing entries.
12. Prepare a postclosing trial balance.

Analyze: Compare the January 31 balance sheet you prepared with the December 31 balance sheet shown in Figure 6.4.

a. What changes occurred in total assets, liabilities, and the owner's ending capital?

b. What changes occurred in the ***Cash*** and ***Accounts Receivable*** accounts?

c. Has there been an improvement in the firm's financial position? Why or why not?

DATE		TRANSACTIONS
Jan.	2	Purchased supplies for $7,000; issued Check 1015.
	2	Purchased a one-year insurance policy for $8,400; issued Check 1016.
	7	Sold services for $20,000 in cash and $5,000 on credit during the first week of January.
	12	Collected a total of $4,000 on account from credit customers during the first week of January.
	12	Issued Check 1017 for $3,600 to pay for special promotional advertising to new businesses on the local radio station during the month.
	13	Collected a total of $4,500 on account from credit customers during the second week of January.
	14	Returned supplies that were damaged for a cash refund of $750.
	15	Sold services for $20,700 in cash and $2,300 on credit during the second week of January.
	20	Purchased supplies for $5,000 from White's, Inc.; received Invoice 2384 payable in 30 days.
	20	Sold services for $12,500 in cash and $3,500 on credit during the third week of January.
	20	Collected a total of $5,600 on account from credit customers during the third week of January.
	21	Issued Check 1018 for $7,065 to pay for maintenance work on the office equipment.
	22	Issued Check 1019 for $3,600 to pay for special promotional advertising to new businesses in the local newspaper.
	23	Received the monthly telephone bill for $1,025 and paid it with Check 1020.
	26	Collected a total of $1,600 on account from credit customers during the fourth week of January.
	27	Issued Check 1021 for $3,000 to Office Plus as payment on account for Invoice 2223.
	28	Sent Check 1022 for $2,675 in payment of the monthly bill for utilities.
	29	Sold services for $19,000 in cash and $2,750 on credit during the fourth week of January.
	31	Issued Checks 1023–1027 for $32,800 to pay the monthly salaries of the regular employees and three part-time workers.
	31	Issued Check 1028 for $12,000 for personal use.
	31	Issued Check 1029 for $4,150 to pay for maintenance services for the month.
	31	Purchased additional equipment for $15,000 from Contemporary Equipment Company; issued Check 1030 for $10,000 and bought the rest on credit. The equipment has a five-year life and no salvage value.
	31	Sold services for $7,600 in cash and $1,620 on credit on January 31.

Accounting for Sales and Accounts Receivable

Chapter 7

© Kristoffer Tripplaar/Alamy Stock Photo

www.mccormickcorporation.com

Variety is the spice of life and McCormick & Company, Incorporated, provides a wide variety of spices to consumer and industrial customers in more than 110 countries. In 1889, Willoughby M. McCormick started the company in a basement and sold his flavors and extracts door to door. The company grew quickly but faced a major setback in 1904 when a fire destroyed all of the company's assets and records. The devastation of losing everything pushed Willoughby McCormick to nearly give up on his company, but his dedication to his employees compelled him to rebuild the company and it has continued to grow since.

However, the contributions of the company are not limited to the sales of spices and extracts. In addition to the continued development and production of innovative new products, McCormick has built a legacy of establishing industry quality standards, improving employee relations and working conditions, and developing a legacy of charitable donations and organizations. McCormick is committed to taking responsibility for its products—and the world around them.

McCormick sells to a rapidly growing base of consumer and industrial customers, earning sales of $4.3 billion during 2014 and having a reported $493.6 million of accounts receivable at the end of 2014. The accuracy and reliability of recording sales and collecting accounts receivable are crucial to the continued success of McCormick and its continued commitment to its employees and the communities it serves.

thinking critically

Do you think that McCormick & Company varies the discounts that it offers to its various industrial customers?

LEARNING OBJECTIVES

- **7-1** Record credit sales in a sales journal.
- **7-2** Post from the sales journal to the general ledger accounts.
- **7-3** Post from the sales journal to the customers' accounts in the accounts receivable subsidiary ledger.
- **7-4** Record sales returns and allowances in the general journal.
- **7-5** Post sales returns and allowances.
- **7-6** Prepare a schedule of accounts receivable.
- **7-7** Compute trade discounts.
- **7-8** Record credit card sales in appropriate journals.
- **7-9** Prepare the state sales tax return.
- **7-10** Define the accounting terms new to this chapter.

NEW TERMS

accounts receivable ledger
charge-account sales
contra revenue account
control account
credit memorandum
invoice
list price
manufacturing business
merchandise inventory
merchandising business
net price
net sales
open-account credit
periodic inventory system
perpetual inventory system
retail business
sales allowance
sales journal
sales return
Sales Returns and Allowances
schedule of accounts receivable
service business
special journal
subsidiary ledger
trade discount
wholesale business

Section 1

SECTION OBJECTIVES	TERMS TO LEARN
>> 7-1 Record credit sales in a sales journal. WHY IT'S IMPORTANT Credit sales are a major source of revenue for many businesses. The sales journal is an efficient option for recording large volumes of credit sales transactions. **>> 7-2 Post from the sales journal to the general ledger accounts.** WHY IT'S IMPORTANT A well-designed accounting system prevents repetitive tasks.	manufacturing business merchandise inventory merchandising business periodic inventory system perpetual inventory system retail business sales journal service business special journal subsidiary ledger

Merchandise Sales

When an accounting system is developed for a firm, one important consideration is the nature of the firm's operations. The three basic types of businesses are a **service business,** which sells services; a **merchandising business,** which sells goods that it purchases for resale; and a **manufacturing business,** which sells goods that it produces.

Trayton Eli's Consulting Services, the firm that was described in Chapters 2 through 6, is a service business. The firm that we will examine next, Maxx-Out Sporting Goods, is a merchandising business that sells the latest sporting goods and sportswear for men, women, and children. It is a **retail business,** which sells goods and services directly to individual consumers. Maxx-Out Sporting Goods is a sole proprietorship owned and operated by Max Ferraro, who was formerly a sales manager for a major retail clothing store.

Maxx-Out Sporting Goods must account for purchases and sales of goods, and for **merchandise inventory**—the stock of goods that is kept on hand. Refer to the chart of accounts for Maxx-Out Sporting Goods nearby. You will learn about the accounts in this and following chapters.

Due to the relatively small size of its operations, Maxx-Out Sporting Goods does not keep track of its inventory daily. Maxx-Out Sporting Goods uses a **periodic inventory system.** In a periodic inventory system, the cost of inventory on hand must be determined by counting merchandise inventory in stock.

Larger businesses need to know the number of units and the unit cost for inventory on hand at all times. These businesses use a perpetual inventory system. In a **perpetual inventory system,** the amount of inventory on hand is adjusted for each sale, purchase, or return. Electronic equipment, such as point-of-sale cash registers and scanners, helps track inventory balances. The accounting for a perpetual system is discussed in the appendix to Chapter 9.

To allow for efficient recording of financial data, the accounting systems of most merchandising businesses include special journals and subsidiary ledgers.

important!

Business Classifications

The term *merchandising* refers to the type of business operation, not the type of legal entity. Maxx-Out Sporting Goods could have been a partnership or a corporation instead of a sole proprietorship.

Special Journals and Subsidiary Ledgers

A **special journal** is a journal that is used to record only one type of transaction. A **subsidiary ledger** is a ledger that contains accounts of a single type. Table 7.1 lists the journals and ledgers that merchandising businesses generally use in their accounting systems. In this chapter, we will discuss the sales journal and the accounts receivable subsidiary ledger.

JOURNALS	
Type of Journal	**Purpose**
Sales	To record sales of merchandise on credit
Purchases	To record purchases of merchandise on credit
Cash receipts	To record cash received from all sources
Cash payments	To record all disbursements of cash
General	To record all transactions that are not recorded in another special journal and all adjusting and closing entries
LEDGERS	
Type of Ledger	**Content**
General	Assets, liabilities, owner's equity, revenue, and expense accounts
Accounts receivable	Accounts for credit customers
Accounts payable	Accounts for creditors

TABLE 7.1

Journals and Ledgers Used by Merchandising Businesses

Maxx-Out Sporting Goods Chart of Accounts

Assets

101 Cash
105 Petty Cash Fund
109 Notes Receivable
111 Accounts Receivable
112 Allowance for Doubtful Accounts
116 Interest Receivable
121 Merchandise Inventory
126 Prepaid Insurance
127 Prepaid Interest
129 Supplies
131 Store Equipment
132 Accumulated Depreciation—Store Equipment
141 Office Equipment
142 Accumulated Depreciation—Office Equipment

Liabilities

201 Notes Payable—Trade
202 Notes Payable—Bank
205 Accounts Payable
216 Interest Payable
221 Social Security Tax Payable
222 Medicare Tax Payable
223 Employee Income Tax Payable
225 Federal Unemployment Tax Payable
227 State Unemployment Tax Payable
229 Salaries Payable
231 Sales Tax Payable

Owner's Equity

301 Max Ferraro, Capital
302 Max Ferraro, Drawing
399 Income Summary

Revenue

401 Sales
451 Sales Returns and Allowances
491 Interest Income
493 Miscellaneous Income

Cost of Goods Sold

501 Purchases
502 Freight In
503 Purchases Returns and Allowances
504 Purchases Discounts

Expenses

611 Salaries Expense—Sales
612 Supplies Expense
614 Advertising Expense
617 Cash Short or Over
626 Depreciation Expense—Store Equipment
634 Rent Expense
637 Salaries Expense—Office
639 Insurance Expense
641 Payroll Taxes Expense
643 Utilities Expense
649 Telephone Expense
651 Uncollectible Accounts Expense
657 Bank Fees Expense
658 Delivery Expense
659 Depreciation Expense—Office Equipment
691 Interest Expense
693 Miscellaneous Expense

The Sales Journal

The **sales journal** is used to record only sales of merchandise on credit. To understand the need for a sales journal, consider how credit sales made at Maxx-Out Sporting Goods would be entered and posted using a general journal and general ledger. Refer to Figure 7.1.

FIGURE 7.1

Journalizing and Posting Credit Sales

GENERAL JOURNAL PAGE 2

DATE		DESCRIPTION	POST. REF.	DEBIT	CREDIT
2019					
Jan.	3	Accounts Receivable	111	702 00	
		Sales Tax Payable	231		52 00
		Sales	401		650 00
		Sold merchandise on			
		credit to Ann Anh,			
		Sales Slip 1101			
	8	Accounts Receivable	111	648 00	
		Sales Tax Payable	231		48 00
		Sales	401		600 00
		Sold merchandise on			
		credit to Cathy Ball,			
		Sales Slip 1102			
	11	Accounts Receivable	111	756 00	
		Sales Tax Payable	231		56 00
		Sales	401		700 00
		Sold merchandise on			
		credit to Barbara Coe, Sales			
		Slip 1103			
	15	Accounts Receivable	111	324 00	
		Sales Tax Payable	231		24 00
		Sales	401		300 00
		Sold merchandise on			
		credit to Amalia Rodriguez,			
		Sales Slip 1104			

ACCOUNT *Accounts Receivable* ACCOUNT NO. 111

DATE		DESCRIPTION	POST. REF.	DEBIT	CREDIT	BALANCE DEBIT	BALANCE CREDIT
2019							
Jan.	1	Balance	✓			3,240 00	
	3		J2	702 00		3,942 00	
	8		J2	648 00		4,590 00	
	11		J2	756 00		5,346 00	
	15		J2	324 00		5,670 00	

(continued)

Note the word "Balance" in the ledger accounts. To record beginning balances, enter the date in the Date column, the word "Balance" in the Description column, a check mark in the Posting Reference column, and the amount in the Debit or Credit Balance column.

Most state and many local governments impose a sales tax on retail sales of certain goods and services. Businesses are required to collect this tax from their customers and send it to the proper tax agency at regular intervals. When goods or services are sold on credit, the sales tax is usually recorded at the time of the sale even though it will not be collected immediately. A liability account called ***Sales Tax Payable*** is credited for the sales tax charged.

FIGURE 7.1 (continued)

ACCOUNT Sales Tax Payable ACCOUNT NO. 231

DATE		DESCRIPTION	POST. REF.	DEBIT	CREDIT	BALANCE DEBIT	BALANCE CREDIT
2019							
Jan.	1	Balance	✓				756 00
	3		J2		52 00		808 00
	8		J2		48 00		856 00
	11		J2		56 00		912 00
	15		J2		24 00		936 00

ACCOUNT Sales ACCOUNT NO. 401

DATE		DESCRIPTION	POST. REF.	DEBIT	CREDIT	BALANCE DEBIT	BALANCE CREDIT
2019							
Jan.	3		J2		650 00		650 00
	8		J2		600 00		1250 00
	11		J2		700 00		1950 00
	15		J2		300 00		2250 00

As you can see, a great amount of repetition is involved in both journalizing and posting these sales. The four credit sales made on January 3, 8, 11, and 15 required four separate entries in the general journal and involved four debits to ***Accounts Receivable,*** four credits to ***Sales Tax Payable,*** four credits to ***Sales*** (the firm's revenue account), and four descriptions. The posting of 12 items to the three general ledger accounts represents still further duplication of effort. This recording procedure is not efficient for a business that has a substantial number of credit sales each month.

RECORDING TRANSACTIONS IN A SALES JOURNAL

>> 7-1 OBJECTIVE

Record credit sales in a sales journal.

A special journal intended only for credit sales provides a more efficient method of recording these transactions. Figure 7.2 shows the January credit sales of Maxx-Out Sporting Goods recorded in a sales journal. Since Maxx-Out Sporting Goods is located in a state that has

FIGURE 7.2

A Sales Journal

SALES JOURNAL PAGE 1

	DATE		SALES SLIP NO.	CUSTOMER'S ACCOUNT DEBITED	POST. REF.	ACCOUNTS RECEIVABLE DEBIT	SALES TAX PAYABLE CREDIT	SALES CREDIT	
1	2019								1
2	Jan.	3	1101	Ann Anh		702 00	52 00	650 00	2
3		8	1102	Cathy Ball		648 00	48 00	600 00	3
4		11	1103	Barbara Coe		756 00	56 00	700 00	4
5		15	1104	Amalia Rodriguez		324 00	24 00	300 00	5
6		18	1105	Fred Wu		810 00	60 00	750 00	6
7		21	1106	Linda Carter		486 00	36 00	450 00	7
8		28	1107	Kim Ramirez		108 00	8 00	100 00	8
9		29	1108	Mesia Davis		1080 00	80 00	1000 00	9
10		31	1109	Alma Sanchez		972 00	72 00	900 00	10
11		31	1110	Ann Anh		270 00	20 00	250 00	11
12									12

FIGURE 7.3

Customer's Sales Slip

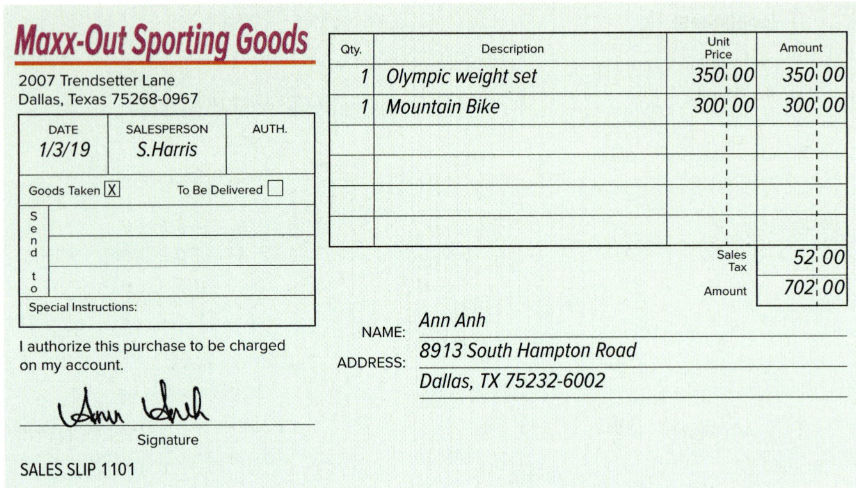

Maxx-Out Sporting Goods
2007 Trendsetter Lane
Dallas, Texas 75268-0967

DATE	SALESPERSON	AUTH.
1/3/19	S.Harris	

Goods Taken [X] To Be Delivered [ ]

Send to

Special Instructions:

I authorize this purchase to be charged on my account.

Signature

SALES SLIP 1101

Qty.	Description	Unit Price	Amount
1	Olympic weight set	350.00	350.00
1	Mountain Bike	300.00	300.00
		Sales Tax	52.00
		Amount	702.00

NAME: Ann Anh
ADDRESS: 8913 South Hampton Road
Dallas, TX 75232-6002

an 8 percent sales tax on retail transactions, its sales journal includes a Sales Tax Payable Credit column. For the sake of simplicity, the sales journal shown here includes a limited number of transactions. The firm actually has many more credit sales each month.

recall

Journals

A journal is a day-to-day record of a firm's transactions.

Notice that the headings and columns in the sales journal speed up the recording process. No general ledger account names are entered. Only one line is needed to record all information for each transaction—date, sales slip number, customer's name, debit to ***Accounts Receivable,*** credit to ***Sales Tax Payable,*** and credit to ***Sales.*** Since the sales journal is used for a single purpose, there is no need to enter any descriptions. Thus, a great deal of repetition is avoided.

Entries in the sales journal are usually made daily. In a retail business such as Maxx-Out Sporting Goods, the data needed for each entry is taken from a copy of the customer's sales slip, as shown in Figure 7.3.

Many small retail firms use a sales journal similar to the one shown in Figure 7.2. However, keep in mind that special journals vary in format according to the needs of individual businesses.

>> 7-2 OBJECTIVE

Post from the sales journal to the general ledger accounts.

POSTING FROM A SALES JOURNAL

A sales journal not only simplifies the initial recording of credit sales, it also eliminates a great deal of repetition in posting these transactions. With a sales journal, it is not necessary to post each credit sale individually to general ledger accounts. Instead, summary postings are made at the end of the month after the amount columns of the sales journal are totaled. See Figure 7.4 for an illustration of posting from the sales journal to the general ledger.

In actual practice, before any posting takes place, the equality of the debits and credits recorded in the sales journal is proved by comparing the column totals. The proof for the sales journal in Figure 7.4 is given below. All multicolumn special journals should be proved in a similar manner before their totals are posted.

Proof of Sales Journal	
	Debits
Accounts Receivable Debit column	$6,156.00
	Credits
Sales Tax Payable Credit column	$ 456.00
Sales Credit column	5,700.00
	$6,156.00

FIGURE 7.4

End-of-Month Postings

SALES JOURNAL PAGE 1

	DATE		SALES SLIP NO.	CUSTOMER'S ACCOUNT DEBITED	POST. REF.	ACCOUNTS RECEIVABLE DEBIT	SALES TAX PAYABLE CREDIT	SALES CREDIT	
1	2019								1
2	Jan.	3	1101	Ann Anh	✓	702 00	52 00	650 00	2
3		8	1102	Cathy Ball	✓	648 00	48 00	600 00	3
4		11	1103	Barbara Coe	✓	756 00	56 00	700 00	4
5		15	1104	Amalia Rodriguez	✓	324 00	24 00	300 00	5
6		18	1105	Fred Wu	✓	810 00	60 00	750 00	6
7		21	1106	Linda Carter	✓	486 00	36 00	450 00	7
8		28	1107	Kim Ramirez	✓	108 00	8 00	100 00	8
9		29	1108	Mesia Davis	✓	1080 00	80 00	1000 00	9
10		31	1109	Alma Sanchez	✓	972 00	72 00	900 00	10
11		31	1110	Ann Anh	✓	270 00	20 00	250 00	11
12		31		Totals		6156 00	456 00	5700 00	12
13						(111)	(231)	(401)	13
14									14
15									
16									
17									

ACCOUNT *Accounts Receivable* ACCOUNT NO. 111

DATE		DESCRIPTION	POST. REF.	DEBIT	CREDIT	BALANCE DEBIT	BALANCE CREDIT
2019							
Jan.	1	Balance	✓			3240 00	
	23		J2		162 00	3078 00	
	25		J2		486 00	2592 00	
	31		S1	6156 00		8748 00	

ACCOUNT *Sales Tax Payable* ACCOUNT NO. 231

DATE		DESCRIPTION	POST. REF.	DEBIT	CREDIT	BALANCE DEBIT	BALANCE CREDIT
2019							
Jan.	1	Balance	✓				756 00
	11		CP1	756 00			–0–
	23		J2	12 00		12 00	
	25		J2	36 00		48 00	
	31		S1		456 00		408 00

ACCOUNT *Sales* ACCOUNT NO. 401

DATE		DESCRIPTION	POST. REF.	DEBIT	CREDIT	BALANCE DEBIT	BALANCE CREDIT
2019							
Jan.	31	Balance	S1		5700 00		5700 00

After the equality of the debits and credits has been verified, the sales journal is ruled and the column totals are posted to the general ledger accounts involved. To indicate that the postings have been made, the general ledger account numbers are entered in parentheses under the column totals in the sales journal. The abbreviation S1 is written in the Posting Reference column of the accounts, showing that the data was posted from page 1 of the sales journal.

The check marks in the sales journal in Figure 7.4 indicate that the amounts have been posted to the individual customer accounts. Posting from the sales journal to the customer accounts in the subsidiary ledger is illustrated later in this chapter.

important!

Posting

When posting from the sales journal, post information moving from left to right across the ledger form.

ADVANTAGES OF A SALES JOURNAL

Using a special journal for credit sales saves time, effort, and recording space. Both the journalizing process and the posting process become more efficient, but the advantage in the posting process is especially significant. If a business used the general journal to record 300 credit sales a month, the firm would have to make 900 postings to the general ledger—300 to ***Accounts Receivable,*** 300 to ***Sales Tax Payable,*** and 300 to ***Sales.*** With a sales journal, the firm makes only three summary postings to the general ledger at the end of each month no matter how many credit sales were entered.

The use of a sales journal and other special journals also allows division of work. In a business with a fairly large volume of transactions, it is essential that several employees be able to record transactions at the same time.

Finally, the sales journal improves the audit trail by bringing together all entries for credit sales in one place and listing them by source document number as well as by date. This procedure makes it easier to trace the details of such transactions.

Section 1 Self Review

QUESTIONS

1. What is a special journal? Give four examples of special journals.
2. What type of transaction is recorded in the sales journal?
3. What is a subsidiary ledger? Give two examples of subsidiary ledgers.

EXERCISES

4. Types of business operations are:
   a. service, merchandising, corporation.
   b. sole proprietorship, merchandising, manufacturing.
   c. service, merchandising, manufacturing.
5. Which of the following is not a reason to use a sales journal?
   a. increases efficiency
   b. allows division of work
   c. increases credit sales
   d. improves audit trail

ANALYSIS

6. All sales recorded in the sales journal below were made on account and are taxable at a rate of 8 percent. What errors have been made in the entries? Assume the Sales Credit column is correct.

Answers to Section 1 Self Review are on page 238.)

SALES JOURNAL PAGE 1

	DATE		SALES SLIP NO.	CUSTOMER'S ACCOUNT DEBITED	POST. REF.	ACCOUNTS RECEIVABLE DEBIT	SALES TAX PAYABLE CREDIT	SALES CREDIT	
12	Apr.	25	4100	Carolyn Harris		642 00	42 00	600 00	12
13		25	4101	Teresa Wells		872 00	72 00	900 00	13

Section 2

SECTION OBJECTIVES	TERMS TO LEARN
>> 7-3 Post from the sales journal to the customers' accounts in the accounts receivable subsidiary ledger. **WHY IT'S IMPORTANT** This ledger contains individual records that reflect all transactions of each customer. **>> 7-4** Record sales returns and allowances in the general journal. **WHY IT'S IMPORTANT** Companies can see how much revenue is lost due to merchandise problems. **>> 7-5** Post sales returns and allowances. **WHY IT'S IMPORTANT** Accurate, up-to-date customer records contribute to overall customer satisfaction. **>> 7-6** Prepare a schedule of accounts receivable. **WHY IT'S IMPORTANT** This schedule provides a snapshot of amounts due from customers.	accounts receivable ledger contra revenue account control account credit memorandum net sales sales allowance sales return *Sales Returns and Allowances* schedule of accounts receivable

Accounts Receivable

A business that extends credit to customers must manage its accounts receivable carefully. Accounts receivable represent a substantial asset for many businesses, and this asset must be converted into cash in a timely manner. Otherwise, a firm may not be able to pay its bills even though it has a large volume of sales and earns a satisfactory profit.

The Accounts Receivable Ledger

The accountant needs detailed information about the transactions with credit customers and the balances owed by such customers at all times. This information is provided by an **accounts receivable ledger** with individual accounts for all credit customers. The accounts receivable ledger is referred to as a subsidiary ledger because it is separate from and subordinate to the general ledger.

Using an accounts receivable ledger makes it possible to verify that customers are paying their balances on time and that they are within their credit limits. The accounts receivable ledger also provides a convenient way to answer questions from credit customers. Customers may ask about their current balances or about a possible billing error.

The accounts for credit customers are maintained in a balance ledger form with three money columns, as shown in Figure 7.5 nearby. Notice that this form does not contain a column for indicating the type of account balance. The balances in the customer accounts are presumed to be debit balances since asset accounts normally have debit balances. However, occasionally there is a credit balance because a customer has overpaid an amount owed or has returned goods that were already paid for. One common procedure for dealing with this situation is to circle the balance in order to show that it is a credit amount.

For a small business such as Maxx-Out Sporting Goods, customer accounts are alphabetized in the accounts receivable ledger. Larger firms and firms that use accounting software programs assign an account number to each credit customer and arrange the customer accounts in numeric order. Postings to the accounts receivable ledger are usually made daily so that the customer accounts can be kept up to date at all times.

POSTING A CREDIT SALE

>> 7-3 OBJECTIVE

Post from the sales journal to the customers' accounts in the accounts receivable subsidiary ledger.

Each credit sale recorded in the sales journal is posted to the appropriate customer's account in the accounts receivable ledger, as shown in Figure 7.5. The date, the sales slip number, and the amount that the customer owes as a result of the sale are transferred from the sales journal to the customer's account. The amount is taken from the Accounts Receivable Debit column of the journal and is entered in the Debit column of the account. Next, the new balance is determined and recorded.

To show that the posting has been completed, a check mark (✓) is entered in the sales journal and the abbreviation S1 is entered in the Posting Reference column of the customer's account. As noted before, this abbreviation identifies page 1 of the sales journal.

POSTING CASH RECEIVED ON ACCOUNT

When the transaction involves cash received on account from a credit customer, the cash collected is first recorded in a cash receipts journal. (The necessary entry in the cash receipts journal is discussed in Chapter 9.) The cash is then posted to the individual customer account in the accounts receivable ledger. Figure 7.6 shows a posting for cash received on January 7 from Ann Anh, a credit customer of Maxx-Out Sporting Goods.

Sales Returns and Allowances

>> 7-4 OBJECTIVE

Record sales returns and allowances in the general journal.

A sale is entered in the accounting records when the goods are sold or the service is provided. If something is wrong with the goods or service, the firm may take back the goods, resulting in a **sales return,** or give the customer a reduction in price, resulting in a **sales allowance.**

When a return or allowance is related to a credit sale, the normal practice is to issue a document called a **credit memorandum** to the customer rather than giving a cash refund. The credit

FIGURE 7.5

Posting from the Sales Journal to the Accounts Receivable Ledger

SALES JOURNAL — PAGE 1

DATE		SALES SLIP NO.	CUSTOMER'S ACCOUNT DEBITED	POST. REF.	ACCOUNTS RECEIVABLE DEBIT	SALES TAX PAYABLE CREDIT	SALES CREDIT
2019							
Jan.	3	1101	Ann Anh	✓	702 00	52 00	650 00

NAME Ann Anh
ADDRESS 8913 South Hampton Road, Dallas, TX 75232-6002

DATE		DESCRIPTION	POST. REF.	DEBIT	CREDIT	BALANCE
2019						
Jan.	1	Balance	✓			432 00
	3	Sales Slip 1101	S1	702 00		1 134 00

FIGURE 7.6

Posting for Cash Received on Account

NAME Ann Anh
ADDRESS 8913 South Hampton Road, Dallas, TX 75232-6002

DATE		DESCRIPTION	POST. REF.	DEBIT	CREDIT	BALANCE
2019						
Jan.	1	Balance	✓			432 00
	3	Sales Slip 1101	S1	702 00		1 134 00
	7		CR1		432 00	702 00

memorandum states that the customer's account is being reduced by the amount of the return or allowance plus any sales tax. A copy of the credit memorandum provides the data needed to enter the transaction in the firm's accounting records.

A debit to the ***Sales Returns and Allowances*** account is preferred to making a direct debit to ***Sales.*** This procedure gives a complete record of sales returns and allowances for each accounting period. Business managers use this record as a measure of operating efficiency. The ***Sales Returns and Allowances*** account is a **contra revenue account** because it has a debit balance, which is contrary, or opposite, to the normal credit balance for a revenue account.

BUSINESS TRANSACTION

On January 23, Maxx-Out Sporting Goods issued Credit Memorandum 101 for a sales allowance to Fred Wu for merchandise purchased on account. The merchandise was damaged but still usable.

Maxx-Out Sporting Goods
2007 Trendsetter Lane, Dallas TX 75268-0967

CREDIT MEMORANDUM **NO. 101**

DATE: *January 23, 2019*
NAME: *Fred Wu*
ADDRESS: *4640 Walnut Hill Lane*
Dallas, TX 75267-6205

CUSTOMER SIGNATURE

ORIGINAL SALES DATE	ORIGINAL SALES SLIP	APPROVAL	X MDSE RET
Jan. 18, 2019	*No. 1105*	*S.H.*	

QTY	DESCRIPTION	AMOUNT
1	*Athletic Suit*	*$150.00*
REASON FOR RETURN: *damaged*	SUB TOTAL	*$150.00*
THE TOTAL SHOWN AT THE RIGHT WILL BE CREDITED TO YOUR ACCOUNT.	SALES TAX	*12.00*
	TOTAL	*$162.00*

ANALYSIS

The contra revenue account ***Sales Returns and Allowances*** is increased by $150. The liability account ***Sales Tax Payable*** is decreased by $12. The asset account ***Accounts Receivable*** is decreased by $162.

DEBIT-CREDIT RULES

DEBIT Increases to a contra revenue account are recorded as debits. Debit ***Sales Returns and Allowances*** for $150. Decreases to liability accounts are recorded as debits. Debit ***Sales Tax Payable*** for $12.

CREDIT Decreases to an asset account are recorded as credits. Credit ***Accounts Receivable*** for $162.

T-ACCOUNT PRESENTATION

Sales Returns and Allowances	
+	−
150	

Sales Tax Payable	
−	+
12	

Accounts Receivable	
+	−
	162

GENERAL JOURNAL ENTRY

GENERAL JOURNAL PAGE *1*

	DATE		DESCRIPTION	POST. REF.	DEBIT	CREDIT	
1	*2019*						1
2	*Jan.*	*23*	*Sales Returns and Allowances*		*150 00*		2
3			*Sales Tax Payable*		*12 00*		3
4			*Accts. Rec.—Fred Wu*			*162 00*	4

THE BOTTOM LINE

Allowance for Damaged Merchandise

Income Statement

Control Revenue	↑	150
Net Income	↓	150

Balance Sheet

Assets	↓	162
Liabilities	↓	12
Equity	↓	150

What is the ultimate effect of this transaction on the financial statements? An increase in contra revenue causes a decrease in net income. Note that the $150 decrease in net income causes a $150 decrease in owner's equity. The asset ***Accounts Receivable*** is decreased, and the liability ***Sales Tax Payable*** is also decreased. The eventual effect of this transaction on the income statement and the balance sheet is summarized in the box titled *The Bottom Line.*

RECORDING SALES RETURNS AND ALLOWANCES

Depending on the volume of sales returns and allowances, a business may use a general journal to record these transactions, or it may use a special sales returns and allowances journal.

Using the General Journal for Sales Returns and Allowances A small firm that has a limited number of sales returns and allowances each month has no need to establish a special journal for such transactions. Instead, the required entries are made in the general journal.

Using a Sales Returns and Allowances Journal In a business having many sales returns and allowances, it is efficient to use a special journal for these transactions. An example of a *sales returns and allowances journal* is shown in Figure 7.7.

>> 7-5 OBJECTIVE

Post sales returns and allowances.

POSTING A SALES RETURN OR ALLOWANCE

Whether sales returns and allowances are recorded in the general journal or in a special sales returns and allowances journal, each of these transactions must be posted from the general ledger to the appropriate customer's account in the accounts receivable ledger. Figure 7.8 shows how a return of merchandise was posted from the general journal to the account of Linda Carter.

FIGURE 7.7

Sales Returns and Allowances Journal

SALES RETURNS AND ALLOWANCES JOURNAL — PAGE 8

	DATE		SALES SLIP NO.	CUSTOMER'S ACCOUNT CREDITED	POST. REF.	ACCOUNTS RECEIVABLE CREDIT	SALES TAX PAYABLE DEBIT	SALES RET. & ALLOW. DEBIT	
1	2019								1
2	Jan.	23	1105	Fred Wu	✓	162 00	12 00	150 00	2
3		25	1106	Linda Carter	✓	486 00	36 00	450 00	3
4									4
17		31		Totals		3,240 00	240 00	3,000 00	17
18						(111)	(231)	(451)	18
19									19

FIGURE 7.8

Posting a Sales Return to the Customer's Account

GENERAL JOURNAL — PAGE 1

	DATE		DESCRIPTION	POST. REF.	DEBIT	CREDIT	
1	2019						1
6	Jan.	25	Sales Returns and Allowances	451	450 00		6
7			Sales Tax Payable	231	36 00		7
8			Accounts Rec./Linda Carter	111/✓		486 00	8
9			Accepted a return of				9
10			defective merchandise,				10
11			Credit Memorandum 102;				11
12			original sale made on Sales				12
13			Slip 1106 of January 21.				13
14							14
15							

NAME Linda Carter

ADDRESS 1819 Belt Line Road, Dallas, Texas 75267-6318

DATE		DESCRIPTION	POST. REF.	DEBIT	CREDIT	BALANCE
2019						
Jan.	1	Balance	✓			54 00
	21	Sales Slip 1106	S1	486 00		540 00
	25	CM 102	J1		486 00	54 00

Because the credit amount in the general journal entry for this transaction requires two postings, the account number 111 and a check mark are entered in the Posting Reference column of the journal. The 111 indicates that the amount was posted to the ***Accounts Receivable*** account in the general ledger, and the check mark indicates that the amount was posted to the customer's account in the accounts receivable ledger. Notice that a diagonal line was used to separate the two posting references.

Refer to Figure 7.7, which shows a special sales returns and allowances journal instead of a general journal. The account numbers at the bottom of each column are the posting references for the three general ledger accounts: ***Accounts Receivable, Sales Tax Payable,*** and ***Sales Returns and Allowances.*** The check marks in the Posting Reference column show that the credits were posted to individual customer accounts in the accounts receivable subsidiary ledger.

Remember that a business can use the general journal or special journals for transactions related to credit sales. A special journal is an efficient option for recording and posting large numbers of transactions.

Figure 7.9 shows the accounts receivable ledger after posting is completed.

REPORTING NET SALES

At the end of each accounting period, the balance of the ***Sales Returns and Allowances*** account is subtracted from the balance of the ***Sales*** account in the Revenue section of the income statement. The resulting figure is the **net sales** for the period.

For example, assume the ***Sales Returns and Allowances*** account contains a balance of $600 at the end of January. Also assume the ***Sales*** account has a balance of $25,700 at the end of January. The Revenue section of the firm's income statement will appear as follows.

Maxx-Out Sporting Goods
Income Statement (Partial)
Month Ended January 31, 2019

Revenue	
Sales	$25,700
Less Sales Returns and Allowances	600
Net Sales	$25,100

ABOUT ACCOUNTING

Investing in Ethics

Are ethical companies—those with a strong internal enforcement policy—really more profitable? Yes, according to a study by Dr. Curtis Verschoor of DePaul University. Dr. Verschoor reports, "of the 87 companies where an ethics code was clearly stated, the average Market Value Added (MVA) was 2.5 times larger than for those not mentioning a code of ethics or conduct."

FIGURE 7.9

Accounts Receivable Ledger

NAME *Ann Anh*
ADDRESS *8913 South Hampton Road, Dallas, Texas 75232-6002*

DATE		DESCRIPTION	POST. REF.	DEBIT	CREDIT	BALANCE
2019						
Jan.	1	Balance	✓			432 00
	3	Sales Slip 1101	S1	702 00		1134 00
	7		CR1		432 00	702 00
	31	Sales Slip 1110	S1	270 00		972 00

NAME *Cathy Ball*
ADDRESS *7517 Woodrow Wilson Lane, Dallas, Texas 75267-6205*

DATE		DESCRIPTION	POST. REF.	DEBIT	CREDIT	BALANCE
2019						
Jan.	8	Sales Slip 1102	S1	648 00		648 00

(continued)

FIGURE 7.9

(continued)

NAME *Vickie Bowman*
ADDRESS *1712 Red Bird Lane, Dallas, Texas 75267-6502*

DATE		DESCRIPTION	POST. REF.	DEBIT	CREDIT	BALANCE
2019						
Jan.	1	Balance	✓			270 00
	11		CR1		270 00	– 0 –

NAME *Linda Carter*
ADDRESS *1819 Belt Line Road, Dallas, Texas 75267-6318*

DATE		DESCRIPTION	POST. REF.	DEBIT	CREDIT	BALANCE
2019						
Jan.	1	Balance	✓			54 00
	21	Sales Slip 1106	S1	486 00		540 00
	25	CM 102	J1		486 00	54 00

NAME *Barbara Coe*
ADDRESS *1864 Elm Street, Dallas, Texas 75267-6205*

DATE		DESCRIPTION	POST. REF.	DEBIT	CREDIT	BALANCE
2019						
Jan.	1	Balance	✓			1 080 00
	11	Sales Slip 1103	S1	756 00		1 836 00
	13		CR1		540 00	1 296 00

NAME *Mesia Davis*
ADDRESS *1008 University Boulevard, Dallas, Texas 75267-6318*

DATE		DESCRIPTION	POST. REF.	DEBIT	CREDIT	BALANCE
2019						
Jan.	1	Balance	✓			216 00
	29	Sales Slip 1108	S1	1 080 00		1 296 00
	31		CR1		275 00	1 021 00

NAME *Kim Ramirez*
ADDRESS *5787 Valley View Lane, Dallas, Texas 75267-6318*

DATE		DESCRIPTION	POST. REF.	DEBIT	CREDIT	BALANCE
2019						
Jan.	1	Balance	✓			216 00
	28	Sales Slip 1107	S1	108 00		324 00
	31		CR1		108 00	216 00

FIGURE 7.9

(continued)

NAME *Amalia Rodriguez*

ADDRESS *8108 Sherman Drive, Dallas, Texas 75267-6205*

DATE		DESCRIPTION	POST. REF.	DEBIT	CREDIT	BALANCE
2019						
Jan.	1	Balance	✓			648 00
	15	Sales Slip 1104	S1	324 00		972 00

NAME *Alma Sanchez*

ADDRESS *1382 Clark Road, Dallas, Texas 75267-6205*

DATE		DESCRIPTION	POST. REF.	DEBIT	CREDIT	BALANCE
2019						
Jan.	1	Balance	✓			108 00
	16		CR1		108 00	–0–
	31	Sales Slip 1109	S1	972 00		972 00

NAME *Fred Wu*

ADDRESS *4640 Walnut Hill Lane, Dallas, Texas 75267-6205*

DATE		DESCRIPTION	POST. REF.	DEBIT	CREDIT	BALANCE
2019						
Jan.	1	Balance	✓			216 00
	18	Sales Slip 1105	S1	810 00		1026 00
	22		CR1		400 00	626 00
	23	CM 101	J1		162 00	464 00

Schedule of Accounts Receivable

>> 7-6 OBJECTIVE

Prepare a schedule of accounts receivable.

The use of an accounts receivable ledger does not eliminate the need for the ***Accounts Receivable*** account in the general ledger. This account remains in the general ledger and continues to appear on the balance sheet at the end of each fiscal period. However, the ***Accounts Receivable*** account is now considered a control account. A **control account** serves as a link between a subsidiary ledger and the general ledger. Its balance summarizes the balances of its related accounts in the subsidiary ledger.

At the end of each month, after all the postings have been made from the sales journal, the cash receipts journal, and the general journal to the accounts receivable ledger, the balances in the accounts receivable ledger must be proved against the balance of the ***Accounts Receivable*** general ledger account. First a **schedule of accounts receivable,** which lists the subsidiary ledger account balances, is prepared. The total of the schedule is compared with the balance of the ***Accounts Receivable*** account. If the two figures are not equal, errors must be located and corrected.

On January 31, the accounts receivable ledger at Maxx-Out Sporting Goods contains the accounts shown in Figure 7.9. To prepare a schedule of accounts receivable, the names of all customers with account balances are listed with the amount of their unpaid balances. Next the figures are added to find the total owed to the business by its credit customers.

Best Buy Co., Inc., reported accounts receivable of approximately $1.2 billion at January 30, 2016.

FIGURE 7.10

Schedule of Accounts Receivable and the Accounts Receivable Account

Maxx-Out Sporting Goods
Schedule of Accounts Receivable
January 31, 2019

Ann Anh	972.00
Cathy Ball	648.00
Linda Carter	54.00
Barbara Coe	1296.00
Mesia Davis	1021.00
Kim Ramirez	216.00
Amalia Rodriguez	972.00
Alma Sanchez	972.00
Fred Wu	464.00
Total	6615.00

ACCOUNT *Accounts Receivable* ACCOUNT NO. *111*

DATE		DESCRIPTION	POST. REF.	DEBIT	CREDIT	BALANCE DEBIT	BALANCE CREDIT
2019							
Jan.	1	Balance	✓			3240.00	
	23		J1		162.00	3078.00	
	25		J1		486.00	2592.00	
	31		S1	6156.00		8748.00	
	31		CR1		2133.00	6615.00	

A comparison of the total of the schedule of accounts receivable prepared at Maxx-Out Sporting Goods on January 31 and the balance of the ***Accounts Receivable*** account in the general ledger shows that the two figures are the same, as shown in Figure 7.10. The posting reference CR1 refers to the cash receipts journal, which is discussed in Chapter 9.

In addition to providing a proof of the subsidiary ledger, the schedule of accounts receivable serves another function. It reports information about the firm's accounts receivable at the end of the month. Management can review the schedule to see exactly how much each customer owes.

Section 2 Self Review

QUESTIONS

1. What are net sales?
2. What is a sales return? What is a sales allowance?
3. Which accounts are kept in the accounts receivable ledger?

EXERCISES

4. Where would you report net sales?
   a. sales general ledger account
   b. general journal
   c. income statement
   d. sales journal
5. Which of the following general ledger accounts would appear in a sales returns and allowances journal?
   a. ***Sales Returns and Allowances, Sales Tax Payable, Accounts Receivable***
   b. ***Sales Returns and Allowances, Sales, Accounts Receivable***
   c. ***Sales Returns, Sales Allowances, Sales***

ANALYSIS

6. Draw a diagram showing the relationship between the accounts receivable ledger, the schedule of accounts receivable, and the general ledger.

Answers to Section 2 Self Review are on page 239.)

Section 3

SECTION OBJECTIVES	TERMS TO LEARN
>> 7-7 Compute trade discounts. WHY IT'S IMPORTANT Trade discounts allow for flexible pricing structures. >> 7-8 Record credit card sales in appropriate journals. WHY IT'S IMPORTANT Credit cards are widely used in merchandising transactions. >> 7-9 Prepare the state sales tax return. WHY IT'S IMPORTANT Businesses are legally responsible for accurately reporting and remitting sales taxes.	charge-account sales invoice list price net price open-account credit trade discount wholesale business

Special Topics in Merchandising

Merchandisers have many accounting concerns. These include pricing, credit, and sales taxes.

Credit Sales for a Wholesale Business

The operations of Maxx-Out Sporting Goods are typical of those of many retail businesses—businesses that sell goods and services directly to individual consumers. In contrast, a **wholesale business** is a manufacturer or distributor of goods that sells to retailers or large consumers such as hotels and hospitals. The basic procedures used by wholesalers to handle sales and accounts receivable are the same as those used by retailers. However, many wholesalers offer cash discounts and trade discounts, which are not commonly found in retail operations.

The procedures used in connection with cash discounts are examined in Chapter 9. The handling of trade discounts is described here.

COMPUTING TRADE DISCOUNTS

>> 7-7 OBJECTIVE
Compute trade discounts.

A wholesale business offers goods to trade customers at less than retail prices. This price adjustment is based on the volume purchased by trade customers and takes the form of a **trade discount,** which is a reduction from the **list price**—the established retail price. There may be a single trade discount or a series of discounts for each type of goods. The **net price** (list price less all trade discounts) is the amount the wholesaler records in its sales journal.

The same goods may be offered to different customers at different trade discounts, depending on the size of the order and the costs of selling to the various types of customers.

Single Trade Discount Suppose the list price of goods is $1,500 and the trade discount is 40 percent. The amount of the discount is $600, and the net price to be shown on the invoice and recorded in the sales journal is $900.

List price	$1,500
Less 40% discount ($1,500 × 0.40)	600
Invoice price	$ 900

important!

Trade Discounts

The amount of sales revenue recorded is the list price minus the trade discount.

important!

Special Journal Format

Special journals such as the sales journal can vary in format from company to company.

Series of Trade Discounts If the list price of goods is $1,500 and the trade discount is quoted in a series such as 25 and 15 percent, a different net price will result.

List price	$1,500.00
Less first discount ($1,500 × 0.25)	375.00
Difference	$1,125.00
Less second discount ($1,125 × 0.15)	168.75
Invoice price	$ 956.25

USING A SALES JOURNAL FOR A WHOLESALE BUSINESS

Since sales taxes apply only to retail transactions, a wholesale business does not need to account for such taxes. Its sales journal may therefore be as simple as the one illustrated in Figure 7.11. This sales journal has a single amount column. The total of this column is posted to the general ledger at the end of the month as a debit to the ***Accounts Receivable*** account and a credit to the ***Sales*** account (Figure 7.12). During the month, the individual entries in the sales journal are posted to the customer accounts in the accounts receivable ledger.

Wholesale businesses issue invoices. An **invoice** is a customer billing for merchandise bought on credit. Copies of the invoices are used to enter the transactions in the sales journal.

The next merchandising topic, credit policies, applies to both wholesalers and retailers. The discussion in this textbook focuses on credit policies and accounting for retail firms.

FIGURE 7.11

Wholesaler's Sales Journal

SALES JOURNAL PAGE 1

	DATE		INVOICE NO.	CUSTOMER'S ACCOUNT DEBITED	POST. REF.	ACCOUNTS RECEIVABLE DR. SALES CR.	
1	2019						1
2	Jan.	3	7099	Gabbert's Hardware Company		18600 00	2
3							3
25		31	7151	Neal's Department Store		4200 00	25
26		31		Total		40875 00	26
27						(111/401)	27
28							28

FIGURE 7.12

General Ledger Accounts

ACCOUNT *Accounts Receivable* ACCOUNT NO. 111

DATE		DESCRIPTION	POST. REF.	DEBIT	CREDIT	BALANCE DEBIT	BALANCE CREDIT
2019							
Jan.	1	Balance	✓			46700 00	
	31		S1	40875 00		87575 00	

ACCOUNT *Sales* ACCOUNT NO. 401

DATE		DESCRIPTION	POST. REF.	DEBIT	CREDIT	BALANCE DEBIT	BALANCE CREDIT
2019							
Jan.	31		S1		40875 00		40875 00

Credit Policies

The use of credit is considered to be one of the most important factors in the rapid growth of modern economic systems. Sales on credit are made by large numbers of wholesalers and retailers of goods and by many professional people and service businesses. The assumption is that the volume of both sales and profits will increase if buyers are given a period of a month or more to pay for the goods or services they purchase.

However, the increase in profits a business expects when it grants credit will be realized only if each customer completes the transaction by paying for the goods or services purchased. If payment is not received, the expected profits become actual losses and the purpose for granting the credit is defeated. Business firms try to protect against the possibility of such losses by investigating a customer's credit record and ability to pay for purchases before allowing any credit to the customer.

Professional people such as doctors, lawyers, architects, and owners of small businesses like Maxx-Out Sporting Goods usually make their own decisions about granting credit. Such decisions may be based on personal judgment or on reports available from credit bureaus, information supplied by other creditors, and credit ratings supplied by national firms such as Dun & Bradstreet.

Dun & Bradstreet is a leader in providing credit information. The company's common stock trades on the New York Stock Exchange. Its ticker symbol is DNB. For the year ended December 31, 2015, the company reported revenues of $1.6 billion.

Larger businesses maintain a credit department to determine the amounts and types of credit that should be granted to customers. In addition to using credit data supplied by institutions, the credit department may obtain financial statements and related reports from customers who have applied for credit. This information is analyzed to help determine the maximum amount of credit that may be granted and suitable credit terms for the customer. Financial statements that have been audited by certified public accountants are used extensively by credit departments.

Even though the credit investigation is thorough, some accounts receivable become uncollectible. Unexpected business developments, errors of judgment, incorrect financial data, and many other causes may lead to defaults in payments by customers. Experienced managers know that some uncollectible accounts are to be expected in normal business operations and that limited losses indicate that a firm's credit policies are sound. Provisions for such limited losses from uncollectible accounts are usually made in budgets and other financial projections.

Each business must develop credit policies that achieve maximum sales with minimum losses from uncollectible accounts:

- A credit policy that is too tight results in a low level of losses at the expense of increases in sales volume.
- A credit policy that is too lenient may result in increased sales volume accompanied by a high level of losses.

Good judgment based on knowledge and experience must be used to achieve a well-balanced credit policy.

Different types of credit have evolved with the growing economy and changing technology. The different types of credit require different accounting treatments.

ACCOUNTING FOR DIFFERENT TYPES OF CREDIT SALES

The most common types of credit sales are:

- open-account credit,
- business credit cards,
- bank credit cards,
- cards issued by credit card companies.

Open-Account Credit The form of credit most commonly offered by professional people and small businesses permits the sale of services or goods to the customer with the understanding that the amount is to be paid at a later date. This type of arrangement is called **open-account credit.** It is usually granted on the basis of personal acquaintance or knowledge of the customer. However, formal credit checks may also be used. The amount involved in each transaction is usually small, and payment is expected within 30 days or on receipt of a monthly statement. Open-account sales are also referred to as **charge-account sales.**

Maxx-Out Sporting Goods uses the open-account credit arrangement. Sales transactions are recorded as debits to the ***Accounts Receivable*** account and credits to the ***Sales*** account. Collections on account are recorded as debits to the ***Cash*** account and credits to the ***Accounts Receivable*** account.

Business Credit Cards Many retail businesses, especially large ones such as department store chains and gasoline companies, provide their own credit cards (sometimes called charge cards) to customers who have established credit. Whenever a sale is completed using a business credit card, a sales slip is prepared in the usual manner. Then the sales slip and the credit card are placed in a mechanical device that prints the customer's name, account number, and other data on all copies of the sales slip. Many companies use computerized card readers and sales registers that print out a sales slip with the customer information and a line for the customer's signature. Some businesses require that the salesclerk contact the credit department by telephone or computer terminal to verify the customer's credit status before completing the transaction.

Business credit card sales are similar to open-account credit sales. A business credit card sale is recorded as:

- a debit to ***Accounts Receivable,***
- a credit to a revenue account such as ***Sales.***

A customer payment is recorded as:

- a debit to ***Cash,***
- a credit to ***Accounts Receivable.***

Bank Credit Cards Retailers can provide credit while minimizing or avoiding the risk of losses from uncollectible accounts by accepting bank credit cards. The most widely accepted bank credit cards are MasterCard and Visa. Many banks participate in one or both of these credit card programs, and other banks have their own credit cards. Bank credit cards are issued to consumers directly by banks.

A business may participate in these credit card programs by meeting conditions set by the bank. Banks review such factors as:

- The business's financial history.
- The industry in which the business operates.
- The type of business: online, physical store, or both.
- Any past merchant account history.

A credit card sale is processed when the customer inserts the chip end of the credit card into an electronic terminal (see Figure 7.13). The terminal transmits information to the bank or credit card company using an Internet connection.

When a business makes a sale to a customer using a bank credit card, it acquires an asset that can be converted into cash immediately without responsibility for later collection from the customer. In most cases, the bank deposits the cash from the sale into the business's bank account the same day.

Banks charge the business a fee, called a *discount,* for processing the sale. The discount is usually between 1.5 and 4 percent of the amount charged. Depending on the arrangements that have been made, the bank will deduct the discount and immediately credit the depositor's checking account with the net amount of the sale, or it will credit the depositor's checking account for the full amount of the sale and deduct the discount at the end of the month. If the second procedure is used, the total discount for the month's sales will appear on the bank statement.

The bank is responsible for collecting from the cardholder. If any amounts are uncollectible, the bank sustains the loss. For the retailer, bank credit card sales are like cash sales. The

© Africa Studio/Shutterstock, RF

FIGURE 7.13

Credit Card Reader

FIGURE 7.14

Credit Card Receipt

MAXX-OUT SPORTING GOODS
DALLAS, TX

****

SWEATSUIT	$125.00
SALES TAX	$10.00
TOTAL	$135.00
NAME :	
CONNORS/JAMES	
TYPE :	
PURCHASED	SWIPED
VISTA	
************222	
INVOICE #	08789798234
AUTH CODE :	12345
DATE :	01/28/19
TIME	17:02

James Connors

Signature :

accounting procedures for such sales are therefore quite similar to the accounting procedures for cash sales, which will be discussed in Chapter 9. If the business is billed once each month for the bank's discount, the total amount involved in the daily deposit of the credit card sales slips is debited to ***Cash*** and credited to ***Sales.***

Credit Card Companies Credit cards such as American Express and Diners Club are issued by business firms or subsidiaries of business firms that are operated for the special purpose of handling credit card transactions. The potential cardholder must submit an application and pay an annual fee to the credit card company. If the credit references are satisfactory, the credit card is issued. It is normally reissued at one-year intervals so long as the company's credit experience with the cardholder remains satisfactory.

Hotels, restaurants, airline companies, many types of retail stores, and a wide variety of other businesses accept these credit cards. When making sales to cardholders, sellers usually prepare their own sales slip or bill and then complete a special sales slip required by the credit card company (see Figure 7.14). As with the sales slips for bank credit cards, the forms must be imprinted with the identifying data on the customer's card and signed by the customer. Such sales slips are sometimes referred to as *sales invoices, sales drafts,* or *sales vouchers.* The term used varies from one credit card company to another.

The seller acquires an account receivable from the credit card company rather than from the customer. At approximately one-month intervals, the credit card company bills the cardholders for all sales slips it has acquired during the period. It is the responsibility of the credit card company to collect from the cardholders.

>> 7-8 OBJECTIVE
Record credit card sales in appropriate journals.

ACCOUNTING FOR CREDIT CARD SALES

The procedure used to account for credit card sales is similar to the procedure for recording open-account credit sales. However, the account receivable is with the credit card company, not with the cardholders who buy the goods or services.

There are two basic methods of recording these sales. Businesses that have few transactions with credit card companies normally debit the amounts of such sales to the usual ***Accounts Receivable*** account in the general ledger and credit them to the same ***Sales*** account that is used for cash sales and other types of credit sales. An individual account for each credit card company is set up in the accounts receivable subsidiary ledger. This method of recording sales is shown in Figure 7.15.

Payment from a credit card company is recorded in the cash receipts journal, a procedure discussed in Chapter 9. Fees charged by the credit card companies for processing these sales are debited to an account called ***Discount Expense on Credit Card Sales.*** For example, assume that American Express charges a 7 percent discount fee on the sale charged by Wilson Davis on January 3 and remits the balance to the firm. This transaction would be recorded in the cash receipts journal by debiting ***Cash*** for $502.20, debiting ***Discount Expense on Credit Card Sales*** for $37.80, and crediting ***Accounts Receivable*** for $540.00.

Firms that do a large volume of business with credit card companies may debit all such sales to a special ***Accounts Receivable from Credit Card Companies*** account in the general ledger, thus separating this type of receivable from the accounts receivable resulting from open-account credit sales. A special account called ***Sales—Credit Card Companies*** is credited for the revenue from these transactions. Figure 7.16 shows how the necessary entries are made in the sales journal.

FIGURE 7.15
Recording Credit Card Company Sales

SALES JOURNAL PAGE 17

DATE		SALES SLIP NO.	CUSTOMER'S ACCOUNT DEBITED	POST. REF.	ACCOUNTS RECEIVABLE DEBIT	SALES TAX PAYABLE CREDIT	SALES CREDIT
2019							
Jan.	3	533	American Express		540 00	40 00	500 00
			(Wilson Davis)				
	11	651	MasterCard		216 00	16 00	200 00
			(Teresa Logan)				

FIGURE 7.16 **Recording Sales for Accounts Receivable from Credit Card Companies**

SALES JOURNAL PAGE 7

DATE		SALES SLIP NO.	CUSTOMER'S ACCOUNT DEBITED	POST. REF.	ACCOUNTS RECEIVABLE DEBIT	ACCT. REC.—CREDIT CARD COMPANIES DEBIT	SALES TAX PAYABLE CREDIT	SALES CREDIT	SALES—CREDIT CARD COMPANIES CREDIT
2019									
Jan.	3		Summary of credit card sales/						
			American Express			9720 00	720 00		9000 00
	11		Summary of credit card sales/						
			MasterCard			5400 00	400 00		5000 00
	31		Totals			48600 00	3600 00		45000 00
						(114)	(231)		(404)

Sales Taxes

Many cities and states impose a tax on retail sales. Sales taxes imposed by city and state governments vary. However, the procedures used to account for these taxes are similar.

A sales tax may be levied on all retail sales, but often certain items are exempt. In most cases, the amount of the sales tax is stated separately and then added to the retail price of the merchandise.

In November 2012, California voters approved an initiative to raise the state sales tax by 0.25% through December 31, 2016.

The retailer is required to collect sales tax from customers, make periodic (usually monthly) reports to the taxing authority, and pay the taxes due when the reports are filed. The government may allow the retailer to retain part of the tax as compensation for collecting it.

PREPARING THE STATE SALES TAX RETURN

>> 7-9 OBJECTIVE

Prepare the state sales tax return.

At the end of each month, after the accounts have all been posted, Maxx-Out Sporting Goods prepares the sales tax return. The information required for the monthly return comes from the accounting data of the current month. Three accounts are involved: ***Sales Tax Payable, Sales,*** and ***Sales Returns and Allowances.*** In some states, the sales tax return is filed quarterly rather than monthly.

The procedures to file a sales tax return are similar to those used by Maxx-Out Sporting Goods on February 7 when it filed the monthly sales tax return for January with the state tax commissioner. The firm's sales are subject to an 8 percent state sales tax. To highlight the data needed, the January postings are shown in the ledger accounts in Figure 7.17.

FIGURE 7.17

Ledger Account Postings for Sales Tax

ACCOUNT *Sales Tax Payable* ACCOUNT NO. *231*

DATE		DESCRIPTION	POST. REF.	DEBIT	CREDIT	BALANCE DEBIT	BALANCE CREDIT
2019							
Jan.	1	Balance	✓				756 00
	11		CP1	756 00			–0–
	23		J1	12 00		12 00	
	25		J1	36 00		48 00	
	31		S1		456 00		408 00
	31		CR1		1,800 00		2,208 00

ACCOUNT *Sales* ACCOUNT NO. *401*

DATE		DESCRIPTION	POST. REF.	DEBIT	CREDIT	BALANCE DEBIT	BALANCE CREDIT
2019							
Jan.	31		S1		5,700 00		5,700 00
	31		CR1		22,500 00		28,200 00

ACCOUNT *Sales Returns and Allowances* ACCOUNT NO. *451*

DATE		DESCRIPTION	POST. REF.	DEBIT	CREDIT	BALANCE DEBIT	BALANCE CREDIT
2019							
Jan.	23		J1	150 00		150 00	
	25		J1	450 00		600 00	

THE BOTTOM LINE
Retail Sales

Income Statement	
Revenue	↑ 27,600
Net Income	↑ 27,600

Balance Sheet	
Assets	↑ 29,808.00
Liabilities	↑ 2,208.00
Equity	↑ 27,600.00

Using these figures as a basis, the amount of the firm's taxable gross sales for January is determined as follows:

Cash Sales	$22,500
Credit Sales	5,700
Total Sales	$28,200
Less Sales Returns and Allowances	600
Taxable Gross Sales for January	$27,600

The 8 percent sales tax on the gross sales of $27,600 amounts to $2,208.00. Note that the firm's increase in assets (***Cash*** and ***Accounts Receivable***) is equal to sales revenue plus the sales tax liability on that revenue.

In the state where Maxx-Out Sporting Goods is located, a retailer who files the sales tax return (see Figure 7.19) on time and who pays the tax when it is due is entitled to a discount. The discount is intended to compensate the retailer, at least in part, for acting as a collection agent for the government. The discount rate depends on the amount of tax to be paid. For amounts over $1,000, the rate is 1 percent of the total tax due. For Maxx-Out Sporting Goods, the discount for January is determined as follows:

Taxable Gross Sales for January	$27,600.00
8% Sales Tax Rate	× 0.08
Sales Tax Due	$ 2,208.00
1% Discount Rate	× 0.01
Discount	$ 22.08
Sales Tax Due	$ 2,208.00
Discount	(22.08)
Net Sales Tax Due	$ 2,185.92

The firm sends a check for the net sales tax due with the sales tax return. The accounting entry made to record this payment includes a debit to ***Sales Tax Payable*** and a credit to ***Cash*** (for $2,185.92 in this case). After the amount of the payment is posted, the balance in the ***Sales Tax Payable*** account should be equal to the discount, as shown in Figure 7.18. Slight differences can arise because the tax collected at the time of the sale is determined by a tax bracket method that can give results slightly more or less than the final computations on the tax return.

FIGURE 7.18

Effect of Paying Sales Tax

ACCOUNT *Sales Tax Payable* ACCOUNT NO. *231*

DATE		DESCRIPTION	POST. REF.	DEBIT	CREDIT	BALANCE DEBIT	BALANCE CREDIT
2019							
Jan.	*1*	*Balance*	✓				*756 00*
	11		*CP1*	*756 00*			*–0–*
	23		*J1*	*12 00*		*12 00*	
	25		*J1*	*36 00*		*48 00*	
	31		*S1*		*456 00*		*408 00*
	31		*CR1*		*1800 00*		*2208 00*
Feb.	*6*		*CP1*	*2185 92*			*22 08*

Tax payment → (Debit 2185 92)

Amount of discount → (Balance Credit 22 08)

FIGURE 7.19

State Sales Tax Return

SALES TAX RETURN

ALWAYS REFER TO THIS NUMBER WHEN WRITING THE DIVISION → LICENSE NUMBER *217539*

—IMPORTANT— ANY CHANGE IN OWNERSHIP REQUIRES A NEW LICENSE: NOTIFY THIS DIVISION IMMEDIATELY.

This return DUE on the 1st day of month following period covered by the return, and becomes DELINQUENT on the 21st day.

37-9462315
FED. E.I. NO. OR S.S NO.

STATE TAX COMMISSION
SALES AND USE TAX DIVISION
DRAWER 20
CAPITAL CITY, STATE 78711
RETURN REQUESTED

January 31, 2019
—Sales for period ending—

MAKE ALL REMITTANCES PAYABLE TO STATE TAX COMMISSIOIN DO NOT SEND CASH STAMPS NOT ACCEPTED

OWNER'S NAME AND LOCATION

Maxx-Out Sporting Goods
2007 Trendsetter Lane
Dallas, Texas 75268-0967

COMPUTATION OF SALES TAX	For Taxpayer's Use	Do Not Use This Column
1. TOTAL Gross proceeds of sales or Gross Receipts (to include rentals)	27,600.00	
2. Add cost of personal property purchased on a RETAIL LICENSE FOR RESALE but USED BY YOU or YOUR EMPLOYEES, including GIFTS and PREMIUMS	–0–	
3. USE TAX—Add cost of personal property purchased outside of STATE for your use, storage, or consumption	–0–	
4. Total (Lines 1, 2, and 3)	27,600.00	
5. LESS ALLOWABLE DEDUCTIONS (Must be itemized on reverse side)	–0–	
6. Net taxable total (Line 4 minus Line 5)	27,600.00	
7. Sales and Use Tax Due (8% of Line 6)	2,208.00	
8. LESS TAXPAYER'S DISCOUNT—(Deductible only when amount of TAX due is not delinquent at time of payment) →	22.08	
IF LINE 7 IS LESS THAN $100.00 —DEDUCT 3% IF LINE 7 IS $100 BUT LESS THAN $1,000.00 —DEDUCT 2% IF LINE 7 IS $1,000.00 OR MORE —DEDUCT 1%		
9. NET AMOUNT OF TAX PAYABLE (Line 7 minus Line 8)	2,185.92	
Add the following penalty and interest if return or remittance is late. 10. Specific Penalty: 25% of tax $____ 11. Interest: 1/2 of 1% per month from due date until paid. $____ TOTAL PENALTY AND INTEREST →		
12. TOTAL TAX, PENALTY AND INTEREST	2,185.92	
13. Subtract credit memo No.		
14. TOTAL AMOUNT DUE (IF NO SALES MADE SO STATE)	2,185.92	

I certify that this return, including the accompanying schedules or statements, has been examined by me and to the best of my knowledge and belief, a true and complete return, made in good faith, for the period stated, pursuant to the provisions of the Code of Laws, 20–, and Acts Amendatory Thereto.

URGENT—SEE THAT LICENSE NUMBER IS ON RETURN

Max Ferraro
SIGNATURE

Owner
Owner, partner or title

February 7, 2019
Date

Division Use Only

Return must be signed by owner or if corporation, authorized person.

THE BOTTOM LINE
Discount on Sales Tax

Income Statement	
Misc. Income	↑ 22.08
Net Income	↑ 22.08

Balance Sheet	
Assets	No effect
Liabilities	↓ 22.08
Equity	↑ 22.08

If there is a balance in the ***Sales Tax Payable*** account after the sales tax liability is satisfied, the balance is transferred to an account called ***Miscellaneous Income*** by a general journal entry. This entry consists of a debit to ***Sales Tax Payable*** and a credit to ***Miscellaneous Income.***

RECORDING SALES TAX IN THE SALES ACCOUNT

In some states, retailers can credit the entire sales price plus tax to the ***Sales*** account. At the end of each month or quarter, they must remove from the ***Sales*** account the amount of tax included and transfer that amount to the ***Sales Tax Payable*** account. Assume that during January a retailer whose sales are all taxable sells merchandise for a total price of $20,250, which includes an 8 percent tax. The entry to record these sales is summarized in general journal form shown here.

GENERAL JOURNAL PAGE 4

	DATE		DESCRIPTION	POST. REF.	DEBIT	CREDIT	
1	2019						1
2	Jan.	31	Accounts Receivable	111	20 250 00		2
3			Sales	401		20 250 00	3
4			To record total sales and				4
5			sales tax collected during				5
6			the month				6
7							7

At the end of the month, the retailer must transfer the sales tax from the ***Sales*** account to the ***Sales Tax Payable*** account. The first step in the transfer process is to determine the amount of tax involved. The sales tax payable is computed as follows.

MANAGERIAL IMPLICATIONS <<

CREDIT SALES

- Credit sales are a major source of revenue in many businesses, and accounts receivable represent a major asset.
- Management needs up-to-date and correct information about both sales and accounts receivable in order to monitor the financial health of the firm.
- Special journals save time and effort and reduce the cost of accounting work.
- In a retail firm that must handle sales tax, the sales journal and the cash receipts journal provide a convenient method of recording the amounts owed for sales tax.
  - When the data is posted to the Sales Tax Payable account in the general ledger, the firm has a complete and systematic record that speeds the completion of the periodic sales tax return.
  - The firm has detailed proof of its sales tax figures in the case of a tax audit.
- An accounts receivable subsidiary ledger provides management and the credit department with up-to-date information about the balances owed by all customers.
  - This information is useful in controlling credit and collections.
  - Detailed information helps in evaluating the effectiveness of credit policies.
  - Management must keep a close watch on the promptness of customer payments because much of the cash needed for day-to-day operations usually comes from payments on accounts receivable.
- A well-balanced credit policy helps increase sales volume but also keeps losses from uncollectible accounts at an acceptable level.
- Retailers are liable for any sales taxes not collected. This situation can be avoided with an efficient control system.

THINKING CRITICALLY

What are some possible consequences of out-of-date accounts receivable records?

Sales + tax	= \$20,250
100% of sales + 8% of sales	= \$20,250
108% of sales	= \$20,250
Sales	= \$20,250/1.08
Sales	= \$18,750
Tax	= \$18,750 × 0.08 = \$1,500

The firm then makes the following entry to transfer the liability from the ***Sales*** account.

GENERAL JOURNAL PAGE 4

	DATE		DESCRIPTION	POST. REF.	DEBIT	CREDIT	
1	2019						1
8	Jan.	31	Sales	401	1 5 0 0 00		8
9			Sales Tax Payable	231		1 5 0 0 00	9
10			To transfer sales tax				10
11			payable from the Sales				11
12			account to the liability				12
13			account				13
14							14
15							15

The retailer in this example originally recorded the entire sales price plus tax in the ***Sales*** account. The sales tax was transferred to the ***Sales Tax Payable*** account at the end of the month.

Section 3 Self Review

QUESTIONS

1. What are four types of credit sales?
2. What is the difference between list price and net price?
3. What account is used to record sales tax owed by a business to a city or state?

EXERCISES

4. A company that buys \$4,000 of goods from a wholesaler offering trade discounts of 20 and 10 percent will pay what amount for the goods?
   a. \$1,760
   b. \$2,800
   c. \$2,880
   d. \$2,780
5. If a wholesale business offers a trade discount of 35 percent on a sale of \$7,200, what is the amount of the discount?
   a. \$240
   b. \$252
   c. \$2,400
   c. \$2,520

ANALYSIS

6. What factors would you consider in deciding whether or not to extend credit to a customer?

Answers to Section 3 Self Review are on page 239.)

7 Chapter REVIEW Chapter Summary

The nature of the operations of a business, the volume of its transactions, and other factors influence the design of an accounting system. In this chapter, you have learned about the use of special journals and subsidiary ledgers suitable for a merchandising business. These additional journals and ledgers increase the efficiency of recording credit transactions and permit the division of labor.

Learning Objectives

7-1 Record credit sales in a sales journal.

The sales journal is used to record credit sales transactions, usually on a daily basis. For sales transactions that include sales tax, the sales tax liability is recorded at the time of the sale to ensure that company records reflect the appropriate amount of sales tax liability.

7-2 Post from the sales journal to the general ledger accounts.

At the end of each month, the sales journal is totaled, proved, and ruled. Column totals are then posted to the general ledger. Using a sales journal rather than a general journal to record sales saves the time and effort of posting individual entries to the general ledger during the month.

7-3 Post from the sales journal to the customers' accounts in the accounts receivable subsidiary ledger.

The accounts of individual credit customers are kept in a subsidiary ledger called the accounts receivable ledger. Daily postings are made to this ledger from the sales journal, the cash receipts journal, and the general journal or the sales returns and allowances journal. The current balance of a customer's account is computed after each posting so that the amount owed is known at all times.

7-4 Record sales returns and allowances in the general journal.

Sales returns and allowances are usually debited to a contra revenue account. A firm with relatively few sales returns and allowances could use the general journal to record these transactions.

7-5 Post sales returns and allowances.

Sales returns and allowances transactions must be posted to the general ledger and to the appropriate accounts receivable subsidiary ledgers. The balance of the ***Sales Returns and Allowances*** account is subtracted from the balance of the ***Sales*** account to show net sales on the income statement.

7-6 Prepare a schedule of accounts receivable.

Each month a schedule of accounts receivable is prepared. It is used to prove the subsidiary ledger against the ***Accounts Receivable*** account. It also reports the amounts due from credit customers.

7-7 Compute trade discounts.

Wholesale businesses often offer goods to trade customers at less than retail prices. Trade discounts are expressed as a percentage off the list price. Multiply the list price by the percentage trade discount offered to compute the dollar amount.

7-8 Record credit card sales in appropriate journals.

Credit sales are common, and different credit arrangements are used. Businesses that have few transactions with credit card companies normally record these transactions in the sales journal by debiting the usual ***Accounts Receivable*** account in the general ledger and crediting the same ***Sales*** account that is used for cash sales.

7-9 Prepare the state sales tax return.

In states and cities that have a sales tax, the retailer must prepare a sales tax return and send the total tax collected to the taxing authority.

7-10 Define the accounting terms new to this chapter.

Glossary

Accounts receivable ledger (p. 203) A subsidiary ledger that contains credit customer accounts

Charge-account sales (p. 214) Sales made through the use of open-account credit or one of various types of credit cards

Contra revenue account (p. 205) An account with a debit balance, which is contrary to the normal balance for a revenue account

Control account (p. 209) An account that links a subsidiary ledger and the general ledger since its balance summarizes the balances of the accounts in the subsidiary ledger

Credit memorandum (p. 204) A note verifying that a customer's account is being reduced by the amount of a sales return or sales allowance plus any sales tax that may have been involved

Invoice (p. 212) A customer billing for merchandise bought on credit

List price (p. 211) An established retail price

Manufacturing business (p. 196) A business that sells goods that it has produced

Merchandise inventory (p. 196) The stock of goods a merchandising business keeps on hand

Merchandising business (p. 196) A business that sells goods purchased for resale

Net price (p. 211) The list price less all trade discounts

Net sales (p. 207) The difference between the balance in the ***Sales*** account and the balance in the ***Sales Returns and Allowances*** account

Open-account credit (p. 214) A system that allows the sale of services or goods with the understanding that payment will be made at a later date

Periodic inventory system (p. 196) An inventory system in which the merchandise inventory balance is only updated when a physical inventory is taken

Perpetual inventory system (p. 196) An inventory system that tracks the inventories on hand at all times

Retail business (p. 196) A business that sells directly to individual consumers

Sales allowance (p. 204) A reduction in the price originally charged to customers for goods or services

Sales journal (p. 197) A special journal used to record sales of merchandise on credit

Sales return (p. 204) A firm's acceptance of a return of goods from a customer

Sales Returns and Allowances (p. 205) A contra revenue account where sales returns and sales allowances are recorded; sales returns and allowances are subtracted from sales to determine net sales

Schedule of accounts receivable (p. 209) A listing of all balances of the accounts in the accounts receivable subsidiary ledger

Service business (p. 196) A business that sells services

Special journal (p. 196) A journal used to record only one type of transaction

Subsidiary ledger (p. 196) A ledger dedicated to accounts of a single type and showing details to support a general ledger account

Trade discount (p. 211) A reduction from list price

Wholesale business (p. 211) A business that manufactures or distributes goods to retail businesses or large consumers such as hotels and hospitals

Comprehensive **Self Review**

1. Name the two different time periods usually covered in sales tax returns.
2. What is a control account?
3. Why does a small merchandising business usually need a more complex set of financial records and statements than a small service business?
4. Why is it useful for a firm to have an accounts receivable ledger?
5. Explain how service, merchandising, and manufacturing businesses differ from each other.

(Answers to Comprehensive Self Review are on page 240.)

Discussion Questions

1. How are the net sales for an accounting period determined?
2. What purposes does the schedule of accounts receivable serve?
3. How do retail and wholesale businesses differ?
4. Why is a sales return or allowance usually recorded in a special ***Sales Returns and Allowances*** account rather than being debited to the ***Sales*** account?
5. How is a multicolumn special journal proved at the end of each month?
6. What kind of account is ***Sales Returns and Allowances***?
7. The sales tax on a credit sale is not collected from the customer immediately. When is this tax usually entered in a firm's accounting records? What account is used to record this tax?
8. In a particular state, the sales tax rate is 5 percent of sales. The retailer is allowed to record both the selling price and the tax in the same account. Explain how to compute the sales tax due when this method is used.
9. What two methods are commonly used to record sales involving credit cards issued by credit card companies?
10. What procedure does a business use to collect amounts owed to it for sales on credit cards issued by credit card companies?
11. When a firm makes a sale involving a credit card issued by a credit card company, does the firm have an account receivable with the cardholder or with the credit card company?
12. What is the discount on credit card sales? What type of account is used to record this item?
13. Why are bank credit card sales similar to cash sales for a business?
14. What is open-account credit?
15. What is a trade discount? Why do some firms offer trade discounts to their customers?

APPLICATIONS

Exercises connect

Exercise 7.1
Objective 7-1

► Identifying the journal to record transactions.

The accounting system of Naturally Healthy Foods includes the journals listed below. Indicate the specific journal in which each of the transactions listed below would be recorded.

JOURNALS

Cash receipts journal
Cash payments journal
Sales journal
General journal
Purchases journal

DATE		TRANSACTIONS
May	1	Purchased merchandise on credit.
	2	Sold merchandise on credit.
	3	Accepted a return of merchandise from a credit customer.
	4	Sold merchandise for cash.
	5	Gave a $400 allowance for damaged merchandise.
	6	Received a payment on account from a credit customer.
	7	Issued a check to pay a creditor on account.
	8	Received an additional cash investment from the owner.

Identifying the accounts used to record sales and related transactions.

Exercise 7.2
Objective 7-1

The transactions below took place at Colorado Outdoor Adventures, a retail business that sells outdoor clothing and camping equipment. Indicate the numbers of the general ledger accounts that would be debited and credited to record each transaction.

GENERAL LEDGER ACCOUNTS

101	Cash	401	Sales
111	Accounts Receivable	451	Sales Returns and Allowances
231	Sales Tax Payable		

DATE		TRANSACTIONS
May	1	Sold merchandise on credit; the transaction involved sales tax.
	2	Received checks from credit customers on account.
	3	Accepted a return of merchandise from a credit customer; the original sale involved sales tax.
	4	Sold merchandise for cash; the transaction involved sales tax.
	5	Gave an allowance to a credit customer for damaged merchandise; the original sale involved sales tax.
	6	Provided a cash refund to a customer who returned merchandise; the original sale was made for cash and involved sales tax.

Recording credit sales.

Exercise 7.3
Objective 7-2

CONTINUING >>> Problem

The following transactions took place at Colorado Outdoor Adventures during June. Enter these transactions in a sales journal like the one shown in Figure 7.2. Use 18 as the page number for the sales journal.

DATE		TRANSACTIONS
June	1	Sold a tent and other items on credit to Bill Justin; issued Sales Slip 1101 for $600 plus sales tax of $48.
	2	Sold a backpack, an air mattress, and other items to Vanessa Chen; issued Sales Slip 1102 for $450 plus sales tax of $36.
	3	Sold a lantern, cooking utensils, and other items to Jim Salazar; issued Sales Slip 1103 for $375 plus sales tax of $30.

Recording sales returns and allowances.

Exercise 7.4
Objective 7-2

Record the general journal entries for the following transactions of Linens and Things that occurred in July. Use 15 as the page number for the general journal.

DATE		TRANSACTIONS
July	5	Accepted a return of damaged merchandise from Terri McDonald, a credit customer; issued Credit Memorandum 301 for $837, which includes sales tax of $62; the original sale was made on Sales Slip 1610 of June 30.
	21	Gave an allowance to Robert Lynch, a credit customer, for merchandise that was slightly damaged but usable; issued Credit Memorandum 302 for $1,026, which includes sales tax of $76; the original sale was made on Sales Slip 1663 of July 17.

Exercise 7.5
Objective 7-2

▶ Posting from the sales journal.

The sales journal for Charleston Company is shown below. Describe how the amounts would be posted to the general ledger accounts.

SALES JOURNAL PAGE 1

	DATE		SALES SLIP NO.	CUSTOMER'S ACCOUNT DEBITED	POST. REF.	ACCOUNTS RECEIVABLE DEBIT	SALES TAX PAYABLE CREDIT	SALES CREDIT	
1	2019								1
2	July	2	1101	Scott Cohen		540 00	40 00	500 00	2
3		7	1102	Julia Hoang		864 00	64 00	800 00	3
11		31	1110	Barbara Baxter		324 00	24 00	300 00	11
12		31		Totals		6 480 00	480 00	6 000 00	12
13						(111)	(231)	(401)	13
14									14

Exercise 7.6
Objective 7-7

▶ Computing a trade discount.

Vicente Wholesalers made sales using the following list prices and trade discounts. What amount will be recorded for each sale in the sales journal?

1. List price of $800 and trade discount of 20 percent
2. List price of $2,080 and trade discount of 40 percent
3. List price of $1,500 and trade discount of 25 percent

Exercise 7.7
Objective 7-7

▶ Computing a series of trade discounts.

Elegant Gardens, a wholesale firm, made sales using the following list prices and trade discounts. What amount will be recorded for each sale in the sales journal?

1. List price of $6,000 and trade discounts of 40 and 15 percent
2. List price of $7,300 and trade discounts of 25 and 8 percent
3. List price of $7,100 and trade discounts of 20 and 10 percent

Exercise 7.8
Objective 7-9

▶ Computing the sales tax due and recording its payment.

The balances of certain accounts of Brittany Corporation on April 30, 2019, were as follows:

Sales	$220,000
Sales Returns and Allowances	2,000

The firm's net sales are subject to a 6 percent sales tax. Prepare the general journal entry to record payment of the sales tax payable on April 30, 2019.

Exercise 7.9
Objective 7-6

▶ Preparing a schedule of accounts receivable.

The accounts receivable ledger for Country Barn Antiques follows below.

1. Prepare a schedule of accounts receivable as of January 31, 2019.
2. What should be the balance in the ***Accounts Receivable*** (control) account?

Exercise 7.10
Objective 7-5

▶ Posting sales returns and allowances.

Post the following journal entries to the appropriate ledger accounts. Assume the following account balances as of March 1, 2019:

Accounts Receivable (control account)	$1,688
Accounts Receivable—Cara Fountain	940
Accounts Receivable—Sadie Palmer	748

NAME *Cindy Anderson*
ADDRESS *917 Broadway, New York, NY 10018*

DATE		DESCRIPTION	POST. REF.	DEBIT	CREDIT	BALANCE
2019						
Jan.	1	Balance	✓			1 4 7 5 00
	2	Sales Slip 1801	S1	5 4 0 00		2 0 1 5 00

NAME *Edward Charleston*
ADDRESS *2022 5th Avenue, New York, NY 10018*

DATE		DESCRIPTION	POST. REF.	DEBIT	CREDIT	BALANCE
2019						
Jan.	1	Balance	✓			3 7 8 00
	27	Sales Slip 1824	S1	1 8 9 00		5 6 7 00
	31		CR1		1 8 4 00	3 8 3 00

NAME *Neal Feingold*
ADDRESS *98 Houston Street, New York, NY 10018*

DATE		DESCRIPTION	POST. REF.	DEBIT	CREDIT	BALANCE
2019						
Jan.	1	Balance	✓			3 2 4 00
	15	Sales Slip 1812	CR1		3 2 4 00	– 0 –
	31		S1	7 5 6 00		7 5 6 00

NAME *Don Peterson*
ADDRESS *5063 Park Avenue, New York, NY 10019*

DATE		DESCRIPTION	POST. REF.	DEBIT	CREDIT	BALANCE
2019						
Jan.	1	Balance	✓			6 4 8 00
	20	Sales Slip 1819	S1	2 1 6 00		8 6 4 00
	21		CR1		4 5 0 00	4 1 4 00
	22	Sales Slip 1822	S1	8 1 0 00		1 2 2 4 00

NAME *Maria Sanchez*
ADDRESS *2111 West 32nd Street, New York, NY 10019*

DATE		DESCRIPTION	POST. REF.	DEBIT	CREDIT	BALANCE
2019						
Jan.	1	Balance	✓			4 8 6 00
	31	Sales Slip 1810	S1	2 2 1 4 00		2 7 0 0 00

NAME *Nickie Wong*
ADDRESS *721 Lexington Avenue, New York, NY 10027*

DATE		DESCRIPTION	POST. REF.	DEBIT	CREDIT	BALANCE
2019						
Jan.	1	Balance	✓			2 3 7 6 00
	12		CR1		1 1 8 8 00	1 1 8 8 00
	17	Sales Slip 1817	S1	9 6 4 00		2 1 5 2 00

GENERAL JOURNAL PAGE 42

DATE		DESCRIPTION	POST. REF.	DEBIT	CREDIT
2019					
Mar.	14	Sales Returns and Allowances		300 00	
		Sales Tax Payable		24 00	
		Accounts Rec.—Cara Fountain			324 00
		Accepted return on defective			
		merchandise, Credit Memo			
		101; original sale of Feb. 23,			
		Sales Slip 1101			
	22	Sales Returns and Allowances		100 00	
		Sales Tax Payable		8 00	
		Accounts Rec.—Sadie Palmer			108 00
		Gave allowance for damaged			
		merchandise, Credit Memo			
		102; original sale Mar. 15,			
		Sales Slip 1150			

PROBLEMS

Problem Set A

Problem 7.1A
Objectives 7-1, 7-2

Recording credit sales and posting from the sales journal.

Superior Appliances is a retail store that sells household appliances. Merchandise sales are subject to an 8 percent sales tax. The firm's credit sales for July are listed below, along with the general ledger accounts used to record these sales. The balance shown for ***Accounts Receivable*** is for the beginning of the month.

DATE		TRANSACTIONS
July	1	Sold a dishwasher to John Martinez; issued Sales Slip 501 for $925 plus sales tax of $74.
	6	Sold a washer to Helen Thai; issued Sales Slip 502 for $1,875 plus sales tax of $150.
	11	Sold a high-definition television set to Richard Jones; issued Sales Slip 503 for $1,625 plus sales tax of $130.
	17	Sold an electric dryer to Mary Schneider; issued Sales Slip 504 for $1,275 plus sales tax of $102.
	23	Sold a trash compactor to Victoria Caramello; issued Sales Slip 505 for $800 plus sales tax of $64.
	27	Sold a home entertainment system to Jeff Budd; issued Sales Slip 506 for $1,725 plus sales tax of $138.
	29	Sold an electric range to Michelle Ly; issued Sales Slip 507 for $1,450 plus sales tax of $116.
	31	Sold a double oven to Peter McVay; issued Sales Slip 508 for $1,350 plus sales tax of $108.

INSTRUCTIONS

1. Open the general ledger accounts and enter the balance of ***Accounts Receivable*** for July 1, 2019.
2. Record the transactions in a sales journal like the one shown in Figure 7.4. Use 8 as the journal page number.
3. Total, prove, and rule the sales journal as of July 31.
4. Post the column totals from the sales journal to the proper general ledger accounts.

GENERAL LEDGER ACCOUNTS

111 Accounts Receivable, $34,500 Dr.
231 Sales Tax Payable
401 Sales

Analyze: What percentage of credit sales was for entertainment items?

Journalizing, posting, and reporting sales transactions.

◄ **Problem 7.2A**
Objectives 7-1, 7-2, 7-4

Towncenter Furniture specializes in modern living room and dining room furniture. Merchandise sales are subject to an 8 percent sales tax. The firm's credit sales and sales returns and allowances for February 2019 are reflected below, along with the general ledger accounts used to record these transactions. The balances shown are for the beginning of the month.

DATE		TRANSACTIONS
Feb.	1	Sold a living room sofa to Sun Yoo; issued Sales Slip 1615 for $4,790 plus sales tax of $383.20.
	5	Sold three recliners to Jacqueline Moore; issued Sales Slip 1616 for $2,350 plus sales tax of $188.
	9	Sold a dining room set to Hazel Tran; issued Sales Slip 1617 for $6,550 plus sales tax of $524.
	11	Accepted a return of one damaged recliner from Jacqueline Moore that was originally sold on Sales Slip 1616 of February 5; issued Credit Memorandum 702 for $1,026, which includes sales tax of $76.00.
	17	Sold living room tables and bookcases to Ann Brown; issued Sales Slip 1618 for $9,550 plus sales tax of $764.
	23	Sold eight dining room chairs to Domingo Salas; issued Sales Slip 1619 for $3,650 plus sales tax of $292.
	25	Gave Ann Brown an allowance for scratches on her bookcases; issued Credit Memorandum 703 for $702, which includes sales tax of $52; the bookcases were originally sold on Sales Slip 1618 of February 17.
	27	Sold a living room sofa and four chairs to Jose Saucedo; issued Sales Slip 1620 for $4,225 plus sales tax of $338.
	28	Sold a dining room table to Mimi Yuki; issued Sales Slip 1621 for $2,050 plus sales tax of $164.
	28	Sold a living room modular wall unit to Alan Baker; issued Sales Slip 1622 for $3,900 plus sales tax of $312.

INSTRUCTIONS

1. Open the general ledger accounts and enter the balances for February 1.
2. Record the transactions in a sales journal and in a general journal. Use 8 as the page number for the sales journal and 24 as the page number for the general journal.
3. Post the entries from the general journal to the general ledger.
4. Total, prove, and rule the sales journal as of February 28.

5. Post the column totals from the sales journal.
6. Prepare the heading and the Revenue section of the firm's income statement for the month ended February 28, 2019.

GENERAL LEDGER ACCOUNTS

111 Accounts Receivable, $16,636 Dr.
231 Sales Tax Payable, $7,270 Cr.
401 Sales
451 Sales Returns and Allowances

Analyze: Based on the beginning balance of the *Sales Tax Payable* account, what was the amount of net sales for January? (Hint: Sales tax returns are filed and paid to the state quarterly.)

Problem 7.3A

Objectives 7-1, 7-2, 7-3, 7-4, 7-6

Recording sales transactions, posting to the accounts receivable ledger, and preparing a schedule of accounts receivable.

The Elegant Table sells china, glassware, and other gift items that are subject to an 8 percent sales tax. The shop uses a general journal and a sales journal similar to those illustrated in this chapter.

DATE		TRANSACTIONS
Nov.	1	Sold china to Pauline Judge; issued Sales Slip 1001 for $1,750 plus $140 sales tax.
	5	Sold a brass serving tray to Janet Hutchison; issued Sales Slip 1002 for $2,350 plus $188 sales tax.
	6	Sold a vase to Charles Brown; issued Sales Slip 1003 for $950 plus $76 sales tax.
	10	Sold a punch bowl and glasses to Lisa Morgan; issued Sales Slip 1004 for $1,950 plus $156 sales tax.
	14	Sold a set of serving bowls to Dorothy Watts; issued Sales Slip 1005 for $800 plus $64 sales tax.
	17	Gave Lisa Morgan an allowance because of a broken glass discovered when unpacking the punch bowl and glasses sold on November 10, Sales Slip 1004; issued Credit Memorandum 102 for $162.00, which includes sales tax of $12.
	21	Sold a coffee table to Teresa Yu; issued Sales Slip 1006 for $3,450 plus $276 sales tax.
	24	Sold sterling silver teaspoons to Henry Okafor; issued Sales Slip 1007 for $850 plus $68 sales tax.
	25	Gave Teresa Yu an allowance for scratches on her coffee table sold on November 21, Sales Slip 1006; issued Credit Memorandum 103 for $378, which includes $28 in sales tax.
	30	Sold a clock to Elaine Brock; issued Sales Slip 1008 for $4,050 plus $324 sales tax.

INSTRUCTIONS

1. Record the transactions for November in the proper journal. Use 6 as the page number for the sales journal and 16 as the page number for the general journal.
2. Immediately after recording each transaction, post to the accounts receivable ledger.
3. Post the amounts from the general journal daily. Post the sales journal amount as a total at the end of the month.
4. Prepare a schedule of accounts receivable. Compare the balance of the ***Accounts Receivable*** control account with the total of the schedule.

Analyze: Which customer has the highest balance owed at November 30, 2016?

Recording sales transactions, posting to the accounts receivable ledger, and preparing a schedule of accounts receivable.

◀ **Problem 7.4A**
Objectives 7-1, 7-2, 7-3, 7-4, 7-6

Bella Floral Designs is a wholesale shop that sells flowers, plants, and plant supplies. The transactions shown below took place during January.

DATE		TRANSACTIONS
Jan.	3	Sold a floral arrangement to Thomas Florist; issued Invoice 1081 for $600.
	8	Sold potted plants to Carter Garden Supply; issued Invoice 1082 for $825.
	9	Sold floral arrangements to Thomasville Flower Shop; issued Invoice 1083 for $482.
	10	Sold corsages to Moore's Flower Shop; issued Invoice 1084 for $630.
	15	Gave Thomasville Flower Shop an allowance because of withered blossoms discovered in one of the floral arrangements sold on Invoice 1083 on January 9; issued Credit Memorandum 101 for $60.
	20	Sold table arrangements to Cedar Hill Floral Shop; issued Invoice 1085 for $580.
	22	Sold plants to Applegate Nursery; issued Invoice 1086 for $780.
	25	Sold roses to Moore's Flower Shop; issued Invoice 1087 for $437.
	27	Sold several floral arrangements to Thomas Florist; issued Invoice 1088 for $975.
	31	Gave Thomas Florist an allowance because of withered blossoms discovered in one of the floral arrangements sold on Invoice 1088 on January 27; issued Credit Memorandum 102 for $200.

INSTRUCTIONS

1. Record the transactions in the proper journal. Use 7 as the page number for the sales journal and 11 as the page number for the general journal.
2. Immediately after recording each transaction, post to the accounts receivable ledger.
3. Post the amounts from the general journal daily. Post the sales journal amount as a total at the end of the month.
4. Prepare a schedule of accounts receivable. Compare the balance of the ***Accounts Receivable*** control account with the total of the schedule.

Analyze: Damaged goods decreased sales by what dollar amount? By what percentage amount?

Problem Set B

Recording credit sales and posting from the sales journal.

◀ **Problem 7.1B**
Objectives 7-1, 7-2

Best Appliances is a retail store that sells household appliances. Merchandise sales are subject to an 8 percent sales tax. The firm's credit sales for June are listed below Instruction 4, along with the general ledger accounts used to record these sales. The balance shown for Accounts Receivable is for the beginning of the month.

INSTRUCTIONS

1. Open the general ledger accounts and enter the balance of ***Accounts Receivable*** for June 1.
2. Record the transactions in a sales journal like the one shown in Figure 7.4. Use 8 as the journal page number.

3. Total, prove, and rule the sales journal as of June 30.
4. Post the column totals from the sales journal to the proper general ledger accounts.

DATE		TRANSACTIONS
June	1	Sold a dishwasher to Omar Achmed; issued Sales Slip 201 for $550 plus sales tax of $44.
	6	Sold a washer to Gilbert Gomez; issued Sales Slip 202 for $925 plus sales tax of $74.
	11	Sold a high-definition television set to Ty James; issued Sales Slip 203 for $2,200 plus sales tax of $176.
	17	Sold an electric dryer to Barbara Odom; issued Sales Slip 204 for $750 plus sales tax of $60.
	23	Sold a trash compactor to Raj Patel; issued Sales Slip 205 for $500 plus sales tax of $40.
	27	Sold a portable television set to June Kim; issued Sales Slip 206 for $300 plus sales tax of $24.
	29	Sold an electric range to Jim Park; issued Sales Slip 207 for $525 plus sales tax of $42.
	30	Sold a microwave oven to Sherry Chavez; issued Sales Slip 208 for $275 plus sales tax of $22.

GENERAL LEDGER ACCOUNTS

111 Accounts Receivable, $83,000 Dr.
231 Sales Tax Payable
401 Sales

Analyze: What percentage of sales was for entertainment items?

Problem 7.2B ► Journalizing, posting, and reporting sales transactions.

Objectives 7-1, 7-2, 7-4

The Furniture Lot is a retail store that specializes in modern living room and dining room furniture. Merchandise sales are subject to an 8 percent sales tax. The firm's credit sales and sales returns and allowances for June are reflected below, along with the general ledger accounts used to record these transactions. The balances shown are for the beginning of the month.

INSTRUCTIONS

1. Open the general ledger accounts and enter the balances for June 1.
2. Record the transactions in a sales journal and a general journal. Use 9 as the page number for the sales journal and 26 as the page number for the general journal.
3. Post the entries from the general journal to the general ledger.
4. Total, prove, and rule the sales journal as of June 30.
5. Post the column totals from the sales journal.
6. Prepare the heading and the Revenue section of the firm's income statement for the month ended June 30, 2016.

GENERAL LEDGER ACCOUNTS

111 Accounts Receivable, $24,150 Dr.
231 Sales Tax Payable, $4,515 Cr.
401 Sales
451 Sales Returns and Allowances

DATE		TRANSACTIONS
June	1	Sold a living room sofa to Kenya Jackson; issued Sales Slip 1601 for $2,525 plus sales tax of $202.
	5	Sold three recliners to Carmen Cruz; issued Sales Slip 1602 for $1,500 plus sales tax of $120.
	9	Sold a dining room set to Lu Chang; issued Sales Slip 1603 for $6,025 plus sales tax of $482.
	11	Accepted a return of a damaged chair from Carmen Cruz; the chair was originally sold on Sales Slip 1602 of June 5; issued Credit Memorandum 215 for $540, which includes sales tax of $40.
	17	Sold living room tables and bookcases to Rick Jones; issued Sales Slip 1604 for $4,000 plus sales tax of $320.
	23	Sold eight dining room chairs to Demitri Brown; issued Sales Slip 1605 for $2,400 plus sales tax of $192.
	25	Gave Rick Jones an allowance for scratches on his bookcases; issued Credit Memorandum 216 for $270, which includes sales tax of $20; the bookcases were originally sold on Sales Slip 1604 of June 17.
	27	Sold a living room sofa and four chairs to Paul Rivera; issued Sales Slip 1606 for $2,575 plus sales tax of $206.
	29	Sold a dining room table to Rosie Seltz; issued Sales Slip 1607 for $1,150 plus sales tax of $92.
	30	Sold a living room modular wall unit to Jim Mayor; issued Sales Slip 1608 for $3,100 plus sales tax of $248.

Analyze: Based on the beginning balance of the ***Sales Tax Payable*** account, what was the amount of total net sales for April and May? (Hint: Sales tax returns are filed and paid to the state quarterly.)

Recording sales transactions, posting to the accounts receivable ledger, and preparing a schedule of accounts receivable.

◄ **Problem 7.3B**

Objectives 7-1, 7-2, 7-3, 7-4, 7-6

Wine Country Gift Shop sells cards, supplies, and various holiday gift items. All sales are subject to a sales tax of 8 percent. The shop uses a sales journal and general journal.

DATE		TRANSACTIONS
Feb.	3	Sold Joel Bennett a box of holiday greeting cards for $75 plus sales tax of $6 on Sales Slip 201.
	4	Sold Ken Hamlett a Valentine's Day party pack for $200 plus sales tax of $16 on Sales Slip 202.
	5	Vickie Neal bought 10 boxes of Valentine's Day gift packs for her office. Sales Slip 203 was issued for $300 plus sales tax of $24.
	8	Sold Amy Peloza a set of crystal glasses for $400 plus sales tax of $32 on Sales Slip 204.
	9	Larry Edwards purchased two statues for $300 plus $24 sales tax on Sales Slip 205.
	9	Gave Vickie Neal an allowance because of incomplete items in two gift packs; issued Credit Memorandum 101 for $54, which includes sales tax of $4.
	10	Sold Gordon Dunn a Valentine Birthday package for $150 plus $12 sales tax on Sales Slip 206.

DATE	TRANSACTIONS
13	Gave Amy Peloza an allowance of $50 because of two broken glasses in the set she purchased on February 8. Credit Memorandum 102 was issued for the allowance plus sales tax of $4.
14	Sold Joel Bennett 12 boxes of gift candy for $200 plus sales tax of $16 on Sales Slip 207.
15	Sold a punch serving set with glasses for $300 to Kerry Goree. Sales tax of $24 was included on Sales Slip 208.
20	Sold Ned Jones a box of holiday greeting cards for $100 plus sales tax of $8 on Sales Slip 209.
22	Sold Stacie Andrews a set of crystal glasses for $400 plus sales tax of $32 on Sales Slip 210.
28	Melissa Thomas purchased three statues for $600 plus $48 sales tax on Sales Slip 211.

INSTRUCTIONS

1. Record the credit sale transactions for February in the proper journal. Use 6 as the page number for the sales journal and 16 as the page number for the general journal.
2. Immediately after recording each transaction, post to the accounts receivable ledger.
3. Post the entries to the appropriate accounts.
4. Prepare a schedule of accounts receivable and compare the balance due with the amount shown in the ***Accounts Receivable*** control account.

Analyze: How many postings were made to the general ledger?

Problem 7.4B
Objectives 7-1, 7-2, 7-3, 7-4, 7-6

▶ Recording sales transactions, posting to the accounts receivable ledger, and preparing a schedule of accounts receivable.

The Vintage Nursery is a wholesale shop that sells flowers, plants, and plant supplies. The transactions shown below took place during February.

DATE	TRANSACTIONS
Feb. 3	Sold a floral arrangement to Thompson Funerals; issued Invoice 2201 for $400.
8	Sold potted plants to Meadows Nursery; issued Invoice 2202 for $800.
9	Sold floral arrangements to DeSoto Flower Shop; issued Invoice 2203 for $1,050.
10	Sold corsages to Lovelace Nursery; issued Invoice 2204 for $700.
15	Gave DeSoto Flower Shop an allowance because of withered blossoms discovered in one of the floral arrangements sold on Invoice 2203 on February 9; issued Credit Memorandum 105 for $100.
20	Sold table arrangements to Lovelace Nursery; issued Invoice 2205 for $650.
22	Sold plants to Southwest Nursery; issued Invoice 2206 for $850.
25	Sold roses to Denton Flower Shop; issued Invoice 2207 for $450.
27	Sold several floral arrangements to Thompson Funerals; issued Invoice 2208 for $750.
28	Gave Thompson Funerals an allowance because of withered blossoms discovered in one of the floral arrangements sold on Invoice 2208 on February 27; issued Credit Memorandum 106 for $75.

INSTRUCTIONS

1. Record the transactions in the proper journal. Use 5 as the page number for the sales journal and 10 as the page number for the general journal.
2. Immediately after recording each transaction, post to the accounts receivable ledger.
3. Post the amounts from the general journal daily. Post the sales journal amount as a total at the end of the month.
4. Prepare a schedule of accounts receivable. Compare the balance of the ***Accounts Receivable*** control account with the total of the schedule.

Analyze: Damaged goods decreased sales by what dollar amount? By what percentage amount?

Critical Thinking Problem 7.1

Wholesaler Transactions

Matrix Toy Company sells toys and games to retail stores. The firm offers a trade discount of 40 percent on toys and 30 percent on games. Its credit sales and sales returns and allowances transactions for August are shown nearby. The general ledger accounts used to record these transactions are listed below. The balance shown for ***Accounts Receivable*** is as of the beginning of August.

INSTRUCTIONS

1. Open the general ledger accounts and enter the balance of ***Accounts Receivable*** for August 1.
2. Set up an accounts receivable subsidiary ledger. Open an account for each of the credit customers listed below and enter the balances as of August 1. Enter n/45 in the blank space after "Terms." This means each customer has 45 days to pay for the merchandise it purchased.

Bombay's Department Store	$28,900
Little Annie's Toy Store	30,500
Reader's Bookstores	
Pinkerton Toy Center	
Super Game Center	19,010
The Game Store	

3. Record the transactions in a sales journal and in a general journal. Use 9 as the page number for the sales journal and 25 as the page number for the general journal. Be sure to enter each sale at its net price.
4. Post the individual entries from the sales journal and the general journal.
5. Total and rule the sales journal as of August 31.
6. Post the column total from the sales journal to the proper general ledger accounts.
7. Prepare the heading and the Revenue section of the firm's income statement for the month ended August 31.
8. Prepare a schedule of accounts receivable for August 31.
9. Check the total of the schedule of accounts receivable against the balance of the ***Accounts Receivable*** account in the general ledger. The two amounts should be equal.

GENERAL LEDGER ACCOUNTS

111	Accounts Receivable, $78,410 Dr.
401	Sales
451	Sales Returns and Allowances

DATE	TRANSACTIONS
August 1	Sold toys to Bombay's Department Store; issued Invoice 1001, which shows a list price of $19,500 and a trade discount of 40 percent.
5	Sold games to the Reader's Bookstores; issued Invoice 1002, which shows a list price of $21,250 and a trade discount of 30 percent.
9	Sold games to the Super Game Center; issued Invoice 1003, which shows a list price of $7,500 and a trade discount of 30 percent.
14	Sold toys to the Little Annie's Toy Store; issued Invoice 1004, which shows a list price of $26,400 and a trade discount of 40 percent.
18	Accepted a return of all the games shipped to the Super Game Center because they were damaged in transit; issued Credit Memo 151 for the original sale made on Invoice 1003 on August 9.
22	Sold toys to The Game Store; issued Invoice 1005, which shows a list price of $16,200 and a trade discount of 40 percent.
26	Sold games to the Bombay's Department Store; issued Invoice 1006, which shows a list price of $20,600 and a trade discount of 30 percent.
30	Sold toys to the Pinkerton Toy Center; issued Invoice 1007, which shows a list price of $22,800 and a trade discount of 40 percent.

Analyze: What is the effect on net sales if the company offers a series of trade discounts on toys (25 percent, 15 percent) instead of a single 40 percent discount?

Critical Thinking Problem 7.2

Retail Store

Tony Zendejas is the owner of Housewares Galore, a housewares store that sells a wide variety of items for the kitchen, bathroom, and home. Housewares Galore offers a company credit card to customers.

The company has experienced an increase in sales since the credit card was introduced. Tony is considering replacing his manual system of recording sales with electronic point-of-sale cash registers that are linked to a computer.

Cash sales are now rung up by the salesclerks on a cash register that generates a tape listing total cash sales at the end of the day. For credit sales, salesclerks prepare handwritten sales slips that are forwarded to the accountant for manual entry into the sales journal and accounts receivable ledger.

The electronic register system Tony is considering would use an optical scanner to read coded labels attached to the merchandise. As the merchandise is passed over the scanner, the code is sent to the computer. The computer is programmed to read the code and identify the item being sold, record the amount of the sale, maintain a record of total sales, update the inventory record, and keep a record of cash received.

If the sale is a credit transaction, the customer's company credit card number is swiped through a card reader connected with the register. The computer updates the customer's account in the accounts receivable ledger stored in computer memory.

If this system is used, many of the accounting functions are done automatically as sales are entered into the register. At the end of the day, the computer prints a complete sales journal, along with up-to-date balances for the general ledger and the accounts receivable ledger accounts related to sales transactions.

Listed below are four situations that Tony is eager to eliminate. Would use of an electronic point-of-sale system as described above reduce or prevent these problems? Why or why not?

1. The accountant did not post a sale to the customer's subsidiary ledger account.
2. The salesclerk did not charge a customer for an item.
3. The customer purchased merchandise using a stolen credit card.
4. The salesclerk was not aware that the item purchased was on sale and did not give the customer the sale price.

BUSINESS CONNECTIONS

Retail Sales

Managerial | FOCUS

1. How does the ***Sales Returns and Allowances*** accountant provide management with a measure of operating efficiency? What problems might be indicated by a high level of returns and allowances?
2. Suppose you are the accountant for a small chain of clothing stores. Up to now, the firm has offered open-account credit to qualified customers but has not allowed the use of bank credit cards. The president of the chain has asked your advice about changing the firm's credit policy. What advantages might there be in eliminating the open-account credit and accepting bank credit cards instead? Do you see any disadvantages?
3. Suppose a manager in your company has suggested that the firm not hire an accountant to advise it on tax matters and to file tax returns. He states that tax matters are merely procedural in nature and that anyone who can read the tax form instructions can do the necessary work. Comment on this idea.
4. During the past year, Cravens Company has had a substantial increase in its losses from uncollectible accounts. Assume that you are the newly hired controller of this firm and that you have been asked to find the reason for the increase. What policies and procedures would you investigate?
5. Why is it usually worthwhile for a business to sell on credit even though it will have some losses from uncollectible accounts?
6. How can a firm's credit policy affect its profitability?
7. How can efficient accounting records help management maintain sound credit and collection policies?
8. Why should management insist that all sales on credit and other transactions affecting the firm's accounts receivable be journalized and posted promptly?

Sales Returns and Allowances

Ethical | DILEMMA

Credit memos are created when a product is returned. A debit to ***Sales Returns and Allowances*** and a credit to ***A/R*** is recorded when a credit memo is created. A credit memo will reduce ***A/R*** and write off the invoice. You have noticed that the A/R clerk, Wes, has created an abnormally high number of credit memos. You notice the inventory does not reflect the additional inventory resulting from the ***Sales Returns and Allowances.*** What would you do and how would you document this decision?

Financial Statement ANALYSIS

Home Depot

Income Statement

An excerpt from the Consolidated Statements of Earnings for The Home Depot, Inc., is presented below. Review the financial data and answer the following analysis questions:

(Amounts in millions except per share data) Fiscal Year	2016	2015	2014
Revenues:			
Net Sales	$88,519	$83,176	$78,812

Analyze:

1. The Home Depot, Inc.'s statement reports one figure for net sales. Name one account whose balance may have been deducted from the ***Sales*** account balance to determine a net sales amount.
2. The data presented demonstrate a steady increase in net sales over the three-year period. By what amount and by what percentage have net sales of 2016 increased from sales of 2014?

Analyze Online: Find the most recent consolidated statements of income on The Home Depot, Inc., website (www.homedepot.com). Click on *Investor Relations* then *Financial Reports* then *Annual Reports,* then select the link for the most recent annual report.

3. What dollar amount is reported for net sales for the most recent year?
4. What is the trend in net sales over the last three years?
5. What are some possible reasons for this trend?

TEAMWORK

Customer to Vendor

Divide into groups of four individuals. Your company is named Cole's Cooking Supplies. Assign one person as Cole's sales associate; one as the company's A/R clerk; one as the customer, Louisa's Cooking School; and one as Louisa's A/P clerk. Record the transaction each individual would record from a sale of $50,000 for cooking supplies.

Internet CONNECTION

Accounting General Ledger Packages

Go to the QuickBooks and Sage websites at quickbooks.com and na.sage.com. Compare products at each site. What are some activities that each program can facilitate?

Answers to **Self Reviews**

Answers to Section 1 Self Review

1. A journal that is used to record only one type of transaction. Examples are the sales journal, the purchases journal, the cash receipts journal, and the cash payments journal.
2. Sales of merchandise on credit.
3. A ledger that contains accounts of a single type. Examples are the accounts receivable ledger and the accounts payable ledger.
4. **c.** service, merchandising, manufacturing.
5. **c.** increases credit sales

6. The sale to Harris was recorded at a taxable rate of 7 percent instead of 8 percent. Therefore, the Sales Tax Payable column should have an entry of $48, not $42. The Accounts Receivable Debit column should have an entry of $648, not $642.

   The sale to Wells should have an entry in the Accounts Receivable Debit column of $972, not $872.

Answers to Section 2 Self Review

1. Sales minus sales returns and allowances.
2. A sales return results when a customer returns goods and the firm takes them back. A sales allowance results when the firm gives a customer a reduction in the price of the good or service.
3. Individual accounts for all credit customers.
4. **c.** income statement
5. **a.** ***Sales Returns and Allowances, Sales Tax Payable, Accounts Receivable***
6.

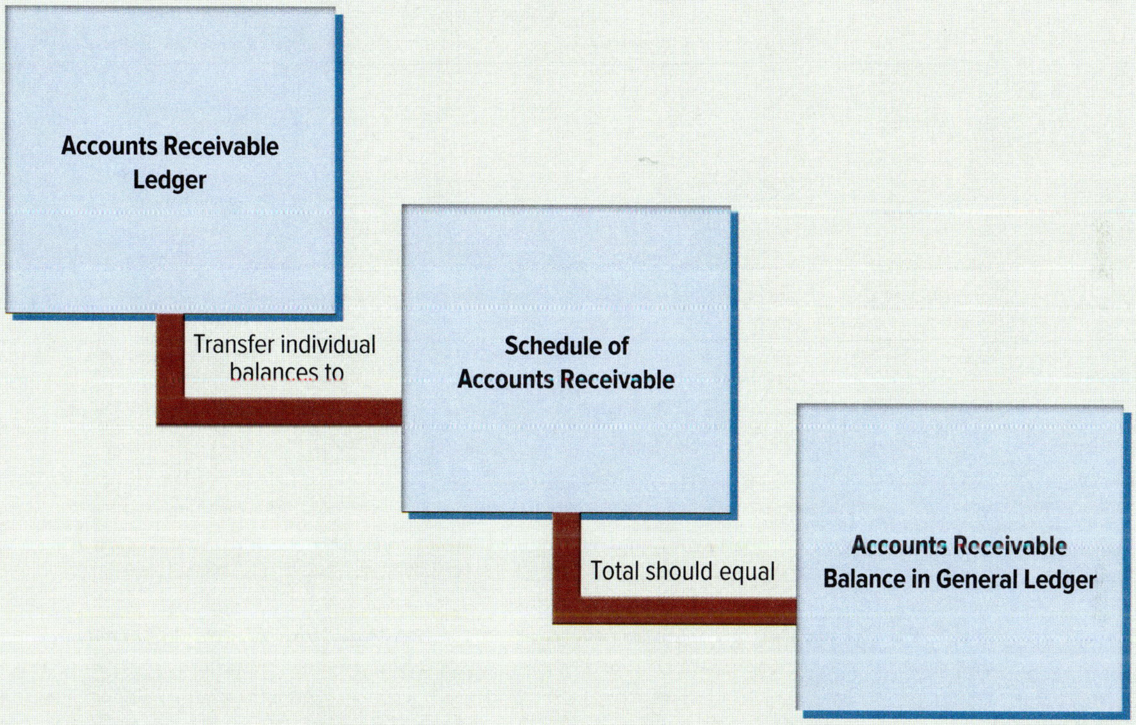

Answers to Section 3 Self Review

1. Four types of credit sales are open-account credit, business credit card sales, bank credit card sales, and credit card company sales.
2. List price is the established retail price of an item; net price is the amount left after all trade discounts are subtracted from the list price.
3. ***Sales Tax Payable*** is the account used to record the liability for sales taxes to be paid in the future.
4. **c.** $2,880
5. **d.** $2,520
6. Possible factors are payment history, amount of current debt, amount of potential debt (available credit cards), employment history, salary, references from other creditors.

Answers to Comprehensive Self Review

1. The month and the quarter.
2. A control account is an account that serves as a link between a subsidiary ledger and the general ledger because its balance summarizes the balances of the accounts in the subsidiary ledger.
3. A merchandising business must account for the purchase and sale of goods and for its merchandise inventory.
4. It contains detailed information about the transactions with credit customers and shows the balances owed by credit customers at all times.
5. A service business sells services; a merchandising business sells goods that it has purchased for resale; and a manufacturing business sells goods that it has produced.

Accounting for Purchases and Accounts Payable

Chapter **8**

© Kristoffer Tripplaar/Alamy Stock Photo

www.bedbathandbeyond.com

Bed Bath & Beyond is a retailer with inventory of a wide selection of domestic merchandise and home furnishings. Starting out, it sold a limited selection of merchandise at its store in Springfield, New Jersey, then called Bed 'n Bath. In response to growing competition in the domestics market, the number of products offered was increased in 1985 and the name was changed to Bed Bath & Beyond. It has since grown to operate several subsidiaries and has further expanded its product selection to include specially commissioned, limited-edition items from emerging fashion and home designers and has expanded its customer base to include institutional customers in the hospitality, cruise line, health care, and other industries.

Bed Bath & Beyond is committed to serving its customers and is dedicated to continually increasing the convenience of its shopping experience and selection of merchandise. It offers extensive breadth, depth, and differentiation of its merchandise to better engage its customers, whatever their interests. Its products can be viewed and purchased in-store, online, and through a mobile device, and it offers in-store pickup or direct shipping.

For the three months ended August 29, 2015, Bed Bath & Beyond reported sales of nearly $3 billion, amounting to an increase of 1.7 percent from the three months ended August 30, 2014. With increasing sales, ever-growing product selection, and multiple distribution channels, meticulous record keeping of purchases and accounts payable is imperative. Knowing amounts due to vendors and payment due dates enables the company to effectively manage its cash flow.

thinking critically

Do you think that companies such as Bed Bath & Beyond pay their bills at the last possible minute? Why or why not?

LEARNING OBJECTIVES

8-1 Record purchases of merchandise on credit in a three-column purchases journal.

8-2 Post from the three-column purchases journal to the general ledger accounts.

8-3 Post credit purchases from the purchases journal to the accounts payable subsidiary ledger.

8-4 Record purchases returns and allowances in the general journal and post them to the *Accounts Payable* account in the general ledger and to the accounts payable subsidiary ledger.

8-5 Prepare a schedule of accounts payable.

8-6 Compute the net delivered cost of purchases.

8-7 Demonstrate a knowledge of the procedures for effective internal control of purchases.

8-8 Define the accounting terms new to this chapter.

NEW TERMS

accounts payable ledger
cash discount
cost of goods sold
Freight In account
purchase allowance
purchase invoice
purchase order
purchase requisition
purchase return
Purchases account
purchases discount
purchases journal
receiving report
sales discount
sales invoice
schedule of accounts payable
Transportation In account

Section 1

SECTION OBJECTIVES	TERMS TO LEARN
>> 8-1 Record purchases of merchandise on credit in a three-column purchases journal. **WHY IT'S IMPORTANT** Most merchandisers purchase goods on credit, and the use of a special journal improves efficiency when recording these transactions. >> 8-2 Post from the three-column purchases journal to the general ledger accounts. **WHY IT'S IMPORTANT** Summary postings from the purchases journal minimize repetitive tasks.	cash discount cost of goods sold *Freight In* account purchase invoice purchase order purchase requisition *Purchases* account purchases discount purchases journal receiving report sales discount sales invoice *Transportation In* account

Merchandise Purchases

In this chapter, you will learn how Maxx-Out Sporting Goods manages its purchases of goods for resale and its accounts payable.

Accounting for Purchases

Most merchandising businesses purchase goods on credit under open-account arrangements. A large firm usually has a centralized purchasing department that is responsible for locating suppliers, obtaining price quotations, negotiating credit terms, and placing orders. In small firms, purchasing activities are handled by a single individual, usually the owner or manager.

PURCHASING PROCEDURES

When a sales department needs goods, it sends the purchasing department a purchase requisition (Figure 8.1). A **purchase requisition** lists the items to be ordered. It is signed by someone with the authority to approve requests for merchandise, usually the manager of the sales department. The purchasing department selects a supplier who can furnish the goods at a competitive price and then issues a purchase order (Figure 8.2). The **purchase order** specifies the exact items, quantity, price, and credit terms. It is signed by someone with authority to approve purchases, usually the purchasing agent.

When the goods arrive at the business, they are inspected. A **receiving report** is prepared to show the quantity and condition of the goods received. The purchasing department receives a copy of the receiving report and compares it to the purchase order. If defective goods or the wrong quantity of goods is received, the purchasing department contacts the supplier and settles the problem.

Figure 8.3 shows the invoice, or *bill,* for items ordered and shipped. The customer, Maxx-Out Sporting Goods, calls it a **purchase invoice.** The supplier, International Sportsman, calls it a **sales invoice.** The customer's accounting department compares the invoice to copies of the purchase order and receiving report. The accounting department checks the quantities, prices, and math on the invoice and then records the purchase. It is important to record purchases in the accounting records as soon as the invoice is verified. Shortly before the due date of the invoice, the accounting department issues a check to the supplier and records the payment.

The purchasing department for The Home Depot, Inc., purchases 30,000 to 40,000 different kinds of home improvement supplies, building materials, and lawn and garden products.

Maxx-Out Sporting Goods
2007 Trendsetter Lane
Dallas, TX 75268-0967

PURCHASE REQUISITION
No. 325

DEPARTMENT Men's
DATE OF REQUEST January 2, 2019
ADVISE ON DELIVERY Max Ferraro
DATE REQUIRED January 25, 2019

QUANTITY	DESCRIPTION
10	Assorted colors men's sweatsuits

APPROVED BY ______ REQUESTED BY ______

FOR PURCHASING DEPARTMENT USE ONLY

PURCHASE ORDER 9001
DATE January 5, 2019
ISSUED TO: International Sportsman
1718 Sherry Lane
Denton, TX 75267-6205

FIGURE 8.1

Purchase Requisition

Maxx-Out Sporting Goods
2007 Trendsetter Lane
Dallas, TX 75268-0967

PURCHASE ORDER

To International Sportsman
1718 Sherry Lane
Denton, TX 75267-6205

Date: January 5, 2019
Order No: 9001
Terms: n/30
FOB: Denton

QUANTITY	ITEM	UNIT PRICE	TOTAL
10	Assorted colors men's sweatsuits	55.00	550.00

APPROVED BY *Max Ferraro*

FIGURE 8.2

Purchase Order

International Sportsman
1718 Sherry Lane
Denton, TX 75267-6205

INVOICE NO. 7985

SOLD TO: Maxx-Out Sporting Goods
2007 Trendsetter Lane
Dallas, TX 75268-0967

DATE: January 23, 2019
ORDER NO.: 9001
SHIPPED BY: Metroplex Express
TERMS: n/30

YOUR ORDER NO.	SALESPERSON	TERMS
9001		n/30
DATE SHIPPED	**SHIPPED BY**	**FOB**
January 23, 2019	Metroplex Express	Denton

QUANTITY	DESCRIPTION	UNIT PRICE	TOTAL
10	Assorted colors men's sweatsuits	55 00	550 00
	Freight		50 00
	Total		600 00

FIGURE 8.3

Invoice

THE PURCHASES ACCOUNT

The purchase of merchandise for resale is a cost of doing business. The purchase of merchandise is debited to the ***Purchases* account.** ***Purchases*** is a temporary account classified as a cost of goods sold account. The **cost of goods sold** is the actual cost to the business of the merchandise sold to customers.

Cost of goods sold accounts follow the debit and credit rules of expense accounts. The ***Purchases*** account is increased by debits and decreased by credits. Its normal balance is a debit. In the chart of accounts, the cost of goods sold accounts appear just before the expense accounts.

> **Walmart purchases private-label products from suppliers and markets these as Walmart brands. Products such as Ol'Roy™ dog food and EverStart® batteries are purchased at lower costs than nationally known brands, enabling Walmart to sell these items at a lower price to its customers.**

FREIGHT CHARGES FOR PURCHASES

Sometimes the buyer pays the freight charge—the cost of shipping the goods from the seller's warehouse to the buyer's location. There are two ways to handle the freight charges paid by the buyer:

- The buyer is billed directly by the transportation company for the freight charge. The buyer issues a check directly to the freight company.
- The seller pays the freight charge and includes it on the invoice. The invoice includes the price of the goods and the freight charge.

important!

Credit Purchases and Freight Charges

The purchases journal is used to record *only credit purchases of merchandise for resale.* Credit purchases of other items used in the business are recorded in the general journal.

Freight In is debited for transportation charges on merchandise inventory that are paid by the buyer. Transportation charges for other asset purchases are not debited to ***Freight In*** but to the asset account charged when the asset was purchased. For example, if freight is paid for purchase of equipment, the ***Equipment*** account would be debited for the freight charges.

The freight charge is debited to the ***Freight In*** or ***Transportation In* account.** This is a cost of goods sold account showing transportation charges for merchandise purchased. The buyer enters three elements in the accounting records:

Price of goods (debit ***Purchases***)	$550.00
Freight charge (debit ***Freight In***)	50.00
Total invoice (credit ***Accounts Payable***)	$600.00

Purchases	
Dr.	Cr.
+	+
550	

Freight In	
Dr.	Cr.
+	−
50	

Accounts Payable	
Dr.	Cr.
−	+
	600

THE PURCHASES JOURNAL

For most merchandising businesses, it is not efficient to enter purchases of goods in the general journal. Instead, credit purchases of merchandise are recorded in a special journal called the **purchases journal.**

The following illustrates how credit purchases appear in a general journal. Each entry involves a debit to ***Purchases*** and ***Freight In*** and a credit to ***Accounts Payable*** plus a detailed explanation.

These 4 general journal entries require 12 separate postings to general ledger accounts: 4 to ***Purchases,*** 4 to ***Freight In,*** and 4 to ***Accounts Payable.*** As you can see from the ledger accounts that follow, it takes a great deal of time and effort to post these entries.

GENERAL JOURNAL PAGE 1

DATE		DESCRIPTION	POST. REF.	DEBIT	CREDIT
2019					
Jan.	3	Purchases	501	2 675 00	
		Freight In	502	190 00	
		Accounts Payable	205		2 865 00
		Purchased merchandise from			
		Active Designs, Invoice 5879,			
		dated January 2, 2019,			
		terms 2/10, n/30			
	5	Purchases	501	3 880 00	
		Freight In	502	175 00	
		Accounts Payable	205		4 055 00
		Purchased merchandise from			
		The Sports Warehouse, Invoice 633,			
		dated January 3, 2019,			
		terms n/30			
	6	Purchases	501	2 900 00	
		Freight In	502	240 00	
		Accounts Payable	205		3 140 00
		Purchased merchandise from			
		The Modern Sportsman,			
		Invoice 8011, dated			
		January 4, 2019, terms n/30			
	7	Purchases	501	3 675 00	
		Freight In	502	260 00	
		Accounts Payable	205		3 935 00
		Purchased merchandise from			
		World of Sports, Invoice 4321,			
		dated January 4, 2019,			
		terms 2/10, n/30			

ACCOUNT *Accounts Payable* ACCOUNT NO. 205

DATE		DESCRIPTION	POST. REF.	DEBIT	CREDIT	BALANCE DEBIT	BALANCE CREDIT
2019							
Jan.	1	Balance	✓				10 800 00
	3		J1		2 865 00		13 665 00
	5		J1		4 055 00		17 720 00
	6		J1		3 140 00		20 860 00
	7		J1		3 935 00		24 795 00

ACCOUNT *Purchases* ACCOUNT NO. 501

DATE		DESCRIPTION	POST. REF.	DEBIT	CREDIT	BALANCE DEBIT	BALANCE CREDIT
2019							
Jan.	3		J1	2 675 00		2 675 00	
	5		J1	3 880 00		6 555 00	
	6		J1	2 900 00		9 455 00	
	7		J1	3 675 00		13 130 00	

>> 8-1 OBJECTIVE
Record purchases of merchandise on credit in a three-column purchases journal.

ACCOUNT Freight In ACCOUNT NO. 502

DATE		DESCRIPTION	POST. REF.	DEBIT	CREDIT	BALANCE DEBIT	BALANCE CREDIT
2019							
Jan.	3		J1	190 00		190 00	
	5		J1	175 00		365 00	
	6		J1	240 00		605 00	
	7		J1	260 00		865 00	

Figure 8.4 shows the purchases journal for Maxx-Out Sporting Goods. Remember that the purchases journal is only for credit purchases of merchandise for resale to customers. Notice how the columns efficiently organize the data about the credit purchases. The purchases journal makes it possible to record each purchase on a single line. In addition, there is no need to enter account names and descriptions.

RECORDING TRANSACTIONS IN A PURCHASES JOURNAL

Use the information on the purchase invoice to make the entry in the purchases journal:

1. Enter the date, supplier name, invoice number, invoice date, and credit terms.
2. In the Accounts Payable Credit column, enter the total owed to the supplier.
3. In the Purchases Debit column, enter the price of the goods purchased.
4. In the Freight In Debit column, enter the freight amount.

The total of the Purchases Debit and Freight In Debit columns must equal the amount entered in the Accounts Payable Credit column.

The invoice date and credit terms determine when payment is due. The following credit terms often appear on invoices:

- *Net 30 days,* or *n/30,* means that payment in full is due 30 days after the date of the invoice.
- *Net 10 days EOM,* or *n/10 EOM,* means that payment in full is due 10 days after the end of the month in which the invoice was issued.
- *2% 10 days, net 30 days,* or *2/10, n/30,* means that if payment is made within 10 days of the invoice date, the customer can take a 2 percent discount. Otherwise, payment in full is due in 30 days.

The 2 percent discount is a **cash discount;** it is a discount offered by suppliers to encourage quick payment by customers. To the customer it is known as a **purchases discount.** To the supplier it is known as a **sales discount.**

FIGURE 8.4 Purchases Journal

PURCHASES JOURNAL PAGE 1

DATE		PURCHASED FROM	INVOICE NUMBER	INVOICE DATE	TERMS	POST. REF.	ACCOUNTS PAYABLE CREDIT	PURCHASES DEBIT	FREIGHT IN DEBIT
2019									
Jan.	3	Active Designs	5879	01/02/19	2/10, n/30		2,865 00	2,675 00	190 00
	5	The Sports Warehouse	633	01/03/19	n/30		4,055 00	3,880 00	175 00
	6	The Modern Sportsman	8011	01/04/19	n/30		3,140 00	2,900 00	240 00
	7	World of Sports	4321	01/04/19	2/10, n/30		3,935 00	3,675 00	260 00
	19	Athletic Equipment, Inc.	8997	01/15/19	2/10, n/30		4,200 00	3,860 00	340 00
	23	International Sportsman	7985	01/22/19	n/30		600 00	550 00	50 00
	31						18,795 00	17,540 00	1,255 00

FIGURE 8.5 Posting to the General Ledger

PURCHASES JOURNAL PAGE 1

DATE		CUSTOMER'S NAME	INVOICE NUMBER	INVOICE DATE	TERMS	POST. REF.	ACCOUNTS PAYABLE CREDIT	PURCHASES DEBIT	FREIGHT IN DEBIT
2019									
Jan.	3	Active Designs	5879	01/02/19	2/10, n/30	✓	2865 00	2675 00	190 00
	5	The Sports Warehouse	633	01/03/19	n/30	✓	4055 00	3880 00	175 00
	6	The Modern Sportsman	8011	01/04/19	n/30	✓	3140 00	2900 00	240 00
	7	World of Sports	4321	01/04/19	2/10, n/30	✓	3935 00	3675 00	260 00
	19	Athletic Equipment, Inc.	8997	01/15/19	2/10, n/30	✓	4200 00	3860 00	340 00
	23	International Sportsman	7985	01/22/19	n/30	✓	600 00	550 00	50 00
	31						18795 00	17540 00	1255 00
							(205)	(501)	(502)

ACCOUNT Accounts Payable ACCOUNT NO. 205

DATE		DESCRIPTION	POST. REF.	DEBIT	CREDIT	BALANCE DEBIT	BALANCE CREDIT
2019							
Jan.	1	Balance	✓				10800 00
	31		P1		18795 00		29595 00

ACCOUNT Purchases ACCOUNT NO. 501

DATE		DESCRIPTION	POST. REF.	DEBIT	CREDIT	BALANCE DEBIT	BALANCE CREDIT
2019							
Jan.	31		P1	17540 00		17540 00	

ACCOUNT Freight In ACCOUNT NO. 502

DATE		DESCRIPTION	POST. REF.	DEBIT	CREDIT	BALANCE DEBIT	BALANCE CREDIT
2019							
Jan.	31		P1	1255 00		1255 00	

POSTING TO THE GENERAL LEDGER

>> 8-2 OBJECTIVE

Post from the three column purchases journal to the general ledger accounts.

The purchases journal simplifies the posting process. Summary amounts are posted at the end of the month. Refer to Figure 8.5 as you learn how to post from the purchases journal to the general ledger accounts.

Total the Accounts Payable Credit, the Purchases Debit, and the Freight In Debit columns. Before posting, prove the equality of the debits and credits recorded in the purchases journal.

Proof of Purchases Journal	
	Debits
Purchases Debit column	$17,540.00
Freight In Debit column	1,255.00
	$18,795.00
	Credits
Accounts Payable Credit column	$18,795.00

important!

Cash Discounts

In the purchases journal, record the amount shown on the invoice. The cash discount is recorded when the payment is made.

After the equality of debits and credits is verified, rule the purchases journal. The steps to post the column totals to the general ledger follow:

1. Locate the ***Accounts Payable*** ledger account.
2. Enter the date.
3. Enter the posting reference, P1. The **P** is for purchases journal. The **1** is the purchases journal page number.
4. Enter the amount from the Accounts Payable Credit column in the purchases journal in the Credit column of the ***Accounts Payable*** ledger account.
5. Compute the new balance and enter it in the Balance Credit column.
6. In the purchases journal, enter the ***Accounts Payable*** ledger account number (205) under the column total.
7. Repeat the steps for the Purchases Debit and Freight In Debit columns.

During the month, the individual entries in the purchases journal are posted to the creditor accounts in the accounts payable ledger. The check marks in the purchases journal in Figure 8.5 indicate that these postings have been completed. This procedure is discussed later in this chapter.

ADVANTAGES OF A PURCHASES JOURNAL

Every business has certain types of transactions that occur over and over again. A well-designed accounting system includes journals that permit efficient recording of such transactions. In most merchandising firms, purchases of goods on credit take place often enough to make it worthwhile to use a purchases journal.

A special journal for credit purchases of merchandise saves time and effort when recording and posting purchases. The use of a purchases journal and other special journals allows for the division of accounting work among different employees. The purchases journal strengthens the audit trail. All credit purchases are recorded in one place, and each entry refers to the number and date of the invoice.

Section 1 Self Review

QUESTIONS

1. What activities does a purchasing department perform?
2. What type of transaction is recorded in the purchases journal?
3. What are the advantages of using a purchases journal?

EXERCISES

4. When the sales department needs goods, what document is sent to the purchasing department?
   a. Purchase invoice
   b. Purchase order
   c. Purchase requisition
   d. Sales requisition
5. What form is sent to the supplier to order goods?
   a. Purchase invoice
   b. Purchase order
   c. Purchase requisition
   d. Sales invoice

ANALYSIS

6. An invoice dated March 15 for $4,000 shows credit terms 2/10, n/30. What do the credit terms mean?

(Answers to Section 1 Self Review are on page 273.)

Section 2

SECTION OBJECTIVES	TERMS TO LEARN
>> 8-3 Post credit purchases from the purchases journal to the accounts payable subsidiary ledger. WHY IT'S IMPORTANT Up-to-date records allow prompt payment of invoices. **>> 8-4** Record purchases returns and allowances in the general journal and post them to the *Accounts Payable* account in the general ledger and to the accounts payable subsidiary ledger. WHY IT'S IMPORTANT For unsatisfactory goods received, an allowance or return is reflected in the accounting records. **>> 8-5** Prepare a schedule of accounts payable. WHY IT'S IMPORTANT This schedule provides a snapshot of amounts owed to suppliers. **>> 8-6** Compute the net delivered cost of purchases. WHY IT'S IMPORTANT This is an important component in measuring operational results. **>> 8-7** Demonstrate a knowledge of the procedures for effective internal control of purchases. WHY IT'S IMPORTANT Businesses try to prevent fraud, errors, and holding excess inventory.	accounts payable ledger purchase allowance purchase return schedule of accounts payable

Accounts Payable

Businesses that buy merchandise on credit can conduct more extensive operations and use financial resources more effectively than if they paid cash for all purchases. It is important to pay invoices on time so that the business maintains a good credit reputation with its suppliers.

The Accounts Payable Ledger

Businesses need detailed records in order to pay invoices promptly. The **accounts payable ledger** provides information about the individual accounts for all creditors. The accounts payable ledger is a subsidiary ledger; it is separate from and subordinate to the general ledger. The accounts payable ledger contains a separate account for each creditor. Each account shows purchases, payments, and returns and allowances. The balance of the account shows the amount owed to the creditor.

Figure 8.6 shows the accounts payable ledger account for International Sportsman. Notice that the Balance column does not indicate whether the balance is a debit or a credit. The form assumes that the balance will be a credit because the normal balance of liability accounts is a credit. A debit balance may exist if more than the amount owed was paid to the creditor or if returned goods were already paid for. If the balance is a debit, circle the amount to show that the account does not have the normal balance.

Small businesses like Maxx-Out Sporting Goods arrange the accounts payable ledger in alphabetical order. Large businesses and businesses that use computerized accounting systems assign an account number to each creditor and arrange the accounts payable ledger in numeric order.

FIGURE 8.6

Accounts Payable Ledger Account

NAME *International Sportsman* TERMS *n/30*

ADDRESS *1718 Sherry Lane, Dallas, Texas 75267-6205*

DATE		DESCRIPTION	POST. REF.	DEBIT	CREDIT	BALANCE
2019						
Jan.	*1*	*Balance*	✓			*1 6 0 0 00*
	23	*Invoice 7985, 01/23/19*	*P1*		*6 0 0 00*	*2 2 0 0 00*

>> 8-3 OBJECTIVE

Post credit purchases from the purchases journal to the accounts payable subsidiary ledger.

POSTING A CREDIT PURCHASE

To keep the accounting records up to date, invoices are posted to the accounts payable subsidiary ledger every day. Refer to Figure 8.6 as you learn how to post to the accounts payable ledger.

1. Locate the accounts payable ledger account for the creditor International Sportsman.
2. Enter the date.
3. In the Description column, enter the invoice number and date.
4. In the Posting Reference column, enter the purchases journal page number.
5. Enter the amount from the Accounts Payable Credit column in the purchases journal in the Credit column of the accounts payable subsidiary ledger.
6. Compute and enter the new balance in the Balance column.
7. In the purchases journal (Figure 8.5), enter a check mark (✓) in the Posting Reference column. This indicates that the transaction is posted in the accounts payable subsidiary ledger.

POSTING CASH PAID ON ACCOUNT

When the transaction involves cash paid on account to a supplier, the payment is first recorded in a cash payments journal. (The cash payments journal is discussed in Chapter 9.) The cash payment is then posted to the individual creditor's account in the accounts payable ledger. Figure 8.7 shows a posting for cash paid to a creditor on January 27.

>> 8-4 OBJECTIVE

Record purchases returns and allowances in the general journal and post them to the ***Accounts Payable*** account in the general ledger and to the accounts payable subsidiary ledger.

Purchases Returns and Allowances

When merchandise arrives, it is examined to confirm that it is satisfactory. Occasionally, the wrong goods are shipped, or items are damaged or defective. A **purchase return** is when the business returns the goods. A **purchase allowance** is when the purchaser keeps the goods but receives a reduction in the price of the goods. The supplier issues a credit memorandum for the return or allowance. The credit memorandum reduces the amount that the purchaser owes.

Purchases returns and allowances are entered in the ***Purchases Returns and Allowances*** account, not in the ***Purchases*** account. The ***Purchases Returns and Allowances*** account is a complete record of returns and allowances. Business managers analyze this account to identify problem suppliers.

Purchases Returns and Allowances is a contra cost of goods sold account. The normal balance of cost of goods sold accounts is a debit. The normal balance of ***Purchases Returns and Allowances,*** a contra cost of goods sold account, is a credit.

recall

Subsidiary Ledger

The total of the accounts in the subsidiary ledger must equal the control account balance.

RECORDING PURCHASES RETURNS AND ALLOWANCES

Maxx-Out Sporting Goods received merchandise from International Sportsman on January 23. Some goods were damaged, and the supplier granted a $100 purchase allowance. Maxx-Out Sporting Goods recorded the full amount of the invoice, $600, in the purchases journal. The purchase allowance was recorded separately in the general journal.

NAME *International Sportsman* TERMS *n/30*
ADDRESS *1718 Sherry Lane, Dallas, Texas 75267-6205*

DATE		DESCRIPTION	POST. REF.	DEBIT	CREDIT	BALANCE
2019						
Jan.	1	Balance	✓			1 6 0 0 00
	23	Invoice 7985, 01/23/19	P1		6 0 0 00	2 2 0 0 00
	27		CP1	1 0 0 0 00		1 2 0 0 00

FIGURE 8.7

Posting a Payment Made on Account

BUSINESS TRANSACTION

On January 30, Maxx-Out Sporting Goods received a credit memorandum for $100 from International Sportsman as an allowance for damaged merchandise.

International Sportsman
1718 Sherry Lane
Dallas, TX 75267-6205

CREDIT MEMORANDUM
NUMBER: 103
DATE: January 30, 2019

TO: Maxx-Out Sporting Goods
2007 Trendsetter Lane
Dallas, TX 75268-0967

ORIGINAL INVOICE: 7985
INVOICE DATE: January 23, 2019
DESCRIPTION: Credit for damaged merchandise: $100.00

ANALYSIS

The liability account ***Accounts Payable*** is decreased by $100. The contra cost of goods sold account ***Purchases Returns and Allowances*** is increased by $100.

DEBIT-CREDIT RULES

DEBIT Decreases to liabilities are debits. Debit ***Accounts Payable*** for $100.

CREDIT Increases to contra cost of goods sold accounts are recorded as credits. Credit ***Purchases Returns and Allowances*** for $100.

T-ACCOUNT PRESENTATION

Accounts Payable	
−	+
100	

Purchases Returns and Allowances	
−	+
	100

GENERAL JOURNAL ENTRY

GENERAL JOURNAL PAGE 1

	DATE		DESCRIPTION	POST. REF.	DEBIT	CREDIT	
15	Jan.	30	Accounts Payable/International Sportsman		1 0 0 00		15
16			Purchases Returns and Allowances			1 0 0 00	16
17			Received Credit Memo 103 for				17
18			damaged merchandise returned;				18
19			original Invoice 7985,				19
20			January 23, 2019				20

THE BOTTOM LINE

Purchase Allowance

Income Statement

Contra Cost of Goods Sold	↑ 100
Net Income	↑ 100

Balance Sheet

Liabilities	↓ 100
Equity	↑ 100

FIGURE 8.8

Posting to a Creditor's Account

GENERAL JOURNAL PAGE 1

	DATE		DESCRIPTION	POST. REF.	DEBIT	CREDIT	
1	*2019*						1
15	*Jan.*	*30*	*Accounts Payable/International Sportsman*	*205* / ✓	*100 00*		16
16			*Purchases Returns and Allowances*	*503*		*100 00*	17
17			*Received Credit Memo 103 for*				18
18			*damaged merchandise*				19
19			*returned; original*				20
20			*Invoice 7985, January 23, 2019*				21
21							22
22							

NAME *International Sportsman* TERMS *n/30*

ADDRESS *1718 Sherry Lane, Dallas, Texas 75267-6205*

DATE		DESCRIPTION	POST. REF.	DEBIT	CREDIT	BALANCE
2019						
Jan.	*1*	*Balance*	✓			*1 6 0 0 00*
	23	*Invoice 7985, 01/23/19*	*P1*		*6 0 0 00*	*2 2 0 0 00*
	27		*CP1*	*1 0 0 0 00*		*1 2 0 0 00*
	30	*CM 103*	*J1*	*1 0 0 00*		*1 1 0 0 00*

recall

Contra Accounts

The ***Purchases Returns and Allowances*** account is a contra account. Contra accounts have normal balances that are the opposite of related accounts. For example, the normal balance of ***Purchases Returns and Allowances*** is credit, where the normal balance of ***Purchases*** is debit.

Notice that this entry includes a debit to ***Accounts Payable*** and a credit to ***Purchases Returns and Allowances.*** In addition, there is a debit to the creditor's account in the accounts payable subsidiary ledger. Businesses that have few returns and allowances use the general journal to record these transactions. Businesses with many returns and allowances use a special journal for purchases returns and allowances.

POSTING A PURCHASES RETURN OR ALLOWANCE

Whether recorded in the general journal or in a special journal, it is important to promptly post returns and allowances to the creditor's account in the accounts payable ledger. Refer to Figure 8.8 to learn how to post purchases returns and allowances to the supplier's account.

1. Enter the date.
2. In the Description column, enter the credit memorandum number.
3. In the Posting Reference column, enter the general journal page number.
4. Enter the amount of the return or allowance in the Debit column.
5. Compute the new balance and enter it in the Balance column.
6. In the general journal, enter a check mark (✓) to show that the transaction was posted to the creditor's account in the accounts payable subsidiary ledger.

After the transaction is posted to the general ledger, enter the ***Purchases Returns and Allowances*** ledger account number in the Posting Reference column.

>> 8-5 OBJECTIVE

Prepare a schedule of accounts payable.

Schedule of Accounts Payable

The total of the individual creditor accounts in the subsidiary ledger must equal the balance of the ***Accounts Payable*** control account. To prove that the control account and the subsidiary ledger are equal, businesses prepare a **schedule of accounts payable**—a list of all balances owed to creditors. Figure 8.9 shows the accounts payable subsidiary ledger for Maxx-Out Sporting Goods on January 31.

Figure 8.10 shows the schedule of accounts payable for Maxx-Out Sporting Goods. Notice that the accounts payable control account balance is $20,245. This equals the total on the schedule of accounts payable. If the amounts are not equal, it is essential to locate and correct the errors.

FIGURE 8.9

The Accounts Payable Ledger

NAME *Active Designs* TERMS *2/10, n/30*
ADDRESS *2313 Belt Line Road, Dallas, Texas 75267-6205*

DATE		DESCRIPTION	POST. REF.	DEBIT	CREDIT	BALANCE
2019						
Jan.	1	Balance	✓			2,200.00
	3	Invoice 5879, 01/02/19	P1		2,865.00	5,065.00
	13		CP1	3,200.00		1,865.00
	30		CP1	800.00		1,065.00

NAME *Athletic Equipment, Inc.* TERMS *2/10, n/30*
ADDRESS *1027 St James Avenue, Dallas, Texas 75267-6205*

DATE		DESCRIPTION	POST. REF.	DEBIT	CREDIT	BALANCE
2019						
Jan.	19	Invoice 8997, 01/15/19	P1		4,200.00	4,200.00

NAME *International Sportsman* TERMS *n/30*
ADDRESS *1718 Sherry Lane, Dallas, Texas 75267-6205*

DATE		DESCRIPTION	POST. REF.	DEBIT	CREDIT	BALANCE
2019						
Jan.	1	Balance	✓			1,600.00
	23	Invoice 7985, 01/23/19	P1		600.00	2,200.00
	27		CP1	1,000.00		1,200.00
	30	CM 103	J1	100.00		1,100.00

NAME *The Modern Sportsman* TERMS *n/30*
ADDRESS *2860 Jackson Drive, Dallas, Texas 75267-6205*

DATE		DESCRIPTION	POST. REF.	DEBIT	CREDIT	BALANCE
2019						
Jan.	1	Balance	✓			1,600.00
	6	Invoice 8011, 01/04/19	P1		3,140.00	4,740.00

NAME *The Sports Warehouse* TERMS *n/30*
ADDRESS *1313 Sunset Drive, Dallas, Texas 75267-6205*

DATE		DESCRIPTION	POST. REF.	DEBIT	CREDIT	BALANCE
2019						
Jan.	1	Balance	✓			2,400.00
	5	Invoice 633, 01/03/19	P1		4,055.00	6,455.00
	17		CP1	4,250.00		2,205.00

NAME *World of Sports* TERMS *2/10, n/30*
ADDRESS *1729 Parker Road, Dallas, Texas 75267-6205*

DATE		DESCRIPTION	POST. REF.	DEBIT	CREDIT	BALANCE
2019						
Jan.	1	Balance	✓			3,000.00
	7	Invoice 4321, 01/04/19	P1		3,935.00	6,935.00

FIGURE 8.10

Schedule of Accounts Payable and the Accounts Payable Account

Maxx-Out Sporting Goods
Schedule of Accounts Payable
January 31, 2019

Active Designs	1 065 00
Athletic Equipment, Inc.	4 200 00
International Sportsman	1 100 00
The Modern Sportsman	4 740 00
The Sports Warehouse	2 205 00
World of Sports	6 935 00
Total	20 245 00

ACCOUNT *Accounts Payable* ACCOUNT NO. *205*

DATE		DESCRIPTION	POST. REF.	DEBIT	CREDIT	BALANCE DEBIT	BALANCE CREDIT
2019							
Jan.	*1*	*Balance*					*10 800 00*
	30		*J1*	*100 00*			*10 700 00*
	31		*P1*		*18 795 00*		*29 495 00*
	31		*CP1*	*9 250 00*			*20 245 00*

>> 8-6 OBJECTIVE

Compute the net delivered cost of purchases.

Determining the Cost of Purchases

The ***Purchases*** account accumulates the cost of merchandise bought for resale. The income statement of a merchandising business contains a section showing the total cost of purchases. This section combines information about the cost of the purchases, freight in, and purchases returns and allowances for the period. Maxx-Out Sporting Goods has the following general ledger account balances at January 31:

Purchases	$17,540
Freight In	1,255
Purchases Returns and Allowances	100

The net delivered cost of purchases for Maxx-Out Sporting Goods for January is calculated as follows:

Purchases	$17,540
Freight In	1,255
Delivered Cost of Purchases	$18,795
Less Purchases Returns and Allowances	100
Net Delivered Cost of Purchases	$18,695

For firms that do not have freight charges, the amount of net purchases is calculated as follows:

Purchases	$17,540
Less Purchases Returns and Allowances	100
Net Purchases	$17,440

In Chapter 13, you will see how the complete income statement for a merchandising business is prepared. You will learn about the Cost of Goods Sold section and how the net delivered cost of purchases is used in calculating the results of operations.

Internal Control of Purchases

>> 8-7 OBJECTIVE
Demonstrate a knowledge of the procedures for effective internal control of purchases.

Internal controls are the company's policies and procedures in place to safeguard assets, ensure reliability of accounting data, and promote compliance with management policies and applicable laws. Because of the large amount of money spent to purchase goods, businesses should develop careful procedures to control purchases and payments. A business should ensure its control process includes sufficient safeguards to:

- create written proof that purchases and payments are authorized;
- ensure that different people are involved in the process of buying goods, receiving goods, and making payments.

internal CONTROL

Separating duties among employees provides a system of checks and balances. In a small business with just a few employees, it might be very difficult to separate duties. This means the owner must be involved in daily operations. Even a small business, however, should design a set of control procedures as effective as resources allow. Effective systems for small businesses should have the following controls in place:

1. All purchases should be made only after proper authorization has been given in writing.
2. Goods should be carefully checked when received. They should then be compared with the purchase order and with the invoice received from the supplier.
3. The purchase order, receiving report, and invoice should be checked to confirm that the information on the documents is in agreement.
4. The computations on the invoice should be checked for accuracy.
5. Authorization for payment should be made by someone other than the person who ordered the goods.
6. Another person should write the check for payment.
7. Prenumbered forms should be used for purchase requisitions, purchase orders, and checks. The numbers on the documents issued should be verified periodically to make sure all forms can be accounted for.

ABOUT **ACCOUNTING**

Employee Fraud

In its 2014 Global Fraud Study, the Association of Certified Fraud Examiners reported that the typical organization loses 5 percent of its revenues to fraud each year. The best defense against fraud is to use good internal controls: Have multiple employees in contact with suppliers and screen employees and vendors to reduce fraud opportunities.

Medium- and large-sized businesses often use the voucher system. As a business grows, the owner finds it increasingly difficult to be involved in all the firm's transactions. The owner cannot personally approve or sign all checks. That's when the internal controls provided by the voucher system become increasingly important.

Controls built into a voucher system include the following:

- All liabilities are authorized. For example, a properly approved purchase order is required for each purchase of merchandise on account.
- All payments are made by check.
- All checks are issued based on a properly approved voucher.
- Vouchers are used to cover bills and invoices received from outside parties.
- All bills and invoices are verified before they are approved for payment.
- Only experienced and responsible employees are allowed to approve bills and invoices for payment.
- Invoices are attached to the vouchers to provide supporting documentation.
- Different employees approve the vouchers, record the vouchers and payments, and sign and mail the checks.
- All paid vouchers, including supporting documentation, are kept on file for a specified period of time.

MANAGERIAL IMPLICATIONS <<

ACCOUNTING FOR PURCHASES

- Management and the accounting staff need to work together to make sure that there are good internal controls over purchasing.
- A carefully designed system of checks and balances protects the business against fraud, errors, and excessive investment in merchandise.
- The accounting staff needs to record transactions efficiently so that up-to-date information about creditors is available.
- Using the purchases journal and the accounts payable subsidiary ledger improves efficiency.
- To maintain a good credit reputation with suppliers, it is important to have an accounting system that ensures prompt payment of invoices.
- A well-run accounting system provides management with information about cash: cash required to pay suppliers, short-term loans needed to cover temporary cash shortages, and cash available for short-term investments.
- Separate accounts for recording purchases, freight charges, and purchases returns and allowances make it easy to analyze the elements in the cost of purchases.

THINKING CRITICALLY

As a manager, what internal controls would you put in your accounting system?

Section 2 Self Review

QUESTIONS

1. What is the purpose of the schedule of accounts payable?
2. A firm has a debit balance of $62,450 in its ***Purchases*** account and a credit balance of $2,875 in its ***Purchases Returns and Allowances*** account. Calculate net purchases for the period.
3. A firm receives an invoice that reflects the price of goods as $1,375 and the freight charge as $92. How is this transaction recorded?

EXERCISES

4. The net delivered cost of purchases for the period appears on the:
   a. balance sheet
   b. income statement
   c. schedule of accounts payable
   d. statement of owner's equity
5. In the accounts payable ledger, a supplier's account has a beginning balance of $4,800. A transaction of $1,600 is posted from the purchases journal. What is the balance of the supplier's account?
   a. $3,200 debit
   b. $3,200 credit
   c. $6,400 debit
   d. $6,400 credit

ANALYSIS

6. In the general ledger, the ***Accounts Payable*** account has a balance of $15,500. The schedule of accounts payable lists accounts totaling $20,500. What could cause this error?

(Answers to Section 2 Self Review are on page 273.)

REVIEW Chapter Summary

Chapter 8

Review and Applications

In this chapter, you have learned about the accounting journals and ledgers required for the efficient processing of purchases for a business. Businesses with strong internal controls establish and follow procedures for approving requests for new merchandise, choosing suppliers, placing orders with suppliers, checking goods after they arrive, identifying invoices, and approving payments.

Learning Objectives

8-1 Record purchases of merchandise on credit in a three-column purchases journal.

Purchases and payments on account must be entered in the firm's accounting records promptly and accurately. Most merchandising businesses normally purchase goods on credit. The most efficient system for recording purchases on credit is the use of a special purchases journal. With this type of journal, only one line is needed to enter all the data.

The purchases journal is used only to record the credit purchase of goods for resale. General business expenses are not recorded in the purchases journal.

8-2 Post from the three-column purchases journal to the general ledger accounts.

The use of the three-column purchases journal simplifies the posting process because nothing is posted to the general ledger until the month's end. Then, summary postings are made to the ***Purchases, Freight In,*** and ***Accounts Payable*** accounts.

8-3 Post credit purchases from the purchases journal to the accounts payable subsidiary ledger.

An accounts payable subsidiary ledger helps a firm keep track of the amounts it owes to creditors. Postings are made to this ledger on a daily basis.

- Each credit purchase is posted from the purchases journal to the accounts payable subsidiary ledger.
- Each payment on account is posted from the cash payments journal to the accounts payable subsidiary ledger.

8-4 Record purchases returns and allowances in the general journal and post them to the *Accounts Payable* account in the general ledger and to the accounts payable subsidiary ledger.

Returns and allowances on purchases of goods are credited to an account called ***Purchases Returns and Allowances.*** These transactions may be recorded in the general journal or in a special purchases returns and allowances journal. Each return or allowance on a credit purchase is posted to the accounts payable subsidiary ledger.

8-5 Prepare a schedule of accounts payable.

At the month's end, a schedule of accounts payable is prepared. The schedule lists the balances owed to the firm's creditors and proves the accuracy of the subsidiary ledger. The total of the schedule of accounts payable is compared with the balance of the ***Accounts Payable*** account in the general ledger, which acts as a control account. The two amounts should be equal.

8-6 Compute the net delivered cost of purchases.

The net delivered cost of purchases is computed by adding the cost of purchases and freight in, then subtracting any purchases returns and allowances. Net delivered cost of purchases is reported in the Cost of Goods Sold section of the income statement.

8-7 Demonstrate a knowledge of the procedures for effective internal control of purchases.

Purchases and payments should be properly authorized and processed with appropriate documentation to provide a system of checks and balances. A division of responsibilities within the purchases process ensures strong internal controls.

8-8 Define the accounting terms new to this chapter.

Glossary

Accounts payable ledger (p. 249) A subsidiary ledger that contains a separate account for each creditor

Cash discount (p. 246) A discount offered by suppliers for payment received within a specified period of time

Cost of goods sold (p. 244) The actual cost to the business of the merchandise sold to customers

***Freight In* account** (p. 244) An account showing transportation charges for items purchased

Purchase allowance (p. 250) A price reduction from the amount originally billed

Purchase invoice (p. 242) A bill received for goods purchased

Purchase order (p. 242) An order to the supplier of goods specifying items needed, quantity, price, and credit terms

Purchase requisition (p. 242) A list sent to the purchasing department showing the items to be ordered

Purchase return (p. 250) Return of unsatisfactory goods

***Purchases* account** (p. 244) An account used to record cost of goods bought for resale during a period

Purchases discount (p. 246) A cash discount offered to the customer for payment within a specified period

Purchases journal (p. 244) A special journal used to record the purchase of goods on credit

Receiving report (p. 242) A form showing quantity and condition of goods received

Sales discount (p. 246) A cash discount offered by the supplier for payment within a specified period

Sales invoice (p. 242) A supplier's billing document

Schedule of accounts payable (p. 252) A list of all balances owed to creditors

Transportation In* account** (p. 244) See ***Freight In account

Comprehensive **Self Review**

1. What type of account is ***Purchases Returns and Allowances***?
2. What is a cash discount and why is it offered?
3. What is the purpose of the ***Freight In*** account?
4. What is the purpose of a purchase requisition? A purchase order?
5. What is the difference between a receiving report and an invoice?

(Answers to Comprehensive Self Review are on page 273.)

Discussion Questions

1. Why are the invoice date and terms recorded in the purchases journal?
2. What major safeguards should be built into a system of internal control for purchases of goods?
3. What is the purpose of a credit memorandum?
4. What is a purchase allowance?
5. What is a purchase return?
6. What is a schedule of accounts payable? Why is it prepared?
7. What is the relationship of the ***Accounts Payable*** account in the general ledger to the accounts payable subsidiary ledger?
8. What type of accounts are kept in the accounts payable ledger?
9. Why is it useful for a business to have an accounts payable ledger?
10. How is the net delivered cost of purchases computed?

11. What journals can be used to enter various merchandise purchase transactions?
12. What is the difference between a purchase invoice and a sales invoice?
13. What is the normal balance of the ***Purchases*** account?
14. On what financial statement do the accounts related to purchases of merchandise appear? In which section of this statement are they reported?
15. Why is the use of a ***Purchases Returns and Allowances*** account preferred to crediting these transactions to ***Purchases***?
16. What do the following credit terms mean?
    - **a.** n/30
    - **b.** 2/10, n/30
    - **c.** n/10 EOM
    - **d.** n/20
    - **e.** 1/10, n/20
    - **f.** 3/5, n/30
    - **g.** n/15 EOM
17. A business has purchased some new equipment for use in its operations, not for resale to customers. The terms of the invoice are n/30. Should this transaction be entered in the purchases journal? If not, where should it be recorded?

APPLICATIONS

Exercises connect

Identifying the journals used to record purchases and related transactions.

Exercise 8.1
Objective 8-1

The accounting system of Suit City includes the following journals. Indicate which journal is used to record each transaction.

JOURNALS

Cash receipts journal
Cash payments journal
Purchases journal
Sales journal
General journal

TRANSACTIONS

1. Purchased merchandise for $3,000; the terms are 2/10, n/30.
2. Returned damaged merchandise to a supplier and received a credit memorandum for $800.
3. Issued a check for $3,600 to a supplier as a payment on account.
4. Purchased merchandise for $2,000 plus a freight charge of $140; the supplier's invoice is payable in 30 days.
5. Received an allowance for merchandise that was damaged but can be sold at a reduced price; the supplier's credit memorandum is for $475.
6. Purchased merchandise for $3,500 in cash.

Exercise 8.2
Objective 8-1

▶ Identifying journals used to record purchases and related transactions.

The following transactions took place at Extreme Bikers. Indicate the general ledger account numbers that would be debited and credited to record each transaction.

GENERAL LEDGER ACCOUNTS

101 Cash

205 Accounts Payable

501 Purchases

502 Freight In

503 Purchases Returns and Allowances

TRANSACTIONS

1. Purchased merchandise for $1,500; the terms are 2/10, n/30.
2. Returned damaged merchandise to a supplier and received a credit memorandum for $300.
3. Issued a check for $800 to a supplier as a payment on account.
4. Purchased merchandise for $2,400 plus a freight charge of $260; the supplier's invoice is payable in 30 days.
5. Received an allowance for merchandise that was damaged but can be sold at a reduced price; the supplier's credit memorandum is for $400.
6. Purchased merchandise for $4,200 in cash.

Exercise 8.3
Objective 8-1

▶ Recording credit purchases.

The following transactions took place at Sonoma Auto Parts and Custom Shop during the first week of July. Indicate how these transactions would be entered in a purchases journal like the one shown in this chapter.

DATE		TRANSACTIONS
July	1	Purchased batteries for $1,890 plus a freight charge of $95 from Batteries Plus Corporation; received Invoice 6812, dated June 27, which has terms of n/30.
	3	Purchased mufflers for $4,250 plus a freight charge of $99 from Performance Mufflers; received Invoice 441, dated June 30, which has terms of 1/10, n/60.
	5	Purchased car radios for $2,470 plus freight of $127 from Harbor Sounds Shop, Inc.; received Invoice 5601, dated July 1, which has terms of 2/10, n/30.
	10	Purchased truck tires for $6,270 from Specialty Tire Company; received invoice 1102, dated July 8, which has terms of 2/10, n/30.

Exercise 8.4
Objective 8-4

▶ Recording a purchase return.

On March 9, Modern Kitchens, a retail store, received Credit Memorandum 244 for $3,420 from J & M Appliance Corporation. The credit memorandum covered a return of damaged trash compactors originally purchased on Invoice 4101 dated February 3. Prepare the general journal entry that Modern Kitchens would make for this transaction.

Exercise 8.5
Objective 8-4

▶ Recording a purchase allowance.

On April 17, New World Appliances was given an allowance of $1,075 by Upscale Kitchens, which issued Credit Memorandum 112. The allowance was for scratches on stoves that were originally purchased on Invoice 911 dated March 20. Prepare the general journal entry that New World Appliances would make for this transaction.

Determining the cost of purchases.

◀ **Exercise 8.6**
Objective 8-4

On June 30 the general ledger of Beverly Hills Clothiers, a clothing store, showed a balance of $63,895 in the ***Purchases*** account, a balance of $2,975 in the ***Freight In*** account, and a balance of $4,280 in the ***Purchases Returns and Allowances*** account. What was the delivered cost of the purchases made during June? What was the net delivered cost of these purchases?

Errors in recording purchase transactions.

◀ **Exercise 8.7**
Objectives 8-1, 8-4

The following errors were made in recording transactions in posting from the purchases journal. How will these errors be detected?

a. A credit of $2,000 to the Thomastown Furniture Company account in the accounts payable ledger was posted as $200.

b. The Accounts Payable column total of the purchases journal was understated by $200.

c. An invoice of $1,680 for merchandise from Johnson Company was recorded as having been received from Baxton Company, another supplier.

d. A $500 payment to Baxton Company was debited to Johnson Company.

Determining the cost of purchases.

◀ **Exercise 8.8**
Objective 8-4

Complete the following schedule by supplying the missing information.

Net Delivered Cost of Purchases	Case A	Case B
Purchases	(a)	95,570
Freight In	4,275	(c)
Delivered Cost of Purchases	97,750	(d)
Less Purchases Returns and Allowances	(b)	3,930
Net Delivered Cost of Purchases	93,825	97,920

PROBLEMS

Problem Set A connect

Journalizing credit purchases and purchases returns and allowances and posting to the general ledger.

◀ **Problem 8.1A**
Objectives 8-1, 8-2, 8-3

Digital World is a retail store that sells cameras and photography supplies. The firm's credit purchases and purchases returns and allowances transactions for June 2019 appear below, along with the general ledger accounts used to record these transactions. The balance shown in ***Accounts Payable*** is for the beginning of June.

INSTRUCTIONS

1. Open the general ledger accounts and enter the balance of ***Accounts Payable*** for June 1, 2019.
2. Record the transactions in a three-column purchases journal and in a general journal. Use 14 as the page number for the purchases journal and 38 as the page number for the general journal.
3. Post entries from the general journal to the general ledger accounts.
4. Total and rule the purchases journal as of June 30.
5. Post the column totals from the purchases journal to the proper general ledger accounts.
6. Compute the net purchases of the firm for the month of June.

GENERAL LEDGER ACCOUNTS

205 Accounts Payable, $14,404 Cr.
501 Purchases
502 Freight In
503 Purchases Returns and Allowances

DATE	TRANSACTIONS
June 1	Purchased instant cameras for $2,050 plus a freight charge of $230 from Pro Photo Equipment, Invoice 4241, dated May 27; the terms are 60 days net.
8	Purchased film for $1,394 from Photo Supplies, Invoice 1102, dated June 3, net payable in 45 days.
12	Purchased lenses for $916 from Nano Glass, Invoice 7282, dated June 9; the terms are 1/10, n/60.
18	Received Credit Memorandum 110 for $400 from Pro Photo Equipment for defective cameras that were returned; they were originally purchased on Invoice 4241, dated May 27.
20	Purchased color film for $1,200 plus freight of $75 from Photo Supplies, Invoice 1148, dated June 15, net payable in 45 days.
23	Purchased camera cases for $1,956 from Hi-Qual Case, Invoice 3108, dated June 18, net due and payable in 45 days.
28	Purchased lens filters for $2,470 plus freight of $120 from Holtz Spectrum, Invoice 5027, dated June 24; the terms are 2/10, n/30.
30	Received Credit Memorandum 1108 for $310 from Hi-Qual Case; the amount is an allowance for damaged but usable goods purchased on Invoice 3108, dated June 18.

(**Note:** Save your working papers for use in Problem 8.2A.)

Analyze: What total purchases were posted to the ***Purchases*** general ledger account for June?

Problem 8.2A ► **Posting to the accounts payable ledger and preparing a schedule of accounts payable.**

Objectives 8-4, 8-6

CONTINUING >>> Problem

This problem is a continuation of Problem 8.1A.

INSTRUCTIONS

1. Set up an accounts payable subsidiary ledger for Digital World. Open an account for each of the creditors listed below and enter the balances as of June 1, 2019. Arrange the accounts payable ledger in alphabetical order.
2. Post the individual entries from the purchases journal and the general journal prepared in Problem 8.1A.
3. Prepare a schedule of accounts payable for June 30.
4. Check the total of the schedule of accounts payable against the balance of the ***Accounts Payable*** account in the general ledger. The two amounts should be equal.

Creditors		
Name	**Terms**	**Balance**
Photo Supplies	n/45	$10,580
Hi-Qual Case	n/45	1,300
Pro Photo Equipment	n/60	
Nano Glass	1/10, n/60	2,524
Holtz Spectrum	2/10, n/30	

Analyze: What amount is owed to Nano Glass on June 30?

Journalizing credit purchases and purchases returns and allowances, computing the net delivered cost of goods, posting to the general ledger, posting to the accounts payable ledger, and preparing a schedule of accounts payable.

◀ **Problem 8.3A**

Objectives 8-1, 8-2, 8-3, 8-4, 8-5, 8-6

The Old English Garden Shop is a retail store that sells garden equipment, furniture, and supplies. Its credit purchases and purchases returns and allowances for July are listed below. The general ledger accounts used to record these transactions are also provided. The balance shown is for the beginning of July 2019.

INSTRUCTIONS

PART I

1. Open the general ledger accounts and enter the balance of ***Accounts Payable*** for July 1.
2. Record the transactions in a three-column purchases journal and in a general journal. Use 8 as the page number for the purchases journal and 20 as the page number for the general journal.
3. Post the entries from the general journal to the proper general ledger accounts.
4. Total, prove, and rule the purchases journal as of July 31.
5. Post the column totals from the purchases journal to the proper general ledger accounts.
6. Compute the net delivered cost of the firm's purchases for the month of July.

GENERAL LEDGER ACCOUNTS

205 Accounts Payable, $35,980 Cr.

501 Purchases

502 Freight In

503 Purchases Returns and Allowances

DATE		TRANSACTIONS
July	1	Purchased lawn mowers for $9,410 plus a freight charge of $269 from Charleston Corporation, Invoice 1011, dated June 26, net due and payable in 60 days.
	5	Purchased outdoor chairs and tables for $4,470 plus a freight charge of $562 from Cedarbrook Garden Center, Invoice 639, dated July 2, net due and payable in 45 days.
	9	Purchased grass seed for $1,525 from Lawn and Gardens Supply, Invoice 8164, dated July 5; the terms are 30 days net.
	16	Received Credit Memorandum 110 for $500 from Cedarbrook Garden Center; the amount is an allowance for scratches on some of the chairs and tables originally purchased on Invoice 639, dated July 2.
	19	Purchased fertilizer for $1,300 plus a freight charge of $266 from Lawn and Gardens Supply, Invoice 9050, dated July 15; the terms are 30 days net.
	21	Purchased hoses from Dunn Rubber Company for $3,790 plus a freight charge of $264, Invoice 1785, dated July 17; terms are 1/15, n/60.
	28	Received Credit Memorandum 223 for $530 from Dunn Rubber Company for damaged hoses that were returned; the goods were purchased on Invoice 1785, dated July 17.
	31	Purchased lawn sprinkler systems for $10,610 plus a freight charge of $298 from Warren industrial Products, Invoice 8985, dated July 26; the terms are 2/10, n/30.

INSTRUCTIONS

PART II

1. Set up an accounts payable subsidiary ledger for The Old English Garden Shop. Open an account for each of the creditors listed below and enter the balances as of July 1.
2. Post the individual entries from the purchases journal and the general journal prepared in Part I.
3. Prepare a schedule of accounts payable for July 31, 2019.
4. Check the total of the schedule of accounts payable against the balance of the ***Accounts Payable*** account in the general ledger. The two amounts should be equal.

Creditors		
Name	**Terms**	**Balance**
Cedarbrook Garden Center	n/45	$11,220
Charleston Corporation	n/60	18,220
Dunn Rubber Company	1/15, n/60	
Lawn and Gardens Supply	n/30	6,540
Warren Industrial Products	2/10, n/30	

Analyze: What total freight charges were posted to the general ledger for the month of July?

Problem 8.4A ► **Journalizing credit purchases and purchases returns and allowances, posting to the general ledger, posting to the accounts payable ledger, and preparing a schedule of accounts payable.**

Objectives 8-1, 8-2, 8-3, 8-4, 8-5, 8-6

Office Plus is a retail business that sells office equipment, furniture, and supplies. Its credit purchases and purchases returns and allowances for September are shown below. The general ledger accounts and the creditors' accounts in the accounts payable subsidiary ledger used to record these transactions are also provided. All balances shown are for the beginning of September.

INSTRUCTIONS

1. Open the general ledger accounts and enter the balance of ***Accounts Payable*** for September 1, 2019.
2. Open the creditors' accounts in the accounts payable subsidiary ledger and enter the balances for September 1.
3. Record the transactions in a three-column purchases journal and in a general journal. Use 5 as the page number for the purchases journal and 14 as the page number for the general journal.
4. Post to the accounts payable subsidiary ledger daily.
5. Post the entries from the general journal to the proper general ledger accounts at the end of the month.
6. Total and rule the purchases journal as of September 30.
7. Post the column totals from the purchases journal to the proper general ledger accounts.
8. Prepare a schedule of accounts payable and compare the balance of the ***Accounts Payable*** control account with the schedule of accounts payable.

GENERAL LEDGER ACCOUNTS

205 Accounts Payable, $28,356 Cr.
501 Purchases
502 Freight In
503 Purchases Returns and Allowances

Creditors		
Name	**Terms**	**Balance**
Apex Office Machines, Inc.	n/60	$11,060
Brown Paper Company	1/10, n/30	2,220
Dalton Office Furniture Company	n/30	9,676
Davis Corporation	n/30	
Zenn Furniture, Inc.	2/10, n/30	5,400

DATE		TRANSACTIONS
Sept.	3	Purchased desks for $8,020 plus a freight charge of $222 from Dalton Office Furniture Company, Invoice 4213, dated August 29; the terms are 30 days net.
	7	Purchased computers for $12,300 from Apex Office Machines, Inc., Invoice 9217, dated September 2, net due and payable in 60 days.
	10	Received Credit Memorandum 511 for $700 from Dalton Office Furniture Company; the amount is an allowance for damaged but usable desks purchased on Invoice 4213, dated August 29.
	16	Purchased file cabinets for $2,656 plus a freight charge of $134 from Davis Corporation, Invoice 8066, dated September 11; the terms are 30 days net.
	20	Purchased electronic desk calculators for $1,100 from Apex Office Machines, Inc., Invoice 11011, dated September 15, net due and payable in 60 days.
	23	Purchased bond paper and copy machine paper for $8,500 plus a freight charge of $100 from Brown Paper Company, Invoice 6498, dated September 18; the terms are 1/10, n/30.
	28	Received Credit Memorandum 312 for $980 from Apex Office Machines, Inc., for defective calculators that were returned; the calculators were originally purchased on Invoice 11011, dated September 15.
	30	Purchased office chairs for $3,940 plus a freight charge of $170 from Zenn Furniture, Inc., Invoice 696, dated September 25, the terms are 2/10, n/30.

Analyze: What total amount was recorded for purchases returns and allowances in the month of September? What percentage of total purchases does this represent?

Problem Set B

Journalizing credit purchases and purchases returns and allowances and posting to the general ledger.

◀ **Problem 8.1B**
Objectives 8-1, 8-2, 8-3

Mountain Ski Shop is a retail store that sells ski equipment and clothing. The firm's credit purchases and purchases returns and allowances during May 2019 follow, along with the general ledger accounts used to record these transactions. The balance shown in ***Accounts Payable*** is for the beginning of May.

INSTRUCTIONS

1. Open the general ledger accounts and enter the balance of ***Accounts Payable*** for May 1, 2019.
2. Record the transactions in a three-column purchases journal and in a general journal. Use 15 as the page number for the purchases journal and 38 as the page number for the general journal.

3. Post the entries from the general journal to the proper general ledger accounts.
4. Total and rule the purchases journal as of May 31.
5. Post the column totals from the purchases journal to the proper general ledger accounts.
6. Compute the net purchases of the firm for the month of May.

GENERAL LEDGER ACCOUNTS

205 Accounts Payable, $21,608 Cr.

501 Purchases

502 Freight In

503 Purchases Returns and Allowances

DATE	TRANSACTIONS
May 1	Purchased ski boots for $6,600 plus a freight charge of $120 from East Coast Snow Shop, Invoice 6572, dated April 28; the terms are 45 days net.
8	Purchased skis for $12,500 from May-Day Ski Shop, Invoice 4916, dated May 2; the terms are net payable in 30 days.
9	Received Credit Memorandum 155 for $1,050 from East Coast Snow Shop for damaged ski boots that were returned; the boots were originally purchased on Invoice 6572, dated April 28.
12	Purchased ski jackets for $5,200 from Fashion Ski Wear, Invoice 986, dated May 11, net due and payable in 60 days.
16	Purchased ski poles for $2,650 from May-Day Ski Shop, Invoice 5011, dated May 15; the terms are n/30.
22	Purchased ski pants for $3,160 from Winter Sports Clothing, Invoice 4019, dated May 16; the terms are 1/10, n/60.
28	Received Credit Memorandum 38 for $480 from May-Day Ski Shop for defective ski poles that were returned; the items were originally purchased on Invoice 5011, dated May 15.
31	Purchased sweaters for $3,630 plus a freight charge of $220 from Golden Skis & Clothing, Invoice 8354, dated May 27; the terms are 2/10, n/30.

(**Note:** Save your working papers for use in Problem 8.2B.)

Analyze: What total accounts payable were posted from the purchases journal to the general ledger for the month?

Problem 8.2B ► Posting to the accounts payable ledger and preparing a schedule of accounts payable.

Objectives 8-4, 8-6

CONTINUING >>> Problem

This problem is a continuation of Problem 8.1B.

INSTRUCTIONS

1. Set up an accounts payable subsidiary ledger for Mountain Ski Shop. Open an account for each of the creditors listed below and enter the balances as of May 1, 2019. Arrange the accounts payable ledger in alphabetical order.
2. Post the individual entries from the purchases journal and the general journal prepared in Problem 8.1B.
3. Prepare a schedule of accounts payable for May 31.

4. Check the total of the schedule of accounts payable against the balance of the ***Accounts Payable*** account in the general ledger. The two amounts should be equal.

Creditors		
Name	**Terms**	**Balance**
May-Day Ski Shop	n/30	$1,700
Fashion Ski Wear	n/60	8,720
Winter Sports Clothing	1/10, n/60	5,000
East Coast Snow Shop	n/45	6,188
Golden Skis & Clothing	2/10, n/30	

Analyze: What amount did Mountain Ski Shop owe to its supplier East Coast Snow Shop on May 31?

Journalizing credit purchases and purchases returns and allowances, computing the net delivered cost of goods, posting to the general ledger, posting to the accounts payable ledger, and preparing a schedule of accounts payable.

◀ **Problem 8.3B**
Objectives 8-1, 8-2, 8-3, 8-4, 8-5, 8-6

The Garden Supply Center is a retail store that sells garden equipment, furniture, and supplies. Its credit purchases and purchases returns and allowances for December are shown below. The general ledger accounts used to record these transactions are also provided. The balance shown is for the beginning of December 2019.

INSTRUCTIONS

PART I

1. Open the general ledger accounts and enter the balance of ***Accounts Payable*** for December 1.
2. Record the transactions in a three-column purchases journal and in a general journal. Use 8 as the page number for the purchases journal and 20 as the page number for the general journal.
3. Post the entries from the general journal to the proper general ledger accounts.
4. Total, prove, and rule the purchases journal as of December 31.
5. Post the column totals from the purchases journal to the proper general ledger accounts.
6. Compute the net delivered cost of the firm's purchases for the month of December.

GENERAL LEDGER ACCOUNTS

205 Accounts Payable, $13,490 Cr.
501 Purchases
502 Freight In
503 Purchases Returns and Allowances

DATE		TRANSACTIONS
Dec.	1	Purchased lawn mowers for $6,780 plus a freight charge of $356 from Shelby Corporation, Invoice 2110, dated November 26, net due and payable in 45 days.
	5	Purchased outdoor chairs and tables for $5,700 plus a freight charge of $100 from Patio Dudes, Invoice 633, dated December 2; the terms are 1/15, n/60.
	9	Purchased grass seed for $1,148 from Summer Lawn Center, Invoice 1127, dated December 4; the terms are 30 days net.

DATE	TRANSACTIONS
16	Received Credit Memorandum 101 for $300 from Patio Dudes; the amount is an allowance for scratches on some of the chairs and tables originally purchased on Invoice 633, dated December 2.
19	Purchased fertilizer for $1,750 plus a freight charge of $166 from Summer Lawn Center, Invoice 1131, dated December 15; the terms are 30 days net.
21	Purchased garden hoses for $860 plus a freight charge of $86 from DHX Rubber Company, Invoice 8517, dated December 17; the terms are n/60.
28	Received Credit Memorandum 210 for $150 from DHX Rubber Company for damaged hoses that were returned; the goods were purchased on Invoice 8517, dated December 17.
31	Purchased lawn sprinkler systems for $3,900 plus a freight charge of $180 from Carson Industries, Invoice 8819, dated December 26; the terms are 2/10, n/30.

INSTRUCTIONS

PART II

1. Set up an accounts payable subsidiary ledger for The Garden Supply Center. Open an account for each of the following creditors and enter the balances as of December 1.
2. Post the individual entries from the purchases journal and the general journal prepared in Part I.
3. Prepare a schedule of accounts payable for December 31.
4. Check the total of the schedule of accounts payable against the balance of the ***Accounts Payable*** account in the general ledger. The two amounts should be equal.

Creditors		
Name	**Terms**	**Balance**
Carson Industries	2/10, n/30	$2,150
DHX Rubber Company	n/60	3,850
Patio Dudes	1/15, n/60	
Shelby Corporation	n/45	4,842
Summer Lawn Center	n/30	2,648

Analyze: By what amount did ***Accounts Payable*** increase during the month of December?

Problem 8.4B ►

Objectives 8-1, 8-2, 8-3, 8-4, 8-5, 8-6

Journalizing credit purchases and purchases returns and allowances, posting to the general ledger, posting to the accounts payable ledger, and preparing a schedule of accounts payable.

Simpson's Card and Novelty Shop is a retail card, novelty, and business supply store. Its credit purchases and purchases returns and allowances for February 2019 appear below. The general ledger accounts and the creditors' accounts in the accounts payable subsidiary ledger used to record these transactions are also provided. The balance shown is for the beginning of February.

INSTRUCTIONS

1. Open the general ledger accounts and enter the balance of ***Accounts Payable*** for February.
2. Open the creditors' accounts in the accounts payable subsidiary ledger and enter the balances for February 1, 2019.

3. Record each transaction in the appropriate journal, purchases or general. Use page 4 in the purchases journal and page 12 in the general journal.
4. Post entries to the accounts payable subsidiary ledger daily.
5. Post entries in the general journal to the proper general ledger accounts at the end of the month.
6. Total and rule the purchases journal as of February 28.
7. Post the totals to the appropriate general ledger accounts.
8. Calculate the net delivered cost of purchases.
9. Prepare a schedule of accounts payable and compare the balance of the ***Accounts Payable*** control account with the schedule of accounts payable.

GENERAL LEDGER ACCOUNTS

203 Accounts Payable, $15,200 credit balance

501 Purchases

502 Freight In

503 Purchases Returns and Allowances

Creditors

Name	Terms	Balance
Business Forms, Inc.	n/30	$8,000
Gifts and Holiday Cards	2/10, n/30	4,000
Packing and Mailing Supply Center	2/10, n/30	3,200
Specialty Business Cards	1/10, n/45	

DATE		TRANSACTIONS
Feb.	5	Purchased copy paper from Packing and Mailing Supply Center for $2,000 plus $100 shipping charges on Invoice 502, dated February 2.
	8	Purchased assorted holiday cards from Gifts and Holiday Cards on Invoice 2808, $1,900, dated February 5.
	12	Purchased five boxes of novelty items from Gifts and Holiday Cards for a total cost of $1,200, Invoice 2904, dated February 8.
	13	Purchased a tray of cards from Specialty Business Cards on Invoice 2013 for $1,100, dated February 9.
	19	Purchased supply of forms from Business Forms, Inc., for $1,980 plus shipping charges of $60 on Invoice 2019, dated February 16.
	20	One box of cards purchased on February 8 from Gifts and Holiday Cards was water damaged. Received Credit Memorandum 102 for $200.
	21	Toner supplies are purchased from Specialty Business Cards for $3,600 plus shipping charges of $110, Invoice 1376, dated February 19.
	27	Received Credit Memorandum 118 for $240 from Gifts and Holiday Cards as an allowance for damaged novelty items purchased on February 12.

Analyze: What total amount did Simpson's Card and Novelty Shop pay in freight charges during the month of February? What percentage of delivered cost of purchases does this represent?

Critical Thinking Problem 8.1

Merchandising: Sales and Purchases

Fashion Standards is a retail clothing store. Sales of merchandise and purchases of goods on account for January 2019, the first month of operations, appear below.

INSTRUCTIONS

1. Record the purchases of goods on account on page 6 of a three-column purchases journal.
2. Record the sales of merchandise on account on page 1 of a sales journal.
3. Post the entries from the purchases journal and the sales journal to the individual accounts in the accounts payable and accounts receivable subsidiary ledgers. Use the following account numbers:

   Accounts Receivable 111

   Accounts Payable 205

   Sales Tax Payable 231

   Sales 401

   Purchases 501

   Freight In 502

   All customers have n/30 credit terms.
4. Total, prove, and rule the journals as of January 31.
5. Post the column totals from the special journals to the proper general ledger accounts.
6. Prepare a schedule of accounts payable for January 31.
7. Prepare a schedule of accounts receivable for January 31.

		PURCHASES OF GOODS ON ACCOUNT
Jan.	3	Purchased dresses for $4,500 plus a freight charge of $120 from Fashion Expo, Invoice 101, dated December 26; the terms are net 30 days.
	5	Purchased handbags for $3,480 plus a freight charge of $89 from Tru Totes & Co., Invoice 223, dated December 28; the terms are 2/10, n/30.
	7	Purchased blouses for $3,000 plus a freight charge of $75 from Extreme Fashions, Invoice 556, dated January 3; the terms are 2/10, n/30.
	9	Purchased casual pants for $2,360 from Comfy Casuals, Invoice 110, dated January 5; terms are n/30.
	12	Purchased business suits for $6,400 plus a freight charge of $150 from Professional Wears, Invoice 104, dated January 9; the terms are 2/10, n/30.
	18	Purchased shoes for $3,120 plus freight of $80 from City Walks, Invoice 118, dated January 14; the terms are n/60.
	25	Purchased hosiery for $1,025 from Silky Legs Express, Invoice 1012, dated January 20; the terms are 2/10, n/30.
	29	Purchased scarves and gloves for $1,600 from Comfy Casuals, Invoice 315, dated January 26; the terms are n/30.
	31	Purchased party dresses for $7,500 plus a freight charge of $250 from Special Occasions Dress Shop, Invoice 1044, dated January 27; the terms are 2/10, n/30.

		SALES OF MERCHANDISE ON ACCOUNT
Jan.	4	Sold two dresses to Vivian Cho; issued Sales Slip 101 for $600 plus $48 sales tax.
	5	Sold a handbag to Dina Bates; issued Sales Slip 102 for $525 plus $42 sales tax.
	6	Sold four blouses to Julia Adams; issued Sales Slip 103 for $400 plus $32 sales tax.
	10	Sold casual pants and a blouse to Cheryl Scott; issued Sales Slip 104 for $350 plus $28 sales tax.
	14	Sold a business suit to Alleen De Revere; issued Sales Slip 105 for $500 plus $40 sales tax.
	17	Sold hosiery, shoes, and gloves to Sasha Ramirez; issued Sales Slip 106 for $625 plus $50 sales tax.
	21	Sold dresses and scarves to Elaine Patterson; issued Sales Slip 107 for $1,500 plus $120 sales tax.
	24	Sold a business suit to Andrea Aguilar; issued Sales Slip 108 for $500 plus $40 sales tax.
	25	Sold shoes to Tracy Mai; issued Sales Slip 109 for $300 plus $24 sales tax.
	29	Sold a casual pants set to Toni Garcia; issued Sales Slip 110 for $600 plus $48 sales tax.
	31	Sold a dress and handbag to Linda Martin; issued Sales Slip 111 for $950 plus $76 sales tax.

Analyze: What is the net delivered cost of purchases for the month of January?

Critical Thinking Problem 8.2

Internal Control

Celeste Renard, owner of Sensual Linens Shop, was preparing checks for payment of the current month's purchase invoices when she realized that there were two invoices from Passionate Linens Company, each for the purchase of 100 red, heart-imprinted king-size linen sets. Alexander thinks that Passionate Linens Company must have billed Sensual Linens Shop twice for the same shipment because she knows the shop would not have needed two orders for 100 red linen sets within a month.

1. How can Renard determine whether Passionate Linens Company billed Sensual Linens Shop in error or whether Sensual Linens Shop placed two identical orders for red, heart-imprinted linen sets?
2. If two orders were placed, how can Renard prevent duplicate purchases from happening in the future?

BUSINESS CONNECTIONS

Cash Management

Managerial | FOCUS

1. Why should management be concerned about paying its invoices on a timely basis?
2. Why is it important for a firm to maintain a satisfactory credit rating?

3. Suppose you are the new controller of a small but growing company and you find that the firm has a policy of paying cash for all purchases of goods even though it could obtain credit. The president of the company does not like the idea of having debts, but the vice president thinks this is a poor business policy that will hurt the firm in the future. The president has asked your opinion. Would you agree with the president or the vice president? Why?
4. How would excessive investment in merchandise harm a business?
5. How can good internal controls over purchases protect a firm from fraud and errors and from excessive investment in merchandise?
6. Why should management be concerned about internal controls over purchases?

Ethical DILEMMA

Adding New Vendors

Anna Abraham is the accounts payable clerk for Jiffy Delivery Service. This company runs 10 branches in the San Diego area. The company pays for a variety of expenses. Anna writes the checks for each of the vendors and the controller signs the checks. Anna has decided she needs a raise and the controller has told her to wait for six months. Anna has devised a plan to get a raise on her own. She creates a new vendor for her friend's business with the name John's Car Detailing. She also creates two purchase orders for car detailing service from John's for $75 and $70. She writes checks to John's Car Detailing to pay these invoices. She knows the controller will sign all checks only looking at the checks over $100. She delivers the checks to John, who will deposit the checks in his bank account. John then writes a check to her for $145. Is this a good way for Anna to obtain a raise? Is it an ethical practice? Eventually what will be the effect of her actions? What can the company do to prevent this type of behavior?

Financial Statement ANALYSIS

Home Depot

Income Statement

The following financial statement excerpt is taken from the *2015 Annual Report (for the fiscal year ended January 31, 2016)* for The Home Depot, Inc.

Consolidated Statements of Earnings

(In millions)	*For the fiscal year ended January 31, 2016*	*February 1, 2015*
Net Sales	*$88,519*	*$83,176*
Cost of Sales	*58,254*	*54,787*
Gross Profit	*$30,265*	*$28,389*

1. The Cost of Sales amount on The Home Depot, Inc., consolidated statements of earnings represents the net cost of the goods that were sold for the period. For the year ended January 31, 2016, what percentage of net sales was the cost of sales? For the year ended February 1, 2015?
2. What factors might affect a merchandising company's cost of sales from one period to another?

Analyze Online: On The Home Depot, Inc., website (www.homedepot.com), locate the Investor Relations' section.

3. Review the consolidated statements of operations found in the current year's annual report.
4. What amount is reported for cost of sales?
5. What amount is reported for net sales?

Payment Terms

TEAMWORK

A company needs to develop an objective for paying bills. Does it want to stretch its cash flow as far as it can? Does it want to have a good reputation of always paying bills on time? Does it want to be sure to get paid by its customers before they pay their vendors? In a group, discuss what would be the best payment terms to use for each objective and its impact on the company.

Computer Check Format

Internet CONNECTION

Go to the QuickBooks and Sage websites at quickbooks.com and na.sage.com. Select product overview and more information. You want to be sure to see a copy of a check and purchase order. Compare and contrast the information contained on each check and purchase order. How many copies can you get of the check and purchase order? How is the form different? How is it the same? What information should be included on a company's check and purchase invoice?

Answers to **Self Reviews**

Answers to Section 1 Self Review

1. Locating suitable suppliers, obtaining price quotations and credit terms, and placing orders.
2. Merchandise purchased on credit for resale.
3. It saves time and effort, and it strengthens the audit trail.
4. **c.** Purchase requisition
5. **b.** Purchase order
6. The business will receive a 2 percent discount if the invoice is paid within 10 days. If the invoice is not paid within 10 days, the total amount is due within 30 days.

Answers to Section 2 Self Review

1. It lists all of the creditors to whom money is owed.
2. $59,575 ($62,450 – $2,875)
3. Journal entry:

Purchases	1,375.00	
Freight In	92.00	
Accounts Payable		1,467.00

4. **b.** income statement
5. **d.** $6,400 credit ($4,800 + $1,600)
6. A payment was made and recorded in the general ledger account but was not recorded in the creditor's subsidiary ledger account.

Answers to Comprehensive Self Review

1. A contra cost of goods sold account.
2. A price reduction offered to encourage quick payment of invoices by customers.
3. To accumulate freight charges paid for purchases.
4. The purchase requisition is used by a sales department to notify the purchasing department of the items wanted. The purchase order is prepared by the purchasing department to order the necessary goods at an appropriate price from the selected supplier.
5. The receiving report shows the quantity of goods received and the condition of the goods. The invoice shows quantities and prices; it is the document from which checks are prepared in payment of purchases.

Cash Receipts, Cash Payments, and Banking Procedures

Chapter 9

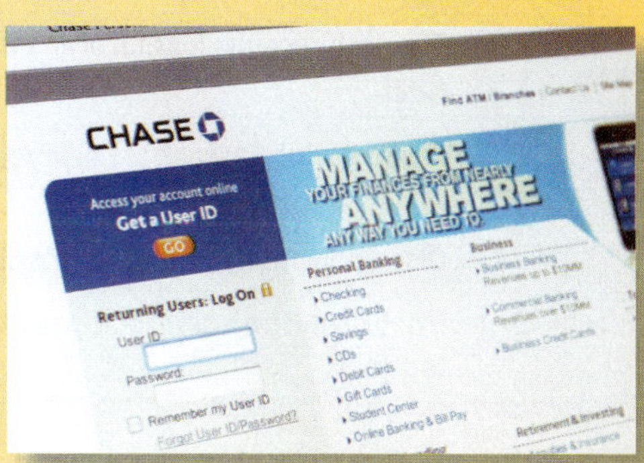

© NetPhotos3/Alamy Stock Photo

www.chase.com

JP Morgan Chase & Co. (Chase) is a leading global financial services firm and one of the largest banking institutions in the United States, with operations worldwide. Chase had $2.4 trillion in assets and $247.6 billion in equity as of December 31, 2015. Under the J.P. Morgan and Chase brands, the company serves millions of customers in the United States and many of the world's largest corporate and institutional clients.

The core strategy for the Consumer and Community Banking Division has been to build lifetime, engaged relationships with customers, according to Matt Zames, Chase's chief operating officer. Key to this strategy has been expanding the firm's digital and online banking offerings. According to Zames, the firm has invested 8 to 9 percent of its annual revenue to fund its global technology capabilities and protection of customer security in recent years.

Chase online banking allows businesses to view account activity, pay bills, transfer funds, receive electronic payments from customers, and view monthly statements from a personal computer.

In addition to online banking via personal computer, the Chase mobile app allows customers to view account balances and history, scan and deposit checks electronically, and pay bills with a mobile device. Chase also offers its customers various account alerts, including e-mail or text alerts when certain transactions exceed a customer-set limit. The number of Chase customers using mobile devices has more than doubled in recent years.

thinking critically

What types of payments could be processed by a small business using electronic banking?

LEARNING OBJECTIVES

- **9-1** Record cash receipts in a cash receipts journal.
- **9-2** Account for cash short or over.
- **9-3** Post from the cash receipts journal to subsidiary and general ledgers.
- **9-4** Record cash payments in a cash payments journal.
- **9-5** Post from the cash payments journal to subsidiary and general ledgers.
- **9-6** Demonstrate a knowledge of procedures for a petty cash fund.
- **9-7** Demonstrate a knowledge of internal control procedures for cash.
- **9-8** Write a check, endorse checks, prepare a bank deposit slip, and maintain a checkbook balance.
- **9-9** Reconcile the monthly bank statement.
- **9-10** Record any adjusting entries required from the bank reconciliation.
- **9-11** Understand how businesses use online banking to manage cash activities.
- **9-12** *Appendix:* Record transactions for a retailer using the perpetual inventory system.
- **9-13** Define the accounting terms new to this chapter.

NEW TERMS

bank reconciliation statement
blank endorsement
bonding
canceled check
cash
cash payments journal
cash receipts journal
cash register proof
***Cash Short or Over* account**
check
credit memorandum
debit memorandum
deposit in transit
deposit slip
dishonored (NSF) check
drawee
drawer
electronic funds transfer (EFT)
endorsement
full endorsement
negotiable
outstanding checks
payee
petty cash analysis sheet
petty cash fund
petty cash voucher
postdated check
promissory note
restrictive endorsement
service charge
statement of account

Section 1

SECTION OBJECTIVES	TERMS TO LEARN
>> 9-1 Record cash receipts in a cash receipts journal. WHY IT'S IMPORTANT The cash receipts journal is an efficient option for recording incoming cash. **>> 9-2 Account for cash short or over.** WHY IT'S IMPORTANT Discrepancies in cash are a possible indication that cash is mismanaged. **>> 9-3 Post from the cash receipts journal to subsidiary and general ledgers.** WHY IT'S IMPORTANT The subsidiary and general ledgers must hold accurate, up-to-date information about cash transactions.	cash cash register proof cash receipts journal *Cash Short or Over account* petty cash fund promissory note statement of account

Cash Receipts

Cash is the business asset that is most easily lost, mishandled, or even stolen. A well-managed business has careful procedures for controlling cash and recording cash transactions.

Cash Transactions

In accounting, the term **cash** is used for currency, coins, checks, money orders, and funds on deposit in a bank. Most cash transactions involve checks.

CASH RECEIPTS

The type of cash receipts depends on the nature of the business. Supermarkets receive checks as well as currency and coins. Department stores receive checks in the mail, or by electronic payment, from charge account customers. Cash received by wholesalers is usually in the form of checks.

CASH PAYMENTS

For safety and convenience, most businesses make payments by check. Sometimes a limited number of transactions are paid with currency and coins. The **petty cash fund** is used to handle payments involving small amounts of money, such as postage stamps, delivery charges, and minor purchases of office supplies. Some businesses maintain a fund to provide cash for business-related travel and entertainment expenses.

The Cash Receipts Journal

To improve the accounting for cash receipts, many businesses use a special **cash receipts journal.** The cash receipts journal simplifies the recording of transactions and eliminates repetition in posting.

FIGURE 9.1 Cash Receipts Journal

CASH RECEIPTS JOURNAL PAGE 1

DATE		DESCRIPTION	POST. REF.	ACCOUNTS RECEIVABLE CREDIT	SALES TAX PAYABLE CREDIT	SALES CREDIT	OTHER ACCOUNTS CREDIT			CASH DEBIT
							ACCOUNT NAME	POST. REF.	AMOUNT	
2019										
Jan.	7	Ann Anh		702 00						702 00
	8	Cash Sales			360 00	4 500 00				4 860 00
	11	Vickie Bowman		270 00						270 00
	12	Investment					M. Ferraro, Capital		15 000 00	15 000 00
	13	Barbara Coe		540 00						540 00
	15	Cash Sales			384 00	4 800 00	Cash Short/Over		(18 00)	5 166 00
	16	Alma Sanchez		108 00						108 00
	17	Cash Refund					Supplies		75 00	75 00
	22	Fred Wu		400 00						400 00
	22	Cash Sales			400 00	5 000 00				5 400 00
	29	Cash Sales			216 00	2 700 00	Cash Short/Over		16 00	2 932 00
	31	Kim Ramirez		108 00						108 00
	31	Mesia Davis		275 00						275 00
	31	Cash Sales			440 00	5 500 00				5 940 00
	31	Note Collection/					Notes Receivable		800 00	
		Stacee Fairley					Interest Income		36 00	836 00

RECORDING TRANSACTIONS IN THE CASH RECEIPTS JOURNAL

>> 9-1 OBJECTIVE

Record cash receipts in a cash receipts journal.

The format of the cash receipts journal varies according to the needs of each business. Figure 9.1 shows the cash receipts journal for Maxx-Out Sporting Goods, which has two major sources of cash receipts: checks from credit customers who are making payments on account and currency and coins from cash sales.

The cash receipts journal has separate columns for the accounts frequently used when recording cash receipts. There are columns for:

- debits to ***Cash,***
- credits to ***Accounts Receivable*** for payments received on account,
- credits to ***Sales*** and ***Sales Tax Payable*** for cash sales.

At the end of the month, the totals of these columns are posted to the general ledger.

Notice the Other Accounts Credit section, which is for entries that do not fit into one of the special columns. Entries in the Other Accounts Credit section are individually posted to the general ledger.

Cash Sales and Sales Taxes Maxx-Out Sporting Goods uses a cash register to record cash sales and to store currency and coins. As each transaction is entered, the cash register prints a receipt for the customer. It also records the sale and the sales tax on an audit tape locked inside the machine. At the end of the day, when the machine is cleared, the cash register prints the transaction totals on the audit tape. The manager of the store removes the audit tape, and a cash register proof is prepared. The **cash register proof** is a verification that the amount in the cash register agrees with the amount shown on the audit tape. The cash register proof is used to record cash sales and sales tax in the cash receipts journal. The currency and coins are deposited in the firm's bank.

ABOUT ACCOUNTING

Automated Teller Machines

The banking industry paved the way for the Internet's self-service applications (such as ordering products online) with ATMs.

Refer to Figure 9.1, the cash receipts journal for Maxx-Out Sporting Goods. To keep it simple, it shows weekly, rather than daily, cash sales entries. Look at the January 8 entry. The steps to record the January 8 sales follow:

1. Enter the sales tax collected, $360.00, in the Sales Tax Payable Credit column.
2. Enter the sales, $4,500.00, in the Sales Credit column.

3. Enter the cash received, $4,860.00, in the Cash Debit column.
4. Confirm that total credits equal total debits ($360.00 + $4,500.00 = $4,860.00).

>> 9-2 OBJECTIVE
Account for cash short or over.

important!

Cash Short or Over
Expect errors when employees make change, but investigate large and frequent errors. They may indicate dishonesty or incompetence, neither of which is a good attribute in employees.

Cash Short or Over Occasionally, errors occur when making change. When errors happen, the cash in the cash register is either more than or less than the cash listed on the audit tape. When cash in the register is more than the audit tape, cash is over. When cash in the register is less than the audit tape, cash is short. Cash tends to be short more often than over because customers are more likely to notice and complain if they receive too little change.

Record short or over amounts in the ***Cash Short or Over* account.** If the account has a credit balance, there is an overage, which is treated as revenue. If the account has a debit balance, there is a shortage, which is treated as an expense.

Figure 9.1 shows how cash overages and shortages appear in the cash receipts journal. Look at the January 29 entry. Cash sales were $2,700. Sales tax collected was $216. The cash drawer was over $16. Overages are recorded as credits. Notice that the account name and the overage are entered in the Other Accounts Credit section.

Now look at the January 15 entry. This time the cash register was short. Shortages are recorded as debits. Debits are not the normal balance of the Other Accounts Credit column, so the debit entry is circled.

Businesses that have frequent entries for cash shortages and overages add a Cash Short or Over column to the cash receipts journal.

Cash Received on Account Maxx-Out Sporting Goods makes sales on account and bills customers once a month. It sends a **statement of account** that shows the transactions during the month and the balance owed. Customers are asked to pay within 30 days of receiving the statement. Checks from credit customers are entered in the cash receipts journal, and then the checks are deposited in the bank.

Figure 9.1 shows how cash received on account is recorded. Look at the January 7 entry for Ann Anh. The check amount is entered in the Accounts Receivable Credit and the Cash Debit columns.

Cash Discounts on Sales Maxx-Out Sporting Goods, like most retail businesses, does not offer cash discounts. However, many wholesale businesses offer cash discounts to customers who pay within a certain time period. For example, a wholesaler may offer a 1 percent discount if the customer pays within 10 days. To the wholesaler this is a *sales discount.* Sales discounts are recorded when the payment is received. Sales discounts are recorded in a contra revenue account, ***Sales Discounts.*** Businesses with many sales discounts add a Sales Discounts Debit column to the cash receipts journal.

Additional Investment by the Owner Figure 9.1 shows that on January 12, owner Max Ferraro invested an additional $15,000 in Maxx-Out Sporting Goods. He intends to use the money to expand the product line. The account name and amount are entered in the Other Accounts Credit section. The debit is entered in the Cash Debit column.

Receipt of a Cash Refund Sometimes a business receives a cash refund for supplies, equipment, or other assets that are returned to the supplier. Figure 9.1 shows that on January 17, Maxx-Out Sporting Goods received a $75 cash refund for supplies that were returned to the seller. The account name and amount are entered in the Other Accounts Credit section. The debit is entered in the Cash Debit column.

Collection of a Promissory Note and Interest A **promissory note** is a written promise to pay a specified amount of money on a certain date. Most notes require that interest is paid at a specified rate. Businesses use promissory notes to extend credit for some sales transactions.

Sometimes promissory notes are used to replace an accounts receivable balance when the account is overdue. For example, on July 31 Maxx-Out Sporting Goods accepted a six-month promissory note from Stacee Fairley, who owed $800 on account (see Figure 9.2). Fairley had asked for more time to pay his balance. Maxx-Out Sporting Goods agreed to grant more time if

FIGURE 9.2

A Promissory Note

$ 800.00 July 31, 2018

Six Months AFTER DATE I PROMISE TO PAY

TO THE ORDER OF Maxx-Out Sporting Goods

Eight Hundred and no/100 DOLLARS

PAYABLE AT First Texas Bank

VALUE RECEIVED with interest at 9%

NO. 30 DUE January 31, 2019 Stacee Fairley

Fairley signed a promissory note with 9 percent annual interest. The note provides more legal protection than an account receivable. The interest is compensation for the delay in receiving payment.

On the date of the transaction, July 31, Maxx-Out Sporting Goods recorded a general journal entry to increase notes receivable and to decrease accounts receivable for $800. The asset account ***Notes Receivable*** was debited and ***Accounts Receivable*** was credited.

GENERAL JOURNAL PAGE 16

	DATE		DESCRIPTION	POST REF.	DEBIT	CREDIT	
1	2018						1
2	July	31	Notes Receivable	109	800 00		2
3			Accounts Receivable/Stacee Fairley	111 / ✓		800 00	3
4			Received a 6-month, 9% note from				4
5			Stacee Fairley to replace open account				5

On January 31, the due date of the note, Maxx-Out Sporting Goods received a check for $836 from Fairley. This sum covered the amount of the note ($800) and the interest owed for the six-month period ($36). Figure 9.1 shows the entry in the cash receipts journal. The account names, ***Notes Receivable*** and ***Interest Income,*** and the amounts are entered on two lines in the Other Accounts Credit section. The debit is in the Cash Debit column.

POSTING FROM THE CASH RECEIPTS JOURNAL

>> 9-3 OBJECTIVE

Post from the cash receipts journal to subsidiary and general ledgers.

During the month, the amounts recorded in the Accounts Receivable Credit column are posted to individual accounts in the accounts receivable subsidiary ledger. Similarly, the amounts that appear in the Other Accounts Credit column are posted individually to the general ledger accounts during the month. The "CR1" posting references in the ***Cash Short or Over*** general ledger account below show that the entries appear on the first page of the cash receipts journal.

ACCOUNT Cash Short or Over ACCOUNT NO. 617

DATE		DESCRIPTION	POST. REF.	DEBIT	CREDIT	BALANCE	
						DEBIT	CREDIT
2019							
Jan.	15		CR1	18 00		18 00	
	29		CR1		16 00	2 00	

Posting the Column Totals At the end of the month, the cash receipts journal is totaled and the equality of debits and credits is proved.

Proof of Cash Receipts Journal	
	Debits
Cash Debit column	$42,612.00
	Credits
Accounts Receivable Credit column	$ 2,403.00
Sales Tax Payable Credit column	1,800.00
Sales Credit column	22,500.00
Other Accounts Credit column	15,909.00
Total Credits	$42,612.00

Figure 9.3 shows the cash receipts journal after all posting is completed.

When the cash receipts journal has been proved, rule the columns and post the totals to the general ledger. Figure 9.4 shows how to post from the cash receipts journal to the general ledger accounts.

To post a column total to a general ledger account, enter "CR1" in the Posting Reference column to show that the entry is from the first page of the cash receipts journal. Enter the column total in the general ledger account Debit or Credit column. Figure 9.4 shows the entries to ***Accounts Receivable*** (1), ***Sales Tax Payable*** (2), ***Sales*** (3), and ***Cash*** (4). Compute the new balance for each account and enter it in the Balance Debit or Balance Credit column.

Enter the general ledger account numbers under the column totals on the cash receipts journal. The (X) in the Other Accounts Credit Amount column indicates that the individual amounts were posted, not the total.

Posting to the Accounts Receivable Ledger To keep customer balances current, accountants post entries from the Accounts Receivable Credit column to the customers' accounts

FIGURE 9.3 **Posted Cash Receipts Journal**

CASH RECEIPTS JOURNAL — PAGE 1

DATE		DESCRIPTION	POST. REF.	ACCOUNTS RECEIVABLE CREDIT	SALES TAX PAYABLE CREDIT	SALES CREDIT	OTHER ACCOUNTS CREDIT: ACCOUNT NAME	POST. REF.	AMOUNT	CASH DEBIT
2019										
Jan.	7	Ann Anh	✓	702 00						702 00
	8	Cash Sales			360 00	4 500 00				4 860 00
	11	Vickie Bowman	✓	270 00						270 00
	12	Investment					M. Ferraro, Capital	301	15 000 00	15 000 00
	13	Barbara Coe	✓	540 00						540 00
	15	Cash Sales			384 00	4 800 00	Cash Short/Over	617	(18 00)	5 166 00
	16	Alma Sanchez	✓	108 00						108 00
	17	Cash Refund					Supplies	129	75 00	75 00
	22	Fred Wu	✓	400 00						400 00
	22	Cash Sales			400 00	5 000 00				5 400 00
	29	Cash Sales			216 00	2 700 00	Cash Short/Over	617	16 00	2 932 00
	31	Kim Ramirez	✓	108 00						108 00
	31	Mesia Davis	✓	275 00						275 00
	31	Cash Sales			440 00	5 500 00				5 940 00
	31	Note Collection/					Notes Receivable	109	800 00	
		Stacee Fairley					Interest Income	491	36 00	836 00
		Totals		2 403 00	1 800 00	22 500 00			15 909 00	42 612 00
				(111)	(231)	(401)			(X)	(101)

FIGURE 9.4 Posting from the Cash Receipts Journal

CASH RECEIPTS JOURNAL PAGE 1

DATE		DESCRIPTION	POST. REF.	ACCOUNTS RECEIVABLE CREDIT	SALES TAX PAYABLE CREDIT	SALES CREDIT	OTHER ACCOUNTS CREDIT: ACCOUNT NAME	POST. REF.	AMOUNT	CASH DEBIT
2019										
Jan.	7	Ann Anh	✓	702 00						702 00
		Totals		2403 00	1800 00	22500 00			15909 00	42612 00
				(111)	(231)	(401)			(X)	(101)

ACCOUNT Cash ACCOUNT NO. 101

DATE		DESCRIPTION	POST. REF.	DEBIT	CREDIT	BALANCE DEBIT	BALANCE CREDIT
2019							
Jan.	1	Balance	✓			12025 50	
	31		CR1	42612 00		54637 50	

ACCOUNT Accounts Receivable ACCOUNT NO. 111

DATE		DESCRIPTION	POST. REF.	DEBIT	CREDIT	BALANCE DEBIT	BALANCE CREDIT
2019							
Jan.	1	Balance	✓			3240 00	
	23		J1		162 00	3078 00	
	25		J1		486 00	2592 00	
	31		S1	6156 00		8748 00	
	31		CR1		2403 00	6345 00	

ACCOUNT Sales Tax Payable ACCOUNT NO. 231

DATE		DESCRIPTION	POST. REF.	DEBIT	CREDIT	BALANCE DEBIT	BALANCE CREDIT
2019							
Jan.	1	Balance	✓				756 00
	11		CP1	756 00			– 0 –
	23		J1	8 00		8 00	
	25		J1	36 00		44 00	
	31		S1		436 00		392 00
	31		CR1		1800 00		2192 00

ACCOUNT Sales ACCOUNT NO. 401

DATE		DESCRIPTION	POST. REF.	DEBIT	CREDIT	BALANCE DEBIT	BALANCE CREDIT
2019							
Jan.	31		S1		5450 00		5450 00
	31		CR1		22500 00		27950 00

in the accounts receivable subsidiary ledger daily. For example, on January 7, $702 was posted to Ann Anh's account in the subsidiary ledger. The "CR1" in the Posting Reference column indicates that the transaction appears on page 1 of the cash receipts journal. The check mark (✓) in the Posting Reference column in the cash receipts journal (Figure 9.4) shows that the amount was posted to Ann Anh's account in the accounts receivable subsidiary ledger.

NAME *Ann Anh*

ADDRESS *8913 South Hampton Road, Dallas, Texas 75232-6002*

DATE		DESCRIPTION	POST. REF.	DEBIT	CREDIT	BALANCE
2019						
Jan.	1	Balance	✓			432 00
	3	Sales Slip 1101	S1	702 00		1134 00
	7		CR1		702 00	432 00
	31	Sales Slip 1110	S1	267 50		699 50

ADVANTAGES OF THE CASH RECEIPTS JOURNAL

The cash receipts journal:

- saves time and effort when recording and posting cash receipts,
- allows for the division of work among the accounting staff,
- strengthens the audit trail by recording all cash receipts transactions in one place.

Section 1 Self Review

QUESTIONS

1. How and when are the amounts in the Accounts Receivable Credit column of the cash receipts journal posted?
2. What is a promissory note? In what situation would a business accept a promissory note?
3. What is a cash shortage? A cash overage? How are they recorded?

EXERCISES

4. Which items are considered cash?
   a. Currency
   b. Funds on deposit in the bank
   c. Money orders
   d. All of the above
5. Collection of a note receivable is recorded in the:
   a. accounts receivable journal.
   b. cash receipts journal.
   c. general journal.
   d. promissory note journal.

ANALYSIS

6. You notice that the ***Cash Short or Over*** account has 15 entries during the month. The ending balance is a $10 shortage for the month. Is this a problem? Why or why not?

(Answers to Section 1 Self Review are on page 342.)

Section 2

SECTION OBJECTIVES	TERMS TO LEARN
>> 9-4 Record cash payments in a cash payments journal. WHY IT'S IMPORTANT The cash payments journal is an efficient option for recording payments by check. >> 9-5 Post from the cash payments journal to subsidiary and general ledgers. WHY IT'S IMPORTANT The subsidiary and general ledgers must hold accurate, up-to-date information about cash transactions. >> 9-6 Demonstrate a knowledge of procedures for a petty cash fund. WHY IT'S IMPORTANT Businesses use the petty cash fund to pay for small operating expenditures. >> 9-7 Demonstrate a knowledge of internal control procedures for cash. WHY IT'S IMPORTANT Internal controls safeguard business assets.	bonding cash payments journal petty cash analysis sheet petty cash voucher

Cash Payments

A good system of internal control requires that payments be made by check. In a good internal control system, one employee approves payments, another employee prepares the checks, and another employee records the transactions.

The Cash Payments Journal

Unless a business has just a few cash payments each month, the process of recording these transactions in the general journal is time consuming. The **cash payments journal** is a special journal used to record transactions involving the payment of cash.

RECORDING TRANSACTIONS IN THE CASH PAYMENTS JOURNAL

>> 9-4 OBJECTIVE
Record cash payments in a cash payments journal.

Refer to Figure 9.5 for Maxx-Out Sporting Goods' cash payments journal. Notice that there are separate columns for the accounts frequently used when recording cash payments— ***Cash, Accounts Payable,*** and ***Purchases Discounts.*** At the end of the month, the totals of these columns are posted to the general ledger.

The Other Accounts Debit section is for entries that do not fit into one of the special columns. Entries in the Other Accounts Debit section are individually posted to the general ledger.

Payments for Expenses Businesses write checks for a variety of expenses each month. In January, Maxx-Out Sporting Goods issued checks for rent, electricity, telephone service,

FIGURE 9.5 Cash Payments Journal

CASH PAYMENTS JOURNAL PAGE 1

DATE		CK. NO.	DESCRIPTION	POST. REF.	ACCOUNTS PAYABLE DEBIT	OTHER ACCOUNTS DEBIT			PURCHASES DISCOUNTS CREDIT	CASH CREDIT
						ACCOUNT TITLE	POST. REF.	AMOUNT		
2019										
Jan.	3	111	January rent			Rent Expense		1500 00		1500 00
	10	112	Store fixtures			Store Equipment		2400 00		2400 00
	11	113	Tax remittance			Sales Tax Payable		756 00		756 00
	11	114	World of Sports		3935 00				78 70	3856 30
	13	115	Active Designs		2865 00				57 30	2807 70
	14	116	Store Supplies			Supplies		900 00		900 00
	15	117	Withdrawal			M. Ferraro, Drawing		3000 00		3000 00
	17	118	Electric bill			Utilities Expense		318 00		318 00
	17	119	The Sports Warehouse		4250 00					4250 00
	21	120	Telephone bill			Telephone Expense		276 00		276 00
	25	121	Newspaper ad			Advertising Expense		840 00		840 00
	27	122	International Sportsman		1000 00					1000 00
	30	123	Active Designs		1135 00					1135 00
	31	124	World of Sports		565 00					565 00
	31	125	January payroll			Salaries Expense		4950 00		4950 00
	31	126	Purchase of goods			Purchases		3200 00		3200 00
	31	127	Freight charge			Freight In		175 00		175 00
	31	128	Cash refund			Sales Returns & Allow.		160 00		
						Sales Tax Payable		12 80		172 80
	31	129	Note Paid to			Notes Payable		6000 00		
			Metroplex Equip. Co.			Interest Expense		300 00		6300 00
	31	130	Establish Petty Cash fund			Petty Cash Fund		175 00		175 00
			TOTALS		13750 00			24962 80	136 00	38576 80

advertising, and salaries. Refer to the January 3 entry for rent expense in Figure 9.5. Notice that the account name and amount are entered in the Other Accounts Debit section. The credit is in the Cash Credit column.

Payments on Account Merchandising businesses usually make numerous payments on account for goods that were purchased on credit. If there is no cash discount, the entry in the cash payments journal is a debit to ***Accounts Payable*** and a credit to ***Cash.*** For an example of a payment without a discount, refer to the January 27 entry for International Sportsman in Figure 9.5.

Purchases Discounts is a contra cost of goods sold account that appears in the Cost of Goods Sold section of the income statement. Purchases discounts are subtracted from purchases to obtain net purchases.

For an example of a payment with a discount, refer to the January 13 entry for Active Designs in Figure 9.5. Maxx-Out Sporting Goods takes a 2 percent discount for paying within the discount period ($\$2,865 \times 0.02 = \$57.30$). When there is a cash discount, three elements must be recorded:

- Debit ***Accounts Payable*** for the invoice amount, $2,865.
- Credit ***Purchases Discounts*** for the amount of the discount, $57.30.
- Credit ***Cash*** for the amount of cash paid, $2,807.70.

recall

Discount Terms

The terms 2/10, n/30 mean that if payment is made within 10 days, the customer can take a 2 percent discount. Otherwise, payment in full is due in 30 days.

> Debit cards (also called check cards) look like credit cards or ATM (automated teller machine) cards but operate like cash or a personal check. In this context, debit means "subtract" so when you use your debit card, you are subtracting your money from your bank account. Funds on deposit with a bank represent a liability from the bank's perspective. By debiting accounts when depositors use their debit cards, the bank reduces the depositors' account balances, thus reducing the bank's liabilities to depositors. Debit cards are accepted almost everywhere including grocery stores, retail stores, gasoline stations, and restaurants. Debit cards are popular because they offer an alternative to carrying checks or cash. Transactions that are completed using a debit card will appear on your bank statement.

Cash Purchases of Equipment and Supplies Businesses use cash to purchase equipment, supplies, and other assets. These transactions are recorded in the cash payments journal. In January, Maxx-Out Sporting Goods issued checks for store fixtures and store supplies. Refer to the entries on January 10 and 14 in Figure 9.5. Notice that the account names and amounts appear in the Other Accounts Debit section. The credits are recorded in the Cash Credit column.

Payment of Taxes Retail businesses collect sales tax from their customers. Periodically, the sales tax is remitted to the taxing authority. Refer to the entry on January 11 in Figure 9.5. Maxx-Out Sporting Goods issued a check for $756 to pay the December sales tax. Notice that the account name and amount appear in the Other Accounts Debit section. The credit is in the Cash Credit column.

Cash Purchases of Merchandise Most merchandising businesses buy their goods on credit. Occasionally, purchases are made for cash. These purchases are recorded in the cash payments journal. Refer to the January 31 entry for the purchase of goods in Figure 9.5.

Payment of Freight Charges Freight charges on purchases of goods are handled in two ways. In some cases, the seller pays the freight charge and then includes it on the invoice. This method was covered in Chapter 8. The other method is for the buyer to pay the transportation company when the goods arrive. The buyer issues a check for the freight charge and records it in the cash payments journal. Refer to the entry on January 31 in Figure 9.5. The account name and amount appear in the Other Accounts Debit section. The credit is in the Cash Credit column.

Payment of a Cash Refund When a customer purchases goods for cash and later returns them or receives an allowance, the customer is usually given a cash refund. Refer to the January 31 entry in Figure 9.5. Maxx-Out Sporting Goods issued a check for $172.80 to a customer who returned a defective item. When there is a cash refund, three elements are recorded:

- Debit ***Sales Returns and Allowances*** for the amount of the purchase, $160.00.
- Debit ***Sales Tax Payable*** for the sales tax, $12.80.
- Credit ***Cash*** for the amount of cash paid, $172.80.

Notice that the debits in the Other Accounts Debit section appear on two lines because two general ledger accounts are debited.

Payment of a Promissory Note and Interest A promissory note can be issued to settle an overdue account or to obtain goods, equipment, or other property. For example, on August 4 Maxx-Out Sporting Goods issued a 180-day promissory note for $6,000 to purchase store fixtures from Metroplex Equipment Company. The note had an interest rate of 10 percent. Maxx-Out Sporting Goods recorded this transaction in the general journal by debiting ***Store Equipment*** and crediting ***Notes Payable,*** a liability account.

GENERAL JOURNAL PAGE 16

	DATE		DESCRIPTION	POST. REF.	DEBIT	CREDIT	
1	2018						1
2	Aug.	4	Store Equipment	131	6 000 00		2
3			Notes Payable	201		6 000 00	3
4			Issued a 6-month, 10% note to				4
5			Metroplex Equipment Company for				5
6			purchase of new store fixtures				6
7							7

On January 31, Maxx-Out Sporting Goods issued a check for $6,300 in payment of the note, $6,000, and the interest, $300. This transaction was recorded in the cash payments journal in Figure 9.5.

- Debit ***Notes Payable,*** $6,000.
- Debit ***Interest Expense,*** $300.
- Credit ***Cash,*** $6,300.

Notice that the debits in the Other Accounts Debit section appear on two lines.

>> 9-5 OBJECTIVE
Post from the cash payments journal to subsidiary and general ledgers.

POSTING FROM THE CASH PAYMENTS JOURNAL

During the month, the amounts recorded in the Accounts Payable Debit column are posted to individual accounts in the accounts payable subsidiary ledger. The amounts in the Other Accounts Debit column are also posted individually to the general ledger accounts during the month. For example, the January 3 entry in the cash payments journal was posted to the ***Rent Expense*** account. The "CP1" indicates that the entry is recorded on page 1 of the cash payments journal.

ACCOUNT Rent Expense ACCOUNT NO. 634

DATE		DESCRIPTION	POST. REF.	DEBIT	CREDIT	BALANCE DEBIT	BALANCE CREDIT
2019							
Jan.	3		CP1	1 500 00		1 500 00	

Posting the Column Totals At the end of the month, the cash payments journal is totaled and proved. The total debits must equal total credits.

Proof of Cash Payments Journal	
	Debits
Accounts Payable Debit column	$13,750.00
Other Accounts Debit column	24,962.80
Total Debits	$38,712.80
	Credits
Purchases Discount Credit column	$ 136.00
Cash Credit column	38,576.80
Total Credits	$38,712.80

FIGURE 9.6 Posted Cash Payments Journal

CASH PAYMENTS JOURNAL PAGE 1

DATE		CK. NO.	DESCRIPTION	POST. REF.	ACCOUNTS PAYABLE DEBIT	OTHER ACCOUNTS DEBIT			PURCHASES DISCOUNTS CREDIT	CASH CREDIT
						ACCOUNT TITLE	POST. REF.	AMOUNT		
2019										
Jan.	3	111	January rent			Rent Expense	634	1500 00		1500 00
	10	112	Store fixtures			Store Equipment	131	2400 00		2400 00
	11	113	Tax remittance			Sales Tax Payable	231	756 00		756 00
	11	114	World of Sports	✓	3935 00				78 70	3856 30
	13	115	Active Designs	✓	2865 00				57 30	2807 70
	14	116	Store Supplies			Supplies	129	900 00		900 00
	15	117	Withdrawal			M. Ferraro, Drawing	302	3000 00		3000 00
	17	118	Electric bill			Utilities Expense	643	318 00		318 00
	17	119	The Sports Warehouse	✓	4250 00					4250 00
	21	120	Telephone bill			Telephone Expense	649	276 00		276 00
	25	121	Newspaper ad			Advertising Expense	614	840 00		840 00
	27	122	International Sportsman	✓	1000 00					1000 00
	30	123	Active Designs	✓	1135 00					1135 00
	31	124	World of Sports	✓	565 00					565 00
	31	125	January payroll			Salaries Expense	637	4950 00		4950 00
	31	126	Purchase of goods			Purchases	501	3200 00		3200 00
	31	127	Freight charge			Freight In	502	175 00		175 00
	31	128	Cash refund			Sales Returns & Allow.	451	160 00		
						Sales Tax Payable	231	12 80		172 80
	31	129	Note Paid to Metroplex			Notes Payable	201	6000 00		
			Equipment Company			Interest Expense	691	300 00		6300 00
	31	130	Establish Petty Cash fund			Petty Cash Fund	105	175 00		175 00
	31		Totals		13750 00			24962 80	136 00	38576 80
					(205)			(X)	(504)	(101)

Figure 9.6 shows the January cash payments journal after posting for Maxx-Out Sporting Goods. Notice that the account numbers appear in the Posting Reference column of the Other Accounts Debit section to show that the amounts were posted.

When the cash payments journal has been proved, rule the columns and post the totals to the general ledger. Figure 9.7 shows how to post from the cash payments journal to the general ledger accounts.

To post a column total to a general ledger account, enter "CP1" in the Posting Reference column to show that the entry is from page 1 of the cash payments journal.

Enter the column total in the general ledger account Debit or Credit column. Figure 9.7 shows the entries to ***Accounts Payable*** (1), ***Purchases Discounts*** (2), and ***Cash*** (3). Compute the new balance and enter it in the Balance Debit or Balance Credit column.

Enter the general ledger account numbers under the column totals on the cash payments journal. The (X) in the Other Accounts Debit column indicates that the individual accounts were posted, not the total.

Posting to the Accounts Payable Ledger To keep balances current, accountants post entries from the Accounts Payable Debit column of the cash payments journal to the vendor accounts in the accounts payable subsidiary ledger daily. For example, on January 13, $2,865 was posted to Active Designs account in the subsidiary ledger. The "CP1" in the Posting Reference column indicates that the entry is recorded on page 1 of the cash payments journal. The check mark (✓) in the Posting Reference column of the cash payments journal (Figure 9.7) shows that the amount was posted to the supplier's account in the accounts payable subsidiary ledger.

NAME *Active Designs* TERMS *2/10, n/30*

ADDRESS *2313 Belt Line Road, Dallas, Texas 75267-6205*

DATE		DESCRIPTION	POST. REF.	DEBIT	CREDIT	BALANCE
2019						
Jan.	1	Balance	✓			2,200.00
	3	Invoice 5879, 01/02/19	P1		2,865.00	5,065.00
	13		CP1	2,865.00		2,200.00
	30		CP1	1,135.00		1,065.00

ADVANTAGES OF THE CASH PAYMENTS JOURNAL

The cash payments journal:

- saves time and effort when recording and posting cash payments,
- allows for a division of labor among the accounting staff,
- improves the audit trail because all cash payments are recorded in one place and listed by check number.

FIGURE 9.7 Posted General Ledger Accounts

CASH PAYMENTS JOURNAL PAGE 1

DATE		CK. NO.	DESCRIPTION	POST. REF.	ACCOUNTS PAYABLE DEBIT	OTHER ACCOUNTS DEBIT: ACCOUNT TITLE	POST. REF.	AMOUNT	PURCHASES DISCOUNTS CREDIT	CASH CREDIT
2019										
Jan.	3	111	January rent			Rent Expense	535	1,500.00		1,500.00
	10	112	Store fixtures			Store Equipment	131	2,400.00		2,400.00
	11	113	Tax remittance			Sales Tax Payable	231	756.00		756.00
	11	114	World of Sports	✓	3,935.00				78.70	3,856.30
	13	115	Active Designs	✓	2,865.00				57.30	2,807.70
			Totals		13,750.00			24,962.80	136.00	38,576.80
					(205)			(X)	(504)	(101)

ACCOUNT *Cash* ACCOUNT NO. *101*

DATE		DESCRIPTION	POST. REF.	DEBIT	CREDIT	BALANCE DEBIT	BALANCE CREDIT
2019							
Jan.	1	Balance	✓			12,025.50	
	31		CR1	42,612.00		54,637.50	
	31		CP1		38,576.80	16,060.70	

ACCOUNT *Accounts Payable* ACCOUNT NO. *205*

DATE		DESCRIPTION	POST. REF.	DEBIT	CREDIT	BALANCE DEBIT	BALANCE CREDIT
2019							
Jan.	1	Balance	✓				10,800.00
	18		J1	476.00			10,324.00
	31		P1		18,795.00		29,119.00
	31		CP1	13,750.00			15,369.00

ACCOUNT *Purchases Discounts* ACCOUNT NO. *504*

DATE		DESCRIPTION	POST. REF.	DEBIT	CREDIT	BALANCE DEBIT	BALANCE CREDIT
2019							
Jan.	31		CP1		136.00		136.00

The Petty Cash Fund

>> **9-6 OBJECTIVE**
Demonstrate a knowledge of procedures for a petty cash fund.

In a well-managed business, most bills are paid by check. However, there are times when small expenditures are made with currency and coins. Most businesses use a petty cash fund to pay for small expenditures. Suppose that in the next two hours the office manager needs a $4 folder for a customer. It is not practical to obtain an approval and write a check for $4 in the time available. Instead, the office manager takes $4 from the petty cash fund to purchase the folder.

ESTABLISHING THE FUND

The amount of the petty cash fund depends on the needs of the business. Usually the office manager, cashier, or assistant is in charge of the petty cash fund. The cashier is responsible for petty cash. To set up the petty cash fund, Maxx-Out Sporting Goods wrote a $175 check to the cashier. She cashed the check and put the currency in a locked cash box.

The establishment of the petty cash fund should be recorded in the cash payments journal. Debit ***Petty Cash Fund*** in the Other Accounts Debit section of the journal and enter the credit in the Cash Credit column.

important!

Petty Cash
Only one person controls the petty cash fund. That person should keep receipts for all expenditures.

MAKING PAYMENTS FROM THE FUND

Petty cash fund payments are limited to small amounts. A **petty cash voucher** is used to record the payments made from the petty cash fund. The petty cash voucher shows the voucher number, amount, purpose of the expenditure, and account to debit. The person receiving the funds signs the voucher, and the person who controls the petty cash fund initials the voucher. Figure 9.8 shows a petty cash voucher for $16.25 for office supplies.

THE PETTY CASH ANALYSIS SHEET

Most businesses use a **petty cash analysis sheet** to record transactions involving petty cash. The Receipts column shows cash put in the fund, and the Payments column shows the cash paid out. There are special columns for accounts that are used frequently, such as ***Supplies, Freight In,*** and ***Miscellaneous Expense.*** There is an Other Accounts Debit column for entries that do not fit in a special column. Figure 9.9 shows the petty cash analysis sheet for Maxx-Out Sporting Goods for February.

Replenishing the Fund The total vouchers plus the cash on hand should always equal the amount of the fund—$175 for Maxx-Out Sporting Goods. Replenish the petty cash fund at the end of each month or sooner if the fund is low. Refer to Figures 9.9 and 9.10 as you learn how to replenish the petty cash fund.

1. Total the columns on the petty cash analysis sheet.
2. Prove the petty cash fund by adding cash on hand and total payments. This should equal the petty cash fund balance ($15.25 + $159.75 = $175.00).

PETTY CASH VOUCHER 1
NOTE: This form must be computer processed or filled out in black ink.

DESCRIPTION OF EXPENDITURE	ACCOUNTS TO BE CHARGED	AMOUNT	
Office supplies	Supplies 129	16	25
	Total	16	25

RECEIVED THE SUM OF Sixteen ---------- DOLLARS AND 25/100 CENTS
SIGNED L.T. Green Metroplex Office Supply Co. DATE 2/3/19 APPROVED BY M.F. DATE 2/3/19

FIGURE 9.8
Petty Cash Voucher

FIGURE 9.9 Petty Cash Analysis Sheet

PETTY CASH ANALYSIS PAGE 1

DATE		VOU. NO.	DESCRIPTION	RECEIPTS	PAYMENTS	SUPPLIES DEBIT	DELIVERY EXPENSE DEBIT	MISC. EXPENSE DEBIT	OTHER ACCOUNTS DEBIT	
									ACCOUNT TITLE	AMOUNT
2019										
Feb.	1		Establish fund	175 00						
	3	1	Office supplies		16 25	16 25				
	6	2	Delivery service		24 00		24 00			
	11	3	Withdrawal		25 00				M. Ferraro, Drawing	25 00
	15	4	Postage stamps		37 00			37 00		
	20	5	Delivery service		17 50		17 50			
	26	6	Window washing		26 00			26 00		
	28	7	Store supplies		14 00	14 00				
	28		Totals	175 00	159 75	30 25	41 50	63 00		25 00
	28		Balance on hand		15 25					
				175 00	175 00					
	28		Balance on hand	15 25						
	28		Replenish fund	159 75						
	28		Carried forward	175 00						

FIGURE 9.10 Reimbursing the Petty Cash Fund

CASH PAYMENTS JOURNAL PAGE 1

DATE		CK. NO.	DESCRIPTION	POST. REF.	ACCOUNTS PAYABLE DEBIT	OTHER ACCOUNTS DEBIT			PURCHASES DISCOUNTS CREDIT	CASH CREDIT
						ACCOUNT TITLE	POST. REF.	AMOUNT		
2019										
Feb.	28	191	Replenish Petty Cash fund			Supplies	129	30 25		
						M. Ferraro, Drawing	302	25 00		
						Delivery Expense	523	41 50		
						Miscellaneous Expense	593	63 00		159 75

3. Write a check to restore the petty cash fund to its original balance.
4. Record the check in the cash payments journal. Refer to the petty cash analysis sheet for the accounts and amounts to debit. Notice that the debits appear on four lines of the Other Accounts Debit section. The credit appears in the Cash Credit column.

INTERNAL CONTROL OF THE PETTY CASH FUND

Whenever there is valuable property or cash to protect, appropriate safeguards must be established. Petty cash is no exception. The following internal control procedures apply to petty cash:

internal CONTROL

1. Use the petty cash fund only for small payments that cannot conveniently be made by check.
2. Limit the amount set aside for petty cash to the approximate amount needed to cover one month's payments from the fund.
3. Write petty cash fund checks to the person in charge of the fund, not to the order of "Cash."

4. Assign one person to control the petty cash fund. This person has sole control of the money and is the only one authorized to make payments from the fund.
5. Keep petty cash in a safe, a locked cash box, or a locked drawer.
6. Prepare a petty cash voucher for each payment. The voucher should be signed by the person who receives the money and should show the payment details. This provides an audit trail for the fund. Additionally, obtain a vendor's invoice or other receipt as documentation for each petty cash voucher.

Internal Control over Cash

>> 9-7 OBJECTIVE

Demonstrate a knowledge of internal control procedures for cash.

In a well-managed business, there are internal control procedures for handling and recording cash receipts and cash payments. The internal control over cash should be tailored to the needs of the business. Accountants play a vital role in designing, establishing, and monitoring the cash control system. In developing internal control procedures for cash, certain basic principles must be followed.

internal CONTROL

CONTROL OF CASH RECEIPTS

As noted already, cash is the asset that is most easily stolen, lost, or mishandled. Yet cash is essential to carrying on business operations. It is important to protect all cash receipts to make sure that funds are available to pay expenses and take care of other business obligations. The following are essential cash receipt controls:

1. Have only designated employees receive and handle cash whether it consists of checks and money orders or currency and coins. These employees should be carefully chosen for reliability and accuracy and should be carefully trained. In some businesses, employees who handle cash are bonded. **Bonding** is the process by which employees are investigated by an insurance company. Employees who pass the background check can be bonded; that is, the employer can purchase insurance on the employees. If the bonded employees steal or mishandle cash, the business is insured against the loss.
2. Keep cash receipts in a cash register, a locked cash drawer, or a safe while they are on the premises.
3. Make a record of all cash receipts as the funds come into the business. For checks, endorse each check when received. For currency and coins, this record is the audit tape in a cash register or duplicate copies of numbered sales slips. The use of a cash register provides an especially effective means of control because the machine automatically produces a tape showing the amounts entered. This tape is locked inside the cash register until it is removed by a supervisor.
4. Before a bank deposit is made, check the funds to be deposited against the record made when the cash was received. The employee who checks the deposit is someone other than the one who receives or records the cash.
5. Deposit cash receipts in the bank promptly—every day or several times a day. Deposit the funds intact—do not make payments directly from the cash receipts. The person who makes the bank deposit is someone other than the one who receives and records the funds.
6. Enter cash receipts transactions in the accounting records promptly. The person who records cash receipts is not the one who receives or deposits the funds.
7. Have the monthly bank statement sent to and reconciled by someone other than the employees who handle, record, and deposit the funds.

One of the advantages of efficient procedures for handling and recording cash receipts is that the funds reach the bank sooner. Cash receipts are not kept on the premises for more than a short time, which means that the funds are safer and are readily available for paying bills owed by the firm.

CONTROL OF CASH PAYMENTS

It is important to control cash payments so that the payments are made only for authorized business purposes. The following are essential cash payment controls:

1. Make all payments by check except for payments from special-purpose cash funds such as a petty cash fund or a travel and entertainment fund.
2. Issue checks only with an approved bill, invoice, or other document that describes the reason for the payment.
3. Have only designated personnel, who are experienced and reliable, approve bills and invoices.
4. Have checks prepared and recorded in the checkbook or check register by someone other than the person who approves the payments.
5. Have still another person sign and mail the checks to creditors. Consider requiring two people to sign all checks greater than a predesignated amount.
6. Use prenumbered check forms. Periodically the numbers of the checks that were issued and the numbers of the blank check forms remaining should be verified to make sure that all check numbers are accounted for.
7. During the bank reconciliation process, compare the canceled checks to the checkbook or check register. The person who does the bank reconciliation should be someone other than the person who prepares or records the checks.
8. Enter promptly in the accounting records all cash payment transactions. The person who records cash payments should not be the one who approves payments or the one who writes the checks.

Small businesses usually cannot achieve the division of responsibility recommended for cash receipts and cash payments. However, no matter what size the firm, efforts should be made to set up effective control procedures for cash.

Section 2 Self Review

QUESTIONS

1. How and when are amounts in the Other Accounts Debit column of the cash payments journal posted?
2. What cash payments journal entry records a cash withdrawal by the owner of a sole proprietorship?
3. Why does a business use a petty cash fund?

EXERCISES

4. To take the discount, what is the payment date for an invoice dated January 20 with terms 3/15, n/30?
   a. February 3
   b. February 4
   c. February 5
   d. February 6
5. Cash purchases of merchandise are recorded in the:
   a. cash receipts journal.
   b. general journal.
   c. cash payments journal.
   d. purchases journal.

ANALYSIS

6. Your employer keeps a $200 petty cash fund. She asked you to replenish the fund. She is missing a receipt for $7.40, which she says she spent on postage. How should you handle this?

(Answers to Section 2 Self Review are on pages 342–343.)

Section 3

SECTION OBJECTIVES	TERMS TO LEARN
>> **9-8** Write a check, endorse checks, prepare a bank deposit slip, and maintain a checkbook balance. WHY IT'S IMPORTANT Banking tasks are basic practices in every business. >> **9-9** Reconcile the monthly bank statement. WHY IT'S IMPORTANT Reconciliation of the bank statement provides a good control of cash. >> **9-10** Record any adjusting entries required from the bank reconciliation. WHY IT'S IMPORTANT Certain items are not recorded in the accounting records during the month. >> **9-11** Understand how businesses use online banking to manage cash activities. WHY IT'S IMPORTANT Many businesses use online banking to manage a significant portion of cash activities.	bank reconciliation statement blank endorsement canceled check check credit memorandum debit memorandum deposit in transit deposit slip dishonored (NSF) check drawee drawer electronic funds transfer (EFT) endorsement full endorsement negotiable outstanding checks payee postdated check restrictive endorsement service charge

Banking Procedures

Businesses with good internal control systems safeguard cash. Many businesses make a daily bank deposit, and some make two or three deposits a day. Keeping excess cash is a dangerous practice. Also, frequent bank deposits provide a steady flow of funds for the payment of expenses.

Writing Checks

A **check** is a written order signed by an authorized person, the **drawer,** instructing a bank, the **drawee,** to pay a specific sum of money to a designated person or business, the **payee.** The checks in Figure 9.11 are **negotiable,** which means that ownership of the checks can be transferred to another person or business.

Before writing the check, complete the check stub. In Figure 9.11, the check stub for Check 111 shows:

- Balance brought forward: $12,025.50
- Check amount: $1,500.00
- Balance: $10,525.50
- Date: January 3, 2019
- Payee: Carter Real Estate Group
- Purpose: January rent

Once the stub has been completed, fill in the check. Carefully enter the date, the payee, and the amount in figures and words. Draw a line to fill any empty space after the payee's name and after the amount in words. To be valid, checks need an authorized signature. For Maxx-Out Sporting Goods, only Max Ferraro, the owner, is authorized to sign checks.

FIGURE 9.11 Checks and Check Stubs

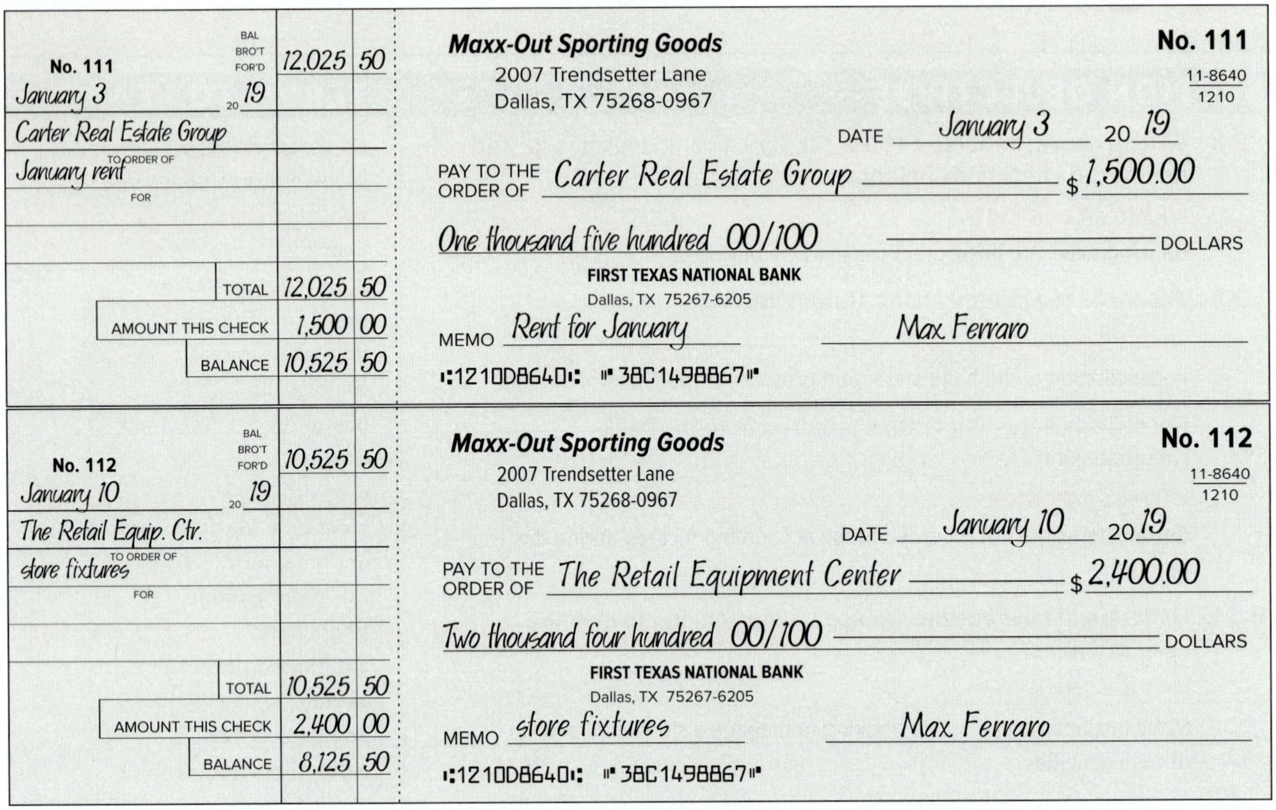
No. 111
BAL BRO'T FOR'D 12,025 50
January 3 20 19
Carter Real Estate Group
TO ORDER OF
January rent
FOR
TOTAL 12,025 50
AMOUNT THIS CHECK 1,500 00
BALANCE 10,525 50

Maxx-Out Sporting Goods
2007 Trendsetter Lane
Dallas, TX 75268-0967
No. 111
11-8640
1210
DATE January 3 20 19
PAY TO THE ORDER OF Carter Real Estate Group $ 1,500.00
One thousand five hundred 00/100 DOLLARS
FIRST TEXAS NATIONAL BANK
Dallas, TX 75267-6205
MEMO Rent for January
Max Ferraro
⑆1210D8640⑆ ⑈38C1498867⑈

No. 112
BAL BRO'T FOR'D 10,525 50
January 10 20 19
The Retail Equip. Ctr.
TO ORDER OF
store fixtures
FOR
TOTAL 10,525 50
AMOUNT THIS CHECK 2,400 00
BALANCE 8,125 50

Maxx-Out Sporting Goods
2007 Trendsetter Lane
Dallas, TX 75268-0967
No. 112
11-8640
1210
DATE January 10 20 19
PAY TO THE ORDER OF The Retail Equipment Center $ 2,400.00
Two thousand four hundred 00/100 DOLLARS
FIRST TEXAS NATIONAL BANK
Dallas, TX 75267-6205
MEMO store fixtures
Max Ferraro
⑆1210D8640⑆ ⑈38C1498867⑈

Figure 9.11 shows the check stub for Check 112, a cash purchase from The Retail Equipment Center for $2,400. After Check 112, the account balance is $8,125.50 ($10,525.50 – $2,400.00).

Endorsing Checks

Each check needs an endorsement to be deposited. The **endorsement** is a written authorization that transfers ownership of a check. After the payee transfers ownership to the bank by an endorsement, the bank has a legal right to collect payment from the drawer, the person or business that issued the check. If the check cannot be collected, the payee guarantees payment to all subsequent holders.

Several forms of endorsement are shown in Figure 9.12. Endorsements are placed on the back of the check, on the left, near the perforated edge where the check was separated from the stub.

A **blank endorsement** is the signature of the payee that transfers ownership of the check without specifying to whom or for what purpose. Checks with a blank endorsement can be further endorsed by anyone who has the check, even if the check is lost or stolen.

A **full endorsement** is a signature transferring a check to a specific person, business, or bank. Only the person, business, or bank named in the full endorsement can transfer it to someone else.

The safest endorsement is the **restrictive endorsement.** A restrictive endorsement is a signature that transfers the check to a specific party for a specific purpose, usually for deposit to a bank account. Most businesses restrictively endorse the checks they receive using a rubber stamp.

>> 9-8 OBJECTIVE

Write a check, endorse checks, prepare a bank deposit slip, and maintain a checkbook balance.

Preparing the Deposit Slip

Businesses prepare a **deposit slip** to record each deposit of cash or checks to a bank account. Usually the bank provides deposit slips preprinted with the account name and number. Figure 9.13 shows the deposit slip for the January 8 deposit for Maxx-Out Sporting Goods.

Notice the printed numbers on the lower edge of the deposit slip. These are the same numbers on the bottom of the checks, Figure 9.11. The numbers are printed using a special magnetic

Full Endorsement

PAY TO THE ORDER OF
FIRST TEXAS NATIONAL BANK
Maxx-Out Sporting Goods
38-14-98867

Blank Endorsement

Max Ferraro
38-14-98867

Restrictive Endorsement

PAY TO THE ORDER OF
FIRST TEXAS NATIONAL BANK
FOR DEPOSIT ONLY
Maxx-Out Sporting Goods
38-14-98867

FIGURE 9.12

Types of Check Endorsement

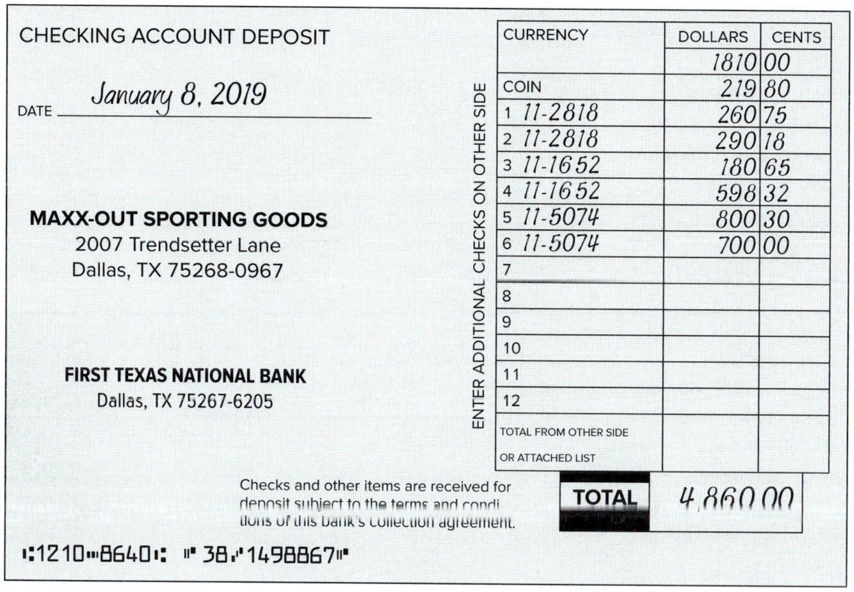
CHECKING ACCOUNT DEPOSIT

DATE January 8, 2019

MAXX-OUT SPORTING GOODS
2007 Trendsetter Lane
Dallas, TX 75268-0967

FIRST TEXAS NATIONAL BANK
Dallas, TX 75267-6205

ENTER ADDITIONAL CHECKS ON OTHER SIDE

	DOLLARS	CENTS
CURRENCY	1810	00
COIN	219	80
1 11-2818	260	75
2 11-2818	290	18
3 11-1652	180	65
4 11-1652	598	32
5 11-5074	800	30
6 11-5074	700	00
7		
8		
9		
10		
11		
12		
TOTAL FROM OTHER SIDE OR ATTACHED LIST		
TOTAL	4,860	00

Checks and other items are received for deposit subject to the terms and conditions of this bank's collection agreement.

⑆1210⑈8640⑆ ⑈38⑉14⑉98867⑈

FIGURE 9.13

Deposit Slip

ink character recognition (MICR) type that can be "read" by machine. Deposit slips and checks encoded with MICR are rapidly and efficiently processed by machine.

- The 12 indicates that the bank is in the 12th Federal Reserve District.
- The 10 is the routing number used in processing the document.
- The 8640 identifies First Texas National Bank.
- The 38 14 98867 is the account number.

The deposit slip for Maxx-Out Sporting Goods shows the date, January 8. Currency is the paper money, $1,810.00. Coin is the amount in coins, $219.80. The checks and money orders are individually listed. Some banks ask that the *American Bankers Association (ABA) transit number* for each check be entered on the deposit slip. The transit number appears on the top part of the fraction that appears in the upper right corner of the check. In Figure 9.11, the transit number is 11-8640.

Many banks now allow businesses to deposit checks to an automated teller machine (ATM) without using deposit slips. The ATM receipt provides the depositor with images of the checks deposited as well as the total amount of the deposit.

Handling Postdated Checks

Occasionally, a business will receive a postdated check. A **postdated check** is dated some time in the future. If the business receives a postdated check, it should not deposit it before the date on the check. Otherwise, the check could be refused by the drawer's bank. Postdated checks are written by drawers who do not have sufficient funds to cover the check. The drawer expects to have adequate funds in the bank by the date on the check. Issuing or accepting postdated checks is not a proper business practice.

>> 9-9 OBJECTIVE

Reconcile the monthly bank statement.

Reconciling the Bank Statement

Once a month, the bank sends a statement of the deposits received and the checks paid for each account. Figure 9.14 shows the bank statement for Maxx-Out Sporting Goods. It shows a day-to-day listing of all transactions during the month. A code, explained at the bottom, identifies

FIGURE 9.14

Bank Statement

FIRST TEXAS NATIONAL BANK

MAXX-OUT SPORTING GOODS 1-877-TEXBANK
2007 Trendsetter Lane
Dallas, TX 75268-0967

Account Number: 38-14-98867 January 1–January 31, 2019
Activity Summary:

Balance, January 1	$ 12,025.50
Deposits and credits	37,672.00
Withdrawals and debits	(25,189.00)
Balance, January 31	$ 24,508.50

DATE	DESCRIPTION	DEPOSITS/ CREDITS	WITHDRAWALS/ DEBITS	BALANCE
1/1/19	Opening balance			$ 12,025.50
1/7/19	Deposit	702.00		12,727.50
1/7/19	Check No. 111		1,500.00	11,227.50
1/8/19	Check No. 112		2,400.00	8,827.50
1/8/19	Deposit	4,860.00		13,687.50
1/11/19	Deposit	270.00		13,957.50
1/11/19	Check No. 113		756.00	13,201.50
1/12/19	Check No. 114		3,856.30	9,345.20
1/12/19	Deposit	15,000.00		24,345.20
1/13/19	Check No. 115		2,807.70	21,537.50
1/13/19	Deposit	540.00		22,077.50
1/15/19	Deposit	5,166.00		27,243.50
1/15/19	Check No. 116		900.00	26,343.50
1/17/19	Deposit	108.00		26,451.50
1/17/19	Check No. 117		3,000.00	23,451.50
1/17/19	Check No. 118		318.00	23,133.50
1/18/19	Deposit	75.00		23,208.50
1/18/19	Check No. 119		4,250.00	18,958.50
1/18/19	Check No. 120		276.00	18,682.50
1/22/19	Deposit	400.00		19,082.50
1/22/19	Deposit	5,400.00		24,482.50
1/22/19	Check No. 121		840.00	23,642.50
1/22/19	Check No. 122		1,000.00	22,642.50
1/22/19	Check No. 10087		1,600.00	21,042.50
1/29/19	Deposit	2,932.00		23,974.50
1/29/19	Debit for NSF Check		525.00	23,449.50
1/31/19	Deposit	108.00		23,557.50
1/31/19	Deposit	275.00		23,832.50
1/31/19	Credit for funds collected	836.00		24,668.50
1/31/19	Service fee for NSF check		25.00	24,643.50
1/31/19	Check No. 123		1,135.00	24,508.50
	Totals	37,672.00	25,189.00	

transactions that do not involve checks or deposits. For example, SC indicates a service charge. The last column of the bank statement shows the account balance at the beginning of the period, after each day's transactions, and at the end of the period.

Often the bank encloses canceled checks with the bank statement. **Canceled checks** are checks paid by the bank during the month. Canceled checks are proof of payment. They are filed after the bank reconciliation is complete.

Usually there is a difference between the ending balance shown on the bank statement and the balance shown in the checkbook. A bank reconciliation determines why the difference exists and brings the records into agreement.

CHANGES IN THE CHECKING ACCOUNT BALANCE

A **credit memorandum** explains any addition, other than a deposit, to the checking account. For example, when a note receivable is due, the bank may collect the note from the maker and place the proceeds in the checking account. The amount collected appears on the bank statement, and the credit memorandum showing the details of the transaction is enclosed with the bank statement.

A **debit memorandum** explains any deduction, other than a check, from the checking account. Service charges and dishonored checks appear as debit memorandums.

Bank **service charges** are fees charged by banks to cover the costs of maintaining accounts and providing services, such as the use of the night deposit box and the collection of promissory notes. The debit memorandum shows the type and amount of each service charge.

Figure 9.15 shows a debit memorandum for a $525.00 dishonored check. A **dishonored check** is one that is returned to the depositor unpaid. Normally, checks are dishonored because there are insufficient funds in the drawer's account to cover the check. The bank usually stamps the letters *NSF* for *Not Sufficient Funds* on the check. The business records a journal entry to debit ***Accounts Receivable*** and credit ***Cash*** for the amount of the dishonored check.

When a check is dishonored, the business contacts the drawer to arrange for collection. The drawer can ask the business to redeposit the check because the funds are now in the account. If so, the business records the check deposit again. Sometimes, the business requests a cash payment.

THE BANK RECONCILIATION PROCESS: AN ILLUSTRATION

When the bank statement is received, it is reconciled with the financial records of the business. On February 5, Maxx-Out Sporting Goods received the bank statement shown in Figure 9.14. The ending cash balance according to the bank is $23,508.50. On January 31, the ***Cash*** account, called the *book balance of cash,* is $16,060.70. The same amount appears on the check stub at the end of January.

Sometimes the difference between the bank balance and the book balance is due to errors. The bank might make an arithmetic error, give credit to the wrong depositor, or charge a check against the wrong account. Some banks require that errors in the bank statement be reported within a short period of time. The errors made by businesses include not recording a check or deposit, or recording a check or deposit for the wrong amount.

Other than errors, there are four reasons why the book balance of cash may not agree with the balance on the bank statement.

DEBIT: **MAXX-OUT SPORTING GOODS** — **FIRST TEXAS NATIONAL BANK**
2007 Trendsetter Lane
Dallas, TX 75268-0967

38-14-98867 — DATE: *January 31, 2019*

NSF Check - David Newhouse	*525*	*00*

APPROVED: *Max Ferraro*

FIGURE 9.15

Debit Memorandum

FIGURE 9.16

Bank Reconciliation Statement

Maxx-Out Sporting Goods Bank Reconciliation Statement January 31, 2019		
Balance on Bank Statement		23 508 50
Additions:		
Deposit of January 31 in transit	5 940 00	
Check incorrectly charged to account	1 600 00	7 540 00
		31 048 50
Deductions for outstanding checks:		
Check 124 of January 31	565 00	
Check 125 of January 31	4 950 00	
Check 126 of January 31	3 200 00	
Check 127 of January 31	175 00	
Check 128 of January 31	172 80	
Check 129 of January 31	6 300 00	
Check 130 of January 31	175 00	
Total Checks Outstanding		15 537 80
Adjusted Bank Balance		15 510 70
Balance in Books		16 060 70
Deductions:		
NSF Check from David Newhouse	525 00	
Bank Service Charge	25 00	550 00
Adjusted Book Balance		15 510 70

1. **Outstanding checks** are checks that are recorded in the cash payments journal but have not been paid by the bank.
2. **Deposit in transit** is a deposit that is recorded in the cash receipts journal but that reaches the bank too late to be shown on the monthly bank statement.
3. Service charges and other deductions are not recorded in the business records.
4. Deposits, such as the collection of promissory notes, are not recorded in the business records.

Figure 9.16 shows a **bank reconciliation statement** that accounts for the differences between the balance on the bank statement and the book balance of cash. The bank reconciliation statement format is:

First Section		Second Section	
	Bank statement balance		Book balance
+	deposits in transit	+	deposits not recorded
−	outstanding checks	−	deductions
+ or −	bank errors	+ or −	errors in the books
	Adjusted bank balance		Adjusted book balance

When the bank reconciliation statement is complete, the adjusted bank balance must equal the adjusted book balance.

Use the following steps to prepare the bank reconciliation statement:

First Section

1. Enter the balance on the bank statement, $23,508.50.
2. Compare the deposits in the checkbook with the deposits on the bank statement. Maxx-Out Sporting Goods had one deposit in transit. On January 31, receipts of $5,940.00 were placed in the bank's night deposit box. The bank recorded the deposit on February 1. The deposit will appear on the February bank statement.

3. List the outstanding checks.
   - Put the canceled checks in numeric order.
   - Compare the canceled checks to the check stubs, verifying the check numbers and amounts.
   - Examine the endorsements to make sure that they agree with the names of the payees.
   - List the checks that have not cleared the bank.
   - Maxx-Out Sporting Goods has seven outstanding checks totaling $15,537.80.
4. While reviewing the canceled checks for Maxx-Out Sporting Goods, Max Ferraro found a $1,600 check issued by The Dress Barn. The $1,600 was deducted from Maxx-Out Sporting Goods' account; it should have been deducted from the account for The Dress Barn. This is a bank error. Max Ferraro contacted the bank about the error. The correction will appear on the next bank statement. The bank error amount is added to the bank statement balance on the bank reconciliation statement.
5. The adjusted bank balance is $15,510.70.

Second Section

1. Enter the balance in books from the ***Cash*** account, $16,060.70.
2. Record any deposits made by the bank that have not been recorded in the accounting records. Maxx-Out Sporting Goods did not have any.
3. Record deductions made by the bank. There are two items:
   - the NSF check for $525,
   - the bank service charge for $25.
4. Record any errors in the accounting records that were discovered during the reconciliation process. Maxx-Out Sporting Goods did not have any errors in January.
5. The adjusted book balance is $15,510.70.

Notice that the adjusted bank balance and the adjusted book balance agree.

important!

Adjusted Book Balance

Journal entries are required to record additions and deductions that appear on the bank statement but have not been recorded in the general ledger. These items are located under the "Balance in Books" section of the bank reconciliation.

Adjusting the Financial Records

>> 9-10 OBJECTIVE

Record any adjusting entries required from the bank reconciliation.

Items in the second section of the bank reconciliation statement include additions and deductions made by the bank that do not appear in the accounting records. Businesses prepare journal entries to record these items in the books.

For Maxx-Out Sporting Goods, two entries must be made. The first entry is for the NSF check from David Newhouse, a credit customer. The second entry is for the bank service charge. The effect of the two items is a decrease in the ***Cash*** account balance.

MANAGERIAL IMPLICATIONS <<

CASH

- It is important to safeguard cash against loss and theft.
- Management and the accountant need to work together:
  - to make sure that there are effective controls for cash receipts and cash payments,
  - to monitor the internal control system to make sure that it functions properly,
  - to develop procedures that ensure the quick and efficient recording of cash transactions.
- To make decisions, management needs up-to-date information about the cash position so that it can anticipate cash shortages and arrange loans or arrange for the temporary investment of excess funds.
- Management and the accountant need to establish controls over the banking activities—depositing funds, issuing checks, recording checking account transactions, and reconciling the monthly bank statement.

THINKING CRITICALLY

How would you determine how much cash to keep in the business checking account, as opposed to in a short-term investment?

BUSINESS TRANSACTION

The January bank reconciliation statement (Figure 9.16) shows an NSF check of $525 and a bank service charge of $25.

ANALYSIS

The asset account ***Accounts Receivable*** is increased by $525 for the returned check. The expense account ***Bank Fees Expense*** is increased by $25 for the service charge. The asset account ***Cash*** is decreased by $550 ($525 + $25).

DEBIT-CREDIT RULES

DEBIT Increases to assets are debits. Debit ***Accounts Receivable*** for $525. Increases to expenses are debits. Debit ***Bank Fees Expense*** for $25.

CREDIT Decreases to assets are credits. Credit ***Cash*** for $550.

T-ACCOUNT PRESENTATION

Accounts Receivable	
+	−
525	

Bank Fees Expense	
+	−
25	

Cash	
+	−
	550

GENERAL JOURNAL ENTRY

GENERAL JOURNAL PAGE 17

	DATE		DESCRIPTION	POST. REF.	DEBIT	CREDIT	
29	Jan.	31	Accounts Receivable/David Newhouse	111/✓	525 00		29
30			Bank Fees Expense	593	25 00		30
31			Cash	101		550 00	31
32			To record NSF check and bank				32
33			service charge				33

THE BOTTOM LINE

Adjusting Entries

Income Statement		
Expenses	↑	25
Net Income	↓	25

Balance Sheet		
Assets	↓	25
Equity	↓	25

After posting, the ***Cash*** account appears as follows.

ACCOUNT Cash ACCOUNT NO. 101

DATE		DESCRIPTION	POST. REF.	DEBIT	CREDIT	BALANCE DEBIT	BALANCE CREDIT
2019							
Jan.	1	Balance	✓			12 025 50	
	31		CR1	42 612 00		54 637 50	
	31		CP1		38 576 80	16 060 70	
	31		J17		550 00	15 510 70	

Notice that $15,510.70 is the adjusted bank balance, the adjusted book balance, and the general ledger ***Cash*** balance. A notation is made on the latest check stub to deduct the amounts ($525 and $25). The notation includes the reasons for the deductions.

Sometimes the bank reconciliation reveals an error in the firm's financial records. For example, the February bank reconciliation for Maxx-Out Sporting Goods found that Check 151 was written for $465. The amount on the bank statement is $465. However, the check was recorded in the accounting records as $445. The business made a $20 error when recording the check. Maxx-Out Sporting Goods prepared the following journal entry to correct the error. The $20 is also deducted on the check stub.

GENERAL JOURNAL PAGE 18

	DATE		DESCRIPTION	POST. REF.	DEBIT	CREDIT	
1	2019						1
2							2
29	Feb.	28	Advertising Expense	514	20 00		29
30			Cash	101		20 00	30
31			To correct error for check				31
32			151 of February 22				32

Internal Control of Banking Activities

Well-run businesses put the following internal controls in place:

internal CONTROL

1. Limit access to the checkbook to designated employees. When the checkbook is not in use, keep it in a locked drawer or cabinet.
2. Use prenumbered check forms. Periodically, verify and account for all checks. Examine checks before signing them. Match each check to an approved invoice or other payment authorization.
3. Separate duties.
   - The person who writes the check should not sign or mail the check.
   - The person who performs the bank reconciliation should not handle or deposit cash receipts or write, record, sign, or mail checks.
4. File all deposit receipts, canceled checks, voided checks, and bank statements for future reference. These documents provide a strong audit trail for the checking account.
5. Require employees working with cash receipts or cash payments to take mandatory annual vacations.

> In November 2012, Rita Crundwell, former comptroller for a small Illinois town, pleaded guilty to stealing $53 million from city funds over a period of several years. These funds were used to support a lavish lifestyle, including purchase of a $2 million custom RV, a Florida vacation home, and a horse-breeding farm. Crundwell was the sole person responsible for managing the town's finances. The crime was uncovered by another employee while Crundwell was on vacation.

Using Online Banking

>> 9-11 OBJECTIVE
Understand how businesses use online banking to manage cash activities.

Many businesses now manage a significant portion of their cash activities using online banking. Online banking offers many features to make businesses more efficient. These features include:

- Businesses can initiate **electronic funds transfers (EFT)** to vendors from a computer instead of writing checks.
- Payments to government agencies for taxes can be submitted online, using the government agency website, to avoid late payment penalties.
- Businesses can receive EFT from customers, rather than receiving checks in the mail. This is especially important in transacting cash receipts from foreign customers. Routine payments, such as those for utilities expenses and loan payments, can be automatically deducted from the company's bank account.
- Many banks offer security alerts for such instances as changes in mailing addresses and ATM and automatic payment withdrawals that exceed specified limits. Such alerts are often sent to the responsible company official via e-mail or phone text messages. When an alert is received, the company should view account activity online to ensure cash transactions are legitimate.

FIGURE 9.17 **Online Account Activity**

Business Checking		Account #987-654321			
Date	**Type**	**Description**	**Additions**	**Payments**	**Balance**
7/31/2019	ATM	ATM withdrawal		$200.00	$27,819.91
7/31/2019	Check	Check #1421 (view)		$1,225.95	$28,019.91
7/30/2019	Bill payment	Online payment		$248.52	$29,245.86
7/30/2019	Check	Check #1420 (view)		$428.20	$29,494.38
7/30/2019	ACH credit	Baden Holding	$10,200.00		$29,922.58
7/30/2019	Deposit	Deposit ID #8989	$5,400.00		$19,722.58
7/30/2019	Loan payment	Online transfer to WC XXX		$3,900.00	$14,322.58
7/29/2019	Check	Check #1422 (view)		$850.00	$18,222.58

There are usually no source documents for the transactions listed above. The accountant should check bank activity online frequently to ensure all EFT and other transactions initiated electronically are recorded in the accounting records.

For example, the online account activity of Western Imports and Exports for July 29, 30, and 31, 2019, is shown in Figure 9.17. The company's accountant was out of town during that period.

In matching these transactions to the company's ***Cash*** account in the general ledger, the accountant identified the following unrecorded transactions:

1. The loan payment on 7/30/2019 was an automatic debit by Western Equipment for the company's monthly payment on an equipment loan. The loan does not bear interest.
2. The ACH credit on 7/30/2019 was an EFT payment sent by Baden Holding, a German customer, on account.
3. The bill payment of 7/30/2019 was an automatic debit by West Communications (telephone).
4. The ATM withdrawal of 7/31/2019 was for personal use by the owner, Susan De Angelis.

The accountant recorded these transactions in the general journal, as follows:

GENERAL JOURNAL PAGE 10

DATE		DESCRIPTION	POST. REF.	DEBIT	CREDIT
2019					
July	30	Notes Payable		3 900 00	
		Cash			3 900 00
		To record loan payment to Western			
		Equipment			
	30	Cash		10 200 00	
		Accounts Receivable/Baden Holding			10 200 00
		To record EFT received on account			
		from Baden Holding			
	30	Telephone Expense		248 52	
		Cash			248 52
		To record online payment to			
		West Communications			
	31	Susan De Angelis, Drawing		200 00	
		Cash			200 00
		To record ATM withdrawal by			
		Susan De Angelis for personal use			

In addition to the internal controls over banking activities discussed earlier, companies using online banking should allow only authorized check signors access to the company's online account. Additionally, log-in information, such as user identification and passwords, should be changed frequently.

Section 3 Self Review

QUESTIONS

1. What is a postdated check? When should postdated checks be deposited?
2. Why does a payee endorse a check before depositing it?
3. Which bank reconciliation items require journal entries?

EXERCISES

4. Which of the following does not require an adjustment to the financial records?
   a. Deposits in transit
   b. Bank service charge
   c. Check that was incorrectly recorded at $115 but was written and paid by the bank as $151
   d. NSF check from a customer
5. On the bank reconciliation statement, you would not find a list of:
   a. deposits in transit.
   b. canceled checks.
   c outstanding checks.
   d. NSF checks.

ANALYSIS

6. James is one of several accounting clerks at Uptown Beverage Company. His job duties include recording invoices as they are received, filing the invoices, and writing the checks for accounts payable. He is a fast and efficient clerk and usually has some time available each day to help other clerks. It has been suggested that reconciling the bank statement should be added to his job duties. Do you agree or disagree? Why or why not?

(Answers to Section 3 Self Review are on page 343.)

>> 9-12 OBJECTIVE

Appendix: Record transactions for a retailer using the perpetual inventory system.

APPENDIX TO CHAPTER 9: The Perpetual Inventory System

Merchandising companies sell products, not services. Their accounting practices are different from those of service companies. We will focus on these differences and explain the general ledger accounts used by merchandising companies.

The distribution channel is the means that manufacturers of products use to sell their products to consumers. A common example of the distribution channel is:

Manufacturer sells to *Wholesaler* who sells to *Retailer* who sells to *Consumer.*

In this appendix, we learn to record transactions for a retailer. We will use a general journal to record transactions.

The accounting for sales and purchases discussed in Chapters 7, 8, and 9 assumed use of the periodic inventory system. When the periodic system is used, the inventory records are only updated when a physical inventory is taken. A physical inventory is an actual count of units on hand. This system is adequate for smaller businesses such as Maxx-Out Sporting Goods.

Larger businesses require up-to-date information of inventories on hand and use the perpetual inventory system. The perpetual inventory system updates both the general ledger merchandise inventory account and inventory items in the inventory ledger with each purchase, sale, and return. Using a perpetual inventory system requires a substantial investment in point-of-sale cash registers, scanning devices, back office hardware, and computer software.

Perpetual inventory management systems give management more control over the company's inventory. Management can use computers to access inventory records to know exactly how much of each item in inventory is on hand. This assists management in inventory control and purchasing activities. The perpetual inventory system also allows for cycle counts of inventory. A cycle count is an inventory management procedure in which only certain inventory items are counted and compared with the perpetual inventory records. Shortages of inventory on hand can be investigated and corrective actions taken.

In this appendix, we will introduce Big 10 Sporting Goods, a multistate retailer selling sporting goods and sporting apparel. Big 10 Sporting Goods must account for purchases, sales, returns of goods, and *merchandise inventory*—the stock of goods on hand.

Big 10 Sporting Goods uses the perpetual inventory method. We will first examine purchasing transactions entered into by Big 10 Sporting Goods, then sales transactions by Big 10 Sporting Goods.

Purchasing Transactions

When the perpetual inventory system is used, the ***Merchandise Inventory*** account is used to record purchases and purchase returns of merchandise inventory. It is also used to record freight costs of merchandise inventory purchased. ***Merchandise Inventory*** is an asset account with a normal debit balance.

The ***Merchandise Inventory*** account replaces the ***Purchases, Purchases Returns,*** and ***Freight In*** accounts used in the periodic inventory system.

Big 10 Sporting Goods engaged in the following purchases transactions during the month of September 2019. The accounting for these transactions is illustrated below. Descriptions have been omitted.

PURCHASES AND CASH PAYMENTS WITH FREIGHT CHARGES

If the freight terms are free on board (FOB) shipping point, the buyer pays the freight charge—the cost of shipping the goods from the seller's warehouse to the buyer's location. If the freight terms are FOB destination, the seller pays the freight charges. There are two ways to handle the freight charges paid by the buyer:

- The buyer is billed directly by the transportation company for the freight charge. The buyer issues a check directly to the freight company.
- The seller pays the freight charge and includes it on the invoice. The invoice includes the price of the goods and the freight charge.

On September 1 and September 2, Big 10 Sporting Goods engaged in purchases of merchandise. The transaction on September 1 involved the purchase of merchandise for cash, with no freight charges. The September 2 transaction was for the purchase of merchandise on account, with freight charges. The accounting for these transactions follows.

BUSINESS TRANSACTION

On September 1, Big 10 Sporting Goods purchased merchandise for cash, $12,000.

GENERAL JOURNAL ENTRY

GENERAL JOURNAL

	DATE		DESCRIPTION	POST. REF.	DEBIT	CREDIT	
1	2019						1
2	Sept.	1	Merchandise Inventory		12 000 00		2
3			Cash			12 000 00	3

BUSINESS TRANSACTION

On September 2, Big 10 Sporting Goods recorded a purchase of weight-lifting equipment for $9,500 plus freight of $250 from Sledge Hammer Strength; the terms are 2/10, n/30.

GENERAL JOURNAL ENTRY

GENERAL JOURNAL

	DATE		DESCRIPTION	POST. REF.	DEBIT	CREDIT	
1	2019						1
5	Sept.	2	Merchandise Inventory ($9,500 + $250)		9 750 00		5
6			Accounts Payable/Sledge Hammer Strength			9 750 00	6

PURCHASE RETURNS AND ALLOWANCES

When merchandise arrives, it is examined to confirm that it is satisfactory. Occasionally, the wrong goods are shipped, or items are damaged or defective. A *purchase return* is when the business returns the goods. A *purchase allowance* is when the purchaser keeps the goods but receives a reduction in the price of the goods. The supplier issues a credit memorandum for the return or allowance. The credit memorandum reduces the amount that the purchaser owes.

A purchase return by Big 10 Sporting Goods to Sledge Hammer Strength follows.

BUSINESS TRANSACTION

On September 5, Big 10 Sporting Goods returned damaged merchandise purchased on September 2 from Sledge Hammer Strength; it received Credit Memorandum 302 for $400.

GENERAL JOURNAL ENTRY

GENERAL JOURNAL

	DATE		DESCRIPTION	POST. REF.	DEBIT	CREDIT	
1	2019						1
8	Sept.	5	Accounts Payable/Sledge Hammer Strength		400 00		8
9			Merchandise Inventory			400 00	9

RECORDING PURCHASES DISCOUNTS

The accounting for purchases discounts received is illustrated below.

BUSINESS TRANSACTION

On September 11, Big 10 Sporting Goods paid the amount due to Sledge Hammer Strength for the purchase of September 2, less the return on September 5, taking the 1 percent discount.

GENERAL JOURNAL ENTRY

GENERAL JOURNAL

	DATE		DESCRIPTION	POST. REF.	DEBIT	CREDIT	
1	2019						1
11	Sept.	11	Accounts Payable/Sledge Hammer Strength ($9,750 – $400)		9 350 00		11
12			Merchandise Inventory [1% × ($9,500 – $400)]			91 00	12
13			Cash ($9,750 – $400 – $91)			9 259 00	13

The 1 percent discount reduces the cost of the merchandise purchased. As ***Merchandise Inventory*** is an asset account, we credit ***Merchandise Inventory*** to reflect the decrease in its cost.

Purchases discounts are calculated only on the cost of the merchandise purchased, less any returns. Purchases discounts are not allowed on freight charges.

RECORDING MERCHANDISE PURCHASED WITH TRADE DISCOUNTS

Many wholesale businesses offer goods to trade customers with the price computed using trade discounts. This is often done to simplify pricing. Publishing separate trade discounts can simplify the pricing structure appearing in product catalogs and brochures, while providing the company the flexibility to change the discounts offered through separate updates. Additionally, companies can raise the discount offered as the volume of the product purchased increases, promoting customer loyalty.

There may be a single trade discount or a series of discounts for each type of goods.

A vendor of Big 10 Sporting Goods, Modern Sportsman, offers merchandise for sale with a list price of $10,000, with trade discounts of 20 percent and 10 percent, terms 2/10, n/30.

On September 15, Big 10 Sporting Goods purchases merchandise with a list price of $10,000 from Modern Sportsman. The amount owed for the purchase is computed as follows:

List price	$10,000.00
Less first discount ($10,000 × 20%)	2,000.00
Difference	$ 8,000.00
Less second discount ($8,000 × 10%)	800.00
Invoice price	$ 7,200.00

The journal entry to record the purchase on September 15 follows:

GENERAL JOURNAL

	DATE		DESCRIPTION	POST. REF.	DEBIT	CREDIT	
1	*2019*						1
15	*Sept.*	*15*	*Merchandise Inventory*		*7 200 00*		15
16			*Accounts Payable/Modern Sportsman*			*7 200 00*	16

On September 24, Big 10 Sporting Goods pays the amount owed to Modern Sportsman, less the 2 percent discount. The entry to record the payment is below.

GENERAL JOURNAL

	DATE		DESCRIPTION	POST. REF.	DEBIT	CREDIT	
1	*2019*						1
18	*Sept.*	*24*	*Accounts Payable/Modern Sportsman*		*7 200 00*		18
19			*Merchandise Inventory (2% × $7,200)*			*1 44 00*	19
20			*Cash ($7,200 − $144)*			*7 056 00*	20

Sales Transactions

There are several new accounts used in accounting for sales transactions when the perpetual inventory method is employed. These new accounts are summarized below.

Name of Account	Type of Account	Normal Balance	Used to Record
Sales	Revenue	CR	Sales of merchandise inventory
Sales Tax Payable	Liability	CR	Sales tax charged to customers
Sales Discounts	Contra revenue	DR	Early payment discounts given to buyer by seller
Sales Returns and Allowance	Contra revenue	DR	Products returned by buyer on the seller's books
Credit Card Expense	Expense	DR	Fees charged by credit card companies to seller
Cost of Goods Sold	Expense	DR	The cost of merchandise sold to companies

Big 10 Sporting Goods engaged in the following sales transactions during the month of September 2019. Big 10 Sporting Goods sells merchandise for cash, on account, and to customers using bank credit cards. The accounting for these transactions is illustrated below. Big 10 Sporting Goods must charge 5 percent sales tax on all purchases. Descriptions have been omitted.

RECORDING SALES WITH SALES TAX PAYABLE FOR CASH AND ON ACCOUNT

For merchandising companies, the revenue account is called ***Sales.*** Revenue is recorded when the product is sold to the customer. Additionally, perpetual inventory accounting requires a second entry when sales are made. This entry debits the ***Cost of Goods Sold*** account and credits the ***Merchandise Inventory*** account. The ***Cost of Goods Sold*** account shows the actual cost of the merchandise sold to customers and is classified as an expense in a perpetual inventory system. ***Merchandise Inventory*** is an asset account whose balance represents the cost of merchandise inventory on hand.

Most state and many local governments impose a sales tax on the sale of certain goods and services. Businesses are required to collect this tax from their customers and pay it to the proper tax agency at regular intervals. When taxable goods and services are sold on account, the sales tax is usually recorded at the time of sale, even though it will be collected from the customer later. A liability account called ***Sales Tax Payable*** is credited for the sales tax charged.

Below are two sales transactions of Big 10 Sporting Goods involving sales tax.

BUSINESS TRANSACTION

On September 1, Big 10 Sporting Goods recorded cash sales, $28,000, plus sales tax of $1,400. The cost of the merchandise sold was $14,000.

GENERAL JOURNAL ENTRY

GENERAL JOURNAL

	DATE		DESCRIPTION	POST. REF.	DEBIT	CREDIT	
1	2019						1
2	Sept.	1	Cash ($28,000 + $1,400)		29 400 00		2
3			Sales			28 000 00	3
4			Sales Tax Payable ($28,000 × 5%)			1 400 00	4
5							5
6		1	Cost of Goods Sold		14 000 00		6
7			Merchandise Inventory			14 000 00	7

BUSINESS TRANSACTION

On September 2, Big 10 Sporting Goods recorded a sale of sporting apparel to Richard Santo on account, terms 1/10, net 30, $1,000, plus $50 tax. The cost of the merchandise sold was $550.

GENERAL JOURNAL ENTRY

GENERAL JOURNAL

	DATE		DESCRIPTION	POST. REF.	DEBIT	CREDIT	
1	2019						1
9	Sept.	2	Accounts Receivable/Richard Santo ($1,000 + $50)		1 050 00		9
10			Sales			1 000 00	10
11			Sales Tax Payable ($1,000 × 5%)			50 00	11
13		2	Cost of Goods Sold		550 00		13
14			Merchandise Inventory			550 00	14

RECORDING SALES RETURNS AND SALES ALLOWANCES

If the customer is dissatisfied with the goods received, the firm may take back the goods, resulting in a *sales return.* Or it may negotiate a reduction in the sales price, resulting in a *sales allowance.*

If the goods returned were initially paid for with cash, the customer will receive a cash refund. When a return or allowance is related to a credit sale, the normal practicc is to issuc a document called a *credit memorandum* to the customer instead of giving the customer a cash refund. The credit memorandum documents the reduction in the customer's account balance, crediting the customer's account receivable for the amount of the return or allowance. If the sale was made with sales tax added, the sales tax paid on the goods returned will also be credited to the customer's account. Both sales returns and sales allowances are recorded in a contra revenue account, ***Sales Returns and Allowances.***

The perpetual inventory method requires two entries to record a return of product by the customer. The first entry records the credit memorandum given to the customer. The second entry records the return of merchandise to stock.

In the case of a sales allowance, only the first entry to record the credit memorandum is recorded, as the customer is keeping the merchandise.

The transaction below describes how Big 10 Sporting Goods would record the issuance of a credit memorandum to a customer for return of damaged goods.

BUSINESS TRANSACTION

On September 5, Big 10 Sporting Goods accepted a return of goods from Richard Santo. The items were originally sold on September 2. Big 10 Sporting Goods issued Credit Memorandum 202 to Richard Santo for $200. The cost of the returned items was $110.

GENERAL JOURNAL ENTRY

GENERAL JOURNAL

	DATE		DESCRIPTION	POST. REF.	DEBIT	CREDIT	
1	2019						1
15	Sept.	5	Sales Tax Payable ($200 × 5%)		10 00		15
16			Sales Returns and Allowances		200 00		16
17			Accounts Receivable ($200 + $10)			210 00	17
19		5	Merchandise Inventory		110 00		19
20			Cost of Goods Sold			110 00	20

CASH DISCOUNTS ON SALES

Many companies selling products offer payment terms to certain customers. Additionally, they may offer discounts if the invoice is paid within a specified time period to encourage quicker payment. This is done to improve a firm's cash flow. The invoice date and credit terms determine when payment is due. The following credit terms often appear on invoices:

- *Net 30 days,* or *n/30,* means that payment in full is due 30 days after the date of the invoice.
- *Net 10 days EOM,* or *n/10 EOM,* means that payment in full is due 10 days after the end of the month in which the invoice was issued.
- *2 percent 10 days, net 30 days,* or *2/10, n/30,* means that if payment is made within 10 days of the invoice date, the customer can take a 2 percent discount. Otherwise, payment in full is due in 30 days. Note that discounts are not allowed on any freight portion of the invoice.

Big 10 Sporting Goods offers a 1 percent discount if the customer pays within 10 days of the invoice; otherwise, the amount is due in whole in 30 days. This credit term is expressed on the invoice as 1/10, n/30. To the seller, this is a *sales discount.* Sales discounts are recorded when the payment is received. Sales discounts are recorded in a contra revenue account, ***Sales Discounts.***

The accounting for sales discounts is illustrated in the transaction below.

BUSINESS TRANSACTION

On September 11, Big 10 Sporting Goods received payment from Richard Santo for the sale of September 2, less the return on September 5 and less the cash discount.

GENERAL JOURNAL ENTRY

GENERAL JOURNAL

	DATE		DESCRIPTION	POST. REF.	DEBIT	CREDIT	
1	2019						1
22	Sept.	11	*Sales Discounts [(1% × ($1,000 − $200)]*		8 00		22
23			*Cash ($1,050 − $210 − $8)*		832 00		23
24			*Accounts Receivable ($1,050 − $210)*			840 00	24

BANK CREDIT CARDS

Retailers can provide credit while minimizing or avoiding the risk of losses from uncollectible accounts by accepting bank credit cards. The most widely accepted bank credit cards are MasterCard and Visa. Many banks participate in one or both of these credit card programs and other banks have their own credit cards. Bank credit cards are issued to consumers directly by banks. A business may participate in these credit card programs by meeting conditions set by the bank. Banks review such factors as:

- The business's financial history.
- The industry in which the business operates.
- The type of business: online, physical store, or both.
- Any past merchant account history.

When a sale is made to a cardholder, the sale is processed electronically. The customer inserts his or her credit card into a card reading device. The card reading device transmits information to the bank using an Internet connection.

Sales made to customers paying with bank credit cards are treated as cash sales. In most cases, the amount processed on the card is transferred to the seller's bank account the same day. Fees charged by the credit card company for processing these sales are debited to an account called ***Credit Card Expense.*** It is important to note these fees are charged on the total amount of the sale plus any sales tax.

For example, assume Big 10 Sporting Goods sells merchandise on September 15 totaling $20,000 to customers using bank credit cards, plus 5 percent sales tax. The bank credit card company charges a 2 percent fee to process the transactions. The cost of the merchandise sold was $13,500.

Cash would be debited for $20,580, computed as follows:

Merchandise sales	$20,000.00
Plus sales tax ($20,000 × 5%)	1,000.00
Subtotal	21,000.00
Less bank fee ($21,000 × 2%)	420.00
Debit to ***Cash***	$20,580.00

The following journal entry records the sales made to customers using bank credit cards on September 15.

GENERAL JOURNAL

	DATE		DESCRIPTION	POST. REF.	DEBIT	CREDIT	
1	*2019*						1
26	*Sept.*	*15*	*Credit Card Expense*		*420 00*		26
27			*Cash*		*20 580 00*		27
28			*Sales*			*20 000 00*	28
29			*Sales Tax Payable*			*1 000 00*	29
31		*15*	*Cost of Goods Sold*		*13 500 00*		31
32			*Merchandise Inventory*			*13 500 00*	32

POSTING TRANSACTIONS TO SUBSIDIARY LEDGERS

The posting of transactions from the general journal to the accounts receivable ledger is discussed in Chapter 7. The posting of transactions from the general journal to the accounts payable ledger is discussed in Chapter 8. When the perpetual inventory method is used, such postings are done in the same manner demonstrated in Chapters 7 and 8.

9 Chapter REVIEW Chapter Summary

In this chapter, you have learned the basic principles of accounting for cash payments and cash receipts.

Learning Objectives

9-1 **Record cash receipts in a cash receipts journal.**

Use of special journals leads to an efficient recording process for cash transactions. The cash receipts journal has separate columns for the accounts used most often for cash receipt transactions.

9-2 **Account for cash short or over.**

Errors can occur when making change. Cash register discrepancies should be recorded using the expense account ***Cash Short or Over.***

9-3 **Post from the cash receipts journal to subsidiary and general ledgers.**

Individual accounts receivable amounts are posted to the subsidiary ledger daily. Figures in the Other Accounts Credit column are posted individually to the general ledger during the month. All other postings are done on a summary basis at month-end.

9-4 **Record cash payments in a cash payments journal.**

The cash payments journal has separate columns for the accounts used most often, eliminating the need to record the same account names repeatedly.

9-5 **Post from the cash payments journal to subsidiary and general ledgers.**

Individual accounts payable amounts are posted daily to the accounts payable subsidiary ledger. Amounts listed in the Other Accounts Debit column are posted individually to the general ledger during the month. All other postings are completed on a summary basis at the end of the month.

9-6 **Demonstrate a knowledge of procedures for a petty cash fund.**

Although most payments are made by check, small payments are often made through a petty cash fund. A petty cash voucher is prepared for each payment and signed by the person receiving the money. The person in charge of the fund records expenditures on a petty cash analysis sheet. The fund is replenished with a check for the sum spent. An entry is made in the cash payments journal to debit the accounts involved.

9-7 **Demonstrate a knowledge of internal control procedures for cash.**

All businesses need a system of internal controls to protect cash from theft and mishandling and to ensure accurate records of cash transactions. A checking account is essential to store cash safely and to make cash payments efficiently. For maximum control over outgoing cash, all payments should be made by check except those from carefully controlled special-purpose cash funds such as a petty cash fund.

9-8 **Write a check, endorse checks, prepare a bank deposit slip, and maintain a checkbook balance.**

Check writing requires careful attention to details. If a standard checkbook is used, the stub should be completed before the check so that it will not be forgotten. The stub gives the data needed to journalize the payment.

9-9 **Reconcile the monthly bank statement.**

A bank statement should be immediately reconciled with the cash balance in the firm's financial records. Usually, differences are due to deposits in transit, outstanding checks, and bank service charges, but many factors can cause lack of agreement between the bank balance and the book balance.

9-10 **Record any adjusting entries required from the bank reconciliation.**

Some differences between the bank balance and the book balance may require that the firm's records be adjusted after the bank statement is reconciled. Journal entries are recorded and then posted to correct the ***Cash*** account balance and the checkbook balance.

9-11 **Understand how businesses use online banking to manage cash activities.**

Many businesses now use online banking to receive cash payments from customers and to initiate cash payments.

9-12 *Appendix:* **Record transactions for a retailer using the perpetual inventory system.**

Perpetual inventory systems give management more control over the company's inventory, and assist management in inventory control and purchasing activities.

9-13 **Define the accounting terms new to this chapter.**

Glossary

Bank reconciliation statement (p. 298) A statement that accounts for all differences between the balance on the bank statement and the book balance of cash

Blank endorsement (p. 294) A signature of the payee written on the back of the check that transfers ownership of the check without specifying to whom or for what purpose

Bonding (p. 291) The process by which employees are investigated by an insurance company that will insure the business against losses through employee theft or mishandling of funds

Canceled check (p. 297) A check paid by the bank on which it was drawn

Cash (p. 276) In accounting, currency, coins, checks, money orders, and funds on deposit in a bank

Cash payments journal (p. 283) A special journal used to record transactions involving the payment of cash

Cash receipts journal (p. 276) A special journal used to record and post transactions involving the receipt of cash

Cash register proof (p. 277) A verification that the amount of currency and coins in a cash register agrees with the amount shown on the cash register audit tape

***Cash Short or Over* account** (p. 278) An account used to record any discrepancies between the amount of currency and coins in the cash register and the amount shown on the audit tape

Check (p. 293) A written order signed by an authorized person instructing a bank to pay a specific sum of money to a designated person or business

Credit memorandum (p. 297) A form that explains any addition, other than a deposit, to a checking account

Debit memorandum (p. 297) A form that explains any deduction, other than a check, from a checking account

Deposit in transit (p. 298) A deposit that is recorded in the cash receipts journal but that reaches the bank too late to be shown on the monthly bank statement

Deposit slip (p. 294) A form prepared to record the deposit of cash or checks to a bank account

Dishonored (NSF) check (p. 297) A check returned to the depositor unpaid because of insufficient funds in the drawer's account; also called an NSF check

Drawee (p. 293) The bank on which a check is written

Drawer (p. 293) The person or firm issuing a check

Electronic funds transfer (EFT) (p. 301) An electronic transfer of money from one account to another

Endorsement (p. 294) A written authorization that transfers ownership of a check

Full endorsement (p. 294) A signature transferring a check to a specific person, firm, or bank

Negotiable (p. 293) A financial instrument whose ownership can be transferred to another person or business

Outstanding checks (p. 298) Checks that have been recorded in the cash payments journal but have not yet been paid by the bank

Payee (p. 293) The person or firm to whom a check is payable

Petty cash analysis sheet (p. 289) A form used to record transactions involving petty cash

Petty cash fund (p. 276) A special-purpose fund used to handle payments involving small amounts of money

Petty cash voucher (p. 289) A form used to record the payments made from a petty cash fund

Postdated check (p. 295) A check dated some time in the future

Promissory note (p. 278) A written promise to pay a specified amount of money on a specific date

Restrictive endorsement (p. 294) A signature that transfers a check to a specific party for a stated purpose

Service charge (p. 297) A fee charged by a bank to cover the costs of maintaining accounts and providing services

Statement of account (p. 278) A form sent to a firm's customers showing transactions during the month and the balance owed

Comprehensive **Self Review**

1. Describe a full endorsement.
2. What is a petty cash voucher?
3. When is the petty cash fund replenished?
4. What are the advantages of using special journals for cash receipts and cash payments?
5. What does the term *cash* mean in business?

(Answers to Comprehensive Self Review are on page 343.)

Discussion Questions

1. Why is a bank reconciliation prepared?
2. Why are journal entries sometimes needed after the bank reconciliation statement is prepared?
3. Give some reasons why the bank balance and the book balance of cash might differ.
4. What is the book balance of cash?
5. What procedures are used to achieve internal control over banking activities?
6. What information is shown on the bank statement?
7. What is a check?
8. What type of information is entered on a check stub? Why should a check stub be prepared before the check is written?
9. Why are MICR numbers printed on deposit slips and checks?
10. Which type of endorsement is most appropriate for a business to use?
11. How are cash shortages and overages recorded?
12. When are petty cash expenditures entered in a firm's accounting records?
13. Describe the major controls for petty cash.
14. What type of account is ***Purchases Discounts***? How is this account presented on the income statement?
15. How does a firm record a payment on account to a creditor when a cash discount is involved? Which journal is used?
16. How does a wholesale business record a check received on account from a customer when a cash discount is involved? Which journal is used?
17. Why do some wholesale businesses offer cash discounts to their customers?
18. What is a promissory note? What entry is made to record the collection of a promissory note and interest? Which journal is used?
19. Describe the major controls for cash payments.
20. Explain what *bonding* means. How does bonding relate to safeguarding cash?

21. Describe the major controls for cash receipts.

22. Explain the meaning of the following terms:

- **a.** Canceled check
- **b.** Outstanding check
- **c.** Deposit in transit
- **d.** Debit memorandum
- **e.** Credit memorandum
- **f.** Dishonored check
- **g.** Blank endorsement
- **h.** Deposit slip
- **i.** Drawee
- **j.** Restrictive endorsement
- **k.** Payee
- **l.** Drawer
- **m.** Service charge

Discussion Questions 23, 24, 25, and 26 refer to the Appendix to this chapter.

23. What account is debited for the purchase of merchandise inventory when (a) the periodic system is used and (b) the perpetual inventory system is used?

24. What account is credited for the return of merchandise inventory when (a) the periodic system is used and (b) the perpetual inventory system is used?

25. What account is debited for freight charges on merchandise inventory purchases when (a) the periodic system is used and (b) the perpetual inventory system is used?

26. What account is credited for a cash discount taken by the purchaser when (a) the periodic system is used and (b) the perpetual system is used?

APPLICATIONS

Exercises connect®

Recording cash receipts.

Exercise 9.1
Objective 9-1

The following transactions took place at Eddie's Sports Gear during the first week of October 2019. Indicate how these transactions would be entered in a cash receipts journal.

DATE		TRANSACTIONS
Oct.	1	Had cash sales of $6,600 plus sales tax of $528; there was a cash overage of $12.
	2	Collected $890 on account from Jerry Lin, a credit customer.
	3	Had cash sales of $5,500 plus sales tax of $440.
	4	Eddie Reynolds, the owner, made an additional cash investment of $24,000.
	6	Had cash sales of $7,400 plus sales tax of $592; there was a cash shortage of $20.

Exercise 9.2 ▶ **Recording cash payments.**

Objective 9-4

CONTINUING >>> Problem

The following transactions took place at Eddie's Sports Gear during the first week of October 2019. Indicate how these transactions would be entered in a cash payments journal.

DATE		TRANSACTIONS
Oct.	1	Issued Check 3850 for $3,600 to pay the monthly rent.
	1	Issued Check 3851 for $3,200 to Fisher Company, a creditor, on account.
	2	Issued Check 3852 for $13,100 to purchase new equipment.
	2	Issued Check 3853 for $1,520 to remit sales tax to the state sales tax authority.
	3	Issued Check 3854 for $1,960 to Sports Emporium, a creditor, on account for invoice of $2,000 less cash discount of $40.
	4	Issued Check 3855 for $3,925 to purchase merchandise.
	6	Issued Check 3856 for $4,906 as a cash withdrawal for personal use by Eddie Reynolds, the owner.

Exercise 9.3 ▶ **Recording the establishment of a petty cash fund.**

Objective 9-6

On January 2, The Public Legal Clinic issued Check 2108 for $500 to establish a petty cash fund. Indicate how this transaction would be recorded in a cash payments journal.

Exercise 9.4 ▶ **Recording the replenishment of a petty cash fund.**

Objective 9-6

On January 2, Jasmine's Floral Supplies Inc. issued Check 3100 for $300 to establish a petty cash fund. On January 31, Check 3159 was issued to replenish the petty cash fund. An analysis of payments from the fund showed these totals: ***Supplies,*** $68; ***Delivery Expense,*** $109; and ***Miscellaneous Expense,*** $14. Indicate how this transaction would be recorded in a cash payments journal.

Exercise 9.5 ▶ **Preparing a bank reconciliation statement.**

Objectives 9-9, 9-10

Teng Corporation received a bank statement showing a balance of $15,700 as of October 31, 2019. The firm's records showed a book balance of $15,262 on October 31. The difference between the two balances was caused by the following items. Prepare the adjusted bank balance section and the adjusted book balance section of the bank reconciliation statement. Also prepare the necessary journal entry.

1. A debit memorandum for an NSF check from Richard Wolf for $332.
2. Three outstanding checks: Check 7017 for $124, Check 7098 for $55, and Check 7107 for $1,560.
3. A bank service charge of $12.
4. A deposit in transit of $957.

Exercise 9.6 ▶ **Analyzing bank reconciliation items.**

Objective 9-9

At Livermore Delivery and Courier Service, the following items were found to cause a difference between the bank statement and the firm's records. Indicate whether each item will affect the bank balance or the book balance when the bank reconciliation statement is prepared. Also indicate which items will require an accounting entry after the bank reconciliation is completed.

1. A deposit in transit.
2. A debit memorandum for a dishonored check.
3. A credit memorandum for a promissory note that the bank collected for Livermore.
4. An error found in Livermore's records, which involves the amount of a check. The firm's checkbook and cash payments journal indicate $808 as the amount, but the canceled check itself and the listing on the bank statement show that $880 was the actual sum.
5. An outstanding check.
6. A bank service charge.
7. A check issued by another firm that was charged to Livermore's account by mistake.

Preparing a bank reconciliation statement.

Exercise 9.7
Objective 9-9

Di Stefano Office Supply Company received a bank statement showing a balance of $70,005 as of March 31, 2019. The firm's records showed a book balance of $71,487 on March 31. The difference between the two balances was caused by the following items. Prepare a bank reconciliation statement for the firm as of March 31 and the necessary journal entries from the statement.

1. A debit memorandum for $40, which covers the bank's collection fee for the note.
2. A deposit in transit of $4,700.
3. A check for $348 issued by another firm that was mistakenly charged to Di Stefano's account.
4. A debit memorandum for an NSF check of $6,145 issued by Wozniak Construction Company, a credit customer.
5. Outstanding checks: Check 3782 for $2,200; Check 3840 for $251.
6. A credit memorandum for a $7,300 noninterest-bearing note receivable that the bank collected for the firm.

Determining the adjusted bank balance.

Exercise 9.8
Objective 9-9

Florence Company received a bank statement showing a balance of $13,550 on November 30, 2019. During the bank reconciliation process, Florence Company's accountant noted the following bank errors:

1. A check for $265 issued by Florentine, Inc., was mistakenly charged to Florence Company's account.
2. Check 2782 was written for $200 but was paid by the bank as $1,200.
3. Check 2920 for $85 was paid by the bank twice.
4. A deposit for $580 on November 22 was credited by the bank for $850.

Assuming outstanding checks total $2,450, prepare the adjusted bank balance section of the November 30, 2019, bank reconciliation.

Journalizing electronic transactions

Exercise 9.9
Objective 9-11

After returning from a three-day business trip, the accountant for Southeast Sales, Johanna Estrada, checked bank activity in the company's checking account online. The activity for the last three days follows.

Business Checking		Account #123456-987			
Date	**Type**	**Description**	**Additions**	**Payments**	**Balance**
09/24/2019	Loan Payment	Online Transfer to HMG XXXX		$3,500.00	$15,675.06
09/24/2019	Deposit	DEPOSIT ID NUMBER 8888	$2,269.60		$19,175.06
09/23/2019	Check	CHECK #1554 (view)		$3,500.00	$16,905.46
09/23/2019	Bill Payment	Online Payment		$36.05	$20,405.46
09/22/2019	Check	CHECK #1553 (view)		$240.00	$20,441.51
09/22/2019	Check	CHECK #1551 (view)		$1,750.00	$20,681.51
09/22/2019	ACH Credit	Edwards UK AP PAYMENT	$8,900.00		$22,431.51
09/22/2019	ATM	ATM WITHDRAWAL		$240.00	$13,531.51

After matching these transactions to the company's ***Cash*** account in the general ledger, Johanna noted the following unrecorded transactions:

1. The ATM withdrawal on 9/22/2019 was for personal use by the owner, Robert Savage.
2. The ACH credit on 9/22/2019 was an electronic funds payment received on account from Edwards UK, a credit customer located in Great Britain.
3. The bill payment made 9/23/2019 was to Waste Control Trash Services (utilities).
4. The loan payment on 9/24/2019 was an automatic debit by Central Motors for the company's monthly payment on a loan for its automobiles. The loan does not bear interest.

Prepare the journal entries in a general journal to record the four transactions above. Use 21 as the page number.

Exercise 9.10 Appendix
Objective 9-12

► Normal balances.

Identify the normal balance of the following accounts. Use "Dr." for debit or "Cr." for credit.

1. _____ Merchandise Inventory
2. _____ Sales Tax Payable
3. _____ Sales
4. _____ Sales Discounts
5. _____ Sales Returns and Allowances
6. _____ Cost of Goods Sold
7. _____ Credit Card Expense

Exercise 9.11 Appendix
Objective 9-12

► Recording purchases made for cash and on account.

Ruby Corporation engaged in the following transactions during June. The company uses the perpetual inventory system. Record these transactions in a general journal.

DATE		TRANSACTIONS
2019		
June	4	Purchased merchandise on account from Salinas Company; Invoice 100 for $1,025; terms n/30.
	15	Recorded purchases for cash, $1,540.
	30	Paid amount due to Salinas Company for the purchase on June 4.

Exercise 9.12 Appendix
Objective 9-12

► Recording purchases with purchases returns and purchases discounts.

Record the following transactions of J. Min Designs in a general journal. The company uses the perpetual inventory system.

DATE		TRANSACTIONS
2019		
April	1	Purchased merchandise on credit from O'Rourke Fabricators, Invoice 885, $3,000, terms 1/10, n/30; freight of $20 was paid by O'Rourke Fabricators and added to the invoice (total invoice amount, $3,020).
	9	Paid amount due to O'Rourke Fabricators for the purchase of April 1, less the 1 percent discount, Check 457.
	15	Purchased merchandise on credit from Kroll Company, Invoice 145, $1,250, terms 1/10, n/30; freight of $75 prepaid by Kroll and added to the invoice.
	17	Returned damaged merchandise purchased on April 15 from Kroll Company; received Credit Memorandum 332 for $50.
	24	Paid the amount due to Kroll Company for the purchase of April 15, less the return on April 17, taking the 1 percent discount, Check 470.

Recording purchases made for cash and on account.

◄ Exercise 9.13 Appendix
Objective 9-12

Tsang Corporation operates in a state with no sales tax. The company uses the perpetual inventory system. Record the following transactions in a general journal.

DATE		TRANSACTIONS
2019		
June	5	Sold merchandise on account to Benson Company; issued Sales Slip 1200 for $975, terms n/30. The cost of the merchandise sold was $683.
	15	Recorded cash sales, $1,940. The cost of merchandise sold was $1,358.
	30	Received payment on account due from Benson Company for the sale on June 5.

Recording sales made for cash and on account, with 8 percent sales tax, and sales returns.

◄ Exercise 9.14 Appendix
Objective 9-12

Record the following transactions of Fashion Park in a general journal. Fashion Park must charge 8 percent sales tax on all sales. The company uses the perpetual inventory system.

DATE		TRANSACTIONS
2019		
April	2	Sold merchandise for cash, $2,500 plus sales tax. The cost of merchandise sold was $1,500.
	3	The customer purchasing merchandise for cash on April 2 returned $250 of the merchandise; provided a cash refund to the customer. The cost of returned merchandise was $150.
	4	Sold merchandise on credit to Jordan Clark; issued Sales Slip 908 for $1,050 plus tax, terms n/30. The cost of the merchandise sold was $630.
	6	Accepted return of merchandise from Jordan Clark; issued Credit Memorandum 302 for $150 plus tax. The original sale was made on Sales Slip 908 of April 4. The cost of returned merchandise was $90.
	30	Received payment on account from Jordan Clark in payment of her purchase of April 4, less the return on April 6.

Recording a sale made on account, with a sales discount.

◄ Exercise 9.15 Appendix
Objective 9-12

On April 1, Moloney Meat Distributors sold merchandise on account to Fronke's Franks for $3,500 on Invoice 1001, terms 2/10, n/30. The cost of merchandise sold was $2,000. Payment was received in full from Fronke's Franks, less discount, on April 10.

Record the transactions for Moloney Meat Distributors on April 1 and April 10. The company uses the perpetual inventory system. Use 14 as the journal page number.

Journalizing merchandising transactions for buyer and seller.

◄ Exercise 9.16 Appendix
Objective 9-12

Bushard Company (buyer) and Schmidt, Inc. (seller), engaged in the following transactions during February 2019.

Bushard Company

DATE		TRANSACTIONS
2019		
Feb.	10	Purchased merchandise for $5,000 from Schmidt, Inc., Invoice 1980, terms 1/10, n/30.
	13	Received Credit Memorandum 230 from Schmidt, Inc., for damaged merchandise totaling $200 that was returned; the goods were purchased on Invoice 1980, dated February 10.
	19	Paid amount due to Schmidt, Inc., for Invoice 1980 of February 10, less the return of February 13 and less the cash discount, Check 2010.

Schmidt, Inc.

DATE		TRANSACTIONS
2019		
Feb.	10	Sold merchandise for $5,000 on account to Bushard Company, Invoice 1980, terms 1/10, n/30. The cost of merchandise sold was $3,000.
	13	Issued Credit Memorandum 230 to Bushard Company for damaged merchandise totaling $200 that was returned; the goods were purchased on Invoice 1980, dated February 10. The cost of the returned goods was $120.
	19	Received payment from Bushard Company for Invoice 1980 of February 10, less the return of February 13 and less the cash discount, Check 2010.

Both companies use the perpetual inventory system. Journalize the transactions above in a general journal for both Bushard Company and Schmidt, Inc. Use 20 as the journal page for both companies.

PROBLEMS

Problem Set A

Problem 9.1A
Objectives 9-1, 9-2, 9-3

Journalizing cash receipts and posting to the general ledger.

Entertainment Inc. is a retail store that rents movies and sells music CDs over the Internet. The firm's cash receipts for February and the general ledger accounts used to record these transactions are shown below.

INSTRUCTIONS

1. Open the general ledger accounts and enter the balances as of February 1, 2019.
2. Record the transactions in a cash receipts journal. Use 4 as the page number.
3. Post the individual entries from the Other Accounts Credit section of the cash receipts journal to the proper general ledger accounts.
4. Total, prove, and rule the cash receipts journal as of February 28, 2019.
5. Post the column totals from the cash receipts journal to the proper general ledger accounts.

GENERAL LEDGER ACCOUNTS

101 Cash	$ 5,060 Dr.
109 Notes Receivable	900 Dr.
111 Accounts Receivable	4,125 Dr.
129 Supplies	710 Dr.
231 Sales Tax Payable	345 Cr.
301 Jason Wilson, Capital	35,000 Cr.
401 Sales	
491 Interest Income	
620 Cash Short or Over	

DATE		TRANSACTIONS
Feb.	3	Received $600 from Danielle Pelzel, a credit customer, on account.
	5	Received a cash refund of $130 for damaged supplies.
	7	Had cash sales of $5,800 plus sales tax of $464 during the first week of February; there was a cash shortage of $70.
	9	Jason Wilson, the owner, invested an additional $16,000 cash in the business.
	12	Received $480 from Kyela Jones, a credit customer, in payment of her account.
	14	Had cash sales of $4,550 plus sales tax of $364 during the second week of February; there was an overage of $38.
	16	Received $550 from Sadie Nelson, a credit customer, to apply toward her account.
	19	Received a check from Ketura Pittman to pay her $900 promissory note plus interest of $36.
	21	Had cash sales of $5,050 plus sales tax of $404 during the third week of February.
	25	Alfred Herron, a credit customer, sent a check for $680 to pay the balance he owes.
	28	Had cash sales of $5,100 plus sales tax of $408 during the fourth week of February; there was a cash shortage of $46.

Analyze: What total accounts receivable were collected in February?

Journalizing cash payments, recording petty cash, and posting to the general ledger.

◄ **Problem 9.2A**
Objectives 9-4, 9-5, 9-6

The cash payments of The Aristocrats Jewels, a retail business, for June and the general ledger accounts used to record these transactions appear below.

INSTRUCTIONS

1. Open the general ledger accounts and enter the balances as of June 1.
2. Record all payments by check in a cash payments journal; use 8 as the page number.
3. Record all payments from the petty cash fund on a petty cash analysis sheet; use 8 as the sheet number.
4. Post the individual entries from the Other Accounts Debit section of the cash payments journal to the proper general ledger accounts.

5. Total, prove, and rule the petty cash analysis sheet as of June 30. Record the replenishment of the fund and the final balance on the sheet.
6. Total, prove, and rule the cash payments journal as of June 30.
7. Post the column totals from the cash payments journal to the proper general ledger accounts.

GENERAL LEDGER ACCOUNTS

101 Cash	$46,740 Dr.
105 Petty Cash Fund	
129 Supplies	1,160 Dr.
201 Notes Payable	4,200 Cr.
205 Accounts Payable	19,880 Cr.
231 Sales Tax Payable	5,200 Cr.
302 Larry Jennings, Drawing	
451 Sales Returns and Allowances	
504 Purchases Discounts	
611 Delivery Expense	
620 Rent Expense	
623 Salaries Expense	
626 Telephone Expense	
634 Interest Expense	
635 Miscellaneous Expense	

DATE		TRANSACTIONS
June	1	Issued Check 4121 for $3,500 to pay the monthly rent.
	2	Issued Check 4122 for $5,200 to remit the state sales tax.
	3	Issued Check 4123 for $2,880 to Perfect Timing Watch Company, a creditor, in payment of Invoice 6808, dated May 5.
	4	Issued Check 4124 for $250 to establish a petty cash fund. (After journalizing this transaction, be sure to enter it on the first line of the petty cash analysis sheet.)
	5	Paid $40 from the petty cash fund for office supplies, Petty Cash Voucher 1.
	7	Issued Check 4125 for $4,368 to Perry Corporation in payment of a $4,200 promissory note and interest of $168.
	8	Paid $30 from the petty cash fund for postage stamps, Petty Cash Voucher 2.
	10	Issued Check 4126 for $604 to a customer as a cash refund for a defective watch that was returned; the original sale was made for cash.
	12	Issued Check 4127 for $286 to pay the telephone bill.
	14	Issued Check 4128 for $5,831 to International Jewelry Company, a creditor, in payment of Invoice 8629, dated May 6 ($5,950), less a cash discount ($119).
	15	Paid $19 from the petty cash fund for delivery service, Petty Cash Voucher 3.
	17	Issued Check 4129 for $960 to purchase store supplies.
	20	Issued Check 4130 for $3,920 to Nelsons Jewelry and Accessories, a creditor, in payment of Invoice 1513, dated June 12 ($4,000), less a cash discount ($80).
	22	Paid $34 from the petty cash fund for a personal withdrawal by Larry Jennings, the owner, Petty Cash Voucher 4.

DATE	9.2A (cont.) TRANSACTIONS
25	Paid $40 from the petty cash fund to have the store windows washed and repaired, Petty Cash Voucher 5.
27	Issued Check 4131 for $3,750 to Classy Creations, a creditor, in payment of Invoice 667, dated May 30.
30	Paid $34 from the petty cash fund for delivery service, Petty Cash Voucher 6.
30	Issued Check 4132 for $7,925 to pay the monthly salaries.
30	Issued Check 4133 for $6,000 to Larry Jennings, the owner, as a withdrawal for personal use.
30	Issued Check 4134 for $197 to replenish the petty cash fund. (Foot the columns of the petty cash analysis sheet in order to determine the accounts that should be debited and the amounts involved.)

Analyze: What total payments were made from the petty cash fund for the month?

Journalizing sales and cash receipts and posting to the general ledger.

◀ **Problem 9.3A**

Objectives 9-1, 9-2, 9-3

Awesome Sounds is a wholesale business that sells musical instruments. Transactions involving sales and cash receipts for the firm during April 2019 follow, along with the general ledger accounts used to record these transactions.

INSTRUCTIONS

1. Open the general ledger accounts and enter the balances as of April 1, 2016.
2. Record the transactions in a sales journal, a cash receipts journal, and a general journal. Use 7 as the page number for each of the special journals and 17 as the page number for the general journal.
3. Post the entries from the general journal to the general ledger.
4. Total, prove, and rule the special journals as of April 30, 2016.
5. Post the column totals from the special journals to the proper general ledger accounts.
6. Prepare the heading and the Revenue section of the firm's income statement for the month ended April 30.

GENERAL LEDGER ACCOUNTS

Account	Balance
101 Cash	$17,400 Dr.
109 Notes Receivable	
111 Accounts Receivable	22,000 Dr.
401 Sales	
451 Sales Returns and Allowances	
452 Sales Discounts	

DATE		TRANSACTIONS
April	1	Sold merchandise for $4,900 to Soprano Music Center; issued Invoice 9312 with terms of 2/10, n/30.
	3	Received a check for $1,960 from Music Supply Store in payment of Invoice 6718 of March 25 ($2,000), less a cash discount ($40).
	5	Sold merchandise for $1,825 in cash to a new customer who has not yet established credit.
	8	Sold merchandise for $5,500 to Music Warehouse; issued Invoice 9313 with terms of 2/10, n/30.

(continued)

DATE	9.3A (cont.) TRANSACTIONS
10	Soprano Music Center sent a check for $4,802 in payment of Invoice 9312 of April 1 ($4,900), less a cash discount ($98).
15	Accepted a return of damaged merchandise from Music Warehouse; issued Credit Memorandum 105 for $900; the original sale was made on Invoice 9313 of April 8.
19	Sold merchandise for $11,500 to Eagleton Music Center; issued Invoice 9314 with terms of 2/10, n/30.
23	Collected $3,225 from Sounds From Yesterday for Invoice 6725 of March 25.
26	Accepted a two-month promissory note for $6,500 from Country Music Store in settlement of its overdue account; the note has an interest rate of 12 percent.
28	Received a check for $11,270 from Eagleton Music Center in payment of Invoice 9314, dated April 19 ($11,500), less a cash discount ($230).
30	Sold merchandise for $10,800 to Contemporary Sounds, Inc.; issued Invoice 9315 with terms of 2/10, n/30.

Analyze: What total sales on account were made in the month of April, prior to any returns or allowances?

Problem 9.4A
Objectives 9-4, 9-5

Journalizing purchases, cash payments, and purchases discounts; posting to the general ledger.

The Bike and Hike Outlet is a retail store. Transactions involving purchases and cash payments for the firm during June 2019 are listed below, as are the general ledger accounts used to record these transactions.

INSTRUCTIONS

1. Open the general ledger accounts and enter the balances as of June 1, 2019.
2. Record the transactions in a purchases journal, a cash payments journal, and a general journal. Use 8 as the page number for each of the special journals and 20 as the page number for the general journal.
3. Post the entries from the general journal and from the Other Accounts Debit section of the cash payments journal to the proper general ledger accounts.
4. Total, prove, and rule the special journals as of June 30.
5. Post the column totals from the special journals to the general ledger.
6. Show how the firm's net cost of purchases would be reported on its income statement for the month ended June 30.

GENERAL LEDGER ACCOUNTS

101 Cash	$21,900 Dr.
131 Equipment	66,000 Dr.
201 Notes Payable	
205 Accounts Payable	4,980 Cr.
501 Purchases	
503 Purchases Ret. and Allow.	
504 Purchases Discounts	
611 Rent Expense	
614 Salaries Expense	
617 Telephone Expense	

DATE		TRANSACTIONS
June	1	Issued Check 1101 for $3,400 to pay the monthly rent.
	3	Purchased merchandise for $3,100 from Perfect Fit Shoe Shop, Invoice 746, dated June 1; the terms are 2/10, n/30.
	5	Purchased new store equipment for $5,500 from Middleton Company, Invoice 9067 dated June 4, net payable in 30 days.
	7	Issued Check 1102 for $1,570 to Leisure Wear Clothing Company, a creditor, in payment of Invoice 3342 of May 9.
	8	Issued Check 1103 for $3,038 to Perfect Fit Shoe Shop, a creditor, in payment of Invoice 746 dated June 1 ($3,100), less a cash discount ($62).
	12	Purchased merchandise for $2,300 from Juandas Coat Shop, Invoice 9922, dated June 9, net due and payable in 30 days.
	15	Issued Check 1104 for $238 to pay the monthly telephone bill.
	18	Received Credit Memorandum 203 for $800 from Juandas Coat Shop for defective goods that were returned; the original purchase was made on Invoice 9922 dated June 9.
	21	Purchased new store equipment for $10,500 from Warren Company; Issued a three-month promissory note with interest at 12 percent.
	23	Purchased merchandise for $6,400 from The Motor Speedway, Invoice 1927, dated June 20; terms of 2/10, n/30.
	25	Issued Check 1105 for $1,500 to Juandas Coat Shop, a creditor, in payment of Invoice 7416 dated May 28.
	28	Issued Check 1106 for $6,272 to The Motor Speedway, a creditor, in payment of Invoice 1927 of June 20 ($6,400), less a cash discount ($128).
	30	Purchased merchandise for $2,080 from Jogging Shoes Store, Invoice 4713, dated June 26; the terms are 1/10, n/30.
	30	Issued Check 1107 for $5,800 to pay the monthly salaries of the employees.

Analyze: Assuming that all relevant information is included in this problem, what total liabilities does the company have at month-end?

Preparing a bank reconciliation statement and journalizing entries to adjust the cash balance.

◄ **Problem 9.5A**
Objectives 9-9, 9-10

On May 2, 2019, PHF Vacations received its April bank statement from First City Bank and Trust. Enclosed with the bank statement, which appears below, was a debit memorandum for $210 that covered an NSF check issued by Doris Fisher, a credit customer. The firm's checkbook contained the following information about deposits made and checks issued during April. The balance of the ***Cash*** account and the checkbook on April 30, 2019, was $3,012.

DATE		TRANSACTIONS	
April	1	Balance	$6,099
	1	Check 1207	110
	3	Check 1208	400
	5	Deposit	450
	5	Check 1209	325
	10	Check 1210	3,000

(continued)

DATE	9.5A (cont.) TRANSACTIONS	
17	Check 1211	60
19	Deposit	200
22	Check 1212	8
23	Deposit	200
26	Check 1213	250
28	Check 1214	18
30	Check 1215	16
30	Deposit	250

FIRST CITY BANK AND TRUST

PHF Vacations
1718 Jade Lane
San Diego, CA 92111-4998

1-877-123-9876

Account Number: 23-11070-08

April 1–30, 2019

Activity Summary:

Balance, April 1	$ 6,099.00
Deposits and credits	850.00
Withdrawals and debits	(4,370.00)
Balance, April 30	$ 2,579.00

DATE	DESCRIPTION	DEPOSITS/CREDITS	WITHDRAWALS/DEBITS	BALANCE
4/1/19	Opening balance			$6,099.00
4/6/19	Deposit	450.00		6,549.00
4/6/19	Check No. 1207		110.00	6,439.00
4/10/19	Check No. 1208		400.00	6,039.00
4/10/19	Check No. 1209		325.00	5,714.00
4/13/19	Check No. 1210		3,000.00	2,714.00
4/14/19	Service fee		7.00	2,707.00
4/20/19	Deposit	200.00		2,907.00
4/22/19	Check No. 1211		60.00	2,847.00
4/25/19	Deposit	200.00		3,047.00
4/26/19	Check No. 1212		8.00	3,039.00
4/29/19	Debit for NSF Check		210.00	2,829.00
4/29/19	Check No. 1213		250.00	2,579.00
	Totals	850.00	4,370.00	

INSTRUCTIONS

1. Prepare a bank reconciliation statement for the firm as of April 30, 2019.
2. Record general journal entries for any items on the bank reconciliation statement that must be journalized. Date the entries April 30, 2019.

Analyze: What checks remain outstanding after the bank statement has been reconciled?

Preparing a bank reconciliation statement and journalizing entries to adjust the cash balance.

◀ **Problem 9.6A**
Objectives 9-9, 9-10

On August 31, 2019, the balance in the checkbook and the ***Cash*** account of the Dry Creek Bed and Breakfast was $12,981. The balance shown on the bank statement on the same date was $13,897.

NOTES

a. The firms records indicate that a $1,500 deposit dated August 30 and a $701 deposit dated August 31 do not appear on the bank statement.

b. A service charge of $8 and a debit memorandum of $270 covering an NSF check have not yet been entered in the firm's records. (The check was issued by Art Corts, a credit customer.)

c. The following checks were issued but have not yet been paid by the bank:

Check 712, $110
Check 713, $125
Check 716, $238
Check 736, $577
Check 739, $78
Check 741, $120

d. A credit memorandum shows that the bank collected a $2,094 note receivable and interest of $53 for the firm. These amounts have not yet been entered in the firm's records.

INSTRUCTIONS

1. Prepare a bank reconciliation statement for the firm as of August 31.
2. Record general journal entries for items on the bank reconciliation statement that must be journalized. Date the entries August 31, 2019.

Analyze: What effect did the journal entries recorded as a result of the bank reconciliation have on the fundamental accounting equation?

Correcting errors revealed by a bank reconciliation.

◀ **Problem 9.7A**
Objectives 9-9, 9-10

During the bank reconciliation process at A. Fontes Consultancy on May 2, 2019, the following two errors were discovered in the firm's records.

1. The checkbook and the cash payments journal indicated that Check 2206 dated April 17 was issued for $695 to make a cash purchase of supplies. However, examination of the canceled check and the listing on the bank statement showed that the actual amount of the check was $14.
2. The checkbook and the cash payments journal indicated that Check 2247 dated April 20 was issued for $130 to pay a utility bill. However, examination of the canceled check and the listing on the bank statement showed that the actual amount of the check was $164.

INSTRUCTIONS

1. Prepare the adjusted book balance section of the firm's bank reconciliation statement. The book balance as of April 30 was $20,275. The errors listed above are the only two items that affect the book balance.
2. Prepare general journal entries to correct the errors. Use page 11 and date the entries April 30, 2019. Check 2206 was correctly debited to ***Supplies*** on April 17, and Check 2247 was debited to ***Utilities Expense*** on April 20.

Analyze: If the errors described had not been corrected, would net income for the period be overstated or understated? By what amount?

Problem 9.8A
Objectives 9-9, 9-10, 9-11

▶ Preparing a bank reconciliation statement and journalizing entries to adjust the cash balance.

On August 1, 2019, the accountant for Western Imports downloaded the company's July 31, 2019, bank statement from the bank's website. The balance shown on the bank statement was $28,760. The July 31, 2019, balance in the ***Cash*** account in the general ledger was $14,242.

Jenny Irvine, the accountant for Western Imports, noted the following differences between the bank's records and the company's ***Cash*** account in the general ledger.

a. An electronic funds transfer for $14,400 from Foncier Ricard, a customer located in France, was received by the bank on July 31.

b. Check 1422 was correctly written and recorded for $1,200. The bank mistakenly paid the check for $1,280.

c. The accounting records indicate that Check 1425 was issued for $60 to make a purchase of supplies. However, examination of the check online showed that the actual amount of the check was for $90.

d. A deposit of $900 made after banking hours on July 31 did not appear on the July 31 bank statement.

e. The following checks were outstanding: Check 1429 for $1,249 and Check 1430 for $141.

f. An automatic debit of $262 on July 31 from CentralComm for telephone service appeared on the bank statement but had not been recorded in the company's accounting records.

INSTRUCTIONS

1. Prepare a bank reconciliation for the firm as of July 31.
2. Record general journal entries for the items on the bank reconciliation that must be journalized. Date the entries July 31, 2019. Use 19 as the page number.

Analyze: What effect on total expenses occurred as a result of the general journal entries recorded?

Problem 9.9A Appendix
Objective 9-12

▶ Recording transactions using the perpetual inventory system.

The following transactions took place at Fine Fashions Outlet during July 2019. Fine Fashions Outlet uses a perpetual inventory system. Record the transactions in a general journal. Use 8 as the page number for the general journal.

DATE		TRANSACTIONS
2019		
July	1	Purchased dresses for $4,750 plus a freight charge of $250 from Fashion Expo, Invoice 101, dated July 1; the terms are 2/10, n/30.
	5	Sold two dresses on account to Alice Chu, terms 1/10, n/30; issued Sales Slip 788 for $600. The cost of the dresses sold was $400.
	7	Received Credit Memorandum 210 for $550 from Fashion Expo for damaged dresses returned; the goods were purchased on Invoice 101 dated July 1.
	9	Accepted a return of a dress from Alice Chu; the dress was originally sold on Sales Slip 788 of July 5; issued Credit Memorandum 89 for $200. The cost of the returned dress was $135.
	10	Issued Check 1255 to pay the amount due to Fashion Expo for Invoice 101, dated July 1, less the return of July 7 and less the cash discount.
	15	Received payment from Alice Chu for the sale of July 5, less the return of July 9 and less the cash discount.
	15	Recorded sales on credit cards for the two-week period ended July 15, $12,000; the bank charges a 3 percent fee on all credit card sales. The cost of merchandise sold was $8,000.

DATE	9.9A (cont.) TRANSACTIONS
17	Purchased merchandise on account from Fashion Wholesalers for $4,500, subject to trade discounts of 40 percent and 10 percent, terms 1/10, n/30, Invoice 2078.
26	Paid amount owed to Fashion Wholesalers for the purchase of July 17, Check 1285.

Analyze: What percentage of the total amount due to Fashion Expo on July 1 is due to the freight charge?

Problem Set B

Journalizing cash receipts and posting to the general ledger.

◄ **Problem 9.1B**

Objectives 9-1, 9-2, 9-3

The Book Peddler is a retail store that sells books, cards, business supplies, and novelties. The firm's cash receipts during June 2019 and the general ledger accounts used to record these transactions appear below.

INSTRUCTIONS

1. Open the general ledger accounts and enter the balances as of June 1.
2. Record the transactions in a cash receipts journal. (Use page 14.)
3. Post the individual entries from the Other Accounts Credit section of the cash receipts journal to the proper general ledger accounts.
4. Total, prove, and rule the cash receipts journal as of June 30.
5. From the cash receipts journal, post the totals to the general ledger.

GENERAL LEDGER ACCOUNTS

102 Cash	$1,200
111 Accounts Receivable	8,400
115 Notes Receivable	1,700
129 Office Supplies	1,000
231 Sales Tax Payable	400
302 Tina Kapoor, Capital	7,600
401 Sales	
791 Interest Income	

DATE	TRANSACTIONS
June 3	Received $500 from Do It Yourself Copy Center, a credit customer.
4	Received a check for $1,802 from Amanda Whitehead to pay her note receivable; the total included $102 of interest.
5	Received a $310 refund for damaged supplies purchased from Books-R-Us.
7	Recorded cash sales of $1,700 plus sales tax payable of $136.
10	Received $1,200 from Linda Park, a credit customer.
13	Tina Kapoor, the owner, contributed additional capital of $13,000 to the business.

(continued)

DATE	9.1B (cont.) TRANSACTIONS
14	Recorded cash sales of $1,600 plus sales tax of $128.
18	Received $1,760 from Karen Cho, a credit customer.
19	Received $1,300 from Nancy Matthews, a credit customer.
21	Recorded cash sales of $1,800 plus sales tax of $144.
27	Received $850 from Alex Holloway, a credit customer.

Analyze: Assuming that all relevant information is included in this problem, what are total assets for The Book Peddler at June 30, 2019?

Problem 9.2B

Objectives 9-4, 9-5, 9-6

Journalizing cash payments and recording petty cash; posting to the general ledger.

The cash payments of European Gift Shop, a retail business, for September and the general ledger accounts used to record these transactions appear below.

INSTRUCTIONS

1. Open the general ledger accounts and enter the balances as of September 1, 2019.
2. Record all payments by check in a cash payments journal. Use 12 as the page number.
3. Record all payments from the petty cash fund on a petty cash analysis sheet with special columns for ***Delivery Expense*** and ***Miscellaneous Expense.*** Use 12 as the sheet number.
4. Post the individual entries from the Other Accounts Debit section of the cash payments journal to the proper general ledger accounts.
5. Total, prove, and rule the petty cash analysis sheet as of September 30, then record the replenishment of the fund and the final balance on the sheet.
6. Total, prove, and rule the cash payments journal as of September 30.
7. Post the column totals from the cash payments journal to the proper general ledger accounts.

GENERAL LEDGER ACCOUNTS

101 Cash	$21,530 Dr.	504 Purchases Discounts
105 Petty Cash Fund		511 Delivery Expense
141 Equipment	43,000 Dr.	611 Interest Expense
201 Notes Payable	1,000 Cr.	614 Miscellaneous Expense
205 Accounts Payable	9,800 Cr.	620 Rent Expense
231 Sales Tax Payable	1,344 Cr.	623 Salaries Expense
302 Fred Lynn, Drawing		626 Telephone Expense
451 Sales Ret. and Allow.		

DATE		TRANSACTIONS
Sept.	1	Issued Check 401 for $1,344 to remit sales tax to the state tax commission.
	2	Issued Check 402 for $1,700 to pay the monthly rent.
	4	Issued Check 403 for $100 to establish a petty cash fund. (After journalizing this transaction, be sure to enter it on the first line of the petty cash analysis sheet.)
	5	Issued Check 404 for $1,470 to Elegant Glassware, a creditor, in payment of Invoice 6793, dated August 28 ($1,500), less a cash discount ($30).

DATE	9.2B (cont.) TRANSACTIONS
6	Paid $12.00 from the petty cash fund for delivery service, Petty Cash Voucher 1.
9	Purchased store equipment for $1,000; issued Check 405.
11	Paid $16 from the petty cash fund for office supplies, Petty Cash Voucher 2 (charge to ***Miscellaneous Expense***).
13	Issued Check 406 for $970 to Taylor Company, a creditor, in payment of Invoice 7925, dated August 15.
14	Issued Check 407 for $425 to a customer as a cash refund for a defective watch that was returned; the original sale was made for cash.
16	Paid $10 from the petty cash fund for a personal withdrawal by Fred Lynn, the owner, Petty Cash Voucher 3.
18	Issued Check 408 for $187 to pay the monthly telephone bill.
21	Issued Check 409 for $833 to African Imports, a creditor, in payment of Invoice 1822, dated September 13 ($850), less a cash discount ($17).
23	Paid $13 from the petty cash fund for postage stamps, Petty Cash Voucher 4 (charge to Miscellaneous Expense).
24	Issued Check 410 for $1,040 to Zachary Corporation in payment of a $1,000 promissory note and interest of $40.
26	Issued Check 411 for $1,240 to Atlantic Ceramics, a creditor, in payment of Invoice 3510, dated August 29.
27	Paid $10 from the petty cash fund for delivery service, Petty Cash Voucher 5.
28	Issued Check 412 for $1,500 to Fred Lynn, the owner, as a withdrawal for personal use.
30	Issued Check 413 for $2,500 to pay the monthly salaries of the employees.
30	Issued Check 414 for $61 to replenish the petty cash fund. (Foot the columns of the petty cash analysis sheet in order to determine the accounts that should be debited and the amounts involved.)

Analyze: What was the amount of total debits to general ledger liability accounts during the month of September?

Journalizing sales and cash receipts and posting to the general ledger.

◀ **Problem 9.3B**
Objectives 9-1, 9-2, 9-3

Royal Construction Company is a wholesale business. The transactions involving sales and cash receipts for the firm during August 2019 and the general ledger accounts used to record these transactions are listed below.

INSTRUCTIONS

1. Open the general ledger accounts and enter the balances as of August 1, 2019.
2. Record the transactions in a sales journal, a cash receipts journal, and a general journal. Use 10 as the page number for each of the special journals and 24 as the page number for the general journal.
3. Post the entries from the general journal to the proper general ledger accounts.
4. Total, prove, and rule the special journals as of August 31, 2019.
5. Post the column totals from the special journals to the proper general ledger accounts.
6. Prepare the heading and the Revenue section of the firm's income statement for the month ended August 31, 2019.

GENERAL LEDGER ACCOUNTS

101 Cash	$15,070 Dr.	401 Sales
109 Notes Receivable		451 Sales Returns and Allowances
111 Accounts Receivable	22,507 Dr.	452 Sales Discounts

DATE		TRANSACTIONS
Aug.	1	Received a check for $6,468 from Construction Supply Company in payment of Invoice 8277 dated July 21 ($6,600), less a cash discount ($132).
	2	Sold merchandise for $19,450 to Jamison Builders; issued Invoice 2978 with terms of 2/10, n/30.
	4	Accepted a three-month promissory note for $12,000 from Davis Custom Homes to settle its overdue account; the note has an interest rate of 12 percent.
	7	Sold merchandise for $18,550 to Branch Construction Company; issued Invoice 2979 with terms of 2/10, n/30.
	11	Collected $19,061 from Jamison Builders for Invoice 2978 dated August 2 ($19,450), less a cash discount ($389.00).
	14	Sold merchandise for $7,050 in cash to a new customer who has not yet established credit.
	16	Branch Construction Company sent a check for $18,179 in payment of Invoice 2979 dated August 7 ($18,550), less a cash discount ($371.00).
	22	Sold merchandise for $6,850 to Contemporary Homes; issued Invoice 2980 with terms of 2/10, n/30.
	24	Received a check for $6,000 from Garcia Homes Center to pay Invoice 2877, dated July 23.
	26	Accepted a return of damaged merchandise from Contemporary Homes; issued Credit Memorandum 101 for $550; the original sale was made on Invoice 2980, dated August 22.
	31	Sold merchandise for $17,440 to Denton County Builders; issued Invoice 2981 with terms of 2/10, n/30.

Analyze: What total sales on account were made in August? Include sales returns and allowances in your computation.

Problem 9.4B
Objectives 9-4, 9-5

Journalizing purchases, cash payments, and purchases discounts; posting to the general ledger.

Contemporary Appliance Center is a retail store that sells a variety of household appliances. Transactions involving purchases and cash payments for the firm during December 2019 and the general ledger accounts used to record these transactions appear below.

INSTRUCTIONS

1. Open the general ledger accounts and enter the balances in these accounts as of December 1, 2019.
2. Record the transactions in a purchases journal, a cash payments journal, and a general journal. Use 12 as the page number for each of the special journals and 30 as the page number for the general journal.
3. Post the entries from the general journal and from the Other Accounts Debit section of the cash payments journal to the proper accounts in the general ledger.
4. Total, prove, and rule the special journals as of December 31, 2019.
5. Post the column totals from the special journals to the general ledger accounts.
6. Show how the firm's cost of purchases would be reported on its income statement for the month ended December 31, 2019.

GENERAL LEDGER ACCOUNTS

101 Cash	$60,700 Dr.
131 Equipment	68,000 Dr.
201 Notes Payable	
205 Accounts Payable	7,600 Cr.
501 Purchases	
503 Purchases Returns and Allowances	
504 Purchases Discounts	
611 Rent Expense	
614 Salaries Expense	
617 Telephone Expense	

DATE	TRANSACTIONS
Dec. 1	Purchased merchandise for $6,600 from Alexis Products for Homes, Invoice 6559, dated November 28; the terms are 2/10, n/30.
2	Issued Check 1801 for $3,000 to pay the monthly rent.
4	Purchased new store equipment for $14,000 from Kesterson Company; issued a two-month promissory note with interest at 10 percent.
6	Issued Check 1802 for $6,468 to Alexis Products for Homes, a creditor, in payment of Invoice 6559, dated November 28 ($6,600), less a cash discount ($132).
10	Purchased merchandise for $9,200 from the Baxter Corporation, Invoice 5119, dated December 7; terms of 2/10, n/30.
13	Issued Check 1803 for $265 to pay the monthly telephone bill.
15	Issued Check 1804 for $9,016 to Baxter Corporation, a creditor, in payment of Invoice 5119, dated December 7 ($9,200), less a cash discount ($184).
18	Purchased merchandise for $12,400 from Household Appliance Center, Invoice 7238, dated December 16; terms of 3/10, n/30.
20	Purchased new store equipment for $6,000 from Safety Security Systems Inc., Invoice 536, dated December 17, net payable in 45 days.
21	Issued Check 1805 for $4,200 to Chain Lighting and Appliances, a creditor, in payment of Invoice 7813, dated November 23.
22	Purchased merchandise for $5,800 from Zale Corporation, Invoice 3161, dated December 19, net due in 30 days.
24	Issued Check 1806 for $12,028 to Household Appliance Center, a creditor, in payment of Invoice 7238, dated December 16 ($12,400), less a cash discount ($372).
28	Received Credit Memorandum 201 for $1,050 from Zale Corporation for damaged goods that were returned; the original purchase was made on Invoice 3161, dated December 19.
31	Issued Check 1807 for $6,500 to pay the monthly salaries of the employees.

Analyze: List the dates for transactions in December that would be categorized as expenses of the business.

Preparing a bank reconciliation statement and journalizing entries to adjust the cash balance.

◀ **Problem 9.5B**
Objectives 9-9, 9-10

On October 7, 2019, Peter Chen, Attorney-at-Law, received his September bank statement from First Texas National Bank. Enclosed with the bank statement was a debit memorandum for $118 that covered an NSF check issued by Annette Cole, a credit customer. The firm's checkbook contained the following information about deposits made and checks issued during September. The balance of the ***Cash*** account and the checkbook on September 30 was $8,134.

INSTRUCTIONS

1. Prepare a bank reconciliation statement for the firm as of September 30, 2019.
2. Record general journal entries for any items on the bank reconciliation statement that must be journalized. Date the entries September 30, 2019.

DATE		TRANSACTIONS	
Sept.	1	Balance	$6,500
	1	Check 104	100
	3	Check 105	10
	3	Deposit	500
	6	Check 106	225
	10	Deposit	410
	11	Check 107	200
	15	Check 108	75
	21	Check 109	60
	22	Deposit	730
	25	Check 110	16
	25	Check 111	80
	27	Check 112	140
	28	Deposit	900

FIRST TEXAS NATIONAL BANK

Peter Chen, Attorney-at-Law
3510 North Central Expressway
Dallas, TX 75232-2709

1-877-987-6543

Account Number: 22-5654-30

September 1–30, 2019

Activity Summary:

Balance, September 1	$ 6,500.00
Deposits and credits	1,640.00
Withdrawals and debits	(816.50)
Balance, September 30	$ 7,323.50

DATE	DESCRIPTION	DEPOSITS/CREDITS	WITHDRAWALS/DEBITS	BALANCE
9/1/19	Opening balance			$6,500.00
9/3/19	Deposit	500.00		7,000.00
9/6/19	Check No. 104		100.00	6,900.00
9/11/19	Deposit	410.00		7,310.00
9/11/19	Check No. 105		10.00	7,300.00
9/11/19	Check No. 107		200.00	7,100.00
9/15/19	Check No. 106		225.00	6,875.00
9/19/19	Check No. 109		60.00	6,815.00
9/23/19	Deposit	730.00		7,545.00
9/25/19	Check No. 110		16.00	7,529.00
9/25/19	Check No. 111		80.00	7,449.00
9/28/19	Debit for NSF Check		118.00	7,331.00
9/28/19	Service charge		7.50	7,323.50
	Totals	1,640.00	816.50	

Analyze: How many checks were paid (cleared the bank) according to the September 30 bank statement?

Preparing a bank reconciliation statement and journalizing entries to adjust the cash balance.

◀ **Exercise 9.6B**
Objectives 9-9, 9-10

On July 31, 2019, the balance in Bay City Appliances' checkbook and ***Cash*** account was $8,318.59. The balance shown on the bank statement on the same date was $9,442.03.

NOTES

a. The following checks were issued but have not yet been paid by the bank: Check 533 for $151.95, Check 535 for $122.50, and Check 537 for $625.40.

b. A credit memorandum shows that the bank has collected a $1,447 note receivable and interest of $30 for the firm. These amounts have not yet been entered in the firm's records.

c. The firm's records indicate that a deposit of $994.07 made on July 31 does not appear on the bank statement.

d. A service charge of $14.34 and a debit memorandum of $245 covering an NSF check have not yet been entered in the firm's records. (The check was issued by Roberta La Follette, a credit customer.)

INSTRUCTIONS

1. Prepare a bank reconciliation statement for the firm as of July 31, 2019.
2. Record general journal entries for any items on the bank reconciliation statement that must be journalized. Date the entries July 31, 2019.

Analyze: After all journal entries have been recorded and posted, what is the balance in the ***Cash*** account at July 31, 2019?

Correcting errors revealed by a bank reconciliation.

◀ **Problem 9.7B**
Objectives 9-9, 9-10

During the bank reconciliation process at Wimpy Dudes Moving Corporation on March 3, 2019, the following errors were discovered in the firm's records.

a. The checkbook and the cash payments journal indicated that Check 1301 dated February 18 was issued for $328 to pay for hauling expenses. However, examination of the canceled check and the listing on the bank statement showed that the actual amount of the check was $308.

b. The checkbook and the cash payments journal indicated that Check 1322 dated February 24 was issued for $504 to pay a telephone bill. However, examination of the canceled check and the listing on the bank statement showed that the actual amount of the check was $540.

INSTRUCTIONS

1. Prepare the adjusted book balance section of the firm's bank reconciliation statement. The book balance as of February 28, 2019, was $20,551. The errors listed are the only two items that affect the book balance.
2. Prepare general journal entries to correct the errors. Date the entries February 28, 2019. Check 1301 was debited to ***Hauling Expense*** on February 18 and Check 1322 was debited to ***Telephone Expense*** on February 24.

Analyze: What net change to the ***Cash*** account occurred as a result of the correcting journal entries?

Preparing a bank reconciliation statement and journalizing entries to adjust the cash balance.

◀ **Problem 9.8B**
Objectives 9-9, 9-10, 9-11

On December 1, 2019, Robert Santo, the accountant for Euro Specialty Products, downloaded the company's November 30, 2019, bank statement from the bank's website. The balance shown on the bank statement was $29,734. The November 30, 2019, balance in the ***Cash*** account in the general ledger was $16,630.

Robert noted the following differences between the bank's records and the company's ***Cash*** account in the general ledger.

a. The following checks were outstanding: Check 4129 for $1,322 and Check 4130 for $239.

b. A deposit of $1,224 made after banking hours on November 30 did not appear on the November 30 bank statement.

c. An automatic debit of $323 on November 30 from ClearComm for telephone service appeared on the bank statement but had not been recorded in the company's accounting records.

d. An electronic funds transfer for $12,800 from Cantori Cucine, a customer located in Italy, was received by the bank on November 30.

e. Check 4122 was correctly written and recorded for $1,200. The bank mistakenly paid the check for $1,000.

f. The accounting records indicate that Check 4125 was issued for $980 to make a purchase of equipment. However, examination of the check online showed that the actual amount of the check was for $890.

INSTRUCTIONS

1. Prepare a bank reconciliation for the firm as of November 30.
2. Record general journal entries for the items on the bank reconciliation that must be journalized. Date the entries November 30, 2019. Use 44 as the page number.

Analyze: What effect did the journal entries recorded as a result of the bank reconciliation have on total assets?

Problem 9.9B Appendix

Objective 9-12

► Recording transactions using the perpetual inventory system.

The following transactions took place at The Garden Center during June 2019. The Garden Center uses a perpetual inventory system. Record the transactions in a general journal. Use 10 as the page number for the general journal.

DATE		TRANSACTIONS
2019		
June	1	Purchased lawn mowers for $5,080 plus a freight charge of $320 from Mow Down Corporation, Invoice 201, dated June 1; the terms are 2/10, n/30.
	5	Sold garden supplies on account to Arthur Gomez, terms 1/10, n/30; issued Sales Slip 888 for $1,000. The cost of the merchandise sold was $500.
	7	Received Credit Memorandum 310 for $550 from Mow Down Corporation for defective lawn mowers returned; the goods were purchased on Invoice 201 dated June 1.
	9	Accepted a return of various garden supplies from Arthur Gomez; the items were originally sold on Sales Slip 888 of June 5. Issued Credit Memorandum 89 for $100. The cost of the returned items was $50.
	10	Issued Check 1555 to pay the amount due to Mow Down Corporation for Invoice 201, dated June 1, less the return of June 7 and less the cash discount.
	15	Received payment from Arthur Gomez for the sale of June 5, less the return of June 9 and less the cash discount.
	15	Recorded sales on credit cards for the two-week period ended June 15, $15,000; the bank charges a 2 percent fee on all credit card sales. The cost of merchandise sold was $7,500.
	17	Purchased merchandise on account from Patio Wholesalers for $9,000, subject to trade discounts of 30 percent and 10 percent, terms 1/10, n/30, Invoice 2178.
	26	Paid amount owed to Patio Wholesalers for the purchase of June 17, Check 1598.

Analyze: Assume 20 lawn mowers were purchased from Mow Down Corporation on June 1. What was the average cost per lawn mower? (Hint: Include the freight charges as part of the cost of the lawn mowers.)

Critical Thinking Problem 9.1

Special Journals

During September 2019, Interior Designs Specialty Shop, a retail store, had the transactions listed below. The general ledger accounts used to record these transactions are also provided below.

INSTRUCTIONS

1. Open the general ledger accounts and enter the balances as of September 1, 2019.
2. Record the transactions in a sales journal, a cash receipts journal, a purchases journal, a cash payments journal, and a general journal. Use page 12 as the page number for each of the special journals and page 32 as the page number for the general journal.
3. Post the entries from the general journal to the proper general ledger accounts.
4. Post the entries from the Other Accounts Credit section of the cash receipts journal to the proper general ledger accounts.
5. Post the entries from the Other Accounts Debit section of the cash payments journal to the proper general ledger accounts.
6. Total, prove, and rule the special journals as of September 30.
7. Post the column totals from the special journals to the proper general ledger accounts.
8. Set up an accounts receivable ledger for Interior Designs Specialty Shop. Open an account for each of the customers listed below and enter the balances as of September 1. All of these customers have terms of n/30.

Credit Customers	
Name	**Balance 9/01/19**
Rachel Carter	
Mesia Davis	$1,260.00
Robert Kent	1,730.00
Pam Lawrence	
David Prater	1,050.00
Henry Tolliver	
Jason Williams	2,100.00

9. Post the individual entries from the sales journal, the cash receipts journal, and the general journal to the accounts receivable subsidiary ledger.
10. Prepare a schedule of accounts receivable for September 30, 2019.
11. Check the total of the schedule of accounts receivable against the balance of the ***Accounts Receivable*** account in the general ledger. The two amounts should be the same.

Creditors		
Name	**Balance 9/01/19**	**Terms**
Booker, Inc.		n/45
McKnight Corporation	$5,500	1/10, n/30
Nelson Craft Products		2/10, n/30
Rocker Company		n/30
Reed Millings Company		2/10, n/30
Sadler Floor Coverings	1,940	n/30
Wells Products	2,120	n/30

12. Set up an accounts payable subsidiary ledger for Interior Designs Specialty Shop. Open an account for each of the creditors listed above and enter the balances as of September 1, 2019.
13. Post the individual entries from the purchases journal, the cash payments journal, and the general journal to the accounts payable subsidiary ledger.
14. Prepare a schedule of accounts payable for September 1, 2019.
15. Check the total of the schedule of accounts payable against the balance of the ***Accounts Payable*** account in the general ledger. The two amounts should be the same.

GENERAL LEDGER ACCOUNTS

101 Cash	$18,945 Dr.	451 Sales Returns and Allowances
109 Notes Receivable		501 Purchases
111 Accounts Receivable	6,140 Dr.	502 Freight In
121 Supplies	710 Dr.	503 Purchases Returns and Allowances
131 Inventory	29,365 Dr.	504 Purchases Discounts
201 Notes Payable		611 Cash Short or Over
205 Accounts Payable	9,560 Cr.	614 Rent Expense
231 Sales Tax Payable		617 Salaries Expense
301 Sergio Cortez, Capital	45,600 Cr.	619 Utilities Expense
401 Sales		

DATE		TRANSACTIONS
Sept.	1	Received a check for $1,050 from David Prater to pay his account.
	1	Issued Check 1401 for $1,940 to Sadler Floor Coverings, a creditor, in payment of Invoice 6325 dated August 3.
	2	Issued Check 1402 for $2,500 to pay the monthly rent.
	3	Sold a table on credit for $650 plus sales tax of $52.00 to Pam Lawrence, Sales Slip 1850.
	5	Sergio Cortez, the owner, invested an additional $15,000 cash in the business in order to expand operations.
	6	Had cash sales of $3,900 plus sales tax of $312 during the period September 1–6; there was a cash shortage of $20.
	6	Purchased carpeting for $4,450 from Reed Millings Company, Invoice 827, dated September 3; terms of 2/10, n/30.
	6	Issued Check 1403 for $158 to Tri-City Trucking Company to pay the freight charge on goods received from Reed Millings Company.
	8	Purchased store supplies for $370 from Rocker Company, Invoice 4204, dated September 6, net amount due in 30 days.
	8	Sold chairs on credit for $950 plus sales tax of $76.00 to Henry Tolliver, Sales Slip 1851.
	11	Accepted a two-month promissory note for $2,100 from Jason Williams to settle his overdue account; the note has an interest rate of 10 percent.
	11	Issued Check 1404 for $4,361 to Reed Millings Company, a creditor, in payment of Invoice 827 dated September 3 ($4,450) less a cash discount ($89).
	13	Had cash sales of $3,850 plus sales tax of $308 during the period September 8–13.
	14	Purchased carpeting for $3,700 plus a freight charge of $84 from Wells Products, Invoice 9453, dated September 11, net due and payable in 30 days.

DATE	TRANSACTIONS (cont.)
15	Collected $1,260 on account from Mesia Davis.
17	Gave a two-month promissory note for $5,500 to McKnight Corporation, a creditor, to settle an overdue balance; the note bears interest at 12 percent.
19	Sold a lamp on credit to Rachel Carter for $250 plus sales tax of $20, Sales Slip 1852.
20	Had cash sales of $4,100 plus sales tax of $328 during the period September 15–20; there was a cash shortage of $9.00.
21	Purchased area rugs for $2,800 from Nelson Craft Products, Invoice 677, dated September 18; the terms are 2/10, n/30.
22	Issued Check 1405 for $306 to pay the monthly utility bill.
23	Granted an allowance to Rachel Carter for scratches on the lamp that she bought on Sales Slip 1852 of September 19; issued Credit Memorandum 151 for $54, which includes a price reduction of $50 and sales tax of $4.
24	Received Credit Memorandum 110 for $300 from Nelson Craft Products for a damaged rug that was returned; the original purchase was made on Invoice 677 dated September 18.
24	Robert Kent sent a check for $1,730 to pay the balance he owes.
25	Issued Check 1406 for $3,600 to make a cash purchase of merchandise.
26	Issued Check 1407 for $2,450 to Nelson Craft Products, a creditor, in payment of Invoice 677 of September 18 ($2,800), less a return ($300) and a cash discount ($50).
27	Purchased hooked rugs for $4,200 plus a freight charge of $128 from Booker, Inc., Invoice 1368, dated September 23, net payable in 45 days.
27	Had cash sales of $4,800 plus sales tax of $384 during the period September 22–27.
28	Issued Check 1408 for $2,120 to Wells Products, a creditor, in payment of Invoice 8984 dated August 30.
29	Sold a cabinet on credit to Mesia Davis for $1,200 plus sales tax of $96, Sales Slip 1853.
30	Had cash sales of $1,500 plus sales tax of $120 for September 29–30; there was a cash overage of $10.
30	Issued Check 1409 for $6,800 to pay the monthly salaries of the employees.

Analyze: What were the total cash payments for September?

Critical Thinking Problem 9.2

Cash Controls

Mike Lucci is the owner of Lucci Contractors, a successful small construction company. He spends most of his time out of the office supervising work at various construction sites, leaving the operation of the office to the company's cashier/bookkeeper, Gloria Harris. Gloria makes bank deposits, pays the company's bills, maintains the accounting records, and prepares monthly bank reconciliations.

Recently a friend told Mike that while he was at a party he overheard Gloria bragging that she paid for her new clothes with money from the company's cash receipts. She said her boss would never know because he never checks the cash records.

Mike admits that he does not check on Gloria's work. He now wants to know if Gloria is stealing from him. He asks you to examine the company's cash records to determine whether Gloria has stolen cash from the business and, if so, how much.

Your examination of the company's cash records reveals the following information:

1. Gloria prepared the following August 31, 2019, bank reconciliation.

Balance in books, August 31, 2019		$18,786
Additions:		
Outstanding checks		
Check 1780	$ 792	
Check 1784	1,819	
Check 1806	384	2,695
		$21,481
Deductions:		
Deposit in transit, August 28, 2019	$4,882	
Bank service charge	10	4,892
Balance on bank statement, August 31, 2019		$16,589

2. An examination of the general ledger shows the ***Cash*** account with a balance of $18,786 on August 31, 2019.
3. The August 31 bank statement shows a balance of $16,589.
4. The August 28 deposit of $4,882 does not appear on the August 31 bank statement.
5. A comparison of canceled checks returned with the August 31 bank statement with the cash payments journal reveals the following checks as outstanding:

Check 1590	$ 263
Check 1680	1,218
Check 1724	486
Check 1780	792
Check 1784	1,819
Check 1806	384

Prepare a bank reconciliation using the format presented in this chapter for the month of August. Assume there were no bank or bookkeeping errors in August. Did Gloria take cash from the company? If so, how much and how did she try to conceal the theft? How can Mike improve his company's internal controls over cash?

BUSINESS CONNECTIONS

Managerial | FOCUS

Cash Management

1. The new accountant for Asheville Hardware Center, a large retail store, found the following weaknesses in the firm's cash-handling procedures. How would you explain to management why each of these procedures should be changed?
   a. No cash register proof is prepared at the end of each day. The amount of money in the register is considered the amount of cash sales for the day.
   b. Small payments are sometimes made from the currency and coins in the cash register. (The store has no petty cash fund.)
   c. During busy periods for the firm, cash receipts are sometimes kept on the premises for several days before a bank deposit is made.
   d. When funds are removed from the cash register at the end of each day, they are placed in an unlocked office cabinet until they are deposited.
   e. The person who makes the bank deposits also records them in the checkbook, journalizes cash receipts, and reconciles the bank statement.

2. Why should management be concerned about having accurate information about the firm's cash position available at all times?
3. Many banks now offer a variety of computer services to clients. Why is it not advisable for a firm to pay its bank to complete the reconciliation procedure at the end of each month?
4. Assume that you are the newly hired controller at Norton Company and that you have observed the following banking procedures in use at the firm. Would you change any of these procedures? Why or why not?
   a. A blank endorsement is made on all checks to be deposited.
   b. The checkbook is kept on the top of a desk so that it will be handy.
   c. The same person prepares bank deposits, issues checks, and reconciles the bank statement.
   d. The reconciliation process usually takes place two or three weeks after the bank statement is received.
   e. The bank statement and the canceled checks are thrown away after the reconciliation process is completed.
   f. As a shortcut in the reconciliation process, there is no attempt to compare the endorsements on the back of the canceled checks with the names of the payees shown on the face of these checks.
5. Why should management be concerned about achieving effective internal control over cash receipts and cash payments?
6. How does management benefit when cash transactions are recorded quickly and efficiently?
7. Why do some companies require that all employees who handle cash be bonded?
8. Why is it a good practice for a business to make all payments by check except for minor payments from a petty cash fund?

Ethical DILEMMA

Borrowing from Petty Cash

Daniel Brown is in charge of the $250 petty cash fund for Metro Auto Repair Service. When an employee needs a special part that is not in inventory, Daniel takes money from petty cash to buy the part. One day Daniel was short of cash and needed some lunch money. He decided to borrow $10 that he would pay back on payday in three days. Daniel continues this practice for three days for a total of $30. He does not have enough to pay the petty cash back. When he reconciles the petty cash, he records this $30 as a cash short/over expense. This is the first time he has done it. Is this an ethical action? What should Daniel do to fix this problem if there is one?

Financial Statement ANALYSIS

Home Depot

Balance Sheet

The following excerpt is taken from The Home Depot, Inc., *2015 Annual Report (for the fiscal year ended January 31, 2016):*

The Home Depot, Inc. Consolidated Balance Sheets		
	As of	
amounts in millions	*January 31, 2016*	*February 1, 2015*
ASSETS		
Current Assets:		
*Cash and cash equivalents**	*$ 2,216*	*$ 1,723*
Total assets	*$42,549*	*$39,946*
** Cash and Cash Equivalents: Short-term investments that have maturities of three months or less when purchased are considered to be cash equivalents.*		

Analyze:

1. What percentage of total assets is made up of cash and cash equivalents at January 31, 2016?
2. Cash receipt and cash payment transactions affect the total value of a company's assets. By what amount did the category "Cash and cash equivalents" change from February 1, 2015, to January 31, 2016?
3. If accountants at The Home Depot, Inc., failed to record cash receipts of $150,000 on January 31, 2016, what impact would this error have on the balance sheet category "Cash and cash equivalents"?

TEAMWORK

Internal Controls of Cash

You and four friends have decided to create a new service company called Unpacking for You. Your company unpacks for families once they have moved into a new house. Your business is primarily a cash business. Each family will pay you $100 for each room that is unpacked on the same day you finish the service. How will your business make sure that the payment from the customer is valid? How will you ensure that you will receive the cash when the customer pays the employee in cash?

Internet CONNECTION

Bank Charges

Many times a negative cash flow is a potential problem in a business. Go to the website for the local banks in your community. Check the requirements for a line of credit or mortgage in case your company needs cash quickly to buy a product you know you will sell for a large profit. Some bank websites could be: www.bankofamerica.com, www.wellsfargo.com, www.chase.com.

Answers to **Self Reviews**

Answers to Section 1 Self Review

1. Amounts from the Accounts Receivable Credit column are posted as credits to the individual customers' accounts in the accounts receivable subsidiary ledger daily. The total of the Accounts Receivable Credit column is posted as a credit to the ***Accounts Receivable*** control account in the general ledger at the end of the accounting period.
2. A written promise to pay a specified amount of money on a specified date. To grant credit in certain sales transactions or to replace open-account credit when a customer has an overdue balance.
3. A cash shortage occurs when cash in the register is less than the audit tape; an overage occurs when cash is more than the audit tape. Debit shortages and credit overages in the ***Cash Short or Over*** account.
4. **d.** all of the above
5. **b.** cash receipts journal
6. The frequency of cash discrepancies indicates that a problem may exist in the handling of the cash. However, depending on the size of the business and the number of registers, 15 entries may not be unusual.

Answers to Section 2 Self Review

1. Amounts in the Other Accounts Debit section are posted individually to the general ledger accounts daily. The total of the Other Accounts Debit column is not posted because the individual amounts were previously posted to the general ledger.
2. Record the name of the owner's drawing account and the amount in the Other Accounts Debit section of the cash payments journal and record the amount in the Cash Credit column.
3. To make small expenditures that require currency and coins.
4. **b.** February 4

5. **c.** cash payments journal
6. You should explain to your employer that she must keep all receipts regardless of the amount. Ask your employer to complete a voucher for that amount, then record the entry in the proper account.

Answers to Section 3 Self Review

1. A check that is dated in the future. It should not be deposited before its date because the drawer of the check may not have sufficient funds in the bank to cover the check at the current time.
2. Endorsement is the legal process by which the payee transfers ownership of the check to the bank.
3. Items in the second section of the bank reconciliation statement require entries in the firm's financial records to correct the ***Cash*** account balance and make it equal to the checkbook balance. These may include bank fees, debit memorandums, NSF checks, and interest income.
4. **a.** Deposits in transit
5. **b.** canceled checks
6. Disagree. Good internal control requires separation of duties.

Answers to Comprehensive Self Review

1. A full endorsement contains the name of the payee plus the name of the firm or bank to whom the check is payable.
2. A record of when a payment is made from petty cash, the amount and purpose of the expenditure, and the account to be charged.
3. Petty cash can be replenished at any time if the fund runs low, but it should be replenished at the end of each month so that all expenses for the month are recorded.
4. They eliminate repetition in postings; the initial recording of transactions is faster.
5. Checks, money orders, and funds on deposit in a bank as well as currency and coins.

Payroll Computations, Records, and Payment

Chapter 10

© Joe Randle/Getty Images

www.hrblock.com

In the 1940s Henry, Leon, and Richard Bloch borrowed $5,000 from a relative and founded United Business Company, an accounting services firm. By the mid-1950s they had 12 employees and were keeping books for various small local businesses in the Kansas City area. Things would change quickly, however. In 1954, based on the recommendation from a client, the Blochs ran an ad for their tax preparation services, and the small office was flooded with calls. It seems just as the IRS was phasing out its free tax preparation services and turning taxpayers away, the Bloch brothers were advertising their services.

United Business Company changed its name to H&R Block and shifted its focus from general accounting services to tax preparation. Today, H&R Block employs quite a few more employees than they did in 1950 and with those added employees, the company's payroll responsibilities have also grown. Not only does it file tax returns for its clients, it also, as an employer, must deduct appropriate taxes from its employees' paychecks.

H&R Block is currently the largest consumer tax services company in the United States. It earned $3.08 billion in revenues in 2015 with in-person and digital tax solutions.

thinking critically

What kinds of taxes and other deductions come out of an H&R Block employee's paycheck? What deductions come out of yours?

LEARNING OBJECTIVES

10-1 Explain the major federal laws relating to employee earnings and withholding.

10-2 Compute gross earnings of employees.

10-3 Determine employee deductions for social security tax.

10-4 Determine employee deductions for Medicare tax.

10-5 Determine employee deductions for income tax.

10-6 Enter gross earnings, deductions, and net pay in the payroll register.

10-7 Journalize payroll transactions in the general journal.

10-8 Maintain an earnings record for each employee.

10-9 Define the accounting terms new to this chapter.

NEW TERMS

- commission basis
- compensation record
- employee
- Employee's Withholding Allowance Certificate (Form W-4)
- exempt employees
- federal unemployment taxes (FUTA)
- hourly rate basis
- independent contractor
- individual earnings record
- Medicare tax
- payroll register
- piece-rate basis
- salary basis
- Social Security Act
- social security (FICA or OASDI) tax
- state unemployment taxes (SUTA)
- tax-exempt wages
- time and a half
- wage-bracket table method
- workers' compensation insurance

Section 1

SECTION OBJECTIVES	TERMS TO LEARN
>> 10-1 Explain the major federal laws relating to employee earnings and withholding. **WHY IT'S IMPORTANT** Tax and labor laws protect the rights of both the employee and the employer. Income tax withholding laws ensure continued funding of certain federal and state programs.	employee federal unemployment taxes (FUTA) independent contractor Medicare tax Social Security Act social security (FICA or OASDI) tax state unemployment taxes (SUTA) time and a half workers' compensation insurance

Payroll Laws and Taxes

A large component of the activity of any business is concerned with payroll work. Payroll accounting is so important that it requires special consideration.

Who Is an Employee?

Payroll accounting relates only to earnings of those individuals classified as employees. An **employee** is hired by and works under the control and direction of the employer. Usually the employer provides the tools or equipment used by the employee, sets the employee's working hours, and determines how the employee completes the job. Examples of employees are the company president, the bookkeeper, the sales clerk, and the warehouse worker. All employee earnings and taxes are reported on a calendar-year basis.

In contrast to an employee, an **independent contractor** is paid by the company to carry out a specific task or job but is not under the direct supervision or control of the company. The independent contractor is told what needs to be done, but the means of doing the job are left to the independent contractor. The IRS has a set of guidelines to determine if a vendor meets the definition of independent contractor. Examples of independent contractors are the accountant who performs the independent audit, the outside attorney who renders legal advice, and the consultant who installs a new accounting system.

This text addresses issues related to employees but not to independent contractors. When dealing with independent contractors, businesses do not have to follow federal labor laws regulating minimum rates of pay and maximum hours of employment. The business is not required to withhold or match payroll taxes on amounts paid to independent contractors. The independent contractor is responsible for paying all payroll taxes related to income.

>> **10-1 OBJECTIVE**
Explain the major federal laws relating to employee earnings and withholding.

Federal Employee Earnings and Withholding Laws

Since the 1930s, many federal and state laws have affected the relationship between employers and employees. Some of these laws deal with working conditions, including hours and earnings. Others relate to income tax withholding. Some concern taxes that are levied against the employer to provide specific employee benefits.

THE FAIR LABOR STANDARDS ACT

The *Fair Labor Standards Act* of 1938, often referred to as the Wage and Hour Law, applies only to firms engaged directly or indirectly in interstate commerce. It sets a minimum hourly rate of pay and maximum hours of work per week to be performed at the regular rate of pay. When this book was printed, the minimum hourly rate of pay was $7.25, and the maximum number of hours at the regular pay rate was 40 hours per week. When an employee works more than 40 hours in a week, the employee earns at least one and one-half times the regular hourly rate of pay for the extra hours. This overtime rate is called **time and a half.** Even if the federal law does not apply to them, many employers pay time and a half for overtime because of union contracts or simply as good business practice.

SOCIAL SECURITY TAX

The *Federal Insurance Contributions Act (FICA)* is commonly referred to as the **Social Security Act.** The act, first passed in the 1930s, has been amended frequently. Social Security's Old-Age, Survivors, and Disability Insurance (OASDI) program provides the following benefits:

- Retirement benefits when a worker reaches the eligible retirement age.
- Benefits for the dependents of the retired worker.
- Benefits for the worker and the worker's dependents when the worker is disabled.

These retirement and disability benefits are paid by the **social security tax,** sometimes called the **FICA** or **OASDI tax.** Both the employer and the employee pay an equal amount of social security tax. The employer is required to withhold social security tax from the employee's pay. On the schedule provided by the IRS, the employer sends the social security tax withheld to the federal government.

The rate of the social security tax has remained constant for many years at 6.2 percent. The earning amount subject to this tax is indexed and so increases each year, according to congressional action. In 2016, the social security tax rate was 6.2 percent of the first $118,500 of salary or wages paid to each employee. In examples and problems, this text uses a social security tax rate of 6.2 percent of the first $122,700 of salary or wages.

MEDICARE TAX

The Medicare tax is closely related to the social security tax. Prior to 1992, it was a part of the social security tax. The **Medicare tax** is a tax levied equally on employees and employers to provide medical care for the employee and the employee's spouse after each has reached 65.

In recent years, the Medicare tax rate has remained constant at 1.45 percent. The Medicare tax applies to all salaries and wages paid during the year. The employer is required to withhold the Medicare tax from the employee's pay and send it to the federal government on the schedule established by the IRS.

Note that the social security tax is paid on a maximum amount of earnings with no additional tax paid on earnings that cross the ceiling limit (in this text we will use $122,700 as the ceiling wage subject to social security). An individual who earns more than $122,700 in a calendar year will not pay any social security tax on earnings above the $122,700 amount (in this text). The Medicare tax does not have an earnings base limit. Therefore, the Medicare tax applies to *all* earnings paid during the year.

FEDERAL INCOME TAX

Employers are required to withhold from employees' earnings an estimated amount of income tax that will be payable by the employee on the earnings. The amount depends on several factors. Later in this chapter you will learn how to determine the amount to withhold from an employee's paycheck.

important!

Changes to FLSA

Two rule changes offered in 2015 included amendments to the Fair Labor Standards Act that would dramatically impact businesses in the U.S. Most employees historically categorized as "Management" have not been eligible for overtime. Effective the end of 2016, many lower-level managers and supervisors become eligible for overtime. The other change is an increase in the federal minimum wage—this proposal has generated much opposition from businesses but much support from employee groups. Worth noting is that states may set their own minimum wage levels.

important!

Wage Base Limit

The social security tax has a wage base maximum ceiling on which taxes are paid and withheld. There is no maximum wage base limit for the Medicare tax. All salaries and wages are subject to the Medicare tax. The Affordable Care Act created an additional Medicare tax of 0.9 percent on individuals with earnings in excess of $200,000 (that means individual high-income earners will pay 1.45 percent in Medicare taxes on all earnings and an additional 0.9 percent of Medicare taxes on earnings in excess of $200,000). Employers will not be taxed on this additional Medicare tax.

State and Local Taxes

Most states, and many local governments, require employers to withhold income taxes from employees' earnings to prepay the employees' state and local income taxes. These rules are generally almost identical to those governing federal income tax withholding, but they require separate general ledger accounts in the firm's accounting system.

Employer's Payroll Taxes and Insurance Costs

Remember that employers withhold social security and Medicare taxes from employees' earnings. In addition, employers pay social security and Medicare taxes on their employees' earnings. Employers are also required to pay federal and state taxes for unemployment benefits and to carry workers' compensation insurance.

SOCIAL SECURITY TAX

The employer's share of the social security tax is 6.2 percent up to the earnings maximum subject to this tax. (In this text, the social security tax is 6.2 percent of the first $122,700 of earnings.) Periodically the employer pays to the federal government the social security tax withheld from gross wages/earnings plus the employer's share of the social security tax.

	Social Security
Employee (pays through withholding)	6.2%
Employer (pays equal amount)	6.2
Total	12.4%

MEDICARE TAX

The employer's share of Medicare tax is 1.45 percent of earnings. Like the social security tax, Medicare taxes must be deposited with the federal government. The Medicare tax withheld from gross earnings plus the employer's share of the Medicare tax is the amount to be deposited.

The Medicare tax rates the employer remits to the federal government are shown below:

	Medicare
Employee (pays through withholding)	1.45%
Employer (pays equal amount)	1.45
Total	2.90%

FEDERAL UNEMPLOYMENT TAX

The *Federal Unemployment Tax Act (FUTA)* provides benefits for employees who become unemployed. Taxes levied by the federal government against employers to benefit unemployed workers are called **federal unemployment taxes (FUTA).** Employers pay the entire amount of these taxes. In this text, we assume that the taxable earnings base is $7,000. That is, the tax applies to the first $7,000 of each employee's earnings for the year. As this text is written, the FUTA tax rate was 6.0 percent, but it can be reduced by the state unemployment tax rate. In examples and problems, this text uses a FUTA tax rate of 6.0 percent. These rates will be used in all payroll examples.

TABLE 10.1

Summary of Payroll Tax Liabilities (Who Pays)

Federal Income Tax	Social Security Tax	Medicare Tax	Unemployment Tax
Employee	Employee Employer	Employee Employer	Employer
The employee pays these taxes by the withholding of the tax from the periodic wage payment.			
The employer pays these taxes through the deposits/filing and reporting on the appropriate forms.			

STATE UNEMPLOYMENT TAX

The federal and state unemployment programs work together to provide benefits for employees who become unemployed. Employers pay all of the **state unemployment taxes (SUTA).** Often, the earnings base for the federal and state unemployment taxes are the same: the first $7,000 of each employee's earnings for the year. For many states the SUTA tax rate is 5.4 percent.

The federal unemployment tax rate (6.0 percent) can be reduced by the rate charged by the state (5.4 percent in this example), so the FUTA rate can be as low as 0.6 percent (6.0 percent – 5.4 percent).

SUTA tax		5.4%
FUTA tax rate	6.0%	
Less SUTA tax	(5.4)	
Net FUTA tax		0.6
Total federal and state unemployment tax		6.0%

WORKERS' COMPENSATION INSURANCE

Workers' compensation insurance is not a tax, but insurance that protects employees against losses from job-related injuries or illnesses, or compensates their families if death occurs in the course of the employment. Workers' compensation requirements are defined by each state, not the federal government. Most states mandate workers' compensation insurance.

Employee Records Required by Law

> Many companies outsource payroll duties to professional payroll companies. ADP, Inc., is the world's largest provider of payroll services and employee information systems.

Federal laws require that certain payroll records be maintained. For each employee the employer must keep a record of:

- the employee's name, address, social security number, and date of birth;
- hours worked each day and week, and wages paid at the regular and overtime rates (certain exceptions exist for employees who earn salaries);
- cumulative wages paid throughout the year;
- amount of income tax, social security tax, and Medicare tax withheld for each pay period;
- proof that the employee is a U.S. citizen or has a valid work permit;
- cost of employer-sponsored health insurance coverage if provided by the employer.

Section 1 Self Review

QUESTIONS

1. What is "time and a half"?
2. How are unemployment insurance benefits financed?
3. How are social security benefits financed?

EXERCISES

4. The purpose of FUTA is to provide benefits for:
   a. employees who become unemployed.
   b. employees who become injured while on the job.
   c. retired workers.
   d. disabled employees.
5. Who pays the social security tax?
   a. Employee only.
   b. Employer only.
   c. Both employee and employer.
   d. None of the above.

ANALYSIS

6. Henri Harvey was hired by Harvey Architects to create three oil paintings for the president's office. Is Henri an employee? Why or why not?

(Answers to Section 1 Self Review are on page 379.)

Section 2

SECTION OBJECTIVES	TERMS TO LEARN
>> 10-2 Compute gross earnings of employees. WHY IT'S IMPORTANT Payroll is a large part of business activity. >> 10-3 Determine employee deductions for social security tax. WHY IT'S IMPORTANT Employers are legally responsible for collecting and remitting this tax. >> 10-4 Determine employee deductions for Medicare tax. WHY IT'S IMPORTANT Employers have legal responsibility. >> 10-5 Determine employee deductions for income tax. WHY IT'S IMPORTANT Employers are legally responsible. >> 10-6 Enter gross earnings, deductions, and net pay in the payroll register. WHY IT'S IMPORTANT The payroll register provides information needed to prepare paychecks.	commission basis Employee's Withholding Allowance Certificate (Form W-4) exempt employees hourly rate basis payroll register piece-rate basis salary basis tax-exempt wages wage-bracket table method

Calculating Earnings and Taxes

Tomlin Furniture Company is a sole proprietorship owned and managed by Sarah Tomlin. Tomlin Furniture Company imports furniture and novelty items to sell over the Internet. It has five employees. The three shipping clerks and the shipping supervisor are paid on an hourly basis. The office clerk is paid a weekly salary. Payday is each Monday; it covers the wages and salaries earned the previous week. The employees are subject to withholding of social security, Medicare, and federal income taxes. The business pays social security and Medicare taxes, and federal and state unemployment insurance taxes. The business is required by state law to carry workers' compensation insurance. Since it is involved in interstate commerce, Tomlin Furniture Company is subject to the Fair Labor Standards Act.

From time to time, Sarah Tomlin, the owner, makes cash withdrawals to cover her personal expenses. The withdrawals by the owner of a sole proprietorship are not treated as salaries or wages but as reductions in owner's equity.

Computing Total Earnings of Employees

The first step in preparing payroll is to compute the gross wages or salary for each employee. There are several ways to compute earnings:

Hourly rate basis workers earn a stated rate per hour. Gross pay depends on the number of hours worked.

Salary basis workers earn an agreed-upon amount for each week, month, or other period.

Commission basis workers, usually salespeople, earn a percentage of net sales.

Piece-rate basis manufacturing workers are paid based on the number of units produced.

> Walmart has approximately 2 million employees in its worldwide operations, which include Walmart discount stores, Sam's Clubs, the distribution centers, and the home office. Fifty-one percent of its stores are in the United States. It is the number 1 retailer in Canada and Mexico. It also has operations in Asia, the United Kingdom, Central America, and South America.

Determining Pay for Hourly Employees

>> **10-2 OBJECTIVE**
Compute gross earnings of employees.

Two pieces of data are needed to compute gross pay for hourly rate basis employees: the number of hours worked during the payroll period and the rate of pay.

HOURS WORKED

At Tomlin Furniture Company, the shipping supervisor keeps a weekly time sheet. Each day she enters the hours worked by each shipping clerk. At the end of the week, the office clerk uses the time sheet to compute the total hours worked and to prepare the payroll.

Many businesses use time clocks for hourly employees. Businesses utilizing time clocks may have a physical time clock near the employee entrance or time may be captured by the computer work location for each person. Those with physical time clocks ask each employee to insert a time card in the time clock to record the times of arrival and departure. The payroll clerk collects this data at the end of the week, determines the hours worked by each employee, and multiplies the number of hours by the pay rate to compute the gross pay and withholdings. Most businesses utilize a payroll software program to calculate earnings, withholdings, and net pay.

recall

Owner Withdrawals

Withdrawals by the owner of a sole proprietorship are debited to a temporary owner's equity account (in this case, ***Sarah Tomlin, Drawing***). Withdrawals are not treated as salary or wages, but serve to reduce the owner's equity or capital. The sole proprietor will pay income and earnings taxes on the net taxable income of the sole proprietor business entity, not the withdrawals.

GROSS PAY

Alicia Martinez, Jorge Rodriguez, and George Dunlap are shipping clerks at Tomlin Furniture Company. They are hourly employees. Their gross pay for the week that ended January 6 is determined as follows:

- Martinez worked 40 hours. She earns \$10 an hour. Her gross pay is \$400 (40 hours × \$10).
- Rodriguez worked 40 hours. He earns \$9.50 an hour. His gross pay is \$380 (40 × \$9.50).
- Dunlap earns \$9 per hour. He worked 45 hours. He is paid 40 hours at regular pay and 5 hours at time and a half. There are two ways to compute Dunlap's gross pay:

  1. The Wage and Hour Law method identifies the *overtime premium,* the amount the firm could have saved if all the hours were paid at the regular rate. The overtime premium rate is \$4.50, one-half of the regular rate (\$9 × ½ = \$4.50).

Total hours × regular rate:	
45 hours × \$9	\$405.00
Overtime premium:	
5 hours × \$4.50	22.50
Gross pay	\$427.50

2. The second method identifies how much the employee earned by working overtime.

Regular earnings:	
40 hours × $9	$360.00
Overtime earnings:	
5 hours × $13.50 ($9 × 1½)	67.50
Gross pay	$427.50

Cecilia Wu is the shipping supervisor at Tomlin Furniture Company. She is an hourly employee. She earns $14 an hour, and she worked 40 hours. Her gross pay is $560 (40 × $14).

WITHHOLDINGS FOR HOURLY EMPLOYEES REQUIRED BY LAW

Recall that three deductions from employees' gross pay are required by federal law: social security tax, Medicare tax, and federal income tax withholding.

>> 10-3 OBJECTIVE
Determine employee deductions for social security tax.

Social Security Tax The social security tax is levied on both the employer and the employee. This text calculates social security tax using a 6.2 percent tax rate on the first $122,700 of wages paid during the calendar year. **Tax-exempt wages** are earnings in excess of the base amount set by the Social Security Act ($122,700). Tax-exempt wages are not subject to social security withholding.

If an employee works for more than one employer during the year, the social security tax is deducted and matched by each employer. When the employee files a federal income tax return, any excess social security tax withheld from the employee's earnings is refunded by the government or applied to payment of the employee's federal income taxes.

To determine the amount of social security tax to withhold from an employee's pay, multiply the taxable wages by the social security tax rate. Round the result to the nearest cent.

The following shows the social security tax deductions for Tomlin Furniture Company's hourly employees.

Employee	Gross Pay	Tax Rate	Tax
Alicia Martinez	$400.00	6.2%	$ 24.80
Jorge Rodriguez	380.00	6.2	23.56
George Dunlap	427.50	6.2	26.51
Cecilia Wu	560.00	6.2	34.72
Total social security tax withheld			$109.59

>> 10-4 OBJECTIVE
Determine employee deductions for Medicare tax.

Medicare Tax The Medicare tax is levied on both the employee and the employer. To compute the Medicare tax to withhold from the employee's paycheck, multiply the wages by the Medicare tax rate, 1.45 percent. The following shows the Medicare tax deduction for the hourly employees.

Employee	Gross Pay	Tax Rate	Tax
Alicia Martinez	$400.00	1.45%	$ 5.80
Jorge Rodriguez	380.00	1.45	5.51
George Dunlap	427.50	1.45	6.20
Cecilia Wu	560.00	1.45	8.12
Total Medicare tax			$25.63

Federal Income Tax A substantial portion of the federal government's revenue comes from the income tax on individuals. Employers are required to withhold federal income tax from employees' pay. Periodically the employer pays the federal income tax withheld to the federal government. After the end of the year, the employee files an income tax return. If the amount of federal income tax withheld does not cover the amount of income tax due, the employee pays the balance. If too much federal income tax has been withheld, the employee receives a refund.

>> **10-5 OBJECTIVE**
Determine employee deductions for income tax.

The federal income tax is a pay-as-you-go tax. There are two ways to pay. If you are an employee, your employer will withhold income tax from your pay based on your instructions in Form W-4. If you do not pay tax through withholdings, or do not pay enough taxes through withholdings because of income from other sources, you might have to pay estimated taxes. Individuals who are in business for themselves generally have to pay taxes through the estimated tax system. The Electronic Federal Tax Payment System (EFTPS) is a free service from the IRS through which taxpayers can use the Internet or telephone to pay their federal taxes, especially 1040 estimated taxes.

Withholding Allowances The amount of federal income tax to withhold from an employee's earnings depends on the:

- earnings during the pay period,
- length of the pay period,
- marital status,
- number of withholding allowances.

Determining the number of withholding allowances for some taxpayers is complex. In the simplest circumstances, a taxpayer claims a withholding allowance for:

- the taxpayer,
- a spouse who does not also claim an allowance,
- each dependent for whom the taxpayer provides more than half the support during the year.

As the number of withholding allowances increases, the amount of federal income tax withheld decreases. The goal is to claim the number of withholding allowances so that the federal income tax withheld is about the same as the employee's tax liability.

To claim withholding allowances, employees complete **Employee's Withholding Allowance Certificate, Form W-4.** The employee gives the completed Form W-4 to the employer. If the number of exemption allowances decreases, the employee must file a new Form W-4 within 10 days. If the number of exemption allowances increases, the employee may, but is not required to, file another Form W-4. If an employee does not file a Form W-4, the employer withholds federal income tax based on zero withholding allowances.

Figure 10.1 shows Form W-4 for Alicia Martinez. Notice that on Line 5, Martinez claims one withholding allowance.

important!

Pay-As-You-Go
Employee income tax withholding is designed to place employees on a pay-as-you-go basis in paying their federal income tax.

Computing Federal Income Tax Withholding Although there are several ways to compute the federal income tax to withhold from an employee's earnings, the **wage bracket table method** is almost universally used. The wage-bracket tables are in *Publication 15, Circular E.* This publication contains withholding tables for weekly, biweekly, semimonthly, monthly, and daily or miscellaneous payroll periods for single and married persons. Figure 10.2 shows partial tables for single and married persons who are paid weekly.

Use the following steps to determine the amount to withhold:

1. Choose the table for the pay period and the employee's marital status.
2. Find the row in the table that matches the wages earned. Find the column that matches the number of withholding allowances claimed on Form W-4. The income tax to withhold is the intersection of the row and the column.

important!

Get It in Writing
Employers need a signed Form W-4 in order to change the employee's federal income tax withholding.

Employee	Gross Pay	Marital Status	Withholding Allowances	Income Tax Withholding
Alicia Martinez	$400.00	Married	1	$ 19.00
Jorge Rodriguez	380.00	Single	1	34.00
George Dunlap	427.50	Single	3	23.00
Cecilia Wu	560.00	Married	2	30.00
				$106.00

As an example, let's determine the amount to withhold from Cecilia Wu's gross pay. Wu is married, claims two withholding allowances, and earned $560 for the week:

1. Go to the table for married persons paid weekly, Figure 10.2B.
2. Find the line covering wages between $560 and $570. Find the column for two withholding allowances. The tax to withhold is $30; this is where the row and the column intersect.

Using the wage-bracket tables, can you find the federal income tax amounts to withhold for Martinez, Rodriguez, and Dunlap?

Other Deductions Required by Law Most states and some local governments require employers to withhold state and local income taxes from earnings. In some states, employers are also required to withhold disability or other taxes. The procedures are similar to those for federal income tax withholding. Apply the tax rate to the earnings, or use withholding tables.

FIGURE 10.1 Form W-4 (Partial)

Cut here and give Form W-4 to your employer. Keep the top part for your records.

Form **W-4** Department of the Treasury Internal Revenue Service

Employee's Withholding Allowance Certificate

▶ Whether you are entitled to claim a certain number of allowances or exemption from withholding is subject to review by the IRS. Your employer may be required to send a copy of this form to the IRS.

OMB No. 1545-0010 **2019**

1 Type or print your first name and middle initial: Alicia | Last name: Martinez | 2 Your social security number: 123 45 6789

Home address (number and street or rural route): 1712 Windmill Hill Lane

3 ☐ Single ☑ Married ☐ Married, but withhold at higher Single rate.
Note. If married, but legally separated, or spouse is a nonresident alien, check the "Single" box.

City or town, state, and ZIP code: Dallas, TX 75232-6002

4 **If your last name differs from that shown on your social security card, check here. You must call 1-800-772-1213 for a new card.** ▶ ☐

5 Total number of allowances you are claiming (from line **H** above **or** from the applicable worksheet on page 2) 5 1

6 Additional amount, if any, you want withheld from each paycheck . . . . 6 $

7 I claim exemption from withholding for 2019, and I certify that I meet **both** of the following conditions for exemption.
- Last year I had a right to a refund of **all** federal income tax withheld because I had **no** tax liability **and**
- This year I expect a refund of **all** federal income tax withheld because I expect to have **no** tax liability.

If you meet both conditions, write "Exempt" here . . . . ▶ 7

Under penalties of perjury, I declare that I have examined this certificate and to the best of my knowledge and belief, it is true, correct, and complete.

Employee's signature (Form is not valid unless you sign it.) ▶ Alicia Martinez   Date ▶ November 5, 2019

8 Employer's name and address (Employer: Complete lines 8 and 10 only if sending to the IRS.) Tomlin Furniture Co. 5910 Lake June Road, Dallas, TX 75232-6017 | 9 Office code (optional) | 10 Employer identification number (EIN) 75 1234567

For Privacy Act and Paperwork Reduction Act Notice, see page 2. Cat. No. 220Q Form **W-4**

FIGURE 10.2A

Sample Federal Withholding Tax Tables (Partial) for Single Persons—Weekly Payroll Period

SINGLE Persons—**WEEKLY** Payroll Period (For Wages Paid Through December 2019)

If the wages are –		And the number of withholding allowances claimed is –										
At least	But less than	0	1	2	3	4	5	6	7	8	9	10
		The amount of income tax to be withheld is –										
$0	**$55**	$0	$0	$0	$0	$0	$0	$0	$0	$0	$0	$0
55	**60**	1	0	0	0	0	0	0	0	0	0	0
60	**65**	1	0	0	0	0	0	0	0	0	0	0
65	**70**	2	0	0	0	0	0	0	0	0	0	0
70	**75**	2	0	0	0	0	0	0	0	0	0	0
75	**80**	3	0	0	0	0	0	0	0	0	0	0
80	**85**	3	0	0	0	0	0	0	0	0	0	0
85	**90**	4	0	0	0	0	0	0	0	0	0	0
90	**95**	4	0	0	0	0	0	0	0	0	0	0
95	**100**	5	0	0	0	0	0	0	0	0	0	0
100	**105**	5	0	0	0	0	0	0	0	0	0	0
105	**110**	6	0	0	0	0	0	0	0	0	0	0
110	**115**	6	0	0	0	0	0	0	0	0	0	0
115	**120**	7	1	0	0	0	0	0	0	0	0	0
120	**125**	7	1	0	0	0	0	0	0	0	0	0
125	**130**	8	2	0	0	0	0	0	0	0	0	0
130	**135**	8	2	0	0	0	0	0	0	0	0	0
135	**140**	9	3	0	0	0	0	0	0	0	0	0
140	**145**	9	3	0	0	0	0	0	0	0	0	0
145	**150**	10	4	0	0	0	0	0	0	0	0	0
150	**155**	10	4	0	0	0	0	0	0	0	0	0
155	**160**	11	5	0	0	0	0	0	0	0	0	0
160	**165**	11	5	0	0	0	0	0	0	0	0	0
165	**170**	12	6	0	0	0	0	0	0	0	0	0
170	**175**	12	6	0	0	0	0	0	0	0	0	0
175	**180**	13	7	1	0	0	0	0	0	0	0	0
180	**185**	13	7	1	0	0	0	0	0	0	0	0
185	**190**	14	8	2	0	0	0	0	0	0	0	0
190	**195**	14	8	2	0	0	0	0	0	0	0	0
195	**200**	15	9	3	0	0	0	0	0	0	0	0
200	**210**	16	9	3	0	0	0	0	0	0	0	0
210	**220**	18	10	4	0	0	0	0	0	0	0	0
220	**230**	19	11	5	0	0	0	0	0	0	0	0
230	**240**	21	12	6	1	0	0	0	0	0	0	0
240	**250**	22	13	7	2	0	0	0	0	0	0	0
250	**260**	24	15	8	3	0	0	0	0	0	0	0
260	**270**	25	16	9	4	0	0	0	0	0	0	0
270	**280**	27	18	10	5	0	0	0	0	0	0	0
280	**290**	28	19	11	6	0	0	0	0	0	0	0
290	**300**	30	21	12	7	1	0	0	0	0	0	0
300	**310**	31	22	13	8	2	0	0	0	0	0	0
310	**320**	33	24	15	9	3	0	0	0	0	0	0
320	**330**	34	25	16	10	4	0	0	0	0	0	0
330	**340**	36	27	18	11	5	0	0	0	0	0	0
340	**350**	37	28	19	12	6	0	0	0	0	0	0
350	**360**	39	30	21	13	7	1	0	0	0	0	0
360	**370**	40	31	22	14	8	2	0	0	0	0	0
370	**380**	42	33	24	15	9	3	0	0	0	0	0
380	**390**	43	34	25	17	10	4	0	0	0	0	0
390	**400**	45	36	27	18	11	5	0	0	0	0	0
400	**410**	46	37	28	20	12	6	0	0	0	0	0
410	**420**	48	39	30	21	13	7	1	0	0	0	0
420	**430**	49	40	31	23	14	8	2	0	0	0	0
430	**440**	51	42	33	24	15	9	3	0	0	0	0
440	**450**	52	43	34	26	17	10	4	0	0	0	0
450	**460**	54	45	36	27	18	11	5	0	0	0	0
460	**470**	55	46	37	29	20	12	6	0	0	0	0
470	**480**	57	48	39	30	21	13	7	1	0	0	0
480	**490**	58	49	40	32	23	14	8	2	0	0	0
490	**500**	60	51	42	33	24	15	9	3	0	0	0
500	**510**	61	52	43	35	26	17	10	4	0	0	0
510	**520**	63	54	45	36	27	18	11	5	0	0	0
520	**530**	64	55	46	38	29	20	12	6	0	0	0
530	**540**	66	57	48	39	30	21	13	7	1	0	0
540	**550**	67	58	49	41	32	23	14	8	2	0	0
550	**560**	69	60	51	42	33	24	15	9	3	0	0
560	**570**	70	61	52	44	35	26	17	10	4	0	0
570	**580**	72	63	54	45	36	27	18	11	5	0	0
580	**590**	73	64	55	47	38	29	20	12	6	0	0
590	**600**	75	66	57	48	39	30	21	13	7	1	0

This table does not contain actual withholding amounts for the year 2019 and should not be used to determine payroll withholdings for 2019.

FIGURE 10.2B

Sample Federal Withholding Tax Tables (Partial) for Married Persons—Weekly Payroll Period

MARRIED Persons—**WEEKLY** Payroll Period (For Wages Paid Through December 2019)

If the wages are –		And the number of withholding allowances claimed is –										
At least	But less than	0	1	2	3	4	5	6	7	8	9	10
		The amount of income tax to be withheld is –										
$0	**$125**	$0	$0	$0	$0	$0	$0	$0	$0	$0	$0	$0
125	**130**	0	0	0	0	0	0	0	0	0	0	0
130	**135**	0	0	0	0	0	0	0	0	0	0	0
135	**140**	0	0	0	0	0	0	0	0	0	0	0
140	**145**	0	0	0	0	0	0	0	0	0	0	0
145	**150**	0	0	0	0	0	0	0	0	0	0	0
150	**155**	0	0	0	0	0	0	0	0	0	0	0
155	**160**	0	0	0	0	0	0	0	0	0	0	0
160	**165**	1	0	0	0	0	0	0	0	0	0	0
165	**170**	1	0	0	0	0	0	0	0	0	0	0
170	**175**	2	0	0	0	0	0	0	0	0	0	0
175	**180**	2	0	0	0	0	0	0	0	0	0	0
180	**185**	3	0	0	0	0	0	0	0	0	0	0
185	**190**	3	0	0	0	0	0	0	0	0	0	0
190	**195**	4	0	0	0	0	0	0	0	0	0	0
195	**200**	4	0	0	0	0	0	0	0	0	0	0
200	**210**	5	0	0	0	0	0	0	0	0	0	0
210	**220**	6	0	0	0	0	0	0	0	0	0	0
220	**230**	7	1	0	0	0	0	0	0	0	0	0
230	**240**	8	2	0	0	0	0	0	0	0	0	0
240	**250**	9	3	0	0	0	0	0	0	0	0	0
250	**260**	10	4	0	0	0	0	0	0	0	0	0
260	**270**	11	5	0	0	0	0	0	0	0	0	0
270	**280**	12	6	0	0	0	0	0	0	0	0	0
280	**290**	13	7	1	0	0	0	0	0	0	0	0
290	**300**	14	8	2	0	0	0	0	0	0	0	0
300	**310**	15	9	3	0	0	0	0	0	0	0	0
310	**320**	16	10	4	0	0	0	0	0	0	0	0
320	**330**	17	11	5	0	0	0	0	0	0	0	0
330	**340**	18	12	6	0	0	0	0	0	0	0	0
340	**350**	19	13	7	1	0	0	0	0	0	0	0
350	**360**	20	14	8	2	0	0	0	0	0	0	0
360	**370**	21	15	9	3	0	0	0	0	0	0	0
370	**380**	22	16	10	4	0	0	0	0	0	0	0
380	**390**	23	17	11	5	0	0	0	0	0	0	0
390	**400**	24	18	12	6	0	0	0	0	0	0	0
400	**410**	25	19	13	7	1	0	0	0	0	0	0
410	**420**	26	20	14	8	2	0	0	0	0	0	0
420	**430**	27	21	15	9	3	0	0	0	0	0	0
430	**440**	28	22	16	10	4	0	0	0	0	0	0
440	**450**	30	23	17	11	5	0	0	0	0	0	0
450	**460**	31	24	18	12	6	0	0	0	0	0	0
460	**470**	33	25	19	13	7	1	0	0	0	0	0
470	**480**	34	26	20	14	8	2	0	0	0	0	0
480	**490**	36	27	21	15	9	3	0	0	0	0	0
490	**500**	37	28	22	16	10	4	0	0	0	0	0
500	**510**	39	30	23	17	11	5	0	0	0	0	0
510	**520**	40	31	24	18	12	6	0	0	0	0	0
520	**530**	42	33	25	19	13	7	1	0	0	0	0
530	**540**	43	34	26	20	14	8	2	0	0	0	0
540	**550**	45	36	27	21	15	9	3	0	0	0	0
550	**560**	46	37	29	22	16	10	4	0	0	0	0
560	**570**	48	39	30	23	17	11	5	0	0	0	0
570	**580**	49	40	32	24	18	12	6	0	0	0	0
580	**590**	51	42	33	25	19	13	7	1	0	0	0
590	**600**	52	43	35	26	20	14	8	2	0	0	0
600	**610**	54	45	36	27	21	15	9	3	0	0	0
610	**620**	55	46	38	29	22	16	10	4	0	0	0
620	**630**	57	48	39	30	23	17	11	5	0	0	0
630	**640**	58	49	41	32	24	18	12	6	0	0	0
640	**650**	60	51	42	33	25	19	13	7	1	0	0
650	**660**	61	52	44	35	26	20	14	8	2	0	0
660	**670**	63	54	45	36	27	21	15	9	3	0	0
670	**680**	64	55	47	38	29	22	16	10	4	0	0
680	**690**	66	57	48	39	30	23	17	11	5	0	0
690	**700**	67	58	50	41	32	24	18	12	6	0	0
700	**710**	69	60	51	42	33	25	19	13	7	1	0
710	**720**	70	61	53	44	35	26	20	14	8	2	0
720	**730**	72	63	54	45	36	27	21	15	9	3	0
730	**740**	73	64	56	47	38	29	22	16	10	4	0

This table does not contain actual withholding amounts for the year 2019 and should not be used to determine payroll withholdings for 2019.

WITHHOLDINGS NOT REQUIRED BY LAW

There are many payroll deductions not required by law but made by agreement between the employee and the employer. Some examples are:

- group life insurance,
- group medical insurance (see requirements under the Affordable Care Act detailed later),

- company retirement plans,
- bank or credit union savings plans or loan repayments,
- U.S. saving bonds purchase plans,
- stocks and other investment purchase plans,
- employer loan repayments,
- union dues.

These and other payroll deductions increase the payroll recordkeeping work but do not involve any new principles or procedures. They are handled in the same way as the deductions for social security, Medicare, and federal income taxes. The amounts withheld from the employee's pay are recorded as liabilities on payday.

Effective in 2015, all employers with 50 or more full-time-equivalent employees are required to provide health insurance under the Affordable Care Act (ACA) or face tax penalties. As the ACA continues to be implemented, additional employer requirements will be phased in. Businesses will be subject to substantial tax penalties if they do not provide health insurance for employees, provided the business is subject to the requirements of the ACA.

Tomlin Furniture Company pays all medical insurance premiums for each employee. If the employee chooses to have medical coverage for a spouse or dependent, Tomlin Furniture Company deducts $40 per week for coverage for the employee. Dunlap and Wu each has $40 per week deducted to obtain the medical coverage.

Determining Pay for Salaried Employees

A salaried employee earns a specific sum of money for each payroll period. The office clerk at Tomlin Furniture Company earns a weekly salary.

HOURS WORKED

Salaried workers who do not hold supervisory jobs are covered by the provisions of the Wage and Hour Law that deal with maximum hours and overtime premium pay. Employers keep time records for all nonsupervisory salaried workers to make sure that their hourly earnings meet the legal requirements.

Salaried employees who hold supervisory or managerial positions are called **exempt employees.** They are not subject to the maximum hour and overtime premium pay provisions of the Wage and Hour Law. As this text is being revised, there is a proposal in Congress to remove many salaried personnel from the exempt classification (those earning up to approximately $50,000 per year) and qualifying those individuals for overtime pay. This text relies on the definitions as provided in this chapter for overtime calculations.

GROSS EARNINGS

Cynthia Booker is the office clerk at Tomlin Furniture Company. During the first week of January, she worked 40 hours, her regular schedule. There are no overtime earnings because she did not work more than 40 hours during the week. Her salary of $480 is her gross pay for the week.

WITHHOLDINGS FOR SALARIED EMPLOYEES REQUIRED BY LAW

The procedures for withholding taxes for salaried employees are the same as for withholding for hourly rate employees. Apply the tax rate to the earnings, or use withholding tables.

Recording Payroll Information for Employees

A payroll register is prepared for each pay period. The **payroll register** shows all the payroll information for the pay period.

FIGURE 10.3 Payroll Register

PAYROLL REGISTER **WEEK BEGINNING** *January 1, 2019*

NAME	NO. OF ALLOW.	MARITAL STATUS	CUMULATIVE EARNINGS	NO. OF HRS.	RATE/ SALARY	EARNINGS REGULAR	EARNINGS OVERTIME	EARNINGS GROSS AMOUNT	CUMULATIVE EARNINGS
Martinez, Alicia	1	M		40	10.00	400 00		400 00	400 00
Rodriguez, Jorge	1	S		40	9.50	380 00		380 00	380 00
Dunlap, George	3	S		45	9.00	360 00	67 50	427 50	427 50
Wu, Cecilia	2	M		40	14.00	560 00		560 00	560 00
Booker, Cynthia	1	S		40	480.00	480 00		480 00	480 00
			0 00			2 180 00	67 50	2 247 50	2 247 50
(A)	*(B)*		*(C)*	*(D)*	*(E)*	*(F)*	*(G)*	*(H)*	*(I)*

>> 10-6 OBJECTIVE

Enter gross earnings, deductions, and net pay in the payroll register.

THE PAYROLL REGISTER

Figure 10.3 shows the payroll register for Tomlin Furniture Company for the week ended January 6. Note that all employees were paid for eight hours on January 1, a holiday. To learn how to complete the payroll register, refer to Figure 10.3 and follow these steps:

1. *Columns A, B, and E.* Enter the employee's name (Column A), number of withholding allowances and marital status (Column B), and rate of pay (Column E). In a computerized payroll system, this information is entered once and is automatically retrieved each time payroll is prepared.
2. *Column C.* The Cumulative Earnings column (Column C) shows the total earnings for the calendar year before the current pay period. This figure is needed to determine whether the employee has exceeded the earnings limit for the social security and FUTA taxes. Since this is the first payroll period of the year, there are no cumulative earnings prior to the current pay period.
3. *Column D.* In Column D, enter the total number of hours worked in the current period. This data comes from the weekly time sheet.
4. *Columns F, G, and H.* Using the hours worked and the pay rate, calculate regular pay (Column F), the overtime earnings (Column G), and gross pay (Column H).
5. *Column I.* Calculate the cumulative earnings after this pay period (Column I) by adding the beginning cumulative earnings (Column C) and the current period's gross pay (Column H).
6. *Columns J, K, and L.* The Taxable Wages columns show the earnings subject to taxes for social security (Column J), Medicare (Column K), and FUTA (Column L). Only the earnings at or under the earnings limit are included in these columns.
7. *Columns M, N, O, and P.* The Deductions columns show the withholding for social security tax (Column M), Medicare tax (Column N), federal income tax (Column O), and medical insurance (Column P).
8. *Column Q.* Subtract the deductions (Columns M, N, O, and P) from the gross earnings (Column H). Enter the results in the Net Amount column (Column Q). This is the amount paid to each employee.
9. *Column R.* Enter the check number in Column R.
10. *Columns S and T.* The payroll register's last two columns classify employee earnings as office salaries (Column S) or shipping wages (Column T).

When the payroll data for all employees has been entered in the payroll register, total the columns. Check the balances of the following columns:

- Total regular earnings plus total overtime earnings must equal the gross amount (Columns F + G = Column H).

AND ENDING *January 6, 2019* **PAID** *January 8, 2019*

TAXABLE WAGES			DEDUCTIONS						DISTRIBUTION	
SOCIAL SECURITY	MEDICARE	FUTA	SOCIAL SECURITY	MEDICARE	INCOME TAX	HEALTH INSURANCE	NET AMOUNT	CHECK NO.	OFFICE SALARIES	SHIPPING WAGES
400 00	400 00	400 00	24 80	5 80	19 00		350 40	1601		400 00
380 00	380 00	380 00	23 56	5 51	34 00		316 93	1602		380 00
427 50	427 50	427 50	26 51	6 20	23 00	40 00	331 79	1603		427 50
560 00	560 00	560 00	34 72	8 12	30 00	40 00	447 16	1604		560 00
480 00	480 00	480 00	29 76	6 96	49 00		394 28	1605	480 00	
2 247 50	2 247 50	2 247 50	139 35	32 59	155 00	80 00	1 840 56		480 00	1 767 50
(J)	*(K)*	*(L)*	*(M)*	*(N)*	*(O)*	*(P)*	*(Q)*	*(R)*	*(S)*	*(T)*

- The total gross amount less total deductions must equal the total net amount.

Gross amount		$2,247.50
Less deductions:		
Social security tax	$139.35	
Medicare tax	32.59	
Income tax	155.00	
Health insurance	80.00	
Total deductions		406.94
Net amount		$1,840.56

- The office salaries and the shipping wages must equal gross earnings (Columns S + T = Column H).

The payroll register supplies all the information to make the journal entry to record the payroll. Journalizing the payroll is discussed in Section 3.

Section 2 Self Review

QUESTIONS

1. What three payroll deductions does federal law require?
2. What factors determine the amount of federal income tax to be withheld from an employee's earnings?
3. List four payroll deductions that are not required by law but can be made by agreement between the employee and the employer.

EXERCISES

4. Which of the following affects the amount of Medicare tax to be withheld from an hourly rate employee's pay?
   a. medical insurance premium
   b. marital status
   c. withholding allowances claimed on Form W-4
   d. hours worked
5. Stacy Carter worked 48 hours during the week ending November 17. Her regular rate is $9 per hour. Calculate her gross earnings for the week.
   a. $432
   b. $492
   c. $468
   d. $444

ANALYSIS

6. Jamie Jones left a voice mail asking you to withhold an additional $40 of federal income tax from her wages each pay period, starting June 1. When should you begin withholding the extra amount?

(Answers to Section 2 Self Review are on page 379.)

Section 3

SECTION OBJECTIVES	TERMS TO LEARN
>> 10-7 Journalize payroll transactions in the general journal. WHY IT'S IMPORTANT Payroll cost is an operating expense. >> 10-8 Maintain an earnings record for each employee. WHY IT'S IMPORTANT Federal law requires that employers maintain records.	**compensation record** **individual earnings record**

Recording Payroll Information

In this section you will learn how to prepare paychecks and journalize and post payroll transactions by following the January payroll activity for Tomlin Furniture Company.

>> **10-7 OBJECTIVE**
Journalize payroll transactions in the general journal.

Recording Payroll

Recording payroll involves two separate entries: one to record the payroll expense and another to pay the employees. The general journal entry to record the payroll expense is based on the payroll register. The gross pay is debited to ***Shipping Wages Expense*** for the shipping clerks and supervisor and to ***Office Salaries Expense*** for the office clerk. Each type of deduction is credited to a separate liability account ***(Social Security Tax Payable, Medicare Tax Payable, Employee Income Tax Payable, Health Insurance Premiums Payable).*** Net pay is credited to the liability account ***Salaries and Wages Payable.***

Refer to Figure 10.3 to see how the data on the payroll register is used to prepare the January 8 payroll journal entry for Tomlin Furniture Company. Following is an analysis of the entry.

BUSINESS TRANSACTION

The information in the payroll register (Figure 10.3) is used to record the payroll expense.

ANALYSIS

The expense account ***Office Salaries Expense*** is increased by $480.00. The expense account ***Shipping Wages Expense*** is increased by $1,767.50. The liability account for each deduction is increased: ***Social Security Tax Payable,*** $139.35; ***Medicare Tax Payable,*** $32.59; ***Employee Income Tax Payable,*** $155.00; ***Health Insurance Premiums Payable,*** $80.00. The liability account ***Salaries and Wages Payable*** is increased by the net amount of the payroll, $1,840.56.

DEBIT-CREDIT RULES

DEBIT Increases in expenses are recorded as debits. Debit ***Office Salaries Expense*** for $480.00. Debit ***Shipping Wages Expense*** for $1,767.50.

CREDIT Increases in liability accounts are recorded as credits. Credit ***Social Security Tax Payable*** for $139.35. Credit ***Medicare Tax Payable*** for $32.59. Credit ***Employee Income Tax Payable*** for $155.00. Credit ***Health Insurance Premiums Payable*** for $80.00. Credit ***Salaries and Wages Payable*** for $1,840.56.

T-ACCOUNT PRESENTATION

Office Salaries Expense	
+	−
480.00	

Social Security Tax Payable	
−	+
	139.35

Medicare Tax Payable	
−	+
	32.59

Shipping Wages Expense	
+	−
1,767.50	

Employee Income Tax Payable	
−	+
	155.00

Health Insurance Premiums Payable	
−	+
	80.00

Salaries and Wages Payable	
−	+
	1,840.56

GENERAL JOURNAL ENTRY

GENERAL JOURNAL PAGE 1

	DATE		DESCRIPTION	POST. REF.	DEBIT	CREDIT	
1	2019						1
2	Jan.	8	Office Salaries Expense		480 00		2
3			Shipping Wages Expense		1 767 50		3
4			Social Security Tax Payable			139 35	4
5			Medicare Tax Payable			32 59	5
6			Employee Income Tax Payable			155 00	6
7			Health Insurance Premiums Payable			80 00	7
8			Salaries and Wages Payable			1 840 56	8
9			Payroll for week ending Jan. 6				9

THE BOTTOM LINE

Record Payroll

Income Statement

Expenses ↑ $2,247.50
Net Income ↓ $2,247.50

Balance Sheet

Liabilities ↑ $2,247.50
Equity ↓ $2,247.50

Southwest Airlines Co. recorded salaries, wages, and benefits of more than $6.38 billion for the year ended December 31, 2015.

Paying Employees

Most businesses pay their employees by check or by direct deposit. By using these methods, the business avoids the inconvenience and risk involved in dealing with currency.

important!

Payroll Liabilities
Deductions from employee paychecks are liabilities for the employer.

PAYING BY CHECK

Paychecks may be deducted on the firm's regular checking account or on a payroll bank account. The check stub, an e-check stub, or deposit information e-mail shows information about the employee's gross earnings, deductions, and net pay. Employees should keep this item as a record of their payroll data. The check number is entered in the Check Number column of the payroll register (Figure 10.3, Column R). The canceled check (or e-record) provides a record of the payment, and the employee's endorsement serves as a receipt. Following is an analysis of the transaction to pay Tomlin Furniture Company's employees.

BUSINESS TRANSACTION

On January 8, Tomlin Furniture Company wrote five checks for payroll, check numbers 1601–1605.

ANALYSIS

The liability account ***Salaries and Wages Payable*** is decreased by $1,840.56. The asset account ***Cash*** is decreased by $1,840.56.

DEBIT-CREDIT RULES

DEBIT Decreases to liability accounts are recorded as debits. Debit ***Salaries and Wages Payable*** for $1,840.56.

CREDIT Decreases to assets are credits. Credit ***Cash*** for $1,840.56.

T-ACCOUNT PRESENTATION

Salaries and Wages Payable –	Salaries and Wages Payable +
1,840.56	

Cash +	Cash –
	1,840.56

GENERAL JOURNAL ENTRY

GENERAL JOURNAL PAGE 1

	DATE		DESCRIPTION	POST. REF.	DEBIT	CREDIT	
11	Jan.	8	Salaries and Wages Payable		1 8 4 0 56		11
12			Cash			1 8 4 0 56	12
13			To record payment of salaries and wages				13
14			for week ended Jan. 6				14

THE BOTTOM LINE
Issue Paychecks

Income Statement
No effect on net income

Balance Sheet
Assets ↓ 1,840.56
Liabilities ↓ 1,840.56
No effect on equity

important!

Separate Payroll Account
Using a separate payroll account facilitates the bank reconciliation and provides better internal control.

Checks Written on a Separate Payroll Account Many businesses write payroll checks (either physically or electronically) from a separate payroll bank account. This is a two-step process:

1. A check is drawn on the regular bank account for the total amount of net pay and deposited in the payroll bank account.
2. Individual payroll checks are issued from the payroll bank account.

MANAGERIAL IMPLICATIONS <<

LAWS AND CONTROLS

- It is management's responsibility to ensure that the payroll procedures and records comply with federal, state, and local laws.
- For most businesses, wages and salaries are a large part of operating expenses. Payroll records help management to keep track of and control expenses.
- Management should investigate large or frequent overtime expenditures.
- To prevent errors and fraud, management periodically should have the payroll records audited and payroll procedures evaluated.
- Two common payroll frauds are the overstatement of hours worked and the issuance of checks to nonexistent employees.

THINKING CRITICALLY

What controls would you put in place to prevent payroll fraud?

Using a separate payroll account simplifies the bank reconciliation of the regular checking account and makes it easier to identify outstanding payroll checks.

PAYING BY DIRECT DEPOSIT

The most popular method of paying employees is the direct deposit method. The bank electronically transfers net pay from the employer's account to the personal account of the employee. On payday, the employee receives a statement or e-mail showing gross earnings, deductions, and net pay.

Individual Earnings Records

>> **10-8 OBJECTIVE**

Maintain an earnings record for each employee.

An **individual earnings record,** also called a **compensation record,** is created for each employee. This record contains the employee's name, address, social security number, date of birth, number of withholding allowances claimed, rate of pay, and any other information needed to compute earnings and complete tax reports.

The payroll register provides the details that are entered on the employee's individual earnings record for each pay period. Figure 10.4 shows the earnings record for Alicia Martinez.

The earnings record shows the payroll period, the date paid, the regular and overtime hours, the regular and overtime earnings, the deductions, and the net pay. The cumulative earnings on the earnings record agree with Column I of the payroll register (Figure 10.3). The earnings records are totaled monthly and at the end of each calendar quarter. This provides information needed to make tax payments and file tax returns.

FIGURE 10.4 An Individual Earnings Record

EARNINGS RECORD FOR 2019

NAME Alicia Martinez RATE $10 per hour SOCIAL SECURITY NO. 123-45-6789

ADDRESS 1712 Windmill Hill Lane, Dallas, TX 75232-6002 DATE OF BIRTH November 23, 1979

WITHHOLDING ALLOWANCES 1 MARITAL STATUS M

PAYROLL NO.	DATE		HOURS		EARNINGS				DEDUCTIONS				NET PAY
	WK. END.	PAID	RG	OT	REGULAR	OVERTIME	TOTAL	CUMULATIVE	SOCIAL SECURITY	MEDICARE	INCOME TAX	OTHER	
1	1/06	1/08	40		400 00		400 00	400 00	24 80	5 80	19 00		350 40
2	1/13	1/15	40		400 00		400 00	800 00	24 80	5 80	19 00		350 40
3	1/20	1/22	40		400 00		400 00	1200 00	24 80	5 80	19 00		350 40
4	1/27	1/29	40		400 00		400 00	1600 00	24 80	5 80	19 00		350 40
	January				1600 00		1600 00		99 20	23 20	76 00		1401 60

Completing January Payrolls

Figure 10.5 shows the entire cycle of computing, paying, journalizing, and posting payroll data. In order to complete the January payroll for Tomlin Furniture Company, assume that all employees worked the same number of hours each week of the month as they did the first week. Thus, they had the same earnings, deductions, and net pay each week.

ENTRY TO RECORD PAYROLL

As illustrated earlier in this section, one general journal entry is made to record the weekly payroll for all employees of Tomlin Furniture Company. This general journal entry records the payroll expense and liability, but not the payments to employees. Since we are assuming an identical payroll for each week of the month, each of the four weekly payrolls requires general journal entries identical to the one shown in Figure 10.5. Notice how the payroll register column totals are recorded in the general journal.

> *ABOUT* **ACCOUNTING**
>
> **Tax Returns**
>
> Research conducted by the Tax Foundation found that approximately 60 percent of Americans pay a tax preparer to complete their federal income tax returns.

ENTRY TO RECORD PAYMENT OF PAYROLL

The weekly entries in the general journal to record payments to employees debit ***Salaries and Wages Payable*** and credit ***Cash.***

POSTINGS TO LEDGER ACCOUNTS

The entries to record the weekly payroll expense and liability amounts are posted from the general journal to the accounts in the general ledger. The total of the Salaries and Wages Payable Debit column in the cash payments journal is posted to the ***Salaries and Wages Payable*** general ledger account.

FIGURE 10.5 **Journalizing and Posting Payroll Data**

AND ENDING *January 6, 2019* **PAID** *January 8, 2019*

TAXABLE WAGES			DEDUCTIONS				DISTRIBUTION			
SOCIAL SECURITY	MEDICARE	FUTA	SOCIAL SECURITY	MEDICARE	INCOME TAX	HEALTH INSURANCE	NET AMOUNT	CHECK NO.	OFFICE SALARIES	SHIPPING WAGES
400 00	400 00	400 00	24 80	5 80	19 00		350 40	1601		400 00
380 00	380 00	380 00	23 56	5 51	34 00		316 93	1602		380 00
427 50	427 50	427 50	26 51	6 20	23 00	40 00	331 79	1603		427 50
560 00	560 00	560 00	34 72	8 12	30 00	40 00	447 16	1604		560 00
480 00	480 00	480 00	29 76	6 96	49 00		394 28	1605	480 00	
2 247 50	2 247 50	2 247 50	139 35	32 59	155 00	80 00	1 840 56		480 00	1 767 50
(J)	*(K)*	*(L)*	*(M)*	*(N)*	*(O)*	*(P)*	*(Q)*	*(R)*	*(S)*	*(T)*

	Date		Description	Post. Ref.	Debit	Credit	
1	*2019*						1
2	*Jan.*	*8*	*Office Salaries Expense*	*541*	*480 00*		2
3			*Shipping Wages Expense*	*542*	*1 767 50*		3
4			*Social Security Tax Payable*	*221*		*139 35*	4
5			*Medicare Tax Payable*	*222*		*32 59*	5
6			*Employee Income Tax Payable*	*223*		*155 00*	6
7			*Health Insurance Premiums Payable*	*224*		*80 00*	7
8			*Salaries and Wages Payable*	*229*		*1 840 56*	8
9			*Payroll for week ending Jan. 6*				9

FIGURE 10.5 (continued)

	Date		Description	Post. Ref.	Debit	Credit	
1	2019						1
2	Jan.	8	Office Salaries Expense	541	480 00		2
3			Shipping Wages Expense	542	1 767 50		3
4			Social Security Tax Payable	221		139 35	4
5			Medicare Tax Payable	222		32 59	5
6			Employee Income Tax Payable	223		155 00	6
7			Health Insurance Premiums Payable	224		80 00	7
8			Salaries and Wages Payable	229		1 840 56	8
9			Payroll for week ending Jan. 6				9
10							10
11							11

Office Salaries Expense

Debit		Credit	
1/08	480.00		
1/15	480.00		
1/22	480.00		
1/29	480.00		

Medicare Tax Payable

Debit		Credit	
		1/08	32.59
		1/15	32.59
		1/22	32.59
		1/29	32.59

Shipping Wages Expense

Debit		Credit	
1/08	1,767.50		
1/15	1,767.50		
1/22	1,767.50		
1/29	1,767.50		

Employee Income Tax Payable

Debit		Credit	
		1/08	155.00
		1/15	155.00
		1/22	155.00
		1/29	155.00

Health Ins. Premiums Payable

Debit		Credit	
		1/08	80.00
		1/15	80.00
		1/22	80.00
		1/29	80.00

Social Security Tax Payable

Debit		Credit	
		1/08	139.35
		1/15	139.35
		1/22	139.35
		1/29	139.35

Salaries and Wages Payable

Debit		Credit	
1/08	1,840.56	1/08	1,840.56
1/15	1,840.56	1/15	1,840.56
1/22	1,840.56	1/22	1,840.56
1/29	1,840.56	1/29	1,840.56

GENERAL JOURNAL PAGE 1

	Date		Description	Post. Ref.	Debit	Credit	
1	2019						1
2	Jan.	8	Salaries and Wages Payable		1 840 56		2
3			Cash			1 840 56	3
4			To record payment of				4
5			salaries and wages				5
6			for week				6
7			ended Jan. 6				7

Section 3 Self Review

QUESTIONS

1. What is the purpose of a payroll bank account?
2. What accounts are debited and credited when individual payroll checks are written on the regular checking account?
3. What appears on an individual earnings record?

EXERCISES

4. Details related to all employees' gross earnings, deductions, and net pay for a period are found in the:
   a. payroll register.
   b. individual earnings record.
   c. general journal.
   d. cash payments journal.
5. Payroll deductions are recorded in a separate:
   a. asset account.
   b. expense account.
   c. liability account.
   d. revenue account.

ANALYSIS

6. This general journal entry was made to record the payroll liability for amounts withheld from the weekly payroll (amounts in parentheses are credit entries, others are debit entries).

Office Salaries Expense	*600.00*
Shipping Wages Expense	*2,586.00*
Health Insurance Premium Expense	*40.00*
Social Security Taxes Expense	*197.41*
Medicare Taxes Payable	*(48.17)*
Employee Income Tax Payable	*(266.00)*
Cash	*(2,634.42)*

What corrections should be made to this journal entry?

(Answers to Section 3 Self Review are on page 379.)

REVIEW Chapter Summary

Chapter 10

The main goal of payroll work is to compute the gross wages or salaries earned by each employee, the amounts to be deducted for various taxes and other purposes, and the net amount payable.

Learning Objectives

10-1 **Explain the major federal laws relating to employee earnings and withholding.**

Several federal laws affect payroll.

- The federal Wage and Hour Law limits to 40 the number of hours per week an employee can work at the regular rate of pay. For more than 40 hours of work a week, an employer involved in interstate commerce must pay one and one-half times the regular rate.
- Federal laws require that the employer withhold at least three taxes from the employee's pay: the employee's share of social security tax, the employee's share of Medicare tax, and federal income tax. Instructions for computing these taxes are provided by the government.
- If required, state disability and other income taxes can also be deducted.
- Voluntary deductions can also be made.

10-2 **Compute gross earnings of employees.**

To compute gross earnings for an employee, it is necessary to know whether the employee is paid using an hourly rate basis, a salary basis, a commission basis, or a piece-rate basis.

10-3 **Determine employee deductions for social security tax.**

The social security tax is levied in an equal amount on both the employer and the employee. The tax is a percentage of the employee's gross wages during a calendar year up to a maximum wage base limit.

10-4 **Determine employee deductions for Medicare tax.**

The Medicare tax is levied in an equal amount on both the employer and the employee. There is no wage base limit for Medicare taxes. Under the ACA, higher income wage earners are now subject to an additional Medicare tax of 0.9 percent in addition to the regular Medicare tax of 1.45 percent. Unlike the regular Medicare tax, this additional tax on high-income wage earners is paid only by the individuals; the business does not match the amount.

10-5 **Determine employee deductions for income tax.**

Income taxes are deducted from an employee's paycheck by the employer and then are paid to the government periodically. Although several methods can be used to compute the amount of federal income tax to be withheld from employee earnings, the wage-bracket table method is most often used. The wage-bracket tables are in *Publication 15, Circular E, Employer's Tax Guide.* Withholding tables for various pay periods for single and married persons are contained in *Circular E.*

10-6 **Enter gross earnings, deductions, and net pay in the payroll register.**

Daily records of the hours worked by each nonsupervisory employee are kept. Using these hourly time sheets, the payroll clerk computes the employees' earnings, deductions, and net pay for each payroll period and records the data in a payroll register.

10-7 **Journalize payroll transactions in the general journal.**

The payroll register is used to prepare a general journal entry to record payroll expense and liability amounts. A separate journal entry is made to record payments to employees.

10-8 **Maintain an earnings record for each employee.**

At the beginning of each year, the employer sets up an individual earnings record for each employee. The amounts in the payroll register are posted to the individual earnings records throughout the year so that the firm has detailed payroll information for each employee. At the end of the year, employers provide reports that show gross earnings and total deductions to each employee.

10-9 **Define the accounting terms new to this chapter.**

Glossary

Commission basis (p. 351) A method of paying employees according to a percentage of net sales (sales less sales returns)

Compensation record (p. 363) See individual earnings record

Employee (p. 346) A person who is hired by and works under the control and direction of the employer

Review and Applications

Employee's Withholding Allowance Certificate, Form W-4 (p. 353) A form used to claim exemption (withholding) allowances

Exempt employees (p. 357) Salaried employees who hold supervisory or managerial positions who are not subject to the maximum hour and overtime pay provisions of the Wage and Hour Law

Federal unemployment taxes (FUTA) (p. 348) Taxes levied by the federal government against employers to benefit unemployed workers

Hourly rate basis (p. 350) A method of paying employees according to a stated rate per hour

Independent contractor (p. 346) One who is paid by a company to carry out a specific task or job but is not under the direct supervision or control of the company

Individual earnings record (p. 363) An employee record that contains information needed to compute earnings and complete tax reports

Medicare tax (p. 347) A tax levied on employees and employers to provide medical care for the employee and the employee's spouse after each has reached age 65

Payroll register (p. 357) A record of payroll information for each employee for the pay period

Piece-rate basis (p. 351) A method of paying employees according to the number of units produced

Salary basis (p. 350) A method of paying employees according to an agreed-upon amount for each week or month

Social Security Act (p. 347) A federal act providing certain benefits for employees and their families; officially the Federal Insurance Contributions Act

Social security (FICA or OASDI) tax (p. 347) A tax imposed by the Federal Insurance Contributions Act and collected on employee earnings to provide retirement and disability benefits

State unemployment taxes (SUTA) (p. 349) Taxes levied by a state government against employers to benefit unemployed workers

Tax-exempt wages (p. 352) Earnings in excess of the base amount set by the Social Security Act

Time and a half (p. 347) Rate of pay for an employee's work in excess of 40 hours a week

Wage-bracket table method (p. 353) A simple method to determine the amount of federal income tax to be withheld using a table provided by the government

Workers' compensation insurance (p. 349) Insurance that protects employees against losses from job-related injuries or illnesses, or compensates their families if death occurs in the course of the employment

Comprehensive Self Review

1. What is the purpose of the payroll register?
2. How does an independent contractor differ from an employee?
3. From an accounting and internal control viewpoint, would it be preferable to pay employees by check or cash? Explain.
4. How is the amount of social security tax to be withheld from an employee's earnings determined?
5. What is the purpose of workers' compensation insurance?

(Answers to Comprehensive Self Review are on page 379.)

Discussion Questions

1. How does the Fair Labor Standards Act affect the wages paid by many firms? What types of firms are regulated by the act?
2. What factors affect how much federal income tax must be withheld from an employee's earnings?

3. What aspects of employment are regulated by the Fair Labor Standards Act? What is another commonly used name for this act?
4. What is an exempt employee?
5. How are the federal and state unemployment taxes related?
6. Does the employee bear any part of the SUTA tax? Explain.
7. Give two examples of common payroll fraud.
8. How are earnings determined when employees are paid on the hourly rate basis?
9. What is the purpose of the Medicare tax?
10. What is the purpose of the social security tax?
11. How does the direct deposit method of paying employees operate?
12. What are the four bases for determining employee gross earnings?
13. What is the simplest method for finding the amount of federal income tax to be deducted from an employee's gross pay?
14. What publication of the Internal Revenue Service provides information about the current federal income tax rates and the procedures that employers should use to withhold federal income tax from an employee's earnings?
15. How does the salary basis differ from the hourly rate basis of paying employees?

APPLICATIONS

Exercises

Computing gross earnings.

Exercise 10.1
Objective 10-2

The hourly rates of four employees of Ernesto's Enterprises follow, along with the hours that these employees worked during one week. Determine the gross earnings of each employee.

Employee No.	Hourly Rate	Hours Worked
1	$9.71	38
2	9.25	30
3	9.92	33
4	9.13	32

Computing regular earnings, overtime earnings, and gross pay.

Exercise 10.2
Objective 10-2

During one week, four production employees of Morgan Manufacturing Company worked the hours shown below. All these employees receive overtime pay at one and one-half times their regular hourly rate for any hours worked beyond 40 in a week. Determine the regular earnings, overtime earnings, and gross earnings for each employee.

Employee No.	Hourly Rate	Hours Worked
1	$11.00	46
2	10.62	47
3	10.46	38
4	10.80	48

Exercise 10.3 ▶ Determining social security withholding.

Objective 10-3

The monthly salaries for December and the year-to-date earnings of the employees of Bush Consulting Company as of November 30 follow.

Employee No.	December Salary	Year-to-Date Earnings Through November 30
1	$ 9,900	$ 99,000
2	10,000	70,000
3	10,709	117,799
4	10,000	100,000

Determine the amount of social security tax to be withheld from each employee's gross pay for December. Assume a 6.2 percent social security tax rate and an earnings base of $122,700 for the calendar year.

Exercise 10.4 ▶ Determining deduction for Medicare tax.

Objective 10-4

CONTINUING >>> Problem

Using the earnings data given in Exercise 10.3, determine the amount of Medicare tax to be withheld from each employee's gross pay for December. Assume a 1.45 percent Medicare tax rate and that all salaries and wages are subject to the tax.

Exercise 10.5 ▶ Determining federal income tax withholding.

Objective 10-5

Data about the marital status, withholding allowances, and weekly salaries of the four office workers at Peter Office Supply Company follow. Use the tax tables in Figure 10.2 to find the amount of federal income tax to be deducted from each employee's gross pay.

Employee No.	Marital Status	Withholding Allowances	Weekly Salary
1	M	2	$675
2	S	1	565
3	M	2	665
4	S	1	495

Exercise 10.6 ▶ Recording payroll transactions in the general journal.

Objective 10-7

Private Publishing has two office employees. A summary of their earnings and the related taxes withheld from their pay for the week ending August 7, 2019, follows.

	Ann Chen	David Kendrick
Gross earnings	$1,420.00	$1,290.00
Social security deduction	(88.04)	(79.98)
Medicare deduction	(20.59)	(18.71)
Income tax withholding	(380.16)	(232.32)
Net pay for week	$ 931.21	$ 958.99

1. Prepare the general journal entry to record the company's payroll for the week. Use the account names given in this chapter. Use 16 as the page number for the general journal.
2. Prepare the general journal entry to summarize the checks to pay the weekly payroll.

Journalizing payroll transactions.

◀ **Exercise 10.7**
Objective 10-7

On July 31, 2019, the payroll register for White Sales Company showed the following totals for the month: gross earnings, $38,950; social security tax, $2,414.90; Medicare tax, $564.78; income tax, $5,842.00; and net amount due, $30,128.32. Of the total earnings, $30,500.00 was for sales salaries and $8,450.00 was for office salaries. Prepare a general journal entry to record the monthly payroll of the firm on July 31, 2019. Use 20 as the page number for the general journal.

PROBLEMS

Problem Set A

Computing gross earnings, determining deductions, journalizing payroll transactions.

◀ **Problem 10.1A**
Objectives 10-2, 10-3, 10-4, 10-5, 10-7

Kathy Burnett works for Triumph Industries. Her pay rate is $13.44 per hour and she receives overtime pay at one and one-half times her regular hourly rate for any hours worked beyond 40 in a week. During the pay period that ended December 31, 2019, Kathy worked 42 hours. Kathy is married and claims three withholding allowances on her W-4 form. Kathy's cumulative earnings prior to this pay period total $29,000. Kathy's wages are subject to the following deductions:

1. Social Security tax at 6.2 percent
2. Medicare tax at 1.45 percent
3. Federal income tax (use the withholding table shown in Figure 10.2B)
4. Health and disability insurance premiums, $161
5. Charitable contribution, $18
6. U.S. Savings Bond, $100

INSTRUCTIONS

1. Compute Kathy's regular, overtime, gross, and net pay.
2. Assuming the weekly payroll has been recorded, journalize the payment of her wages for the week ended December 31, 2019. Use 54 as the page number for the general journal.

Analyze: Based on Kathy's cumulative earnings through December 31, how much overtime pay did she earn this year?

Computing gross earnings, determining deductions, preparing payroll register, journalizing payroll transactions.

◀ **Problem 10.2A**
Objectives 10-2, 10-3, 10-4, 10-5

City Place Movie Theaters has four employees and pays them on an hourly basis. During the week beginning June 24 and ending June 30, 2019, these employees worked the hours shown below. Information about hourly rates, marital status, withholding allowances, and cumulative earnings prior to the current pay period also appears below.

Employee	Regular Hours Worked	Hourly Rate	Marital Status	Withholding Allowances	Cumulative Earnings
Andy Anderson	48	$12.70	M	1	$17,640
Roma Benson	48	11.50	M	4	16,975
Frank Cortez	40	11.20	M	1	16,080
Winter Wise	50	10.70	S	2	14,660

INSTRUCTIONS

1. Enter the basic payroll information for each employee in a payroll register. Record the employee's name, number of withholding allowances, marital status, total and overtime hours, and regular hourly rate. Consider any hours worked beyond 40 in the week as overtime hours.
2. Compute the regular, overtime, and gross earnings for each employee. Enter the figures in the payroll register.
3. Compute the amount of social security tax to be withheld from each employee's earnings. Assume a 6.2 percent social security rate on the first $122,700 earned by the employee during the year. Enter the figures in the payroll register.
4. Compute the amount of Medicare tax to be withheld from each employee's earnings. Assume a 1.45 percent Medicare tax rate on all salaries and wages earned by the employee during the year. Enter the figures in the payroll register.
5. Determine the amount of federal income tax to be withheld from each employee's total earnings. Use the tax tables in Figure 10.2. Enter the figures in the payroll register.
6. Compute the net pay of each employee and enter the figures in the payroll register.
7. Total and prove the payroll register.
8. Prepare a general journal entry to record the payroll for the week ended June 30, 2019. Use 15 as the page number for the general journal.
9. Record the general journal entry to summarize payment of the payroll on July 3, 2019.

Analyze: What are Andy Anderson's cumulative earnings on June 30, 2019?

Problem 10.3A

Objectives 10-2, 10-3, 10-4, 10-5

Computing gross earnings, determining deductions, preparing payroll register, journalizing payroll transactions.

Alexander Wilson operates Metroplex Courier and Delivery Service. He has four employees who are paid on an hourly basis. During the workweek beginning December 15 and ending December 21, 2019, his employees worked the number of hours shown below. Information about their hourly rates, marital status, and withholding allowances also appears below, along with their cumulative earnings for the year prior to the December 15–21 payroll period.

Employee	Hours Worked	Regular Hourly Rate	Marital Status	Withholding Allowances	Cumulative Earnings
Gloria Bahamon	47	$16.70	M	4	$32,860
Alex Garcia	43	28.50	S	1	57,300
Ron Price	49	26.90	M	3	53,972
Sara Russell	40	13.70	S	0	26,620

INSTRUCTIONS

1. Enter the basic payroll information for each employee in a payroll register. Record the employee's name, number of withholding allowances, marital status, total and overtime hours, and regular hourly rate. Consider any hours worked beyond 40 in the week as overtime hours.
2. Compute the regular, overtime, and gross earnings for each employee. Enter the figures in the payroll register.
3. Compute the amount of social security tax to be withheld from each employee's gross earnings. Assume a 6.2 percent social security rate on the first $122,700 earned by the employee during the year. Enter the figures in the payroll register.
4. Compute the amount of Medicare tax to be withheld from each employee's gross earnings. Assume a 1.45 percent Medicare tax rate on all salaries and wages earned by the employee during the year. Enter the figures in the payroll register.

5. Determine the amount of federal income tax to be withheld from each employee's total earnings. Use the tax tables in Figure 10.2 to determine the withholding for Russell. Withholdings are $112.00 for Bahamon, $323.00 for Garcia, and $258 for Price. Enter the figures in the payroll register.
6. Compute the net amount due each employee and enter the figures in the payroll register.
7. Total and prove the payroll register. Bahamon and Russell are office workers. Garcia and Price are delivery workers.
8. Prepare a general journal entry to record the payroll for the week ended December 21, 2019. Use 32 as the page number for the general journal.
9. Prepare a general journal entry on December 23 to summarize payment of wages for the week.

Analyze: What percentage of total taxable wages was delivery wages?

Computing gross earnings, determining deductions and net amount due, journalizing payroll transactions.

◄ **Problem 10.4A**
Objectives 10-2, 10-3, 10-4, 10-5, 10-6, 10-7

Nashville Publishing Company pays its employees monthly. Payments made by the company on October 31, 2019, follow. Cumulative amounts paid to the persons named prior to October 31 are also given.

1. Paul Parker, president, gross monthly salary of $20,000; gross earnings prior to October 31, $160,000.
2. Carolyn Wells, vice president, gross monthly salary of $15,000; gross earnings paid prior to October 31, $150,000.
3. Michelle Clark, independent accountant who audits the company's accounts and performs consulting services, $16,500; gross amounts paid prior to October 31, $42,500.
4. James Wu, treasurer, gross monthly salary of $6,000; gross earnings prior to October 31, $60,000.
5. Payment to Editorial Publishing Services for monthly services of Betty Jo Bradley, an editorial expert, $6,000; amount paid to Editorial Publishing Services prior to October 31, 2019, $34,000.

INSTRUCTIONS

1. Use an earnings ceiling of $122,700 for social security taxes and a tax rate of 6.2 percent and a tax rate of 1.45 percent on all earnings for Medicare taxes. Prepare a schedule showing the following information:
   a. Each employee's cumulative earnings prior to October 31.
   b. Each employee's gross earnings for October.
   c. The amounts to be withheld for each payroll tax from each employee's earnings; the employee's income tax withholdings are Paul Parker, $5,600; Carolyn Wells, $4,200; James Wu, $1,320.
   d. The net amount due each employee.
   e. The total gross earnings, the total of each payroll tax deduction, and the total net amount payable to employees.
2. Prepare the general journal entry to record the company's payroll on October 31. Use journal page 22. Omit explanations.
3. Prepare the general journal entry to record payments to employees on October 31.

Analyze: What distinguishes an employee from an independent contractor?

Problem Set B

Computing gross earnings, determining deductions, journalizing payroll transactions.

◄ **Problem 10.1B**
Objectives 10-2, 10-3, 10-4, 10-5, 10-7

Juan Padronas works for H&C Commercial Builders, Inc. His pay rate is $13.00 per hour and he receives overtime pay at one and one-half times his regular hourly rate for any hours worked beyond

40 in a week. During the pay period ended December 31, 2019, Juan worked 48 hours. Juan is married and claims three withholding allowances on his W-4 form. Juan's cumulative earnings prior to this pay period total $28,000. Juan's wages are subject to the following deductions:

1. Social security tax at 6.2 percent
2. Medicare tax at 1.45 percent
3. Federal income tax (use the withholding table shown in Figure 10.2B)
4. Health insurance premiums, $150
5. Charitable contribution, $20
6. Credit Union Savings, $25

INSTRUCTIONS

1. Compute Juan's regular, overtime, gross, and net pay.
2. Assuming the weekly payroll has been recorded, journalize the payment of his wages for the week ended December 31, 2019. Use journal page 18.

Analyze: Based on Juan's cumulative earnings through December 31, how much overtime pay did he earn this year?

Problem 10.2B

Objectives 10-2, 10-3, 10-4, 10-5

► Computing earnings, determining deductions and net amount due, preparing payroll register, journalizing payroll transactions.

The four employees for ACWorks are paid on an hourly basis. During the week of December 25–31, 2019, these employees worked the hours indicated. Information about their hourly rates, marital status, withholding allowances, and cumulative earnings prior to the current pay period also appears below.

Employee	Hours Worked	Regular Hourly Rate	Marital Status	Withholding Allowances	Cumulative Earnings
Betty Brooks	45	$12.80	M	3	$ 44,179.00
Cynthia Carter	48	13.40	M	2	53,015.00
Mary Easley	44	29.50	M	4	82,748.00
James Periot	30	37.00	S	2	104,486.00

INSTRUCTIONS

1. Enter the basic payroll information for each employee in a payroll register. Record the employee's name, number of withholding allowances, marital status, total hours, overtime hours, and regular hourly rate. Consider any hours worked beyond 40 in the week as overtime hours.
2. Compute the regular earnings, overtime premium, and gross earnings for each employee. Enter the figures in the payroll register.
3. Compute the amount of social security tax to be withheld from each employee's gross earnings. Assume a 6.2 percent social security tax rate on the first $122,700 earned by each employee during the year. Enter the figures in the payroll register.
4. Compute the amount of Medicare tax to be withheld from each employee's gross earnings. Assume a 1.45 percent Medicare tax rate on all earnings for each employee during the year. Enter the figure on the payroll register.
5. Determine the amount of federal income tax to be withheld from each employee's gross earnings. Income tax withholdings are $235 for Easley and $238 for Periot. Enter these figures in the payroll register.
6. Compute the net amount due each employee and enter the figures in the payroll register.
7. Complete the payroll register for the store employees.

8. Prepare a general journal entry to record the payroll for the week ended December 31, 2019. Use page 18 for the journal.
9. Record the general journal entry to summarize the payment on December 31, 2019, of the net amount due employees.

Analyze: What is the difference between the amount credited to the ***Cash*** account on December 31, 2019, for the payroll week ended December 31 and the amount debited to ***Wages Expense*** for the same payroll period? What causes the difference between the two figures?

Computing earnings, determining deductions and net amount due, preparing payroll register, journalizing payroll transactions.

◀ **Problem 10.3B**

Objectives 10-2, 10-3, 10-4, 10-5

Barbara Merino operates Merino Consulting Services. She has four employees and pays them on an hourly basis. During the week ended November 12, 2019, her employees worked the number of hours shown below. Information about their hourly rates, marital status, withholding allowances, and cumulative earnings for the year prior to the current pay period also appears below.

Employee	Hours Worked	Regular Hourly Rate	Marital Status	Withholding Allowances	Cumulative Earnings
Kathryn Allen	43	$10.50	M	3	$26,565
Calvin Cooke	36	10.25	S	2	25,933
Maria Vasquez	45	29.75	M	4	75,268
Hollie Visage	41	32.75	S	2	82,858

INSTRUCTIONS

1. Enter the basic payroll information for each employee in a payroll register. Record the employee's name, number of withholding allowances, marital status, total hours, overtime hours, and regular hourly rate. Consider any hours worked beyond 40 in the week as overtime hours.
2. Compute the regular earnings, overtime premium, and gross earnings for each employee. Enter the figures in the payroll register.
3. Compute the amount of social security tax to be withheld from each employee's gross earnings. Assume a 6.2 percent social security rate on the first $122,700 earned by the employee during the year. Enter the figures in the payroll register.
4. Compute the amount of Medicare tax to be withheld from each employee's gross earnings. Assume a 1.45 percent Medicare tax rate on all earnings paid during the year. Enter the figures in the payroll register.
5. Use the tax tables in Figure 10.2 to determine the federal income tax to be withheld. Federal income tax to be withheld from Vasquez's pay is $192 and from Visage's pay is $267. Enter the figures in the payroll register.
6. Compute the net amount due each employee and enter the figures in the payroll register.
7. Complete the payroll register. Allen and Cooke are office workers. Earnings for Vasquez and Visage are charged to consulting wages.
8. Prepare a general journal entry to record the payroll for the week ended November 12, 2019. Use the account titles given in this chapter. Use journal page 32.
9. Prepare the general journal entry to summarize payment of amounts due employees on November 15, 2019.

Analyze: What total deductions were taken from employee paychecks for the pay period ended November 12?

Computing gross earnings, determining deductions and net amount due, journalizing payroll transactions.

◀ **Problem 10.4B**

Objectives 10-2, 10-3, 10-4, 10-5, 10-7

Universal Operations pays its employees monthly. Payments made by the company on November 30, 2019, follow. Cumulative amounts paid to the persons named prior to November 30 are also given.

1. Tony Orlando, president, gross monthly salary of $17,000; gross earnings prior to November 30, $170,000.
2. Chris Stamos, vice president, gross monthly salary of $12,000; gross earnings paid prior to November 30, $120,000.
3. Caley Marie, independent media buyer who purchases media contracts for companies and performs other public relations consulting services, $15,650; gross amounts paid prior to November 30, $52,850.
4. Claire Hayakawa, treasurer, gross monthly salary of $6,400; gross earnings prior to November 30, $57,600.
5. Payment to the Canal Marketing Group for monthly services of Anna Canal, a marketing and public relations expert, $15,500; amount paid to the Canal Marketing Group prior to November 30, $46,500.

INSTRUCTIONS

1. Use an earnings ceiling of $122,700 and a tax rate of 6.2 percent for social security taxes and a tax rate of 1.45 percent on all earnings for Medicare taxes. Prepare a schedule showing the following information:
   a. Each employee's cumulative earnings prior to November 30.
   b. Each employee's gross earnings for November.
   c. The amounts to be withheld for each payroll tax from each employee's earnings; the employee's income tax withholdings are Tony Orlando, $4,760; Chris Stamos, $3,000; Claire Hayakawa, $1,200.
   d. The net amount due each employee.
   e. The total gross earnings, the total of each payroll tax deduction, and the total net amount payable to employees.
2. Give the general journal entry to record the company's payroll on November 30. Use journal page 24. Omit explanations.
3. Give the general journal entry to record payments to employees on November 30.

Analyze: In what month in 2019 did Chris Stamos reach the withholding limit for social security?

Critical Thinking Problem 10.1

Payroll Accounting

Charlie Company pays salaries and wages on the last day of each month. Payments made on December 31, 2019, for amounts incurred during December are shown below. Cumulative amounts paid prior to December 31 to the persons named are also shown.

a. Charlie Fisher, president, gross monthly salary, $11,000; gross earnings paid prior to December 31, $121,000.
b. Carol Swartz, vice president, gross monthly salary, $10,000; gross earnings paid prior to December 31, $100,000.
c. Juan Rios, independent accountant who audits the company's accounts and performs certain consulting services, $15,000; gross amount paid prior to December 31, $25,000.
d. Henry House, treasurer, gross monthly salary, $6,500; gross earnings paid prior to December 31, $71,500.
e. Payment to Wright Security Services for Eddie Wright, a security guard who is on duty on Saturdays and Sundays, $1,000; amount paid to Wright Security Services prior to December 31, $11,000.

INSTRUCTIONS

1. Using the tax rates and earnings ceilings given in this chapter, prepare a schedule showing the following information:
   a. Each employee's cumulative earnings prior to December 31.

b. Each employee's gross earnings for December.
c. The amounts to be withheld for each payroll tax from each employee's earnings (employee income tax withholdings for Fisher are $3,080; for Swartz, $2,500; and for House, $1,300).
d. The net amount due each employee.
e. The total gross earnings, the total of each payroll tax deduction, and the total net amount payable to employees.

2. Record the general journal entry for the company's payroll on December 31. Use journal page 32.
3. Record the general journal entry for payments to employees on December 31.

Analyze: What is the balance of the ***Salaries Payable*** account after all payroll entries have been posted for the month?

Critical Thinking Problem 10.2

Payroll Internal Controls

Several years ago, Paul Rivera opened Casa Tacos, a restaurant specializing in homemade tacos. The restaurant was so successful that Rivera was able to expand, and his company now operates eight restaurants in the local area.

Rivera tells you that when he first started, he handled all aspects of the business himself. Now that there are eight Casa Tacos, he depends on the managers of each restaurant to make decisions and oversee day-to-day operations. Paul oversees operations at the company's headquarters, which is located at the first Casa Tacos.

Each manager interviews and hires new employees for a restaurant. The new employee is required to complete a W-4, which is sent by the manager to the headquarters office. Each restaurant has a time clock and employees are required to clock in as they arrive or depart. Blank time cards are kept in a box under the time clock. At the beginning of each week, employees complete the top of the card they will use during the week. The manager collects the cards at the end of the week and sends them to headquarters.

Paul hired his cousin Anna to prepare the payroll instead of assigning this task to the accounting staff. Because she is a relative, Paul trusts her and has confidence that confidential payroll information will not be divulged to other employees.

When Anna receives a W-4 for a new employee, she sets up an individual earnings record for the employee. Each week, using the time cards sent by each restaurant's manager, she computes the gross pay, deductions, and net pay for all the employees. She then posts details to the employees' earnings records and prepares and signs the payroll checks. The checks are sent to the managers, who distribute them to the employees.

As long as Anna receives a time card for an employee, she prepares a paycheck. If she fails to get a time card for an employee, she checks with the manager to see if the employee was terminated or has quit. At the end of the month, Anna reconciles the payroll bank account and prepares quarterly and annual payroll tax returns.

1. Identify any weaknesses in Casa Tacos's payroll system.
2. Identify one way a manager could defraud Casa Tacos under the present payroll system.
3. What internal control procedures would you recommend to Paul to protect against the fraud you identified above?

BUSINESS CONNECTIONS

Cash Management

Managerial | FOCUS

1. Why should managers check the amount spent for overtime?
2. The new controller for CAR Company, a manufacturing firm, has suggested to management that the business change from paying the factory employees in cash to paying them by check. What reasons would you offer to support this suggestion?

3. Why should management make sure that a firm has an adequate set of payroll records?
4. How can detailed payroll records help managers control expenses?

Ethical DILEMMA

Salary vs. Hourly

Susie's Sweater Factory employs two managers for the factory. These managers work 12 hours per day at $16 per hour. After eight hours, they receive overtime pay. Management is trying to cut costs. They have decided to promote the managers to a salary position. The managers will be offered a daily salary of $200. Since they would be promoted to a salary position, they will not receive overtime. The company has required they accept the promotion or find employment elsewhere. Is it ethical for the company to offer the managers a salary position? Is it ethical to require the employee to accept the promotion? Should the managers accept the promotion?

Financial Statement ANALYSIS

Home Depot

Balance Sheet

The Home Depot, Inc., reported the following data in its FY 2015 10-K *(for the fiscal year ended January 31, 2016)*:

The Home Depot, Inc. and Subsidiaries
Consolidated Balance Sheets

(in millions except per share amounts)	***Jan. 31, 2016***	***Feb. 1, 2015***
Current liabilities:		
Accrued salaries and related expenses	*1,515*	*1,391*
Total current liabilities	*12,526*	*11,269*

Analyze:

1. What percentage of total current liabilities is made up of accrued salaries and related expenses at January 31, 2016?
2. By what amount did accrued salaries and related expenses change from fiscal 2014 to fiscal 2015?

TEAMWORK

Cycle to Pay Employee

There are many approvals needed to create a paycheck for an employee. Divide into groups of five to identify the jobs necessary to create a paycheck for an employee. Describe the function and, if necessary, the journal entry for each job.

Internet CONNECTION

Certified Payroll Professional

Log onto the Certified Payroll Professional (CPP) website at www.americanpayroll.org. Find the requirements to become a CPP. How many years of experience are required? What is the fee to take the exam? Describe the testing procedure.

Answers to **Self Reviews**

Answers to Section 1 Self Review

1. The federal requirement that covered employees be paid at a rate equal to one and one-half times their normal hourly rate for each hour worked in excess of 40 hours per week.
2. By state and federal taxes levied on the employer.
3. By a tax levied equally on both employers and employees. The tax amount is based on the earnings.
4. **a.** employees who become unemployed.
5. **c.** Both employee and employer.
6. He is not an employee. He is an independent contractor because he has been hired to complete a specific job and is not under the control of the employer.

Answers to Section 2 Self Review

1. Social security tax, Medicare tax, and federal income tax.
2. Amount of earnings, period covered by the payment, employee's marital status, and the number of withholding allowances.
3. Health insurance premiums, life insurance premiums, union dues, retirement plans.
4. **d.** hours worked
5. **c.** $468
6. When you receive a signed Form W-4 for the change in withholding.

Answers to Section 3 Self Review

1. Using a separate payroll account simplifies the bank reconciliation procedure and makes it easier to identify outstanding payroll checks.
2. Debit ***Salaries and Wages Payable*** and credit ***Cash.***
3. Employee's name, address, social security number, date of birth, number of withholding allowances claimed, marital status, rate of pay, and any other information needed to compute earnings and complete tax reports.
4. **a.** payroll register
5. **c.** liability account
6. ***Health Insurance Premiums Expense*** Dr. 40.00 should be ***Health Insurance Premiums Payable*** Cr. 40.00; ***Social Security Taxes Expense*** Cr. 197.41 should be ***Social Security Tax Payable*** Cr. 197.41; ***Cash*** Cr. 2,634.42 should be ***Salaries and Wages Payable*** Cr. 2,634.42

Answers to Comprehensive Self Review

1. To record in one place all information about an employee's earnings and withholdings for the period.
2. An employee is one who is hired by the employer and who is under the control and direction of the employer. An independent contractor is paid by the company to carry out a specific task or job and is not under the direct supervision and control of the employer.
3. By check because there is far less possibility of mistake, lost money, or fraud. The check serves as a receipt and permanent record of the transaction.
4. Social security taxes are determined by multiplying the amount of taxable earnings by the social security tax rate.
5. To compensate workers for losses suffered from job-related injuries or to compensate their families if the employee's death occurs in the course of employment.

Payroll Taxes, Deposits, and Reports

Chapter **11**

www.ford.com

© Kristoffer Tripplaar/Alamy Stock Photo

The American multinational auto manufacturer Ford Motor Company was incorporated by Henry Ford on June 16, 1903. Henry Ford is credited with producing the Model T, one of the best-selling vehicles of all time; with producing the F-150 truck, which has been the best-selling vehicle in the United States for the past 32 years; and with introducing the assembly-line manufacturing process. But did you know Ford is also responsible for establishing the eight-hour workday?

In 1914, Ford increased his factory workers' pay to $5 per day, which was double the existing pay rate for factory workers at the time. At the same time, he reduced the assembly-line workers' workday from nine hours to eight. These two changes benefited both the workers and the company; the combination of higher pay and fewer working hours significantly decreased employee turnover and increased vehicle production. With eight-hour shifts, the Ford factory could operate 24 hours per day with three eight-hour shifts instead of only two nine-hour shifts. The increase in wages enabled many of the employees to purchase Ford vehicles.

As of November 2015, Ford Motor Company employed approximately 197,000 people at 67 manufacturing plants across six continents. Sales for the third quarter of 2015 totaled $35.8 billion. But as Henry Ford said, "A business that makes nothing but money is a poor business." Ford Motor Company continues to be dedicated to Henry Ford's legacy of corporate responsibility and volunteerism. Executive Chairman Bill Ford echoes Ford's founder, saying, "I want us to be the company that makes a difference in people's lives, one that inspires its employees, delights its customers, rewards it shareholders, and makes the world a better place."

thinking critically

What types of benefits do you think are important to people working in industries such as manufacturing? What would be important to you?

LEARNING OBJECTIVES

11-1 Explain how and when payroll taxes are paid to the government.

11-2 Compute and record the employer's social security and Medicare taxes.

11-3 Record deposit of social security, Medicare, and employee income taxes.

11-4 Prepare an Employer's Quarterly Federal Tax Return, Form 941.

11-5 Prepare Wage and Tax Statement (Form W-2) and Annual Transmittal of Wage and Tax Statements (Form W-3).

11-6 Compute and record liability for federal and state unemployment taxes and record payment of the taxes.

11-7 Prepare an Employer's Federal Unemployment Tax Return, Form 940.

11-8 Compute and record workers' compensation insurance premiums.

11-9 Define the accounting terms new to this chapter.

NEW TERMS

Employer's Annual Federal Unemployment Tax Return, Form 940
Employer's Quarterly Federal Tax Return, Form 941
experience rating system
merit rating system
Transmittal of Wage and Tax Statements, Form W-3
unemployment insurance program
Wage and Tax Statement, Form W-2
withholding statement

Section 1

SECTION OBJECTIVES	TERMS TO LEARN
>> 11-1 Explain how and when payroll taxes are paid to the government. WHY IT'S IMPORTANT Employers are required by law to deposit payroll taxes. >> 11-2 Compute and record the employer's social security and Medicare taxes. WHY IT'S IMPORTANT Accounting records should reflect all liabilities. >> 11-3 Record deposit of social security, Medicare, and employee income taxes. WHY IT'S IMPORTANT Payments decrease the payroll tax liability. >> 11-4 Prepare an Employer's Quarterly Federal Tax Return, Form 941. WHY IT'S IMPORTANT Completing a federal tax return is part of the employer's legal obligation. >> 11-5 Prepare Wage and Tax Statement (Form W-2) and Annual Transmittal of Wage and Tax Statements (Form W-3). WHY IT'S IMPORTANT Employers are legally required to provide end-of-year payroll information.	Employer's Quarterly Federal Tax Return, Form 941 Transmittal of Wage and Tax Statements, Form W-3 Wage and Tax Statement, Form W-2 withholding statement

Social Security, Medicare, and Employee Income Tax

In Chapter 10, you learned that the law requires employers to act as collection agents for certain taxes due from employees. In this chapter, you will learn how to compute the employer's taxes, make tax payments, and file the required tax returns and reports.

>> 11-1 OBJECTIVE
Explain how and when payroll taxes are paid to the government.

Payment of Payroll Taxes

The payroll register provides information about wages subject to payroll taxes. Figure 11.1 shows a portion of the payroll register for Tomlin Furniture Company for the week ending January 6.

Employers make tax deposits for the following taxes that are withheld from employee gross wages: federal income tax, social security tax, and Medicare tax. In addition, the employer must also deposit an amount equal to the social security and Medicare taxes withheld from employees' wages. If a check is written to cover these taxes, the deposits are made in a Federal Reserve Bank or other authorized financial institution (businesses usually make these payroll tax deposits at their own bank).

If the business makes the deposit electronically (the preferred method), the *Electronic Federal Tax Payment System (EFTPS)* is used. This is a system for electronically depositing employment taxes using a telephone or a computer. Electronic filing of taxes due is now required in most instances. An employer *must* use EFTPS if the annual federal tax deposits are more than $200,000. Employers who are required to make electronic deposits and do not do so can be subject to a 10 percent penalty.

FIGURE 11.1 Portion of a Payroll Register

AND ENDING *January 6, 2019* **PAID** *January 8, 2019*

TAXABLE WAGES			DEDUCTIONS				DISTRIBUTION			
SOCIAL SECURITY	MEDICARE	FUTA	SOCIAL SECURITY	MEDICARE	INCOME TAX	HEALTH INSURANCE	NET AMOUNT	CHECK NO.	OFFICE SALARIES	SHIPPING WAGES
400 00	400 00	400 00	24 80	5 80	19 00		350 40	1601		400 00
380 00	380 00	380 00	23 56	5 51	34 00		316 93	1602		380 00
427 50	427 50	427 50	26 51	6 20	23 00	40 00	331 79	1603		427 50
560 00	560 00	560 00	34 72	8 12	30 00	40 00	447 16	1604		560 00
480 00	480 00	480 00	29 76	6 96	19 00		394 28	1605	480 00	
2 247 50	2 247 50	2 247 50	139 35	32 59	155 00	80 00	1 840 56		480 00	1 767 50

The frequency of deposits depends on the amount of tax liability. The amount currently owed is compared to the tax liability threshold. For simplicity, this textbook uses $2,500 as the tax liability threshold.

The deposit schedules are not related to how often employees are paid. The deposit schedules are based on the amount currently owed and the amount reported in the lookback period. The *lookback period* is a four-quarter period ending on June 30 of the preceding year.

1. If the amount owed is less than $2,500, payment is due quarterly with the payroll tax return (Form 941).

Example. An employer's tax liability is as follows:

January	$ 580
February	640
March	620
	$1,840

Since at no time during the quarter is the accumulated tax liability $2,500 or more, no deposit is required during the quarter. The employer may pay the amount with the payroll tax returns.

2. If the amount owed is $2,500 or more, the schedule is determined from the total taxes reported on Form 941 during the lookback period.

a. If the amount reported in the lookback period was $50,000 or less, the employer is subject to the *Monthly Deposit Schedule Rule.* Monthly payments are due on the 15th day of the following month. For example, the January payment is due by February 15.

b. If the amount reported in the lookback period was more than $50,000, the employer is subject to the *Semiweekly Deposit Schedule Rule.* "Semiweekly" refers to the fact that deposits are due on either Wednesdays or Fridays, depending on the employer's payday.

- If payday is a Wednesday, Thursday, or Friday, the deposit is due on the following Wednesday.
- If payday is a Saturday, Sunday, Monday, or Tuesday, the deposit is due on the following Friday.

c. For new employers with no lookback period, if the amount owed is $2,500 or more, payments are due under the Monthly Deposit Schedule Rule.

3. If the total accumulated tax liability reaches $100,000 or more on any day, a deposit is due on the next banking day. This applies even if the employer is on a monthly or a semiweekly deposit schedule.

important!

In addition to keeping good records on taxes withheld from employees, the Affordable Care Act provisions are requiring businesses with a designated number of minimum employees to report on health insurance benefits. Many of these reporting requirements (and taxes) will be tracked and reported through the summary earnings report and other federal filings.

EMPLOYER'S SOCIAL SECURITY AND MEDICARE TAX EXPENSES

>> 11-2 OBJECTIVE

Compute and record the employer's social security and Medicare taxes.

Remember that both employers and employees pay social security and Medicare taxes. Figure 11.1 shows the *employee's* share of these payroll taxes. The *employer* pays the same amount of payroll taxes. At the assumed rate of 6.2 percent for social security and 1.45 percent for Medicare tax, the employer's tax liability is $343.88.

important!

Tax Liability

The employer's tax liability is the amount owed for:

- employee withholdings (income tax, social security tax, Medicare tax);
- employer's matching amounts of social security and Medicare taxes withheld from employees.

	Employee (Withheld)	Employer (Matched)
Social security	$139.35	$139.35
Medicare	32.59	32.59
	$171.94	$171.94
Total	$343.88	

In Chapter 10, you learned how to record employee payroll deductions. The entry to record the employer's share (commonly called "matching") of social security and Medicare taxes is made at the end of each payroll period. The debit is to the ***Payroll Taxes Expense*** account. The credits are to the same liability accounts used to record the employee's share of payroll taxes.

BUSINESS TRANSACTION

On January 8, Tomlin Furniture Company recorded the employer's share of social security and Medicare taxes. The information on the payroll register (Figure 11.1) is used to record the payroll taxes expense.

ANALYSIS

The expense account ***Payroll Taxes Expense*** is increased by the employer's share of social security and Medicare taxes, $171.94. The liability account ***Social Security Tax Payable*** is increased by $139.35. The liability account ***Medicare Tax Payable*** is increased by $32.59.

DEBIT-CREDIT RULES

DEBIT Increases to expense accounts are recorded as debits. Debit ***Payroll Taxes Expense*** for $171.94.

CREDIT Increases to liability accounts are recorded as credits. Credit ***Social Security Tax Payable*** for $139.35. Credit ***Medicare Tax Payable*** for $32.59.

T-ACCOUNT PRESENTATION

Payroll Taxes Expense	
+	−
171.94	

Social Security Tax Payable	
−	+
	139.35

Medicare Tax Payable	
−	+
	32.59

THE BOTTOM LINE

Employer's Payroll Taxes

Income Statement	
Expenses	↑ 171.94
Net Income	↓ 171.94

Balance Sheet	
Liabilities	↑ 171.94
Equity	↓ 171.94

GENERAL JOURNAL ENTRY

GENERAL JOURNAL PAGE 1

	DATE		DESCRIPTION	POST. REF.	DEBIT	CREDIT	
1	2019						1
2	Jan.	8	Payroll Taxes Expense		171 94		2
3			Social Security Tax Payable			139 35	3
4			Medicare Tax Payable			32 59	4
5			To record social security and				5
6			Medicare taxes for Jan. 8 payroll				6

According to the Social Security Administration, benefits were being paid to approximately 65 million men, women, and children in 2015. It is essential that earnings are correctly reported so that future benefits can be calculated accurately.

RECORDING THE PAYMENT OF TAXES WITHHELD

>> 11-3 OBJECTIVE

Record deposit of social security, Medicare, and employee income taxes.

At the end of January, the accounting records for Tomlin Furniture Company contained the following information:

	Employee (Withheld)	Employer (Matched)	Total
Social security	$ 557.40	$557.40	$1,114.80
Medicare	130.36	130.36	260.72
Federal income tax	620.00	—	620.00
Total	$1,307.76	$687.76	$1,995.52

Tomlin Furniture Company is on a monthly payment schedule. The amount reported in the lookback period is less than $50,000. The payroll tax liability for the quarter ending March 31, 2019, is more than $2,500. (Recall that this textbook uses $2,500 as the tax liability threshold.) A tax payment is due on the 15th day of the following month, February 15.

The tax liability for the first quarter is deposited electronically.

The entry to record the tax deposit is shown below. The entry is shown in general journal form for illustration purposes only. (Tomlin Furniture Company actually uses a cash payments journal.)

GENERAL JOURNAL PAGE 2

	DATE		DESCRIPTION	POST. REF.	DEBIT	CREDIT	
1	2019						1
21							21
22	Feb.	15	Social Security Tax Payable		1 114 80		22
23			Medicare Tax Payable		260 72		23
24			Employee Income Tax Payable		620 00		24
25			Cash			1 995 52	25
26			Deposit of payroll taxes withholding				26
27			at First State Bank				27
28							28

FEBRUARY PAYROLL RECORDS

There were four weekly payroll periods in February. Each hourly employee worked the same number of hours each week and had the same gross pay and deductions as in January. The office clerk earned her regular salary and had the same deductions as in January. At the end of the month:

- the individual earnings records were updated;
- the taxes were deposited before March 15;
- the tax deposit was recorded in the cash payments journal.

MARCH PAYROLL RECORDS

There were five weekly payroll periods in March. Assume that the payroll period ended on March 31, and the payday was on March 31. Also assume that the earnings and deductions of the employees were the same for each week as in January and February. At the end of the month, the individual earnings records were updated, the taxes were deposited, and the tax deposit was recorded in the cash payments journal.

QUARTERLY SUMMARY OF EARNINGS RECORDS

At the end of each quarter, the individual earnings records are totaled. This involves adding the columns in the Earnings, Deductions, and Net Pay sections. Figure 11.2 shows the earnings record, posted and summarized, for Alicia Martinez for the first quarter.

Table 11.1 shows the quarterly totals for each employee of Tomlin Furniture Company. This information is taken from the individual earnings records. Through the end of the first quarter, no employee has exceeded the social security earnings limit ($122,700) and the FUTA/SUTA limit ($7,000) has only been exceeded by Cecilia Wu.

>> 11-4 OBJECTIVE

Prepare an Employer's Quarterly Federal Tax Return, Form 941.

EMPLOYER'S QUARTERLY FEDERAL TAX RETURN

Each quarter an employer files an **Employer's Quarterly Federal Tax Return, Form 941** with the Internal Revenue Service. Form 941 must be filed by all employers subject to federal income tax withholding, social security tax, or Medicare tax, with certain exceptions as specified in *Publication 15, Circular E.* This tax return provides information about employee earnings, the tax liability for each month in the quarter, and the deposits made.

FIGURE 11.2 Individual Earnings Record

EARNINGS RECORD FOR 2019

NAME Alicia Martinez RATE $10 per hour SOCIAL SECURITY NO. 123-45-6789
ADDRESS 1712 Windmill Hill Lane, Dallas TX 75232-6002 DATE OF BIRTH October 31, 1979
WITHHOLDING ALLOWANCES 1 MARITAL STATUS M

PAYROLL NO.	DATE		HOURS		EARNINGS				DEDUCTIONS				NET PAY
	WK. END.	PAID	RG	OT	REGULAR	OVERTIME	TOTAL	CUMULATIVE	SOCIAL SECURITY	MEDICARE	INCOME TAX	OTHER	
1	1/06	1/08	40		400 00		400 00	400 00	24 80	5 80	19 00		350 40
2	1/13	1/15	40		400 00		400 00	400 00	24 80	5 80	19 00		350 40
3	1/20	1/22	40		400 00		400 00	400 00	24 80	5 80	19 00		350 40
4	1/27	1/29	40		400 00		400 00	400 00	24 80	5 80	19 00		350 40
	January				1600 00		1600 00	1600 00	99 20	23 20	76 00		1401 60
1	2/03	2/05	40		400 00		400 00	400 00	24 80	5 80	19 00		350 40
2	2/10	2/12	40		400 00		400 00	400 00	24 80	5 80	19 00		350 40
3	2/17	2/19	40		400 00		400 00	400 00	24 80	5 80	19 00		350 40
4	2/24	2/25	40		400 00		400 00	400 00	24 80	5 80	19 00		350 40
	February				1600 00		1600 00	1600 00	99 20	23 20	76 00		1401 60
1	3/03	3/05	40		400 00		400 00	400 00	24 80	5 80	19 00		350 40
2	3/10	3/12	40		400 00		400 00	400 00	24 80	5 80	19 00		350 40
3	3/17	3/19	40		400 00		400 00	400 00	24 80	5 80	19 00		350 40
4	3/24	3/26	40		400 00		400 00	400 00	24 80	5 80	19 00		350 40
5	3/31	3/31	40		400 00		400 00	400 00	24 80	5 80	19 00		350 40
	March				2000 00		2000 00	2000 00	124 00	29 00	95 00		1752 00
	First Quarter				5200 00		5200 00	5200 00	322 40	75 40	247 00		4555 20

	Taxable Earnings				Deductions		
Employee	Total Earnings	Social Security	Medicare	SUTA & FUTA	Social Security	Medicare Tax	Income Tax
Alicia Martinez	5,200.00	5,200.00	5,200.00	5,200.00	322.40	75.40	247.00
Jorge Rodriguez	4,940.00	4,940.00	4,940.00	4,940.00	306.28	71.63	442.00
George Dunlap	5,557.50	5,557.50	5,557.50	5,557.50	344.57	80.58	299.00
Cecilia Wu	7,280.00	7,280.00	7,280.00	7,000.00	451.36	105.56	390.00
Cynthia Booker	6,240.00	6,240.00	6,240.00	6,240.00	386.88	90.48	637.00
Totals	29,217.50	29,217.50	29,217.50	28,937.50	1,811.49	423.65	2,015.00

TABLE 11.1

Summary of Earnings, Quarter Ended March 31, 2019

> The Social Security Administration administers the Old Age and Survivors, Disability Insurance, and Supplemental Security Income programs. These programs are funded by the social security taxes collected from employees and matched by employers. The system currently takes in more in revenue from the 12.4 percent payroll taxes than it pays out in benefits. The trust fund is expected to begin paying out more in benefits than it collects in 2032.

When to File Form 941 The due date for Form 941 is the last day of the month following the end of each calendar quarter. If the taxes for the quarter were deposited when due, the due date is extended by 10 days.

Completing Form 941 Figure 11.3 shows Form 941 for Tomlin Furniture Company. Form 941 is prepared using the data on the quarterly summary of earnings records shown in Table 11.1. Let's examine Form 941.

- Use the preprinted form if it is available. Otherwise, enter the employer's name, address, and identification number at the top of Form 941. Check the applicable quarter.
- *Line 1* is completed for each quarter. Enter the number of employees for the pay periods indicated.
- *Line 2* shows total wages and tips subject to withholding. For Tomlin Furniture Company the total subject to withholdings is $29,217.50.
- *Line 3* shows the total employee income tax withheld during the quarter, $2,015.00.
- *Line 4* is checked if no wages or tips are subject to social security or Medicare tax.
- *Line 5a* shows the total amount of wages that are subject to social security taxes, $29,217.50. The amount is multiplied by the combined social security rate, 12.4 percent.

Social Security Tax:	
Employee's share	6.2%
Employer's share	6.2
Total	12.4%

The amount of taxes is $3,622.97 ($29,217.50 × 12.4%).

- *Line 5b* is left blank since no employees at Tomlin Furniture Company had taxable social security tips.

important!

Quarters

A quarter is a three-month period. There are four quarters in a year:

- 1st quarter: January, February, March
- 2nd quarter: April, May, June
- 3rd quarter: July, August, September
- 4th quarter: October, November, December

FIGURE 11.3 Employer's Quarterly Federal Tax Return, Form 941

Form **941 for 2019: Employer's QUARTERLY Federal Tax Return**
Department of the Treasury — Internal Revenue Service

950114
OMB No. 1545-0029

Employer identification number (EIN) 7 5 – 1 2 3 4 5 6 7

Name *(not your trade name)* Sarah Tomlin

Trade name *(if any)* Tomlin Furniture Company

Address 5910 Lake June Road
Number Street Suite or room number

Dallas TX 75232-6017
City State ZIP code

Foreign country name Foreign province/county Foreign postal code

Report for this Quarter . . .
(Check one.)

☒ **1:** January, February, March
☐ **2:** April, May, June
☐ **3:** July, August, September
☐ **4:** October, November, December

Instructions and prior year forms are available at *www.irs.gov/form941.*

Read the separate instructions before you complete Form 941. Type or print within the boxes.

Part 1: Answer these questions for this quarter.

Line	Description	Column 1		Column 2	Line	Amount
1	**Number of employees who received wages, tips, or other compensation for the pay period including:** ***Mar. 12*** **(Quarter 1),** ***June 12*** **(Quarter 2),** ***Sept. 12*** **(Quarter 3), or** ***Dec. 12*** **(Quarter 4)**				1	5
2	**Wages, tips, and other compensation**				2	29,217.50
3	**Federal income tax withheld from wages, tips, and other compensation**				3	2,015.00
4	**If no wages, tips, and other compensation are subject to social security or Medicare tax**					☐ **Check and go to line 6.**
5a	**Taxable social security wages**	29,217.50	× .124 =	3,622.97		
5b	**Taxable social security tips**	.	× .124 =	.		
5c	**Taxable Medicare wages & tips**	29,217.50	× .029 =	847.31		
5d	**Taxable wages & tips subject to Additional Medicare Tax withholding**	.	× .009 =	.		
5e	**Add Column 2 from lines 5a, 5b, 5c, and 5d**				5e	4,470.28
5f	**Section 3121(q) Notice and Demand—Tax due on unreported tips** (see instructions)				5f	.
6	**Total taxes before adjustments.** Add lines 3, 5e, and 5f				6	6,485.28
7	**Current quarter's adjustment for fractions of cents**				7	.
8	**Current quarter's adjustment for sick pay**				8	.
9	**Current quarter's adjustments for tips and group-term life insurance**				9	.
10	**Total taxes after adjustments.** Combine lines 6 through 9				10	6,485.28
11	**Total deposits for this quarter, including overpayment applied from a prior quarter and overpayments applied from Form 941-X, 941-X (PR), 944-X, 944-X (PR), or 944-X (SP) filed in the current quarter**				11	6,485.28
12	**Balance due.** If line 10 is more than line 11, enter the difference and see instructions				12	
13	**Overpayment.** If line 11 is more than line 10, enter the difference	.				Check one: ☐ Apply to next return. ☐ Send a refund.

▶ **You MUST complete both pages of Form 941 and SIGN it.** Next ▶

For Privacy Act and Paperwork Reduction Act Notice, see the back of the Payment Voucher. Cat. No. 17001Z Form **941**

FIGURE 11.3 (concluded)

950214

Name (not your trade name)	Employer identification number (EIN)
Sarah Tomlin	75-1234567

Part 2: Tell us about your deposit schedule and tax liability for this quarter.

If you are unsure about whether you are a monthly schedule depositor or a semiweekly schedule depositor, see Pub. 15 (Circular E), section 11.

14 Check one: ☐ **Line 10 on this return is less than $2,500 or line 10 on the return for the prior quarter was less than $2,500, and you did not incur a $100,000 next-day deposit obligation during the current quarter.** If line 10 for the prior quarter was less than $2,500 but line 10 on this return is $100,000 or more, you must provide a record of your federal tax liability. If you are a monthly schedule depositor, complete the deposit schedule below; if you are a semiweekly schedule depositor, attach Schedule B (Form 941). Go to Part 3.

☒ **You were a monthly schedule depositor for the entire quarter.** Enter your tax liability for each month and total liability for the quarter, then go to Part 3.

Tax liability: Month 1	1995 . 52	
Month 2	1995 . 52	
Month 3	2494 . 24	
Total liability for quarter	6485 . 28	**Total must equal line 10.**

☐ **You were a semiweekly schedule depositor for any part of this quarter.** Complete Schedule B (Form 941), Report of Tax Liability for Semiweekly Schedule Depositors, and attach it to Form 941.

Part 3: Tell us about your business. If a question does NOT apply to your business, leave it blank.

15 If your business has closed or you stopped paying wages . . . . ☐ Check here, and

enter the final date you paid wages / / .

16 If you are a seasonal employer and you do not have to file a return for every quarter of the year . . ☐ Check here.

Part 4: May we speak with your third-party designee?

Do you want to allow an employee, a paid tax preparer, or another person to discuss this return with the IRS? See the instructions for details.

☐ Yes. Designee's name and phone number

Select a 5-digit Personal Identification Number (PIN) to use when talking to the IRS.

☒ No.

Part 5: Sign here. You MUST complete both pages of Form 941 and SIGN it.

Under penalties of perjury, I declare that I have examined this return, including accompanying schedules and statements, and to the best of my knowledge and belief, it is true, correct, and complete. Declaration of preparer (other than taxpayer) is based on all information of which preparer has any knowledge.

Sign your name here	Sarah Tomlin	Print your name here	Sarah Tomlin
		Print your title here	Owner
Date	04 / 30 / 2019	Best daytime phone	972-709-4567

Paid Preparer Use Only Check if you are self-employed . . . ☐

Preparer's name		PTIN	
Preparer's signature		Date	/ /
Firm's name (or yours if self-employed)		EIN	
Address		Phone	
City	State	ZIP code	

- *Line 5c* shows the total amount of wages that are subject to Medicare taxes, $29,217.50. The amount is multiplied by the combined Medicare tax rate, 2.9 percent.

Medicare Tax:	
Employee's share	1.45%
Employer's share	1.45
Total	2.90%

  The amount of taxes is $847.31 ($29,217.50 × 2.90%).
- *Line 5d* is left blank since no employees at Tomlin Furniture Company were subject to the additional Medicare tax withholding.
- *Line 5e* shows the total social security and Medicare taxes, $4,470.28.
- *Line 5f* is left blank since no employees at Tomlin Furniture Company had taxable social security tips.
- *Line 6* shows the total tax liability for withheld income taxes, social security, and Medicare Taxes, $6,485.28.
- *Line 7* is for adjustments due to rounding. Tomlin Furniture Company had no rounding adjustments this quarter.
- *Line 8* is for adjustments due to sick pay. Tomlin Furniture Company had no sick pay adjustments this quarter.
- *Line 9* is for adjustments for tips and group-term life insurance. Tomlin Furniture Company had no adjustments this quarter.
- *Line 10* shows total taxes after adjustments, $6,485.28.
- *Line 11* shows total deposits made during the quarter including overpayments applied from a prior quarter, $6,485.28.
- Any balance due is entered on *Line 12* or an overpayment is entered on *Line 13.*
- *Line 14* shows the monthly deposits made by Tomlin Furniture Company.

recall

Tax Calculations

Social security and Medicare taxes are calculated by multiplying the taxable wages by the tax rate.

Notice that on Line 14 if the amount of taxes is less than $2,500, the amount may be paid with the return or with a financial depositor. There is no need to complete the record of monthly deposits. Since the amount of taxes due for Tomlin Furniture Company is greater than $2,500, and Tomlin is a monthly depositor, the record of monthly tax deposits must be completed on Line 14. The total deposits shown on Line 14 must equal the taxes shown on Line 10.

If the employer did not deduct enough taxes from an employee's earnings, the business pays the difference. The deficiency is debited to ***Payroll Taxes Expense.***

>> 11-5 OBJECTIVE

Prepare Wage and Tax Statement (Form W-2) and Annual Transmittal of Wage and Tax Statements (Form W-3).

Wage and Tax Statement, Form W-2

Employers provide a **Wage and Tax Statement, Form W-2** to each employee by January 31 for the previous calendar year's earnings. Form W-2 is sometimes called a **withholding statement.** Form W-2 contains information about the employee's earnings and tax withholdings for the year. The information for Form W-2 comes from the employee's earnings record.

Employees who stop working for the business during the year may ask that a Form W-2 be issued early. The Form W-2 must be issued within 30 days after the request or after the final wage payment, whichever is later.

important!

Form W-2

The employer must provide each employee with a Wage and Tax Statement, Form W-2, by January 31 of the following year. All payroll forms are revised each year. Those used in the text are illustrative of current forms at the time of publication.

Figure 11.4 shows Form W-2 for Alicia Martinez. This is the standard form provided by the Internal Revenue Service (IRS). Some employers use a "substitute" Form W-2 that is approved by the IRS. The substitute form permits the employer to list total deductions and to reconcile the gross earnings, the deductions, and the net pay. If the firm issues 250 or more Forms W-2, the returns must be filed electronically.

At least four copies of each of Form W-2 are prepared:

1. One copy for the employer to send to the Social Security Administration, which shares the information with the IRS.
2. One copy for the employee to attach to the federal income tax return.

FIGURE 11.4 Wage and Tax Statement, Form W-2

22222 | Void ☐ | a Employee's social security number 123-45-6789 | For Official Use Only ▶ OMB No. 1545-0008

b Employer identification number (EIN)	75-1234567
c Employer's name, address, and ZIP code	Tomlin Furniture Company 5910 Lake June Road Dallas, TX 75232-6017
d Control number	
e Employee's first name and initial	Alicia
Last name	Martinez
Suff.	
f Employee's address and ZIP code	1712 Windmill Hill Lane Dallas, Texas 75232-6002
1 Wages, tips, other compensation	20,800.00
2 Federal income tax withheld	988.00
3 Social security wages	20,800.00
4 Social security tax withheld	1,289.60
5 Medicare wages and tips	20,800.00
6 Medicare tax withheld	301.60
7 Social security tips	
8 Allocated tips	
9	
10 Dependent care benefits	
11 Nonqualified plans	
12a See instructions for box 12	
13 Statutory employee ☐ Retirement plan ☐ Third-party sick pay ☐	
12b	
14 Other	
12c	
12d	

15 State	Employer's state ID number	16 State wages, tips, etc.	17 State income tax	18 Local wages, tips, etc.	19 Local income tax	20 Locality name
TX	12-9876500	20800.00				

Form **W-2** **Wage and Tax Statement** **2019**

Department of the Treasury—Internal Revenue Service

For Privacy Act and Paperwork Reduction Act Notice, see the separate instructions.

Copy A For Social Security Administration — Send this entire page with Form W-3 to the Social Security Administration; photocopies are **not** acceptable.

Cat. No. 10134D

Do Not Cut, Fold, or Staple Forms on This Page

3. One copy for the employee's records.
4. One copy for the employer's records.

If there is a state income tax, two more copies of Form W-2 are prepared:

5. One copy for the employer to send to the state tax department.
6. One copy for the employee to attach to the state income tax return.

Additional copies are prepared if there is a city or county income tax.

Annual Transmittal of Wage and Tax Statements, Form W-3

The **Transmittal of Wage and Tax Statements, Form W-3,** is submitted with Forms W-2 to the Social Security Administration. Form W-3 reports the total social security wages; total Medicare wages; total social security tax withheld; total Medicare tax withheld; total wages, tips, and other compensation; total federal income tax withheld; and other information.

A copy of Form W-2 for each employee is attached to Form W-3. Form W-3 is due by the last day of February following the end of the calendar year. The Social Security Administration shares the tax information on Forms W-2 with the Internal Revenue Service. Figure 11.5 shows the completed Form W-3 for Tomlin Furniture Company.

The amounts on Form W-3 must equal the sums of the amounts on the attached Forms W-2. For example, the amount entered in Box 1 of Form W-3 must equal the sum of the amounts entered in Box 1 of all the Forms W-2.

The amounts on Form W-3 also must equal the sums of the amounts reported on the Forms 941 during the year. For example, the social security wages reported on the Form W-3 must equal the sum of the social security wages reported on the four Forms 941.

The filing of Form W-3 marks the end of the routine procedures needed to account for payrolls and for payroll tax withholdings.

ABOUT **ACCOUNTING**

IRS Electronic Filing

While filing of individual and business income tax returns is steadily increasing (approximately 86.3% for individuals in 2015), the IRS reported in late 2015 that the e-filing of all Form 94x series was only 33.3%. The stated goal is 80% of employment tax returns to be filed electronically.

FIGURE 11.5 Transmittal of Wage and Tax Statements, Form W-3

DO NOT STAPLE

33333	a Control number	For Official Use Only ▶ OMB No. 1545-0008	
b Kind of Payer (Check one): 941 [X]; Military [ ]; 943 [ ]; 944 [ ]; CT-1 [ ]; Hshld. emp. [ ]; Medicare govt. emp. [ ]		Kind of Employer (Check one): None apply [X]; 501c non-govt. [ ]; State/local non-501c [ ]; State/local 501c [ ]; Federal govt. [ ]	Third-party sick pay (Check if applicable) [ ]
c Total number of Forms W-2 5	d Establishment number	1 Wages, tips, other compensation 116,870.00	2 Federal income tax withheld 8,060.00
e Employer identification number (EIN) 75-1234567		3 Social security wages 116,870.00	4 Social security tax withheld 7,245.96
f Employer's name Tomlin Furniture Company		5 Medicare wages and tips 116,870.00	6 Medicare tax withheld 1,697.60
5910 Lake June Road Dallas, TX 75232-6017 g Employer's address and ZIP code		7 Social security tips	8 Allocated tips
		9	10 Dependent care benefits
		11 Nonqualified plans	12a Deferred compensation
h Other EIN used this year		13 For third-party sick pay use only	12b
15 State TX	Employer's state ID number 12-9876500	14 Income tax withheld by payer of third-party sick pay	
16 State wages, tips, etc.	17 State income tax	18 Local wages, tips, etc.	19 Local income tax
Employer's contact person Sarah Tomlin		Employer's telephone number 972-709-4567	For Official Use Only
Employer's fax number		Employer's email address	

Under penalties of perjury, I declare that I have examined this return and accompanying documents and, to the best of my knowledge and belief, they are true, correct, and complete.

Signature ▶ *Sarah Tamlin* Title ▶ OWNER Date ▶ 2/10/2020

Form **W-3 Transmittal of Wage and Tax Statements** 2019 Department of the Treasury Internal Revenue Service

Section 1 Self Review

QUESTIONS

1. What is the purpose of Form W-2?
2. How does a business deposit federal payroll taxes?
3. What is the purpose of Form 941?

EXERCISES

4. Which tax is paid equally by the employee and employer?
   a. federal income tax
   b. state income tax
   c. social security tax
   d. federal unemployment tax
5. Employers usually record social security taxes in the accounting records at the end of:
   a. each payroll period.
   b. each month.
   c. each quarter.
   d. the year.

ANALYSIS

6. Your business currently owes $2,910 in payroll taxes. During the lookback period, your business paid $10,000 in payroll taxes. How often does your business need to make payroll tax deposits?

(Answers to Section 1 Self Review are on page 414.)

Section 2

SECTION OBJECTIVES	TERMS TO LEARN
>> 11-6 Compute and record liability for federal and state unemployment taxes and record payment of the taxes. WHY IT'S IMPORTANT Businesses need to record all payroll tax liabilities. >> 11-7 Prepare an Employer's Federal Unemployment Tax Return, Form 940. WHY IT'S IMPORTANT The unemployment insurance programs provide support to individuals during temporary periods of unemployment. >> 11-8 Compute and record workers' compensation insurance premiums. WHY IT'S IMPORTANT Businesses need insurance to cover workplace injury claims.	Employer's Annual Federal Unemployment Tax Return, Form 940 experience rating system merit rating system unemployment insurance program

Unemployment Tax and Workers' Compensation

In Section 1, we discussed taxes that are withheld from employees' earnings and, in some cases, matched by the employer. In this section, we will discuss payroll-related expenses that are paid solely by the employer.

Unemployment Compensation Insurance Taxes

The unemployment compensation tax program, often called the **unemployment insurance program,** provides unemployment compensation through a tax levied on employers.

COORDINATION OF FEDERAL AND STATE UNEMPLOYMENT RATES

The unemployment insurance program is a federal program that encourages states to provide unemployment insurance for employees working in the state. The federal government allows a credit—or reduction—in the federal unemployment tax for amounts charged by the state for unemployment taxes.

This text assumes that the federal unemployment tax rate is 6.0 percent less a state unemployment tax credit of 5.4 percent; thus, the federal tax rate is reduced to 0.6 percent (6.0 percent −5.4 percent). The earnings limits for the federal and the state unemployment taxes are usually the same, $7,000.

A few states levy an unemployment tax on the employee. The tax is withheld from employee pay and remitted by the employer to the state.

For businesses that provide steady employment, the state unemployment tax rate may be lowered based on an **experience rating system,** or a **merit rating system.** Under the experience rating system, the state tax rate may be reduced to less than 1 percent for businesses that provide steady employment. In contrast, some states levy penalty rates as high as 10 percent for employers with poor records of providing steady employment.

The reduction of state unemployment taxes because of favorable experience ratings does not affect the credit allowable against the federal tax. An employer may take a credit against the federal unemployment tax as though it were paid at the normal state rate even though the employer actually pays the state a lower rate.

Because of its experience rating, Tomlin Furniture Company pays state unemployment tax of 4.0 percent, which is less than the standard rate of 5.4 percent. Note that the business may take the credit for the full amount of the state rate (5.4 percent) against the federal rate, even though the business actually pays a state rate of 4.0 percent.

>> 11-6 OBJECTIVE

Compute and record liability for federal and state unemployment taxes and record payment of the taxes.

COMPUTING AND RECORDING UNEMPLOYMENT TAXES

Tomlin Furniture Company records its state and federal unemployment tax expense at the end of each payroll period. The unemployment taxes for the payroll period ending January 6 are as follows:

Federal unemployment tax	($2,247.50 × 0.006)	=	$ 13.49
State unemployment tax	($2,247.50 × 0.040)	=	89.90
Total unemployment taxes		=	$103.39

The entry to record the employer's unemployment payroll taxes follows.

GENERAL JOURNAL PAGE 1

	DATE		DESCRIPTION	POST. REF.	DEBIT	CREDIT	
1	2019						1
8	Jan.	8	Payroll Taxes Expense		103 39		8
9			Federal Unemployment Tax Payable			13 49	9
10			State Unemployment Tax Payable			89 90	10
11			Unemployment taxes on				11
12			weekly payroll				12

REPORTING AND PAYING STATE UNEMPLOYMENT TAXES

In most states, the due date for the state unemployment tax return is the last day of the month following the end of the quarter. Generally, the tax is paid, electronically, with the return.

Employer's Quarterly Report Each state requires reporting of wages for unemployment tax purposes. Since Tomlin Furniture Company is located in Texas, it will complete the Texas state unemployment tax form and submit the tax due. Generally, each state requires quarterly reporting of wages and depositing of state unemployment taxes due. Amounts of wages subject to tax and the state tax rate are determined by each state.

Tomlin Furniture Company submits the report and issues a check payable to the state tax authority for the amount due. The entry is recorded in the cash payments journal. The transaction is shown here in general journal form for purposes of illustration:

GENERAL JOURNAL PAGE ______

	DATE		DESCRIPTION	POST. REF.	DEBIT	CREDIT	
1	2019						1
2	Apr.	29	State Unemployment Tax Payable		1 157 50		2
3			Cash			1 157 50	3
4			Paid SUTA taxes for quarter				4
5			ending March 31				5
6							6

Earnings in Excess of Base Amount State unemployment tax is paid on the first $7,000 of annual earnings for each employee. Earnings over $7,000 are not subject to state unemployment tax.

For example, Cecilia Wu earns $560 every week of the year. Table 11.1 shows that she earned $7,280 at the end of the first quarter. In the four weeks of January, February, and March, she earned $2,240 ($560 × 4).

	Earnings	Cumulative Earnings
January	$2,240	$2,240
February	2,240	4,480
March	2,240	6,720
March, week 5	560	7,280

In the fifth week of March, Wu earned $560, but only $280 of it is subject to state unemployment tax ($7,000 earnings limit – $6,720 cumulative earnings = $280). For the rest of the calendar year, Wu's earnings are not subject to state unemployment tax.

REPORTING AND PAYING FEDERAL UNEMPLOYMENT TAXES

The rules for reporting and depositing federal unemployment taxes differ from those used for social security and Medicare taxes.

Depositing Federal Unemployment Taxes Generally, federal unemployment tax payments are electronically deposited through EFTPS. Deposits are made quarterly and are due on the last day of the month following the end of the quarter.

The federal unemployment tax is calculated at the end of each quarter. It is computed by multiplying the first $7,000 of each employee's wages by 0.006. A deposit is required when more than $500 of federal unemployment tax is owed. If $500 or less is owed, no deposit is due. Any deposit due of $500 or more should be electronically deposited.

For example, suppose that a business calculates its federal unemployment tax to be $325 at the end of the first quarter. Since it is not more than $500, no deposit is due. At the end of the second quarter, it calculates its federal unemployment taxes on second quarter wages to be $200. The total undeposited unemployment tax now is more than $500, so a deposit is required.

First quarter undeposited tax	$325
Second quarter undeposited tax	200
Total deposit due	$525

In the case of Tomlin Furniture Company, the company owed $173.63 in federal unemployment tax at the end of March. Since this is less than $500, no deposit is due.

Month	Taxable Earnings Paid	Rate	Tax Due	Deposit Due Date
January	$8,990.00	0.006	$53.94	April 30
February	8,990.00	0.006	53.94	April 30
March	10,957.50	0.006	65.75	April 30
Total	$28,937.50		$173.63	

The payment of federal unemployment tax is recorded by debiting the ***Federal Unemployment Tax Payable*** account and crediting the ***Cash*** account.

>> 11-7 OBJECTIVE
Prepare an Employer's Federal Unemployment Tax Return, Form 940.

Reporting Federal Unemployment Tax, Form 940 Tax returns are not due quarterly for the federal unemployment tax. The employer submits an annual return. The **Employer's Annual Federal Unemployment Tax Return, Form 940,** is a preprinted government form used to report unemployment taxes for the calendar year. It is due by January 31 of the following year. The due date is extended to February 10 if all tax deposits were made on time.

The information needed to complete Form 940 comes from the annual summary of individual earnings records and from the state unemployment tax returns filed during the year.

Figure 11.6 shows Form 940 prepared for Tomlin Furniture Company. Refer to it as you learn how to complete Form 940.

PART 1: Asks the filer if he or she was required to pay SUTA tax in more than one state.

PART 2: Determine your FUTA tax before adjustments.

- *Line 3* shows the total compensation paid to employees, $116,870.00.
- *Line 4* is blank because there were no exempt payments for Tomlin Furniture Company.
- *Line 5* shows the compensation that exceeds the $7,000 earnings limit, $81,870 ($116,870 – $35,000).
- *Line 6* shows the wages not subject to federal unemployment tax, $81,870.
- *Line 7* shows the taxable wages for the year, $35,000. This amount must agree with the total taxable FUTA wages shown on the individual employee earnings records for the year.
- *Line 8* shows the FUTA tax, $210 ($35,000 × 0.006).

PART 3: Determine your adjustments.

- *Lines 9, 10, and 11* are blank because Tomlin Furniture Company had no adjustments.

PART 4: Determine your FUTA tax and balance due or overpayment.

- *Line 12* shows the total FUTA tax, after adjustments, $210.
- *Line 13* shows the FUTA tax deposited during the year, $0.
- *Line 14* shows the balance due, $210.
- *Line 15* is blank because there is no overpayment.

PART 5: Report your FUTA tax liability by quarter. This section is not applicable to Tomlin Furniture Company because its total FUTA liability is less than $500.

>> 11-8 OBJECTIVE

Compute and record workers' compensation insurance premiums.

WORKERS' COMPENSATION INSURANCE

Workers' compensation provides benefits for employees who are injured on the job. The insurance premium, which is paid by the employer, depends on the risk involved with the work performed. It is important to classify earnings according to the type of work the employees perform and to summarize labor costs according to the insurance premium classifications.

For instance, workers' compensation insurance will cost much more for workers in a coal mine or on an oil rig than it will for workers in an office setting. Insurance companies will have different rates for each category of risk of a company's workers.

There are two ways to handle workers' compensation insurance. The method a business uses depends on the number of its employees.

Estimated Annual Premium in Advance Employers who have few employees pay an estimated premium in advance. At the end of the year, the employer calculates the actual premium. If the actual premium is more than the estimated premium paid, the employer pays the balance due. If the actual premium is less than the estimated premium paid, the employer receives a refund.

Tomlin Furniture Company has two work classifications: office work and shipping work. The workers' compensation premium rates are:

Office workers	$0.45 per $100 of labor costs
Shipping workers	1.25 per $100 of labor costs

The insurance premium rates recognize that injuries are more likely to occur to shipping workers than to office workers. Based on employee earnings for the previous year, Tomlin Furniture Company paid an estimated premium of $1,000 for the new year. The payment was made on January 15.

FIGURE 11.6 Employer's Annual Federal Unemployment Tax Return, Form 940

Form **940 for 2019: Employer's Annual Federal Unemployment (FUTA) Tax Return** 850113

Department of the Treasury — Internal Revenue Service OMB No. 1545-0028

Employer identification number (EIN) 7 5 – 1 2 3 4 5 6 7

Name *(not your trade name)* Sarah Tomlin

Trade name *(if any)* Tomlin Furniture Company

Address 5910 June Lake Road

Number Street Suite or room number

Dallas TX 75322-6017

City State ZIP code

Foreign country name Foreign province/county Foreign postal code

Type of Return
(Check all that apply.)

- ☐ **a.** Amended
- ☐ **b.** Successor employer
- ☐ **c.** No payments to employees in 2019
- ☐ **d.** Final: Business closed or stopped paying wages

Instructions and prior-year forms are available at *www.irs.gov/form940.*

Read the separate instructions before you complete this form. Please type or print within the boxes.

Part 1: Tell us about your return. If any line does NOT apply, leave it blank. See instructions before completing Part 1.

1a	**If you had to pay state unemployment tax in one state only, enter the state abbreviation** .	1a	T X
1b	**If you had to pay state unemployment tax in more than one state, you are a multi-state employer** . . .	1b	☐ Check here. Complete Schedule A (Form 940).
2	**If you paid wages in a state that is subject to CREDIT REDUCTION** . . .	2	☐ Check here. Complete Schedule A (Form 940).

Part 2: Determine your FUTA tax before adjustments. If any line does NOT apply, leave it blank.

3	**Total payments to all employees** . . .	3	116870. 00
4	**Payments exempt from FUTA tax** . . . 4 [.]		
	Check all that apply: 4a ☐ Fringe benefits; 4b ☐ Group-term life insurance; 4c ☐ Retirement/Pension; 4d ☐ Dependent care; 4e ☐ Other		
5	**Total of payments made to each employee in excess of $7,000** . . . 5 [81870. 00]		
6	**Subtotal** (line 4 + line 5 = line 6) . . .	6	81870. 00
7	**Total taxable FUTA wages** (line 3 – line 6 = line 7) (see instructions) . . .	7	35000. 00
8	**FUTA tax before adjustments** (line 7 × .006 = line 8) . . .	8	210. 00

Part 3: Determine your adjustments. If any line does NOT apply, leave it blank.

9	**If ALL of the taxable FUTA wages you paid were excluded from state unemployment tax, multiply line 7 by .054** (line 7 × .054 = line 9). Go to line 12 . . .	9	.
10	**If SOME of the taxable FUTA wages you paid were excluded from state unemployment tax, OR you paid ANY state unemployment tax late** (after the due date for filing Form 940), complete the worksheet in the instructions. Enter the amount from line 7 of the worksheet . .	10	.
11	**If credit reduction applies,** enter the total from Schedule A (Form 940) . . .	11	.

Part 4: Determine your FUTA tax and balance due or overpayment. If any line does NOT apply, leave it blank.

12	**Total FUTA tax after adjustments** (lines 8 + 9 + 10 + 11 = line 12) . . .	12	210. 00
13	**FUTA tax deposited for the year, including any overpayment applied from a prior year** .	13	0. 00
14	**Balance due** (If line 12 is more than line 13, enter the excess on line 14.) • If line 14 is more than $500, you must deposit your tax. • If line 14 is $500 or less, you may pay with this return. (see instructions) . . .	14	210. 00
15	**Overpayment** (If line 13 is more than line 12, enter the excess on line 15 and check a box below.) . . .	15	.

▶ You **MUST** complete both pages of this form and **SIGN** it. Check one: ☐ Apply to next return. ☐ Send a refund.

Next ▶

For Privacy Act and Paperwork Reduction Act Notice, see the back of Form 940-V, Payment Voucher. Cat. No. 11234O Form **940**

FIGURE 11.6 (concluded)

850212

Name (not your trade name)	Employer identification number (EIN)
Sarah Tomlin	75-123456

Part 5: Report your FUTA tax liability by quarter only if line 12 is more than $500. If not, go to Part 6.

16 Report the amount of your FUTA tax liability for each quarter; do NOT enter the amount you deposited. If you had no liability for a quarter, leave the line blank.

16a	**1st quarter** (January 1 – March 31)	**16a**	.
16b	**2nd quarter** (April 1 – June 30)	**16b**	.
16c	**3rd quarter** (July 1 – September 30)	**16c**	.
16d	**4th quarter** (October 1 – December 31)	**16d**	.

17 **Total tax liability for the year** (lines 16a + 16b + 16c + 16d = line 17) **17** . **Total must equal line 12.**

Part 6: May we speak with your third-party designee?

Do you want to allow an employee, a paid tax preparer, or another person to discuss this return with the IRS? See the instructions for details.

☐ **Yes.** Designee's name and phone number

Select a 5-digit Personal Identification Number (PIN) to use when talking to IRS

☒ **No.**

Part 7: Sign here. You MUST complete both pages of this form and SIGN it.

Under penalties of perjury, I declare that I have examined this return, including accompanying schedules and statements, and to the best of my knowledge and belief, it is true, correct, and complete, and that no part of any payment made to a state unemployment fund claimed as a credit was, or is to be, deducted from the payments made to employees. Declaration of preparer (other than taxpayer) is based on all information of which preparer has any knowledge.

✗ **Sign your name here**	*Sarah Tomlin*
Print your name here	Sarah Tomlin
Print your title here	Owner
Date	01 / 31 / 2020
Best daytime phone	972-123-8766

Paid Preparer Use Only Check if you are self-employed . ☐

Preparer's name		PTIN	
Preparer's signature		Date	/ /
Firm's name (or yours if self-employed)		EIN	
Address		Phone	
City	State	ZIP code	

GENERAL JOURNAL PAGE ______

	DATE		DESCRIPTION	POST. REF.	DEBIT	CREDIT	
1	2019						1
14	Jan.	15	Prepaid Workers' Compensation Insurance		1 000 00		14
15			Cash			1 000 00	15
16			Estimated workers' compensation				16
17			insurance for 2019				17
18							18

At the end of the year, the actual premium was computed to be $1,261.20. The actual premium was computed by applying the proper rates to the payroll data for the year:

- The office wages were $24,960.
  ($24,960 ÷ $100) × $0.45 =
  249.60 × $0.45 = $112.32
- The shipping wages were $91,910.
  ($91,910 ÷ $100) × $1.25 =
  919.1 × $1.25 = $1,148.88
- Total premium for year = $1,261.20

Classification	Payroll	Rate	Premium
Office work	$24,960	$0.45 per $100	$ 112.32
Shipping work	91,910	1.25 per $100	1,148.88
Total premium for year			$1,261.20
Less estimated premium paid			1,000.00
Balance of premium due			$ 261.20

On December 31, the balance due to the insurance company is recorded as a liability by an adjusting entry. Tomlin Furniture Company owes $261.20 ($1,261.20 $1,000.00) for the workers' compensation insurance.

MANAGERIAL IMPLICATIONS <<

PAYROLL TAXES

- Management must ensure that payroll taxes are computed properly and paid on time.
- In order to avoid penalties, it is essential that a business prepares its payroll tax returns accurately and files the returns and required forms promptly.
- The payroll system should ensure that payroll reports are prepared in an efficient manner.
- Managers need to be familiar with all payroll taxes and how they impact operating expenses.
- Managers must be knowledgeable about unemployment tax regulations in their state because favorable experience ratings can reduce unemployment tax expense.
- Management is responsible for developing effective internal control procedures over payroll operations and ensuring that they are followed.

THINKING CRITICALLY

What accounting records are used to prepare Form 941?

GENERAL JOURNAL PAGE ______

	DATE		DESCRIPTION	POST. REF.	DEBIT	CREDIT	
1	2019						1
2	Dec.	31	Workers' Compensation Insurance Expense		261 20		2
3			Workers' Compensation Insurance Payable			261 20	3
4							4

Additionally, an adjusting journal would be recorded on December 31, 2019, for prepaid workers' compensation insurance expired.

Suppose that on January 15, Tomlin Furniture Company had paid an estimated premium of $1,400 instead of $1,000. The actual premium at the end of the year was $1,261.20. Tomlin Furniture Company would be due a refund from the insurance company for the amount overpaid, $138.80 ($1,400.00 – $1,261.20).

THE BOTTOM LINE

Workers' Compensation Refund Receivable

Income Statement	
Expenses	↓ 138.80
Net Income	↑ 138.80

Balance Sheet	
Assets	↑ 138.80
Equity	↑ 138.80

Deposit and Monthly Premium Payments Employers with many employees use a different method to handle workers' compensation insurance. At the beginning of the year, they make large deposits, often 25 percent of the estimated annual premium. From January through November, they pay the actual premium due based on an audit of the month's wages. The premium for the last month is deducted from the deposit. Any balance is refunded or applied toward the following year's deposit.

Internal Control over Payroll Operations

internal CONTROL

Now that we have examined the basic accounting procedures used for payrolls and payroll taxes, let's look at some internal control procedures that are recommended to protect payroll operations.

1. Assign only highly responsible, well-trained employees to work in payroll operations.
2. Keep payroll records in secured location. Train payroll employees to maintain confidentiality about pay rates and other information in the payroll records.
3. Add new employees to the payroll system and make all changes in employee pay rates only with proper written authorization from management.
4. Make changes to an employee's withholding allowances based only on a Form W-4 properly completed and signed by the employee.
5. Make voluntary deductions from employee earnings based only on a signed authorization from the employee.
6. Have the payroll authorizations examined by someone other than the person who prepares them. Compare each check/deposit to the entry for the employee in the payroll register.
7. If still issuing actual payroll checks, have them distributed to the employees by someone other than the person who prepares them.
8. Have the monthly payroll bank account statement received and reconciled by someone other than the person who prepares the payroll checks.
9. Use prenumbered forms for the payroll checks. Periodically the numbers of the checks issued and the numbers of the unused checks should be verified to make sure that all checks can be accounted for.
10. Maintain files of all authorization forms for adding new employees, changing pay rates, and making voluntary deductions. Also retain all Forms W-4.

Section 2 Self Review

QUESTIONS

1. Why is it important for workers' compensation wages to be classified according to the type of work performed?
2. Who pays the federal unemployment tax? The state unemployment tax?
3. How does a favorable experience rating affect the state unemployment tax rate?

EXERCISES

4. State unemployment taxes are filed:
   a. monthly.
   b. quarterly.
   c. yearly.
   d. at the end of each pay period.
5. The federal unemployment taxes are reported on:
   a. Form 941.
   b. Form 8109.
   c. Form W-3.
   d. Form 940.

ANALYSIS

6. At the end of the year, the business has a balance due for workers' compensation insurance. If no adjusting entry is made, will the amount of net income reported be correct? If not, how will it be wrong?

(Answers to Section 2 Self Review are on page 414.)

11 Chapter REVIEW Chapter Summary

Employers must pay social security, SUTA, FUTA, and Medicare taxes. They must also collect federal and state taxes from their employees and then remit those taxes to the appropriate taxing authorities. In this chapter, you have learned how to compute the employer's taxes and how to file the required tax returns and reports.

Learning Objectives

11-1 Explain how and when payroll taxes are paid to the government.

Employers act as collection agents for social security, Medicare, and federal income taxes withheld from employee earnings. Employers must remit these sums that are withheld from employee earnings but also must make a deposit for the business matching the amounts withheld from employees for social security and Medicare taxes to the government. These taxes must be deposited in an authorized depository, usually a commercial bank. The methods and schedules for deposits vary according to the sums involved.

11-2 Compute and record the employer's social security and Medicare taxes.

Employers should multiply the social security and Medicare tax rates by taxable wages to compute the employer's portion of taxes due.

11-3 Record deposit of social security, Medicare, and employee income taxes.

As taxes are paid to the government, the accounting records should be updated to reflect the payment, thereby reducing tax liability accounts.

11-4 Prepare an Employer's Quarterly Federal Tax Return, Form 941.

The Form 941 reports wages paid, federal employee income tax withheld, and applicable social security and Medicare taxes.

11-5 Prepare Wage and Tax Statement (Form W-2) and Annual Transmittal of Wage and Tax Statements (Form W-3).

By the end of January, each employee must be given a Wage and Tax Statement, Form W-2, showing the previous year's earnings and withholdings for social security, Medicare, and employee income tax. The employer files a Transmittal of Wage and Tax Statements, Form W-3, with copies of employees' Forms W-2. Form W-3 is due by the last day of February following the end of the calendar year.

11-6 Compute and record liability for federal and state unemployment taxes and record payment of the taxes.

Unemployment insurance taxes are paid by the employer to both state and federal governments. State unemployment tax returns differ from state to state but usually require a list of employees, their social security numbers, and taxable wages paid. The rate of state unemployment tax depends on the employer's experience rating. The net federal unemployment tax rate can be as low as 0.6 percent based on assumptions in this chapter.

11-7 Prepare an Employer's Federal Unemployment Tax Return, Form 940.

An Employer's Annual Federal Unemployment Tax Return, Form 940, must be filed in January for the preceding calendar year. The form shows the total wages paid, the amount of wages subject to unemployment tax, and the federal unemployment tax owed for the year. A credit is allowed against gross federal tax for unemployment tax charged under state plans, up to 5.4 percent of wages subject to the federal tax.

11-8 Compute and record workers' compensation insurance premiums.

By state law, employers might be required to carry workers' compensation insurance. For companies with a few employees, an estimated premium is paid at the start of the year. A final settlement is made with the insurance company on the basis of an audit of the payroll after the end of the year. Premiums vary according to the type of work performed by each employee. Other premium payment plans can be used for larger employers.

11-9 Define the accounting terms new to this chapter.

Glossary

Employer's Annual Federal Unemployment Tax Return, Form 940 (p. 395) Preprinted government form used by the employer to report unemployment taxes for the calendar year

Employer's Quarterly Federal Tax Return, Form 941 (p. 386) Preprinted government form used by the employer to report payroll tax information relating to social security, Medicare, and employee income tax withholding to the Internal Revenue Service

Experience rating system (p. 393) A system that rewards an employer for maintaining steady employment conditions by reducing the firm's state unemployment tax rate

Merit rating system (p. 393) See Experience rating system

Transmittal of Wage and Tax Statements, Form W-3 (p. 391) Preprinted government form submitted with Forms W-2 to the Social Security Administration

Unemployment insurance program (p. 393) A program that provides unemployment compensation through a tax levied on employers

Wage and Tax Statement, Form W-2 (p. 390) Preprinted government form that contains information about an employee's earnings and tax withholdings for the year

Withholding statement (p. 390) See Wage and Tax Statement, Form W-2

Comprehensive **Self Review**

1. What is Form W-3?
2. Is the ceiling on earnings subject to unemployment taxes larger than or smaller than the ceiling on earnings subject to the social security tax?
3. How do the FUTA and SUTA taxes relate to each other?
4. Under the monthly deposit schedule rule, when must deposits for employee income tax and other withheld taxes be made?
5. Which of the following factors determine the frequency of deposits of social security, Medicare, and income tax withholdings?
   - **a.** Experience rating.
   - **b.** Amount of taxes reported in the lookback period.
   - **c.** Company's net income.
   - **d.** Amount of taxes currently owed.
   - **e.** How often employees are paid.

(Answers to Comprehensive Self Review are on page 414.)

Discussion Questions

1. Which of the following are withheld from employees' earnings?
   - **a.** FUTA
   - **b.** income tax
   - **c.** Medicare
   - **d.** social security
   - **e.** SUTA
   - **f.** workers' compensation
2. What does "monthly" refer to in the Monthly Deposit Schedule Rule?
3. What does "semiweekly" refer to in the Semiweekly Deposit Schedule Rule?

4. What is EFTPS? When is EFTPS required?
5. What is a business tax identification number?
6. What are the four taxes levied on employers?
7. What is the lookback period?
8. What is the purpose of Form W-3? When must it be issued? To whom is it sent?
9. When must Form W-2 be issued? To whom is it sent?
10. What happens if the employer fails to deduct enough employee income tax or FICA tax from employee earnings?
11. How can an employer keep informed about changes in the rates and bases for the social security, Medicare, and FUTA taxes?
12. When is the premium for workers' compensation insurance usually paid?
13. Who pays for workers' compensation insurance?
14. What is Form 941? How often is the form filed?
15. Is the employer required to deposit the federal unemployment tax during the year? Explain.
16. A state charges a basic SUTA tax rate of 5.4 percent. Because of an excellent experience rating, an employer in the state has to pay only 1.0 percent of the taxable payroll as state tax. What is the percentage to be used in computing the credit against the federal unemployment tax?
17. What is the purpose of Form 940? How often is it filed?
18. What is the purpose of allowing a credit against the FUTA for state unemployment taxes?
19. Why was the unemployment insurance system established?

APPLICATIONS

Exercises

Exercise 11.1
Objective 11-1

Depositing payroll taxes.

The amounts of employee income tax withheld and social security and Medicare taxes (both employee and employer shares) shown below were owed by different businesses on the specified dates. In each case, decide whether the firm is required to deposit the sum in an authorized financial institution. If a deposit is necessary, give the date by which it should be made. The employers are monthly depositors.

1. Total taxes of $550 owed on July 31, 2019.
2. Total taxes of $1,650 owed on April 30, 2019.
3. Total taxes of $1,200 owed on March 31, 2019.
4. Total taxes of $8,750 owed on February 28, 2019.

Exercise 11.2
Objective 11-3

Recording deposit of social security, Medicare, and income taxes.

After Beam Corporation paid its employees on July 15, 2019, and recorded the corporation's share of payroll taxes for the payroll paid that date, the firm's general ledger showed a balance of $20,700 in the ***Social Security Tax Payable*** account, a balance of $4,246 in the ***Medicare Tax Payable*** account, and a balance of $19,260 in the ***Employee Income Tax Payable*** account. On July 16, the business issued a check to deposit the taxes owed in the First Texas Bank. Record this transaction in general journal form. Use 24 as the page number for the general journal.

Computing employer's payroll taxes.

◀ **Exercise 11.3**
Objectives 11-2, 11-6

At the end of the weekly payroll period on June 30, 2019, the payroll register of Concord Consultants showed employee earnings of $62,500. Determine the firm's payroll taxes for the period. Use a social security rate of 6.2 percent, Medicare rate of 1.45 percent, FUTA rate of 0.6 percent, and SUTA rate of 5.4 percent. Consider all earnings subject to social security tax and Medicare tax and $35,000 subject to FUTA and SUTA taxes.

Depositing federal unemployment tax.

◀ **Exercise 11.4**
Objective 11-6

On March 31, 2019, the ***Federal Unemployment Tax Payable*** account in the general ledger of The Argosy Company showed a balance of $1,507. This represents the FUTA tax owed for the first quarter of the year. On April 30, 2019, the firm issued a check to deposit the amount owed in the First Security National Bank. Record this transaction in general journal form. Use 14 as the page number for the general journal.

Computing SUTA tax.

◀ **Exercise 11.5**
Objective 11-6

On April 30, 2019, Chung Furniture Company prepared its state unemployment tax return for the first quarter of the year. The firm had taxable wages of $100,050. Because of a favorable experience rating, Chung pays SUTA tax at a rate of 1.4 percent. How much SUTA tax did the firm owe for the quarter?

Paying SUTA tax.

◀ **Exercise 11.6**
Objective 11-6

On June 30, 2019, the ***State Unemployment Tax Payable*** account in the general ledger of Alan Office Supplies showed a balance of $2,148. This represents the SUTA tax owed for the second quarter of the year. On July 31, 2019, the business issued a check to the state unemployment insurance fund for the amount due. Record this payment in general journal form. Use 30 as the page number for the general journal.

Computing FUTA tax.

◀ **Exercise 11.7**
Objective 11-6

On January 31, AC Baking Company prepared its Employer's Annual Federal Unemployment Tax Return, Form 940. During the previous year, the business paid total wages of $462,150 to its 14 employees. Of this amount, $98,000 was subject to FUTA tax. Using a rate of 0.6 percent, determine the FUTA tax owed and the balance due on January 31, 2020, when Form 940 was filed. A deposit of $300 was made during the year.

Computing workers' compensation insurance premiums.

◀ **Exercise 11.8**
Objective 11-8

Kazana Medical Supplies estimates that its office employees will earn $215,000 next year and its factory employees will earn $970,000. The firm pays the following rates for workers' compensation insurance: $0.60 per $100 of wages for the office employees and $8.40 per $100 of wages for the factory employees. Determine the estimated premium for each group of employees and the total estimated premium for next year.

PROBLEMS

Problem Set A

Computing and recording employer's payroll tax expense.

◀ **Problem 11.1A**
Objectives 11-2, 11-6

The payroll register of Big House Cleaning Company showed total employee earnings of $4,500 for the payroll period ended July 14, 2019.

INSTRUCTIONS

1. Compute the employer's payroll taxes for the period. Use rates of 6.2 percent for the employer's share of the social security tax, 1.45 percent for Medicare tax, 0.6 percent for FUTA tax, and 5.4 percent for SUTA tax. All earnings are taxable.
2. Prepare a general journal entry to record the employer's payroll taxes for the period. Use journal page 30.

Analyze: Which of the above taxes are paid by the employee and matched by the employer?

Problem 11.2A
Objectives 11-2, 11-3

Computing employer's social security tax, Medicare tax, and unemployment taxes.

A payroll summary for Mark Consulting Company, owned by Mark Fronke, for the quarter ending June 30, 2019, appears below. The firm made the required tax deposits as follows:

a. For April taxes, paid on May 15.

b. For May taxes, paid on June 17.

Date Wages Paid		Total Earnings	Social Security Tax Deducted	Medicare Tax Deducted	Income Tax Withheld
April	8	$ 3,400.00	$ 210.80	$ 49.30	$ 338.00
	15	3,700.00	229.40	53.65	365.00
	22	4,100.00	254.20	59.45	338.00
	29	4,400.00	272.80	63.80	436.00
		$15,600.00	$ 967.20	$226.20	$1,477.00
May	5	$ 3,200.00	$ 198.40	$ 46.40	$ 318.00
	12	3,400.00	210.80	49.30	338.00
	19	3,400.00	210.80	49.30	338.00
	26	4,400.00	272.80	63.80	436.00
		$14,400.00	$ 892.80	$208.80	$1,430.00
June	2	$ 3,700.00	$ 229.40	$ 53.65	$ 365.00
	9	3,400.00	210.80	49.30	338.00
	16	4,400.00	272.80	63.80	436.00
	23	3,400.00	210.80	49.30	338.00
	30	3,200.00	198.40	46.40	318.00
		$18,100.00	$1,122.20	$262.45	$1,795.00
Total		$48,100.00	$2,982.20	$697.45	$4,702.00

INSTRUCTIONS

1. Using the tax rates given below, and assuming that all earnings are taxable, make the general journal entry on April 8, 2019, to record the employer's payroll tax expense on the payroll ending that date. Use journal page 12.

Social security	6.2 percent
Medicare	1.45
FUTA	0.6
SUTA	5.4

2. Prepare the entries in general journal form to record deposit of the employee income tax withheld and the social security and Medicare taxes (employee and employer shares) on May 15 for April taxes and on June 17 for May taxes.

Analyze: How were the amounts for ***Income Tax Withheld*** determined?

◄ **Problem 11.3A**
Objectives 11-4, 11-6
CONTINUING >>> Problem

This is a continuation of Problem 11.2A for Mark Consulting Company; recording payment of taxes and preparing employer's quarterly federal tax return.

1. On July 15, the firm issued a check to deposit the federal income tax withheld and the FICA tax (both employee and employer shares for the third month [June]). Based on your computations in Problem 11.2A, record the issuance of the check in general journal form. Use journal page 24.
2. Complete Form 941 in accordance with the discussions in this chapter. Use a 12.4 percent social security rate and a 2.9 percent Medicare rate in computations. Use the following address for the company: 2300 East Ocean Blvd., Long Beach, CA 90802. Use 75-4444444 as the employer identification number. Date the return July 31, 2019. Mr. Fronke's phone number is 562-709-3654.

Analyze: Based on the entries that you have recorded, what is the balance of the ***Employee Income Tax Payable*** account at July 15?

◄ **Problem 11.4A**
Objectives 11-6, 11-7

Computing and recording unemployment taxes; completing Form 940.

Certain transactions and procedures relating to federal and state unemployment taxes follow for Fancy Nancy LLC, a retail store owned by Nancy Roberts. The firm's address is 2007 Trendsetter Lane, Dallas, TX 75268-0967. The firm's phone number is 972-456-1200. The employer's federal and state identification numbers are 75-9462315 and 37-9462315, respectively. Carry out the procedures as instructed in each of the following steps.

INSTRUCTIONS

1. Compute the state unemployment insurance tax owed on the employees' wages for the quarter ended March 31, 2019. This information will be shown on the employer's quarterly report to the state agency that collects SUTA tax. The employer has recorded the tax on each payroll date. Although the state charges a 5.4 percent unemployment tax rate, Fancy Nancy LLC's rate is only 1.7 percent because of its experience rating. The employee earnings for the first quarter are shown below. All earnings are subject to SUTA tax.

Name of Employee	Total Earnings
Terri Roma	$5,500
Jo Guyton	4,050
Gloria Dermudez	4,800
Susie Scott	5,600
Anita Thomas	4,550
Terri Wong	3,000
Total	$27,500

2. On April 30, 2019, the firm issued a check to the state employment commission for the amount computed above. In general journal form, record the issuance of the check. Use journal page 82.

Analyze: Why is the business experience rating important with regard to the state unemployment tax rate?

Problem 11.5A ►
Objectives 11-6, 11-7

CONTINUING >>> Problem

This is a continuation of Problem 11.4A for Fancy Nancy LLC; computing and recording unemployment taxes; completing Form 940.

1. Complete Form 940, the Employer's Annual Federal Unemployment Tax Return. Assume that all wages have been paid and that all quarterly payments have been submitted to the state as required. The payroll information for 2019 appears below. The federal tax deposits were submitted as follows: a deposit of $165.00 on April 21, a deposit of $76.80 on July 22, and a deposit of $52.20 on October 21. Date the unemployment tax return January 28, 2020. A check for the balance due as per line 14, Part 4, will be sent with Form 940.

Quarter Ended	Total Wages Paid	Wages Paid in Excess of $7,000	State Unemployment Tax Paid
Mar. 31	$ 27,500.00	–0–	$ 467.50
June 30	30,800.00	$18,000.00	217.60
Sept. 30	38,700.00	30,000.00	147.90
Dec. 31	49,000.00	45,000.00	68.00
Totals	$146,000.00	$93,000.00	$ 901.00

2. In general journal form, record issuance of a check on January 28, 2020, for the balance of FUTA tax due for 2019. Use journal page 15.

Analyze: What total debits were made to liability accounts for entries you recorded in Problem 11.4A and Problem 11.5A?

Problem 11.6A ►
Objective 11-8

Computing and recording workers' compensation insurance premiums.

The following information relates to Ponte Manufacturing Company's workers' compensation insurance premiums for 2019. On January 15, 2019, the company estimated its premium for workers' compensation insurance for the year on the basis of that data.

Work Classification	Amount of Estimated Wages	Insurance Rates
Office work	$ 64,000	$0.30/$100
Shop work	308,000	$6.00/$100

INSTRUCTIONS

1. Compute the estimated premiums.
2. Record in general journal form payment of the estimated premium on January 15, 2019. Use 8 as the page number.
3. On January 4, 2020, an audit of the firm's payroll records showed that it had actually paid wages of $69,960 to its office employees and wages of $315,320 to its shop employees. Compute the actual premium for the year and the balance due the insurance company or the credit due the firm.
4. Prepare the general journal entry on December 31, 2019, to adjust the ***Workers' Compensation Insurance Expense*** account. Use 98 as the page number.

Analyze: If all wages were attributable to shop employees, what premium estimate would have been calculated and recorded on January 15, 2019?

Problem Set B

Computing and recording employer's payroll tax expense.

◄ Problem 11.1B
Objectives 11-2, 11-6

The payroll register of Cliff's Auto Detailers showed total employee earnings of $4,000 for the week ended April 8, 2019.

INSTRUCTIONS

1. Compute the employer's payroll taxes for the period. The tax rates are as follows:

Social security	6.2 percent
Medicare	1.45
FUTA	0.6
SUTA	2.2

2. Prepare a general journal entry to record the employer's payroll taxes for the period. Use journal page 28.

Analyze: If the SUTA tax rate had been 1.2 percent, what total employer payroll taxes would have been recorded?

Computing employer's social security tax, Medicare tax, and unemployment taxes.

◄ Problem 11.2B
Objectives 11-2, 11-3

A payroll summary for Today's Teen owned by Nikki Davis, for the quarter ending September 30, 2019, appears below. The business made the following electronic deposits of payroll taxes:

a. August 15 for July taxes.

b. September 15 for August taxes.

Date Wages Paid		Total Earnings	Social Security Tax Withheld	Medicare Tax Withheld	Federal Income Tax Withheld
July	7	$ 2,000.00	$ 124.00	$ 29.00	$ 175.00
	14	2,000.00	124.00	29.00	175.00
	21	2,100.00	130.20	30.45	190.00
	28	1,980.00	122.76	28.71	160.00
		$ 8,080.00	$ 500.96	$117.16	$ 700.00
Aug.	4	$ 2,100.00	$ 130.20	$ 30.45	190.00
	11	2,400.00	148.80	34.80	210.00
	18	2,400.00	148.80	34.80	210.00
	25	2,600.00	161.20	37.70	230.00
		$ 9,500.00	$ 589.00	$137.75	$ 840.00
Sept.	2	$ 2,000.00	$ 124.00	$ 29.00	$ 175.00
	9	2,100.00	130.20	30.45	190.00
	16	2,100.00	130.20	30.45	190.00
	23	2,200.00	136.40	31.90	200.00
	30	1,900.00	117.80	27.55	160.00
		$10,300.00	$ 638.60	$149.35	$ 915.00
Totals		$27,880.00	$1,728.56	$404.26	$2,455.00

INSTRUCTIONS

1. Prepare the general journal entry on July 7, 2019, to record the employer's payroll tax expense on the payroll ending that date. Use journal page 31. All earnings are subject to the following taxes:

Social security	6.2 percent
Medicare	1.45
FUTA	0.6
SUTA	2.2

2. Make the entries in general journal form to record deposit of the employee income tax withheld and the social security and Medicare taxes (both employees' withholding and employer's matching portion) on August 15 for July taxes and on September 15 for the August taxes.

Analyze: How much would a SUTA rate of 1.5 percent reduce the tax for the payroll of July 7?

Problem 11.3B ▶ This is a continuation of Problem 11.2B for Today's Teen; recording payment of taxes and preparing employer's quarterly federal tax return.

Objectives 11-4, 11-6

CONTINUING >>> Problem

1. On October 15, the firm made a deposit through EFTPS for the federal income tax withheld and the FICA tax (both employees' withholding and employer's matching portion). Based on your computations in Problem 11.2B, record the issuance of the check in general journal form. Use journal page 31.
2. Complete Form 941 in accordance with the discussions in this chapter and the instructions on the form. Use a 12.4 percent social security rate and a 2.9 percent Medicare rate in computations. Use the following address for the company: 12001 Pioneer Blvd., Artesia, CA 90650. The firm's phone number is 562-860-5451. Use 75-5555555 as the employer identification number. Date the return October 31, 2019.

Analyze: What total taxes were deposited with the IRS for the quarter ended September 30, 2019?

Problem 11.4B ▶ Computing and recording unemployment taxes; completing Form 940.

Objectives 11-6, 11-7

Certain transactions and procedures relating to federal and state unemployment taxes are given below for AppMan Wizard, a retail store owned by John Marion. The firm's address is 4560 LBJ Freeway, Dallas, TX 75232-6002. The firm's phone number is 972-456-1201. The employer's federal and state identification numbers are 75-9999999 and 37-6789015, respectively. Carry out the procedures as instructed in each step.

INSTRUCTIONS

1. Compute the state unemployment insurance tax owed for the quarter ended March 31, 2019. This information will be shown on the employer's quarterly report to the state agency that collects SUTA tax. The employer has recorded the tax expense and liability on each payroll date. Although the state charges a 5.4 percent unemployment tax rate, AppMan Wizard has received a favorable experience rating and therefore pays only a 2.3 percent state tax rate. The employee earnings for the first quarter are given below. All earnings are subject to SUTA tax.

Name of Employee	Total Earnings
Brian Morris	$ 4,000
Stan Cantori	3,850
Cailey Marie	3,850
Yvonne Martinez	3,500
Court Caz	3,000
John Phan	3,000
Total	$21,200

2. On April 30, 2019, the firm issued a check for the amount computed above. Record the transaction in general journal form. Use journal page 21.

Analyze: If Brian Morris made the same amount for the quarter ended June 30, 2019, how much of his earnings would be subject to the federal unemployment tax?

This is a continuation of Problem 11.4B for AppMan Wizard; computing and recording unemployment taxes; completing Form 940.

◀ **Problem 11.5B**
Objectives 11-6, 11-7
CONTINUING >>> Problem

1. Complete Form 940, the Employer's Annual Federal Unemployment Tax Return. Assume that all wages have been paid and that all quarterly payments have been submitted to the state as required. The payroll information for 2019 appears below. The firm's FUTA tax liability by quarter follows: first quarter, \$127.20; second quarter, \$127.50; third quarter, \$72.00; and fourth quarter, \$12.00. The firm made no FUTA deposits in 2019. Date the unemployment tax return January 27, 2020. A check for the balance due will be sent with Form 940.

Quarter Ended	Total Wages Paid	Wages Paid in Excess of \$7,000	State Unemployment Tax Paid
Mar. 31	\$ 21,200.00	–0–	\$ 487.60
June 30	21,250.00	–0–	488.75
Sept. 30	24,500.00	\$12,500.00	276.00
Dec. 31	34,800.00	32,800.00	46.00
Totals	\$101,750.00	\$45,300.00	\$1,298.35

2. On January 27, 2020, the firm paid the amount shown on line 14, Part 4 of Form 940. In general journal form, record the payment. Use journal page 48.

Analyze: What is the balance of the ***Federal Unemployment Tax Payable*** account after paying the FUTA amount due on January 27, 2020?

Computing and recording premiums on workers' compensation insurance.

◀ **Problem 11.6B**
Objective 11-8

The following information is for Union Express Delivery Service's workers' compensation insurance premiums. On January 15, 2019, the company estimated its premium for workers' compensation insurance for the year on the basis of the following data:

Work Classification	Amount of Estimated Wages	Insurance Rates
Office work	\$ 50,000	\$0.50/\$100
Delivery work	308,000	\$6.00/\$100

INSTRUCTIONS

1. Use the information to compute the estimated premium for the year.
2. A check was issued to pay the estimated premium on January 17, 2019. Record the transaction in general journal form. Use 7 as the page number.
3. On January 19, 2020, an audit of the firm's payroll records showed that it had actually paid wages of \$52,970 to its office employees and wages of \$316,240 to its delivery employees. Compute the actual premium for the year and the balance due the insurance company or the credit due the firm.
4. Give the general journal entry to adjust the ***Workers' Compensation Insurance Expense*** account. Date the entry December 31, 2019. Use 88 as the page number.

Analyze: What is the balance of the ***Workers' Compensation Insurance Expense*** account at December 31, 2019, after all journal entries have been posted?

Critical Thinking Problem 11.1

Determining Employee Status

In each of the following independent situations, decide whether the business organization should treat the person being paid as an employee and should withhold social security, Medicare, and employee income taxes from the payment made.

1. Tiny Jacobs owns and operates a cigar shop as a sole proprietor. Jacobs withdraws $2,000 a week from the cigar shop.
2. Sam Brandon is a court reporter. He has an office at the Metro Court Reporting Center but pays no rent. The manager of the center receives requests from attorneys for court reporters to take depositions at legal hearings. The manager then chooses a court reporter who best meets the needs of the client and contacts the court reporter chosen. The court reporter has the right to refuse to take on the job, and the court reporter controls his or her working hours and days. Clients make payments to the center, which deducts a 25 percent fee for providing facilities and rendering services to support the court reporter. The balance is paid to the court reporter. During the current month, the center collected fees of $40,000 for Brandon, deducted $10,000 for the center's fee, and remitted the remainder to Brandon.
3. Ken, a registered nurse, has retired from full-time work. However, because of his experience and special skills, on each Monday, Wednesday, and Thursday afternoon he assists Dr. Grace Sue, a dermatologist. Ken is paid an hourly fee by Dr. Sue. During the current week, his hourly fees totaled $700.
4. After working several years as an editor for a trade magazine, Lisa quit her job to stay at home with her two small children. Later, the magazine asked her to work in her home performing editorial work as needed. Lisa is paid an hourly fee for the work she performs. In some cases, she goes to the company's offices to pick up or return a manuscript. In other cases the firm sends a manuscript to her, or she returns one by e-mail. During the current month, Lisa's hourly earnings totaled $1,500.
5. Investor Corporation carries on very little business activity. It merely holds land and certain assets. The board of directors has concluded that it needs no employees. It has decided instead to pay David John, one of the shareholders, a consulting fee of $12,000 per year to serve as president, secretary, and treasurer and to manage all the affairs of the company. John spends an average of one hour per week on the corporation's business affairs. However, his fee is fixed regardless of how few or how many hours he works.

Analyze: What characteristics do the persons you identified as "employees" have in common?

Critical Thinking Problem 11.2

Comparing Employees and Independent Contractors

The *Valley Voice* is a local newspaper that is published Monday through Friday. It sells 90,000 copies daily. The paper is currently in a profit squeeze, and the publisher, Tom Turkey, is looking for ways to reduce expenses.

A review of current distribution procedures reveals that the *Valley Voice* employs 100 truck drivers to drop off bundles of newspapers to 1,300 teenagers who deliver papers to individual homes. The drivers are paid an hourly wage while the teenagers receive 4 cents for each paper they deliver.

Turkey is considering an alternative method of distributing the papers, which he says has worked in other cities the size of Flower Mound (where the *Valley Voice* is published). Under the new system, the newspaper would retain 20 truck drivers to transport papers to five distribution centers around the city. The distribution centers are operated by independent contractors who would be responsible for making their own arrangements to deliver papers to subscribers' homes. The 20 drivers retained by the *Valley Voice* would receive the same hourly rate as they currently earn, and the independent contractors would receive 20 cents for each paper delivered.

1. What payroll information does Turkey need in order to make a decision about adopting the alternative distribution method?

2. Assume the following information:
   a. The average driver earns $42,000 per year.
   b. Average employee income tax withholding is 15 percent.
   c. The social security tax is 6.2 percent of the first $122,700 of earnings.
   d. The Medicare tax is 1.45 percent of all earnings.
   e. The state unemployment tax is 5 percent, and the federal unemployment tax is 0.6 percent of the first $7,000 of earnings.
   f. Workers' compensation insurance is 70 cents per $100 of wages.
   g. The paper pays $300 per month for health insurance for each driver and contributes $250 per month to each driver's pension plan.
   h. The paper has liability insurance coverage for all teenage carriers that costs $100,000 per year.

   Prepare a schedule showing the costs of distributing the newspapers under the current system and the proposed new system. Based on your analysis, which system would you recommend to Turkey?
3. What other factors, monetary and nonmonetary, might influence your decision?

BUSINESS CONNECTIONS

Payroll

Managerial | FOCUS

1. Carolina Company recently discovered that a payroll clerk had issued checks to nonexistent employees for several years and cashed the checks himself. The firm does not have any internal control procedures for its payroll operations. What specific controls might have led to the discovery of this fraud more quickly or discouraged the payroll clerk from even attempting the fraud?
2. Johnson Company has 20 employees. Some employees work in the office, others in the warehouse, and still others in the retail store. In the company's records, all employees are simply referred to as "general employees." Explain to management why this is not an acceptable practice.
3. Why should management be concerned about the accuracy and promptness of payroll tax deposits and payroll tax returns?
4. What is the significance to management of the experience rating system used to determine the employer's tax under the state unemployment insurance laws?

Ghost Employee

Ethical | DILEMMA

Johan Jordan owns a dress shop that has been very successful. He employs 3 sales associates who get paid $10 per hour for a 40-hour week. He decides to open up another dress shop on the other side of town. He hires three more sales associates with the same pay arrangements. After three months, Johan notices he is not making the same profit he did. His sales have doubled and his expenses are the same proportion except for wages. He knows that each sales associate should receive $1,720 each month, yet his total wages expense for the month is $12,040. He worries that he is not paying close enough attention to the old store. What is his problem? Should he discuss this problem with all the sales associates?

Employee Data

Financial Statement ANALYSIS

Home Depot

The Home Depot, Inc. reported the following data in its Form 10-K filing *(for the fiscal year ended January 31, 2016)*:

Number of employees at January 31, 2016	385,000
Contributions to employees' retirement plans during the year ended January 31, 2016	$186 million

Analyze: Assume all employees receive contributions to their retirement plan. What was the average retirement plan contribution made by The Home Depot for full-time employees?

TEAMWORK

Determining Information

Wages and payroll tax expense are the largest cost that a company incurs. At times, a company has a problem paying wages and cash deposits for payroll taxes. Your company has a cash flow problem. In a group of four employees, brainstorm ways to cut the costs of wages and payroll taxes.

Internet | CONNECTION

Internal Revenue Service

Go to the Internal Revenue website at www.irs.gov. Does the website contain the necessary federal forms? Can you use these forms to submit your report? What reports must be obtained from the IRS in an original, not downloaded, form?

Answers to **Self Reviews**

Answers to Section 1 Self Review

1. Form W-2 provides information to enable the employees to complete their federal income tax return. Copies are given to the employee and to the federal government (and to other governmental units that levy an income tax).
2. The preferred method of depositing payroll taxes is through the EFTPS (Electronic Federal Tax Payment System.
3. Form 941 shows income taxes withheld, social security and Medicare taxes due for the quarter, and tax deposits. The form is due on the last day of the month following the end of the quarter.
4. **c.** social security tax
5. **a.** each payroll period
6. Monthly

Answers to Section 2 Self Review

1. The amount of the premium depends on the type of work the employee performs.
2. The employer pays FUTA. Usually the employer pays SUTA, although a few states also levy SUTA on employees.
3. It reduces the rate of SUTA tax that must actually be paid.
4. **b.** quarterly
5. **d.** Form 940
6. Expenses will be understated. Net income will be overstated.

Answers to Comprehensive Self Review

1. Form W-3 is sent to the Social Security Administration. It reports the total social security wages; total Medicare wages; total social security and Medicare taxes withheld; total wages, tips, and other compensation; total employee income tax withheld; and other information.
2. Smaller
3. A credit, with limits, is allowed against the federal tax for unemployment tax charged by the state.
4. By the 15th day of the following month.
5. **b.** Amount of taxes reported in the lookback period

   d. Amount of taxes currently owed

Accruals, Deferrals, and the Worksheet

Chapter **12**

www.starbucks.com

© McGraw-Hill Education/Jill Braaten

The mission of Starbucks is to inspire and nurture the human spirit—one person, one cup, and one neighborhood at a time. Starting out as a single storefront opened in 1971 in Seattle, Washington, it has expanded to 23,043 stores across 68 countries over just a mere 44 years. Starbucks opened 1,677 new stores in fiscal year 2015 alone and served over 72 million more customers in fiscal 2015 over the prior year.

From its start as a roaster and retailer of coffee, tea, and spices, Starbucks' product offerings have expanded to include more than 30 blends of coffee, handcrafted beverages, coffee- and tea-brewing equipment, mugs, packaged edibles, books, and more. Starbucks' beverages and merchandise are also sold at other retail establishments, such as grocery stores.

Starbucks offers a staple menu of coffee and tea beverages year round, as well as a seasonal menu that it continually updates, in addition to developing new flavors and products to offer variety to existing customers and to appeal to new customers. For fiscal year 2015, Starbucks reported net revenues of $19.2 billion, an increase of 17 percent over fiscal year 2014.

With increasing sales and ever-expanding distribution channels, managing inventory levels and purchasing requirements is crucial. Starbucks must order merchandise with enough lead time to have it in stores ahead of demand. At the same time, it must closely monitor in-store inventory levels so as to not have excess inventory and still have the ability to stock new incoming products.

thinking critically

What types of inventory issues do you think Starbucks reflects upon at the end of each year?

LEARNING OBJECTIVES

12-1 Determine the adjustment for merchandise inventory, and enter the adjustment on the worksheet.

12-2 Compute adjustments for accrued and prepaid expense items, and enter the adjustments on the worksheet.

12-3 Compute adjustments for accrued and deferred income items, and enter the adjustments on the worksheet.

12-4 Complete a 10-column worksheet.

12-5 Define the accounting terms new to this chapter.

NEW TERMS

- accrual basis
- accrued expenses
- accrued income
- deferred expenses
- deferred income
- inventory sheet
- net income line
- property, plant, and equipment
- unearned income
- updated account balances

Section 1

SECTION OBJECTIVES	TERMS TO LEARN
>> 12-1 Determine the adjustment for merchandise inventory, and enter the adjustment on the worksheet. **WHY IT'S IMPORTANT** **The change in merchandise inventory affects the financial statements.** >> 12-2 Compute adjustments for accrued and prepaid expense items, and enter the adjustments on the worksheet. **WHY IT'S IMPORTANT** **Each expense item needs to be assigned to the accounting period in which it helped to earn revenue.** >> 12-3 Compute adjustments for accrued and deferred income items, and enter the adjustments on the worksheet. **WHY IT'S IMPORTANT** **The accrual basis of accounting states that income is recognized in the period it is earned.**	accrual basis accrued expenses accrued income deferred expenses deferred income inventory sheet property, plant, and equipment unearned income

Calculating and Recording Adjustments

In Chapter 5, you learned how to make adjustments so that all revenue and expenses that apply to a fiscal period appear on the income statement for that period. In this chapter, you will learn more about adjustments and how they affect Whiteside Antiques, a retail merchandising business owned by Bill Whiteside.

The Accrual Basis of Accounting

Financial statements usually are prepared using the **accrual basis** of accounting because it most nearly attains the goal of matching expenses and revenue in an accounting period.

- *Revenue is recognized when earned, not necessarily when the cash is received.* Revenue is recognized when the sale is complete. A sale is complete when title to the goods passes to the customer or when the service is provided. For sales on account, revenue is recognized when the sale occurs even though the cash is not collected immediately.
- *Expenses are recognized when incurred or used, not necessarily when cash is paid.* Each expense is assigned to the accounting period in which it helped to earn revenue for the business, even if cash is not paid at that time. This is often referred to as *matching revenues and expenses.*

Sometimes cash changes hands before the revenue or expense is recognized. For example, insurance premiums are normally paid in advance, and the coverage extends over several accounting periods. In other cases, cash changes hands after the revenue or expense has been recognized. For example, employees might work during December but be paid in January of the following year. Because of these timing differences, adjustments are made to ensure that revenue and expenses are recognized in the appropriate period.

Using the Worksheet to Record Adjustments

The worksheet is used to assemble data about adjustments and to organize the information for the financial statements. The worksheet for Whiteside Antiques will be prepared in the same manner as covered in Chapter 5. Figure 12.1 shows the first two sections of the worksheet for Whiteside Antiques. Let's review how to prepare the worksheet:

- Enter the trial balance in the Trial Balance section. Total the columns. Be sure that total debits equal total credits.
- Enter the adjustments in the Adjustments section. Use the same letter to identify the debit part and the credit part of each adjustment. Total the columns. Be sure that total debits equal total credits.
- For each account, combine the amounts in the Trial Balance section and the Adjustments section. Enter the results in the Adjusted Trial Balance section, total the columns, and make sure that total debits equal total credits.
- Extend account balances to the Income Statement and Balance Sheet sections and complete the worksheet.

important!

Recognize

The word "recognize" means to record in the accounting records.

ADJUSTMENT FOR MERCHANDISE INVENTORY

>> 12-1 OBJECTIVE

Determine the adjustment for merchandise inventory, and enter the adjustment on the worksheet.

Merchandise inventory consists of the goods that a business has on hand for sale to customers. An asset account for merchandise inventory is maintained in the general ledger. During the accounting period, all purchases of merchandise are debited to the ***Purchases*** account. All sales of merchandise are credited to the revenue account ***Sales.***

Notice that no entries are made directly to the ***Merchandise Inventory*** account during the accounting period. Consequently, when the trial balance is prepared at the end of the period, the ***Merchandise Inventory*** account still shows the *beginning* inventory for the period.

At the end of each period, a business determines the *ending* balance of the ***Merchandise Inventory*** account. The first step in determining the ending inventory is to count the number of units of each type of item on hand. As the merchandise is counted, the quantity on hand is entered on an inventory sheet. The **inventory sheet** lists the quantity of each type of goods a firm has in stock. This process is called a physical inventory. For each item, the quantity is multiplied by the unit cost to find the totals per item. The totals for all items are added to compute the total cost of merchandise inventory.

The trial balance for Whiteside Antiques shows ***Merchandise Inventory*** of $52,000. Based on a count taken on December 31, merchandise inventory at the end of the year actually totaled $47,000. Whiteside Antiques needs to adjust the ***Merchandise Inventory*** account to reflect the balance at the end of the year.

The adjustment is made in two steps, using the accounts ***Merchandise Inventory*** and ***Income Summary.***

recall

Income Summary

The ***Income Summary*** account is a temporary owner's equity account used in the closing process.

1. The beginning inventory ($52,000) is taken off the books by transferring the account balance to the ***Income Summary*** account. This entry is labeled **(a)** on the worksheet in Figure 12.1 and is illustrated in T-account form below.

Merchandise Inventory			
Bal.	52,000	Adj.	52,000 (a)

Income Summary			
Adj.	(a) 52,000		

2. The ending inventory ($47,000) is placed on the books by debiting ***Merchandise Inventory*** and crediting ***Income Summary.*** This entry is labeled **(b)** on the worksheet in Figure 12.1.

Merchandise Inventory			
Bal.	52,000	Adj.	52,000 (a)
Adj.	47,000 (b)		

Income Summary			
Adj.	(a) 52,000	Adj.	(b) 47,000

FIGURE 12.1 10-Column Worksheet—Partial

Whiteside Antiques
Worksheet
Year Ended December 31, 2019

	ACCOUNT NAME	TRIAL BALANCE DEBIT	TRIAL BALANCE CREDIT	ADJUSTMENTS DEBIT	ADJUSTMENTS CREDIT
1	*Cash*	13,136.00			
2	*Petty Cash Fund*	100.00			
3	*Notes Receivable*	1,200.00			
4	*Accounts Receivable*	32,000.00			
5	*Allowance for Doubtful Accounts*		250.00		(c) 800.00
6	*Interest Receivable*			(m) 30.00	
7	*Merchandise Inventory*	52,000.00		(b) 47,000.00	(a) 52,000.00
8	*Prepaid Insurance*	7,350.00			(k) 2,450.00
9	*Prepaid Interest*	225.00			(l) 150.00
10	*Supplies*	6,300.00			(j) 4,975.00
11	*Store Equipment*	30,000.00			
12	*Accumulated Depreciation—Store Equipment*				(d) 2,400.00
13	*Office Equipment*	5,000.00			
14	*Accumulated Depreciation—Office Equipment*				(e) 700.00
15	*Notes Payable—Trade*		2,000.00		
16	*Notes Payable—Bank*		9,000.00		
17	*Accounts Payable*		24,129.00		
18	*Interest Payable*				(i) 20.00
19	*Social Security Tax Payable*		1,084.00		(g) 74.40
20	*Medicare Tax Payable*		250.00		(g) 17.40
21	*Employee Income Taxes Payable*		990.00		
22	*Federal Unemployment Tax Payable*				(h) 7.20
23	*State Unemployment Tax Payable*				(h) 64.80
24	*Salaries Payable*				(f) 1,200.00
25	*Sales Tax Payable*		7,200.00		
26	*Bill Whiteside, Capital*		61,221.00		
27	*Bill Whiteside, Drawing*	27,600.00			
28	*Income Summary*			(a) 52,000.00	(b) 47,000.00
29	*Sales*		561,650.00		
30	*Sales Returns and Allowances*	12,500.00			
31	*Interest Income*		136.00		(m) 30.00
32	*Miscellaneous Income*		366.00		
33	*Purchases*	321,500.00			
34	*Freight In*	9,800.00			
35	*Purchases Returns and Allowances*		3,050.00		
36	*Purchases Discounts*		3,130.00		
37	*Salaries Expense—Sales*	78,490.00		(f) 1,200.00	
38	*Advertising Expense*	7,425.00			
39	*Cash Short or Over*	125.00			
40	*Supplies Expense*			(j) 4,975.00	

FIGURE 12.1 (continued)

	ACCOUNT NAME	TRIAL BALANCE DEBIT	TRIAL BALANCE CREDIT	ADJUSTMENTS DEBIT		ADJUSTMENTS CREDIT
41	*Depreciation Expense—Store Equipment*			*(d)*	2,400.00	
42	*Rent Expense*	27,600.00				
43	*Salaries Expense—Office*	26,500.00				
44	*Insurance Expense*			*(k)*	2,450.00	
45	*Payroll Taxes Expense*	7,205.00		*(g)*	91.80	
46				*(h)*	72.00	
47	*Telephone Expense*	1,875.00				
48	*Uncollectible Accounts Expense*			*(c)*	800.00	
49	*Utilities Expense*	5,925.00				
50	*Depreciation Expense—Office Equipment*			*(e)*	700.00	
51	*Interest Expense*	600.00		*(i)*	20.00	
52				*(l)*	150.00	
53	*Totals*	674,456.00	674,456.00		111,888.80	111,888.80

The effect of this adjustment is to remove the beginning merchandise inventory balance and replace it with the ending merchandise inventory balance. Merchandise inventory is adjusted in two steps on the worksheet because both the beginning and the ending inventory figures appear on the income statement, which is prepared directly from the worksheet.

The merchandise inventory adjustment is not necessary if the perpetual inventory system is used.

ADJUSTMENT FOR LOSS FROM UNCOLLECTIBLE ACCOUNTS

>> 12-2 OBJECTIVE

Compute adjustments for accrued and prepaid expense items, and enter the adjustments on the worksheet.

Credit sales are made with the expectation that the customers will pay the amount due later. Sometimes the account receivable is never collected. Losses from uncollectible accounts are classified as operating expenses.

Under accrual accounting, the expense for uncollectible accounts is recorded in the same period as the related sale. The expense is estimated because the actual amount of uncollectible accounts is not known until later periods. To match the expense for uncollectible accounts with the sales revenue for the same period, the estimated expense is debited to an account named ***Uncollectible Accounts Expense.***

Several methods exist for estimating the expense for uncollectible accounts. Whiteside Antiques uses the *percentage of net credit sales* method. The rate used is based on the company's past experience with uncollectible accounts and management's assessment of current business conditions. Whiteside Antiques estimates that four-fifths of 1 percent (0.80 percent) of net credit sales will be uncollectible. Net credit sales for the year were $100,000. The estimated expense for uncollectible accounts is $800 ($100,000 × 0.0080).

The entry to record the expense for uncollectible accounts includes a credit to a contra asset account, ***Allowance for Doubtful Accounts.*** This account appears on the balance sheet as follows:

Accounts Receivable	$32,000
Allowance for Doubtful Accounts ($800 + $250)	1,050
Net Accounts Receivable	$30,950

THE BOTTOM LINE

Uncollectible Accounts Expense

Income Statement

Expenses	↑ 800
Net Income	↓ 800

Balance Sheet

Assets	↓ 800
Equity	↓ 800

Adjustment **(c)** appears on the worksheet in Figure 12.1 for the expense for uncollectible accounts.

Uncollectible Accounts Expense	
Adj. 800	

Allowance for Doubtful Accounts	
	Bal. 250
	Adj. 800

(c)

When a specific account becomes uncollectible, it is written off:

- The entry is a debit to ***Allowance for Doubtful Accounts*** and a credit to ***Accounts Receivable.***
- The customer's account in the accounts receivable subsidiary ledger is also reduced.

Uncollectible Accounts Expense is not affected by the write-off of individual accounts identified as uncollectible. It is used only when the end-of-period adjustment is recorded.

Notice that net income is decreased at the end of the period when the adjustment for *estimated* expense for uncollectible accounts is made. When a specific customer account is written off, net income is *not* affected. The write-off of a specific account affects only the balance sheet accounts ***Accounts Receivable*** (asset) and ***Allowance for Doubtful Accounts*** (contra asset).

The balance of ***Allowance for Doubtful Accounts*** is reduced throughout the year as customer accounts are written off. Notice that ***Allowance for Doubtful Accounts*** already has a credit balance of $250 in the Trial Balance section of the worksheet. When the estimate of uncollectible accounts expense is based on sales, any remaining balance from previous periods is not considered when recording the adjustment.

ADJUSTMENTS FOR DEPRECIATION

Most businesses have long-term assets that are used in the operation of the business. These are often referred to as **property, plant, and equipment.** Property, plant, and equipment includes buildings, trucks, automobiles, machinery, furniture, fixtures, office equipment, and land.

Property, plant, and equipment costs are not charged to expense accounts when purchased. Instead, the cost of a long-term asset is allocated over the asset's expected useful life by depreciation. This process involves the gradual transfer of acquisition cost to expense. This concept was first introduced in Chapter 5. There is one exception. Land is not depreciated.

There are many ways to calculate depreciation. Whiteside Antiques uses the straight-line method, so an equal amount of depreciation is taken in each year of the asset's useful life. The formula for straight-line depreciation is:

$$\frac{\text{Cost} - \text{Salvage value}}{\text{Estimated useful life}} = \text{Depreciation}$$

Salvage value is an estimate of the amount that could be obtained from the sale or disposition of an asset at the end of its useful life. Cost minus salvage value is called the *depreciable base.*

Depreciation of Store Equipment The trial balance shows that Whiteside Antiques has $30,000 of store equipment. Estimated salvage value is $6,000. What is the amount of annual depreciation expense using the straight-line method?

Cost of store equipment	$30,000
Salvage value	(6,000)
Depreciable base	$24,000
Estimated useful life	10 years

$$\frac{\$30,000 - \$6,000}{10 \text{ years}} = \$2,400 \text{ per year}$$

The annual depreciation expense is $2,400. Adjustment **(d)** appears on the worksheet in Figure 12.1 for the depreciation expense for store equipment.

Depr. Expense—Store Equipment	
Adj. 2,400	

Accum. Depr.—Store Equipment	
	Adj. 2,400

(d)

Depreciation of Office Equipment Whiteside Antiques reports $5,000 of office equipment on the trial balance. What is the amount of annual depreciation expense using the straight-line method if estimated salvage value is $800 and estimated life is 6 years?

Cost of office equipment	$5,000
Salvage value	(800)
Depreciable base	$4,200
Estimated useful life	6 years

$$\frac{\$5{,}000 - \$800}{6 \text{ years}} = \$700 \text{ per year}$$

Annual depreciation expense is $700. Adjustment **(e)** appears on the worksheet in Figure 12.1 for depreciation expense for office equipment.

Depr. Expense—Office Equipment	
Adj. 700	

Accum. Depr.—Office Equipment	
	Adj. 700

(e)

As discussed in Chapter 5, ***Accumulated Depreciation*** is a contra asset account. It has a normal credit balance, which is opposite the normal balance of an asset account.

Most companies do not purchase items of property, plant, or equipment at the beginning of the year, but as needed. In this case, a partial year of depreciation must be calculated and recorded.

For example, assume a company purchased store equipment for $30,000 on October 1, 2019. The store equipment has a useful life of 10 years and an estimated salvage value of $6,000. The depreciation expense for the year ended December 31, 2019, for the store equipment is $600, calculated as follows.

important!

Depreciation

To calculate monthly straight-line depreciation, divide the depreciable base by the number of months in the useful life.

Cost of store equipment	$30,000
Salvage value	(6,000)
Depreciable base	$24,000
Divided by useful life, in months (10 years × 12)	120
Depreciation per month	$ 200
Multiplied by months used in 2019 (Oct., Nov., Dec.)	3
Depreciation for 2019	$ 600

ADJUSTMENTS FOR ACCRUED EXPENSES

Many expense items are paid for, recorded, and used in the same accounting period. However, some expense items are paid for and recorded in one period but used in a later period. Other expense items are used in one period and paid for in a later period. In these situations, adjustments are made so that the financial statements show all expenses in the appropriate period.

Accrued expenses are expenses that relate to (are used in) the current period but have not yet been paid and do not yet appear in the accounting records. Whiteside Antiques makes adjustments for three types of accrued expenses:

- accrued salaries
- accrued payroll taxes
- accrued interest on notes payable

Because accrued expenses involve amounts that must be paid in the future, the adjustment for each item is a debit to an expense account and a credit to a liability account.

Accrued Salaries At Whiteside Antiques, all full-time sales and office employees are paid semimonthly—on the 15th and the last day of the month. The trial balance in Figure 12.1 shows the correct salaries expense for the full-time employees for the year. From December 28 to January 3, the firm hired several part-time sales clerks for the year-end sale. Through December 31, 2019, these employees earned $1,200. The part-time salaries expense has not yet been recorded because the employees will not be paid until January 3, 2020. An adjustment is made to record the amount owed, but not yet paid, as of the end of December.

Adjustment **(f)** appears on the worksheet in Figure 12.1 for accrued salaries.

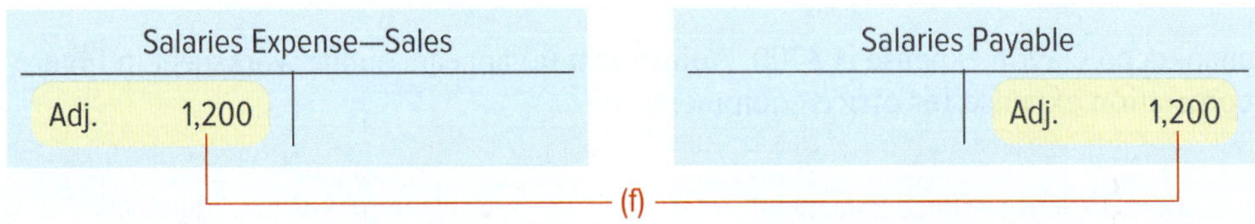

Accrued Payroll Taxes Payroll taxes are not legally owed until the salaries are paid. Businesses that want to match revenue and expenses in the appropriate period make adjustments to accrue the employer's payroll taxes even though the taxes are technically not yet due. Whiteside Antiques makes adjustments for accrued employer's payroll taxes.

important!

Matching

Adjustments for accrued expenses match the expense to the period in which the expense took place.

The payroll taxes related to the full-time employees of Whiteside Antiques have been recorded and appear on the trial balance. However, the payroll taxes for the part-time sales clerks have not been recorded. None of the part-time clerks have reached the social security wage base limit. The entire $1,200 of accrued salaries is subject to the employer's share of social security and Medicare taxes. The accrued employer's payroll taxes are:

Social security tax	$1,200	×	0.0620	=	$74.40
Medicare tax	$1,200	×	0.0145	=	17.40
Total accrued payroll taxes					$91.80

Adjustment **(g)** appears on the worksheet in Figure 12.1 for accrued payroll taxes.

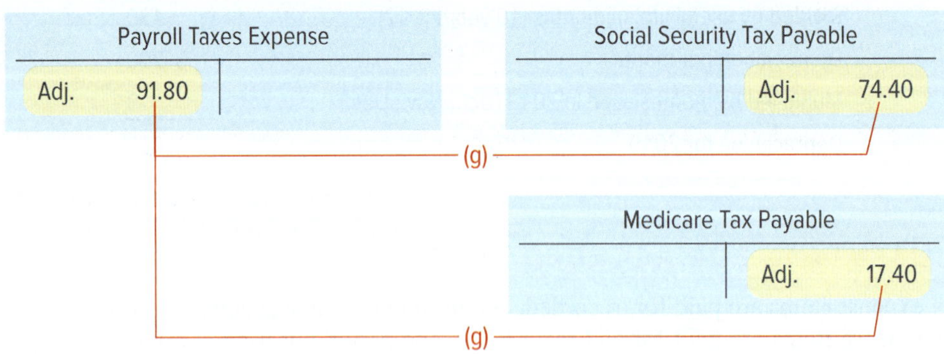

The entire $1,200 of accrued salaries is also subject to unemployment taxes. The unemployment tax rates for Whiteside Antiques are 0.6 percent for federal and 5.4 percent for state.

Federal unemployment tax	$1,200	×	0.006	=	$ 7.20
State unemployment tax	$1,200	×	0.054	=	64.80
Total accrued taxes					$72.00

Adjustment **(h)** appears on the worksheet in Figure 12.1 for accrued unemployment taxes.

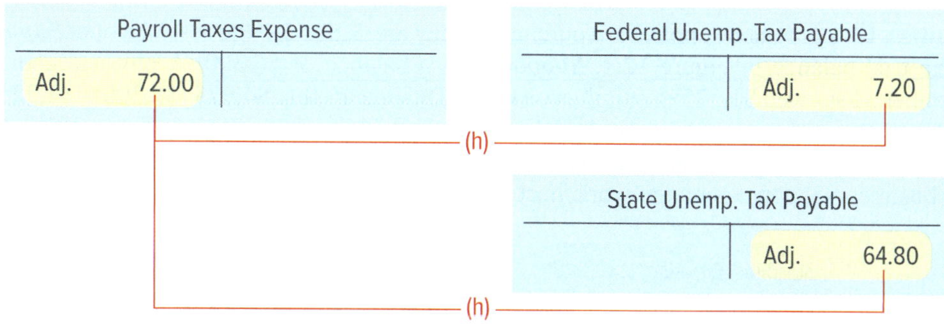

Accrued Interest on Notes Payable On December 1, 2019, Whiteside Antiques issued a two-month note for $2,000, with annual interest of 12 percent. The note was recorded in the ***Notes Payable—Trade*** account. Whiteside Antiques will pay the interest when the note matures on February 1, 2020. However, the interest expense is incurred day by day and should be allocated to each fiscal period involved in order to obtain a complete and accurate picture of expenses. The accrued interest amount is determined by using the interest formula Principal × Rate × Time.

Principal	×	**Rate**	×	**Time**		
$2,000	×	0.12	×	1/12	=	$20

The fraction 1/12 represents one month, which is 1/12 of a year.

Adjustment **(i)** appears on the worksheet in Figure 12.1 for the accrued interest expense.

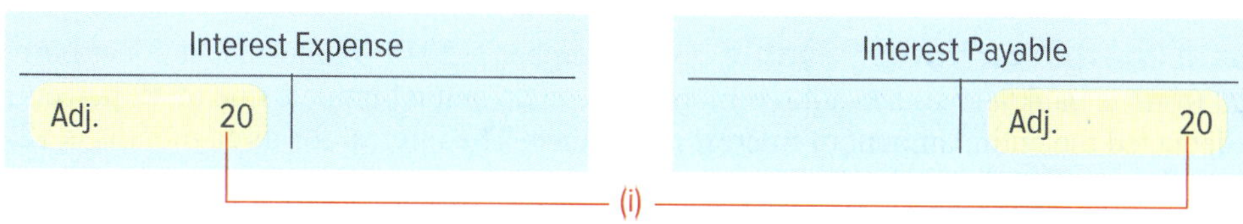

Other Accrued Expenses Most businesses pay property taxes to state and local governments. They accrue these taxes at the end of the accounting period. Adjustments might also be necessary for commissions, professional services, and many other accrued expenses.

> In its December 31, 2014, balance sheet, JetBlue Airways Corporation reported the following current liabilities (all in millions of dollars): Accounts payable, $208; Air traffic liability, $973; Accrued salaries, wages, and benefits, $203; Other accrued liabilities, $287; and Current maturities of long-term debt and capital leases, $265.

ADJUSTMENTS FOR PREPAID EXPENSES

Prepaid expenses, or **deferred expenses**, are expenses that are paid for and recorded before they are used. Often a portion of a prepaid item remains unused at the end of the period; it is applicable to future periods. When paid for, these items are recorded as assets. At the end of the period, an adjustment is made to recognize as an expense the portion used during the period. Whiteside Antiques makes adjustments for three types of prepaid expenses:

- prepaid supplies
- prepaid insurance
- prepaid interest on notes payable

The adjusting entries for supplies used and insurance expired were introduced in Chapter 5. The adjusting entry for prepaid interest on notes payable is new to this chapter.

Supplies Used When supplies are purchased, they are debited to the asset account ***Supplies.*** On the trial balance in Figure 12.1, ***Supplies*** has a balance of $6,300. A physical count on December 31 showed $1,325 of supplies on hand. This means that $4,975 ($6,300 – $1,325) of supplies were used during the year. An adjustment is made to charge the cost of supplies used to the current year's operations and to reflect the value of the supplies on hand.

Adjustment **(j)** appears on the worksheet in Figure 12.1 for supplies expense.

Supplies Expense			
Adj.	4,975		

Supplies			
Bal.	6,300	Adj.	4,975

(j)

Expired Insurance On January 2, 2019, Whiteside Antiques wrote a check for $7,350 for a three-year insurance policy. The asset account ***Prepaid Insurance*** was debited for $7,350. On December 31, 2019, one year of insurance had expired. An adjustment for $2,450 ($7,350 × 1/3) was made to charge the cost of the expired insurance to operations and to decrease ***Prepaid Insurance*** to reflect the prepaid insurance premium that remains.

Adjustment **(k)** appears on the worksheet in Figure 12.1 for the insurance.

Insurance Expense			
Adj.	2,450		

Prepaid Insurance			
Bal.	7,350	Adj.	2,450

(k)

Prepaid Interest on Notes Payable On November 1, 2019, Whiteside Antiques borrowed $9,000 from its bank and signed a three-month note at an annual interest rate of 10 percent. The bank deducted the entire amount of interest in advance. The interest for three months is $225.

Principal	×	**Rate**	×	**Time**		
$9,000	×	0.10	×	3/12	=	$225

Whiteside Antiques received $8,775 ($9,000 – $225). The transaction was recorded as a debit to ***Cash*** for $8,775, a debit to ***Prepaid Interest*** for $225, and a credit to ***Notes Payable—Bank*** for $9,000.

important!

Some assets and liabilities always require adjustments

Although prepaid expenses are usually charged to an asset account when they are paid, some businesses charge most prepayments to expense. In either case, at the time financial statements are prepared, the accounts must be adjusted to show the correct expense and prepayment.

On December 31, two months of prepaid interest ($225 × 2/3 = $150) had been incurred and needed to be recorded as an expense. The adjustment consists of a debit to ***Interest Expense*** and a credit to ***Prepaid Interest.***

Adjustment **(l)** appears on the worksheet in Figure 12.1 for the interest expense.

Interest Expense			
Adj.	150		

Prepaid Interest			
Bal.	225	Adj.	150

(l)

Other Prepaid Expenses Other common prepaid expenses are prepaid rent, prepaid advertising, and prepaid taxes. When paid, the amounts are debited to the asset accounts ***Prepaid Rent, Prepaid Advertising,*** and ***Prepaid Taxes.*** At the end of each period, an adjustment is made to transfer the portion used from the asset account to an expense account. For example, the adjustment for expired rent would be a debit to ***Rent Expense*** and a credit to ***Prepaid Rent.***

Alternative Method Some businesses use a different method for prepaid expenses. At the time cash is paid, they debit an expense account (not an asset account). At the end of each period, they make an adjustment to transfer the portion that is not used from the expense account to an asset account.

Suppose that Whiteside used this alternative method when purchasing the two-year insurance policy. On January 1, 2019, the transaction would have been recorded as a debit to ***Insurance Expense*** for $7,350 and a credit to ***Cash*** for $7,350. On December 31, 2019, after the insurance coverage for one year had expired, coverage for two years remained. The adjustment would be recorded as a debit to ***Prepaid Insurance*** for $4,900 ($7,350 × 2/3) and a credit to ***Insurance Expense*** for $4,900.

Identical amounts appear on the financial statements at the end of each fiscal period, no matter which method is used to handle prepaid expenses.

ADJUSTMENTS FOR ACCRUED INCOME

>> 12-3 OBJECTIVE

Compute adjustments for accrued and deferred income items, and enter the adjustments on the worksheet.

Accrued income is income that has been earned but not yet received and recorded. On December 31, 2019, Whiteside Antiques had accrued interest on notes receivable.

Accrued Interest on Notes Receivable Interest-bearing notes receivable are recorded at face value and are carried in the accounting records at this value until they are collected. The interest income is recorded when it is received, which is normally when the note matures. However, interest income is earned day by day. At the end of the period, an adjustment is made to recognize interest income earned but not yet received or recorded.

On November 1, 2019, Whiteside Antiques accepted a four-month, 15 percent note for $1,200 from a customer. The note and interest are due on March 1, 2020. As of December 31, 2019, interest income for two months (November and December) was earned but not received. The amount of earned interest income is $30.

Principal	×	Rate	×	Time		
$1,200	×	0.15	×	2/12	=	$30

Adjustment **(m)** appears on the worksheet in Figure 12.1 for the interest income. To record the interest income of $30 earned, but not yet received, an adjustment debiting the asset account ***Interest Receivable*** and crediting a revenue account called ***Interest Income*** is made.

Interest Receivable

Debit		Credit	
Adj.	30		

Interest Income

Debit		Credit	
		Bal.	136
		Adj.	30

(m)

ADJUSTMENTS FOR UNEARNED INCOME

Unearned income, or **deferred income**, exists when cash is received before income is earned. Under the accrual basis of accounting, only income that has been earned appears on the income statement. Whiteside Antiques has no unearned income. The following is an example of unearned income for another business.

Unearned Subscription Income for a Publisher Magazine publishers receive cash in advance for subscriptions. When the publisher receives the cash, it is unearned income and is a liability. It is a liability because the publisher has an obligation to provide magazines during the subscription period. As the magazines are sent to the subscribers, income is earned and the liability decreases.

Tech Publishing Corporation publishes *Consumer Technology Today*. When subscriptions are received, ***Cash*** is debited and ***Unearned Subscription Income,*** a liability account, is credited. At the end of the year, ***Unearned Subscription Income*** had a balance of $450,000. During the year, $184,000 of magazines were delivered; income was earned in the amount of $184,000. The adjustment to recognize income is a debit to ***Unearned Subscription Income*** for $184,000 and a credit to ***Subscription Income*** for $184,000.

After the adjustment, the ***Unearned Subscription Income*** account has a balance of $266,000, which represents subscriptions for future periods.

recall

Two Ways to Record Transactions

Earlier in this chapter you learned that prepaid expenses are usually charged to an asset account when paid, but may be charged to an expense account at that time. Likewise, unearned income is usually credited to a liability account when received, but may be credited to an income account. Be sure to understand how the transaction was originally entered before you begin making the adjusting entry.

Unearned Subscription Income

12/31 Adj.	184,000	12/31 Bal.	450,000
		12/31 Bal.	266,000

Other Unearned Income Items Other types of unearned income include management fees, rental income, legal fees, architectural fees, construction fees, and advertising income. The cash received in advance is recorded as unearned income. As the income is earned, the amount is transferred from the liability account to a revenue account.

Alternative Method Some businesses use a different method to handle unearned income. At the time the cash is received, a credit is made to a revenue account (not a liability account). At the end of each period, the adjustment transfers the portion that is not earned to a liability account. For example, suppose Tech Publishing Corporation uses this method. When cash for subscriptions is received, it is credited to ***Subscription Income.*** At the end of the period, an adjustment is made to transfer the unearned income to a liability account. The entry is a debit to ***Subscription Income*** and a credit to ***Unearned Subscription Income.***

Identical amounts appear on the financial statements at the end of each fiscal period no matter which method is used to handle unearned income.

Section 1 Self Review

QUESTIONS

1. Why is a 10-column worksheet used as part of the procedures for adjusting and closing accounts and preparing financial statements?
2. Why are there two amounts (a debit and a credit) in the adjustments column on the line for Merchandise Inventory in the 10-column worksheet?
3. Why are adjusting entries necessary?

EXERCISES

4. In Caymus Company's December 31 trial balance, a credit balance of $31,500 appears in Unearned Fee Income. This amount represents cash received from a customer on November 1 covering work to be performed by Caymus in November through January. At December 31, Caymus had earned $10,500 of the amount received on November 1. What account will be debited and what account will be credited in the adjusting entry on December 31? What is the amount of the adjustment?
5. Caymus Company adjusts and closes its accounts and prepares financial statements each month. In the December 31 Trial Balance column for debit balances, a balance of $9,000 is found in the *Prepaid Rent* account. A payment of $18,000 for prepayment of six months' rent was made on September 1.
   a. What is the amount of the adjusting entry for this item?
   b. What account would be debited and what account would be credited in the December 31 adjustments?

ANALYSIS

6. Your company prepares financial statements each month, using a 10-column worksheet to assemble data. What is the primary difference between the adjustments made on a monthly basis and those made on an annual basis?

(Answers to Section 1 Self Review are on page 453.)

Section 2

SECTION OBJECTIVES	TERMS TO LEARN
>> 12-4 Complete a 10-column worksheet. WHY IT'S IMPORTANT Using the worksheet is a convenient way to gather the information needed for the financial statements.	net income line updated account balances

Completing the Worksheet

After all adjustments have been entered on the worksheet, total the Adjustments Debit and Credit columns and verify that debits and credits are equal. The next step in the process is to prepare the Adjusted Trial Balance section.

Preparing the Adjusted Trial Balance Section

>> **12-4 OBJECTIVE**
Complete a 10-column worksheet.

Figure 12.2 shows the completed worksheet for Whiteside Antiques. The Adjusted Trial Balance section of the worksheet is completed as follows:

1. Combine the amount in the Trial Balance section and the Adjustments section for each account.
2. Enter the results in the Adjusted Trial Balance section. The accounts that do not have adjustments are simply extended from the Trial Balance section to the Adjusted Trial Balance section. For example, the balance of the ***Cash*** account is recorded in the Debit column of the Adjusted Trial Balance section without change.
3. The accounts that are affected by adjustments are recomputed. Follow these rules to combine amounts on the worksheet:

Trial Balance Section	Adjustments Section	Action
Debit	Debit	Add
Debit	Credit	Subtract
Credit	Credit	Add
Credit	Debit	Subtract

- If the account has a debit balance in the Trial Balance section and a debit entry in the Adjustments section, add the two amounts. Look at the ***Salaries Expense—Sales*** account. It has a $78,490 debit balance in the Trial Balance section and a $1,200 debit entry in the Adjustments section. The new balance is $79,690 ($78,490 + $1,200). It is entered in the Debit column of the Adjusted Trial Balance section.
- If the account has a debit balance in the Trial Balance section and a credit entry in the Adjustments section, subtract the credit amount. Look at the ***Supplies*** account. It has a $6,300 debit balance in the Trial Balance section and a $4,975 credit entry in the Adjustments section. The new balance is $1,325 ($6,300 – $4,975). It is entered in the Debit column of the Adjusted Trial Balance section.
- If the account has a credit balance in the Trial Balance section and a credit entry in the Adjustments section, add the two amounts. Look at ***Allowance for Doubtful Accounts.*** It has a $250 credit balance in the Trial Balance section and an $800 credit entry in the Adjustments section. The new balance is $1,050 ($250 + $800). It is entered in the Credit column of the Adjusted Trial Balance section.

FIGURE 12.2 Ten-Column Worksheet—Complete

Whiteside Antiques
Worksheet
Year Ended December 31, 2019

	ACCOUNT NAME	TRIAL BALANCE DEBIT	TRIAL BALANCE CREDIT	ADJUSTMENTS DEBIT	ADJUSTMENTS CREDIT
1	*Cash*	13 136 00			
2	*Petty Cash Fund*	100 00			
3	*Notes Receivable*	1 200 00			
4	*Accounts Receivable*	32 000 00			
5	*Allowance for Doubtful Accounts*		250 00		(c) 800 00
6	*Interest Receivable*			(m) 30 00	
7	*Merchandise Inventory*	52 000 00		(b) 47 000 00	(a) 52 000 00
8	*Prepaid Insurance*	7 350 00			(k) 2 450 00
9	*Prepaid Interest*	225 00			(l) 150 00
10	*Supplies*	6 300 00			(j) 4 975 00
11	*Store Equipment*	30 000 00			
12	*Accumulated Depreciation—Store Equipment*				(d) 2 400 00
13	*Office Equipment*	5 000 00			
14	*Accumulated Depreciation—Office Equipment*				(e) 700 00
15	*Notes Payable—Trade*		2 000 00		
16	*Notes Payable—Bank*		9 000 00		
17	*Accounts Payable*		24 129 00		
18	*Interest Payable*				(i) 20 00
19	*Social Security Tax Payable*		1 084 00		(g) 74 40
20	*Medicare Tax Payable*		250 00		(g) 17 40
21	*Employee Income Taxes Payable*		990 00		
22	*Federal Unemployment Tax Payable*				(h) 7 20
23	*State Unemployment Tax Payable*				(h) 64 80
24	*Salaries Payable*				(f) 1 200 00
25	*Sales Tax Payable*		7 200 00		
26	*Bill Whiteside, Capital*		61 221 00		
27	*Bill Whiteside, Drawing*	27 600 00			
28	*Income Summary*			(a) 52 000 00	(b) 47 000 00
29	*Sales*		561 650 00		
30	*Sales Returns and Allowances*	12 500 00			
31	*Interest Income*		136 00		(m) 30 00
32	*Miscellaneous Income*		366 00		
33	*Purchases*	321 500 00			
34	*Freight In*	9 800 00			
35	*Purchases Returns and Allowances*		3 050 00		
36	*Purchases Discounts*		3 130 00		
37	*Salaries Expense—Sales*	78 490 00		(f) 1 200 00	
38	*Advertising Expense*	7 425 00			
39	*Cash Short or Over*	125 00			
40	*Supplies Expense*			(j) 4 975 00	

ADJUSTED TRIAL BALANCE		INCOME STATEMENT		BALANCE SHEET		
DEBIT	CREDIT	DEBIT	CREDIT	DEBIT	CREDIT	
13,136.00				13,136.00		1
100.00				100.00		2
1,200.00				1,200.00		3
32,000.00				32,000.00		4
	1,050.00				1,050.00	5
30.00				30.00		6
47,000.00				47,000.00		7
4,900.00				4,900.00		8
75.00				75.00		9
1,325.00				1,325.00		10
30,000.00				30,000.00		11
	2,400.00				2,400.00	12
5,000.00				5,000.00		13
	700.00				700.00	14
	2,000.00				2,000.00	15
	9,000.00				9,000.00	16
	24,129.00				24,129.00	17
	20.00				20.00	18
	1,158.40				1,158.40	19
	267.40				267.40	20
	990.00				990.00	21
	7.20				7.20	22
	64.80				64.80	23
	1,200.00				1,200.00	24
	7,200.00				7,200.00	25
	61,221.00				61,221.00	26
27,600.00				27,600.00		27
52,000.00	47,000.00	52,000.00	47,000.00			28
	561,650.00		561,650.00			29
12,500.00		12,500.00				30
	166.00		166.00			31
	366.00		366.00			32
321,500.00		321,500.00				33
9,800.00		9,800.00				34
	3,050.00		3,050.00			35
	3,130.00		3,130.00			36
79,690.00		79,690.00				37
7,425.00		7,425.00				38
125.00		125.00				39
4,975.00		4,975.00				40

FIGURE 12.2 (continued)

ACCOUNT NAME	TRIAL BALANCE		ADJUSTMENTS	
	DEBIT	CREDIT	DEBIT	CREDIT
Depreciation Expense—Store Equipment			(d) 2 400 00	
Rent Expense	27 600 00			
Salaries Expense—Office	26 500 00			
Insurance Expense			(k) 2 450 00	
Payroll Taxes Expense	7 205 00		(g) 91 80	
			(h) 72 00	
Telephone Expense	1 875 00			
Uncollectible Accounts Expense			(c) 800 00	
Utilities Expense	5 925 00			
Depreciation Expense—Office Equipment			(e) 700 00	
Interest Expense	600 00		(i) 20 00	
			(l) 150 00	
Totals	674 456 00	674 456 00	111 888 80	111 888 80
Net Income				

- If the account has a credit balance in the Trial Balance section and a debit entry in the Adjustments section, subtract the debit amount. Whiteside Antiques had no such adjustments.

The Adjusted Trial Balance section now contains the **updated account balances** that will be used in preparing the financial statements.

Look at the ***Income Summary*** account. Recall that the debit entry in this account removed the *beginning* balance from ***Merchandise Inventory*** and the credit entry added the *ending* balance to ***Merchandise Inventory.*** Notice that the debit and credit amounts in ***Income Summary*** are not combined in the Adjusted Trial Balance section.

The ***Merchandise Inventory*** adjustments were required as Whiteside Antiques uses the periodic inventory method. If Whiteside Antiques used the perpetual inventory method, these inventory adjustments would not have been entered in the worksheet.

Once all the updated account balances have been entered in the Adjusted Trial Balance section, total and rule the columns. Confirm that total debits equal total credits.

Preparing the Income Statement and Balance Sheet Sections

To complete the Income Statement and Balance Sheet sections of the worksheet, identify the accounts that appear on the balance sheet. On Figure 12.2, the accounts from ***Cash*** through ***Bill Whiteside, Drawing*** appear on the balance sheet. For each account, enter the amount in the appropriate Debit or Credit column of the Balance Sheet section of the worksheet.

For accounts that appear on the income statement, ***Sales*** through ***Interest Expense,*** enter the amounts in the appropriate Debit or Credit column of the Income Statement section. The ***Income Summary*** debit and credit amounts are also entered in the Income Statement section of the worksheet. Notice that the debit and credit amounts in ***Income Summary*** are not combined in the Income Statement section.

Calculating Net Income or Net Loss

Once all account balances have been entered in the financial statement sections of the worksheet, the net income or net loss for the period is determined.

1. Total the Debit and Credit columns in the Income Statement section. For Whiteside Antiques, the debits total \$564,403.80 and the credits total \$615,362.00. Since the credits exceed the debits, the difference represents net income of \$50,958.20.

ADJUSTED TRIAL BALANCE		INCOME STATEMENT		BALANCE SHEET	
DEBIT	CREDIT	DEBIT	CREDIT	DEBIT	CREDIT
2 400 00		2 400 00			
27 600 00		27 600 00			
26 500 00		26 500 00			
2 450 00		2 450 00			
7 368 80		7 368 80			
1 875 00		1 875 00			
800 00		800 00			
5 925 00		5 925 00			
700 00		700 00			
770 00		770 00			
726 769 80	726 769 80	564 403 80	615 362 00	162 366 00	111 407 80
		50 958 20			50 958 20
		615 362 00	615 362 00	162 366 00	162 366 00

2. To balance the Debit and Credit columns in the Income Statement section, enter $50,958.20 in the Debit column of the Income Statement section. Total each column again and record the final total of each column ($615,362.00) on the worksheet.
3. Total the columns in the Balance Sheet section. Total debits are $162,366.00 and total credits are $111,407.80. The difference must equal the net income for the year, $50,958.20.
4. Enter $50,958.20 in the Credit column of the Balance Sheet section. Total each column again and record the final total in each column ($162,366.00).
5. Rule the Debit and Credit columns in all sections to show that the worksheet is complete.

MANAGERIAL IMPLICATIONS <<

EFFECT OF ADJUSTMENTS ON FINANCIAL STATEMENTS

- If managers are to know the true revenue, expenses, and net income or net loss for a period, the matching process is necessary.
- If accounts are not adjusted, the financial statements will be incomplete, misleading, and of little help in evaluating operations.
- Managers need to be familiar with the procedures and underlying assumptions used by the accountant to make adjustments because adjustments increase or decrease net income.
- Managers need information about uncollectible accounts expense in order to review the firm's credit policy. If losses are too high, management might tighten the requirements for obtaining credit. If losses are very low, management might investigate whether easing credit requirements would increase net income.
- The worksheet is a useful device for gathering data about adjustments and for preparing the financial statements.
- Managers are keenly interested in receiving timely financial statements, especially the income statement, which shows the results of operations.
- Managers are also interested in the prompt preparation of the balance sheet because it shows the financial position of the business at the end of the period.

THINKING CRITICALLY

What are some possible consequences of not making adjusting entries?

Notice that the net income is recorded in two places on the **net income line** of the worksheet. It is recorded in the Credit column of the Balance Sheet section because net income *increases* owner's equity. It is recorded in the Debit column of the Income Statement section to balance the two columns in that section.

Section 2 Self Review

QUESTIONS

1. In the adjusting entry for depreciation, is the ***Depreciation Expense*** account increased or decreased? Is the book value of the asset being depreciated increased or is it decreased?
2. In its December 31, 2019, financial reports, St. Claire Company's accountant made two errors: (1) failed to record interest of $600 accrued on a note payable and (2) failed to record interest of $1,600 accrued on a note receivable. What is the net effect of these two errors on assets, on liabilities, on expenses, on income, and on owner's equity?
3. The trial balance in the first two columns of the worksheet balances and the adjustments in the next two columns balance. However, the adjusted trial balance does not balance. What is the likely source of the trouble?

EXERCISES

4. What account is debited and what account is credited to accrue interest on notes payable?
5. The amount of net income appears on the worksheet in the:
   a. Credit column of the adjusted trial balance section.
   b. Debit column of the balance sheet section.
   c. Credit column of the income statement section.
   d. Debit column of the income statement section.

ANALYSIS

6. Explain why an error in the amount of an adjusting entry usually affects at least two accounting periods.

(Answers to Section 2 Self Review are on page 453.)

REVIEW Chapter Summary

Chapter 12

Review and Applications

Accrual basis accounting requires that all revenue and expenses for a fiscal period be matched and reported on the income statement to determine net income or net loss for the period. In this chapter, you have learned the techniques used to adjust accounts so that they accurately reflect the operations of the period.

Learning Objectives

12-1 **Determine the adjustment for merchandise inventory, and enter the adjustment on the worksheet.**

Merchandise inventory consists of goods that a business has on hand for sale to customers. When the trial balance is prepared at the end of the period, the ***Merchandise Inventory*** account still reflects the beginning inventory. Before the financial statements can be prepared, ***Merchandise Inventory*** must be updated to reflect the ending inventory for the period. The actual quantity of the goods on hand at the end of the period must be counted. Then the adjustment is completed in two steps:

1. Remove the beginning inventory balance from the ***Merchandise Inventory*** account. Debit ***Income Summary;*** credit ***Merchandise Inventory.***
2. Add the ending inventory to the ***Merchandise Inventory*** account. Debit ***Merchandise Inventory;*** credit ***Income Summary.***

12-2 **Compute adjustments for accrued and prepaid expense items, and enter the adjustments on the worksheet.**

Expense accounts are adjusted at the end of the period so that they correctly reflect the current period. Examples of adjustments include provision for uncollectible accounts and depreciation. Other typical adjustments of expense accounts involve accrued expenses and prepaid expenses.

- Accrued expenses are expense items that have been incurred or used but not yet paid or recorded. They include salaries, payroll taxes, interest on notes payable, and property taxes.
- Prepaid expenses are expense items that a business pays for and records before it actually uses the items. Rent, insurance, and advertising paid in advance are examples.

12-3 **Compute adjustments for accrued and deferred income items, and enter the adjustments on the worksheet.**

Revenue accounts are adjusted at the end of the period so that they correctly reflect the current period.

- Adjustments can affect either accrued income or deferred income.
- Accrued income is income that has been earned but not yet received and recorded.
- Deferred, or unearned, income is income that has not yet been earned but has been received.

12-4 **Complete a 10-column worksheet.**

When all adjustments have been entered on the worksheet, the worksheet is completed so that the financial statements can be prepared easily.

1. Figures in the Trial Balance section are combined with the adjustments to obtain an adjusted trial balance.
2. Each item in the Adjusted Trial Balance section is extended to the Income Statement or the Balance Sheet section of the worksheet.
3. The Income Statement columns are totaled and the net income or net loss is determined and entered in the net income line.
4. The amount of net income or net loss is entered in the net income line in the Balance Sheet section. After net income or net loss is added, the total debits must equal the total credits in the Balance Sheet section columns.

12-5 **Define the accounting terms new to this chapter.**

Glossary

Accrual basis (p. 416) A system of accounting by which all revenues and expenses are matched and reported on financial statements for the applicable period, regardless of when the cash related to the transaction is received or paid

Accrued expenses (p. 421) Expense items that relate to the current period but have not yet been paid and do not yet appear in the accounting records

Accrued income (p. 425) Income that has been earned but not yet received and recorded

Deferred expenses (p. 423) See Prepaid expenses

Deferred income (p. 425) See Unearned income

Inventory sheet (p. 417) A form used to list the quantity and type of goods a firm has in stock

Net income line (p. 432) The worksheet line immediately following the column totals on which net income (or net loss) is recorded in two places: the Income Statement section and the Balance Sheet section

Property, plant, and equipment (p. 420) Long-term assets that are used in the operation of a business and that are subject to depreciation (except for land, which is not depreciated)

Unearned income (p. 425) Income received before it is earned

Updated account balances (p. 430) The amounts entered in the Adjusted Trial Balance section of the worksheet

Comprehensive Self Review

1. Why is the accrual basis of accounting favored?
2. What is meant by the term "accrued income"?
3. How, if at all, does "accrued income" differ from "unearned income"?
4. A completed worksheet for Holiday Company on December 31, 2019, showed a total of $930,000 in the debit column of the Income Statement section and a total credit of $902,000 in the credit column. Does this represent a profit or a loss for the year? How much?
5. On July 1, 2019, a landlord received $36,000 cash from a tenant, covering rent from July 1, 2019, through June 30, 2020. The payment received was credited to ***Unearned Rent Income.*** Assuming no entry has been made in the ***Unearned Rent Income*** account since the payment was received, what would be the adjusting entry on December 31, 2019?
6. On July 1, 2019, a landlord received $36,000 cash from a tenant, covering rent from that date through June 30, 2020. The payment was credited to ***Rent Income.*** Assuming no entry has been made in the income account since receipt of the payment, what would be the adjusting entry on December 31, 2019?

(Answers to Comprehensive Self Review are on page 454.)

Discussion Questions

1. What adjustment is made to record the estimated expense for uncollectible accounts?
2. When a specific account receivable is deemed uncollectible, it is written off by debiting __________ and crediting __________.
3. ***Income Summary*** amounts are extended to which statement columns on the worksheet?
4. Why is depreciation recorded?
5. What types of assets are subject to depreciation? Give three examples of such assets.
6. Explain the meaning of the following terms that relate to depreciation:
   a. Salvage value
   b. Depreciable base
   c. Useful life
   d. Straight-line method
7. What adjustment is made for depreciation on office equipment?
8. What is an accrued expense? Give three examples of items that often become accrued expenses.
9. What adjustment is made to record accrued salaries?
10. What is a prepaid expense? Give three examples of prepaid expense items.

11. How is the cost of an insurance policy recorded when the policy is purchased?
12. What adjustment is made to record expired insurance?
13. What is the alternative method of handling prepaid expenses?
14. What is accrued income? Give an example of an item that might produce accrued income.
15. What adjustment is made for accrued interest on a note receivable?
16. What is unearned income? Give two examples of items that would be classified as unearned income.
17. How is unearned income recorded when it is received?
18. What adjustment is made to record income earned during a period?
19. What is the alternative method of handling unearned income?
20. ***Unearned Fees Income*** is classified as which type of account?
21. How does the worksheet help the accountant to prepare financial statements more efficiently?

APPLICATIONS

Exercises

Determining the adjustments for inventory.

Exercise 12.1
Objective 12-1

The beginning inventory of Norcal Wholesalers was $141,000, and the ending inventory is $118,519. What entries are needed at the end of the fiscal period to adjust ***Merchandise Inventory***?

Determining the adjustments for inventory.

Exercise 12.2
Objective 12-1

The Income Statement section of the Johnson Company worksheet for the year ended December 31, 2019, has $199,000 recorded in the Debit column and $215,345 in the Credit column on the line for the ***Income Summary*** account. What were the beginning and ending balances for ***Merchandise Inventory***?

Computing adjustments for uncollectible accounts, depreciation, and payroll items.

Exercise 12.3
Objective 12-2

For each of the following independent situations, indicate the adjusting entry that must be made on the December 31, 2019, worksheet. Omit descriptions.

a. During the year 2019, Sampson Company had net credit sales of $1,950,000. Past experience shows that 1.5 percent of the firm's net credit sales result in uncollectible accounts.

b. Equipment purchased by Park Consultancy for $38,220 on January 2, 2019, has an estimated useful life of 10 years and an estimated salvage value of $2,700. What adjustment for depreciation should be recorded on the firm's worksheet for the year ended December 31, 2019?

c. On December 31, 2019, Giant Plumbing Supply owed wages of $11,400 to its factory employees, who are paid weekly.

d. On December 31, 2019, Giant Plumbing Supply owed the employer's social security (6.2 percent) and Medicare (1.45 percent) taxes on the entire $11,400 of accrued wages for its factory employees.

e. On December 31, 2019, Giant Plumbing Supply owed federal (0.6 percent) and state (5.4 percent) unemployment taxes on the entire $11,400 of accrued wages for its factory employees.

Computing adjustments for accrued and prepaid expense items.

Exercise 12.4
Objective 12-2

For each of the following independent situations, indicate the adjusting entry that must be made on the December 31, 2019, worksheet. Omit descriptions.

a. On December 31, 2019, the ***Notes Payable*** account at Northwood Manufacturing Company had a balance of $16,000. This balance represented a three-month, 7.5 percent note issued on November 1.

b. On January 2, 2019, Hitech Computer Consultants purchased flash drives, paper, and other supplies for $5,230 in cash. On December 31, 2019, an inventory of supplies showed that items costing $1,590 were on hand. The ***Supplies*** account has a balance of $5,230.

c. On September 1, 2019, North Dakota Manufacturing paid a premium of $14,640 in cash for a one-year insurance policy. On December 31, 2019, an examination of the insurance records showed that coverage for a period of four months had expired.

d. On May 1, 2019, Headcase Beauty Salon signed a one-year advertising contract with a local radio station and issued a check for $10,800 to pay the total amount owed. On December 31, 2019, the ***Prepaid Advertising*** account has a balance of $10,800.

Exercise 12.5
Objective 12-2

Recording adjustments for prepaid interest.

On December 1, 2019, Jim's Java Joint borrowed $50,000 from its bank in order to expand its operations. The firm issued a four-month, 6 percent note for $50,000 to the bank and received $49,000 in cash because the bank deducted the interest for the entire period in advance. In general journal form, show the entry that would be made to record this transaction and the adjustment for prepaid interest that should be recorded on the firm's worksheet for the year ended December 31, 2019. Omit descriptions. Round your answers to the nearest dollar.

Exercise 12.6
Objective 12-2

Recording adjustments for accrued interest.

On December 31, 2019, the ***Notes Payable*** account at Vanessa's Boutique Shop had a balance of $90,000. This amount represented funds borrowed on a six-month, 8 percent note from the firm's bank on December 1. Record the journal entry for interest expense on this note that should be recorded on the firm's worksheet for the year ended December 31, 2019. Omit descriptions.

Exercise 12.7
Objective 12-3

Recording adjustments for accrued and deferred income items.

For each of the following independent situations, indicate the adjusting entry that must be made on the December 31, 2019, worksheet. Omit descriptions.

a. On December 31, 2019, the ***Notes Receivable*** account at P. Davis Materials Corporation had a balance of $40,000, which represented a six-month, 5 percent note received from a customer on October 1.

b. During the week ended June 7, 2019, McCormick Media received $75,000 from customers for subscriptions to its magazine *Modern Business.* On December 31, 2019, an analysis of the ***Unearned Subscription Revenue*** account showed that half of the subscriptions were earned in 2019.

c. On November 1, 2019, Perez Realty Company rented a commercial building to a new tenant and received $36,000 in advance to cover the rent for six months. Upon receipt, the $36,000 was recorded in the ***Unearned Rent*** account.

d. On November 1, 2019, the Mighty Bucks Hockey Club sold season tickets for 50 home games, receiving $9,000,000. Upon receipt, the $9,000,000 was recorded in the ***Unearned Season Tickets Income*** account. At December 31, 2019, the Mighty Bucks Hockey Club had played 5 home games.

PROBLEMS

Problem Set A

Problem 12.1A
Objectives 12-2, 12-3
GL

Recording adjustments for accrued and prepaid items and unearned income.

Based on the information below, record the adjusting journal entries that must be made for Sufen Consulting on June 30, 2019. The company has a June 30 fiscal year-end. Use 18 as the page number for the general journal.

a.–b. ***Merchandise Inventory,*** before adjustment, has a balance of $8,300. The newly counted inventory balance is $8,800.

c. ***Unearned Seminar Fees*** has a balance of $6,800, representing prepayment by customers for five seminars to be conducted in June, July, and August 2019. Two seminars had been conducted by June 30, 2019.

d. ***Prepaid Insurance*** has a balance of $16,800 for six months' insurance paid in advance on May 1, 2019.

e. Store equipment costing $11,380 was purchased on March 31, 2019. It has a salvage value of $580 and a useful life of four years.

f. Employees have earned $330 that has not been paid at June 30, 2019.

g. The employer owes the following taxes on wages not paid at June 30, 2019: SUTA, $9.90; FUTA, $1.98; Medicare, $4.79; and social security, $20.46.

h. Management estimates uncollectible accounts expense at 1 percent of sales. This year's sales were $2,800,000.

i. ***Prepaid Rent*** has a balance of $7,800 for six months' rent paid in advance on March 1, 2019.

j. The ***Supplies*** account in the general ledger has a balance of $480. A count of supplies on hand at June 30, 2019, indicated $190 of supplies remain.

k. The company borrowed $8,200 from First Bank on June 1, 2019, and issued a four-month note. The note bears interest at 6 percent.

Analyze: After all adjusting entries have been journalized and posted, what is the balance of the ***Prepaid Rent*** account?

Recording adjustments for accrued and prepaid expense items and unearned income.

◀ **Problem 12.2A**
Objectives 12-2, 12-3

GL

On July 1, 2019, Tim Stein established his own accounting practice. Selected transactions for the first few days of July follow.

INSTRUCTIONS

1. Record the transactions on page 1 of the general journal. Omit descriptions. Assume that the firm initially records prepaid expenses as assets and unearned income as a liability. Omit explanations.
2. Record the adjusting journal entries that must be made on July 31, 2019, on page 2 of the general journal. Omit descriptions.

DATE		TRANSACTIONS
2019		
July	1	Signed a lease for an office and issued Check 101 for $14,400 to pay the rent in advance for six months.
	1	Borrowed money from Second National Bank by issuing a four month, 6 percent note for $33,600; received $32,928 because the bank deducted the interest in advance.
	1	Signed an agreement with Carter Corp. to provide accounting and tax services for one year at $6,800 per month; received the entire fee of $81,600 in advance.
	1	Purchased office equipment for $20,400 from Office Outfitters; issued a two-month, 9 percent note in payment. The equipment is estimated to have a useful life of four years and a $2,160 salvage value. The equipment will be depreciated using the straight line method.
	1	Purchased a one-year insurance policy and issued Check 102 for $1,716 to pay the entire premium.
	3	Purchased office furniture for $23,200 from Furniture Warehouse; issued Check 103 for $13,400 and agreed to pay the balance in 60 days. The equipment has an estimated useful life of six years and a $1,600 salvage value. The office furniture will be depreciated using the straight-line method.
	5	Purchased office supplies for $1,970 with Check 104. Assume $880 of supplies are on hand July 31, 2019.

Analyze: What balance should be reflected in ***Unearned Accounting Fees*** at July 31, 2019?

Problem 12.3A
Objectives 12-2, 12-3

GL

Recording adjustments for accrued and prepaid expense items and earned income.

On July 31, 2019, after one month of operation, the general ledger of Michael Domenici, Consultant, contained the accounts and balances given below.

INSTRUCTIONS

1. Prepare a partial worksheet with the following sections: Trial Balance, Adjustments, and Adjusted Trial Balance. Use the data about the firm's accounts and balances to complete the Trial Balance section.
2. Enter the adjustments described below in the Adjustments section. Identify each adjustment with the appropriate letter.
3. Complete the Adjusted Trial Balance section.

ACCOUNTS AND BALANCES

Cash	$25,510	Dr.
Accounts Receivable	1,440	Dr.
Supplies	960	Dr.
Prepaid Rent	10,500	Dr.
Prepaid Insurance	2,220	Dr.
Prepaid Interest	400	Dr.
Furniture	14,760	Dr.
Accumulated Depreciation—Furniture		
Equipment	7,250	Dr.
Accumulated Depreciation—Equipment		
Notes Payable	17,700	Cr.
Accounts Payable	5,500	Cr.
Interest Payable		
Unearned Consulting Fees	6,000	Cr.
Michael Domenici, Capital	32,520	Cr.
Michael Domenici, Drawing	3,000	Dr.
Consulting Fees	9,000	Cr.
Salaries Expense	4,200	Dr.
Utilities Expense	270	Dr.
Telephone Expense	210	Dr.
Supplies Expense		
Rent Expense		
Insurance Expense		
Depreciation Expense—Furniture		
Depreciation Expense—Equipment		
Interest Expense		

ADJUSTMENTS

a. On July 31, an inventory of the supplies showed that items costing $630 were on hand.

b. On July 1, the firm paid $10,500 in advance for six months of rent.

c. On July 1, the firm purchased a one-year insurance policy for $2,220.

d. On July 1, the firm paid $400 interest in advance on a four-month note that it issued to the bank.

e. On July 1, the firm purchased office furniture for $14,760. The furniture is expected to have a useful life of eight years and a salvage value of $1,800.

f. On July 1, the firm purchased office equipment for $7,250. The equipment is expected to have a useful life of five years and a salvage value of $1,850.

g. On July 1, the firm issued a three-month, 6 percent note for $9,800.

h. On July 1, the firm received a consulting fee of $6,000 in advance for a one-year period.

Analyze: By what total amount were the expense accounts of the business adjusted?

Recording adjustments and completing the worksheet.

◀ **Problem 12.4A**
Objectives 12-1, 12-2, 12-3, 12-4

The Green Thumb Gardener is a retail store that sells plants, soil, and decorative pots. On December 31, 2019, the firm's general ledger contained the accounts and balances that appear below.

INSTRUCTIONS

1. Prepare the Trial Balance section of a 10-column worksheet. The worksheet covers the year ended December 31, 2019.
2. Enter the adjustments below in the Adjustments section of the worksheet. Identify each adjustment with the appropriate letter.
3. Complete the worksheet.

ACCOUNTS AND BALANCES

Cash	$ 6,700	Dr.
Accounts Receivable	3,600	Dr.
Allowance for Doubtful Accounts	62	Cr.
Merchandise Inventory	12,300	Dr.
Supplies	1,300	Dr.
Prepaid Advertising	1,080	Dr.
Store Equipment	8,700	Dr.
Accumulated Depreciation—Store Equipment	1,600	Cr.
Office Equipment	2,200	Dr.
Accumulated Depreciation—Office Equipment	380	Cr.
Accounts Payable	2,725	Cr.
Social Security Tax Payable	530	Cr.
Medicare Tax Payable	88	Cr.
Federal Unemployment Tax Payable		
State Unemployment Tax Payable		
Salaries Payable		
Beth Argo, Capital	30,677	Cr.
Beth Argo, Drawing	21,000	Dr.
Sales	95,048	Cr.
Sales Returns and Allowances	1,200	Dr.
Purchases	49,400	Dr.
Purchases Returns and Allowances	530	Cr.
Rent Expense	7,000	Dr.
Telephone Expense	690	Dr.
Salaries Expense	15,100	Dr.
Payroll Taxes Expense	1,370	Dr.
Income Summary		
Supplies Expense		
Advertising Expense		
Depreciation Expense—Store Equipment		
Depreciation Expense—Office Equipment		
Uncollectible Accounts Expense		

ADJUSTMENTS

a.–b. Merchandise inventory on December 31, 2019, is $13,321.

c. During 2019, the firm had net credit sales of $45,000; the firm estimates that 0.5 percent of these sales will result in uncollectible accounts.

d. On December 31, 2019, an inventory of the supplies showed that items costing $325 were on hand.

e. On October 1, 2019, the firm signed a six-month advertising contract for $1,080 with a local newspaper and paid the full amount in advance.

f. On January 2, 2018, the firm purchased store equipment for $8,700. At that time, the equipment was estimated to have a useful life of five years and a salvage value of $700.

g. On January 2, 2018, the firm purchased office equipment for $2,200. At that time, the equipment was estimated to have a useful life of five years and a salvage value of $300.

h. On December 31, 2019, the firm owed salaries of $1,930 that will not be paid until 2020.

i. On December 31, 2019, the firm owed the employer's social security tax (assume 6.2 percent) and Medicare tax (assume 1.45 percent) on the entire $1,930 of accrued wages.

j. On December 31, 2019, the firm owed federal unemployment tax (assume 0.6 percent) and state unemployment tax (assume 5.4 percent) on the entire $1,930 of accrued wages.

Analyze: By what amount were the assets of the business affected by adjustments?

Problem 12.5A ► Recording adjustments and completing the worksheet.

Objectives 12-1, 12-2, 12-3, 12-4

GL

CONTINUING >>> Problem

Healthy Eating Foods Company is a distributor of nutritious snack foods such as granola bars. On December 31, 2019, the firm's general ledger contained the accounts and balances that follow.

INSTRUCTIONS

1. Prepare the Trial Balance section of a 10-column worksheet. The worksheet covers the year ended December 31, 2019.
2. Enter the adjustments in the Adjustments section of the worksheet. Identify each adjustment with the appropriate letter.
3. Complete the worksheet.

Note: This problem will be required to complete Problem 13.4A in Chapter 13.

ACCOUNTS AND BALANCES

Cash	$ 30,100	Dr.
Accounts Receivable	35,200	Dr.
Allowance for Doubtful Accounts	420	Cr.
Merchandise Invento ry	86,000	Dr.
Supplies	10,400	Dr.
Prepaid Insurance	5,400	Dr.
Office Equipment	8,300	Dr.
Accum. Depreciation—Office Equipment	2,650	Cr.
Warehouse Equipment	28,000	Dr.
Accum. Depreciation—Warehouse Equipment	9,600	Cr.
Notes Payable—Bank	32,000	Cr.
Accounts Payable	12,200	Cr.
Interest Payable		
Social Security Tax Payable	1,680	Cr.
Medicare Tax Payable	388	Cr.
Federal Unemployment Tax Payable		
State Unemployment Tax Payable		

ACCOUNTS AND BALANCES (CONT.)

Salaries Payable		
Phillip Tucker, Capital	108,684	Cr.
Phillip Tucker, Drawing	56,000	Dr.
Sales	653,778	Cr.
Sales Returns and Allowances	10,000	Dr.
Purchases	350,000	Dr.
Purchases Returns and Allowances	9,200	Cr.
Income Summary		
Rent Expense	36,000	Dr.
Telephone Expense	2,200	Dr.
Salaries Expense	160,000	Dr.
Payroll Taxes Expense	13,000	Dr.
Supplies Expense		
Insurance Expense		
Depreciation Expense—Office Equip.		
Depreciation Expense—Warehouse Equip.		
Uncollectible Accounts Expense		
Interest Expense		

ADJUSTMENTS

a.–b. Merchandise inventory on December 31, 2019, is $78,000.

c. During 2019, the firm had net credit sales of $560,000; past experience indicates that 0.5 percent of these sales should result in uncollectible accounts.

d. On December 31, 2019, an inventory of supplies showed that items costing $1,180 were on hand.

e. On May 1, 2019, the firm purchased a one-year insurance policy for $5,400.

f. On January 2, 2017, the firm purchased office equipment for $8,300. At that time, the equipment was estimated to have a useful life of six years and a salvage value of $350.

g. On January 2, 2017, the firm purchased warehouse equipment for $28,000. At that time, the equipment was estimated to have a useful life of five years and a salvage value of $4,000.

h. On November 1, 2019, the firm issued a four-month, 12 percent note for $32,000.

i. On December 31, 2019, the firm owed salaries of $5,000 that will not be paid until 2020.

j. On December 31, 2019, the firm owed the employer's social security tax (assume 6.2 percent) and Medicare tax (assume 1.45 percent) on the entire $5,000 of accrued wages.

k. On December 31, 2019, the firm owed the federal unemployment tax (assume 0.6 percent) and the state unemployment tax (assume 5.4 percent) on the entire $5,000 of accrued wages.

Analyze: When the financial statements for Healthy Eating Foods Company are prepared, what net income will be reported for the period ended December 31, 2019?

Recording adjustments and completing the worksheet. ◀ **Problem 12.6A**

Objectives 12-1, 12-2, 12-3, 12-4

The Artisan Wines is a retail store selling vintage wines. On December 31, 2019, the firm's general ledger contained the accounts and balances below. All account balances are normal.

Cash	$ 28,386
Accounts Receivable	500
Prepaid Advertising	480

Supplies	300
Merchandise Inventory	15,000
Store Equipment	25,000
Accumulated Depreciation—Store Equipment	3,000
Office Equipment	5,000
Accumulated Depreciation—Office Equipment	1,500
Notes Payable, due 2020	20,000
Accounts Payable	2,705
Wages Payable	
Social Security Tax Payable	
Medicare Tax Payable	
Unearned Seminar Fees	6,000
Interest Payable	
Vincent Arroyo, Capital	32,700
Vincent Arroyo, Drawing	14,110
Income Summary	
Sales	153,970
Sales Discounts	200
Seminar Fee Income	
Purchases	91,000
Purchases Returns and Allowances	1,000
Freight In	225
Rent Expense	13,200
Wages Expense	24,000
Payroll Taxes Expense	3,324
Depreciation Expense—Store Equipment	
Depreciation Expense—Office Equipment	
Advertising Expense	
Supplies Expense	
Interest Expense	150

INSTRUCTIONS:

1. Prepare the Trial Balance section of a 10-column worksheet. The worksheet covers the year ended December 31, 2019.
2. Enter the adjustments below in the Adjustments section of the worksheet. Identify each adjustment with the appropriate letter.
3. Complete the worksheet.

ADJUSTMENTS:

a.–b. Merchandise inventory at December 31, 2019, was counted and determined to be $13,000.

c. The amount recorded as prepaid advertising represents $480 paid on September 1, 2019, for 12 months of advertising.

d. The amount of supplies on hand at December 31 was $160.

e. Depreciation on store equipment was $3,000 for 2019.

f. Depreciation on office equipment was $1,125 for 2019.

g. Unearned seminar fees represent $6,000 received on November 1, 2019, for six seminars. At December 31, four of these seminars had been conducted.

h. Wages owed but not paid at December 31 were $500.

i. On December 31, 2019, the firm owed the employer's social security tax ($31.00) and Medicare tax ($7.25).

j. The note payable bears interest at 6 percent per annum. One month's interest is owed at December 31, 2019.

Analyze: What was the amount of revenue earned by conducting seminars during the year ended December 31, 2019?

Problem Set B

Recording adjustments for accrued and prepaid items and unearned income.

Problem 12.1B
Objectives 12-2, 12-3

Based on the information below, record the adjusting journal entries that must be made for Belle Fleur Consulting Services on December 31, 2019. The company has a December 31 fiscal year-end. Use 18 as the page number for the general journal.

a.–b. ***Merchandise Inventory,*** before adjustment, has a balance of $9,700. The newly counted inventory balance is $10,800.

c. ***Unearned Seminar Fees*** has a balance of $18,000, representing prepayment by customers for four seminars to be conducted in December 2019 and January 2020. Three seminars had been conducted by December 31, 2019.

d. ***Prepaid Insurance*** has a balance of $12,000 for six months' insurance paid in advance on October 1, 2019.

e. Store equipment costing $12,000 was purchased on September 1, 2019. It has a salvage value of $600 and a useful life of five years.

f. Employees have earned $1,000 of wages not paid at December 31, 2019.

g. The employer owes the following taxes on wages not paid at December 31, 2019: SUTA, $30.00; FUTA, $6.00; Medicare, $14.50; and social security, $62.00.

h. Management estimates uncollectible accounts expense at 1.5 percent (0.015) of sales. This year's sales were $3,000,000.

i. ***Prepaid Rent*** has a balance of $13,500 for nine months' rent paid in advance on October 1, 2019.

j. The ***Supplies*** account in the general ledger has a balance of $600. A count of supplies on hand at December 31, 2019, indicated $150 of supplies remain.

k. The company borrowed $15,000 on a two-month note payable dated December 1, 2019. The note bears interest at 8 percent.

Analyze: After all adjusting entries have been journalized and posted, what is the balance of the ***Unearned Seminar Fees*** account?

Recording adjustments for accrued and prepaid expense items and unearned income.

Problem 12.2B
Objectives 12-2, 12-3

On June 1, 2019, Raquel Ramirez established her own advertising firm. Selected transactions for the first few days of June follow.

1. Record the transactions on page 1 of the general journal. Omit descriptions. Assume that the firm initially records prepaid expenses as assets and unearned income as a liability.
2. Record the adjusting journal entries that must be made on June 30, 2019, on page 2 of the general journal. Omit descriptions.

DATE		TRANSACTIONS
2019		
June	1	Signed a lease for an office and issued Check 101 for $15,000 to pay the rent in advance for one year.
	1	Borrowed money from National Trust Bank by issuing a three-month, 10 percent note for $18,000; received $17,550 because the bank deducted interest in advance.
	1	Signed an agreement with Michelle's Party Supplies to provide advertising consulting for one year at $6,500 per month; received the entire fee of $78,000 in advance.
	1	Purchased office equipment for $17,200 from The Equipment Depot; issued a three-month, 6 percent note in payment. The equipment is estimated to have a useful life of five years and a $1,000 salvage value and will be depreciated using the straight-line method.
	1	Purchased a one-year insurance policy and issued Check 102 for $1,680 to pay the entire premium.
	3	Purchased office furniture for $17,400 from Office Gallery; issued Check 103 for $10,000 and agreed to pay the balance in 60 days. The furniture is estimated to have a useful life of five years and a $1,200 salvage value and will be depreciated using the straight-line method.
	5	Purchased office supplies for $1,910 with Check 104; assume $850 of supplies are on hand June 30, 2019.

Analyze: At the end of calendar year 2019, how much of the rent paid on June 1 will have been charged to expense?

Problem 12.3B

Objectives 12-2, 12-3

Recording adjustments for accrued and prepaid expense items and unearned income.

On September 30, 2019, after one month of operation, the general ledger of Cross Timbers Company contained the accounts and balances shown below.

INSTRUCTIONS

1. Prepare a partial worksheet with the following sections: Trial Balance, Adjustments, and Adjusted Trial Balance. Use the data about the firm's accounts and balances to complete the Trial Balance section.
2. Enter the adjustments described below in the Adjustments section. Identify each adjustment with the appropriate letter. (Some items may not require adjustments.)
3. Complete the Adjusted Trial Balance section.

ACCOUNTS AND BALANCES

Cash	$26,460	Dr.
Supplies	740	Dr.
Prepaid Rent	4,200	Dr.
Prepaid Advertising	3,750	Dr.
Prepaid Interest	450	Dr.
Furniture	4,840	Dr.
Accumulated Depreciation—Furniture		
Equipment	9,000	Dr.
Accumulated Depreciation—Equipment		

ACCOUNTS AND BALANCES (CONT.)

Notes Payable	20,250	Cr.
Accounts Payable	4,400	Cr.
Interest Payable		
Unearned Course Fees	22,000	Cr.
Scott Nelson, Capital	6,730	Cr.
Scott Nelson, Drawing	2,000	Dr.
Course Fees		
Salaries Expense	1,600	Dr.
Telephone Expense	120	Dr.
Entertainment Expense	220	Dr.
Supplies Expense		
Rent Expense		
Advertising Expense		
Depreciation Expense—Furniture		
Depreciation Expense—Equipment		
Interest Expense		

ADJUSTMENTS

a. On September 30, an inventory of the supplies showed that items costing $705 were on hand.

b. On September 1, the firm paid $4,200 in advance for six months of rent.

c. On September 1, the firm signed a six-month advertising contract for $3,750 and paid the full amount in advance.

d. On September 1, the firm paid $450 interest in advance on a three-month note that it issued to the bank.

e. On September 1, the firm purchased office furniture for $4,840. The furniture is expected to have a useful life of five years and a salvage value of $340.

f. On September 3, the firm purchased equipment for $9,000. The equipment is expected to have a useful life of five years and a salvage value of $1,200.

g. On September 1, the firm issued a two-month, 8 percent note for $5,250.

h. During September, the firm received $22,000 of fees in advance. An analysis of the firm's records shows that $7,000 applies to services provided in September and the rest pertains to future months.

Analyze: What was the net dollar effect on income of the adjustments to the accounting records of the business?

Recording adjustments and completing the worksheet.

◀ **Problem 12.4B**
Objectives 12-1, 12-2, 12-3, 12-4

Fun Depot is a retail store that sells toys, games, and bicycles. On December 31, 2019, the firm's general ledger contained the following accounts and balances.

INSTRUCTIONS

1. Prepare the Trial Balance section of a 10-column worksheet. The worksheet covers the year ended December 31, 2019.
2. Enter the adjustments below in the Adjustments section of the worksheet. Identify each adjustment with the appropriate letter.
3. Complete the worksheet.

ACCOUNTS AND BALANCES

Account	Balance	
Cash	$ 26,400	Dr.
Accounts Receivable	22,700	Dr.
Allowance for Doubtful Accounts	320	Cr.
Merchandise Inventory	138,000	Dr.
Supplies	11,600	Dr.
Prepaid Advertising	5,280	Dr.
Store Equipment	32,500	Dr.
Accumulated Depreciation—Store Equipment	5,760	Cr.
Office Equipment	8,400	Dr.
Accumulated Depreciation—Office Equipment	1,440	Cr.
Accounts Payable	8,600	Cr.
Social Security Tax Payable	5,920	Cr.
Medicare Tax Payable	1,368	Cr.
Federal Unemployment Tax Payable		
State Unemployment Tax Payable		
Salaries Payable		
Janie Fielder, Capital	112,250	Cr.
Janie Fielder, Drawing	100,000	Dr.
Sales	1,043,662	Cr.
Sales Returns and Allowances	17,200	Dr.
Purchases	507,600	Dr.
Purchases Returns and Allowances	5,040	Cr.
Rent Expense	125,000	Dr.
Telephone Expense	4,280	Dr.
Salaries Expense	164,200	Dr.
Payroll Taxes Expense	15,200	Dr.
Income Summary		
Supplies Expense		
Advertising Expense	6,000	Dr.
Depreciation Expense—Store Equipment		
Depreciation Expense—Office Equipment		
Uncollectible Accounts Expense		

ADJUSTMENTS

a.–b. Merchandise inventory on December 31, 2019, is $148,000.

c. During 2019, the firm had net credit sales of $440,000. The firm estimates that 0.7 percent of these sales will result in uncollectible accounts.

d. On December 31, 2019, an inventory of the supplies showed that items costing $2,960 were on hand.

e. On September 1, 2019, the firm signed a six-month advertising contract for $5,280 with a local newspaper and paid the full amount in advance.

f. On January 2, 2018, the firm purchased store equipment for $32,500. At that time, the equipment was estimated to have a useful life of five years and a salvage value of $3,700.

g. On January 2, 2018, the firm purchased office equipment for $8,400. At that time, the equipment was estimated to have a useful life of five years and a salvage value of $1,200.

h. On December 31, 2019, the firm owed salaries of $8,000 that will not be paid until 2020.

i. On December 31, 2019, the firm owed the employer's social security tax (assume 6.2 percent) and Medicare tax (assume 1.45 percent) on the entire $8,000 of accrued wages.

j. On December 31, 2019, the firm owed federal unemployment tax (assume 0.6 percent) and state unemployment tax (assume 5.4 percent) on the entire $8,000 of accrued wages.

Analyze: If the adjustment for advertising had not been recorded, what would the reported net income have been?

Problem 12.5B

Objectives 12-1, 12-2, 12-3, 12-4

CONTINUING >>> Problem

Recording adjustments and completing the worksheet.

Whatnots is a retail seller of cards, novelty items, and business products. On December 31, 2019, the firm's general ledger contained the following accounts and balances.

INSTRUCTIONS

1. Prepare the Trial Balance section of a 10-column worksheet. The worksheet covers the year ended December 31, 2019.
2. Enter the adjustments in the Adjustments section of the worksheet. Identify each adjustment with the appropriate letter.
3. Complete the worksheet.

Note: This problem will be required to complete Problem 13.4B in Chapter 13.

ACCOUNTS AND BALANCES

Account	Balance	
Cash	$ 3,235	Dr.
Accounts Receivable	6,910	Dr.
Allowance for Doubtful Accounts	600	Cr.
Merchandise Inventory	16,985	Dr.
Supplies	750	Dr.
Prepaid Insurance	2,400	Dr.
Store Equipment	6,000	Dr.
Accumulated Depreciation—Store Equip.	2,000	Cr.
Store Fixtures	15,760	Dr.
Accumulated Depreciation—Store Fixtures	4,100	Cr.
Notes Payable	4,000	Cr.
Accounts Payable	600	Cr.
Interest Payable		
Social Security Tax Payable		
Medicare Tax Payable		
Federal Unemployment Tax Payable		
State Unemployment Tax Payable		
Salaries Payable		
Preston Allen, Capital	39,780	Cr.
Preston Allen, Drawing	8,000	Dr.
Sales	236,560	Cr.
Sales Returns and Allowances	6,000	Dr.
Purchases	160,000	Dr.
Purchases Returns and Allowances	2,000	Cr.
Income Summary		
Rent Expense	18,000	Dr.

ACCOUNTS AND BALANCES (CONT.)

Telephone Expense	2,400	Dr.
Salaries Expense	40,000	Dr.
Payroll Tax Expense	3,200	Dr.
Supplies Expense		
Insurance Expense		
Depreciation Expense—Store Equipment		
Depreciation Expense—Store Fixtures		
Uncollectible Accounts Expense		
Interest Expense		

ADJUSTMENTS

a.–b. Merchandise inventory on hand on December 31, 2019, is $15,840.

c. During 2019, the firm had net credit sales of $160,000. Past experience indicates that 0.8 percent of these sales should result in uncollectible accounts.

d. On December 31, 2019, an inventory of supplies showed that items costing $245 were on hand.

e. On July 1, 2019, the firm purchased a one-year insurance policy for $2,400.

f. On January 2, 2017, the firm purchased store equipment for $6,000. The equipment was estimated to have a five-year useful life and a salvage value of $1,000.

g. On January 4, 2017, the firm purchased store fixtures for $15,760. At the time of the purchase, the fixtures were assumed to have a useful life of seven years and a salvage value of $1,410.

h. On October 1, 2019, the firm issued a six-month, $4,000 note payable at 9 percent interest with a local bank.

i. At year-end (December 31, 2019), the firm owed salaries of $1,450 that will not be paid until January 2020.

j. On December 31, 2019, the firm owed the employer's social security tax (assume 6.2 percent) and Medicare tax (assume 1.45 percent) on the entire $1,450 of accrued wages.

k. On December 31, 2019, the firm owed federal unemployment tax (assume 0.6 percent) and state unemployment tax (assume 5.0 percent) on the entire $1,450 of accrued wages.

Analyze: After all adjustments have been recorded, what is the net book value of the company's assets?

Problem 12.6B ► **Recording adjustments and completing the worksheet.**

Objectives 12-1, 12-2, 12-3, 12-4

The Game Place is a retail store that sells computer games, owned by Matt Huffman. On December 31, 2019, the firm's general ledger contained the accounts and balances below. All account balances are normal.

Cash	$ 34,465
Accounts Receivable	1,669
Prepaid Advertising	480
Supplies	425
Merchandise Inventory	18,500
Store Equipment	30,000
Accumulated Depreciation—Store Equipment	3,000
Office Equipment	4,800
Accumulated Depreciation—Office Equipment	1,500
Notes Payable, due 2020	22,500

Accounts Payable	5,725
Wages Payable	
Social Security Tax Payable	
Medicare Tax Payable	
Unearned Seminar Fees	7,500
Interest Payable	
Matt Huffman, Capital	43,000
Matt Huffman, Drawing	18,000
Income Summary	
Sales	163,660
Sales Discounts	180
Seminar Fee Income	
Purchases	92,500
Purchases Returns and Allowances	770
Freight In	275
Rent Expense	26,400
Wages Expense	18,000
Payroll Taxes Expense	1,811
Depreciation Expense—Store Equipment	
Depreciation Expense—Office Equipment	
Advertising Expense	
Supplies Expense	
Interest Expense	150

INSTRUCTIONS

1. Prepare the Trial Balance section of a 10-column worksheet. The worksheet covers the year ended December 31, 2019.
2. Enter the adjustments below in the Adjustments section of the worksheet. Identify each adjustment with the appropriate letter.
3. Complete the worksheet.

ADJUSTMENTS

a.–b. Merchandise inventory at December 31, 2019, was counted and determined to be $21,200.

c. The amount recorded as prepaid advertising represents $480 paid on September 1, 2019, for six months of advertising.

d. The amount of supplies on hand at December 31 was $125.

e. Depreciation on store equipment was $4,500 for 2019.

f. Depreciation on office equipment was $1,500 for 2019.

g. Unearned seminar fees represent $7,500 received on November 1, 2019, for five seminars. At December 31, three of these seminars had been conducted.

h. Wages owed but not paid at December 31 were $800.

i. On December 31, 2019, the firm owed the employer's social security tax ($49.60) and Medicare tax ($11.60).

j. The note payable bears interest at 8 percent per annum. One month's interest is owed at December 31, 2016.

Analyze: How did the balance of merchandise inventory change during the year ended December 31, 2019?

Critical Thinking Problem 12.1

Completing the Worksheet

The unadjusted trial balance of Ben's Jewelers on December 31, 2019, the end of its fiscal year, appears below.

INSTRUCTIONS

1. Copy the unadjusted trial balance onto a worksheet and complete the worksheet using the following information:
   - **a.–b.** Ending merchandise inventory, $98,700.
   - **c.** Uncollectible accounts expense, $1,000.
   - **d.** Store supplies on hand December 31, 2019, $625.
   - **e.** Office supplies on hand December 31, 2019, $305.
   - **f.** Depreciation on store equipment, $11,360.
   - **g.** Depreciation on office equipment, $3,300.
   - **h.** Accrued sales salaries, $4,000, and accrued office salaries, $1,000.
   - **i.** Social security tax on accrued salaries, $326; Medicare tax on accrued salaries, $76. (Assumes that tax rates have increased.)
   - **j.** Federal unemployment tax on accrued salaries, $56; state unemployment tax on accrued salaries, $270.
2. Journalize the adjusting entries on page 30 of the general journal. Omit descriptions.
3. Journalize the closing entries on page 32 of the general journal. Omit descriptions.
4. Compute the following:
   - **a.** net sales
   - **b.** net delivered cost of purchases
   - **c.** cost of goods sold
   - **d.** net income or net loss
   - **e.** balance of ***Ben Waites, Capital*** on December 31, 2019.

Analyze: What change(s) to ***Ben Waites, Capital*** will be reported on the statement of owner's equity?

BEN'S JEWELERS Trial Balance December 31, 2019		
Cash	$ 13,050	Dr
Accounts Receivable	49,900	Dr.
Allowance for Doubtful Accounts	2,000	Cr.
Merchandise Inventory	105,900	Dr.
Store Supplies	4,230	Dr.
Office Supplies	2,950	Dr.
Store Equipment	113,590	Dr.
Accumulated Depreciation—Store Equipment	13,010	Cr.
Office Equipment	27,640	Dr.
Accumulated Depreciation—Office Equipment	4,930	Cr.
Accounts Payable	4,390	Cr.

BEN'S JEWELERS Trial Balance December 31, 2019		
Salaries Payable		
Social Security Tax Payable		
Medicare Tax Payable		
Federal Unemployment Tax Payable		
State Unemployment Tax Payable		
Ben Waites, Capital	166,310	Cr.
Ben Waites, Drawing	30,000	Dr.
Income Summary		
Sales	862,230	Cr.
Sales Returns and Allowances	7,580	Dr.
Purchases	504,810	Dr.
Purchases Returns and Allowances	4,240	Cr.
Purchases Discounts	10,770	Cr.
Freight In	7,000	Dr.
Salaries Expense—Sales	75,950	Dr.
Rent Expense	35,500	Dr.
Advertising Expense	12,300	Dr.
Store Supplies Expense		
Depreciation Expense—Store Equipment		
Salaries Expense—Office	77,480	Dr.
Payroll Taxes Expense		
Uncollectible Accounts Expense		
Office Supplies Expense		
Depreciation Expense—Office Equipment		

Critical Thinking Problem 12.2

Net Profit

When Sara Yu's father died suddenly, Sara had just completed the semester in college, so she stepped in to run the family business, AAA Couriers, until it could be sold. Under her father's direction, the company was a successful operation and provided ample money to meet the family's needs.

Sara was majoring in biology in college and knew little about business or accounting, but she was eager to do a good job of running the business so it would command a good selling price. Since all of the services performed were paid in cash, Sara figured that she would do all right as long as the ***Cash*** account increased. Thus, she was delighted to watch the cash balance increase from $24,800 at the beginning of the first month to $63,028 at the end of the second month—an increase of $38,228 during the two months she had been in charge. When she was presented an income statement for the two months by the company's bookkeeper, she could not understand why it did not show that amount as income but instead reported only $21,100 as net income.

Knowing that you are taking an accounting class, Sara brings the income statement, shown below, to you and asks if you can help her understand the difference.

AAA COURIERS Income Statement Months of June and July, 2019		
Operating Revenues		
Delivery Fees		$205,018
Operating Expenses		
Salaries and Related Taxes	$128,224	
Gasoline and Oil	31,000	
Repairs Expense	6,570	
Supplies Expense	2,268	
Insurance Expense	2,856	
Depreciation Expense	13,000	
Total Operating Expense		183,918
Net Income		$ 21,100

In addition, Sara permits you to examine the accounting records, which show that the balance of ***Salaries Payable*** was $2,680 at the beginning of the first month but had increased to $4,240 at the end of the second month. Most of the balance in the ***Insurance Expense*** account reflects monthly insurance payments covering only one month each. However, the ***Prepaid Insurance*** account had decreased $300 during the two months, and all supplies had been purchased before Sara took over. The balances of the company's other asset and liability accounts showed no changes.

1. Explain the cause of the difference between the increase in the ***Cash*** account balance and the net income for the two months.
2. Prepare a schedule that accounts for this difference.

BUSINESS CONNECTIONS

Ethical DILEMMA

Out of Balance

The president of Murray Stainless Steel Corporation has told you to go out to the factory and count merchandise inventory. He said the stockholders were coming for a meeting and he wanted to put on a good show. He asked you to make the inventory a bit heavy by counting one row twice. The higher ending inventory will show a higher net income. What should you do?

Financial Statement ANALYSIS

Balance Sheet

McCormick and Company, Incorporated reported the following in its *2014 Annual Report:*

Consolidated Balance Sheet

at November 30 (millions)	*2014*	*2013*
Assets		
Cash and cash equivalents	*$ 77.3*	*$ 63.0*
Trade accounts receivable, less allowances	*493.6*	*495.5*
Inventories	*713.8*	*676.9*
Prepaid expenses and other current assets	*131.5*	*134.8*
Total current assets	*1,416.2*	*1,370.2*
Property, plant, and equipment, net	*602.7*	*576.6*

Analyze:

1. Based on the information presented above, which categories might require adjusting entries at the end of an operating period?
2. List the potential adjusting entries. Disregard dollar amounts.
3. By what percentage did McCormick's cash and cash equivalents increase from 2013 to 2014?

Both Sellers and Servers Adjust

TEAMWORK

Accruals and deferrals can vary for each company. The adjusting entries for a service company will differ from those of a merchandising company. Brainstorm the adjusting entries' similarities and differences for a service company and a merchandising company.

There Is Help for Preparing a Trial Balance

Internet CONNECTION

The trial balance worksheet is an organizational tool to view the accruals and deferrals on one piece of paper. Use your search engine to search for *Trial Balance Worksheet Templates.* Download several different forms of worksheets and notice the number of helpful Excel templates available to download.

Answers to **Self Reviews**

Answers to Section 1 Self Review

1. The worksheet facilitates the end-of-period activities by assembling all data needed in one document. The worksheet provides a place for the trial balance and for entering the necessary adjusting entries, an adjusted trial balance to greatly reduce the chance for mathematical errors, and all the information necessary for closing entries and preparing the income statement, statement of owner's equity, and balance sheet.
2. Both the beginning and ending inventory are presented in the income statement, so both should ultimately appear in the Income Statement columns. In the adjusting entries, the beginning balance is closed and transferred to the ***Income Summary.*** The ending inventory is entered in the ***Inventory*** account by a debit in the Adjustments column and a credit to ***Income Summary*** because it reduces the cost of goods sold.
3. Adjusting entries are necessary because the amounts shown for many accounts in the trial balance reflect old data that ignore the fact that assets shown have been partially consumed, that expenses and incomes have not been entered in the accounts even though they have been incurred or earned, and that some liabilities and assets are not reflected in the accounts.
4. ***Unearned Fee Income*** will be debited for $10,500 and ***Fee Income*** will be credited for that amount.
5. **a.** The amount of adjustments is $3,000 ($18,000 ÷ 6).
   b. ***Rent Expense*** will be debited and ***Prepaid Rent*** will be credited.
6. There is no difference except that the amounts will be different because in one case they reflect only one month's activities and in the other case they reflect 12 months' activities.

Answers to Section 2 Self Review

1. The ***Depreciation Expense*** account is increased. The book value of the asset is decreased.
2. The net effects are:
   a. Assets are understated by $1,600.
   b. Liabilities are understated by $600.
   c. Expenses are understated by $600.
   d. Income is understated by $1,600.
   e. Owner's equity is understated by $1,000.

3. It appears that there is an error in adding the adjustment amount to, or subtracting that amount from, some trial balance amount(s).
4. ***Interest Expense*** is debited and ***Interest Payable*** is credited.
5. **d.** Debit column of the income statement
6. Adjusting entries almost invariably involve the assignment of revenues or expenses to a specific accounting period. If the revenue or expense is not assigned to the correct period, it is assigned to an incorrect period. Thus, both periods are incorrectly stated.

Answers to Comprehensive Self Review

1. The accrual method properly matches expenses with revenues in each accounting period so that statement users can rely on the financial statements prepared for each period.
2. Accrued income is income that has been earned but that has not yet been received in cash or other assets.
3. Accrued income is income earned but not yet received. Unearned income is the reverse of accrued income: It is an amount that has been received but has not yet been earned.
4. This represents a loss because expenses are greater than income. The loss is $28,000.
5. ***Unearned Rent Income*** will be debited for $18,000 and ***Rent Income*** will be credited for $18,000.
6. ***Rent Income*** will be debited for $18,000 and ***Unearned Rent Income*** will be credited for that amount.

Financial Statements and Closing Procedures

Chapter 13

www.sprouts.com

© Calamy stock images/Alamy Stock Photo

Sprouts Farmers Market, Inc., is a chain of specialty grocery stores offering fresh, natural, and organic foods. While Sprouts stores are usually smaller than a typical supermarket grocery store, they offer a complete shopping experience that includes fresh produce, bulk foods, vitamins and supplements, packaged groceries, meat and seafood, baked goods, dairy products, frozen foods, natural body care, and household items. On August 1, 2013, Sprouts Farmers Market, which is headquartered in Phoenix, Arizona, raised $333 million in its initial public offering on NASDAQ.

Sprouts reported net sales of $903.1 million for the third quarter ending September 27, 2015, which amounted to an 18 percent increase from the third quarter of 2014; for the 39-week period ending the same day, net sales totaled $2.7 billion, a 19 percent increase compared to the same period in 2014. The third quarter of 2015 marked 34 consecutive quarters of positive comparable store sales growth for Sprouts. The company opened 26 new stores during the first three quarters of 2015, with eight new stores during the third quarter alone. This brings the total store count to 216 across 13 states employing more than 20,000 team members as of November 5, 2015.

To support long-term growth, Sprouts is investing in product innovation, business intelligence, and its human resources to build on its sales momentum into 2016. The company is focused on remaining an innovator in the natural and organic grocery sector and increasing its relevance to customers. However, before it can move into recording its operations for 2016, the company must close out fiscal year 2015. By doing so, Sprouts will have complete revenue and expense results for the fiscal year ending 2015 against which to measure its performance in the years to come.

thinking critically

What types of revenues and expenses do you think Sprouts would include on its income statement that would be typical for a grocery store?

LEARNING OBJECTIVES

- **13-1** Prepare a classified income statement from the worksheet.
- **13-2** Prepare a statement of owner's equity from the worksheet.
- **13-3** Prepare a classified balance sheet from the worksheet.
- **13-4** Journalize and post the adjusting entries.
- **13-5** Journalize and post the closing entries.
- **13-6** Prepare a postclosing trial balance.
- **13-7** Journalize and post reversing entries.
- **13-8** Define the accounting terms new to this chapter.

NEW TERMS

- accounts receivable turnover
- classified financial statement
- current assets
- current liabilities
- current ratio
- gross profit
- gross profit percentage
- inventory turnover
- liquidity
- long-term liabilities
- multiple-step income statement
- plant and equipment
- reversing entries
- single-step income statement
- working capital

Section 1

SECTION OBJECTIVES	TERMS TO LEARN
>> 13-1 Prepare a classified income statement from the worksheet. WHY IT'S IMPORTANT To help decision makers, financial information needs to be presented in a meaningful and easy-to-use way. >> 13-2 Prepare a statement of owner's equity from the worksheet. WHY IT'S IMPORTANT The statement of owner's equity reports changes to and balances in the owner's equity account. >> 13-3 Prepare a classified balance sheet from the worksheet. WHY IT'S IMPORTANT Grouping accounts helps financial statement users to identify total assets, equity, and financial obligations of the business.	classified financial statement current assets current liabilities gross profit liquidity long-term liabilities multiple-step income statement plant and equipment single-step income statement

Preparing the Financial Statements

The information needed to prepare the financial statements is on the worksheet in the Income Statement and Balance Sheet sections. At the end of the period, Whiteside Antiques prepares three financial statements: income statement, statement of owner's equity, and balance sheet, based on the worksheet you studied in Chapter 12. The income statement and the balance sheet are arranged in a classified format. On **classified financial statements,** revenues, expenses, assets, and liabilities are divided into groups of similar accounts and a subtotal is given for each group. This makes the financial statements more useful to the readers.

> The annual report of the Coca-Cola Company includes Consolidated Balance Sheets, Consolidated Statements of Income, and Consolidated Statements of Shareowners' Equity. The annual report also contains a table of Selected Financial Data that reports five consecutive years of summarized financial information.

The Classified Income Statement

A classified income statement is sometimes called a **multiple-step income statement** because several subtotals are computed before net income is calculated. The simpler income statement you learned about in previous chapters is called a **single-step income statement.** It lists all revenues in one section and all expenses in another section. Only one computation is necessary to determine the net income (Total Revenue − Total Expenses = Net Income).

Figure 13.1 shows the classified income statement for Whiteside Antiques. Refer to it as you learn how to prepare a multiple-step income statement.

>> **13-1 OBJECTIVE**
Prepare a classified income statement from the worksheet.

OPERATING REVENUE

The first section of the classified income statement contains the revenue from operations. This is the revenue earned from normal business activities. Other income is presented separately near the bottom of the statement. For Whiteside Antiques, all operating revenue comes from sales of merchandise.

FIGURE 13.1 Classified Income Statement

Whiteside Antiques
Income Statement
Year Ended December 31, 2019

Operating Revenue				
Sales				561,650.00
Less Sales Returns and Allowances				12,500.00
Net Sales				549,150.00
Cost of Goods Sold				
Merchandise Inventory, Jan. 1, 2019			52,000.00	
Purchases		321,500.00		
Freight In		9,800.00		
Delivered Cost of Purchases		331,300.00		
Less Purchases Returns and Allowances	3,050.00			
Purchases Discounts	3,130.00	6,180.00		
Net Delivered Cost of Purchases			325,120.00	
Total Merchandise Available for Sale			377,120.00	
Less Merchandise Inventory, Dec. 31, 2019			47,000.00	
Cost of Goods Sold				330,120.00
Gross Profit on Sales				219,030.00
Operating Expenses				
Selling Expenses				
Salaries Expense—Sales		79,690.00		
Advertising Expense		7,425.00		
Cash Short or Over		125.00		
Supplies Expense		4,975.00		
Depreciation Expense—Store Equipment		2,400.00		
Total Selling Expenses			94,615.00	
General and Administrative Expenses				
Rent Expense		27,600.00		
Salaries Expense—Office		26,500.00		
Insurance Expense		2,450.00		
Payroll Taxes Expense		7,368.80		
Telephone Expense		1,875.00		
Uncollectible Accounts Expense		800.00		
Utilities Expense		5,925.00		
Depreciation Expense—Office Equipment		700.00		
Total General and Administrative Expenses			73,218.80	
Total Operating Expenses				167,833.80
Net Income from Operations				51,196.20
Other Income				
Interest Income		166.00		
Miscellaneous Income		366.00		
Total Other Income			532.00	
Other Expenses				
Interest Expense			770.00	
Net Nonoperating Expense				238.00
Net Income for Year				50,958.20

Because Whiteside Antiques is a retail firm, it does not offer sales discounts to its customers. If it did, the sales discounts would be deducted from total sales in order to compute net sales. The net sales amount is computed as follows:

Sales
(Sales Returns and Allowances)
(Sales Discounts)

Net Sales

The parentheses indicate that the amount is subtracted. Net sales for Whiteside Antiques are $549,150 for 2019.

COST OF GOODS SOLD

The Cost of Goods Sold section contains information about the cost of the merchandise that was sold during the period. Three elements are needed to compute the cost of goods sold: beginning inventory, net delivered cost of purchases, and ending inventory. The format is:

Purchases
+ Freight In
(Purchases Returns and Allowances)
(Purchases Discounts)

Net Delivered Cost of Purchases

Beginning Merchandise Inventory
+ Net Delivered Cost of Purchases

Total Merchandise Available for Sale
(Ending Merchandise Inventory)

Cost of Goods Sold

For Whiteside Antiques, the net delivered cost of purchases is $325,120 and the cost of goods sold is $330,120. ***Merchandise Inventory*** is the one account that appears on both the income statement and the balance sheet. Beginning and ending merchandise inventory balances appear on the income statement. Ending merchandise inventory also appears on the balance sheet in the Assets section.

GROSS PROFIT ON SALES

The **gross profit** on sales is the difference between the net sales and the cost of goods sold. For Whiteside, net sales is the revenue earned from selling antique items. Cost of goods sold is what Whiteside paid for the antiques that were sold during the fiscal period. Gross profit is what is left to cover operating expenses and provide a profit. The format is:

Net Sales
(Cost of Goods Sold)

Gross Profit on Sales

The gross profit on sales is $219,030.

OPERATING EXPENSES

Operating expenses are expenses that arise from normal business activities. Whiteside Antiques separates operating expenses into two categories: *Selling Expenses* and *General and Administrative Expenses.* The selling expenses relate directly to the marketing, sale, and delivery of goods. The general and administrative expenses are necessary for business operations but are not directly connected with the sales function. Rent, utilities, and salaries for office employees are examples of general and administrative expenses.

Merchandising firms often use warehouses to store inventory. These firms would have an additional operating expense category: *Warehouse Expenses.*

FIGURE 13.2

Statement of Owner's Equity

Whiteside Antiques Statement of Owner's Equity Year Ended December 31, 2019		
Bill Whiteside, Capital, January 1, 2019		*61 2 2 1 00*
Net Income for Year	*50 9 5 8 20*	
Less Withdrawals for the Year	*27 6 0 0 00*	
Increase in Capital		*23 3 5 8 20*
Bill Whiteside, Capital, December 31, 2019		*84 5 7 9 20*

NET INCOME OR NET LOSS FROM OPERATIONS

Keeping operating and nonoperating income separate helps financial statement users learn about the operating efficiency of the firm. The format for determining net income (or net loss) from operations is:

Gross Profit on Sales
(Total Operating Expenses)

Net Income (or Net Loss) from Operations

For Whiteside Antiques, net income from operations is $51,196.20.

OTHER INCOME AND OTHER EXPENSES

Income that is earned from sources other than normal business activities appears in the Other Income section. For Whiteside Antiques, other income includes interest on notes receivable and one miscellaneous income item.

Expenses that are not directly connected with business operations appear in the Other Expenses section. The only other expense for Whiteside Antiques is interest expense.

NET INCOME OR NET LOSS

Net income is all the revenue minus all the expenses. For Whiteside Antiques, net income is $50,958.20. If there is a net loss, it appears in parentheses. Net income or net loss is used to prepare the statement of owner's equity.

CONDENSED INCOME STATEMENT

Many companies provide condensed financial statements to vendors and creditors. A condensed income statement summarizes much of the detail into a few lines of information. A condensed income statement for Whiteside Antiques is prepared below, in whole dollars.

Whiteside Antiques Income Statement Year Ended December 31, 2019		
Net Sales		*549,150*
Cost of Goods Sold		*330,120*
Gross Profit		*219,030*
Operating Expenses:		
Selling Expenses	*94,615*	
General and Administrative Expenses	*73,219*	
Total Operating Expenses		*167,834*
Net Income from Operations		*51,196*
Other Expense, Net		*238*
Net Income for Year		*50,958*

>> 13-2 OBJECTIVE

Prepare a statement of owner's equity from the worksheet.

THE STATEMENT OF OWNER'S EQUITY

The statement of owner's equity reports the changes that occurred in the owner's financial interest during the period. Figure 13.2 on the previous page shows the statement of owner's equity for Whiteside Antiques. The ending capital balance for Bill Whiteside, $84,579.20, is used to prepare the balance sheet.

>> 13-3 OBJECTIVE

Prepare a classified balance sheet from the worksheet.

THE CLASSIFIED BALANCE SHEET

The classified balance sheet divides the various assets and liabilities into groups. Figure 13.3 below shows the balance sheet for Whiteside Antiques. Refer to it as you learn how to prepare a classified balance sheet.

FIGURE 13.3

Classified Balance Sheet

Whiteside Antiques
Balance Sheet
December 31, 2019

Assets			
Current Assets			
Cash			13 136 00
Petty Cash Fund			100 00
Notes Receivable			1 200 00
Accounts Receivable		32 000 00	
Less Allowance for Doubtful Accounts		1 050 00	30 950 00
Interest Receivable			30 00
Merchandise Inventory			47 000 00
Prepaid Expenses			
Supplies		1 325 00	
Prepaid Insurance		4 900 00	
Prepaid Interest		75 00	6 300 00
Total Current Assets			98 716 00
Plant and Equipment			
Store Equipment	30 000 00		
Less Accumulated Depreciation	2 400 00	27 600 00	
Office Equipment	5 000 00		
Less Accumulated Depreciation	700 00	4 300 00	
Total Plant and Equipment			31 900 00
Total Assets			130 616 00
Liabilities and Owner's Equity			
Current Liabilities			
Notes Payable—Trade		2 000 00	
Notes Payable—Bank		9 000 00	
Accounts Payable		24 129 00	
Interest Payable		20 00	
Social Security Tax Payable		1 158 40	
Medicare Tax Payable		267 40	
Employee Income Tax Payable		990 00	
Federal Unemployment Tax Payable		7 20	
State Unemployment Tax Payable		64 80	
Salaries Payable		1 200 00	
Sales Tax Payable		7 200 00	
Total Current Liabilities			46 036 80
Owner's Equity			
Bill Whiteside, Capital			84 579 20
Total Liabilities and Owner's Equity			130 616 00

ABOUT **ACCOUNTING**

Financial Reports

Most large companies present comparative condensed income statements and balance sheets. The Securities and Exchange Commission requires most publicly traded corporations to present three years of income statements and two years of balance sheets. This provides users information that helps assess the progress in profit and financial strength of the company.

CURRENT ASSETS

Current assets consist of cash, items that will normally be converted into cash within one year, and items that will be used up within one year. Current assets are usually listed in order of liquidity. **Liquidity** is the ease with which an item can be converted into cash. Current assets are vital to the survival of a business because they provide the funds needed to pay bills and meet expenses. The current assets for Whiteside Antiques total $98,716.

recall

Book Value

Book value is the portion of the original cost that has not been depreciated. Usually, book value bears no relation to the market value of the asset.

PLANT AND EQUIPMENT

Noncurrent assets are called *long-term assets.* An important category of long-term assets is plant and equipment. **Plant and equipment** consists of property that will be used in the business for longer than one year. For many businesses, plant and equipment represents a sizable investment. The balance sheet shows three amounts for each category of plant and equipment:

Asset
(Accumulated depreciation)

Book value

For Whiteside Antiques, total plant and equipment is $31,900.

CURRENT LIABILITIES

Current liabilities are the debts that must be paid within one year. They are usually listed in order of priority of payment. Management must ensure that funds are available to pay current liabilities when they become due in order to maintain the firm's good credit reputation. For Whiteside Antiques, total current liabilities are $46,036.80.

LONG-TERM LIABILITIES

Long-term liabilities are debts of the business that are due more than one year in the future. Although repayment of long-term liabilities might not be due for several years, management must make sure that periodic interest is paid promptly. Long-term liabilities include mortgages, notes payable, and loans payable. Whiteside Antiques had no long-term liabilities on December 31, 2019.

OWNER'S EQUITY

Whiteside Antiques prepares a separate statement of owner's equity that reports all information about changes that occurred in Bill Whiteside's financial interest during the period. The ending balance from that statement is transferred to the Owner's Equity section of the balance sheet.

Section 1 Self Review

QUESTIONS

1. Why are financial statements prepared in classified form?
2. What is the distinction between current liabilities and long-term liabilities?
3. What is gross profit on sales?

EXERCISES

4. Which of the following is not a current asset?
   a. Merchandise inventory
   b. A note receivable due in 11 months
   c. Prepaid insurance covering the next eight months
   d. A note receivable due in 13 months
5. How should purchases returns and allowances be shown on the income statement?
   a. As Other Income
   b. As an addition to the delivered cost of purchases
   c. As a deduction from the delivered cost of purchases
   d. As Other Expenses

ANALYSIS

6. Assume that a business listed the *Freight In* account in the Operating Expense section of the income statement. What is the effect on net purchases? On total operating expenses? On net income from operations?

(Answers to Section 1 Self Review are on page 497.)

Section 2

SECTION OBJECTIVES	TERMS TO LEARN
>> 13-4 Journalize and post the adjusting entries. WHY IT'S IMPORTANT Adjusting entries match revenue and expenses to the proper periods. >> 13-5 Journalize and post the closing entries. WHY IT'S IMPORTANT The temporary accounts are closed in order to prepare for the next accounting period. >> 13-6 Prepare a postclosing trial balance. WHY IT'S IMPORTANT The general ledger must remain in balance. >> 13-7 Journalize and post reversing entries. WHY IT'S IMPORTANT Reversing entries are made so that transactions can be recorded in the usual way in the next accounting period.	accounts receivable turnover current ratio gross profit percentage inventory turnover reversing entries working capital

Completing the Accounting Cycle

The complete accounting cycle was presented in Chapter 6. In this section, we will complete the accounting cycle for Whiteside Antiques.

>> 13-4 OBJECTIVE
Journalize and post the adjusting entries.

Journalizing and Posting the Adjusting Entries

All adjustments are shown on the worksheet. After the financial statements have been prepared, the adjustments are made a permanent part of the accounting records. They are recorded in the general journal as adjusting journal entries and are posted to the general ledger.

JOURNALIZING THE ADJUSTING ENTRIES

Figure 13.4 shows the adjusting journal entries for Whiteside Antiques. Each adjusting entry shows how the adjustment was calculated. Supervisors and auditors need to understand, without additional explanation, why the adjustment was made.

Let's review the types of adjusting entries made by Whiteside Antiques:

Type of Adjustment	Worksheet Reference	Purpose
Inventory	(a–b)	Removes beginning inventory and adds ending inventory to the accounting records.
Expense	(c–e)	Matches expense to revenue for the period; the credit is to a contra asset account.
Accrued Expense	(f–i)	Matches expense to revenue for the period; the credit is to a liability account.
Prepaid Expense	(j–l)	Matches expense to revenue for the period; the credit is to an asset account.
Accrued Income	(m)	Recognizes income earned in the period. The debit is to an asset account.

FIGURE 13.4

Adjusting Entries in the General Journal

GENERAL JOURNAL PAGE 25

DATE		DESCRIPTION	POST. REF.	DEBIT	CREDIT
		Adjusting Entries			
2019		*(Adjustment a)*			
Dec.	*31*	*Income Summary*	*399*	*52000 00*	
		Merchandise Inventory	*121*		*52000 00*
		To transfer beginning inventory			
		to Income Summary			
		(Adjustment b)			
	31	*Merchandise Inventory*	*121*	*47000 00*	
		Income Summary	*399*		*47000 00*
		To record ending inventory			
		(Adjustment c)			
	31	*Uncollectible Accounts Expense*	*685*	*800 00*	
		Allowance For Doubtful Accounts	*112*		*800 00*
		To record estimated loss			
		from uncollectible accounts			
		based on 0.80% of net			
		credit sales of $100,000			
		(Adjustment d)			
	31	*Depreciation Expense—Store Equip.*	*620*	*2400 00*	
		Accum. Depreciation—Store Equip.	*132*		*2400 00*
		To record depreciation			
		for 2019 as shown by			
		schedule on file			
		(Adjustment e)			
	31	*Depreciation Expense—Office Equip.*	*689*	*700 00*	
		Accum. Depreciation—Office Equip.	*142*		*700 00*
		To record depreciation			
		for 2019 as shown by			
		schedule on file			
		(Adjustment f)			
	31	*Salaries Expense—Sales*	*602*	*1200 00*	
		Salaries Payable	*229*		*1200 00*
		To record accrued salaries			
		of part-time sales clerks			
		for Dec. 28–31			

(continued)

FIGURE 13.4

Adjusting Entries in the General Journal (continued)

GENERAL JOURNAL PAGE *26*

DATE		DESCRIPTION	POST. REF.	DEBIT	CREDIT
		Adjusting Entries			
2019		*(Adjustment g)*			
Dec.	*31*	*Payroll Taxes Expense*	*665*	*91 80*	
		Social Security Tax Payable	*221*		*74 40*
		Medicare Tax Payable	*223*		*17 40*
		To record accrued payroll			
		taxes on accrued salaries			
		for Dec. 28–31			
		(Adjustment h)			
	31	*Payroll Taxes Expense*	*665*	*72 00*	
		Fed. Unemployment Tax Payable	*225*		*7 20*
		State Unemployment Tax Payable	*227*		*64 80*
		To record accrued payroll			
		taxes on accrued salaries			
		for Dec. 28–31			
		(Adjustment i)			
	31	*Interest Expense*	*695*	*20 00*	
		Interest Payable	*216*		*20 00*
		To record interest on a			
		2-month, $2,000, 12%			
		note payable dated			
		Dec. 1, 2019			
		(Adjustment j)			
	31	*Supplies Expense*	*615*	*4 975 00*	
		Supplies	*129*		*4 975 00*
		To record supplies used			
		(Adjustment k)			
	31	*Insurance Expense*	*660*	*2 450 00*	
		Prepaid Insurance	*126*		*2 450 00*
		To record expired			
		insurance on 3-year			
		policy purchased for			
		$7,350 on Jan. 2, 2019			

FIGURE 13.4

Adjusting Entries in the General Journal (continued)

GENERAL JOURNAL PAGE 27

	DATE		DESCRIPTION	POST. REF.	DEBIT	CREDIT	
1	2019		(Adjustment l)				1
2	Dec.	31	Interest Expense	695	150 00		2
3			Prepaid Interest	127		150 00	3
4			To record transfer of 2/3				4
5			of prepaid interest of				5
6			$225 for a 3-month,				6
7			10% note payable issued				7
8			to bank on Nov. 1, 2019				8
9							9
10			(Adjustment m)				10
11		31	Interest Receivable	116	30 00		11
12			Interest Income	491		30 00	12
13			To record accrued interest				13
14			earned on a 4-month,				14
15			15% note receivable				15
16			dated Nov. 1, 2019				16
17			($1,200 x 0.15 x 2/12)				17
18							18

POSTING THE ADJUSTING ENTRIES

After the adjustments have been recorded in the general journal, they are promptly posted to the general ledger. The word *Adjusting* is entered in the Description column of the general ledger account. This distinguishes it from entries for transactions that occurred during that period. After the adjusting entries have been posted, the general ledger account balances match the amounts shown in the Adjusted Trial Balance section of the worksheet in Figure 12.2.

Journalizing and Posting the Closing Entries

At the end of the period, the temporary accounts are closed. The temporary accounts are the revenue, cost of goods sold, expense, and drawing accounts.

JOURNALIZING THE CLOSING ENTRIES

>> 13-5 OBJECTIVE

Journalize and post the closing entries.

We were first introduced to closing journal entries in Chapter 6. Due to the additional accounts required for merchandising companies, the closing journal entries are more complex for a merchandising firm.

The Income Statement section of the worksheet in Figure 12.2 provides the data needed to prepare closing entries. There are four steps in the closing process:

1. Close revenue accounts and cost of goods sold accounts with credit balances to ***Income Summary.***
2. Close expense accounts and cost of goods sold accounts with debit balances to ***Income Summary.***
3. Close ***Income Summary,*** which now reflects the net income or loss for the period, to owner's capital.
4. Close the drawing account to owner's capital.

Step 1: Closing the Revenue Accounts and the Cost of Goods Sold Accounts with Credit Balances. The first entry closes the revenue accounts and other temporary income statement accounts with credit balances. Look at the Income Statement section of the worksheet in Figure 12.2. There are five items listed in the Credit column, not including ***Income Summary.*** Debit each account, except ***Income Summary,*** for its balance. Credit ***Income Summary*** for the total, $568,362.

GENERAL JOURNAL PAGE 28

	DATE		DESCRIPTION	POST. REF.	DEBIT	CREDIT	
1	2019		Closing Entries				1
2	Dec.	31	Sales	401	561 650 00		2
3			Interest Income	491	166 00		3
4			Miscellaneous Income	493	366 00		4
5			Purchases Returns and Allowances	503	3 050 00		5
6			Purchases Discounts	504	3 130 00		6
7			Income Summary			568 362 00	7

Step 2: Closing the Expense Accounts and the Cost of Goods Sold Accounts with Debit Balances. The Debit column of the Income Statement section of the worksheet in Figure 12.2 shows the expense accounts and the cost of goods sold accounts with debit balances. Credit each account, *except* ***Income Summary,*** for its balance. Debit ***Income Summary*** for the total, $512,403.80.

GENERAL JOURNAL PAGE 28

	DATE		DESCRIPTION	POST. REF.	DEBIT	CREDIT	
1	2019						1
9	Dec.	31	Income Summary	399	512 403 80		9
10			Sales Returns and Allowances	451		12 500 00	10
11			Purchases	501		321 500 00	11
12			Freight In	502		9 800 00	12
13			Salaries Expense—Sales	602		79 690 00	13
14			Advertising Expense	605		7 425 00	14
15			Cash Short or Over	610		125 00	15
16			Supplies Expense	615		4 975 00	16
17			Depreciation Expense—Store Equip.	620		2 400 00	17
18			Rent Expense	640		27 600 00	18
19			Salaries Expense—Office	645		26 500 00	19
20			Insurance Expense	660		2 450 00	20
21			Payroll Taxes Expense	665		7 368 80	21
22			Telephone Expense	680		1 875 00	22
23			Uncollectible Accounts Expense	685		800 00	23
24			Utilities Expense	687		5 925 00	24
25			Depreciation Expense—Office Equip.	689		700 00	25
26			Interest Expense	695		770 00	26

Step 3: Closing the Income Summary Account. After the first two closing entries have been posted, the balance of the ***Income Summary*** account is equal to the net income or net loss for the period. The third closing entry transfers the ***Income***

Summary balance to the owner's capital account. ***Income Summary*** after the second closing entry has a balance of $50,958.20.

Income Summary			
12/31	52,000.00	12/31	47,000.00
12/31	512,403.80	12/31	568,362.00
	564,403.80		615,362.00
		Bal.	50,958.20

Adjusting Entries (a–b)
Closing Entries

Keep in mind the first debit and the first credit in the ***Income Summary*** account above resulted from the adjusting journal entries for ***Merchandise Inventory*** discussed in Chapter 12. For Whiteside Antiques, the third closing entry is as follows. This closes the ***Income Summary*** account, which remains closed until it is used in the end-of-period process for the next year.

GENERAL JOURNAL PAGE 28

	DATE		DESCRIPTION	POST. REF.	DEBIT	CREDIT	
28	Dec.	31	Income Summary	399	50 958 20		28
29			Bill Whiteside, Capital	301		50 958 20	29

Step 4: Closing the Drawing Account. This entry closes the drawing account and updates the capital account so that its balance agrees with the ending capital reported on the statement of owner's equity and on the balance sheet.

GENERAL JOURNAL PAGE 28

	DATE		DESCRIPTION	POST. REF.	DEBIT	CREDIT	
31	Dec.	31	Bill Whiteside, Capital	301	27 600 00		31
32			Bill Whiteside, Drawing	302		27 600 00	32

POSTING THE CLOSING ENTRIES

The closing entries are posted from the general journal to the general ledger. The word *Closing* is entered in the Description column of each account that is closed. After the closing entry is posted, each temporary account balance is zero.

Preparing a Postclosing Trial Balance

>> 13-6 OBJECTIVE
Prepare a postclosing trial balance.

After the closing entries have been posted, prepare a postclosing trial balance to confirm that the general ledger is in balance. Only the accounts that have balances—the asset, liability, and owner's capital accounts—appear on the postclosing trial balance. The postclosing trial balance matches the amounts reported on the balance sheet. To verify this, compare the postclosing trial balance, Figure 13.5, with the balance sheet, Figure 13.3.

If the postclosing trial balance shows that the general ledger is out of balance, find and correct the error or errors immediately. Any necessary correcting entries must be journalized and posted so that the general ledger is in balance before any transactions can be recorded for the new period.

FIGURE 13.5

Postclosing Trial Balance

Whiteside Antiques
Postclosing Trial Balance
December 31, 2019

ACCOUNT NAME	DEBIT	CREDIT
Cash	13 136 00	
Petty Cash Fund	100 00	
Notes Receivable	1 200 00	
Accounts Receivable	32 000 00	
Allowance for Doubtful Accounts		1 050 00
Interest Receivable	30 00	
Merchandise Inventory	47 000 00	
Supplies	1 325 00	
Prepaid Insurance	4 900 00	
Prepaid Interest	75 00	
Store Equipment	30 000 00	
Accumulated Depreciation—Store Equipment		2 400 00
Office Equipment	5 000 00	
Accumulated Depreciation—Office Equipment		700 00
Notes Payable—Trade		2 000 00
Notes Payable—Bank		9 000 00
Accounts Payable		24 129 00
Interest Payable		20 00
Social Security Tax Payable		1 158 40
Medicare Tax Payable		267 40
Employee Income Taxes Payable		990 00
Federal Unemployment Tax Payable		7 20
State Unemployment Tax Payable		64 80
Salaries Payable		1 200 00
Sales Tax Payable		7 200 00
Bill Whiteside, Capital		84 579 20
Totals	134 766 00	134 766 00

Interpreting the Financial Statements

Interested parties analyze the financial statements to evaluate the results of operations and to make decisions. Interpreting financial statements requires an understanding of the business and the environment in which it operates as well as the nature and limitations of accounting information. Ratios and other measurements are used to analyze and interpret financial statements. Four such measurements are used by Whiteside Antiques.

The **gross profit percentage** reveals the amount of gross profit from each sales dollar. The gross profit percentage is calculated by dividing gross profit by net sales. For Whiteside Antiques, gross profit was almost 40 cents for every dollar of net sales.

$$\frac{\text{Gross profit}}{\text{Net sales}} = \frac{\$219{,}030}{\$549{,}150} = 0.3988 = 39.9\%$$

Working capital is the difference between total current assets and total current liabilities. It is a measure of the firm's ability to pay its current obligations. Whiteside Antiques' working capital is $52,679.20, calculated as follows:

important!

Current Ratio

Banks and other lenders look closely at the current ratio of each loan applicant.

$$\text{Current assets} - \text{Current liabilities} = \$98{,}716.00 - \$46{,}036.80 = \$52{,}679.20$$

The **current ratio** is a relationship between current assets and current liabilities that provides a measure of a firm's ability to pay its current debts. Whiteside has $2.14 in current assets for every dollar of current liabilities. The current ratio may also be compared to that of other firms in the same business. The current ratio is calculated in the following manner:

$$\frac{\text{Current assets}}{\text{Current liabilities}} = \frac{\$98{,}716.00}{\$46{,}036.80} = 2.14 \text{ to } 1$$

Microsoft reported current assets of $124.7 billion and current liabilities of $49.9 billion on June 30, 2015. The current ratio shows that the business has $2.50 of current assets for each dollar of current liabilities.

Inventory turnover shows the number of times inventory is replaced during the accounting period. Inventory turnover is calculated in the following manner:

$$\text{Inventory turnover} = \frac{\text{Cost of goods sold}}{\text{Average inventory}}$$

$$\text{Average inventory} = \frac{\text{Beginning inventory} + \text{Ending inventory}}{2}$$

$$\text{Average inventory} = \frac{\$52{,}000 + \$47{,}000}{2} = \$49{,}500$$

$$\text{Inventory turnover} = \frac{\$330{,}120}{\$49{,}500} = 6.67 \text{ times}$$

For Whiteside Antiques, the average inventory for the year was $49,500. The inventory turnover was 6.67; that is, inventory was replaced about seven times during the year.

A company needs to collect accounts receivable promptly. This minimizes the amount of working capital tied up in receivables and improves cash flow. The **accounts receivable turnover** measures the reasonableness of accounts receivable outstanding, and can be used to estimate the average collection period of accounts receivable.

The accounts receivable turnover is computed as follows:

$$\text{Accounts receivable turnover} = \frac{\text{Net credit sales}}{\text{Average accounts receivable}}$$

Assume the net credit sales for Whiteside Antiques were $326,975 in 2019 and that the balance of accounts receivable at December 31, 2018, was $28,500. The average accounts receivable are $29,725, calculated as:

$$\text{Average accounts receivable} = \frac{\$28{,}500 + \$30{,}950}{2} = \$29{,}725$$

The accounts receivable turnover is 11. The calculation follows.

$$\text{Accounts receivable turnover} = \frac{\$326{,}975}{\$29{,}725} = 11.0 \text{ times}$$

We can use the accounts receivable turnover to estimate the average collection period. The average collection period is computed by dividing 365 days by the accounts receivable turnover. For Whiteside Antiques, its average collection period in 2016 was 33.2 days, calculated as:

$$\text{Average collection period} = \frac{365 \text{ days}}{11.0} = 33.2 \text{ days.}$$

If Whiteside Antiques grants credit terms of n/30 days, its average collection period would be considered satisfactory.

Journalizing and Posting Reversing Entries

>> 13-7 OBJECTIVE

Journalize and post reversing entries.

Some adjustments made at the end of one period can cause problems in the next period. **Reversing entries** are made to reverse the effect of certain adjustments. This helps prevent errors in recording payments or cash receipts in the new accounting period.

Let's use adjustment **(f)** as an illustration of how reversing entries are helpful. On December 31, Whiteside Antiques owed $1,200 of salaries to its part-time sales clerks. The salaries will be paid in January. To recognize the salaries expense in December, adjustment **(f)** was made to debit ***Salaries Expense—Sales*** for $1,200 and credit ***Salaries Payable*** for $1,200. The adjustment was recorded and posted in the accounting records.

By payday on January 3, the part-time sales clerks have earned $1,700:

$1,200	earned in December
$ 500	earned in January

recall

Accrual Basis

Revenues are recognized when earned, and expenses are recognized when incurred or used, regardless of when cash is received or paid.

The entry to record the January 3 payment of the salaries is a debit to ***Salaries Expense—Sales*** for $500, a debit to ***Salaries Payable*** for $1,200, and a credit to ***Cash*** for $1,700. This entry recognizes the salary expense for January and reduces the ***Salaries Payable*** account to zero.

Salaries Expense—Sales

Debit		Credit	
1/3	500		

Cash

Debit		Credit	
12/31	13,136	1/3	1,700
Bal.	11,436		

Salaries Payable

Debit		Credit	
1/3	1,200	12/31	1,200
		Bal.	0

To record this transaction, the accountant had to review the adjustment in the end-of-period records and divide the amount paid between the expense and liability accounts. This review is time consuming, can cause errors, and is sometimes forgotten.

Reversing entries provide a way to guard against oversights, eliminate the review of accounting records, and simplify the entry made in the new period. As an example of a reversing entry, we will analyze the same transaction (January 3 payroll of $1,700) if reversing entries are made.

First, record the adjustment on December 31. Then record the reversing entry on January 1. Note that the reversing entry is the exact opposite (the reverse) of the adjustment. After the reversing entry is posted, the ***Salaries Payable*** account shows a zero balance and the ***Salaries Expense—Sales*** account has a credit balance. This is unusual because the normal balance of an expense account is a debit.

GENERAL JOURNAL PAGE 25

	DATE		DESCRIPTION	POST. REF.	DEBIT	CREDIT	
1	2019		Adjusting Entries				1
35			(Adjustment f)				35
36	Dec.	31	Salaries Expense—Sales	602	1 200 00		36
37			Salaries Payable	229		1 200 00	37

GENERAL JOURNAL PAGE 29

	DATE		DESCRIPTION	POST. REF.	DEBIT	CREDIT	
1	2020		Reversing Entries				1
2	Jan.	1	Salaries Payable	229	1 200 00		2
3			Salaries Expense—Sales	602		1 200 00	3

ACCOUNT *Salaries Payable* ACCOUNT NO. *229*

DATE		DESCRIPTION	POST. REF.	DEBIT	CREDIT	BALANCE DEBIT	BALANCE CREDIT
2019							
Dec.	31	Adjusting	J25		1,200.00		1,200.00
2020							
Jan.	1	Reversing	J29	1,200.00			–0–

ACCOUNT *Salaries Expense—Sales* ACCOUNT NO. *602*

DATE		DESCRIPTION	POST. REF.	DEBIT	CREDIT	BALANCE DEBIT	BALANCE CREDIT
2019							
Dec.	31	Balance				78,490.00	
	31	Adjusting	J25	1,200.00		79,690.00	
	31	Closing	J28		79,690.00	–0–	
2020							
Jan.	1	Reversing	J29		1,200.00		1,200.00

On January 3, the payment of $1,700 of salaries is recorded in the normal manner. Notice that this entry reduces cash and increases the expense account for the entire $1,700. It does not allocate the $1,700 between the expense and liability accounts.

GENERAL JOURNAL PAGE *30*

	DATE		DESCRIPTION	POST. REF.	DEBIT	CREDIT	
1	2020						1
2	Jan.	3	Salaries Expense—Sales	602	1,700.00		2
3			Cash	101		1,700.00	3

After this entry is posted, the expenses are properly divided between the two periods: $1,200 in December and $500 in January. The ***Salaries Payable*** account has a zero balance. The accountant did not have to review the previous records or allocate the payment between two accounts when the salaries were paid.

ACCOUNT *Salaries Expense—Sales* ACCOUNT NO. *602*

DATE		DESCRIPTION	POST. REF.	DEBIT	CREDIT	BALANCE DEBIT	BALANCE CREDIT
2019							
Dec.	31	Balance				78,490.00	
	31	Adjusting	J25	1,200.00		79,690.00	
	31	Closing	J28		79,690.00	–0–	
2020							
Jan.	1	Reversing	J29		1,200.00		1,200.00
	3		J30	1,700.00		500.00	

IDENTIFYING ITEMS FOR REVERSAL

Not all adjustments need to be reversed. Normally, reversing entries are made for accrued items that involve future payments or receipts of cash. Reversing entries are not made for uncollectible accounts, depreciation, and prepaid expenses—if they are initially recorded as assets. However, when prepaid expenses are initially recorded as expenses (the alternative method), the end-of-period adjustment needs to be reversed.

Whiteside Antiques makes reversing entries for:

- accrued salaries—adjustment **(f),**
- accrued payroll taxes—adjustments **(g)** and **(h),**
- interest payable—adjustment **(i),**
- interest receivable—adjustment **(m).**

JOURNALIZING REVERSING ENTRIES

We just analyzed the reversing entry for accrued salaries, adjustment **(f).** The next two reversing entries are for accrued payroll taxes. Making these reversing entries means that the accountant does not have to review the year-end adjustments before recording the payment of payroll taxes in the next year.

GENERAL JOURNAL PAGE 29

	DATE		DESCRIPTION	POST. REF.	DEBIT	CREDIT	
1	2020						1
6	Jan.	1	Social Security Tax Payable	221	74 40		6
7			Medicare Tax Payable	223	17 40		7
8			Payroll Taxes Expense	665		91 80	8
9			To reverse adjusting entry				9
10			(g) made Dec. 31, 2019				10
11							11
12		1	Federal Unemployment Tax Payable	225	7 20		12
13			State Unemployment Tax Payable	227	64 80		13
14			Payroll Taxes Expense	665		72 00	14
15			To reverse adjusting entry				15
16			(h) made Dec. 31, 2019				16

The next reversing entry is for accrued interest expense. The reversing entry that follows prevents recording difficulties when the note is paid on February 1.

GENERAL JOURNAL PAGE 29

	DATE		DESCRIPTION	POST. REF.	DEBIT	CREDIT	
18	Jan.	1	Interest Payable	216	20 00		18
19			Interest Expense	695		20 00	19
20			To reverse adjusting entry				20
21			(i) made Dec. 31, 2019				21

In addition to adjustments for accrued expenses, Whiteside Antiques made two adjustments for accrued income items. The next reversing entry is for accrued interest income on the note receivable. Whiteside will receive cash for the note and the interest on March 1. The reversing entry eliminates any difficulties in recording the interest income when the note is paid on March 1.

GENERAL JOURNAL PAGE 29

	DATE		DESCRIPTION	POST. REF.	DEBIT	CREDIT	
23	Jan.	1	Interest Income	491	30 00		23
24			Interest Receivable	116		30 00	24
25			To reverse adjusting entry				25
26			(m) made Dec. 31, 2019				26

After the reversing entry has been posted, the ***Interest Receivable*** account has a zero balance and the ***Interest Income*** account has a debit balance of $30. This is unusual because the normal balance of ***Interest Income*** is a credit.

On March 1, Whiteside Antiques received a check for $1,260 in payment of the note ($1,200) and the interest ($60). The transaction is recorded in the normal manner as a debit to ***Cash*** for $1,260, a credit to ***Notes Receivable*** for $1,200, and a credit to ***Interest Income*** for $60.

Refer to the ***Interest Income*** general ledger account below. After this entry has been posted, interest income is properly divided between the two periods, $30 in the previous year and $30 in the current year. The balance of ***Interest Receivable*** is zero. The accountant does not have to review the year-end adjustments before recording the receipt of the principal and interest relating to the note receivable on March 1.

ACCOUNT *Interest Receivable* ACCOUNT NO. *116*

DATE		DESCRIPTION	POST. REF.	DEBIT	CREDIT	BALANCE DEBIT	BALANCE CREDIT
2019							
Dec.	31	Adjusting	J27	30 00		30 00	
2020							
Jan.	1	Reversing	J29		30 00	–0–	

ACCOUNT *Interest Income* ACCOUNT NO. *491*

DATE		DESCRIPTION	POST. REF.	DEBIT	CREDIT	BALANCE DEBIT	BALANCE CREDIT
2019							
Dec.	31	Balance					136 00
	31	Adjusting	J27		30 00		166 00
	31	Closing	J28	166 00			–0–
2020							
Jan.	1	Reversing	J29	30 00		30 00	
Mar.	1		CR3		60 00		30 00

Review of the Accounting Cycle

In Chapters 7, 8, and 9, Maxx-Out Sporting Goods was used to introduce accounting procedures, records, and statements for merchandising businesses. In Chapters 12 and 13, Whiteside Antiques was used to illustrate the end-of-period activities for merchandising businesses. Underlying the various procedures described were the steps in the accounting cycle. Let's review the accounting cycle.

1. ***Analyze transactions.*** Transaction data comes into an accounting system from a variety of source documents—sales slips, purchase invoices, credit memorandums, check stubs, and so on. Each document is analyzed to determine the accounts and amounts affected.
2. ***Journalize the data about transactions.*** Each transaction is recorded in either a special journal or the general journal.
3. ***Post the data about transactions.*** Each transaction is transferred from the journal to the ledger accounts. Merchandising businesses typically maintain several subsidiary ledgers in addition to the general ledger.
4. ***Prepare a worksheet.*** At the end of each period, a worksheet is prepared. The Trial Balance section of the worksheet is used to prove the equality of the debits and credits in the general ledger. Adjustments are entered in the Adjustments section so that the financial statements will be prepared using the accrual basis of accounting. The Adjusted Trial Balance section is used to prove the equality of the debits and credits of the updated

ABOUT ACCOUNTING

Professional Conduct

In September 1998, the Securities and Exchange Commission (SEC) defined improper professional conduct by accountants. The new rule allowed the SEC to censure, suspend, or bar accountants who violate it. The American Institute of Certified Public Accountants (AICPA) supported the rule. The rule led to the dissolution of Arthur Andersen, one of the nation's "big five" firms of certified public accountants, in 2003 following the imposition of severe sanctions on the firm in the "Enron Affair," in which Arthur Andersen was the auditor for Enron. The Sarbanes-Oxley Act has further strengthened the SEC's power over professional conduct by accountants that audit publicly traded companies.

account balances. The Income Statement and Balance Sheet sections are used to arrange data in an orderly manner.

5. ***Prepare financial statements.*** A formal set of financial statements is prepared to report information to interested parties.
6. ***Journalize and post adjusting entries.*** Adjusting entries are journalized and posted in the accounting records. This creates a permanent record of the changes shown on the worksheet.
7. ***Journalize and post closing entries.*** Closing entries are journalized and posted in order to transfer the results of operations to owner's equity and to prepare the temporary accounts for the next period. The closing entries reduce the temporary account balances to zero.
8. ***Prepare a postclosing trial balance.*** The postclosing trial balance confirms that the general ledger is still in balance and that the temporary accounts have zero balances.
9. ***Interpret the financial information.*** The accountant, owners, managers, and other interested parties interpret the information shown in the financial statements and other less-formal financial reports that might be prepared. This information is used to evaluate the results of operations and the financial position of the business and to make decisions.

In addition to the nine steps listed here, some firms record reversing entries. Reversing entries simplify the recording of cash payments for accrued expenses and cash receipts for accrued income.

Figure 13.6 shows the flow of data through an accounting system that uses special journals and subsidiary ledgers. The system is composed of subsystems that perform specialized functions.

The accounts receivable area records transactions involving sales and cash receipts and maintains the individual accounts for credit customers. This area also handles billing for credit customers.

The accounts payable area records transactions involving purchases and cash payments and maintains the individual accounts for creditors.

The general ledger and financial reporting area records transactions in the general journal, maintains the general ledger accounts, performs the end-of-period procedures, and prepares financial statements. This area is the focal point for the accounting system because all transactions eventually flow into the general ledger. In turn, the general ledger provides the data that appear in the financial statements.

MANAGERIAL IMPLICATIONS <<

FINANCIAL STATEMENTS

- Managers carefully study the financial statements to evaluate the operating efficiency and financial strength of the business.
- A common analysis technique is to compare the data on current statements with the data from previous statements. This can reveal developing trends.
- In large businesses, financial statements are compared with the published financial reports of other companies in the same industry.
- In order to evaluate information on classified financial statements, managers need to understand the nature and significance of the groupings.
- Management ensures that closing entries are promptly made so that transactions for the new period can be recorded. Any significant delay means that valuable information, such as the firm's cash position, may not be available or up to date.
- The efficiency and effectiveness of the adjusting and closing procedures can have a positive effect on the annual independent audit. For example, detailed descriptions in the general journal make it easy for the auditor to understand the adjusting entries.

THINKING CRITICALLY

How can managers use the financial statements to learn about a company's operating efficiency?

FIGURE 13.6 Flow of Financial Data through an Accounting System

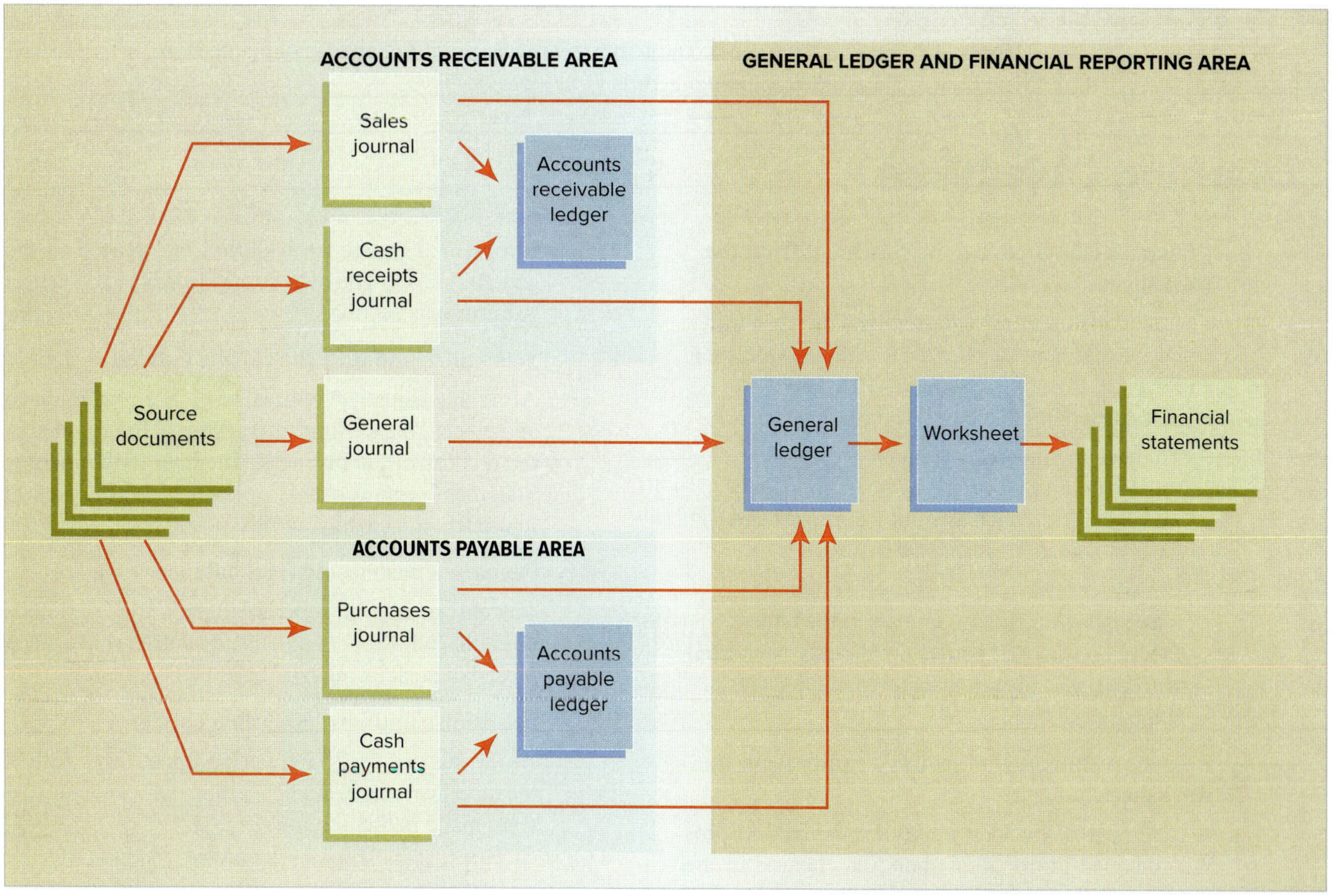

Section 2 Self Review

QUESTIONS

1. Why do adjusting entries need detailed explanations in the general journal?
2. Which adjusting entries should be reversed?
3. What do the four steps in the closing process accomplish?

EXERCISES

4. A reversing entry is made for an end-of-period adjustment that recorded:
   a. estimated bad debts for the period.
   b. an accrued expense that involves future cash payments.
   c. a transfer of an amount from a prepaid expense account to an expense account.
   d. the change in merchandise inventory.
5. The current ratio is:
   a. current liabilities divided by current assets.
   b. the sum of cash, accounts receivable, and notes receivable divided by current liabilities.
   c. current assets divided by current liabilities.
   d. current assets divided by total liabilities.

ANALYSIS

6. At the end of the previous accounting period, an adjusting entry to record accrued employer's payroll taxes was made. Reversing entries were not made for the current accounting period. What effect will this have on the current period's financial statements?

(Answers to Section 2 Self Review are on page 498.)

Review and Applications

13 Chapter REVIEW Chapter Summary

In this chapter, you have learned how to prepare classified financial statements from the worksheet and how to close the accounting records for the period.

Learning Objectives

13-1 **Prepare a classified income statement from the worksheet.**

- A classified income statement for a merchandising business usually includes these sections: Operating Revenue, Cost of Goods Sold, Gross Profit on Sales, Operating Expenses, and Net Income.
- To make the income statement even more useful, operating expenses may be broken down into categories, such as selling expenses and general and administrative expenses.
- Income earned from sources other than normal business activities appears in the Other Income section. Expenses not directly connected with business operations appear in the Other Expenses section.

13-2 **Prepare a statement of owner's equity from the worksheet.**

A statement of owner's equity is prepared to provide detailed information about the changes in the owner's financial interest during the period. The ending owner's capital balance is used to prepare the balance sheet.

13-3 **Prepare a classified balance sheet from the worksheet.**

- Assets are usually presented in two groups: current assets, and plant and equipment. Current assets consist of cash, items to be converted into cash within one year, and items to be used up within one year. Plant and equipment consists of property that will be used for a long time in the operations of the business.
- Liabilities are also divided into two groups: current liabilities and long-term liabilities. Current liabilities will normally be paid within one year. Long-term liabilities are due in more than one year.

13-4 **Journalize and post the adjusting entries.**

When the year-end worksheet and financial statements have been completed, adjusting entries are recorded in the general journal and posted to the general ledger. The data comes from the worksheet Adjustments section.

13-5 **Journalize and post the closing entries.**

After the adjusting entries have been journalized and posted, the closing entries should be recorded in the records of the business. The data in the Income Statement section of the worksheet can be used to journalize the closing entries.

13-6 **Prepare a postclosing trial balance.**

To confirm that the general ledger is still in balance after the adjusting and closing entries have been posted, a postclosing trial balance is prepared.

13-7 **Journalize and post reversing entries.**

At the start of each new period, most firms follow the practice of reversing certain adjustments that were made in the previous period.

- This is done to avoid recording problems with transactions that will occur in the new period.
- Usually, only adjusting entries for accrued expenses and accrued income need to be reversed. Of these, usually only accrued expense and income items involving future payments and receipts of cash can cause difficulties later and should be reversed.
- The use of reversing entries is optional. Reversing entries save time, promote efficiency, and help to achieve a proper matching of revenue and expenses in each period.
- With reversing entries, there is no need to examine each transaction to see whether a portion applies to the past period and then divide the amount of the transaction between the two periods.

13-8 **Define the accounting terms new to this chapter.**

Glossary

Accounts receivable turnover (p. 469) A measure of the speed with which sales on account are collected; the ratio of net credit sales to average receivables

Classified financial statement (p. 456) A format by which revenues and expenses on the income statement, and assets and liabilities on the balance sheet, are divided into groups of similar accounts and a subtotal is given for each group

Current assets (p. 461) Assets consisting of cash, items that normally will be converted into cash within one year, and items that will be used up within one year

Current liabilities (p. 461) Debts that must be paid or otherwise satisfied within one year

Current ratio (p. 468) A relationship between current assets and current liabilities that provides a measure of a firm's ability to pay its current debts (current ratio = current assets ÷ current liabilities)

Gross profit (p. 458) The difference between net sales and the cost of goods sold (gross profit = net sales − cost of goods sold)

Gross profit percentage (p. 468) The amount of gross profit from each dollar of sales (gross profit percentage = gross profit ÷ net sales)

Inventory turnover (p. 469) The number of times inventory is purchased and sold during the accounting period (inventory turnover = cost of goods sold ÷ average inventory)

Liquidity (p. 461) The ease with which an item can be converted into cash

Long-term liabilities (p. 461) Debts of a business that are due more than one year in the future

Multiple-step income statement (p. 456) A type of income statement on which several subtotals are computed before the net income is calculated

Plant and equipment (p. 461) Property that will be used in the business for longer than one year

Reversing entries (p. 469) Journal entries made to reverse the effect of certain adjusting entries involving accrued income or accrued expenses to avoid problems in recording future payments or receipts of cash in a new accounting period

Single-step income statement (p. 456) A type of income statement where only one computation is needed to determine the net income (total revenue − total expenses = net income)

Working capital (p. 468) The difference between current assets and current liabilities. It is a measure of the firm's ability to pay current obligations.

Comprehensive **Self Review**

1. Explain the difference between a single-step income statement and a multiple-step income statement. Which is normally favored?
2. What journal entry(ies) is (are) made in the adjustment column for beginning and ending inventories?
3. Why would a fax machine used in the office not be considered a current asset?
4. Immediately after closing entries are posted, which of the following types of accounts will have zero balances? Select all that apply.
   - **a.** asset accounts
   - **b.** expense accounts
   - **c.** liability accounts
   - **d.** owner's drawing account
   - **e.** ***Income Summary*** account
   - **f.** owner's capital account
   - **g.** revenue accounts
5. Which of the following should have a debit balance in the adjusted trial balance?
   - **a.** ***Sales Returns and Allowances***
   - **b.** ***Purchases Discounts***
   - **c.** ***Salaries Payable***
   - **d.** ***Unearned Rental Income***

6. Describe the entry that would be made to close the ***Income Summary*** account in each of the following cases. The owner of the firm is Jan Hanson.
   - **a.** There is net income of $58,000.
   - **b.** There is a net loss of $8,000.
7. Give the sequence in which the following journal entries are posted to the accounts.
   - **a.** adjusting entries
   - **b.** entries to close expense accounts
   - **c.** entries to close revenue accounts
   - **d.** reversing entries

(Answers to Comprehensive Self Review are on page 498.)

Discussion Questions

1. Give an example of an expense that is classified as Other Expense in the income statement.
2. Which section of the income statement contains information about the purchases made during the period and the beginning and ending inventories?
3. What are operating expenses?
4. What is the purpose of the balance sheet?
5. Give examples of some current assets that usually are classified as Current Assets on the balance sheet.
6. How do current liabilities and long-term liabilities differ?
7. What information is provided by the statement of owner's equity?
8. What account balances or other amounts are included on two different financial statements for the period? Which statements are involved?
9. What is the purpose of the postclosing trial balance?
10. What types of accounts, permanent or temporary, appear on the postclosing trial balance?
11. If the totals of the adjusted trial balance Debit and Credit columns are equal, but the postclosing trial balance does not balance, what is the likely cause of the problem?
12. What types of adjustments are reversed?
13. On December 31, Klien Company made an adjusting entry debiting ***Interest Receivable*** and crediting ***Interest Income*** for $300 of accrued interest. What reversing entry, if any, should be recorded for this item on January 1?
14. Various adjustments made at Acres Company are listed below. Which of the adjustments would normally be reversed?
    - **a.** Adjustment for accrued payroll taxes expense
    - **b.** Adjustment for supplies used
    - **c.** Adjustment for depreciation on the building
    - **d.** Adjustment for estimated uncollectible accounts
    - **e.** Adjustment for accrued interest income
    - **f.** Adjustment for beginning inventory
    - **g.** Adjustment for ending inventory
    - **h.** Adjustment to record portion of insurance premiums that have expired
15. If the owner invests additional capital in the business during the month, how would that new investment be shown in the financial statements?
16. What are the steps in the accounting cycle?

17. Kagan Company's inventory turnover ratio was nine times in 2018 and eight times in 2019. Did Kagan Company sell its inventory more quickly, or more slowly, in 2019 compared to 2018?
18. Gomez Company had a current ratio of 2.0 in 2018 and 2.2 in 2019. Does this signify an improvement or decline in Gomez Company's liquidity from 2018 to 2019?

APPLICATIONS

Exercises connect

Classifying income statement items.

◀ **Exercise 13.1**
Objective 13-1

The accounts listed below appear on the worksheet of Heritage Crafts. Indicate the section of the classified income statement in which each account will be reported.

SECTIONS OF CLASSIFIED INCOME STATEMENT

a. Operating Revenue
b. Cost of Goods Sold
c. Operating Expenses
d. Other Income
e. Other Expenses

ACCOUNTS

1. Purchases Returns and Allowances
2. Telephone Expense
3. Sales Returns and Allowances
4. Purchases
5. Interest Income
6. Merchandise Inventory
7. Interest Expense
8. Sales
9. Depreciation Expense—Store Equipment
10. Rent Expense
11. Sales Discounts
12. Supplies Expense
13. Freight In
14. Purchases Discounts
15. Uncollectible Accounts Expense

Classifying balance sheet items.

◀ **Exercise 13.2**
Objective 13-3

The following accounts appear on the worksheet of Heritage Crafts at December 31, 2019. Indicate the section of the classified balance sheet in which each account will be reported.

SECTIONS OF CLASSIFIED BALANCE SHEET

a. Current Assets
b. Plant and Equipment
c. Current Liabilities

d. Long-Term Liabilities
e. Owner's Equity

ACCOUNTS

1. Accounts Receivable
2. Delivery Van
3. Prepaid Insurance
4. Notes Payable, due 2025
5. Store Supplies
6. Accounts Payable
7. Merchandise Inventory
8. David Stafford, Capital
9. Cash
10. Unearned Subscriptions Income
11. Notes Receivable, due 2020
12. Accumulated Depreciation—Delivery Van
13. Notes Payable, due 2020
14. David Stafford, Drawing
15. Interest Payable

Exercise 13.3
Objective 13-1

Preparing a classified income statement.

The worksheet of Bridget's Office Supplies contains the following revenue, cost, and expense accounts. Prepare a classified income statement for this firm for the year ended December 31, 2019. The merchandise inventory amounted to $59,775 on January 1, 2019, and $52,725 on December 31, 2019. The expense accounts numbered 611 through 617 represent selling expenses, and those numbered 631 through 646 represent general and administrative expenses.

ACCOUNTS

401	Sales	$248,900	Cr.
451	Sales Returns and Allowances	4,350	Dr.
491	Miscellaneous Income	400	Cr.
501	Purchases	103,600	Dr.
502	Freight In	1,975	Dr.
503	Purchases Returns and Allowances	3,600	Cr.
504	Purchases Discounts	1,800	Cr.
611	Salaries Expense—Sales	45,300	Dr.
614	Store Supplies Expense	2,310	Dr.
617	Depreciation Expense—Store Equipment	1,510	Dr.
631	Rent Expense	13,500	Dr.
634	Utilities Expense	3,000	Dr.
637	Salaries Expense—Office	21,100	Dr.
640	Payroll Taxes Expense	6,000	Dr.
643	Depreciation Expense—Office Equipment	570	Dr.
646	Uncollectible Accounts Expense	720	Dr.
691	Interest Expense	740	Dr.

Preparing a statement of owner's equity.

Exercise 13.4
Objective 13-2

The worksheet of Bridget's Office Supplies contains the following owner's equity accounts. Use this data and the net income determined in Exercise 13.3 to prepare a statement of owner's equity for the year ended December 31, 2019. No additional investments were made during the period.

ACCOUNTS

301	Bridget Swanson, Capital	$63,760	Cr.
302	Bridget Swanson, Drawing	40,700	Dr.

Preparing a classified balance sheet.

Exercise 13.5
Objective 13-3

The worksheet of Bridget's Office Supplies contains the following asset and liability accounts. The balance of the ***Notes Payable*** account consists of notes that are due within a year. Prepare a balance sheet dated December 31, 2019. Obtain the ending capital for the period from the statement of owner's equity completed in Exercise 13.4.

ACCOUNTS

101	Cash	$ 5,605	Dr.
107	Change Fund	500	Dr.
111	Accounts Receivable	5,140	Dr.
112	Allowance for Doubtful Accounts	860	Cr.
121	Merchandise Inventory	52,725	Dr.
131	Store Supplies	1,100	Dr.
133	Prepaid Interest	130	Dr.
141	Store Equipment	11,200	Dr.
142	Accum. Depreciation—Store Equipment	1,180	Cr.
151	Office Equipment	3,400	Dr.
152	Accum. Depreciation—Office Equipment	500	Cr.
201	Notes Payable	5,500	Cr.
203	Accounts Payable	3,725	Cr.
216	Interest Payable	110	Cr.
231	Sales Tax Payable	1,890	Cr.

Recording closing entries.

Exercise 13.6
Objective 13-5

On December 31, 2019, the Income Statement section of the worksheet for Capeletti Distributors contained the following information. Give the entries that should be made in the general journal to close the revenue, cost of goods sold, expense, and other temporary accounts. Use journal page 16.

INCOME STATEMENT SECTION

	Debit	Credit
Income Summary	$ 39,600	$ 42,900
Sales		261,500
Sales Returns and Allowances	4,400	
Sales Discounts	1,600	
Interest Income		220
Purchases	137,200	

ACCOUNTS (CONT.)

	Debit	Credit
Freight In	2,700	
Purchases Returns and Allowances		1,500
Purchases Discounts		1,630
Rent Expense	12,000	
Utilities Expense	3,030	
Telephone Expense	1,740	
Salaries Expense	67,100	
Payroll Taxes Expense	5,370	
Supplies Expense	1,280	
Depreciation Expense	3,000	
Interest Expense	420	
Totals	$279,440	$307,750

Assume further that the owner of the firm is John Capeletti and that the ***John Capeletti, Drawing*** account had a balance of $30,700 on December 31, 2019.

Exercise 13.7
Objective 13-7

Journalizing reversing entries.

Examine the following adjusting entries and determine which ones should be reversed. Show the reversing entries that should be recorded in the general journal as of January 1, 2020. Include appropriate descriptions.

2019	(Adjustment a)		
Dec. 31	Uncollectible Accounts Expense	2,940.00	
	Allowance for Doubtful Accounts		2,940.00
	To record estimated loss from uncollectible accounts based on 0.4% of net credit sales, $735,000		
	(Adjustment b)		
31	Supplies Expense	5,700.00	
	Supplies		5,700.00
	To record supplies used during the year		
	(Adjustment c)		
31	Insurance Expense	1,650.00	
	Prepaid Insurance		1,650.00
	To record expired insurance on 1-year $6,600 policy purchased on Oct. 1		
	(Adjustment d)		
31	Depreciation. Exp.—Store Equipment	15,300.00	
	Accum. Depreciation—Store Equip.		15,300.00
	To record depreciation		
	(Adjustment e)		
31	Salaries Expense—Office	3,800.00	
	Salaries Payable		3,800.00
	To record accrued salaries for Dec. 29–31		
	(Adjustment f)		

31	Payroll Taxes Expense	290.70	
	Social Security Tax Payable		235.60
	Medicare Tax Payable		55.10
	To record accrued payroll taxes on accrued salaries: social security, 6.2% × 3,800 = $235.60; Medicare, 1.45% × 3,800 = $55.10		
	(Adjustment g)		
31	Interest Expense	300.00	
	Interest Payable		300.00
	To record accrued interest on a 4-month, 6% trade note payable dated Nov. 1: $30,000 × 0.06 × 2/12 = $300		
	(Adjustment h)		
31	Interest Receivable	188.00	
	Interest Income		188.00
	To record interest earned on 6-month, 8% note receivable dated Oct. 1: $9,400 × 0.08 × 3/12 = $188		

Preparing a postclosing trial balance.

◄ **Exercise 13.8**
Objective 13-6

The Adjusted Trial Balance section of the worksheet for Van Zant Janitorial Supplies follows. The owner made no additional investments during the year. Prepare a postclosing trial balance for the firm on December 31, 2019.

ACCOUNTS

	Debit	Credit
Cash	$ 21,600	
Accounts Receivable	62,800	
Allowance for Doubtful Accounts		$ 220
Merchandise Inventory	187,200	
Supplies	6,240	
Prepaid Insurance	3,160	
Equipment	52,000	
Accumulated Depreciation—Equipment		22,800
Accounts Payable		8,700
Social Security Tax Payable		1,490
Medicare Tax Payable		410
Steven Van Zant, Capital		281,640
Steven Van Zant, Drawing	75,000	
Income Summary	181,000	187,200
Sales		778,000
Sales Returns and Allowances	15,400	
Purchases	487,900	
Freight In	6,400	
Purchases Returns and Allowances		9,500

ACCOUNTS (CONT.)

	Debit	Credit
Purchases Discounts		6,300
Rent Expense	34,800	
Telephone Expense	6,340	
Salaries Expense	124,140	
Payroll Taxes Expense	12,700	
Supplies Expense	7,600	
Insurance Expense	1,660	
Depreciation Expense—Equipment	9,100	
Uncollectible Accounts Expense	1,220	
Totals	$1,296,260	$1,296,260

Exercise 13.9 ▶ **Calculating ratios.**
Objective 13-6

The following selected accounts were taken from the financial records of Los Olivos Distributors at December 31, 2019. All accounts have normal balances.

Cash	$ 33,340
Accounts receivable	47,700
Note receivable, due 2020	9,500
Merchandise inventory	35,700
Prepaid insurance	2,350
Supplies	1,410
Equipment	43,500
Accumulated depreciation, equipment	23,500
Note payable to bank, due 2020	35,000
Accounts payable	13,050
Interest payable	350
Sales	535,000
Sales discounts	3,200
Cost of goods sold	348,540

Accounts Receivable at December 31, 2018, was $52,550. Merchandise inventory at December 31, 2018, was $58,500. Based on the account balances above, calculate the following:

a. The gross profit percentage
b. Working capital
c. The current ratio
d. The inventory turnover
e. The accounts receivable turnover. All sales were on credit.

Exercise 13.10 ▶ **Calculating the accounts receivable turnover and the inventory turnover.**
Objective 13-6

Solomon Company reports the following in its most recent year of operations:

- Sales, $1,000,000 (all on account)
- Cost of goods sold, $490,000
- Gross profit, $510,000

- Accounts receivable, beginning of year, $110,000
- Accounts receivable, end of year, $140,000
- Merchandise inventory, beginning of year, $55,000
- Merchandise inventory, end of year, $60,000.

Based on these balances, compute:

a. the accounts receivable turnover

b. the inventory turnover

PROBLEMS

Problem Set A

Preparing classified financial statements.

◄ **Problem 13.1A**

Objectives 13-1, 13-2, 13-3

Superior Hardwood Company distributes hardwood products to small furniture manufacturers. The adjusted trial balance data given below is from the firm's worksheet for the year ended December 31, 2019.

INSTRUCTIONS

1. Prepare a classified income statement for the year ended December 31, 2019. The expense accounts represent warehouse expenses, selling expenses, and general and administrative expenses.
2. Prepare a statement of owner's equity for the year ended December 31, 2019. No additional investments were made during the period.
3. Prepare a classified balance sheet as of December 31, 2019. The mortgage payable extends for more than a year.

ACCOUNTS

	Debit	Credit
Cash	$ 34,100	
Petty Cash Fund	500	
Notes Receivable, due 2020	11,800	
Accounts Receivable	86,000	
Allowance for Doubtful Accounts		$ 6,000
Merchandise Inventory	234,000	
Warehouse Supplies	2,860	
Office Supplies	1,420	
Prepaid Insurance	10,200	
Land	46,000	
Building	178,000	
Accumulated Depreciation—Building		54,000
Warehouse Equipment	37,000	
Accumulated Depreciation—Warehouse Equipment		17,400
Delivery Equipment	51,000	
Accumulated Depreciation—Delivery Equipment		19,600
Office Equipment	25,000	
Accumulated Depreciation—Office Equipment		12,000

ACCOUNTS (CONT.)

	Debit	Credit
Notes Payable, due 2020		20,200
Accounts Payable		49,000
Interest Payable		580
Mortgage Payable		61,000
Loans Payable, Long-term		17,000
Charles Ronie, Capital (Jan. 1)		452,460
Charles Ronie, Drawing	127,000	
Income Summary	244,000	234,000
Sales		1,685,000
Sales Returns and Allowances	18,200	
Interest Income		1,580
Purchases	767,000	
Freight In	13,800	
Purchases Returns and Allowances		8,440
Purchases Discounts		11,160
Warehouse Wages Expense	199,600	
Warehouse Supplies Expense	7,100	
Depreciation Expense—Warehouse Equipment	5,800	
Salaries Expense—Sales	269,200	
Travel and Entertainment Expense	21,500	
Delivery Wages Expense	60,330	
Depreciation Expense—Delivery Equipment	9,800	
Salaries Expense—Office	70,600	
Office Supplies Expense	4,000	
Insurance Expense	6,200	
Utilities Expense	9,290	
Telephone Expense	6,520	
Payroll Taxes Expense	59,000	
Property Taxes Expense	5,600	
Uncollectible Accounts Expense	5,800	
Depreciation Expense—Building	9,000	
Depreciation Expense—Office Equipment	4,000	
Interest Expense	8,200	
Totals	$2,649,420	$2,649,420

Analyze: What is the current ratio for this business?

Problem 13.2A ► **Preparing classified financial statements.**

Objectives 13-1, 13-2, 13-3

GL

Good to Go Auto Products distributes automobile parts to service stations and repair shops. The adjusted trial balance data that follows is from the firm's worksheet for the year ended December 31, 2019.

INSTRUCTIONS

1. Prepare a classified income statement for the year ended December 31, 2019. The expense accounts represent warehouse expenses, selling expenses, and general and administrative expenses.
2. Prepare a statement of owner's equity for the year ended December 31, 2019. No additional investments were made during the period.
3. Prepare a classified balance sheet as of December 31, 2019. The mortgage payable extends for more than one year.

ACCOUNTS

	Debit	Credit
Cash	$ 99,000	
Petty Cash Fund	600	
Notes Receivable, due 2020	15,000	
Accounts Receivable	140,200	
Allowance for Doubtful Accounts		$ 3,800
Interest Receivable	150	
Merchandise Inventory	128,500	
Warehouse Supplies	3,300	
Office Supplies	700	
Prepaid Insurance	4,640	
Land	16,000	
Building	107,000	
Accumulated Depreciation—Building		16,700
Warehouse Equipment	19,800	
Accumulated Depreciation—Warehouse Equipment		9,500
Office Equipment	9,400	
Accumulated Depreciation—Office Equipment		3,900
Notes Payable, due 2020		15,000
Accounts Payable		56,900
Interest Payable		400
Notes Payable, Long-term		17,000
Mortgage Payable		20,000
Colin O'Brien, Capital (Jan. 1)		326,870
Colin O'Brien, Drawing	70,650	
Income Summary	131,400	128,500
Sales		1,110,300
Sales Returns and Allowances	8,400	
Interest Income		580
Purchases	463,000	
Freight In	9,800	
Purchases Returns and Allowances		13,650
Purchases Discounts		9,240
Warehouse Wages Expense	108,600	

ACCOUNTS (CONT.)

	Debit	Credit
Warehouse Supplies Expense	5,800	
Depreciation Expense—Warehouse Equipment	3,400	
Salaries Expense—Sales	151,700	
Travel Expense	24,000	
Delivery Expense	37,425	
Salaries Expense—Office	85,000	
Office Supplies Expense	1,220	
Insurance Expense	9,875	
Utilities Expense	8,000	
Telephone Expense	3,280	
Payroll Taxes Expense	31,600	
Building Repairs Expense	3,700	
Property Taxes Expense	16,400	
Uncollectible Accounts Expense	3,580	
Depreciation Expense—Building	5,600	
Depreciation Expense—Office Equipment	1,620	
Interest Expense	4,000	
Totals	$1,732,340	$1,732,340

Analyze: What percentage of total operating expenses is attributable to warehouse expenses?

Problem 13.3A ▶ **Preparing classified financial statements.**

Objectives 13-1, 13-2, 13-3

CONTINUING >>> Problem

Obtain all data necessary from the worksheet prepared for Artisan Wines in Problem 12.6A at the end of Chapter 12. Then follow the instructions to complete this problem.

INSTRUCTIONS

1. Prepare a classified income statement for the year ended December 31, 2019. The company does not classify its operating expenses as selling expenses and general and administrative expenses.
2. Prepare a statement of owner's equity for the year ended December 31, 2019. No additional investments were made during the year.
3. Prepare a classified balance sheet as of December 31, 2019.

Analyze: What is the inventory turnover for Artisan Wines?

Problem 13.4A ▶ **Journalizing adjusting, closing, and reversing entries.**

Objectives 13-4, 13-5, 13-7

CONTINUING >>> Problem

GL

Obtain all data that is necessary from the worksheet prepared for Healthy Eating Foods Company in Problem 12.5A at the end of Chapter 12. Then follow the instructions to complete this problem.

INSTRUCTIONS

1. Record adjusting entries in the general journal as of December 31, 2019. Use 25 as the first journal page number. Include descriptions for the entries.
2. Record closing entries in the general journal as of December 31, 2019. Include descriptions.
3. Record reversing entries in the general journal as of January 1, 2020. Include descriptions.

Analyze: Assuming that the firm did not record a reversing entry for salaries payable, what entry is required when salaries of $6,000 are paid on January 3?

Journalizing adjusting and reversing entries.

◀ **Problem 13.5A**
Objectives 13-4, 13-7

The data below concerns adjustments to be made at Coffee Bean Importers.

INSTRUCTIONS

1. Record the adjusting entries in the general journal as of December 31, 2019. Use 25 as the first journal page number. Include descriptions.
2. Record reversing entries in the general journal as of January 1, 2020. Include descriptions.

ADJUSTMENTS

a. On November 1, 2019, the firm signed a lease for a warehouse and paid rent of $21,000 in advance for a six-month period.

b. On December 31, 2019, an inventory of supplies showed that items costing $1,940 were on hand. The balance of the ***Supplies*** account was $11,880.

c. A depreciation schedule for the firm's equipment shows that a total of $10,750 should be charged off as depreciation in 2019.

d. On December 31, 2019, the firm owed salaries of $6,100 that will not be paid until January 2020.

e. On December 31, 2019, the firm owed the employer's social security (6.2 percent) and Medicare (1.45 percent) taxes on all accrued salaries.

f. On October 1, 2019, the firm received a five-month, 8 percent note for $6,500 from a customer with an overdue balance.

Analyze: After the adjusting entries have been posted, what is the balance of the ***Prepaid Rent*** account on January 1, 2020?

Problem Set B

Preparing classified financial statements.

◀ **Problem 13.1B**
Objectives 13-1, 13-2, 13-3

ComputerGeeks.com is a retail store that sells computers, laptops, supplies, and other electronic devices. The adjusted trial balance data given below is from the firm's worksheet for the year ended December 31, 2019.

INSTRUCTIONS

1. Prepare a classified income statement for the year ended December 31, 2019. The expense accounts represent warehouse expenses, selling expenses, and general and administrative expenses.
2. Prepare a statement of owner's equity for the year ended December 31, 2019. No additional investments were made during the period.
3. Prepare a classified balance sheet as of December 31, 2019. The mortgage payable extends for more than one year.

ACCOUNTS

	Debit	Credit
Cash	$12,200	
Petty Cash Fund	100	
Notes Receivable, due 2020	3,200	
Accounts Receivable	19,250	
Allowance for Doubtful Accounts		$2,250

ACCOUNTS (CONT.)

	Debit	Credit
Merchandise Inventory	35,400	
Warehouse Supplies	775	
Office Supplies	780	
Prepaid Insurance	2,200	
Land	7,642	
Building	48,500	
Accumulated Depreciation—Building		13,000
Warehouse Equipment	8,000	
Accumulated Depreciation—Warehouse Equipment		2,300
Delivery Equipment	16,400	
Accumulated Depreciation—Delivery Equipment		3,600
Office Equipment	6,000	
Accumulated Depreciation—Office Equipment		2,500
Notes Payable, due 2020		4,000
Accounts Payable		14,140
Interest Payable		240
Mortgage Payable		15,950
Loans Payable, Long-term		4,000
Bruce Zaro, Capital (Jan. 1)		60,940
Bruce Zaro, Drawing	24,000	
Income Summary	33,125	35,400
Sales		429,800
Sales Returns and Allowances	3,150	
Interest Income		462
Purchases	179,600	
Freight In	2,200	
Purchases Returns and Allowances		2,520
Purchases Discounts		2,350
Warehouse Wages Expense	38,900	
Warehouse Supplies Expense	1,790	
Depreciation Expense—Warehouse Equipment	1,400	
Salaries Expense—Sales	67,200	
Travel and Entertainment Expense	6,300	
Delivery Wages Expense	26,900	
Depreciation Expense—Delivery Equipment	2,440	
Salaries Expense—Office	15,900	
Office Supplies Expense	1,150	
Insurance Expense	1,500	
Utilities Expense	2,400	
Telephone Expense	1,380	

ACCOUNTS (CONT.)

	Debit	Credit
Payroll Taxes Expense	15,250	
Property Taxes Expense	1,750	
Uncollectible Accounts Expense	1,050	
Depreciation Expense—Building	3,000	
Depreciation Expense—Office Equipment	1,020	
Interest Expense	1,600	
Totals	$593,452	$593,452

Analyze: What is the gross profit percentage for the period ended December 31, 2019?

Preparing classified financial statements.

◀ **Problem 13.2B**

Objectives 13-1, 13-2, 13-3

Hog Wild is a retail firm that sells motorcycles, parts, and accessories. The adjusted trial balance data given below is from the firm's worksheet for the year ended December 31, 2019.

INSTRUCTIONS

1. Prepare a classified income statement for the year ended December 31, 2019. The expense accounts represent warehouse expenses, selling expenses, and general and administrative expenses.
2. Prepare a statement of owner's equity for the year ended December 31, 2019. No additional investments were made during the period.
3. Prepare a classified balance sheet as of December 31, 2019. The mortgage payable extends for more than one year.

ACCOUNTS

	Debit	Credit
Cash	$14,350	
Petty Cash Fund	200	
Notes Receivable, due 2020	6,000	
Accounts Receivable	54,600	
Allowance for Doubtful Accounts		$ 5,000
Interest Receivable	200	
Merchandise Inventory	87,915	
Warehouse Supplies	3,700	
Office Supplies	1,800	
Prepaid Insurance	6,900	
Land	20,400	
Building	53,100	
Accumulated Depreciation—Building		8,400
Warehouse Equipment	24,000	
Accumulated Depreciation—Warehouse Equipment		4,000
Office Equipment	12,800	
Accumulated Depreciation—Office Equipment		1,800
Notes Payable, due 2020		8,000
Accounts Payable		32,500

ACCOUNTS (CONT.)

	Debit	Credit
Interest Payable		1,800
Notes Payable, Long-term		6,000
Mortgage Payable		35,875
Nick Henry, Capital (Jan. 1)		198,710
Nick Henry, Drawing	56,000	
Income Summary	88,980	87,915
Sales		608,417
Sales Returns and Allowances	9,400	
Interest Income		720
Purchases	230,050	
Freight In	9,600	
Purchases Returns and Allowances		6,420
Purchases Discounts		5,760
Warehouse Wages Expense	64,300	
Warehouse Supplies Expense	4,300	
Depreciation Expense—Warehouse Equipment	2,400	
Salaries Expense—Sales	78,900	
Travel Expense—Sales	21,000	
Delivery Expense	35,400	
Salaries Expense—Office	57,500	
Office Supplies Expense	1,360	
Insurance Expense	9,500	
Utilities Expense	6,912	
Telephone Expense	4,370	
Payroll Taxes Expense	19,200	
Building Repairs Expense	3,100	
Property Taxes Expense	11,700	
Uncollectible Accounts Expense	2,900	
Depreciation Expense—Building	3,200	
Depreciation Expense—Office Equipment	1,680	
Interest Expense	3,600	
Totals	$1,011,317	$1,011,317

Analyze: What is the inventory turnover for Hog Wild?

Problem 13.3B

Objectives 13-1, 13-2, 13-3

CONTINUING >>> Problem

Preparing classified financial statements.

Obtain all data necessary from the worksheet prepared for The Game Place in Problem 12.6B at the end of Chapter 12. Then follow the instructions to complete this problem.

INSTRUCTIONS

1. Prepare a classified income statement for the year ended December 31, 2019. The company does not classify its operating expenses as selling expenses and general and administrative expenses.
2. Prepare a statement of owner's equity for the year ended December 31, 2019. No additional investments were made during the year.
3. Prepare a classified balance sheet as of December 31, 2019.

Analyze: What is the amount of working capital for The Game Place?

Journalizing adjusting, closing, and reversing entries.

◀ Problem 13.4B
Objectives 13-4, 13-5, 13-7
CONTINUING >>> Problem

Obtain all data that is necessary from the worksheet prepared for Whatnots in Problem 12.5B at the end of Chapter 12. Then follow the instructions to complete this problem.

INSTRUCTIONS

1. Record adjusting entries in the general journal as of December 31, 2019. Use 29 as the first journal page number. Include descriptions for the entries.
2. Record closing entries in the general journal as of December 31, 2019. Include descriptions.
3. Record reversing entries in the general journal as of January 1, 2020. Include descriptions.

Analyze: Assuming that the company did not record a reversing entry for salaries payable, what entry is required when salaries of $2,600 are paid on January 4? (Ignore payroll taxes withheld.)

Journalizing adjusting and reversing entries.

◀ Problem 13.5B
Objectives 13-4, 13-7

The data below concerns adjustments to be made at Amador Creek Wine Company.

INSTRUCTIONS

1. Record the adjusting entries in the general journal as of December 31, 2019. Use 25 as the first journal page number. Include descriptions.
2. Record reversing entries in the general journal as of January 1, 2020. Include descriptions.

ADJUSTMENTS

a. On August 1, 2019, the firm signed a six-month advertising contract with a trade magazine and paid the entire amount, $18,600, in advance. ***Prepaid Advertising*** had a balance of $18,600 on December 31, 2019.

b. On December 31, 2019, an inventory of supplies showed that items costing $1,040 were on hand. The balance of the ***Supplies*** account was $9,680.

c. A depreciation schedule for the firm's store equipment shows that a total of $12,250 should be charged off as depreciation for 2019.

d. On December 31, 2019, the firm owed salaries of $8,800 that will not be paid until January 2020.

e. On December 31, 2019, the firm owed the employer's social security (6.2 percent) and Medicare (1.45 percent) taxes on all accrued salaries.

f. On December 1, 2019, the firm received a five-month, 6 percent note for $6,000 from a customer with an overdue balance.

Analyze: After the adjusting entries have been posted, what is the balance of the Prepaid Advertising account on December 31?

Critical Thinking Problem 13.1

Year-End Processing

Programs Plus is a retail firm that sells computer programs for home and business use. On December 31, 2019, its general ledger contained the accounts and balances shown below:

ACCOUNTS	BALANCES	
Cash	$ 15,280	Dr.
Accounts Receivable	26,600	Dr.
Allowance for Doubtful Accounts	95	Cr.
Merchandise Inventory	62,375	Dr.
Supplies	6,740	Dr.
Prepaid Insurance	2,380	Dr.
Equipment	34,000	Dr.
Accumulated Depreciation—Equipment	10,100	Cr.
Notes Payable	7,264	Cr.
Accounts Payable	6,500	Cr.
Social Security Tax Payable	560	Cr.
Medicare Tax Payable	130	Cr.
Yasser Tousson, Capital	93,620	Cr.
Yasser Tousson, Drawing	50,000	Dr.
Sales	514,980	Cr.
Sales Returns and Allowances	9,600	Dr.
Purchases	319,430	Dr.
Freight In	3,600	Dr.
Purchases Returns and Allowances	7,145	Cr.
Purchases Discounts	5,760	Cr.
Rent Expense	14,500	Dr.
Telephone Expense	2,164	Dr.
Salaries Expense	92,000	Dr.
Payroll Taxes Expense	7,300	Dr.
Interest Expense	185	Dr.

The following accounts had zero balances:

Interest Payable
Salaries Payable
Income Summary
Supplies Expense
Insurance Expense
Depreciation Expense—Equipment
Uncollectible Accounts Expense

The data needed for the adjustments on December 31 are as follows:

a.–b. Ending merchandise inventory, $67,850.

c. Uncollectible accounts, 0.5 percent of net credit sales of $245,000.

d. Supplies on hand December 31, $1,020.

e. Expired insurance, $1,190.

f. ***Depreciation Expense—Equipment,*** $5,600.

g. Accrued interest expense on notes payable, $325.

h. Accrued salaries, $2,100.

i. ***Social Security Tax Payable*** (6.2 percent) and ***Medicare Tax Payable*** (1.45 percent) of accrued salaries.

INSTRUCTIONS

1. Prepare a worksheet for the year ended December 31, 2019.
2. Prepare a classified income statement. The firm does not divide its operating expenses into selling and administrative expenses.
3. Prepare a statement of owner's equity. No additional investments were made during the period.
4. Prepare a classified balance sheet. All notes payable are due within one year.
5. Journalize the adjusting entries. Use 25 as the first journal page number.
6. Journalize the closing entries.
7. Journalize the reversing entries.

Analyze: By what percentage did the owner's capital account change in the period from January 1, 2019, to December 31, 2019?

Critical Thinking Problem 13.2

Classified Balance Sheet

Teagan Fitzgerald is the owner of Newport Jewelry, a store specializing in gold, platinum, and special stones. During the past year, in response to increased demand, Teagan doubled her selling space by expanding into the vacant building space next door to her store. This expansion has been expensive because of the need to increase inventory and to purchase new store fixtures and equipment, including carpeting and state-of-the-art built-in fixtures. Teagan notes that the company's cash position has gone down and she is worried about future demands on cash to finance the growth.

Teagan presents you with a statement showing the assets, liabilities, and her equity for year-end 2018 and 2019, and asks your opinion on the company's ability to pay for the recent expansion. She did not have income and expense data available at the time. She commented that she had not made any new investment in the business in the past two years and was not financially able to do so presently. The information presented is shown below:

	December 31, 2018		December 31, 2019	
Assets				
Cash	$150,000		$ 30,000	
Accounts Receivable	45,000		91,500	
Inventory	105,000		234,000	
Prepaid Expenses	6,000		9,000	
Store Fixtures and Equipment	180,000		390,000	
Total Assets		$486,000		$754,500
Liabilities and Owner's Equity				

(continued)

	December 31, 2018		December 31, 2019	
Liabilities				
Notes Payable (due in 4 years)	$ 90,000		$240,000	
Accounts Payable	132,000		171,000	
Salaries Payable	18,000		19,500	
Total Liabilities		$240,000		$430,500
Owner's Equity				
Teagan Fitzgerald, Capital		246,000		324,000
Total Liabilities and Owner's Equity		$486,000		$754,500

INSTRUCTIONS

1. Prepare classified balance sheets for Newport Jewelry for December 31, 2018, and December 31, 2019. (Ignore depreciation.)
2. Based on the information presented in the classified balance sheets, what is your opinion of Newport Jewelry's ability to pay its current bills in a timely manner?
3. What is the advantage of a classified balance sheet over a balance sheet that is not classified?

BUSINESS CONNECTIONS

Managerial | FOCUS

Understanding Financial Statements

1. Why should management be concerned about the efficiency of the end-of-period procedures?
2. Spectrum Company had an increase in sales and net income during its last fiscal year, but cash decreased and the firm was having difficulty paying its bills by the end of the year. What factors might cause a shortage of cash even though a firm is profitable?
3. For the last three years, the balance sheet of Smith Hardware Center, a large retail store, has shown a substantial increase in merchandise inventory. Why might management be concerned about this development?
4. Why is it important to compare the financial statements of the current year with those of prior years?
5. Should a manager be concerned if the balance sheet shows a large increase in current liabilities and a large decrease in current assets? Explain your answer.
6. The latest income statement prepared at Patel Company shows that net sales increased by 10 percent over the previous year and selling expenses increased by 25 percent. Do you think that management should investigate the reasons for the increase in selling expenses? Why or why not?
7. Why is it useful for management to compare a firm's financial statements with financial information from other companies in the same industry?

Ethical | DILEMMA

Helping Your Boss May Be Wrong

It is standard accounting procedures, or GAAP, to make a journal entry to remove the current year's principle from the long-term liabilities. This entry reduces the long-term liabilities and increases the current liabilities. You are the bookkeeper for Biker's Business. Biker's Business has a bank loan that requires a current ratio of 1.5 times. The owner has asked that you not make the adjusting entry to take the current portion from the long-term liabilities. You know if you make the adjusting entry Biker's Business's loan will need to be repaid immediately (or the loan called). What should you do?

Balance Sheet

Financial Statement ANALYSIS

McCormick & Company, Incorporated, is a global leader in the manufacture, marketing, and distribution of spices, seasoning mixes, condiments, and other products to the food industry. McCormick & Company, Incorporated, reported the following in its *2014 Annual Report:*

Consolidated Balance Sheet

	November 30	
(in millions)	***2014***	***2013***
Total Current Assets	*$1,416.2*	*$1,370.2*
Total Assets	*$4,413.3*	*$4,449.7*
Total Current Liabilities	*$1,122.0*	*$1,063.1*
Total Liabilities	*$2,604.9*	*$2,502.0*

Analyze:

1. What is the current ratio for both 2014 and 2013?
2. Did the current ratio improve or decline from 2013 to 2014?
3. The company reported net sales of $4,243.2 million and gross profit of $1,730.2 million for its fiscal year ended November 30, 2014. What is the gross profit percentage for this period?

Analyzing Home Depot

TEAMWORK

Home Depot

Ratios are an important part of financial analysis. Divide into groups of two or three. Each person should choose one year from the Home Depot *2015 Annual Report* in Appendix A. Calculate the current ratio, gross profit percentage, and inventory turnover. Is Home Depot doing better or worse than the previous year? What account is causing this change?

Using Financial Statements from the Internet

Internet CONNECTION

Choose the website of a corporation. You can find most corporate websites by typing the corporation's name after www., then .com. Find the 10K or annual report. Locate the income statement, balance sheet, and cash flow statement for the corporation. Notice the current assets and current liabilities. Calculate the current ratio, gross profit percentage, and inventory turnover.

Answers to **Self Reviews**

Answers to Section 1 Self Review

1. Classified statements permit users to better interpret the statements and analyze operations and financial conditions.
2. Current liabilities are those that fall due within one year. Long-term liabilities are those that will be due in more than one year.
3. Gross profit is the difference between net sales and the cost of goods sold.
4. **d.** A note receivable due in 13 months
5. **c.** As a deduction from the delivered cost of purchases
6. Net delivered cost of purchases is understated. Operating expenses are overstated. The net income from operations is unchanged.

Answers to Section 2 Self Review

1. So that anyone who needs to examine the entries at a later date will understand how and why the adjustments were made.
2. Adjustments that include entries in asset and liability accounts that have not been used during the period.
3. They provide a systematic and uniform method for closing all accounts that affect profit or loss for the period and transferring that profit or loss, adjusted for owner's withdrawals, to the owner's capital account.
4. **b.** an accrued expense that involves future cash payments.
5. **c.** current assets divided by current liabilities.
6. If the accountant correctly allocates the entire future payment to the payroll taxes expense account and the accrued liability account, there will be no effects on the proper allocation of expense between periods. If the accountant debits the payment in the subsequent month to the payroll taxes expense account, payroll tax expense will be correctly stated in the earlier period and overstated in the current period. ***Payroll Taxes Payable*** will be overstated during the later period.

Answers to Comprehensive Self Review

1. Single-step: all revenues listed in one section and all related costs and expenses in another section. Multiple-step: various sections in which subtotals and totals are computed in arriving at net income. Multistep statements are generally preferred.
2. An entry in the debit column on the ***Income Summary*** line and a credit to ***Merchandise Inventory*** for the amount of beginning inventory closes the beginning inventory. A debit on the ***Merchandise Inventory*** line and a credit to ***Income Summary*** for the amount of ending inventory sets up the ending inventory.
3. It generally has a life of more than one year and is used in business operations.
4. **b.** expense accounts **e.** ***Income Summary*** account
   d. owner's drawing account **g.** revenue accounts
5. **a.** ***Sales Returns and Allowances***
6. **a.** Debit ***Income Summary*** and credit ***Jan Hanson, Capital*** for $58,000.
   b. Debit ***Jan Hanson, Capital*** and credit ***Income Summary*** for $8,000.
7. **a.** adjusting entries; **c.** entries to close revenue accounts; **b.** entries to close expense accounts; **d.** reversing entries

Mini-Practice Set 2

Merchandising Business Accounting Cycle

The Fashion Rack

The Fashion Rack is a retail merchandising business that sells brand-name clothing at discount prices. The firm is owned and managed by Teresa Lojay, who started the business on April 1, 2019. This project will give you an opportunity to put your knowledge of accounting into practice as you handle the accounting work of The Fashion Rack during the month of October 2019.

INTRODUCTION

The Fashion Rack has a monthly accounting period. The firm's chart of accounts is shown below. The journals used to record transactions are the sales journal, purchases journal, cash receipts journal, cash payments journal, and general journal. Postings are made from the journals to the accounts receivable ledger, accounts payable ledger, and general ledger. The employees are paid at the end of the month. A computerized payroll service prepares all payroll records and checks.

INSTRUCTIONS

1. Open the general ledger accounts and enter the balances for October 1, 2019. Obtain the necessary figures from the postclosing trial balance prepared on September 30, 2019, which is shown below. (If you are using the *Study Guide & Working Papers,* you will find that the general ledger accounts are already open.)
2. Open the subsidiary ledger accounts and enter the balances for October 1, 2019. Obtain the necessary figures from the schedule of accounts payable and schedule of accounts receivable prepared on September 30, 2019, which appears below. (If you are using the *Study Guide & Working Papers,* you will find that the subsidiary ledger accounts are already open.)
3. Analyze the transactions for October and record each transaction in the proper journal. (Use 10 as the number for the first page of each special journal and 16 as the number for the first page of the general journal.)
4. Post the individual entries that involve customer and creditor accounts from the journals to the subsidiary ledgers on a daily basis. Post the individual entries that appear in the general journal and in the Other Accounts sections of the cash receipts and cash payments journals to the general ledger on a daily basis.
5. Total, prove, and rule the special journals as of October 31, 2019.
6. Post the column totals from the special journals to the general ledger accounts.

The Fashion Rack
Chart of Accounts

Assets		**Liabilities**	
101	Cash	203	Accounts Payable
111	Accounts Receivable	221	Social Security Tax Payable
112	Allowance for Doubtful Accounts	222	Medicare Tax Payable
121	Merchandise Inventory	223	Employee Income Tax Payable
131	Supplies	225	Federal Unemployment Tax Payable
133	Prepaid Insurance	227	State Unemployment Tax Payable
135	Prepaid Advertising	229	Salaries Payable
141	Equipment	231	Sales Tax Payable
142	Accumulated Depreciation—Equipment		

The Fashion Rack Chart of Accounts (continued)			
Owners Equity		**Expenses**	
301	Teresa Lojay, Capital	611	Advertising Expense
302	Teresa Lojay, Drawing	614	Depreciation Expense—Equipment
399	Income Summary	617	Insurance Expense
Revenues		620	Uncollectible Accounts Expense
401	Sales	623	Janitorial Services Expense
402	Sales Returns and Allowances	626	Payroll Taxes Expense
Cost of Goods Sold		629	Rent Expense
501	Purchases	632	Salaries Expense
502	Freight In	635	Supplies Expense
503	Purchases Returns and Allowances	638	Telephone Expense
504	Purchases Discounts	644	Utilities Expense

7. Check the accuracy of the subsidiary ledgers by preparing a schedule of accounts receivable and a schedule of accounts payable as of October 31, 2019. Compare the totals with the balances of the ***Accounts Receivable*** account and the ***Accounts Payable*** account in the general ledger.
8. Check the accuracy of the general ledger by preparing a trial balance in the first two columns of a 10-column worksheet. Make sure that the total debits and the total credits are equal.
9. Complete the Adjustments section of the worksheet. Use the following data. Identify each adjustment with the appropriate letter.
   - **a.** During October, the firm had net credit sales of $9,810. From experience with similar businesses, the previous accountant had estimated that 1.0 percent of the firm's net credit sales would result in uncollectible accounts. Record an adjustment for the expected loss from uncollectible accounts for the month of October.
   - **b.** On October 31, an inventory of the supplies showed that items costing $3,240 were on hand. Record an adjustment for the supplies used in October.
   - **c.** On September 30, 2019, the firm purchased a six-month insurance policy for $8,400. Record an adjustment for the expired insurance for October.
   - **d.** On October 1, 2019, the firm signed a three-month advertising contract for $4,800 with a local cable television station and paid the full amount in advance. Record an adjustment for the expired advertising for October.
   - **e.** On April 1, 2019, the firm purchased equipment for $83,000. The equipment was estimated to have a useful life of five years and a salvage value of $12,500. Record an adjustment for depreciation on the equipment for October.
   - **f.–g.** Based on a physical count, ending merchandise inventory was determined to be $81,260.
10. Complete the Adjusted Trial Balance section of the worksheet.
11. Determine the net income or net loss for October and complete the worksheet.
12. Prepare a classified income statement for the month ended October 31, 2019. (The firm does not divide its operating expenses into selling and administrative expenses.)
13. Prepare a statement of owner's equity for the month ended October 31, 2019.
14. Prepare a classified balance sheet as of October 31, 2019.
15. Journalize and post the adjusting entries using general journal page 17.
16. Prepare and post the closing entries using general journal page 18.
17. Prepare a postclosing trial balance.

DATE		TRANSACTIONS
Oct.	1	Issued Check 601 for $4,200 to pay City Properties the monthly rent.
	1	Signed a three-month radio advertising contract with Cable Station KOTU for $4,800; issued Check 602 to pay the full amount in advance.
	2	Received $520 from Megan Greening, a credit customer, in payment of her account.
	2	Issued Check 603 for $17,820 to remit the sales tax owed for July through September to the State Tax Commission.
	2	Issued Check 604 for $7,673.40 to A Fashion Statement, a creditor, in payment of Invoice 9387 ($7,830), less a cash discount ($156.60).
	3	Sold merchandise on credit for $2,480 plus sales tax of $124 to Dimitri Sayegh, Sales Slip 241.
	4	Issued Check 605 for $1,050 to BMX Supply Co. for supplies.
	4	Issued Check 606 for $8,594.60 to Today's Woman, a creditor, in payment of Invoice 5671 ($8,770), less a cash discount ($175.40).
	5	Collected $1,700.00 on account from Emily Tran, a credit customer.
	5	Accepted a return of merchandise from Dimitri Sayegh. The merchandise was originally sold on Sales Slip 241, dated October 3; issued Credit Memorandum 18 for $630, which includes sales tax of $30.
	5	Issued Check 607 for $1,666 to Classy Threads, a creditor, in payment of Invoice 3292 ($1,700), less a cash discount ($34).
	6	Had cash sales of $18,600 plus sales tax of $930 during October 1–6.
	8	Received a check from James Helmer, a credit customer, for $832 to pay the balance he owes.
	8	Issued Check 608 for $1,884 to deposit social security tax ($702), Medicare tax ($162), and federal income tax withholding ($1,020) from the September payroll. Record this check in the cash payments journal.
	9	Sold merchandise on credit for $2,050 plus sales tax of $102.50 to Emma Maldonado, Sales Slip 242.
	10	Issued Check 609 for $1,445 to pay *The City Daily* for a newspaper advertisement that appeared in October.
	11	Purchased merchandise for $4,820 from A Fashion Statement, Invoice 9422, dated October 8; the terms are 2/10, n/30.
	12	Issued Check 610 for $375 to pay freight charges to Ace Freight Company, the trucking company that delivered merchandise from A Fashion Statement on September 27 and October 11.
	13	Had cash sales of $12,300 plus sales tax of $615 during October 8–13.
	15	Sold merchandise on credit for $1,940 plus sales tax of $97 to James Helmer, Sales Slip 243.
	16	Purchased discontinued merchandise from Acme Jobbers; paid for it immediately with Check 611 for $6,420.
	16	Received $510 on account from Dimitri Sayegh, a credit customer.
	16	Issued Check 612 for $4,723.60 to A Fashion Statement, a creditor, in payment of Invoice 9422 ($4,820.00), less cash discount ($96.40).
	18	Issued Check 613 for $7,200 to Teresa Lojay as a withdrawal for personal use.
	20	Had cash sales of $13,500 plus sales tax of $675 during October 15–20.
	22	Issued Check 614 to City Utilities for $1,112 to pay the monthly electric bill.

(continued)

DATE	TRANSACTIONS
24	Sold merchandise on credit for $820 plus sales tax of $41 to Megan Greening, Sales Slip 244.
25	Purchased merchandise for $3,380 from Classy Threads, Invoice 3418, dated October 23; the terms are 2/10, n/30.
26	Issued Check 615 to Regional Telephone for $780 to pay the monthly telephone bill.
27	Had cash sales of $14,240 plus sales tax of $712 during October 22–27.
29	Received Credit Memorandum 175 for $430 from Classy Threads for defective goods that were returned. The original purchase was recorded on October 25.
29	Sold merchandise on credit for $3,120 plus sales tax of $156 to Emily Tran, Sales Slip 245.
29	Recorded the October payroll. The records prepared by the payroll service show the following totals: earnings, $10,800; social security, $702.00; Medicare, $162.00; income tax, $1,020; and net pay, $8,916. The excess withholdings corrected an error made in withholdings in September.
29	Recorded the employer's payroll taxes, which were calculated by the payroll service: social security, $702; Medicare, $162; federal unemployment tax, $118; and state unemployment tax, $584. This, too, reflects an understatement of taxes recorded in September and corrected in this month.
30	Purchased merchandise for $4,020 from Today's Woman, Invoice 5821, dated October 26; the terms are 1/10, n/30.
31	Issued Checks 616 through 619, totaling $8,916.00, to employees to pay October payroll. For the sake of simplicity, enter the total of the checks on a single line in the cash payments journal.
31	Issued Check 620 for $475 to Handy Janitors for October janitorial services.
31	Had cash sales of $1,700 plus sales tax of $85 for October 29–31.

The Fashion Rack
Postclosing Trial Balance
September 30, 2019

ACCOUNT NAME	DEBIT	CREDIT
Cash	59,800.00	
Accounts Receivable	6,210.00	
Allowance for Doubtful Accounts		420.00
Merchandise Inventory	88,996.00	
Supplies	4,100.00	
Prepaid Insurance	8,400.00	
Equipment	83,000.00	
Accumulated Depreciation—Equipment		7,050.00
Accounts Payable		18,300.00
Social Security Tax Payable		702.00
Medicare Tax Payable		162.00
Employee Income Tax Payable		1,020.00
Federal Unemployment Tax Payable		512.00
State Unemployment Tax Payable		1,268.00
Sales Tax Payable		17,820.00
Teresa Lojay, Capital		203,252.00
Totals	250,506.00	250,506.00

The Fashion Rack
Schedule of Accounts Payable
September 30, 2019

A Fashion Statement	7 8 3 0 00
Classy Threads	1 7 0 0 00
Today's Woman	8 7 7 0 00
Total	18 3 0 0 00

The Fashion Rack
Schedule of Accounts Receivable
September 30, 2019

Jennifer Brown	7 9 5 00
Megan Greening	5 2 0 00
James Helmer	8 3 2 00
Emma Maldonado	2 3 2 00
Jim Price	1 6 2 1 00
Dimitri Sayegh	5 1 0 00
Emily Tran	1 7 0 0 00
Total	6 2 1 0 00

Appendix A

The Home Depot 2015 Financial Statements (for the fiscal year ended January 31, 2016)

Item 8. Financial Statements and Supplementary Data.

Management's Responsibility for Financial Statements

The financial statements presented in this Annual Report have been prepared with integrity and objectivity and are the responsibility of the management of The Home Depot, Inc. These financial statements have been prepared in conformity with U.S. generally accepted accounting principles and properly reflect certain estimates and judgments based upon the best available information.

The financial statements of the Company have been audited by KPMG LLP, an independent registered public accounting firm. Their accompanying report is based upon an audit conducted in accordance with the standards of the Public Company Accounting Oversight Board (United States).

The Audit Committee of the Board of Directors, consisting solely of independent directors, meets five times a year with the independent registered public accounting firm, the internal auditors and representatives of management to discuss auditing and financial reporting matters. In addition, a telephonic meeting is held prior to each quarterly earnings release. The Audit Committee retains the independent registered public accounting firm and regularly reviews the internal accounting controls, the activities of the independent registered public accounting firm and internal auditors and the financial condition of the Company. Both the Company's independent registered public accounting firm and the internal auditors have free access to the Audit Committee.

Management's Report on Internal Control Over Financial Reporting

Our management is responsible for establishing and maintaining adequate internal control over financial reporting, as such term is defined in Rule 13a-15(f) promulgated under the Securities Exchange Act of 1934, as amended (the "Exchange Act"). Under the supervision and with the participation of our management, including our Chief Executive Officer and Chief Financial Officer, we conducted an evaluation of the effectiveness of our internal control over financial reporting as of January 31, 2016 based on the framework in *Internal Control – Integrated Framework (2013)* issued by the Committee of Sponsoring Organizations of the Treadway Commission (COSO). Based on our evaluation, our management concluded that our internal control over financial reporting was effective as of January 31, 2016 in providing reasonable assurance regarding the reliability of financial reporting and the preparation of financial statements for external purposes in accordance with U.S. generally accepted accounting principles. The effectiveness of our internal control over financial reporting as of January 31, 2016 has been audited by KPMG LLP, an independent registered public accounting firm, as stated in their report which is included on page 30 in this Form 10-K.

/s/ CRAIG A. MENEAR	/s/ CAROL B. TOMÉ
Craig A. Menear **Chairman, Chief Executive Officer and President**	**Carol B. Tomé** **Chief Financial Officer and** **Executive Vice President – Corporate Services**

Report of Independent Registered Public Accounting Firm

The Board of Directors and Stockholders
The Home Depot, Inc.:

We have audited The Home Depot, Inc.'s internal control over financial reporting as of January 31, 2016, based on criteria established in *Internal Control – Integrated Framework (2013)* issued by the Committee of Sponsoring Organizations of the Treadway Commission (COSO). The Home Depot, Inc.'s management is responsible for maintaining effective internal control over financial reporting and for its assessment of the effectiveness of internal control over financial reporting, included in the accompanying Management's Report on Internal Control Over Financial Reporting. Our responsibility is to express an opinion on the Company's internal control over financial reporting based on our audit.

We conducted our audit in accordance with the standards of the Public Company Accounting Oversight Board (United States). Those standards require that we plan and perform the audit to obtain reasonable assurance about whether effective internal control over financial reporting was maintained in all material respects. Our audit included obtaining an understanding of internal control over financial reporting, assessing the risk that a material weakness exists, and testing and evaluating the design and operating effectiveness of internal control based on the assessed risk. Our audit also included performing such other procedures as we considered necessary in the circumstances. We believe that our audit provides a reasonable basis for our opinion.

A company's internal control over financial reporting is a process designed to provide reasonable assurance regarding the reliability of financial reporting and the preparation of financial statements for external purposes in accordance with generally accepted accounting principles. A company's internal control over financial reporting includes those policies and procedures that (1) pertain to the maintenance of records that, in reasonable detail, accurately and fairly reflect the transactions and dispositions of the assets of the company; (2) provide reasonable assurance that transactions are recorded as necessary to permit preparation of financial statements in accordance with generally accepted accounting principles, and that receipts and expenditures of the company are being made only in accordance with authorizations of management and directors of the company; and (3) provide reasonable assurance regarding prevention or timely detection of unauthorized acquisition, use, or disposition of the company's assets that could have a material effect on the financial statements.

Because of its inherent limitations, internal control over financial reporting may not prevent or detect misstatements. Also, projections of any evaluation of effectiveness to future periods are subject to the risk that controls may become inadequate because of changes in conditions, or that the degree of compliance with the policies or procedures may deteriorate.

In our opinion, The Home Depot, Inc. maintained, in all material respects, effective internal control over financial reporting as of January 31, 2016, based on criteria established in *Internal Control – Integrated Framework (2013)* issued by the Committee of Sponsoring Organizations of the Treadway Commission (COSO).

We also have audited, in accordance with the standards of the Public Company Accounting Oversight Board (United States), the Consolidated Balance Sheets of The Home Depot, Inc. and subsidiaries as of January 31, 2016 and February 1, 2015, and the related Consolidated Statements of Earnings, Comprehensive Income, Stockholders' Equity, and Cash Flows for each of the fiscal years in the three-year period ended January 31, 2016, and our report dated March 24, 2016 expressed an unqualified opinion on those consolidated financial statements.

/s/ KPMG LLP

Atlanta, Georgia
March 24, 2016

Report of Independent Registered Public Accounting Firm

The Board of Directors and Stockholders
The Home Depot, Inc.:

We have audited the accompanying Consolidated Balance Sheets of The Home Depot, Inc. and subsidiaries as of January 31, 2016 and February 1, 2015, and the related Consolidated Statements of Earnings, Comprehensive Income, Stockholders' Equity, and Cash Flows for each of the fiscal years in the three-year period ended January 31, 2016. These Consolidated Financial Statements are the responsibility of the Company's management. Our responsibility is to express an opinion on these Consolidated Financial Statements based on our audits.

We conducted our audits in accordance with the standards of the Public Company Accounting Oversight Board (United States). Those standards require that we plan and perform the audit to obtain reasonable assurance about whether the financial statements are free of material misstatement. An audit includes examining, on a test basis, evidence supporting the amounts and disclosures in the financial statements. An audit also includes assessing the accounting principles used and significant estimates made by management, as well as evaluating the overall financial statement presentation. We believe that our audits provide a reasonable basis for our opinion.

In our opinion, the Consolidated Financial Statements referred to above present fairly, in all material respects, the financial position of The Home Depot, Inc. and subsidiaries as of January 31, 2016 and February 1, 2015, and the results of their operations and their cash flows for each of the fiscal years in the three-year period ended January 31, 2016, in conformity with U.S. generally accepted accounting principles.

As discussed in Note 2 to the Consolidated Financial Statements, the Company has changed its accounting policy to include shipping and handling costs from the Company's stores, locations or distribution centers to customers and for online fulfillment center costs within cost of sales, beginning in the first quarter of fiscal 2015. This change in accounting principle has been retrospectively applied to the accompanying Consolidated Financial Statements for the fiscal years ended February 1, 2015 and February 2, 2014.

We also have audited, in accordance with the standards of the Public Company Accounting Oversight Board (United States), The Home Depot, Inc.'s internal control over financial reporting as of January 31, 2016, based on criteria established in *Internal Control – Integrated Framework (2013)* issued by the Committee of Sponsoring Organizations of the Treadway Commission (COSO), and our report dated March 24, 2016 expressed an unqualified opinion on the effectiveness of the Company's internal control over financial reporting.

/s/ KPMG LLP

Atlanta, Georgia
March 24, 2016

THE HOME DEPOT, INC. AND SUBSIDIARIES
CONSOLIDATED BALANCE SHEETS

amounts in millions, except share and per share data	January 31, 2016	February 1, 2015
ASSETS		
Current Assets:		
Cash and Cash Equivalents	$ 2,216	$ 1,723
Receivables, net	1,890	1,484
Merchandise Inventories	11,809	11,079
Other Current Assets	1,078	1,016
Total Current Assets	16,993	15,302
Property and Equipment, at cost	39,266	38,513
Less Accumulated Depreciation and Amortization	17,075	15,793
Net Property and Equipment	22,191	22,720
Goodwill	2,102	1,353
Other Assets	1,263	571
Total Assets	$ 42,549	$ 39,946
LIABILITIES AND STOCKHOLDERS' EQUITY		
Current Liabilities:		
Short-Term Debt	$ 350	$ 290
Accounts Payable	6,565	5,807
Accrued Salaries and Related Expenses	1,515	1,391
Sales Taxes Payable	476	434
Deferred Revenue	1,566	1,468
Income Taxes Payable	34	35
Current Installments of Long-Term Debt	77	38
Other Accrued Expenses	1,943	1,806
Total Current Liabilities	12,526	11,269
Long-Term Debt, excluding current installments	20,888	16,869
Other Long-Term Liabilities	1,965	1,844
Deferred Income Taxes	854	642
Total Liabilities	36,233	30,624
STOCKHOLDERS' EQUITY		
Common Stock, par value $0.05; authorized: 10 billion shares; issued: 1.772 billion shares at January 31, 2016 and 1.768 billion shares at February 1, 2015; outstanding: 1.252 billion shares at January 31, 2016 and 1.307 billion shares at February 1, 2015	88	88
Paid-In Capital	9,347	8,885
Retained Earnings	30,973	26,995
Accumulated Other Comprehensive Loss	(898)	(452)
Treasury Stock, at cost, 520 million shares at January 31, 2016 and 461 million shares at February 1, 2015	(33,194)	(26,194)
Total Stockholders' Equity	6,316	9,322
Total Liabilities and Stockholders' Equity	$ 42,549	$ 39,946

See accompanying Notes to Consolidated Financial Statements.

THE HOME DEPOT, INC. AND SUBSIDIARIES
CONSOLIDATED STATEMENTS OF EARNINGS

	Fiscal Year Ended(1)		
amounts in millions, except per share data	January 31, 2016	February 1, 2015	February 2, 2014
NET SALES	**$ 88,519**	$ 83,176	$ 78,812
Cost of Sales	**58,254**	54,787	51,897
GROSS PROFIT	**30,265**	28,389	26,915
Operating Expenses:			
Selling, General and Administrative	**16,801**	16,280	16,122
Depreciation and Amortization	**1,690**	1,640	1,627
Total Operating Expenses	**18,491**	17,920	17,749
OPERATING INCOME	**11,774**	10,469	9,166
Interest and Other (Income) Expense:			
Interest and Investment Income	**(166)**	(337)	(12)
Interest Expense	**919**	830	711
Interest and Other, net	**753**	493	699
EARNINGS BEFORE PROVISION FOR INCOME TAXES	**11,021**	9,976	8,467
Provision for Income Taxes	**4,012**	3,631	3,082
NET EARNINGS	**$ 7,009**	$ 6,345	$ 5,385
Weighted Average Common Shares	**1,277**	1,338	1,425
BASIC EARNINGS PER SHARE	**$ 5.49**	$ 4.74	$ 3.78
Diluted Weighted Average Common Shares	**1,283**	1,346	1,434
DILUTED EARNINGS PER SHARE	**$ 5.46**	$ 4.71	$ 3.76

(1) Fiscal years ended January 31, 2016, February 1, 2015 and February 2, 2014 include 52 weeks.

See accompanying Notes to Consolidated Financial Statements.

THE HOME DEPOT, INC. AND SUBSIDIARIES
CONSOLIDATED STATEMENTS OF COMPREHENSIVE INCOME

	Fiscal Year Ended(1)		
amounts in millions	January 31, 2016	February 1, 2015	February 2, 2014
Net Earnings	**$ 7,009**	$ 6,345	$ 5,385
Other Comprehensive Loss:			
Foreign Currency Translation Adjustments	**(412)**	(510)	(329)
Cash Flow Hedges, net of tax	**(34)**	11	(12)
Other	—	1	(10)
Total Other Comprehensive Loss	**(446)**	(498)	(351)
COMPREHENSIVE INCOME	**$ 6,563**	$ 5,847	$ 5,034

(1) Fiscal years ended January 31, 2016, February 1, 2015 and February 2, 2014 include 52 weeks.

See accompanying Notes to Consolidated Financial Statements.

THE HOME DEPOT, INC. AND SUBSIDIARIES
CONSOLIDATED STATEMENTS OF STOCKHOLDERS' EQUITY

amounts in millions, except per share data	Common Stock		Paid-In Capital	Retained Earnings	Accumulated Other Comprehensive Income (Loss)	Treasury Stock		Stockholders' Equity
	Shares	Amount				Shares	Amount	
Balance, February 3, 2013	**1,754**	**$ 88**	**$ 7,948**	**$ 20,038**	**$ 397**	**(270)**	**$ (10,694)**	**$ 17,777**
Net Earnings	—	—	—	5,385	—	—	—	5,385
Shares Issued Under Employee Stock Plans	7	—	103	—	—	—	—	103
Tax Effect of Stock-Based Compensation	—	—	123	—	—	—	—	123
Foreign Currency Translation Adjustments	—	—	—	—	(329)	—	—	(329)
Cash Flow Hedges, net of tax	—	—	—	—	(12)	—	—	(12)
Stock Options, Awards and Amortization of Restricted Stock	—	—	228	—	—	—	—	228
Repurchases of Common Stock	—	—	—	—	—	(111)	(8,500)	(8,500)
Cash Dividends ($1.56 per share)	—	—	—	(2,243)	—	—	—	(2,243)
Other	—	—	—	—	(10)	—	—	(10)
Balance, February 2, 2014	**1,761**	**$ 88**	**$ 8,402**	**$ 23,180**	**$ 46**	**(381)**	**$ (19,194)**	**$ 12,522**
Net Earnings	—	—	—	6,345	—	—	—	6,345
Shares Issued Under Employee Stock Plans	7	—	122	—	—	—	—	122
Tax Effect of Stock-Based Compensation	—	—	136	—	—	—	—	136
Foreign Currency Translation Adjustments	—	—	—	—	(510)	—	—	(510)
Cash Flow Hedges, net of tax	—	—	—	—	11	—	—	11
Stock Options, Awards and Amortization of Restricted Stock	—	—	225	—	—	—	—	225
Repurchases of Common Stock	—	—	—	—	—	(80)	(7,000)	(7,000)
Cash Dividends ($1.88 per share)	—	—	—	(2,530)	—	—	—	(2,530)
Other	—	—	—	—	1	—	—	1
Balance, February 1, 2015	**1,768**	**$ 88**	**$ 8,885**	**$ 26,995**	**$ (452)**	**(461)**	**$ (26,194)**	**$ 9,322**
Net Earnings	—	—	—	7,009	—	—	—	7,009
Shares Issued Under Employee Stock Plans	4	—	73	—	—	—	—	73
Tax Effect of Stock-Based Compensation	—	—	145	—	—	—	—	145
Foreign Currency Translation Adjustments	—	—	—	—	(412)	—	—	(412)
Cash Flow Hedges, net of tax	—	—	—	—	(34)	—	—	(34)
Stock Options, Awards and Amortization of Restricted Stock	—	—	244	—	—	—	—	244
Repurchases of Common Stock	—	—	—	—	—	(59)	(7,000)	(7,000)
Cash Dividends ($2.36 per share)	—	—	—	(3,031)	—	—	—	(3,031)
Balance, January 31, 2016	**1,772**	**$ 88**	**$ 9,347**	**$ 30,973**	**$ (898)**	**(520)**	**$ (33,194)**	**$ 6,316**

See accompanying Notes to Consolidated Financial Statements.

THE HOME DEPOT, INC. AND SUBSIDIARIES
CONSOLIDATED STATEMENTS OF CASH FLOWS

amounts in millions	Fiscal Year Ended(1) January 31, 2016	February 1, 2015	February 2, 2014
CASH FLOWS FROM OPERATING ACTIVITIES:			
Net Earnings	$ **7,009**	$ 6,345	$ 5,385
Reconciliation of Net Earnings to Net Cash Provided by Operating Activities:			
Depreciation and Amortization	**1,863**	1,786	1,757
Stock-Based Compensation Expense	**244**	225	228
Gain on Sales of Investments	**(144)**	(323)	—
Changes in Assets and Liabilities, net of the effects of acquisitions:			
Receivables, net	**(181)**	(81)	(15)
Merchandise Inventories	**(546)**	(124)	(455)
Other Current Assets	**(5)**	(199)	(5)
Accounts Payable and Accrued Expenses	**888**	244	605
Deferred Revenue	**109**	146	75
Income Taxes Payable	**154**	168	119
Deferred Income Taxes	**15**	159	(31)
Other	**(33)**	(104)	(35)
Net Cash Provided by Operating Activities	**9,373**	8,242	7,628
CASH FLOWS FROM INVESTING ACTIVITIES:			
Capital Expenditures, net of $165, $217 and $46 of non-cash capital expenditures in fiscal 2015, 2014 and 2013, respectively	**(1,503)**	(1,442)	(1,389)
Proceeds from Sales of Investments	**144**	323	—
Payments for Businesses Acquired, net	**(1,666)**	(200)	(206)
Proceeds from Sales of Property and Equipment	**43**	48	88
Net Cash Used in Investing Activities	**(2,982)**	(1,271)	(1,507)
CASH FLOWS FROM FINANCING ACTIVITIES:			
Proceeds from Short-Term Borrowings, net	**60**	290	—
Proceeds from Long-Term Borrowings, net of discounts	**3,991**	1,981	5,222
Repayments of Long-Term Debt	**(39)**	(39)	(1,289)
Repurchases of Common Stock	**(7,000)**	(7,000)	(8,546)
Proceeds from Sales of Common Stock	**228**	252	241
Cash Dividends Paid to Stockholders	**(3,031)**	(2,530)	(2,243)
Other Financing Activities	**4**	(25)	(37)
Net Cash Used in Financing Activities	**(5,787)**	(7,071)	(6,652)
Change in Cash and Cash Equivalents	**604**	(100)	(531)
Effect of Exchange Rate Changes on Cash and Cash Equivalents	**(111)**	(106)	(34)
Cash and Cash Equivalents at Beginning of Year	**1,723**	1,929	2,494
Cash and Cash Equivalents at End of Year	$ **2,216**	$ 1,723	$ 1,929
SUPPLEMENTAL DISCLOSURE OF CASH PAYMENTS MADE FOR:			
Interest, net of interest capitalized	$ **874**	$ 782	$ 639
Income Taxes	$ **3,853**	$ 3,435	$ 2,839

(1) Fiscal years ended January 31, 2016, February 1, 2015 and February 2, 2014 include 52 weeks.

See accompanying Notes to Consolidated Financial Statements.

NOTES TO CONSOLIDATED FINANCIAL STATEMENTS

1. SUMMARY OF SIGNIFICANT ACCOUNTING POLICIES

Business, Consolidation and Presentation

The Home Depot, Inc., together with its subsidiaries (the "Company"), is a home improvement retailer that sells a wide assortment of building materials, home improvement products and lawn and garden products and provides a number of services. The Home Depot stores, which are full-service, warehouse-style stores averaging approximately 104,000 square feet of enclosed space, with approximately 24,000 additional square feet of outside garden area, stock approximately 30,000 to 40,000 different kinds of products that are sold to do-it-yourself customers, do-it-for-me customers and professional customers. The Company also offers a significantly broader product assortment through its Home Depot, Home Decorators Collection and Blinds.com websites. At the end of fiscal 2015, the Company was operating 2,274 The Home Depot stores, which included 1,977 stores in the United States, including the Commonwealth of Puerto Rico and the territories of the U.S. Virgin Islands and Guam ("U.S."), 182 stores in Canada and 115 stores in Mexico. The Consolidated Financial Statements include the accounts of the Company and its wholly-owned subsidiaries. All significant intercompany transactions have been eliminated in consolidation.

Fiscal Year

The Company's fiscal year is a 52- or 53-week period ending on the Sunday nearest to January 31. Fiscal years ended January 31, 2016 ("fiscal 2015"), February 1, 2015 ("fiscal 2014") and February 2, 2014 ("fiscal 2013") include 52 weeks.

Use of Estimates

Management of the Company has made a number of estimates and assumptions relating to the reporting of assets and liabilities, the disclosure of contingent assets and liabilities, and reported amounts of revenues and expenses in preparing these financial statements in conformity with U.S. generally accepted accounting principles. Actual results could differ from these estimates.

Fair Value of Financial Instruments

The carrying amounts of Cash and Cash Equivalents, Receivables, Short-Term Debt and Accounts Payable approximate fair value due to the short-term maturities of these financial instruments. The fair value of the Company's Long-Term Debt is discussed in Note 11.

Cash Equivalents

The Company considers all highly liquid investments purchased with original maturities of three months or less to be cash equivalents. The Company's cash equivalents are carried at fair market value and consist primarily of money market funds.

Accounts Receivable

The Company has an agreement with a third-party service provider who directly extends credit to customers, manages the Company's private label credit card program and owns the related receivables. The Company evaluated the third-party entities holding the receivables under the program and concluded that they should not be consolidated by the Company. The agreement with the third-party service provider expires in January 2018, with the Company having the option, but no obligation, to purchase the receivables at the end of the agreement. The deferred interest charges incurred by the Company for its deferred financing programs offered to its customers are included in Cost of Sales. The interchange fees charged to the Company for the customers' use of the cards and any profit sharing with the third-party service provider are included in Selling, General and Administrative expenses ("SG&A"). The sum of the three is referred to by the Company as "the cost of credit" of the private label credit card program.

In addition, certain subsidiaries of the Company, including Interline Brands, Inc. ("Interline"), extend credit directly to customers in the ordinary course of business. The receivables due from customers were $253 million and $68 million as of January 31, 2016 and February 1, 2015, respectively. The Company's valuation reserve related to accounts receivable was not material to the Consolidated Financial Statements of the Company as of the end of fiscal 2015 or 2014.

Merchandise Inventories

The majority of the Company's Merchandise Inventories are stated at the lower of cost (first-in, first-out) or market, as determined by the retail inventory method. As the inventory retail value is adjusted regularly to reflect market conditions, the inventory valued using the retail method approximates the lower of cost or market. Certain subsidiaries, including retail operations in Canada and Mexico, distribution centers and Interline, record Merchandise Inventories at the lower of cost or market, as determined by a cost method. These Merchandise Inventories represent approximately 29% of the total Merchandise Inventories balance. The Company evaluates the inventory valued using a cost method at the end of each quarter to ensure that it is carried at the lower of cost or market. The valuation allowance for Merchandise Inventories valued under a cost method was not material to the Consolidated Financial Statements of the Company as of the end of fiscal 2015 or 2014.

Independent physical inventory counts or cycle counts are taken on a regular basis in each store and distribution center to ensure that amounts reflected in the accompanying Consolidated Financial Statements for Merchandise Inventories are properly stated. During the period between physical inventory counts in stores, the Company accrues for estimated losses related to shrink on a store-by-store basis based on recent shrink results and current trends in the business. Shrink (or in the case of excess inventory, "swell") is the difference between the recorded amount of inventory and the physical inventory. Shrink may occur due to theft, loss, inaccurate records for the receipt of inventory or deterioration of goods, among other things.

Income Taxes

Income taxes are accounted for under the asset and liability method. The Company provides for federal, state and foreign income taxes currently payable, as well as for those deferred due to timing differences between reporting income and expenses for financial statement purposes versus tax purposes. Deferred tax assets and liabilities are recognized for the future tax consequences attributable to temporary differences between the financial statement carrying amounts of existing assets and liabilities and their respective tax bases. Deferred tax assets and liabilities are measured using enacted income tax rates expected to apply to taxable income in the years in which those temporary differences are expected to be recovered or settled. The effect of a change in income tax rates is recognized as income or expense in the period that includes the enactment date.

The Company recognizes the effect of income tax positions only if those positions are more likely than not of being sustained. Recognized income tax positions are measured at the largest amount that is greater than 50% likely of being realized. Changes in recognition or measurement are reflected in the period in which the change in judgment occurs.

The Company and its eligible subsidiaries file a consolidated U.S. federal income tax return. Non-U.S. subsidiaries and certain U.S. subsidiaries, which are consolidated for financial reporting purposes, are not eligible to be included in the Company's consolidated U.S. federal income tax return. Separate provisions for income taxes have been determined for these entities. The Company intends to reinvest substantially all of the unremitted earnings of its non-U.S. subsidiaries and postpone their remittance indefinitely. Accordingly, no provision for U.S. income taxes on these earnings was recorded in the accompanying Consolidated Statements of Earnings.

Depreciation and Amortization

The Company's Buildings, Furniture, Fixtures and Equipment are recorded at cost and depreciated using the straight-line method over the estimated useful lives of the assets. Leasehold Improvements are amortized using the straight-line method over the original term of the lease or the useful life of the improvement, whichever is shorter. The Company's Property and Equipment is depreciated using the following estimated useful lives:

	Life
Buildings	5 – 45 years
Furniture, Fixtures and Equipment	2 – 20 years
Leasehold Improvements	5 – 45 years

Capitalized Software Costs

The Company capitalizes certain costs related to the acquisition and development of software and amortizes these costs using the straight-line method over the estimated useful life of the software, which is three to six years. Certain development costs not meeting the criteria for capitalization are expensed as incurred.

Revenues

The Company recognizes revenue, net of estimated returns and sales tax, at the time the customer takes possession of merchandise or receives services. The liability for sales returns is estimated based on historical return levels. When the Company receives payment from customers before the customer has taken possession of the merchandise or the service has been performed, the amount received is recorded as Deferred Revenue in the accompanying Consolidated Balance Sheets until the sale or service is complete. The Company also records Deferred Revenue for the sale of gift cards and recognizes this revenue upon the redemption of gift cards in Net Sales. Gift card breakage income is recognized based upon historical redemption patterns and represents the balance of gift cards for which the Company believes the likelihood of redemption by the customer is remote. During fiscal 2015, 2014 and 2013, the Company recognized $27 million, $32 million and $30 million, respectively, of gift card breakage income. This income is included in the accompanying Consolidated Statements of Earnings as a reduction in SG&A.

Services Revenue

Net Sales include services revenue generated through a variety of installation, home maintenance and professional service programs. In these programs, the customer selects and purchases material for a project, and the Company provides or arranges professional installation. These programs are offered through the Company's stores and in-home sales programs. Under certain programs, when the Company provides or arranges the installation of a project and the subcontractor provides material as part of the installation, both the material and labor are included in services revenue. The Company recognizes this revenue when the service for the customer is complete.

All payments received prior to the completion of services are recorded in Deferred Revenue in the accompanying Consolidated Balance Sheets. Services revenue was $4.0 billion, $3.8 billion and $3.5 billion for fiscal 2015, 2014 and 2013, respectively.

Self-Insurance

The Company is self-insured for certain losses related to general liability (including product liability), workers' compensation, employee group medical and automobile claims. The expected ultimate cost for claims incurred as of the balance sheet date is not discounted and is recognized as a liability. The expected ultimate cost of claims is estimated based upon analysis of historical data and actuarial estimates. The Company maintains network security and privacy liability insurance coverage to limit the Company's exposure to losses such as those that may be caused by a significant compromise or breach of the Company's data security. This coverage is discussed further in Note 13.

Prepaid Advertising

Television and radio advertising production costs, along with media placement costs, are expensed when the advertisement first appears. Amounts included in Other Current Assets in the accompanying Consolidated Balance Sheets relating to prepayments of production costs for print and broadcast advertising as well as sponsorship promotions were not material at the end of fiscal 2015 and 2014.

Vendor Allowances

Vendor allowances primarily consist of volume rebates that are earned as a result of attaining certain purchase levels and advertising co-op allowances for the promotion of vendors' products that are typically based on guaranteed minimum amounts with additional amounts being earned for attaining certain purchase levels. These vendor allowances are accrued as earned, with those allowances received as a result of attaining certain purchase levels accrued over the incentive period based on estimates of purchases.

Volume rebates and certain advertising co-op allowances earned are initially recorded as a reduction in Merchandise Inventories and a subsequent reduction in Cost of Sales when the related product is sold. Certain advertising co-op allowances that are reimbursements of specific, incremental and identifiable costs incurred to promote vendors' products are recorded as an offset against advertising expense. In fiscal 2015, 2014 and 2013, gross advertising expense was $868 million, $884 million and $865 million, respectively, and is included in SG&A. Specific, incremental and identifiable advertising co-op allowances were $129 million, $125 million and $114 million for fiscal 2015, 2014 and 2013, respectively, and are recorded as an offset to advertising expense in SG&A.

Cost of Sales

Cost of Sales includes the actual cost of merchandise sold and services performed, the cost of transportation of merchandise from vendors to the Company's stores, locations or customers, shipping and handling costs from the Company's stores, locations or distribution centers to customers, the operating cost of the Company's sourcing and distribution network, online fulfillment center costs and the cost of deferred interest programs offered through the Company's private label credit card programs.

Impairment of Long-Lived Assets

The Company evaluates its long-lived assets each quarter for indicators of potential impairment. Indicators of impairment include current period losses combined with a history of losses, management's decision to relocate or close a store or other location before the end of its previously estimated useful life or when changes in other circumstances indicate the carrying amount of an asset may not be recoverable. The evaluation for long-lived assets is performed at the lowest level of identifiable cash flows, which is generally the individual store level.

The assets of a store with indicators of impairment are evaluated by comparing its undiscounted cash flows with its carrying value. The estimate of cash flows includes management's assumptions of cash inflows and outflows directly resulting from the use of those assets in operations, including gross margin on Net Sales, payroll and related items, occupancy costs, insurance allocations and other costs to operate a store. If the carrying value is greater than the undiscounted cash flows, an impairment loss is recognized for the difference between the carrying value and the estimated fair market value. Impairment losses are recorded as a component of SG&A in the accompanying Consolidated Statements of Earnings. When a leased location closes, the Company also recognizes in SG&A the net present value of future lease obligations less estimated sublease income. The Company recorded impairments and lease obligation costs on closings and relocations in the ordinary course of business, which were not material to the Consolidated Financial Statements in fiscal 2015, 2014 or 2013.

Goodwill and Other Intangible Assets

Goodwill represents the excess of purchase price over the fair value of net assets acquired. The Company does not amortize goodwill but does assess the recoverability of goodwill in the third quarter of each fiscal year, or more often if indicators warrant, by determining whether the fair value of each reporting unit supports its carrying value. Each year the Company may assess qualitative factors to determine whether it is more likely than not that the fair value of each reporting unit is less than its carrying amount as a basis for determining whether it is necessary to complete quantitative impairment assessments, with a quantitative assessment completed at least once every three years. The Company's most recent quantitative assessment was completed in fiscal 2013.

In fiscal 2015, the Company completed its annual assessment of the recoverability of goodwill for its U.S., Canada and Mexico reporting units. The Company performed qualitative assessments, concluding that the fair value of the reporting units was not more likely than not less than the carrying value. There were no impairment charges related to goodwill for fiscal 2015, 2014 or 2013.

The Company amortizes the cost of other intangible assets over their estimated useful lives, which range up to 12 years, unless such lives are deemed indefinite. Intangible assets with indefinite lives are tested in the third quarter of each fiscal year for impairment, or more often if indicators warrant. There were no impairment charges related to other intangible assets for fiscal 2015, 2014 or 2013.

Stock-Based Compensation

The per share weighted average fair value of stock options granted during fiscal 2015, 2014 and 2013 was $18.54, $14.13 and $13.10, respectively. The fair value of these options was determined at the date of grant using the Black-Scholes option-pricing model with the following assumptions:

	Fiscal Year Ended		
	January 31, 2016	**February 1, 2015**	**February 2, 2014**
Risk-free interest rate	**1.4%**	1.7%	0.8%
Assumed volatility	**20.8%**	22.7%	26.3%
Assumed dividend yield	**2.0%**	2.3%	2.2%
Assumed lives of options	**5 years**	5 years	5 years

Derivatives

The Company uses derivative financial instruments from time to time in the management of its interest rate exposure on long-term debt and its exposure on foreign currency fluctuations. The Company accounts for its derivative financial instruments in accordance with the Financial Accounting Standards Board Accounting Standards Codification ("FASB ASC") Subtopic 815-10. The fair value of the Company's derivative financial instruments is discussed in Note 11.

Comprehensive Income

Comprehensive Income includes Net Earnings adjusted for certain gains and losses that are excluded from Net Earnings under U.S. generally accepted accounting principles. Adjustments to Net Earnings and Accumulated Other Comprehensive Income consist primarily of foreign currency translation adjustments.

Foreign Currency Translation

Assets and liabilities denominated in a foreign currency are translated into U.S. dollars at the current rate of exchange on the last day of the reporting period. Revenues and expenses are generally translated using average exchange rates for the period and equity transactions are translated using the actual rate on the day of the transaction.

Segment Information

The Company operates within a single reportable segment primarily within North America. Net Sales for the Company outside the U.S. were $8.0 billion, $8.5 billion and $8.5 billion for fiscal 2015, 2014 and 2013, respectively. Long-lived assets outside the U.S. totaled $2.3 billion and $2.5 billion as of January 31, 2016 and February 1, 2015, respectively.

The following table presents the Net Sales of each major product category (and related services) for each of the last three fiscal years (dollar amounts in millions):

	Fiscal Year Ended					
Product Category	**January 31, 2016**		**February 1, 2015**		**February 2, 2014**	
	Net Sales	**% of Net Sales**	**Net Sales**	**% of Net Sales**	**Net Sales**	**% of Net Sales**
Indoor Garden	**$ 8,298**	**9.4%**	$ 7,560	9.1%	$ 7,022	8.9%
Paint	**7,465**	**8.4**	7,299	8.8	7,018	8.9
Kitchen and Bath	**6,874**	**7.8**	6,607	7.9	6,301	8.0
Outdoor Garden	**6,565**	**7.4**	6,385	7.7	6,140	7.8
Appliances	**6,534**	**7.4**	5,708	6.9	5,382	6.8
Building Materials	**6,396**	**7.2**	6,054	7.3	5,728	7.3
Plumbing	**6,346**	**7.2**	5,740	6.9	5,435	6.9
Lumber	**6,278**	**7.1**	6,050	7.3	5,820	7.4
Flooring	**6,194**	**7.0**	5,987	7.2	5,721	7.3
Tools	**6,060**	**6.8**	5,388	6.5	5,038	6.4
Electrical	**5,833**	**6.6**	5,653	6.8	5,378	6.8
Hardware	**5,296**	**6.0**	4,975	6.0	4,718	6.0
Millwork	**4,924**	**5.6**	4,694	5.6	4,389	5.6
Décor	**2,757**	**3.1**	2,577	3.1	2,343	3.0
Lighting	**2,699**	**3.0**	2,499	3.0	2,379	3.0
Total	**$ 88,519**	**100.0%**	$ 83,176	100.0%	$ 78,812	100.0%

Note: Certain percentages may not sum to totals due to rounding.

Recent Accounting Pronouncements

In February 2016, the Financial Accounting Standards Board ("FASB") issued Accounting Standards Update No. 2016-02, "Leases (Topic 842)" ("ASU No. 2016-02"), which requires an entity that is a lessee to recognize the assets and liabilities arising from leases on the balance sheet. This guidance also requires disclosures about the amount, timing and uncertainty of cash flows arising from leases. This guidance is effective for annual reporting periods beginning after December 15, 2018, and interim periods within those annual periods, using a modified retrospective approach, and early adoption is permitted. The Company is evaluating the effect that ASU No. 2016-02 will have on its Consolidated Financial Statements and related disclosures.

In April 2015, the FASB issued Accounting Standards Update No. 2015-03, "Interest – Imputation of Interest (Subtopic 835-30): Simplifying the Presentation of Debt Issuance Costs" ("ASU No. 2015-03"), which requires an entity to present debt issuance costs related to a recognized debt liability as a direct deduction from the carrying amount of that debt liability, consistent with debt discounts. The recognition and measurement guidance for debt issuance costs are not affected by this ASU. This guidance is effective for annual reporting periods beginning after December 15, 2015 and for interim and annual reporting periods thereafter, and retrospective application is required. Early adoption is permitted for financial statements that have not been previously issued. The Company does not believe that ASU No. 2015-03 will have a material impact on its Consolidated Financial Statements and related disclosures.

In August 2015, the FASB issued Accounting Standards Update No. 2015-15, "Interest – Imputation of Interest (Subtopic 835-30): Presentation and Subsequent Measurement of Debt Issuance Costs Associated with Line-of-Credit Arrangements" ("ASU No. 2015-15"), which states that ASU No. 2015-03 does not address debt issuance costs for line-of-credit arrangements, and therefore the SEC staff would not object to an entity deferring and presenting these related debt issuance costs as an asset and subsequently amortizing the deferred issuance costs ratably over the term of the line-of-credit arrangement, regardless of whether there are any outstanding borrowings on the line-of-credit arrangement. The Company does not believe that ASU No. 2015-15 will have a material impact on its Consolidated Financial Statements and related disclosures.

In November 2015, the FASB issued Accounting Standards Update No. 2015-17, "Income Taxes (Topic 740): Balance Sheet Classification of Deferred Taxes" ("ASU No. 2015-17"), which requires an entity to present deferred tax assets and liabilities as noncurrent in a classified balance sheet. This guidance is effective for annual reporting periods beginning after December 15, 2016, and interim periods within those annual periods. Early adoption is permitted as of the beginning of an interim or annual reporting period. The guidance in this ASU may be applied either prospectively to all deferred tax assets and liabilities or retrospectively to all periods presented. The Company does not believe that ASU No. 2015-17 will have a material impact on its Consolidated Financial Statements and related disclosures.

In May 2014, the FASB issued Accounting Standards Update No. 2014-09, "Revenue from Contracts with Customers (Topic 606)" ("ASU No. 2014-09"), which requires an entity to recognize revenue to depict the transfer of promised goods or services to customers in an amount that reflects the consideration to which it expects to be entitled in exchange for those goods or services. ASU No. 2014-09 supersedes most existing revenue recognition guidance in U.S. GAAP, and it permits the use of either the retrospective or cumulative effect transition method. In August 2015, the FASB issued Accounting Standards Update No. 2015-14, "Revenue from Contracts with Customers (Topic 606): Deferral of the Effective Date" ("ASU No. 2015-14"), which delayed the effective date of ASU No. 2014-09 by one year. As a result, ASU No. 2014-09 is effective for annual reporting periods beginning after December 15, 2017, including interim periods within that reporting period. Early adoption is permitted for annual reporting periods beginning after December 15, 2016, including interim periods within that reporting period. The Company is evaluating the effect that ASU No. 2014-09 will have on its Consolidated Financial Statements and related disclosures.

Reclassifications

Certain amounts in prior fiscal years have been reclassified to conform with the presentation adopted in the current fiscal year. See Note 2 to the Consolidated Financial Statements included in this report

Five-Year Summary of Financial and Operating Results
The Home Depot, Inc. and Subsidiaries

amounts in millions, except where noted	2015	2014	2013	2012(1)	2011
STATEMENT OF EARNINGS DATA					
Net sales	**$ 88,519**	$ 83,176	$ 78,812	$ 74,754	$ 70,395
Net sales increase (%)	**6.4**	5.5	5.4	6.2	3.5
Earnings before provision for income taxes	**11,021**	9,976	8,467	7,221	6,068
Net earnings	**7,009**	6,345	5,385	4,535	3,883
Net earnings increase (%)	**10.5**	17.8	18.7	16.8	16.3
Diluted earnings per share ($)	**5.46**	4.71	3.76	3.00	2.47
Diluted earnings per share increase (%)	**15.9**	25.3	25.3	21.5	22.9
Diluted weighted average number of common shares	**1,283**	1,346	1,434	1,511	1,570
Gross margin – % of sales(2)	**34.2**	34.1	34.2	34.0	33.9
Total operating expenses – % of sales(2)	**20.9**	21.5	22.5	23.6	24.4
Interest and other, net – % of sales	**0.9**	0.6	0.9	0.7	0.8
Earnings before provision for income taxes – % of sales	**12.5**	12.0	10.7	9.7	8.6
Net earnings – % of sales	**7.9**	7.6	6.8	6.1	5.5
BALANCE SHEET DATA AND FINANCIAL RATIOS					
Total assets	**$ 42,549**	$ 39,946	$ 40,518	$ 41,084	$ 40,518
Working capital	**4,467**	4,033	4,530	3,910	5,144
Merchandise inventories	**11,809**	11,079	11,057	10,710	10,325
Net property and equipment	**22,191**	22,720	23,348	24,069	24,448
Long-term debt	**20,888**	16,869	14,691	9,475	10,758
Stockholders' equity	**6,316**	9,322	12,522	17,777	17,898
Long-term debt-to-equity (%)	**330.7**	181.0	117.3	53.3	60.1
Total debt-to-equity (%)	**337.5**	184.5	117.6	60.7	60.3
Current ratio	**1.36:1**	1.36:1	1.42:1	1.34:1	1.55:1
Inventory turnover(2)	**4.9x**	4.7x	4.6x	4.5x	4.3x
Return on invested capital (%)	**28.0**	24.9	20.9	17.0	14.9
STATEMENT OF CASH FLOWS DATA					
Depreciation and amortization	**$ 1,863**	$ 1,786	$ 1,757	$ 1,684	$ 1,682
Capital expenditures	**1,503**	1,442	1,389	1,312	1,221
Cash dividends per share ($)	**2.360**	1.880	1.560	1.160	1.040
STORE DATA					
Number of stores	**2,274**	2,269	2,263	2,256	2,252
Square footage at fiscal year-end	**237**	236	236	235	235
Average square footage per store (in thousands)	**104**	104	104	104	104
STORE SALES AND OTHER DATA					
Comparable store sales increase (%)(3)(4)	**5.6**	5.3	6.8	4.6	3.4
Sales per square foot ($)(4)	**371**	352	334	319	299
Number of customer transactions(4)	**1,501**	1,442	1,391	1,364	1,318
Average ticket ($)(4)	**58.77**	57.87	56.78	54.89	53.28
Number of associates at fiscal year-end (in thousands)	**385**	371	365	340	331

(1) Fiscal year 2012 includes 53 weeks; all other fiscal years reported include 52 weeks.

(2) In fiscal 2015, the Company changed its accounting policy for shipping and handling costs from the Company's stores, locations or distribution centers to customers and for online fulfillment center costs. This change in accounting policy has been applied retrospectively. See Note 2 to the Consolidated Financial Statements included in Item 8, "Financial Statements and Supplementary Data".

(3) Includes Net Sales at locations open greater than 12 months, including relocated and remodeled stores and online sales, and excluding closed stores. Retail stores become comparable on the Monday following their 365th day of operation. Comparable store sales is intended only as supplemental information and is not a substitute for Net Sales or Net Earnings presented in accordance with generally accepted accounting principles. Net Sales for the 53rd week of fiscal 2012 are not included in comparable store sales results for fiscal 2012.

(4) These amounts do not include results for the Interline acquisition that was completed in the third quarter of fiscal 2015.

Appendix B

Combined Journal

Most small businesses have just a few employees and can devote only a limited amount of time to the preparation of accounting records. To serve the needs of these businesses, accountants have developed certain types of record systems that have special time-saving and labor-saving features but still produce all the necessary financial information for management. One example of such a system is the combined journal discussed in this appendix.

Small firms play an important role in our economy today. In fact, almost one-half of the businesses in the United States are classified as small entities. Despite their limited size, these businesses need good accounting systems that can produce accurate and timely information.

Systems Involving the Combined Journal

The **combined journal,** also called the *combination journal,* provides the cornerstone for a simple yet effective accounting system in many small firms. As its name indicates, this journal combines features of the general journal and the special journals in a single record.

If a small business has enough transactions to make the general journal difficult to use but too few transactions to make it worthwhile to set up special journals, the combined journal offers a solution. It has many of the advantages of special journals but provides the simplicity of a single journal. Like the special journals, the combined journal contains separate money columns for the accounts used most often to record a firm's transactions. This speeds up the initial entry of transactions and permits summary postings at the end of the month. Most transactions can be recorded on a single line, and the need to write account names is minimized.

Other Accounts columns allow the recording of transactions that do not fit into any of the special columns. These columns are also used for entries that would normally appear in the general journal, such as adjusting and closing entries.

Some small firms just use a combined journal and a general ledger in their accounting systems. Others need one or more subsidiary ledgers in addition to the general ledger.

DESIGNING A COMBINED JOURNAL

To function effectively, a combined journal must be designed to meet the specific needs of a firm. For a new business, the accountant first studies the proposed operations and develops an appropriate chart of accounts. Then the accountant decides which accounts are likely to be used often enough in recording daily transactions to justify special columns in the combined journal.

Consider the combined journal shown in Figure B.1, which belongs to Quality Lawn Care and Landscaping Services, a small business that provides lawn and landscaping services. In designing this journal before the firm opened, the accountant established a Cash section with Debit and Credit columns because it was known that the business would constantly be receiving cash from customers and paying out cash for expenses and other obligations. Debit and Credit columns were also set up in the Accounts Receivable and Accounts Payable sections because the firm planned to offer credit to qualified customers and would make credit purchases of supplies and other items.

After further analysis it was realized that the business would have numerous entries for the sale of services, the payment of employee salaries, and the purchase of supplies. Therefore, columns were established for recording credits to *Sales,* debits to *Salaries Expense,* and debits to *Supplies.* Finally, a column was set up for an Other Accounts section to take care of transactions that cannot be entered in the special columns.

FIGURE B.1 Combined Journal

COMBINED JOURNAL

DATE		CK. NO.	DESCRIPTION	POST. REF.	CASH DEBIT	CASH CREDIT	ACCOUNTS RECEIVABLE DEBIT	ACCOUNTS RECEIVABLE CREDIT
2019								
Jan.	3	711	Rent for month			1050 00		
	5		Treschell Seymore	✓			250 00	
	6		C & M Garden Supply	✓				
	7		Cash sales		2300 00			
	7	712	Payroll			780 00		
	10		Annie McGowan	✓	150 00			150 00
	12		The Greenery	✓				
	13		Allen Clark	✓	440 00			440 00
	14		Cash sales		2770 00			
	14	713	Payroll			780 00		
	17		Jessica Savage	✓			175 00	
	18		Lawn and Garden Supply	✓				
	19	714	Telephone service			201 00		
	20		Ned Jones	✓	125 00			125 00
	20		Starlene Neal	✓			110 00	
	21		Cash sales		2540 00			
	21	715	Payroll	✓		780 00		
	24		Lawn and Garden Supply	✓				
	25		Jeraldine Wells	✓			225 00	
	26	716	Ace Garden Supply			460 00		
	28		Cash sales		2200 00			
	28	717	Payroll			780 00		
	30		Note issued for purchase					
			of landscape equipment					
	31		Juanda Fischer	✓			98 00	
	31		Totals		10525 00	4831 00	858 00	715 00
					(101)	(101)	(111)	(111)

RECORDING TRANSACTIONS IN THE COMBINED JOURNAL

The combined journal shown in Figure B.1 contains the January 2019 transactions of Quality Lawn Care and Landscaping Services. Notice that most of these transactions require only a single line and involve the use of just the special columns. The entries for major types of transactions are explained in the following paragraphs.

Payment of Expenses During January, Quality Lawn Care and Landscaping Services issued checks to pay three kinds of expenses: rent, telephone service, and employee salaries. Notice how the payment of the monthly rent on January 3 was recorded in the combined journal. Since there is no special column for rent expense, the debit part of this entry appears in the Other Accounts section. The offsetting credit appears in the Cash Credit column. The payment of the monthly telephone bill on January 19 was recorded in a similar manner. However, when employee salaries were paid on January 7, 14, 21, and 28, both parts of the entries could be made in special columns. Because the firm has a weekly payroll period, a separate column in the combined journal was set up for debits to Salaries Expense.

PAGE 1

ACCOUNTS PAYABLE DEBIT	ACCOUNTS PAYABLE CREDIT	SALES CREDIT	SUPPLIES DEBIT	SALARIES EXPENSE DEBIT	OTHER ACCOUNTS ACCOUNT TITLE	POST REF.	OTHER ACCOUNTS DEBIT	OTHER ACCOUNTS CREDIT	
									1
					Rent Expense	*511*	*1 0 5 0 00*		2
		2 5 0 00							3
	4 5 0 00		*4 5 0 00*						4
		2 3 0 0 00							5
				7 8 0 00					6
									7
	2 2 5 00		*2 2 5 00*						8
									9
		2 7 7 0 00							10
				7 8 0 00					11
		1 7 5 00							12
	1 2 0 0 00				*Equipment*	*131*	*1 2 0 0 00*		13
					Telephone Exp.	*514*	*2 0 1 00*		14
									15
		1 1 0 00							16
		2 5 4 0 00							17
				7 8 0 00					18
	2 9 0 00		*2 9 0 00*						19
		2 2 5 00							20
4 6 0 00									21
		2 2 0 0 00							22
				7 8 0 00					23
					Equipment	*131*	*8 5 0 0 00*		24
					Notes Payable	*201*		*8 5 0 0 00*	25
		9 8 00							26
4 6 0 00	*2 1 6 5 00*	*10 6 6 8 00*	*9 6 5 00*	*3 1 2 0 00*			*10 9 5 1 00*	*8 5 0 0 00*	27
(202)	*(202)*	*(401)*	*(121)*	*(517)*			*(X)*	*(X)*	28

Sales on Credit On January 5, 17, 20, 25, and 31, Quality Lawn Care and Landscaping Services sold services on credit. The necessary entries were made in two special columns of the combined journal: the Accounts Receivable Debit column and the Sales Credit column.

Cash Sales Entries for the firm's weekly cash sales were recorded on January 7, 14, 21, and 28. Again, special columns were used: the Cash Debit column and the Sales Credit column.

Cash Received on Account When Quality Lawn Care and Landscaping Services collected cash on account from credit customers on January 10, 13, and 20, the transactions were entered in the Cash Debit column and the Accounts Receivable Credit column.

Purchases of Supplies on Credit Because the firm's combined journal includes a Supplies Debit column and an Accounts Payable Credit column, all purchases of supplies on credit can be recorded in special columns. Refer to the entries made on January 6, 12, and 24.

Purchases of Equipment on Credit On January 18, Quality Lawn Care and Landscaping Services bought some store equipment on credit. Since there is no special column for equipment, the debit part of the entry was made in the Other Accounts section. The offsetting credit appears in the Accounts Payable Credit column.

Payments on Account Any payments made on account to creditors are recorded in two special columns: Accounts Payable Debit and Cash Credit, as shown in the entry of January 26.

Issuance of a Promissory Note On January 30, the business purchased new cleaning equipment and issued a promissory note to the seller. Notice that both the debit to *Equipment* and the credit to *Notes Payable* had to be recorded in the Other Accounts section.

POSTING FROM THE COMBINED JOURNAL

One of the advantages of the combined journal is that it simplifies the posting process. All amounts in the special columns can be posted to the general ledger on a summary basis at the end of the month. Only the figures that appear in the Other Accounts section require individual postings to the general ledger during the month. Of course, if the firm has subsidiary ledgers, individual postings must also be made to these ledgers.

Daily Postings The procedures followed at Quality Lawn Care and Landscaping Services will illustrate the techniques used to post from the combined journal. Each day any entries appearing in the Other Accounts section are posted to the proper accounts in the general ledger. For example, refer to the combined journal shown in Figure B.1. The five amounts listed in the Other Accounts Debit and Credit columns were posted individually during the month. The account numbers recorded in the Posting Reference column of the Other Accounts section show that the postings have been made.

Because Quality Lawn Care and Landscaping Services has subsidiary ledgers for accounts receivable and accounts payable, individual postings were also made on a daily basis to these ledgers. As each amount was posted, a check mark was placed in the Posting Reference column of the combined journal.

End-of-Month Postings At the end of the month, the combined journal is totaled, proved, and ruled. Then the totals of the special columns are posted to the general ledger. Proving the combined journal involves a comparison of the column totals to make sure that the debits and credits are equal. The following procedure is used:

Proof of Combined Journal	
	Debits
Cash Debit Column	10,525
Accounts Receivable Debit Column	858
Accounts Payable Debit Column	460
Supplies Debit Column	965
Salaries Expense Debit Column	3,120
Other Accounts Debit Column	10,951
	26,879
	Credits
Cash Credit Column	4,831
Accounts Receivable Credit Column	715
Accounts Payable Credit Column	2,165
Sales Credit Column	10,668
Other Accounts Credit Column	8,500
	26,879

After the combined journal is proved, all column totals except those in the Other Accounts section are posted to the appropriate general ledger accounts. As each total is posted, the account number is entered beneath the column in the journal. Notice that an X is used to indicate that the column totals in the Other Accounts section are not posted since the individual amounts were posted on a daily basis.

TYPICAL USES OF THE COMBINED JOURNAL

The combined journal is used most often in small professional offices and small service businesses. It is less suitable for merchandising businesses but is sometimes used in firms of this type if they are very small and have only a limited number of transactions.

Professional Offices The combined journal can be ideal to record the transactions that occur in a professional office, such as the office of a doctor, lawyer, accountant, or architect. However, special journals are more efficient if transactions become very numerous or are too varied.

Service Businesses The use of the combined journal to record the transactions of Quality Lawn Care and Landscaping Services has already been illustrated. The combined journal may be advantageous for a small service business, provided that the volume of transactions does not become excessive and the nature of the transactions does not become too complex.

Merchandising Businesses The combined journal can be used by a merchandising business, but only if the firm is quite small and has a limited number and variety of transactions involving few accounts. However, even for a small merchandising business, the use of special journals might prove more advantageous.

Disadvantages of the Combined Journal

If the variety of transactions is so great that many different accounts are required, the combined journal will not work well. Either the business will have to set up so many columns that the journal will become unwieldy, or it will be necessary to record so many transactions in the Other Accounts columns that little efficiency will result. As a general rule, if the transactions of a business are numerous enough to merit the use of special journals, any attempt to substitute the combined journal is a mistake. Remember that each special journal can be designed for maximum efficiency in recording transactions.

Glossary

Absorption costing The accounting procedure whereby all manufacturing costs, including fixed costs, are included in the cost of goods manufactured

Accelerated method of depreciation A method of depreciating an asset's cost that allocates greater amounts of depreciation to an asset's early years of useful life

Account balance The difference between the amounts recorded on the two sides of an account

Account form balance sheet A balance sheet that lists assets on the left and liabilities and owner's equity on the right (*see also* Report form balance sheet)

Accounting The process by which financial information about a business is recorded, classified, summarized, interpreted, and communicated to owners, managers, and other interested parties

Accounting cycle A series of steps performed during each accounting period to classify, record, and summarize data for a business and to produce needed financial information

Accounting Standards Codification The source of authoritative U.S. GAAP

Accounting Standards Update Changes to Accounting Standards Codification are communicated through Accounting Standards Update covering approximately 90 topics

Accounting system A process designed to accumulate, classify, and summarize financial data

Accounts Written records of the assets, liabilities, and owner's equity of a business

Accounts payable Amounts a business must pay in the future

Accounts payable ledger A subsidiary ledger that contains a separate account for each creditor

Accounts receivable Claims for future collection from customers

Accounts receivable ledger A subsidiary ledger that contains credit customer accounts

Accounts receivable turnover A measure of the speed with which sales on account are collected; the ratio of net credit sales to average receivables

Accrual basis A system of accounting by which all revenues and expenses are matched and reported on financial statements for the applicable period, regardless of when the cash related to the transaction is received or paid

Accrued expenses Expense items that relate to the current period but have not yet been paid and do not yet appear in the accounting records

Accrued income Income that has been earned but not yet received and recorded

Acid-test ratio A measure of immediate liquidity; the ratio of quick assets to current liabilities

Adjusting entries Journal entries made to update accounts for items that were not recorded during the accounting period

Adjustments *See* Adjusting entries

Aging the accounts receivable Classifying accounts receivable balances according to how long they have been outstanding

Allowance method A method of recording uncollectible accounts that estimates losses from uncollectible accounts and charges them to expense in the period when the sales are recorded

Amortization The process of periodically transferring the acquisition cost of intangible assets with estimated useful lives to an expense account

Appropriation of retained earnings A formal declaration of an intention to restrict dividends

Articles of partnership *See* Partnership agreement

Asset turnover A measure of the effective use of assets in making sales; the ratio of net sales to total assets

Assets Property owned by a business

Audit trail A chain of references that makes it possible to trace information, locate errors, and prevent fraud

Auditing The review of financial statements to assess their fairness and adherence to generally accepted accounting principles

Auditor's report An independent accountant's review of a firm's financial statements

Authorized capital stock The number of shares authorized for issue by the corporate charter

Average collection period The ratio of 365 days to the accounts receivable turnover; also called the *number of days' sales in receivables*

Average cost method A method of inventory costing using the average cost of units of an item available for sale during the period to arrive at cost of the ending inventory

Average method of process costing A method of costing that combines the cost of beginning inventory for each cost element with the costs during the current period

Balance ledger form A ledger account form that shows the balance of the account after each entry is posted

Balance sheet A formal report of a business's financial condition on a certain date; reports the assets, liabilities, and owner's equity of the business

Bank draft A check written by a bank that orders another bank to pay the stated amount to a specific party

Bank reconciliation statement A statement that accounts for all differences between the balance on the bank statement and the book balance of cash

Banker's year A 360-day period used to calculate interest on a note

Bill of lading A business document that lists goods accepted for transportation

Blank endorsement A signature of the payee written on the back of the check that transfers ownership of the check without specifying to whom or for what purpose

Bond indenture A bond contract

Bond issue costs Costs incurred in issuing bonds, such as legal and accounting fees and printing costs

Bond retirement When a bond is paid and the liability is removed from the company's balance sheet

Bond sinking fund investment A fund established to accumulate assets to pay off bonds when they mature

Bonding The process by which employees are investigated by an insurance company that will insure the business against losses through employee theft or mishandling of funds

Bonds payable Long-term debt instruments that are written promises to repay the principal at a future date; interest is due at a fixed rate payable over the life of the bond

Book value That portion of an asset's original cost that has not yet been depreciated

Book value (stock) The total equity applicable to a class of stock divided by the number of shares outstanding

Brand name *See* Trade name

Break even A point at which revenue equals expenses

Break-even point (BEP) The sales volume when total revenue equals total expenses

Budget An operating plan expressed in monetary units

Budget performance report A comparison of actual costs and budgeted costs

Business transaction A financial event that changes the resources of a firm

Bylaws The guidelines for conducting a corporation's business affairs

Call price The amount the corporation must pay for the bond when it is called

Callable bonds Bonds that allow the issuing corporation to require the holder to surrender the bonds for payment before their maturity date

Callable preferred stock Stock that gives the issuing corporation the right to repurchase the preferred shares from the stockholders at a specific price

Canceled check A check paid by the bank on which it was drawn

Capacity A facility's ability to produce or use

Capital Financial investment in a business; equity

Capital stock ledger A subsidiary ledger that contains a record of each stockholder's purchases, transfers, and current balance of shares owned; also called stockholders' ledger

Capital stock transfer journal A record of stock transfers used for posting to the stockholders' ledger

Capitalized costs All costs recorded as part of an asset's costs

Carrying value of bonds The balance of the ***Bonds Payable*** account plus the ***Premium on Bonds Payable*** account minus the ***Discount on Bonds Payable*** account; also called *book value of bonds*

Cash In accounting, currency, coins, checks, money orders, and funds on deposit in a bank

Cash discount A discount offered by suppliers for payment received within a specified period of time

Cash equivalents Assets that are easily convertible into known amounts of cash

Cash payments journal A special journal used to record transactions involving the payment of cash

Cash receipts journal A special journal used to record and post transactions involving the receipt of cash

Cash register proof A verification that the amount of currency and coins in a cash register agrees with the amount shown on the cash register audit tape

Cash Short or Over **account** An account used to record any discrepancies between the amount of currency and coins in the cash register and the amount shown on the audit tape

Cashier's check A draft on the issuing bank's own funds

Certified public accountant (CPA) An independent accountant who provides accounting services to the public for a fee

Charge-account sales Sales made through the use of open-account credit or one of various types of credit cards

Chart of accounts A list of the accounts used by a business to record its financial transactions

Check A written order signed by an authorized person instructing a bank to pay a specific sum of money to a designated person or business

Chronological order Organized in the order in which the events occur

Classification A means of identifying each account as an asset, liability, or owner's equity

Classified financial statement A format by which revenues and expenses on the income statement, and assets and liabilities on the balance sheet, are divided into groups of similar accounts and a subtotal is given for each group

Closing entries Journal entries that transfer the results of operations (net income or net loss) to owner's equity and reduce the revenue, expense, and drawing account balances to zero

Collateral trust bonds Bonds secured by the pledge of securities, such as stocks or bonds of other companies

Combined journal A journal that combines features of the general journal and the special journals in a single record

Commercial draft A note issued by one party that orders another party to pay a specified sum on a specified date

Commission basis A method of paying employees according to a percentage of net sales

Common costs Costs not directly traceable to a specific segment of a business

Common stock The general class of stock issued when no other class of stock is authorized; each share carries the same rights and privileges as every other share. Even if preferred stock is issued, common stock will also be issued

Common Stock Dividend Distributable **account** Equity account used to record par, or stated, value of shares to be issued as the result of the declaration of a stock dividend

Common-size statements Financial statements with items expressed as percentages of a base amount

Comparative statements Financial statements presented side by side for two or more years

Compensation record *See* Individual earnings record

Compound entry A journal entry with more than one debit or credit

Computer software An intangible asset; written programs that instruct a computer's hardware to do certain tasks

Conceptual framework A basic framework developed by the FASB to provide conceptual guidelines for financial statements. The most important features are statements of qualitative features of statements, basic assumptions underlying statements, basic accounting principles, and modifying constraints

Conservatism The concept that revenue and assets should be understated rather than overstated if GAAP allows alternatives.

Similarly, expenses and liabilities should be overstated rather than understated

Contingent liability An item that can become a liability if certain things happen

Contra account An account with a normal balance that is opposite that of a related account

Contra asset account An asset account with a credit balance, which is contrary to the normal balance of an asset account

Contra revenue account An account with a debit balance, which is contrary to the normal balance for a revenue account

Contribution margin Gross profit on sales minus direct expenses; revenues minus variable costs

Control account An account that links a subsidiary ledger and the general ledger since its balance summarizes the balances of the accounts in the subsidiary ledger

Controllable fixed costs Costs that the segment manager can control

Convertible bonds Bonds that give the owner the right to convert the bonds into common stock under specified conditions

Convertible preferred stock Preferred stock that conveys the right to convert that stock to common stock after a specified date or during a period of time

Copyright An intangible asset; an exclusive right granted by the federal government to produce, publish, and sell a literary or artistic work for a period equal to the creator's life plus 70 years

Corporate charter A document issued by a state government that establishes a corporation

Corporation A publicly or privately owned business entity that is separate from its owners and has a legal right to own property and do business in its own name; stockholders are not responsible for the debts or taxes of the business

Correcting entry A journal entry made to correct an erroneous entry

Cost center A business segment that incurs costs but does not produce revenue

Cost of goods sold The actual cost to the business of the merchandise sold to customers

Cost of production report Summarizes all costs charged to each department and shows the costs assigned to the goods transferred out of the department and to the goods still in process

Cost variance The difference between the total standard cost and the total actual cost

Cost-benefit test If accounting concepts suggest a particular accounting treatment for an item but it appears that the theoretically correct treatment would require an unreasonable amount of work, the accountant may analyze the benefits and costs of the preferred treatment to see if the benefit gained from its adoption is justified by the cost

Coupon bonds Unregistered bonds that have coupons attached for each interest payment; also called *bearer bonds*

Credit An entry on the right side of an account

Credit memorandum (accounts receivable) A note verifying that a customer's account is being reduced by the amount of a sales return or sales allowance plus any sales tax that may have been involved

Credit memorandum (banking) A form that explains any addition, other than a deposit, to a checking account

Creditor One to whom money is owed

Cumulative preferred stock Stock that conveys to its owners the right to receive the preference dividend for the current year and any prior years in which the preference dividend was not paid before common stockholders receive any dividends

Current assets Assets consisting of cash, items that normally will be converted into cash within one year, and items that will be used up within one year

Current liabilities Debts that must be paid or otherwise satisfied within one year

Current ratio A relationship between current assets and current liabilities that provides a measure of a firm's ability to pay its current debts (current ratio = current assets ÷ current liabilities)

Debentures Unsecured bonds backed only by a corporation's general credit

Debit An entry on the left side of an account

Debit memorandum A form that explains any deduction, other than a check or other electronic payment transaction, from a checking account

Declaration date The date on which the board of directors declares a dividend

Declining-balance method An accelerated method of depreciation in which an asset's book value at the beginning of a year is multiplied by a constant percentage (such as 125%, 150%, or 200%) to determine depreciation for the year

Deferred expenses *See* Prepaid expenses

Deferred income *See* Unearned income

Deferred income taxes The amount of income taxes that will be payable or an amount that may benefit the corporation in the future as a result of the difference between the current year's taxable income and financial statement net income

Departmental income statement Income statement that shows each department's contribution margin and net income from operations after all expenses are allocated

Depletion Allocating the cost of a natural resource to expense over the period in which the resource produces revenue

Deposit in transit A deposit that is recorded in the cash receipts journal but that reaches the bank too late to be shown on the monthly bank statement

Deposit slip A form prepared to record the deposit of cash or checks to a bank account

Depreciation Allocation of the cost of a long-term asset to operations during its expected useful life

Differential cost The difference in cost between one alternative and another

Direct charge-off method A method of recording uncollectible account losses as they occur

Direct costing The accounting procedure whereby only variable costs are included in the cost of goods manufactured, and fixed manufacturing costs are written off as expenses in the period in which they are incurred

Direct expenses Operating expenses that are identified directly with a department and are recorded by department

Direct labor The costs attributable to personnel who work directly on the product being manufactured

Direct materials All items that go into a product and become a part of it

Direct method A means of reporting sources and uses of cash under which all revenue and expenses reported on the income statement appear in the operating section of the statement of cash flows and show the cash received or paid out for each type of transaction

Discount on bonds payable The excess of the face value over the price received by the corporation for a bond

Discounting Deducting the interest from the principal on a note payable or receivable in advance

Discussion memorandum An explanation of a topic under consideration by the Financial Accounting Standards Board

Dishonored check A check returned to the depositor unpaid because of insufficient funds in the drawer's account; also called an NSF check

Dissolution The legal term for termination of a partnership

Distributive share The amount of net income or net loss allocated to each partner

Dividends Distributions of the profits of a corporation to its shareholders

Donated capital Capital resulting from the receipt of gifts by a corporation

Double-declining-balance (DDB) method A method of depreciation that uses a rate equal to twice the straight-line rate and applies that rate to the book value of the asset at the beginning of the year

Double-entry system An accounting system that involves recording the effects of each transaction as debits and credits

Draft A written order that requires one party (a person or business) to pay a stated sum of money to another party

Drawee The bank on which a check is written

Drawer The person or firm issuing a check

Drawing account A special type of owner's equity account set up to record the owner's withdrawal of cash from the business

Economic entity A business or organization whose major purpose is to produce a profit for its owners

Electronic funds transfer (EFT) An electronic transfer of money from one account to another

Employee A person who is hired by and works under the control and direction of the employer

Employee's Withholding Allowance Certificate, Form W-4 A form used to claim exemption (withholding) allowances

Employer's Annual Federal Unemployment Tax Return, Form 940 Preprinted government form used by the employer to report unemployment taxes for the calendar year

Employer's Quarterly Federal Tax Return, Form 941 Preprinted government form used by the employer to report payroll tax information relating to social security, Medicare, and employee income tax withholding to the Internal Revenue Service

Endorsement A written authorization that transfers ownership of a check

Entity Anything having its own separate identity, such as an individual, a town, a university, or a business

Equity An owner's financial interest in a business

Equivalent production The estimated number of units that could have been started and completed with the same effort and costs incurred in the department during the same time period

Exempt employees Salaried employees who hold supervisory or managerial positions who are not subject to the maximum hour and overtime pay provisions of the Wage and Hour Law

Expense An outflow of cash, use of other assets, or incurring of a liability

Experience rating system A system that rewards an employer for maintaining steady employment conditions by reducing the firm's state unemployment tax rate

Exposure draft A proposed solution to a problem being considered by the Financial Accounting Standards Board

Face interest rate The contractual interest rate specified on the bond

Face value An amount of money indicated to be paid, exclusive of interest or discounts

Fair market value The current worth of an asset or the price the asset would bring if sold on the open market

Federal unemployment taxes (FUTA) Taxes levied by the federal government against employers to benefit unemployed workers

Financial statements Periodic reports of a firm's financial position or operating results

Financing activities Transactions with those who provide cash to the business to carry on its activities

Finished goods inventory The cost of completed products ready for sale; corresponds to the *Merchandise Inventory* account of a merchandising business

Finished goods subsidiary ledger A ledger containing a record for each of the different types of finished products

First-in, first-out (FIFO) method A method of inventory costing that assumes the oldest merchandise is sold first

Fixed budget A budget representing only one level of activity

Fixed costs Costs that do not change in total as the level of activity changes

Flexible budget A budget that shows the budgeted costs at various levels of activity

Footing A small pencil figure written at the base of an amount column showing the sum of the entries in the column

Franchise An intangible asset; a right to exclusive dealership granted by a governmental unit or a business entity

***Freight In* account** An account showing transportation charges for items purchased

Full disclosure principle The requirement that all information that might affect the user's interpretation of the profitability and financial position of a business be disclosed in the financial statements or in notes to the statements

Full endorsement A signature transferring a check to a specific person, firm, or bank

Fundamental accounting equation The relationship between assets and liabilities plus owner's equity

Gain The disposition of an asset for more than its book value

General journal A financial record for entering all types of business transactions; a record of original entry

General ledger A permanent, classified record of all accounts used in a firm's operation; a record of final entry

General partner A member of a partnership who has unlimited liability

Generally accepted accounting principles (GAAP) Accounting standards developed and applied by professional accountants

Going concern assumption The assumption that a firm will continue to operate indefinitely

Goodwill An intangible asset; the value of a business in excess of the net value of its identifiable assets

Governmental accounting Accounting work performed for a federal, state, or local governmental unit

Gross profit The difference between net sales and the cost of goods sold (gross profit = net sales — cost of goods sold)

Gross profit method A method of estimating inventory cost based on the assumption that the rate of gross profit on sales and the ratio of cost of goods sold to net sales are relatively constant from period to period

Gross profit percentage The amount of gross profit from each dollar of sales (gross profit percentage = gross profit ÷ net sales)

High-low point method A method to determine the fixed and variable components of a semivariable cost

Historical cost basis principle The principle that requires assets and services to be recorded at their cost at the time they are acquired and that, generally, long-term assets remain at historical costs in the asset accounts

Horizontal analysis Computing the percentage change for individual items in the financial statements from year to year

Hourly rate basis A method of paying employees according to a stated rate per hour

Impairment A situation that occurs when the asset is determined to have a fair market value less than its book value

Income statement A formal report of business operations covering a specific period of time; also called a profit and loss statement or a statement of income and expenses

***Income Summary* account** A special owner's equity account that is used only in the closing process to summarize the results of operations

Income tax method A method of recording the trade-in of an asset for income tax purposes. It does not permit a gain or loss to be recognized on the transaction

Independent contractor One who is paid by a company to carry out a specific task or job but is not under the direct supervision or control of the company

Indirect expenses Operating expenses that cannot be readily identified and are not closely related to activity within a department

Indirect labor Costs attributable to personnel who support production but are not directly involved in the manufacture of a product; for example, supervisory, repair and maintenance, and janitorial staff

Indirect materials and supplies Materials used in manufacturing a product that may not become a part of the product and are not a significant material cost factor

Indirect method A means of reporting cash generated from operating activities by treating net income as the primary source of cash in the operating section of the statement of cash flows and adjusting that amount for changes in current assets and liabilities associated with net income, noncash transactions, and other items

Individual earnings record An employee record that contains information needed to compute earnings and complete tax reports

Industry averages Financial ratios and percentages reflecting averages for similar companies

Industry practice constraint In a few limited cases unusual operating characteristics of an industry, usually based on risk, for which special accounting principles and procedures have been developed. These may not conform completely with GAAP for other industries

Intangible assets Assets that lack a physical substance, such as goodwill, patents, copyrights, and computer software, although software has, in a sense, a physical attribute

Interest The fee charged for the use of money

International accounting The study of accounting principles used by different countries

Interpret To understand and explain the meaning and importance of something (such as financial statements)

Inventory sheet A form used to list the quantity and type of goods a firm has in stock

Inventory turnover The number of times inventory is purchased and sold during the accounting period (inventory turnover = cost of goods sold ÷ average inventory)

Investing activities Transactions that involve the acquisition or disposal of long-term assets

Invoice A customer billing for merchandise bought on credit

Job order A specific order for a specific batch of manufactured items

Job order cost accounting A cost accounting system that determines the unit cost of manufactured items for each separate production order

Job order cost sheet A record of all manufacturing costs charged to a specific job

Journal The record of original entry

Journalizing Recording transactions in a journal

Just-in-time system An inventory system in which raw materials are ordered so they arrive just in time to be placed into production

Labor efficiency variance *See* Labor time variance

Labor rate variance The difference between the actual labor rate per hour and the standard labor rate per hour multiplied by the actual number of hours worked on the job

Labor time variance The difference between the actual hours worked and the standard labor hours allowed for the job multiplied by the standard cost per hour

Last-in, first-out (LIFO) method A method of inventory costing that assumes that the most recently purchased merchandise is sold first

Ledger The record of final entry

Leveraged buyout Purchasing a business by acquiring the stock and obligating the business to pay the debt incurred

Leveraging Using borrowed funds to earn a profit greater than the interest that must be paid on the borrowing

Liabilities Debts or obligations of a business

Limited liability company (LLC) Provides limited liability to the owners, who can elect to have the profits taxed at the LLC level or on their individual tax returns

Limited liability partnership (LLP) A partnership that provides some limited liability for all partners

Limited partner A member of a partnership whose liability is limited to his or her investment in the partnership

Limited partnership A partnership having one or more limited partners

Liquidation Termination of a business by distributing all assets and discontinuing the business

Liquidation value Value of assets to be applied to preferred stock, usually par value or an amount in excess of par value, if the corporation is liquidated

Liquidity The ease with which an item can be converted into cash; the ability of a business to pay its debts when due

List price An established retail price

Long-term liabilities Debts of a business that are due more than one year in the future

Loss The disposition of an asset for less than its book value

Lower of cost or net realizable value rule The principle by which inventory is reported at either its original cost or its net realizable value, whichever is lower

Management advisory services Services designed to help clients improve their information systems or their business performance

Managerial accounting Accounting work carried on by an accountant employed by a single business in industry; the branch of accounting that provides financial information about business segments, activities, or products

Manufacturing business A business that sells goods that it has produced

Manufacturing cost budget A budget made for each manufacturing cost

Manufacturing margin Sales minus the variable cost of goods sold

Manufacturing overhead All manufacturing costs that are not classified as direct materials or direct labor

Manufacturing overhead ledger A subsidiary ledger that contains a record for each overhead item

Manufacturing Summary* account** The account to which all items on the statement of cost of goods manufactured are closed; similar to the ***Income Summary account

Marginal income The manufacturing margin minus variable operating expenses

Markdown Price reduction below the original markon

Market interest rate The interest rate a corporation is willing to pay and investors are willing to accept at the current time

Market value The price per share at which stock is bought and sold

Markon The difference between the cost and the initial retail price of merchandise

Markup A price increase above the original markon

Matching principle The concept that revenue and the costs incurred in earning the revenue should be matched in the appropriate accounting periods

Materiality constraint The significance of an item in relation to a particular situation or set of facts

Materials price variance The difference between the actual price and the standard cost for materials multiplied by the actual quantity of materials used

Materials quantity variance The difference between the actual quantity used and the quantity of materials allowed multiplied by the standard cost of the materials

Materials requisition A form that describes the item and quantity needed and shows the job or purpose

Materials usage variance *See* Materials quantity variance

Maturity value The total amount (principal plus interest) that must be paid when a note comes due

Medicare tax A tax levied on employees and employers to provide medical care for the employee and the employee's spouse after each has reached age 65

Memorandum entry An informational entry in the general journal

Merchandise inventory The stock of goods a merchandising business keeps on hand

Merchandising business A business that sells goods purchased for resale

Merit rating system *See* Experience rating system

Minute book A book in which accurate and complete records of all meetings of stockholders and directors are kept

Monetary unit assumption It is assumed that only those items and events that can be measured in monetary terms are included in the financial statements. An inherent part of this assumption is that the monetary unit is stable

Mortgage loan A long-term debt created when a note is given as part of the purchase price for land or buildings

Multiple-step income statement A type of income statement on which several subtotals are computed before the net income is calculated

Mutual agency The characteristic of a partnership by which each partner is empowered to act as an agent for the partnership, binding the firm by his or her acts

Negotiable A financial instrument whose ownership can be transferred to another person or business

Negotiable instrument A financial document containing a promise or order to pay that meets all requirements of the Uniform Commercial Code in order to be transferable to another party

Net book value The cost of an asset minus its accumulated depreciation, depletion, or amortization, also known as book value

Net income The result of an excess of revenue over expenses

Net income line The worksheet line immediately following the column totals on which net income (or net loss) is recorded in two places: the Income Statement section and the Balance Sheet section

Net loss The result of an excess of expenses over revenue

Net price The list price less all trade discounts

Net realizable value The estimated selling price of an inventory item in the ordinary course of business, less reasonably predictable costs of completion, disposal, and transportation

Net sales The difference between the balance in the ***Sales*** account and the balance in the ***Sales Returns and Allowances*** account

Net salvage value The salvage value of an asset less any costs to remove or sell the asset

Neutrality concept The concept that information in financial statements cannot be selected or presented in a way to favor one set of interested parties over another

No-par-value stock Stock that is not assigned a par value in the corporate charter

Noncumulative preferred stock Stock that conveys to its owners the stated preference dividend for the current year but no rights to dividends for years in which none were declared

Nonparticipating preferred stock Stock that conveys to its owners the right to only the preference dividend amount specified on the stock certificate

Normal balance The increase side of an account

Note payable A liability representing a written promise by the maker of the note (the debtor) to pay another party (the creditor) a specified amount at a specified future date

Note receivable An asset representing a written promise by another party (the debtor) to pay the note holder (the creditor) a specified amount at a specified future date

On account An arrangement to allow payment at a later date; also called a charge account or open-account credit

Open-account credit A system that allows the sale of services or goods with the understanding that payment will be made at a later date

Operating activities Routine business transactions—selling goods or services and incurring expenses

Operating assets and liabilities Current assets and current liabilities

Opportunity cost Potential earnings or benefits that are given up because a certain course of action is taken

Organization costs The costs associated with establishing a corporation

Outstanding checks Checks that have been recorded in the cash payments journal but have not yet been paid by the bank

Overapplied overhead The result of applied overhead exceeding the actual overhead costs

Overhead application rate The rate at which the estimated cost of overhead is charged to each job

Owner's equity The financial interest of the owner of a business; also called proprietorship or net worth

Paid-in capital Capital acquired from capital stock transactions (also known as contributed capital)

Par value An amount assigned by the corporate charter to each share of stock for accounting purposes

Participating preferred stock Stock that conveys the right not only to the preference dividend amount but also to a share of other dividends paid

Partnership A business entity owned by two or more people who carry on a business for profit and who are legally responsible for the debts and taxes of the business

Partnership agreement A legal contract forming a partnership and specifying certain details of operation

Patent An intangible asset; an exclusive right given by the U.S. Patent and Trademark Office to manufacture and sell an invention for a period of 20 years from the date the patent is granted

Payee The person or firm to whom a check is payable

Payment date The date that dividends are paid

Payroll register A record of payroll information for each employee for the pay period

Periodic inventory Inventory based on a periodic count of goods on hand

Periodic inventory system An inventory system in which the merchandise inventory balance is only updated when a physical inventory is taken

Periodicity of income assumption The concept that economic activities of an entity can be divided logically and identified with specific time periods, such as the year or quarter

Permanent account An account that is kept open from one accounting period to the next

Perpetual inventory Inventory based on a running total of number of units

Perpetual inventory system An inventory system that tracks the inventories on hand at all times

Petty cash analysis sheet A form used to record transactions involving petty cash

Petty cash fund A special-purpose fund used to handle payments involving small amounts of money

Petty cash voucher A form used to record the payments made from a petty cash fund

Physical inventory An actual count of the number of units of each type of good on hand

Piece-rate basis A method of paying employees according to the number of units produced

Plant and equipment Property that will be used in the business for longer than one year

Postclosing trial balance A statement that is prepared to prove the equality of total debits and credits after the closing process is completed

Postdated check A check dated some time in the future

Posting Transferring data from a journal to a ledger

Preemptive right A shareholder's right to purchase a proportionate amount of any new stock issued at a later date

Preference dividend A basic or stated dividend rate for preferred stock that must be paid before dividends can be paid on common stock

Preferred stock A class of stock that has special claims on the corporate profits or, in case of liquidation, on corporate assets

Premium on bonds payable The excess of the price paid over the face value of a bond

Prepaid expenses Expense items acquired, recorded, and paid for in advance of their use

Price-earnings ratio The ratio of the current market value of common stock to earnings per share of that stock

Principal The amount shown on the face of a note

Private sector The business sector, which is represented in developing accounting principles by the Financial Accounting Standards Board (FASB)

Process cost accounting A cost accounting system whereby unit costs of manufactured items are determined by totaling unit costs in each production department

Process cost accounting system A method of accounting in which costs are accumulated for each process or department and then transferred on to the next process or department

Production order *See* Job order

Profit center A business segment that produces revenue

Promissory note A written promise to pay a specified amount of money on a specific date

Property, plant, and equipment Long-term assets that are used in the operation of a business and that are subject to depreciation (except for land, which is not depreciated)

Public accountants Members of firms that perform accounting services for other companies

Public sector The government sector, which is represented in developing accounting principles by the Securities and Exchange Commission (SEC)

Purchase allowance A price reduction from the amount originally billed

Purchase invoice A bill received for goods purchased

Purchase order An order to the supplier of goods specifying items needed, quantity, price, and credit terms

Purchase requisition A list sent to the purchasing department showing the items to be ordered

Purchase return Return of unsatisfactory goods

***Purchases* account** An account used to record cost of goods bought for resale during a period

Purchases discount A cash discount offered to customers for payment within a specified period

Purchases journal A special journal used to record the purchase of goods on credit

Qualitative characteristics Traits necessary for credible financial statements: relevance (confirmatory and predictive value), faithful representation (completeness, neutrality, and freedom from error), comparability, timeliness, verifiability, and understandability.

Quick assets Cash, receivables, and marketable securities

Ratio analysis Computing the relationship between various items in the financial statements

Raw materials The materials placed into production

Raw materials ledger record A record showing details of receipts and issues for a type of raw material

Raw materials subsidiary ledger A ledger containing the raw materials ledger records

Real property Assets such as land, land improvements, buildings, and other structures attached to the land

Realization The concept that revenue occurs when goods or services, merchandise, or other assets are exchanged for cash or claims to cash

Receiving report A form showing quantity and condition of goods received

Record date The date on which the specific stockholders to receive a dividend are determined

Recoverability test Test for possible impairment that compares the asset's net book value with the estimated net cash flows from future use of the asset

Registered bonds Bonds issued to a party whose name is listed in the corporation's records

Registrar A person or institution in charge of the issuance and transfer of a corporation's stock

Relevant range of activity The different levels of activity at which a factory is expected to operate

Report form balance sheet A balance sheet that lists the asset accounts first, followed by liabilities and owner's equity

Residual value The estimate of the amount that could be obtained from the sale or disposition of an asset at the end of its useful life; also called salvage or scrap value

Responsibility accounting The process that allows management to evaluate the performance of each segment of the business and assign responsibility for its financial results

Restrictive endorsement A signature that transfers a check to a specific party for a stated purpose

Retail business A business that sells directly to individual consumers

Retail method A method of estimating inventory cost by applying the ratio of cost to selling price in the current accounting period to the retail price of the inventory

Retained earnings The cumulative profits and losses of the corporation not distributed as dividends

Return on common stockholders' equity A measure of how well the corporation is making a profit for its shareholders; the ratio of net income available for common stockholders to common stockholders' equity

Revenue An inflow of money or other assets that results from the sales of goods or services or from the use of money or property; also called income

Revenue recognition principle Revenue is recognized when it has been earned and realized

Reversing entries Journal entries made to reverse the effect of certain adjusting entries involving accrued income or accrued expenses to avoid problems in recording future payments or receipts of cash in a new accounting period

Salary basis A method of paying employees according to an agreed-upon amount for each week or month

Sales allowance A reduction in the price originally charged to customers for goods or services

Sales discount A cash discount offered by the supplier for payment within a specified period

Sales invoice A supplier's billing document

Sales journal A special journal used to record sales of merchandise on credit

Sales return A firm's acceptance of a return of goods from a customer

Sales Returns and Allowances A contra revenue account where sales returns and sales allowances are recorded; sales returns and allowances are subtracted from sales to determine net sales

Salvage value An estimate of the amount that could be received by selling or disposing of an asset at the end of its useful life

Schedule of accounts payable A list of all balances owed to creditors

Schedule of accounts receivable A listing of all balances of the accounts in the accounts receivable subsidiary ledger

Schedule of operating expenses A schedule that supplements the income statement, showing the selling and general and administrative expenses in greater detail

Scrap value *See* Residual value

Secured bonds Bonds for which property is pledged to secure the claims of bondholders

Semidirect expenses Operating expenses that cannot be directly assigned to a department but are closely related to departmental activities

Semivariable costs Costs that vary with, but not in direct proportion to, the volume of activity

Separate entity assumption The concept that a business is separate from its owners; the concept of keeping a firm's financial records separate from the owner's personal financial records

Serial bonds Bonds issued at one time but payable over a period of years

Service business A business that sells services

Service charge A fee charged by a bank to cover the costs of maintaining accounts and providing services

Shareholder A person who owns shares of stock in a corporation; also called a stockholder

Sight draft A commercial draft that is payable on presentation

Single-step income statement A type of income statement where only one computation is needed to determine the net income (total revenue − total expenses = net income)

Slide An accounting error involving a misplaced decimal point

Social entity A nonprofit organization, such as a city, public school, or public hospital

Social security (FICA or OASDI) tax A tax imposed by the Federal Insurance Contributions Act and collected on employee earnings to provide retirement and disability benefits

Social Security Act A federal act providing certain benefits for employees and their families; officially the Federal Insurance Contributions Act

Sole proprietorship A business entity owned by one person, who is legally responsible for the debts and taxes of the business

Special journal A journal used to record only one type of transaction

Specific identification method A method of inventory costing based on the actual cost of each item of merchandise

Standard cost card A form that shows the per-unit standard costs for materials, labor, and overhead

Standard costs A measure of what costs should be in an efficient operation

State unemployment taxes (SUTA) Taxes levied by a state government against employers to benefit unemployed workers

Stated value The value that can be assigned to no-par-value stock by a board of directors for accounting purposes

Statement of account A form sent to a firm's customers showing transactions during the month and the balance owed

Statement of cash flows A financial statement that provides information about the cash receipts and cash payments of a business

Statement of cost of goods manufactured A financial report showing details of the cost of goods completed for a manufacturing business

Statement of owner's equity A formal report of changes that occurred in the owner's financial interest during a reporting period

Statement of partners' equities A financial statement prepared to summarize the changes in the partners' capital accounts during an accounting period

Statement of retained earnings A financial statement that shows all changes that have occurred in retained earnings during the period

Statement of stockholders' equity A financial statement that provides an analysis reconciling the beginning and ending balance of each of the stockholders' equity accounts

Statements of Financial Accounting Standards Accounting principles established by the Financial Accounting Standards Board

Stock Certificates that represent ownership of a corporation

Stock certificate The form by which capital stock is issued; the certificate indicates the name of the corporation, the name of the stockholder to whom the certificate was issued, the class of stock, and the number of shares

Stock dividend Distribution of the corporation's own stock on a pro rata basis that results in conversion of a portion of the firm's retained earnings to permanent capital

Stock split When a corporation issues two or more shares of new stock to replace each share outstanding without making any changes in the capital accounts

Stockholders The owners of a corporation; also called shareholders

Stockholders of record Stockholders in whose name shares are held on date of record and who will receive a declared dividend

Stockholders' equity The corporate equivalent of owners' equity; also called shareholders' equity

Stockholders' ledger *See* Capital stock ledger

Straight-line amortization Amortizing the premium or discount on bonds payable in equal amounts each month over the life of the bond

Straight-line depreciation Allocation of an asset's cost in equal amounts to each accounting period of the asset's useful life

Subchapter S corporation (S corporation) An entity formed as a corporation that meets the requirements of subchapter S of the Internal Revenue Code to be treated essentially as a partnership, so that the corporation pays no income tax

Subscribers' ledger A subsidiary ledger that contains an account receivable for each stock subscriber

Subscription book A list of the stock subscriptions received

Subsidiary ledger A ledger dedicated to accounts of a single type and showing details to support a general ledger account

Sum-of-the-years'-digits method A method of depreciating asset costs by allocating as expense each year a fractional part of the asset's depreciable cost, based on the sum of the digits of the number of years in the asset's useful life

Sunk cost A cost that has been incurred and will not change as a result of a decision

T account A type of account, resembling a T, used to analyze the effects of a business transaction

Tangible personal property Assets such as machinery, equipment, furniture, and fixtures that can be removed and used elsewhere

Tax accounting A service that involves tax compliance and tax planning

Tax-exempt wages Earnings in excess of the base amount set by the Social Security Act

Temporary account An account whose balance is transferred to another account at the end of an accounting period

Time and a half Rate of pay for an employee's work in excess of 40 hours a week

Time draft A commercial draft that is payable during a specified period of time

Time ticket Form used to record hours worked and jobs performed

Total equities The sum of a corporation's liabilities and stockholders' equity

Trade acceptance A form of commercial time draft used in transactions involving the sale of goods

Trade discount A reduction from list price

Trade name An intangible asset; an exclusive business name registered with the U.S. Patent and Trademark Office; also called brand name

Trademark An intangible asset; an exclusive business symbol registered with the U.S. Patent and Trademark Office

Trading on the equity *See* Leveraging

Transfer agent A person or institution that handles all stock transfers and transfer records for a corporation

Transfer price The price at which one segment's goods are transferred to another segment of the company

Transmittal of Wage and Tax Statements, Form W-3 Preprinted government form submitted with Forms W-2 to the Social Security Administration

Transparency Information provided in the financial statements and notes accompanying them should provide a clear and accurate picture of the financial affairs of the company

Transportation In* account** *See* ***Freight In account

Transposition An accounting error involving misplaced digits in a number

Treasury stock A corporation's own capital stock that has been issued and reacquired; the stock must have been previously paid in full and issued to a stockholder

Trend analysis Comparing selected ratios and percentages over a period of time

Trial balance A statement to test the accuracy of total debits and credits after transactions have been recorded

Underapplied overhead The result of actual overhead costs exceeding applied overhead

Unearned income Income received before it is earned

Unemployment insurance program A program that provides unemployment compensation through a tax levied on employers

Units-of-output method *See* Units-of-production method

Units-of-production method A method of depreciating asset cost at the same rate for each unit produced during each period

Unlimited liability The implication that a creditor can look to all partners' personal assets as well as the assets of the partnership for payment of the firm's debts

Updated account balances The amounts entered in the Adjusted Trial Balance section of the worksheet

Valuation account An account, such as *Allowance for Doubtful Accounts*, whose balance is revalued or reappraised in light of reasonable expectations

Variable costing *See* Direct costing

Variable costs Costs that vary in total in direct proportion to changes in the level of activity

Variance analysis Explains the difference between standard cost and actual cost

Vertical analysis Computing the relationship between each item on a financial statement to some base amount on the statement

Wage and Tax Statement, Form W-2 Preprinted government form that contains information about an employee's earnings and tax withholdings for the year

Wage-bracket table method A simple method to determine the amount of federal income tax to be withheld using a table provided by the government

Weighted average method *See* Average cost method

Wholesale business A business that manufactures goods for or distributes goods to retail businesses or large consumers such as hotels and hospitals

Withdrawals Funds taken from the business by the owner for personal use

Withholding statement *See* Wage and Tax Statement, Form W-2

Work in process Partially completed units in the production process

Work in process subsidiary ledger A ledger containing the job order cost sheets

Workers' compensation insurance Insurance that protects employees against losses from job-related injuries or illnesses, or compensates their families if death occurs in the course of the employment

Working capital The measure of the ability of a company to meet its current obligations; the excess of current assets over current liabilities

Worksheet A form used to gather all data needed at the end of an accounting period to prepare financial statements

Index

Key terms and page numbers where defined in the text are in **bold**.

N

O

P

SAMPLE GENERAL LEDGER ACCOUNTS

Account Name	Classification	Permanent or Temporary	Normal Balance
INCOME STATEMENT			
Fees Income	Revenue	Temporary	Credit
Sales	Revenue	Temporary	Credit
Sales Discounts	Contra Revenue	Temporary	Debit
Sales Returns and Allowances	Contra Revenue	Temporary	Debit
Purchases	Cost of Goods Sold	Temporary	Debit
Freight In	Cost of Goods Sold	Temporary	Debit
Purchases Discounts	Contra Cost of Goods Sold	Temporary	Credit
Purchases Returns and Allowances	Contra Cost of Goods Sold	Temporary	Credit
Direct Labor	Cost of Goods Manufactured	Temporary	Debit
Indirect Labor	Cost of Goods Manufactured	Temporary	Debit
Indirect Materials and Supplies	Cost of Goods Manufactured	Temporary	Debit
Payroll Taxes—Factory	Cost of Goods Manufactured	Temporary	Debit
Repairs and Maintenance—Factory	Cost of Goods Manufactured	Temporary	Debit
Depreciation—Factory	Cost of Goods Manufactured	Temporary	Debit
Insurance—Factory	Cost of Goods Manufactured	Temporary	Debit
Property Taxes—Factory	Cost of Goods Manufactured	Temporary	Debit
Advertising Expense	Operating Expense	Temporary	Debit
Amortization Expense	Operating Expense	Temporary	Debit
Bank Fees Expense	Operating Expense	Temporary	Debit
Cash Short or Over	Operating Expense	Temporary	Debit
Delivery Expense	Operating Expense	Temporary	Debit
Depreciation Expense	Operating Expense	Temporary	Debit
Insurance Expense	Operating Expense	Temporary	Debit
Payroll Taxes Expense	Operating Expense	Temporary	Debit
Property Tax Expense	Operating Expense	Temporary	Debit
Rent Expense	Operating Expense	Temporary	Debit
Research and Development Expense	Operating Expense	Temporary	Debit
Salaries Expense	Operating Expense	Temporary	Debit
Supplies Expense	Operating Expense	Temporary	Debit
Telephone Expense	Operating Expense	Temporary	Debit
Uncollectible Accounts Expense	Operating Expense	Temporary	Debit
Utilities Expense	Operating Expense	Temporary	Debit
Workers' Compensation Insurance Expense	Operating Expense	Temporary	Debit
Gain/Loss on Sale of Assets	Other Income/Expense	Temporary	—
Interest Income/Expense	Other Income/Expense	Temporary	—
Miscellaneous Income/Expense	Other Income/Expense	Temporary	—
Income Tax Expense	Other Expense	Temporary	Debit
STATEMENT OF OWNER'S EQUITY			
*(Owner's Name), Capital	Owner's Equity	Permanent	Credit
(Owner's Name), Drawing	Owner's Equity	Temporary	Debit
STATEMENT OF PARTNERS' EQUITY			
*(Partner's Name), Capital	Partners' Equity	Permanent	Credit
(Partner's Name), Drawing	Partners' Equity	Temporary	Debit
STATEMENT OF RETAINED EARNINGS			
*Retained Earnings—Appropriated	Stockholders' Equity	Permanent	Credit
*Retained Earnings	Stockholders' Equity	Permanent	Credit

*Account also appears on the balance sheet.

SAMPLE GENERAL LEDGER ACCOUNTS

Account Name	Classification	Permanent or Temporary	Normal Balance
BALANCE SHEET			
Cash	Current Asset	Permanent	Debit
Petty Cash Fund	Current Asset	Permanent	Debit
Notes Receivable	Current Asset	Permanent	Debit
Notes Receivable—Discounted	Contra Current Asset	Permanent	Credit
Accounts Receivable	Current Asset	Permanent	Debit
Allowance for Doubtful Accounts	Contra Current Asset	Permanent	Credit
Interest Receivable	Current Asset	Permanent	Debit
Stock Subscriptions Receivable	Current Asset	Permanent	Debit
Prepaid Expenses	Current Asset	Permanent	Debit
Merchandise Inventory	Current Asset	Permanent	Debit
Raw Materials Inventory	Current Asset	Permanent	Debit
Work in Process Inventory	Current Asset	Permanent	Debit
Finished Goods Inventory	Current Asset	Permanent	Debit
Building	Property, Plant & Equipment	Permanent	Debit
Equipment	Property, Plant & Equipment	Permanent	Debit
Land	Property, Plant & Equipment	Permanent	Debit
Land Improvements	Property, Plant & Equipment	Permanent	Debit
Accumulated Depreciation	Contra Property, Plant & Equipment	Permanent	Credit
Goodwill	Intangible Asset	Permanent	Debit
Organization Costs	Intangible Asset	Permanent	Debit
Patent	Intangible Asset	Permanent	Debit
Notes Payable	Current Liability	Permanent	Credit
Accounts Payable	Current Liability	Permanent	Credit
Dividends Payable—Preferred	Current Liability	Permanent	Credit
Dividends Payable—Common	Current Liability	Permanent	Credit
Salaries Payable	Current Liability	Permanent	Credit
Social Security Tax Payable	Current Liability	Permanent	Credit
Medicare Tax Payable	Current Liability	Permanent	Credit
Employee Income Tax Payable	Current Liability	Permanent	Credit
Federal Unemployment Tax Payable	Current Liability	Permanent	Credit
State Unemployment Tax Payable	Current Liability	Permanent	Credit
Health Insurance Premiums Payable	Current Liability	Permanent	Credit
Workers' Compensation Insurance Payable	Current Liability	Permanent	Credit
Interest Payable	Current Liability	Permanent	Credit
Sales Tax Payable	Current Liability	Permanent	Credit
Income Tax Payable	Current Liability	Permanent	Credit
Accrued Expenses Payable	Current Liability	Permanent	Credit
Unearned Income	Current Liability	Permanent	Credit
Bonds Payable	Long-Term Liability	Permanent	Credit
Premium on Bonds Payable	Long-Term Liability	Permanent	Credit
Discount on Bonds Payable	Contra Long-Term Liability	Permanent	Debit
(Owner's Name), Capital	Owner's Equity	Permanent	Credit
(Partner's Name), Capital	Partners' Equity	Permanent	Credit
Preferred Stock	Stockholders' Equity	Permanent	Credit
Preferred Stock Subscribed	Stockholders' Equity	Permanent	Credit
Paid-in Capital in Excess of Par—Preferred	Stockholders' Equity	Permanent	Credit
Common Stock	Stockholders' Equity	Permanent	Credit
Common Stock Dividend Distributable	Stockholders' Equity	Permanent	Credit
Common Stock Subscribed	Stockholders' Equity	Permanent	Credit
Paid-in Capital in Excess of Par—Common	Stockholders' Equity	Permanent	Credit
Donated Capital	Stockholders' Equity	Permanent	Credit
Retained Earnings—Appropriated	Stockholders' Equity	Permanent	Credit
Retained Earnings	Stockholders' Equity	Permanent	Credit
Treasury Stock	Contra Stockholders' Equity	Permanent	Debit

RULES OF DEBIT AND CREDIT

PERMANENT ACCOUNTS

Assets	
Debit	**Credit**
+	**–**
Increase	**Decrease**
Normal Balance	

Examples: Cash
Accounts Receivable
Building
Equipment

Contra Assets	
Debit	**Credit**
–	**+**
Decrease	**Increase**
	Normal Balance

Examples: Allowance for Doubtful Accounts
Accumulated Depreciation—Building

Liabilities	
Debit	**Credit**
–	**+**
Decrease	**Increase**
	Normal Balance

Examples: Accounts Payable
Notes Payable
Bonds Payable

Contra Liabilities	
Debit	**Credit**
+	**–**
Increase	**Decrease**
Normal Balance	

Example: Discount on Bonds Payable

Equity	
Debit	**Credit**
–	**+**
Decrease	**Increase**
	Normal Balance

Examples: Linda Carter, Capital *(Sole Proprietorship)*
Ted West, Capital *(Partnership)*
Capital Stock *(Corporation)*
Retained Earnings *(Corporation)*

RULES OF DEBIT AND CREDIT

TEMPORARY ACCOUNTS

Withdrawals (Sole Proprietorship/Partnership)

Debit	Credit
+	–
Increase	Decrease
Normal Balance	

Example: Linda Carter, Withdrawals

Revenue

Debit	Credit
–	+
Decrease	Increase
	Normal Balance

Examples: Fees Income
Sales

Contra Revenue

Debit	Credit
+	–
Increase	Decrease
Normal Balance	

Examples: Sales Discounts
Sales Returns and Allowances

Cost of Goods Sold

Debit	Credit
+	–
Increase	Decrease
Normal Balance	

Examples: Purchases
Freight In

Contra Cost of Goods Sold

Debit	Credit
–	+
Decrease	Increase
	Normal Balance

Examples: Purchases Discounts
Purchases Returns and Allowances

Expenses

Debit	Credit
+	–
Increase	Decrease
Normal Balance	

Examples: Advertising Expense
Utilities Expense
Rent Expense